Other title authored by Dr P.C. Bansil:

Agricultural Statistics in India, fourth edn

Economic Problems of Indian Agriculture

SIXTH EDITION

Techno Economic Research Institute Publication

SIXTH EDITION

Economic Problems of Indian Agriculture

P.C. Bansil
Techno Economic Research Institute
New Delhi

CBS

CBS PUBLISHERS & DISTRIBUTORS
4596/1A, 11 Darya Ganj, New Delhi-110 002 (INDIA)

Economic Problems of Indian Agriculture
Sixth edition

First edition 1969
Second edition 1975
Third edition 1977
Fourth edition 1981
Fifth edition 1986
Sixth edition 2002

ISBN:81-239-0836-9

Edited by Y.N. Arjuna and
Published by S.K. Jain for CBS Publishers & Distributors,
4596/1-A, 11 Darya Ganj, New Delhi 110002 (India).

Printed at Asia Printograph, Shahdara, Delhi-110032.

to
my mother
Jamna Devi

A pious soul,
though she could not receive
formal education,
I owe everything I have today
to her sacrifices and
inspiration

Preface to the Sixth Edition

Indian economy, particularly the agriculture sector, has undergone vast changes since the fifth edition of this book was published in 1986. The situation prevailing today needs to be analysed and understood in the context of relationships and dynamics of changed ground situation. Achievement of near self-sufficiency in foodgrains during the eighties has led today to unprecedented levels of public sector stocks of foodgrains. This, in turn, has created difficult supply–demand imbalances in both internal and external markets. The green revolution has reached a plateau. Negative externalities and second generation environmental problems such as decline in water table, changes in biodiversity and soil salinity, etc. are very much in evidence.

Following the liberalisation and implementation of WTO regulations in 1995, Indian agriculture is being increasingly integrated with global markets leading to competitive exports and imports. Already imports of vegetable oils have reached very high levels, cotton prices have crashed under threat of cheaper imports, and similar problems may have to be confronted even in foodgrains and sugar. All these factors have to be taken into account in designing new agricultural strategies and policies. Each factor has to address not only the question of diversification of agriculture but also that of the rural economy where the vast army of unemployed or underemployed persons have to be provided jobs without causing any significant rural–urban migration. Questions arising from the potential of GM crops have also to be examined carefully in terms of their impact on production relations.

All these and many more issues called for not only rewriting all the existing chapters but also addition of ten new chapters dealing with (1) Agricultural Development—An Overview, Labour Policy, (3) Economics of Farm Size, (4) Agricultural Subsidies, (5) Labour Policy, (6) Hunger, Poverty and Malnutrition, (7) Demand for Foodgrains by 2020 AD, (8) Indian Farmer in the New Millennium, (9) Post-Harvest Management, and Food Processing Industry, and (10) Globalisation of Agriculture and World Trade Organization. It is hoped that this new edition, completely rewritten and expanded, will be able to meet the requirements of students, researchers and policy makers alike.

It would not have been possible to complete this task, but for the contribution of Mr. K.R.. Dasgupta and Mr. C.P. Sharma who were fully involved. Faculty Members Mr. S.P. Malhotra, Ex. Commodity Specialist (FAO), Prof. S.K. Ray, Dr. P.N. Radhakrishnan and Dr. S.R.

Mohnot went through the draft of various chapters and offered valuable comments. The whole material was edited by Mr. Y.N. Arjuna for the publisher. His unflinching interest in the study has really been a motivating factor to give it a final shape of the book which is before the readers. Last but not the least, my thanks are due to Mrs. Ajitha Gangadharan and Mrs. Vasantha R. Pillai who were responsible to prepare and computerise the entire draft.

New Delhi
February 2002

P.C. Bansil

Preface to the Fifth Edition

The Census Commissioner, 1951 had declared the period after 1981 as Doomsday for Indian Agriculture. Strange are the ways of Nature. We are in the mid-eighties and with about 30 million tonnes of foodgrains in stock, the country is faced with the problem of their disposal. All the same there are problems in so far as the production of oilseeds, pulses and coarse grains is concerned. The production of sugar continues to be subject to cyclical variations and above all a substantial part of the irrigation potential already created at such a heavy cost, still remains unutilised. These and many other problems can be expected to find a solution in the Seventh Plan being launched now.

In the light of these fast developments, a study of the agricultural problems of India assumes great importance and this book is intended to meet this urgent demand. Almost all the chapters have been updated or rewritten. New data have been added.

It is hoped that this revised and updated edition will come up to the expectations of the large number of readers of Indian agriculture in India and abroad. Any suggestions for further improvement are always welcome.

New Delhi

P.C. Bansil

Contents

CHAPTER 1

The Setting

Located in the southern peninsula of the Asian continent and lying entirely in the northern hemisphere, India covers an area of 3,288 thousand sq. km. It is the seventh largest and the second most populous country in the world. With a land frontier of 15,200 km and a coastline of 5,700 km, India is rightly called a subcontinent.

In the north, India is separated from Tibet by high mountain ranges of the Himalayas. Nepal, an independent country, is also situated in the north. On the eastern side mountains separate India from Myanmar (formerly Burma). Wedged in between the Indian States of Assam, Tripura and West Bengal, is Bangladesh. In the northwest lies Pakistan. In the south, the country stretches crossing the Tropic of Cancer, forming into a peninsula with the Arabian Sea to the west and the Bay of Bengal to the east. On the south eastern tip is Sri Lanka separated by the Palk Strait.

The Indian subcontinent is an important centre of origin and diversity for more than 20 major agro-horticultural crop species and their wild relatives — rice, beans, sugarcane, cotton pigeonpea, citrus fruits, mango, banana, yams, several vegetables, spices, condiments (turmeric and ginger) and a variety of medicinal and aromatic plants. Nearly 160 domesticated species of economic importance, more than 350 species of their wild relatives, and above 800 species of ethno-botanic interest are natives to this region. They constitute an invaluable reservoir of genes needed by plant breeders for the development of superior crop varieties. For collecting, conserving and utilizing plant genetic resources, a systematic effort was initiated in 1945 in the erstwhile Botany Division of the Indian Agricultural Research Institute, New Delhi. The National Bureau of Plant Genetic Resources (NBPGR), New Delhi, came in existence in 1976, as a nodal office, to cater to a wider mandate — to plan and execute exploration, collection and evaluation of germplasm; to facilitate import-export of germplasm and plant quarantine, and also for safe conservation of both indigenous; and introduced genetic variability in crop plants and their wild relatives.

AGRICULTURE SCENARIO

Our agricultural work force, 70 per cent of the total population, inhabits 600,000 villages, and cultivates 184 million hectares broadly demarcated into 20 agroclimatic zones, that cater to incredibly diverse habitats. Our natural endowments are: the largest population of livestock in the world and a tropical coastline 8,129 km long and an Exclusive Economic Zone of 2.02 million km² vast that permits year-round fish harvest. We are also the home for more than 20 major agro-horticultural crops. In 1965, we were supplementing our bread basket with imports. During nineties, we were ready for meaningful export of our agricultural produce generally. India today occupies the first three positions in world in various agricultural commodities (Table 1.1).

Table 1.1 India's Position in World Agriculture-1997

Item India	*India*	*World*	*India's Share %*	*India's Rank*	*Next to*
1	2	3	4	5	6
1. Area **(Million ha.)					
Total Area	329	13387	2.4	Seventh	Canada, U.S.A., China, Brazil, Australia Russian Fed.
Land Area	297	13048	2.3	Seventh	U.S.A., China, Canada, Brazil, Australia, Russian Fed.
Arable Land	163 F	1382	11.8	Second	U.S.A.
Irrigated Area	57 F	242	23.6	First	
2. Population (Million)					
Total	960	5849	16.4	Second	China
Agriculture	541	2564	21.1	Second	China
3. Economically Active Population (Million)					
Total	420	2827	14.9	Second	China
Agriculture	256	1302	19.3	Second	China
4. Crop Production (Million Tonnes)					
Cereals	223	2096	10.6	Third	China, USA
Wheat	69*	610	11.3	Second	China
Rice	123*	573	21.5	Second	China
Coarse grains	31	914	3.5	Fifth	USA, China, Brazil, Russian Fed.
Potatoes	19 F	295	6.5	Sixth	China, Russian Fed., Poland, USA, Ukraine

Table 1.1 India's Position in World Agriculture-1997 (Contd.)

Item India		India	World	India's Share %	Rank	Next to
1		2	3	4	5	6
	Total Pulses	15	58	25.9	First	
	Groundnut	8*	30	26.7	Second	China
	Tobacco Leaves	0.56 F	8.24	6.8	Third	China, U.S.A.
	Rapessed	7	35	20.0	Second	China
	Coffee (green)	0.21*	5.56	3.8	Ninth	Brazil, Colombia, Indonesia, Mexico, Ethiopia, Uganda, Vietnam, Guatemala
	Sugarcane	265	1241	21.4	Second	Brazil
	Tea	0.79 F	2.73	28.9	First	
	Jute & Allied Fibres	1.72 F	3.27	52.6	First	
	Cotton (lint)	286*	19.7	14.5	Third	USA, China
5.	Livestock Numbers Million Head)					
	Cattle	209	1334	15.7	First	—
	Buffaloes	92 *	167	55.1	First	—
	Camels	1.52 F	19.50	7.8	Third	Somalia, Sudan
	Sheep	56*	1064	5.3	Third	Australia, China
	Goats	121*	703	17.2	Second	China
	Chicken	343*	13413	2.6	Seventh	China, USA, Brazil, Russian Fed., Mexico, Indonesia
6.	Implements (Thousands numbers)**					
	Tractors-in-use	1400 F	26345	5.3	Fourth	USA, Japan, Italy
7.	Vegetables (including Melon)	54.97 F	595.56	9.2	Second	China
8.	Fruits (excluding Melon)	37.13 F	429.45	8.6	Third	China
9.	Milk	72	546.64*	13.2	First	
10.	Eggs	1.61*	51.76	3.1	Fifth	China, U.S.A., Japan, Russian Fed.

F: DAO Estimate
*: Unofficial Figure
**: Figures relate to 1996

SOURCE: FAO Production Year Book 1997 and P.C. Bansil, Agricultural Statistical Compendium, Foodgrains, Techno Economic Research Institute, New Delhi.

In India, in the past 50 years, production has increased fourfold, faster than population growth. Still productivity in the major parts of the country is substantially lower than what has been achieved in other parts of the country. There are areas like Punjab, where yield of wheat is over 4000 kgs per hectare which is comparable with the best in the region. However, about Rs. 50,000 crore worth of food produced in India is wasted every year due to inefficient handling. This is more than Australia's annual food production. Of this, lack of infrastructure causes a loss of approximately Rs. 35,000 crore. Nearly Rs. 20,000 crore is wasted in transit. To stem this rot, India needs huge investment, say to the tune of Rs. 100,000 crore in farm infrastructure alone. Of this, around Rs. 25,000 crore is needed to build an effective transportation system.

Mention may be made in this context that the US food processing industry generates $100 billion in revenue every year. Against this, India, which produces nearly the same amount of food as the US, generates an insignificant fraction of this amount from food processing. Big Indian business houses are still shy in making large investment in agricultural sector that employs 64 per cent of the workforce but contributes 29 per cent to the national income. On the other hand, the software sector, employs only 0.07 per cent of the workforce and generates 1.3 per cent of the national income, yet its market capital is a whopping $55 billion.

Consumption of fresh horticultural produce has been the Indian mindset contrary to the West, where the lifestyle has prompted intake of processed foodstuffs. In India, interestingly regional preferences have also dominated for long due to inadequate and improper provision for transport and storage. The horticulture produce is highly perishable. Late starters scientifically, taking off only in the Fourth Plan in the mid-sixties (the task of self-sufficiency in foodgrains being overriding till then), the horticultural crops offer abundant opportunities for export since the nineties. The crops are also capable of fulfilling the nutritional and social objectives before the nation. Broadly they cover: fruits, vegetables, potato, tuber crops, plantation crops, spices, ornamental crops, medicinal and aromatic crops, and mushrooms. India is at present globally one of the largest producers of fruits and vegetables, and has virtually held monopoly in the trade of spices and condiments for centuries.

India has a large population of livestock: 200 million cattle, 76 million buffaloes, 46 million sheep, 110 million goats, 11 million pigs, 1.9 million equines, 1 million camel and 310 million poultry. Extreme agroclimatic and socioeconomic diversity has resulted into unique evolution of these animal species. Nature's own perfect food, milk, despite odds has witnessed upward trend in production over the years. From 17 million tonnes in 1950, milk production has surpassed 74 million tonnes in 2000. Egg and broiler production has also increased from 5 million to

30,000 million eggs and from 1 million to 400 million broilers over the past 3 decades.

Sustainable animal husbandry over the years has been a part of man-animal-plant-soil relationship where the animal has been an important integrating link sustaining animal and agriculture. Our agricultural operations have been traditionally much dependent on the animal draught power and would continue to be the mainstay of Indian agriculture. A large animal population in relation to available feed and fodder resources coupled with inadequate reach of transfer of technology programmes especially in the hinterland has been the main constraint in animal production.

India now feeds over one billion people and 760 million livestock from about 190 million hectares of cultivable land. Mixed farming systems have been a traditional practice. Better arable land is used more and more for food and cash crops. The grassland and fodder crops not only receive a low priority in the quality of land available for cultivation but also in the use of fertilizer. In India, scientific range management began with the setting up of the Indian Grassland and Fodder Research Institute (IGRRI) in 1962. Over years, the IGFRI has concentrated on: evolving improved varieties of pasture and fodder crops; developing soil-enriching forage crops in order to use neglected lands; providing quality seed to ensure sown pastures in the rangelands for the livestock to browse; bringing about adjustments of soil nutrients by matching biofertilizer affinities and by balancing management to integrate the growth cycle of the plant for animal requirements. Additionally, to improve productivity of such land, and to raise and diversify total production, complementary land-use systems have been suggested.

Fish is a dynamic and renewable resource with considerable potential. It is also a very economical and rich source of animal protein. Out of the 23% of India's total animal protein supply in the diet, fish accounts for a mere 2.3% even when a wide variety of species contribute to the total production. Fish-eating population is generally restricted. India ranks seventh in the world and first among Commonwealth countries in fish production. However, only 10% of the produce is exported. India is the second largest fish producer from inland sources after China.

HOSPITAL FOR PLANTS

With the Green Revolution the consumption of various agricultural inputs have increased to a considerable extent. The consumption of fertilisers and pesticides has increased tremendously. These high consumption of inputs and intensive cultivation of crops along with the high yielding varieties accentuated the problems of pests, diseases and other disorders. The pests and diseases, which were of secondary importance before, have proved to be of prime concern. Similarly, soil fertility has been reduced, resulting in deficiency of nutrients in major food crops although intensity varied from place to place. Plants can't talk. They can't tell us about their problems and diseases. So it is not easy to diagnose their diseases. Keeping this in mind a plant clinic was set up in 1998 managed by the Department of Plant pathology, Punjab Agricultural University (PAU). It was the first clinic of its kind in the whole of the North. As so many people were coming to the plant clinic with their problems, the need was felt to broadbase the clinic and to appoint experts so that better advice could be given to the farmers. Experts from the Departments of Entomology, Plant Pathology, Soil Science and Agronomy are appointed to render expert advice to farmers. Entomologist are engaged in the identification of insects and the symptoms of damage, whereas pathologists deal with plant disorders due to pathogens, soil scientists lock into the disorders due to the nutrient deficiencies or toxicity and other physiological aspects of plant health. Agronomic experts provide knowledge to the farmers in crop production technology including need management with particular reference to integrated weed management. These clinics function directly under the Director of Extension Education.

The plant clinic has a full-fledged laboratory which is equipped with scientific equipment for immediate diagnosis of a disorder. Apart from common diseases, which farmers are aware of, there are more complex problems beyond the understanding of farmers. The diagnosis of these problems requires expertise. The function of the experts starts as soon as the farmers come to purchase the seeds. When they come to buy seeds, experts at the clinic advise the farmers about the variety of the crop to be sown, when it should be sown, which fertilisers have to be used and in what quantity. They also advise farmers about the deficiency of the nutrients, seed treatment for the control of seed-borne diseases and spray schedule to be followed for the control of diseases which appear later on, especially for vegetables crops.

A useful purpose of plant clinic is that the university is getting necessary feedback for reorienting its research programmes and fixing research priorities in agriculture. The clinic also conducts a practical course for the students on B.Sc. Agriculture so that they don't face any difficulty when they go to the field as it brings interaction between students and farmers and inculcates the abilities of good extension workers in the students and gives them practical training in diagnosing the plant disorder.

New Seed Policy

As part of an all-encompassing Seeds Policy 2001, the government proposes to take a series of initiatives including plant variety protection, setting up of a national gene fund, accelerating seed production and exports and ensure seed quality through National Seed

Board (NSB). The seeds sales, imports and export would be regulated by a new Seeds Act under which for quality control, all seeds would have to be compulsorily registered with National Seed Board. Part of the policy is expected to get Union Cabinet's clearance by December 2001, NSB would then replace the Central Seed Committee and Central Seed Certification Board. The policy envisages increase in share of global seeds export market to 10 per cent from one per cent and simultaneous import of the best planting material.

It also concedes that genetically-modified seeds would increase productivity and improve quality, but would have to adhere to safety norms set by the government like environmental, health and biodiversity safety under the Environment Protection Act before commercial release. Transgenic seeds varieties would be imported only after clearance from Genetic Engineering Approval Committee and tested to determine their agronomic value by the Indian Council of Agricultural Research. The export initiative includes encouraging custom production of seeds, strengthening of seeds export promotion zones, quality promotional programmes and creation of a data bank on international marker information and potential.

Referral Laboratory after the introduction of new seeds it was realised that the productivity improvements achieved as a result of Green Revolution were plateauing and there was need for a holistic approach for agriculture while continuing emphasis on marketing and income to farmers. It was perceived that our soils are getting depleted of nutrients, particularly of micronutrients and there is unnecessary use of pesticides. National Agro Foundation established for bringing awareness of the emerging needs to the farming community. This is the first project in the country that is a Referral Laboratory. This was established on October 7, 2000, the *Vijayadasami* day to make a lasting contribution to agriculture.

AGRICULTURE IN THE NATIONAL ECONOMY

India's 72 per cent of the population (about 700 million people) lives in rural areas. Among them about 400 million are in the age group of 16 to 59 years, which is about 67 per cent of the total labour force in the country. An estimated 135 million cultivators operate 142 million hectares of land area (net sown area). Besides the cultivator households, about 90 million agricultural labourers derive their livelihood from the prosperity of agriculture. The fortunes of remaining non-agricultural workers in the rural area, though not directly dependent on agriculture, are also influenced by agricultural growth to a considerable extent. Indian agriculture has changed in numerous ways: it is not any more dominated by subsistence farming. It is not merely producing foodgrains. Chemical fertilisers, tractors, tillers, combine harvesters, and diesel/electric pump sets are a fairly common part of agricultural landscape in the country today. The increase in crop area—

a major contributor to the crop output quite some time back—stopped. It is the increase in double cropped area and yield per hectare of land, a result of green revolution that has sustained crop output growth in the 1980s and 1990s.

Investments in irrigation facilities and expansion of credit facilities, marketing and processing facilities have led to the increased use of purchased inputs and hence higher productivity. These developments have also led to increased supplies of agricultural produce to the market rather than for own consumption by the farm households. Green revolution has been followed by White revolution, Yellow revolution, and then Blue revolution, leading to increase in the growth of milk production, oilseeds production, and production of fish and fish products. Despite these changes, the challenge in the agricultural sector however remains stiff. Increased investments are needed to accelerate the growth in productivity. Investments in providing better technology to the farmers for production, storage, and transportation and processing facilities are the need of the hour.

Opportunities for increasing the agricultural output are enormous, but the higher agricultural output has to be of better quality and will have to be achieved with greater efficiency. Inputs supplied to agriculture also need to be better and more efficient. Within agriculture, returns to improved overall efficiency can be gauged from the fact that estimated post-harvest losses of output in storage and transit are as high as 10 per cent on an average for many crops and 30 to 40 per cent in the case of fruits and vegetables. There are challenges to policy makers to create an environment that will enable full exploitation of the true potential of the agricultural sector to improve incomes of rural households. Clearly the government alone cannot achieve this goal and there has to be a partnership between the farmers, industry, and the government.

As agriculture is the main source of employment in rural areas, the share of income derived from farming (including agricultural wages) is about 56 per cent. Given that farm income accounts for a little over half the purchasing power in rural areas, rapid growth in the agricultural sector is essential to raise household income in rural areas. Faster growth in agriculture not only increases the income derived from agriculture but also supports growth in non-farm income due to its linkages with demand for inputs, marketing services, and industrial goods. This is more so in a situation in which majority of the producers of goods and services depend heavily on domestic demand and exports constitute a relatively small share of total sales, which is evident from the share of exports of gross domestic product (GDP). Currently, the ratio of exports to GDP is roughly 10.2 per cent (2001-01).

Keeping the above in view, the importance of rural sector in influencing the growth of industry and services hardly needs any emphasis. Yet it is useful to draw attention to some basic facts about agriculture and industry linkages. Linkages between agricultural and the non-agricultural sectors are manifold. Agricultural sector, including the allied activities such as livestock, forestry and fisheries, purchases manufactured goods worth Rs 33,400 crore as inputs (NationalAccounts Statistics). This includes fertilisers, pesticides, tractors, and pump-sets besides other products such as agricultural implements. The sector also purchases infrastructure services worth Rs 23,500 crore and other services worth Rs 24,000 crore. The manufacturing sector purchased agricultural output worth Rs 80,000 crore for further processing.

Both urban and rural households purchase 28 per cent of the manufacturing sector's output as consumer goods. And rural households account for 57 per cent of the total consumer expenditures on manufactured products, which means that rural households purchase over Rs 100,000 crore worth of manufactured consumer goods every year. Apart from these national aggregates the data gathered at the National Council of Applied Economic Research (NCAER) shows that the rural market for consumer durable and consumables is increasing at a much faster rate than the urban market. For some products the rural market is already much bigger than the urban market. For instance, the share of rural areas in the market for items such as bicycles, mechanical wristwatches, radios, and black and white televisions is more than 75 per cent. For other items such as cassette recorders, pressure cookers, table fans, sewing machines, quartz wristwatches, ceiling fans, and motorcycles too the rural market dominates the urban market with share ranging between 50 and 75 per cent.

The same is the case with consumables as well. In the case of toothpowder, the share of rural areas is above 75 per cent and for washing cake, washing powder, edible oil, *vanaspati*, toilet soap, cigarettes, soap, footwear, tea and hair oil, the share of rural areas varies between 50 and 75 per cent. Despite such high shares, rural market also has a huge untapped potential, which is indicated by the penetration rates defined as the number of products owned/purchased per 1000 households. For most of the items, with the exceptions of products such as transistors and bicycles in the case of durable items and washing cakes, toothpowder, edible oils and toilet soaps in the case of consumables, rural penetration rates continue to remain lower than urban penetration rates. These vast differences between the rural and urban areas are also evident from ownership pattern of durable products.

The reasons for such low rates of penetration in rural areas include low levels of income, weak rural infrastructure, differences in lifestyles and also inefficient distribution networks, which are a consequence of weak infrastructure. The inadequacy of basic infrastructure (such as roads and power) is reflected in statistics, which reveal that close to 40 per cent of the country's villages are without proper roads. The rural market is scattered and goods are usually bought in the nearby small towns. As distances between villages and small towns are very large, reaching these consumers is very expensive and involves huge costs.

The state of affairs on rural electrification is no better either. After 54 years of independence, close to 17 per cent of the villages are still without electricity (statewise details are shown in the Table 1.2). The record of connecting every rural household with electricity is equally poor, with only 40 per cent of the households having electricity connections. Lack of electricity connections could be the single-most

Table 1.2 Current Status of Rural Infrastructure (Selected Variables)

State	Road length in km[1] (year 2000)	Villages covered by rural telephone exchanges[2] (year 1999)	Percentage of habitations covered under accelerated rural water supply programme (ARWSP) (ARWSP) and minimum needs programme (MNP)[3] (year 1999)	Number of villages electrified as a per centage of the total number of villages[4] (year 1999)
Andhra Pradesh	3542.60	79.30	100.00	100.00
Bihar	3493.82	25.70	99.50	67.20
Gujarat	3556.13	76.80	98.60	99.80
Haryana	3459.02	99.40	99.60	100.00
Himachal Pradesh	3268.24	45.80	91.73	97.40
Karnataka	3528.66	86.30	97.30	100.00
Kerala	3451.44	100.00	91.00	100.00
Madhya Pradesh	3534.26	60.10	98.80	95.43
Maharashtra	3679.47	73.90	*	100.00
Orissa	3418.61	44.30	98.27	73.30
Punjab	3491.33	95.20	56.54	100.00
Rajasthan	3511.43	60.00	95.50	92.22
Tamil Nadu	3562.59	99.10	*	100.00
Uttar Pradesh	3613.59	49.70	*	78.58
West Bengal	3579.51	43.00	*	77.56

Notes: *Maharashtra, Tamil Nadu, Uttar Pradesh and West Bengal had reached the 100 per cent mark in 1997 and till (as on 1999) maintaining the level.

SOURCES: 1. Projections as part of SRTT Rural Infrastructure based on primary district level data collected by International Crop Research Institute for the Semi Arid Tropics, (ICRISAT) Pattancheru, Hyderabad (1998-99).

2. Government of India (1999), Indian Telecommunications Statistics 1999, Ministry of Communications, Department of Telecommunications, Economic Research Unit.

3. Government of India (1993), Annual Reports, Ministry of Rural Development, Government of India.

4. Tata Energy Research Institute (2000-01), TERI Energy Data Directory and Yearbook, Tata Energy Research Institute (TERI), New Delhi.

OUR SOURCE: Facts For You, November 2001.

important explanatory variable accounting for huge rural-urban differentials in penetration levels for some of the products that run on electricity.

The changes in income distribution as tracked by the NCAER's consumer surveys reveal that there is an increasing trend in the share of higher-income categories over time. For instance, the proportion of households in the category of less than Rs 30,000 annual income declined from 67 per cent in 1989-90 to 48 per cent in 1998-99. Taking this trend and the rate of change in household income by 4 per cent per year, the proportion of rural households below Rs 30,000 annual income (in 1997-98 prices) drops further to 35 per cent by 2005-06. The decline in lower-income groups and the rise in higher-income groups clearly have significance to the pattern of demand for goods and services originating from the rural areas.

THE DEMOGRAPHIC BACKGROUND

Census

The first all-India census, though not synchronously taken, was completed in 1872. Since 1881, census in India has been taken up regularly every ten years. The 1981 census marked the completion of 100 years of regular decennial census-taking in the country. According to the 1991 census, the total population of India was 846,303 millions. As compared to the 1981 census, it showed an increase of 23.85 per cent indicating an annual growth rate of 2.4 per cent as against almost 2.5 per cent in the previous decade. This has been possible by reducing the birth rate through sustained family welfare programmes and spread of education. By the end of 1999, however, India's population had touched 1 billion mark, which is one-sixth of world's population. Projected population of India by 2025 is 1330 million. Table 1.3 shows

Table 1.3 Population of India 1901-2001

Year	*Number in million*
1901	238.4
1921	251.3
1941	318.7
1951	361.1
1961	439.2
1971	548.2
1981	683.3
1991	843.9
2001	1027.0

SOURCE: Registrar General and Census Commissioner for India.

Note: For State-wise population data refer to BANSIL, PC: *Agricultural Statistical Compendium — Foodgrains.*

population growth since 1901. The average density of population per sq.km in 1991 was 274. It varied considerably from state to state, being as high as 6352 (Goa, Daman & Diu) and as low as 10 (Arunachal Pradesh) and 33 (Mizoram) as shown in Tables 1.4 and 1.4A.

Table 1.4 1991 Census Highlights

			2001	*1991*	*1981*
Population of India	Millions	Persons	1027.0	846.3 (1)	685.2
	"	Males	531.3	439.2	354.4
	"	Females	495.7	407.1	330.8
Sex Ratio			933	929	933
Density of Population (persons/sq km)			324	267	221
Birth rate (per 1000)				29.5	37.2
Death rate (per 1000)				9.8	15.0
Life expectancy at birth	Years	Total		60.8	50.4
	Years	Male		61.2	50.0
	"	Female		60.4	50.9
Decennial Growth Rate	Percent		21.34	21.4	22.2
Literacy rate (percentage)		Total	65.38	52.2	43.56
		Male	75.85	64.1	56.37
		Female	54.16	39.3	29.75
Proportion of urban population to total population	Percent			25.71	23.31
Percentage of workers to total population (Main activity only)		Total		32.95	32.21
		Males		49.18	49.66
		Females		15.46	13.54

NB 1. Final figure after accounting for adjustment for under enumeration is 861.4 million. Distribution of this into male/female and rural/urban etc. is not available.

SOURCE: Office of the Registrar general, Census, Ministry of Home affairs.

For every 1000 males, India has 927 females. Only Kerala among the states have more women (1036) than men. The lowest female ratio among the states is in Arunachal Pradesh (859). Among the union territories, the lowest female ratio is in Chandigarh where it is 790 (Table 1.5). In some parts of Bihar and Rajasthan, there are only 600 women per 1000 men. The unfavourable sex ratio in the country indicates neglect of girl child and illiteracy among the people. Female literacy rate is the highest in Kerala (86.17 %) as per data shown in Table 1.6.

Rural and Urban Population

A very interesting feature of the population growth is its distribution between rural and urban areas. During the last three decades rural

Table 1.4A Highlights of 1991 Census: State-Wise

State	Annual exponential growth rate 1981-91 (Per cent)	Population aged 0-6 years as percentage of total population	Density population per Sq Km
India	2.14	17.94	274
Andhra Pradesh	2.17	16.49	242
Arunachal Pradesh	3.14	21.12	10
Assam	2.17	19.73	286
Bihar	2.11	20.57	497
Goa	1.49	11.74	316
Gujarat	1.92	16.53	211
Haryana	2.42	18.98	372
Himachal Pradesh	1.89	16.25	93
Jammu & Kashmir	2.54	NA	NA
Karnataka	1.92	16.63	235
Kerala	1.34	13.19	749
Madhya Pradesh	2.38	19.78	149
Maharashtra	2.29	17.11	257
Manipur	2.57	16.69	82
Meghalaya	2.84	22.18	79
Mizoram	3.34	18.60	33
Nagaland	4.45	17.15	73
Orissa	1.83	16.89	203
Punjab	1.89	16.30	403
Rajasthan	2.50	20.13	129
Sikkim	2.51	18.37	57
Tamil Nadu	1.43	13.33	429
Tripura	2.95	18.03	263
Uttar Pradesh	2.27	20.27	473
West Bengal	2.21	16.98	767
Andaman & Nicobar Islands	3.97	16.51	34
Chandigarh	3.52	14.92	5632
Dadra & Nagar Haveli	2.89	20.46	282
Daman & Diu	2.52	15.53	907
Delhi	4.15	17.06	6352
Lakshadweep	2.51	18.30	1616
Pondicherry	2.90	13.67	1642

SOURCE: Census of India 1991, Series-1, Paper 2 of 1992—Final Population Totals—Brief Analysis of Primary Census Abstracts.

population has declined from 82.03 per cent of the total in 1961 to 72.0 per cent in 2001 (Table 1.7). Out of 3696 Urban agglomerations/* towns in the country (excluding Jammu & Kashmir) according to the 1991 Census, in 300, the population exceeds 100,000 each. The range

* According the new definition (79th Constitutional Amendment 1993), the total of towns and agglomerations according to 2001 Census is 4368.

Table 1.5 State-wise Sex Ratio (Females/1000 Males)

State	1971	1981	1991
Andhra Pradesh	977	975	972
Arunachal Pradesh	860	862	996
Assam	897	NA	922
Bihar	953	945	910
Goa	989	981	966
Gujarat	934	941	934
Haryana	866	870	865
Himachal Pradesh	958	972	975
Jammu & Kashmir	877	891	NA
Karnataka	956	962	959
Kerala	1016	1031	1036
Maharashtra	930	936	933
Manipur	980	970	957
Meghalaya	941	953	955
Mizoram	945	919	921
Madhya Pradesh	941	940	931
Nagaland	870	863	886
Orissa	987	981	970
Punjab	864	878	881
Rajasthan	910	918	909
Sikkim	862	834	878
Tamil Nadu	978	976	973
Tripura	942	946	944
Uttar Pradesh	878	884	878
West Bengal	890	911	917
All India	930	934	927

SOURCE: CMIE, India's Social Sectors, February 1996.

of variation in the population of these 300 cities is quite high being 12.57 million in Greater Bombay Urban Agglomeration of Maharashtra and 1,00,109 in Haldia Notified Area in Medinipur district of West-Bengal. The average population per city works out to 467,000. There are 13 urban agglomerations (UA) which have a population of more than 15 lakhs. They are; Greater Bombay (12, 571, 720), Calcutta (10,916,272), Delhi (8,375,188), Hyderabad (4280,261), Bangalore (4,086,548), Ahmedabad (3,297,625), Pune (2485,014), Kanpur (2,111,284), Nagpur (1,661,409), Lucknow (1,642,134), Surat (1,517,076) and Jaipur (1,514,425). Other basic demographic indicators like density, life expectation etc. are as in Tables 1.8 to 1.10.

Population Policy

Maharaja Krishna Rajendra Wodeyar of Mysore was the first ruler of a state in the world to introduce family planning as a state policy in

Table 1.6 Literacy Rate: Population—1991

(Per cent)

State	Total	Male	Female
India	52.21	64.13	39.29
Andhra Pradesh	44.09	55.13	32.72
Arunachal Pradesh	41.59	51.45	29.69
Assam	52.89	61.87	43.03
Bihar	38.48	52.49	22.89
Goa	75.51	83.64	67.09
Gujarat	61.29	73.13	48.64
Haryana	55.85	69.10	40.47
Himachal Pradesh	63.86	75.36	52.13
Jammu & Kashmir	NA	NA	NA
Karnataka	56.04	67.26	44.34
Kerala	89.81	93.62	86.17
Madhya Pradesh	44.20	58.42	28.85
Maharashtra	64.87	76.56	52.32
Manipur	59.89	71.63	47.60
Meghalaya	49.10	53.12	44.85
Mizoram	82.27	85.61	78.60
Nagaland	61.67	67.62	54.75
Orissa	49.09	63.09	34.68
Punjab	58.51	65..66	50.41
Rajasthan	38.55	54.99	20.44
Sikkim	56.94	65.74	46.69
Tamil Nadu	62.66	73.75	51.33
Tripura	60.44	70.58	49.65
Uttar Pradesh	41.60	55.73	25.31
West Bengal	57.70	67.81	46.56
Andaman & Nicobar Islands	73.02	78.99	65.46
Chandigarh	77.81	82.04	72.34
Dadra & Nagar Haveli	40.71	53.66	26.98
Daman & Diu	71.20	82.66	59.40
Delhi	75.29	82.01	66.99
Lakshadweep	81.78	90.18	72.89
Pondicherry	74.74	83.68	65.63

SOURCE: Census of India 1991, Series-1, Paper 2 of 1992—Final Population Totals—Brief Analysis of Primary Census Abstracts.

1932 and India was the first nation to proclaim it as a national policy in 1950. Yet our population growth rate has not dropped below 1.8 per cent annually. There are several impediments but the methods of implementing the programme are also varied and each method has its own effectiveness. Actually the world over, family planning methods are wide ranging from adopting a "one child norm" in China to giving cash incentives in several countries and promoting consciousness

Table 1.7 Rural and Urban Population in India

(Million)

Year	Rural	Urban	Total
1951	298.7	62.4	361.1 (100)
1961	360.3	78.9	439.2 (100)
1971	439.1	109.1	548.2 (100)
1981	525.5	159.7	685.2 (100)
1991	628.7	217.6	846.3 (100)
2001	742.0	285.0	1027.0

Table 1.8 Density and Increase of Population

Year	Density per sq.km	Decade	Percentage increase in population
1921	81		
1931	90	1921-31	11.0
1941	103	1931-41	14.2
1951	117	1941-51	13.3
1961	142	1951-61	21.6
1971	177	1961-71	24.6*
1981	221	1971-81	25.0*
1991	274	1981-91	23.8

through education in all countries. According to present demographic trends, India is expected to reach the critical transition point of a total fertility rate of 2.1 by the year 2026. A generation, after this is reached, around 2050, the population is likely to stabilise. There are, however, major state-level variations which must be taken into account in formulating population policy. Thus, Rajasthan is expected to reach the transition point in 2048, Bihar in 2039, Madhya Pradesh beyond 2060 and Uttar Pradesh beyond 2100.

With this ground situation, this is a time for reflection, introspection and a more responsible and responsive behaviour by the government as well as the civil society. Rightly so, as food requirements, public health measures and inequalities in nutrition, drinking water availability will be amongst the major challenges before the country. The scenario is already bleak:

(i) The under-five mortality in India is 115 compared to 10 in the US.

(ii) The per cent of underweight children in India is 53 compared to less than 1 per cent in the US.
(iii) There are as many illiterate and poor persons as the entire population of India in 1947.
(iv) Only two-thirds of children aged 6-14 attended school in 1992-93 and just over half the population completes more than four years of education.
(v) More than 300 million women do not have access to contraceptives.
(vi) About six lakh women die as a result of pregnancy and 70,000 lives are lost in a year due to unsafe abortions.

Table 1.9 Birth and Death Rates and Life Expectancy

Decade	*Per thousand*		*Expectation of life at birth*	
	Birth rate (estimated)	*Death rate (estimated)*	*Males*	*Female*
1921-31	46.4	36.3	26.91	26.56
1931-41[1]	45.2	31.2	32.09	31.37
1941-51	39.9	27.4	32.45	31.66
1951-61	41.7	22.8	41.90	40.60
1961-71	41.2	19.0	47.10[2]	45.60[2]
1971-81	37.2	15.0	N.A.	N.A.
1981-91	32.5	11.4	N.A.	N.A.

1. Unofficial estimates
Provisional, based on one per cent sample data.
N.A. -Not available.

Table 1.10 Expection of Life at Birth by Sex

Year	*Male*	*Female*	*Person*
1971-81	50.9	50.0	50.5
1981-85	55.4	55.7	55.4
1981-86	55.6	56.4	56.0
1981-88	55.9	55.9	55.9*
1986-91	58.1	59.1	58.6
1991-96	60.6	61.7	61.1
1996-2001	62.8	64.2	63.5
2001	64.1	65.6	64.9
2006	64.8	65.6	65.1

Note: The data for the years marked with (*) are the Projected Values. Office of the Registrar General, India.

SOURCE: Census of India 1981, Series-1, Occasional, Paper-1 of 1984 and Report of the Expert Committee on Population.

The objective of population policy has to be to advance the stabilisation date for the country as a whole as early as possible. It is believed that the spread of female literacy, the empowerment of women, the provision for late marriage, availability of many health facilities and an innovative communications campaign constitute the key components of a strategy aimed at drastically reducing the growth in our population—which is the most serious challenge which the nation is confronted with. Real solution, however, will lie to empower the people, specially the young ones, and they will take care of themselves. Effectively implement the population policy which should focus on health, education and reversible contraceptive methods, laying greater emphasis on women.

Population Commission

The Central Government has announced the composition of the National Population Commission to be headed by the Prime Minister. The Commission will review implementation of the family welfare programme in the country and coordinate the various reproductive health programme, Besides political representatives, the Commission will include demographic and public health experts, NGOs and media professionals. The latest National Family Health Survey (NFHS-2) says that if the country implements its recently framed National Population Policy then its population in 2045 could be 1.3 billion, instead of 1.5 billion. Proper implementation of the Population Policy, linked to the success of the reproductive and child health programme, could prevent 0.2 billion births. The Survey says that two-thirds of the country's population growth in the 20th Century took place after 1971. The growth rate peaked during 1961-1981 and has since shown a gradual decline with a decline in fertility.

The setting up of the Commission is justified for better coordination among various departments such as Planning Commission, Health and Family Welfare, Women and Child Development, Education and Rural Development. More than anything else, the Commission would emphasise a "political will" to tackle the population problem, in a coordinated manner. The Ministry for Family Welfare, planned a four-pronged strategy: rapid reduction of infant and child mortality; sustained reduction in maternal mortality; meeting the unmet needs of family planning and related services such as primary health care and contraceptives; and quality of care.

World Situation

As the world population crossed the six billion mark on October 12, 1999, it was even more significant for the country as India contributes nearly one sixth of it. Almost 78 million people are being added globally every year and the growth is concentrated in some of the poorest countries. This is the first time in history that the human population reached this figure. In the last quarter of a century, the population has increased by 50 per cent from 4 billion. A four fold increase in just this century! Before that it had taken about 400 years for the population to triple to about 1.5 billion in 1900. And in the preceding 500 years, between 1000 and 1500 AD, the population was estimated to have merely doubled from around 250-300 million to 500-550 million.

The world population growth rate was running at a record high of 2 per cent annually, even reaching 2.5 per cent in the poorer nations. Today the average rate is 1.33 per cent. The pessimists have often been proved wrong, among them 18th century Englishman Robert Malthus, one of the early pioneers of the science of economics, who direly warned about the situation in his "essay of the Principle of Population" back in 1798. Malthus' warning regarding population growth and declining farm yields due to soil depletion. Without "abstinence from sexual intercourse", he warned, there would be misery, hunger and diseases, resulting in rising mortality rates. At the time, there were just around one billion people on earth. There are both positive and negative aspects of population growth. The half century, from 1950, has seen more growth in the human population than in the four million years since the beginning of the human race. It is estimated that in the next 50 years anything from two to four billion people shall be added to the current six billion population of the Earth.

Basically population growth depends on two factors: decreasing birth rates and increasing death rates. The latter is what is known as `demographic fatigue' when more people die than are born. Even near-historically it has happened several times. The Black Death plague in the 14th century wiped out 25 million people, or one-fourth of the then population of Europe; smallpox in the 16th century decimated Inca, Aztec and native American civilizations in the New World, killing an estimated 15 million; the influenza pandemic of 1918-19 took a toll of 25-40 million worldwide, with 12.5 million deaths in India alone.

Today the situation is that AIDS has already claimed over 12 million lives since 1980 with more than 35 million people additionally infected with the HIV virus. Unless an effective and cheap vaccine and drug is developed in the next 10 years or so, they too will remain near-death events. Also, according to one source, if the epidemic continues for even a few more years, it would claim more lives in the early 21st century than World War II did. What is alarming in all this is, cash-strapped governance in non-developed countries could unwittingly create situations in the future which could force such demographic fatigue in order to check their burgeoning populations.

Life expectancy is rising: It is 65 years today, 20 years more than it was in 1950. The problem of care for the elderly will also increase. People never could be taught to accept the "abstinence from sexual intercourse", which Malthus, a clergyman, preached as the most effective all-purpose cure. But there have been efforts, despite the Vatican mandate which strictly reject artificial birth control no matter what the population growth might be, by the humankind to try to reduce the number of births.

China, with its 1.3 billion people, has achieved considerable success with its stringent one-child per family policy. India, which already has one billion people, wanted to adopt a different path. First Prime Minister Jawaharlal Nehru worried more about the buildup of large-scale industry than about the population growth. When his daughter Indira Gandhi tried to make up for the time lost with a programme of mass sterilization in the 1970s, she was voted out of power. "Our masses will accept no forced methods of family planning." Indian politicians also know this, and as a result, India's population is growing by 18 million annually. By UN data, the average woman in Asia bears 2.6 children. In Latin America the figure is 2.7, while in North America it is 1.9 and in Europe, 1.4.

Half the world is under 25 years of age and there are over a billion young people in the 15–24 age group parents of the next generation. So the world population will continue to grow in the next few decades due to both improved health care and the large base of the reproductive group. The population division of the UN. Department for Social and Economic Affairs projects it to reach 8.9 billion in 2050 lower than the 9.4 billion that was predicted in 1996. Unfortunately, most of the growth takes place in the poorest and least-prepared countries. The fastest growth regions are sub-Saharan Africa and parts of South and Western Asia. Of the 4.8 billion people living in the developing countries, three-fifths lack basic sanitation, one-third have no access to clean water; one-fourth do not have adequate housing and one-fifth have no access to modern health services.

Demographic factors such as the presence of an unprecedented number of young people, an aging population, urbanization and international migration assume importance in planning for poverty alleviation, provision of the basic social services, ensuring food security, conserving resources and protecting the environment. According to the UNFPA's `State of the World Population' report for 1999, "a demographic transition from high to low fertility and mortality is under way and has already occurred in much of the world. Global life expectancy has risen from 46 to 66 years in the past half century." But progress varies widely from region to region and within a country too.

It is believed that the food production may fail to meet the demands from a growing a population. If this comes true, then at least farmers of the world would have something to celebrate because of the rising food prices. However, today farmers world over are more concerned about falling prices of their produce. In some parts of the world governments are paying farmers not to produce. Among current arguments against biotechnology lies the fear that productivity may increase still further and force the prices down even more.

It is said that the high consumption pattern in the developed world deprives the poorer countries, although the falling prices clearly indicate that there is no scarcity of natural resources. After all, humans do not just consume; they also produce. In fact, greater the number of people, greater the demand for goods and services. But, in an open market characterised by free trade and competition, this also provides incentives to producers to discover new knowledge and innovate cheaper and better means of meeting the demand. And then as economics of scale strikes from larger demand, the prices per unit of the product fall. It seems paradoxical, more people lead to increased demand, but also an opportunity to produce more. Consequently the more one consumes, the more there is to consume !

The only thing which in a free market actually appreciates in value is the price of human labour. More number of human beings—free, enterprising and skilled—far from lowering the wage rate actually pushes it up. The reason we see is a rising standard of living. More significant than 6 billion, perhaps is the period sometime in the middle of the next decade, when 50 per cent of the world's population is projected to be living in urban area. Urbanisation not only improves the quality of life, mortality and infant mortality is much better in cities than in the countryside, for instance, but it also helps in increasing the rural productivity as fewer people depend on land for their survival. Labour becomes more mobile and therefore, available for more productive purposes.

No doubt there are may problems. Environmental problem is at the top of the agenda today. But environmental quality is just like any other valuable resource. The problem, therefore, stems primarily from the failure to bring environmental resources to the discipline of the market forces by instituting property rights and market prices. If there are no physical shortages, why does poverty persist? The answer lies in the policies. It is not population but policies that are the cause of poverty. These have curtailed people's opportunity to seek newer, better and cheaper economic options. The resulting misallocation of resources is manifested in the problem of poverty amidst plenty.

Economic Structure

There has been a steady growth in the GDP and per capita income from 1950-51 onwards. The new 1993-94 based GDP series released lately by the Central Statistical Organisation (CSO) shows that GDP growth decelerated significantly in 1997-98. The real GDP growth rate in 2000-01 is estimated at 6 per cent compared with the growth rate of 6.4 par cent achieved in 1999-2000 and 6.6 per cent in 1998-99. Despite deceleration of growth rate for the second consecutive year, India has the distinction of being one of the fastest growing economies in the world. The reduction of overall growth rate of GDP to 6 per cent in 2001-01 is mainly due to a decline in the growth rate of service sector from 9.6 per cent in 1999-2000 to 8.3 per cent (Table 1.11).

Agriculture, forestry and fisheries play a dominant part in the national economy of the country. With an accelerated developmental activity, particularly in the manufacturing and transport sectors, it is a healthy sign that the share of agriculture in gross domestic product has come down from 39.7 per cent in 1981-82 (at 1993-94 prices) to 28.7 per cent in 1999-2000 and 29.0 per cent in 1998-99. (Table 1.11A) Increases in the GNP and per capita incomes both at constant (1993-94) and current prices (Table 1.12) also indicate a steady growth.

RECENT ECONOMIC DEVELOPMENTS AND PROSPECTS

Indian economy has shown remarkable resilience in the face of substantial increase in the international price of crude oil over the last two years. But the prosperity of agricultural production in 2000-01 is not considered bright-due to erratic behaviour of monsoon rainfall over time and space. However, in terms of growth of value added, the agriculture and allied sector taken as a whole is expected to show a marginal increase from 0.7 per cent in 1999-2000 to 0.9 per cent in 2001-01. Production of foodgrains recovered a sharp decline from the record level of 208.9 million tonnes in 1999-2000 to only 199 million tonnes in 2000-01.

After a turnaround in 1999-2000, industrial growth (measured by the Index of Industrial Production) has again slowed down during the year 2000-01 (April–December). Overall industrial growth during 2000-01 (April–December) at 5.7 per cent is lower than 6.4 per cent during the corresponding period of 1999-2000. The factors responsible for the showdown of industrial growth during 2000-01 include lack of domestic demand for intermediate goods, low inventory demand for capital goods, high oil prices, existence of excess capacity in some sectors, business cycle, inherent adjustment lags in industrial restructuring and infrastructure constraints particularly power, roads and transport and a high interest rate environment due to continued high fiscal deficit.

Industrial production measured by the Index of Industrial Production registered a growth rate of 6.6 per cent in 1999-2000 compared to 4.1 per cent in 1998-99. This was due to better performance of the manufacturing sector which recorded a higher growth rate of 7.1 per cent in 1999-2000 when compared to 4.4 per cent in 1998-99. The mining sector recorded a positive growth rate of 1.0 per cent in 1999-2000 compared to a 0.8 per cent decline in 1998-99. Electricity sector in 1999-2000 recorded a growth rate of 6.6 per cent, marginally

Table 1.11 Sectoral Real Growth Rates in GDP (at Factor Cost)

Percentage change over the previous year

	1980-81 to 1991-92	1992-93 to 2000-01	1993-94	1994-95	1995-96	1996-97	1997-98	1998-99 (P)	1999-2000 (Q)	2000-2001 (A)
I. Agriculture and allied	3.9	3.3	4.1	5.0	–0.9	9.6	–2.4	7.1	0.7	0.9
II. Industry	6.3	6.6	5.2	10.2	11.6	7.1	4.3	3.4	6.4	6.5
1. Mining and quarrying	8.4	4.0	1.4	9.3	5.9	0.5	9.8	1.3	1.7	4.5
2. Manufacturing	6.1	7.4	8.5	12.0	14.9	9.7	1.5	2.5	6.8	6.4
3. Electricity, gas & water supply	9.0	5.9	–0.8	9.4	6.8	5.4	7.9	6.4	5.2	5.6
4. Construction	5.2	5.7	0.6	5.5	6.2	2.1	10.2	6.1	8.1	8.7
III. Services	6.4	8.2	7.6	7.1	10.5	7.2	9.8	8.2	9.6	8.3
5. Trade, hotels, transport and communications	5.5	8.3	7.1	10.4	13.3	7.8	7.7	7.1	8.0	8.0
6. Financial, real estate & business services	9.4	8.8	13.1	5.6	8.2	7.0	11.6	8.4	10.1	9.6
7. Community, social and personal services	5.6	7.4	3.5	3.2	7.9	6.3	11.7	9.9	11.8	7.6
IV. Total GDP	5.4	6.4	5.9	7.3	7.3	7.8	4.8	6.6	6.4	6.0

A: Advance estimates Q: Quick estimates P: Provisional

SOURCE: Central Statistical Organisation.

Table 1.11A Estimates of Gross Domestic Product by Industry of Origin-Percentage Distribution (At 1980-81 Prices Till 1992-93 and at 1993-94 Prices Thereafter)

Industry Group	1981-82	1985-86	1986-87	1988-99	1989-90	1990-91	1991-92	1992-93	1993-94	1994-95	1995-96	1996-97	1997-98	1998-99	1999-2000
1. Agriculture, forestry and logging, fishing, mining and quarrying	39.7	36.3	33.2	34.9	33.3	32.9	32.0	32.2	32.8	32.2	30.1	30.4	28.7	29.0	27.5
2. Manufacturing, consumption, electricity gas and water supply	24.7	25.9	27.2	26.7	27.6	28.0	27.3	27.1	23.4	23.6	24.8	24.4	24.7	24.5	24.6
3. Transport, communication and trade	16.7	17.6	18.2	17.6	17.8	17.8	18.1	18.2	21.2	22.1	22.9	23.1	23.3	21.6	21.9
4. Banking and insurance, real estate and ownarship of dwellings and business services	8.7	9.4	9.9	9.8	10.1	10.2	11.2	11.0	11.2	11.0	11.1	11.1	11.4	12.3	12.7
5. Public administration and defence and other services	10.2	10.7	11.5	11.0	11.2	11.1	11.4	11.5	11.6	11.1	11.1	11.0	11.9	12.6	13.2
6. Gross domestic product at factor cost.	100.0	100.0	100.0	100.0	100.0	100.0	100.0	100.0	100.0	100.0	100.0	100.0	100.0	100.0	100.0

SOURCE: National Accounts Statistics Q = Quick estimates

Table 1.12 **Gross National Product and Net National Product**
(New Series Base 1993-94)

Year	Gross national product at factor cost (Rs. crore)		Net national product at factor cost (Rs. crore)		Per capita net national product (Rs.)		Index numbers (1950-51 = 100): Net national product		Index numbers (1950-51 = 100): Per capita net national product	
	At current prices	At 1993-94 prices	At current prices	At 1993-94 prices	At current prices	At 1993-94 prices	At current prices	At 1993-94 prices	At current prices	At 1993-94 prices
1	2	3	4	5	6	7	8	9	10	11
1950-51	9508	139924	9144	132379	254.7	3687.4	100.0	100.0	100.0	100.0
1951-52	10046	143411	9635	135563	264.0	3714.1	105.4	102.4	103.6	100.7
1952-53	9917	147556	9476	139392	254.7	3747.1	103.6	105.3	100.0	101.6
1953-54	10807	156603	10342	148172	272.9	3909.6	113.1	111.9	107.1	106.0
1954-55	10141	163140	9630	154198	249.5	3994.8	105.3	116.5	98.0	108.3
1955-56	10323	167549	9777	158015	248.8	4020.7	106.9	119.4	97.7	109.0
1956-57	12319	177021	11708	166808	292.0	4159.8	128.0	126.0	114.6	112.8
1957-58	12591	174771	11929	163917	291.7	4007.7	130.5	123.8	114.5	108.7
1958-59	14073	187941	13301	176499	318.2	4222.5	145.5	133.3	124.9	114.5
1969-60	14761	191734	13918	179609	326.7	4216.2	152.2	135.7	128.3	114.3
1960-61	16150	205214	15206	192253	350.4	4429.8	166.3	145.2	137.6	120.1
1961-62	17020	211305	15962	197532	359.5	4448.9	174.6	149.2	141.1	120.7
1962-63	18196	215619	17032	200914	375.1	4425.4	186.3	151.8	147.3	120.0

Table 1.12 Gross National Product and Net National Product (Contd.) (New Series Base 1993-94)

Year	Gross national product at factor cost (Rs. crore)		Net national product at factor cost (Rs. crore)		Per capita net national product (Rs.)		Index numbers (1950-51 = 100)			
							Net national product		Per capita net national product	
	At current prices	At 1993-94 prices	At current prices	At 1993-94 prices	At current prices	At 1993-94 prices	At current prices	At 1993-94 prices	At current prices	At 1993-94 prices
1	2	3	4	5	6	7	8	9	10	11
1963-64	20807	226596	19494	210965	420.1	4546.7	213.2	159.4	165.0	123.3
1964-65	24294	243493	22817	226660	481.9	4781.9	249.5	171.2	189.0	129.7
1965-66	25426	234414	23755	216264	489.8	4459.0	259.8	163.4	192.3	120.9
1966-67	28897	236867	26921	217447	543.9	4392.9	294.4	164.3	213.5	119.1
1967-68	33971	255865	31749	235440	627.5	4653.0	347.2	177.9	246.4	126.2
1968-69	35841	262709	33426	241257	645.3	4657.5	365.6	182.2	253.4	126.3
1969-70	39425	279815	36747	257383	694.7	4865.5	401.9	194.4	272.7	131.9
1970-71	41943	293959	38973	270623	720.4	5002.3	426.2	204.4	282.8	135.7
1971-72	44637	296714	41345	272277	746.3	4914.8	452.2	205.7	293.0	133.3
1972-73	49119	295777	45398	270086	800.7	4763.4	496.5	204.0	314.4	129.2
1973-74	60242	309976	55903	283088	963.8	4880.8	611.4	213.8	378.4	132.4
1974-75	71001	314536	65441	286443	1103.6	4830.4	715.7	216.4	433.3	131.0
1975-76	75463	343202	69014	313673	1137.0	5167.6	754.8	237.0	446.4	140.1

Table 1.12 Gross National Product and Net National Product (Contd.)
(New Series Base 1993-94)

Year	Gross national product at factor cost (Rs. crore)		Net national product at factor cost (Rs. crore)		Per capita net national product (Rs.)		Index numbers (1950-51 = 100)			
							Net national product		Per capita net national product	
	At current prices	At 1993-94 prices	At current prices	At 1993-94 prices	At current prices	At 1993-94 prices	At current prices	At 1993-94 prices	At current prices	At 1993-94 prices
1	2	3	4	5	6	7	8	9	10	11
1976-77	81158	347560	74252	316387	1197.6	5103.0	812.1	239.0	470.2	138.4
1977-78	92659	373496	85163	340782	1343.3	5375.1	931.4	257.4	527.4	145.8
1978-79	99680	394368	91106	359765	1406.0	5551.9	996.4	271.8	552.0	150.6
1979-80	109094	374671	98645	338156	1485.6	5092.7	1078.8	255.4	583.3	138.1
1980-81	130539	402004	118252	363451	1741.6	5352.7	1293.3	274.6	683.8	145.2
1981-82	152118	425206	137410	384430	1985.7	5555.3	1502.8	290.4	779.6	150.7
1982-83	168917	436136	151742	392833	2143.3	5548.5	1659.6	296.7	841.5	150.5
1983-84	197717	468742	178152	422714	2464.1	5846.7	1948.4	319.3	967.5	158.6
1984-85	221317	487156	198830	438069	2690.5	5927.9	2174.6	330.9	1056.4	160.8
1985-86	248161	511129	221444	459256	2933.0	6082.9	2421.9	346.9	1151.6	165.0
1986-87	276502	532102	246113	477239	3192.1	6189.9	2691.7	360.5	1253.3	167.9
1987-88	313432	551505	279458	493408	3546.4	6261.4	3056.4	372.7	1392.4	169.8
1988-89	374064	607315	334371	545680	4153.7	6778.6	3656.9	412.2	1630.9	183.8

Table 1.12 Gross National Product and Net National Product (Contd.)
(New Series Base 1993-94)

Year	Gross national product at factor cost (Rs. crore)		Net national product at factor cost (Rs. crore)		Per capita net national product (Rs.)		Index numbers (1950-51 = 100) Net national product		Index numbers (1950-51 = 100) Per capita net national product	
	At current prices	At 1993-94 prices	At current prices	At 1993-94 prices	At current prices	At 1993-94 prices	At current prices	At 1993-94 prices	At current prices	At 1993-94 prices
1	2	3	4	5	6	7	8	9	10	11
1989-90	432383	648246	385823	582656	4693.7	7088.3	4219.6	440.1	1842.9	192.2
1990-91	503544	683850	450280	614386	5366.9	7322.8	4924.6	464.1	2107.2	198.6
1991-92	579196	691347	514794	617576	6014.0	7214.7	5630.2	466.5	2361.2	195.7
1992-93	661763	726586	587251	648393	6734.5	7435.7	6422.6	489.8	2644.2	201.6
1993-94	769265	769265	685912	685912	7698.2	7698.2	7501.6	518.1	3022.5	208.8
1994-95	903975	824816	805981	734358	8876.4	8087.6	8814.8	554.7	3485.1	219.3
1995-96	1059787	886961	941861	787809	10160.3	8498.5	10300.9	595.1	3989.2	230.5
1996-97	1230464	959360	1093961	852085	11600.9	9035.9	11964.3	643.7	4554.8	245.0
1997-98	1376837	1005617	1224787	890712	12771.5	9287.9	13395.1	672.8	5014.5	251.9
1998-99	1601065	1071073	1434456	948982	14712.4	9733.1	15688.2	716.9	5776.5	264.0
1999-2000Q	1771028	1140389	1590301	1011224	16047.4	10204.1	17392.7	763.9	6300.7	276.7

Q: Quick estimates.
SOURCE: Central Statistical Organisation.

higher than 6.5 per cent in 1998-99. During 2000-01 (April–December) industrial production registered a growth rate of 5.7 per cent, contributed by 5.9 per cent in manufacturing, 4.8 per cent in electricity and 4.1 per cent in mining as compared to 6.4 per cent overall contributed by 7.0 per cent, 7.7 per cent and 0.5 per cent respectively during the corresponding period of last-year.

In services sector, trade, hotels, transport & communications are projected to have same growth and business services are expected to experience a lower growth of 9.6 per cent in 2000-01 as against 10.1 per cent in 1999-2000. The community social and personal services group is envisaged to experience the sharpest decline in this sector by recording a growth of 7.6 per cent in 2000-01 compared with 11.8 per cent in 1999-2000. What the economy is now witnessing-low expectations, limited investment and a slow growth in industry—a return to the situation of the mid-late 1990s. This phenomenon has been obscured in recent years by the growth in the service sector and the occasional rebound in agriculture, both of which helped to maintain annual GDP growth at 5 per cent and more. The obsession with information technology has also hidden the deep-seated problems faced by the so-called "old economy" of manufacturing.

What is now becoming apparent is that even as the software industry continues to record growth rates of over 50 per cent, the performance of the manufacturing sector is falling off. The one positive feature so far has been the very healthy growth of merchandise exports. But exports cannot provide all the buoyancy for the industrial sector since they still account for less than 10 per cent of total production in manufacturing. The return of a slowdown in domestic manufacturing highlights once again the continuing importance of government capital expenditure/public sector investment in the economy. The pent-up demand for manufactured goods that could express itself in the first flush of liberalisation boosted industrial growth in the mid-1990s. But once that effect was exhausted, industrial growth began to peter out. That was also when the effects of a continued cut back in government capital expenditure began to bite. Such outlays boost private investment and thereby maintain the momentum in the industrial sector. But central government capital expenditure-mainly in infrastructure-which averaged 6.8 per cent of GDP in 1985-90 declined to an average of 4.6 per cent in 1990-95.

Investment revival and capital goods production are critically dependent on expectation about the future growth of the economy, expected competition (domestic as well as imports), cost structure, technical capabilities and expected profitability of the investment. The high growth in the consumer goods sector is a latest asset and with some restructuring and favourable internal and external environment it has the potential in contributing to a higher growth momentum in all sectors of the industry.

Scenario 2001-02

The latest round of assessments of the economy by different institutions have scaled down the growth forecast for the GDP in 2001-02 to 5.2-5.25 per cent.* A sharp decline in industrial growth seems to be responsible for this downward revision. However, a closer scrutiny reveals that the services sector with a weight of about 50 per cent in the GDP may well be the eventual culprit (Table 1.13). Over the last three years, either the industry or the agriculture had done badly. But a strong growth in services in these years had saved the day as cyclical downturns in agriculture or industry was well compensated for by services. This year, according to CII estimates, while agriculture looks good at 5 per cent, industry is a major let down with only 3 per cent growth expected. If services had grown at its recent average growth rate of 8.3 per cent, it would have made up for industrial slowdown. But that looks almost impossible now.

Table 1.13 GDP Growth by Sectors (1993-94 Prices)

(Per cent)

	Primary	*Industrial*	*Services*	*GDP*
1991-92	– 1.1	– 1.0	4.8	1.3
1992-93	5.4	4.3	5.4	5.1
1993-94	3.9	5.6	7.6	5.9
1994-95	5.3	10.3	7.1	7.3
1995-96	– 0.3	12.3	10.5	7.3
1996-97	8.8	7.7	7.2	7.8
1997-98	– 1.5	3.8	9.8	4.8
1998-99	6.6	3.6	8.2	6.6
1999-00	0.8	6.9	9.6	6.4
2000-01	0.5	5.5	7.7	5.2

SOURCE: CII

Hongkong & Shanghai Banking Corporation Ltd. (HSBC) has captured this importance of services in its recent report 'End of services-pumped GDP growth.' In fact, the HSBC assessment of the economy is very gloomy as it feels that high growth in services in 1990s was a turnout of fortuitous circumstances, occurring one after another. In reasons that in the mid-nineties, the growth in services was due to growth in industry made possible by reforms. When industrial growth started declining due to lack of follow-up reforms, the Fifth Pay Commission grants maintained services on the high growth path. It

* Even this growth is doubtful. This may actually turn out to be below 4-45 per cent.

seems the Indian economy has run out of luck now. It is obvious that services hold the key to Indian economy not only because of the weight it has in the GDP but also for its impact on the current account deficit. While India's trade deficit has steadily increased from 1.5 per cent of GDP in 1993-94 to 3.8 per cent in 1999-2000, the current account deficit has declined from a high of 1.7 per cent in 1995-96 to 9 per cent in 1999-2000. Invisibles, a high portion of which is services are responsible for imparting stability to current account. It is time reforms are undertaken to rule out the chance factor and put services on high growth path.

Despite ten consecutive favourable monsoons, there has been a sharp deceleration in the contribution of agriculture to the Gross Domestic Product at constant prices during the last two years while services, internal trade and insurance and real estate continue to show high growth rates ranging from eight per cent to 10 per cent. While in the first quarter of the current year, agriculture, forestry and fishing registered an increase of 2.3 per cent in its contribution to the GDP compared to 0.5 per cent increase in the first-quarter of 2000-2001, trade, hotels, transport and communication witnessed a 5.2 per cent increase compared with 9.7 per cent in the first quarter of 2000-01. In financing, insurance, real estate and business services, the increase in contribution of the GDP was 9.9 per cent and 9.5 per cent. Production of rice, wheat, coarse cereals and pulses during the rabi season ending June 2001-01 declined by 6.9 , 9.4, 14 and 24.4 per cent over the corresponding season of the previous year. Among commercial crops, oilseeds and cotton registered a negative growth rate of 22.6 and 19.3 per cent respectively during the rabi of 2000-01, while sugarcane registered a marginal positive growth of 0.4 per cent in production during 2000-01. Among the services sectors, the key indicators of railways, namely, the net tonne kilometres and passenger kilometres have shown growth rate of zero per cent and 12.6 per cent in Q1 of 2001-02 as against their respective growth rates of 7 per cent and 5.9 per cent in the corresponding period of 2000-01.

No doubt, in terms of purchasing power parity (which adjusts for the international differences in the prices of goods and services), India ranks among the top ten rich countries in the world. However, when one looks at the per person GDP, India slips down to the bottom. According to the recently released World Bank data, per person GDP is the highest in US, which is almost $ 35,000, followed by Japan, Hong Kong and Singapore. But in case of India, the figure is abysmal at around $ 2,500. Very few countries have per person income which is less than India's. Despite all this, we have no hesitation to say that the gloom and doom are being overdone, that India's current performance is actually pretty good in a global recession. India is an elephant that can neither accelerate nor slow down as much as nimbler neighbours. It is certainly not an Asian tiger. Yet it is currently outperforming all

Table 1.14 Growth Indicators % Change Over Last Year

	GDP	Industrial
China	7.0	9.5
India	4.4	1.8
Indonesia	3.5	7.5
Philippines	3.3	- 2.1
S. Korea	2.7	- 4.7
Thailand	1.9	1.4
Malaysia	0.5	- 7.3
Hong Kong	0.05	- 0.11
Taiwan	- 2.4	- 14.1
Singapore	- 5.6	- 21.4
Japan	- 3.2	- 11.7
USA	0.3	- 5.8
Euro area	0.2	0.4

the Asian tigers (Table 1.14). That has rarely happened in the last fifty years.

India's GDP growth in the second quarter (2001-02) estimated at an annual rate of just 4.4 per cent is barely half of 8-9 per cent of the desired Govt. levels. Industrial growth decelerated in August 2001 to just 1.8 per cent. Yet, if a comparison of India's industrial and GDP growth is made with that of other Asian countries, it becomes evident that India was doing relatively well. Its performance was second only to that of China. The global recession has slowed even China's growth significantly—a falling tide lowers all boats. The data come from The Economist, and are not strictly comparable across countries, yet are good enough to convey the overall picture. Many former superstars of Asia are suffering near-stagnation or even negative growth rates. Singapore's industrial output registered a massive decline of 21.4 per cent in August 2001, and its GDP had fallen to 5.6 per cent in the third quarter. It did not suffer such a severe downturn even in the Asian financial crisis of 1997-99. Taiwan is also reeling, with negative industrial growth of 14 per cent. Malaysia's industrial growth is minus 7.3 per cent, and South Korea's is minus 4.7 per cent. India looks pretty good in comparison.

Japan, the dominant economy in the region and second-largest in the world, is in the doldrums too. Its GDP performance in the last quarter was minus 3.2 per cent. In many past recessions like 1990-91 and 1979-82. Japan's economy rolled on like a juggernaut even the economies of Europe and America sank. That kept the world economy and the Asian economy buoyant. Japan has stagnated for a decade, has lost all confidence in itself, and is the worst performer in the OECD. Not since the Great Depression has there been such a slump simultaneously in all the major world economics.

The impact has been greatest on Asian economies, and the four tigers have seen their exports drop by 20 to 30 per cent. They have suffered from the downturn in their two top customers, the United States of America and Japan. Having based their miraculous growth on labour-intensive goods in the 1960s and 1970s, they graduated to high-tech goods—notably semiconductors, memory chips and computer components—in the 1990s. The technology slump has now left them in dire straits. They cannot return to low-wage industries, nor can they immediately diversify into other areas. Besides, for decades they took advantage of the rapid growth of neighbouring Japan, sharing its prosperity. They are now sharing its stagnation.

The other successful Asian economies—sometimes called mini-tigers or cubs—have been hit by not just the recession but a more long-term problem: the rise of China. Indian businessmen are not alone in feeling they cannot compete with China. That feeling is shared by businessmen in the length and breadth of Asia. After the Asian financial crisis of 1997, all countries in the region devalued relative to the Chinese yuan. Despite that, China continues to beat them comfortably in all labour-intensive lines of production, and increasingly in goods with higher technological levels. The Asian countries that compete most directly with China are Indonesia. Thailand and Malaysia. All three are now in deep trouble.

In sum, we have both good news and bad news. The good news is that, despite its slowdown. India continues to be one of the fastest-growing economies in the world. The bad news is that India cannot hope to kick-start its way out of problems rooted in global phenomena like the recession and rise of China as a super-manufacturer. What can India do in such circumstances? It needs to abandon quick-fix solutions, and focus on various long-term reforms which will improve its competitiveness once the recession is over. Much needs to be done in overhauling infrastructure (especially power), judicial and administrative processes, labour laws, and much else. These reforms will yield no immediate dividends, yet they are vital for improving long-term health. Basic parameters of the Indian economy are presented in Appendices—Appendix 1.1 and 1.2.

Foreign Trade

Development in India's trade and payments over the past five years mark a noticeable structural change towards a more and sustainable balance of payments. During the post liberalisation period, there has been a sharp improvement in the coverage of import payments through export earnings. The coverage ratio has averaged around 88 per cent since 1992-93, compared with only 52.4 per cent at the beginning of the 1980's and about 70 per cent at the end of the 1980s. Over the years there has been notable changes in the volume, composition and direction of our foreign trade. However, a disquieting feature is that exports have been showing a decelerating trend since 1996-97. After three successive years of robust growth at an annual average of 19.7 per cent (in U.S. Dollars) during 1993-94 to 1995-96, export momentum slowed down in 1996-97, with exports registering a modest growth of 5.3 per cent and decelerating further to 1.5 per cent. Both global and domestic factors have contributed to the slow down in export growth in India since 1996-97.

The country's exports forming about 8-9 per cent of GDP, witnessed a noticeable recovery during 1999-2000 registering a growth of 13.2 per cent in dollar terms against the targeted average growth rate of 11.8 per cent in Ninth Plan. Except agriculture & allied products and leather & leather products all major sectors like chemicals & allied products, gems and jewellery, engineering goods, electronics, textiles, readymade garments, etc. have performed well and contributed quite substantially in the export front. The buoyancy in exports is explained partly by the revival of world trade, recovery in the South-East. Asian economics, upward movement in global commodity prices apart from low domestic inflation and a relatively stable exchange rate.

The composition of exports reveals a gradual shift during the nineties. The share of ores and minerals has declined progressively from 4.6 per cent in 1991-92 to 3.1 per cent in 1997-98 and this trend continued in 1998-99 also. The share of manufactured exports, the dominant sector, had been fluctuating in a narrow range around 75 per cent, the share of agriculture had been more variable, declining during 1991-92 to during 1994-95, then rising during the subsequent two years and dropping again since 1997-98. This is in part, due to lack of consistent agricultural export policy and frequent supply constraints restraining aggressive trade promotion efforts.

The OCED region (including USA, E.U. and Japan), Asia and Latin America are the main destinations of our export. While OCED Countries as a group maintained their share (around 56 per cent) in our total exports in 1997-98, the share of advanced industrial economics as a whole declined due to depressed demand in Western Europe and Japan. During the last two to three decades, the fastest-growing economies of the world also had fast growth of (manufactured) exports and employment. Most of these countries have built a much more positive environment of exports (and investment), than we have been able to do. This has two aspects: a liberal and flexible policy regime for export production and marketing and simplified rules and procedures for exporters. The increased opportunity in the area of software and other service exports and knowledge based industries has thrown up additional areas for policy reform and procedural simplification..

Agri-Exports

India's agri-exports can be divided into three broad categories, i.e. export of (a) raw products, (b) semi raw products (c) processed and ready-to-eat products. Raw products exported are essentially of low value high volume nature, while processed products are of intermediate value and limited volume and processed ready-to-eat products are of high value but low volume nature. The major agri-exports of India are cereals (mostly rice-Basmati and non-Basmati), spices, cashew, oilcake/meals, tobacco, tea, coffee and marine products. Value of agri-exports to total exports of the country has been ranging between 15 to 20 per cent. Whereas marine products export has exhibited some uptrend, this advantage was more than offset by sharp decline in export prices of soya meal which of late has been a major export item (Table 1.15).

India's agri-exports face certain constraints that arise from conflicting domestic policies relating to production, storage, distribution, food security, pricing concerns etc. Unwillingness to decide on basic minimum quantities for export makes Indian supply sources unreliable. Higher domestic prices in comparison to international prices of products of bulk exports like sugar, wheat, rice etc. make our exports commercially less competitive. Market intelligence and creating awareness in international market about quality of products need to be strengthened to boost agricultural exports.

Strategy for Doubling Agri Exports by 2007

The Centre has devised a strategy to double agri-exports from the current Rs 10,000 crore within the next five years and is speeding up its commodity specific zones project. The structure envisaged for these zones was dovetailed to the overall strategy of doubling agri exports by end of the tenth five year plan. The emphasis was on convergence of all the existing schemes under one umbrella, coordinated partnership of centre, state governments and private sector and increased focus on each agro-commodity. To achieve the Rs 20,000 crore target all the points in the value chain from seeds to market intervention would be addressed within the zone. The strategy was for end-to-end development of a product and 70 points had been identified including availability of inputs, pre-harvest technology, infrastructure and marketing. To cultivate inherent strength of a commodity in the international market micro-details were being looked into like reducing starch content in potatoes and proper plucking of mangoes from trees so that they did not turn black. Another component was fiscal interventions like concessional duty on capital goods imported for agri-exports.

The agri export zone scheme is being expanded with the number of zones being doubled from ten to 20. The concept of the agri-export zone was introduced in the Exim Policy in March 2001 and ten such zones are now being set up in several States at an estimated investment of Rs. 200 crores. According to the Commerce Ministry, the scheme has become popular and another ten AEZs will be set up in the current financial year. The ten AEZs already sanctioned include those for

Table 1.15 India's Export of Agricultural Products

(Million dollars)

	1996-97	per cent to total Agri.	1997-98	per cent to total Agri.	1998-99	per cent to total Agri.	1999-2000	per cent to total Agri.
Tea	292	4.3	505	7.7	538	9.0	407	7.4
Coffee	402	5.9	456	6.9	411	6.8	315	5.7
Cereals	1104	16.2	910	13.8	1495	24.9	718	13.1
Tobacco	213	3.1	288	4.4	181	3.0	229	4.2
Spices	339	5.0	379	5.8	388	6.5	393	7.2
Cashew	362	5.3	377	5.7	387	6.4	566	10.3
Sesame and niger seeds	78	1.1	81	1.2	78	1.3	86	1.6
Guargum meal	100	1.5	147	2.2	173	2.9	189	3.5
Oil meals	985	14.4	924	14.0	461	7.7	370	6.8
Fruits and vegetables	208	3.0	204	3.1	183	3.1	202	3.7
Processed fruits and juices	59	0.9	73	1.1	69	1.1	113	2.1
Meal and preparations	200	2.9	217	3.3	187	3.1	180	3.3
Marine Products	1129	16.5	1207	18.3	1038	17.3	1180	21.6
Others	1359	19.9	824	12.5	422	7.0	527	9.6
Total agri-exports	6828	100.0	6594	100.0	6014	100.0	5475	100.0
Total country export	33470		35006		33218		37599	
Per cent of agri. to total export	20.4		18.8		18.1		14.6	

pineapple in West Bengal, litchi in Uttranchal, gherkins in Karnataka vegetables in Punjab, mangoes and potatoes in Uttar Pradesh, grapes and wines in Maharashtra, flowers in Tamil Nadu and potatoes in Punjab.

The aim of the AEZ is to take a comprehensive look at a particular product located in contiguous area for the purpose of developing and sourcing the raw materials, their processing and packaging, leading to final exports. Thus, the entire effort is centred around a cluster approach of identifying the potential products, the geographical region in which these are grown and adopting an end to end approach of integrating the entire process from production to market.

After the signing of memoranda of understanding between the representative bodies of the Central and State governments, it is expected that potato exports will commence from Punjab and U.P. shortly. Exports of litchi from Uttaranchal will begin from the next season—June 2002—as necessary preparations are already under way. Similarly, in the case of West Bengal, the State Government is finalising the entrepreneurs with whom the MOUs will be signed soon. Exports from this greenfield AEZ is likely to commence in 2003.

In the case of AEZ for mangoes in U.P., the exports are likely to begin the next season. An overall marketing strategy has already been worked out to promote export of mangoes in specific destinations. Gherkins from Karnataka and vegetables from Punjab are already being exported but the process is being strengthened through interventions under the AEZ scheme.

Agri-Imports

Agri-imports constitute only a small proportion of the country's total imports. During the period 1996-97 to 1999-2000, agri-imports have been in the range of 4 to 7 per cent of the total imports of the country. In recent years, edible oil has become the single largest agri-import accounting for more than 50 per cent of the value of total agri-imports. In 1999-2000, it accounted for as high as 70 per cent of total agri-imports. It zoomed to 4.5 million tonnes during, 2000-01 from 4.19 million tonnes previous year. Another item, which has been accounting for around 10 per cent of total agri-imports is raw cashewnut. Each of the other agricultural and allied products imported into the country—cereals, pulses, spices, sugar, milk and milk products, chicken meat etc.-account for very small proportion of total agri-import, except in some climatically abnormal years warranting relatively larger import of a particular commodity—cereals (mostly wheat) in 1997-98, pulses in 1996-97 and 1997-98 (Table 1.16). Pulses which are primarily imported from Myanmar, Australia, Canada and New Zealand, accounted for 6 per cent of total agri imports valued at $ 10.9 million during 2000-01.

It is generally the policy that import duties should be low for those sensitive essential products where there is a large domestic shortfall

Table 1.16 Import of Agricultural Products

(Million dollars)

	1996-97	Per cent to Agri.	1997-98	Per cent to total Agri.	1998-99	Per cent to total Agri.	1999-2000	Per cent to total Agri.
Cereal	137.2	9.6	291.5	15.8	287.7	9.9	133.6	5.1
Pulses	250.8	17.6	321.4	17.4	168.5	5.8	63.2	2.4
Milk and cream	0.7	—	1.4	0.1	2.9	0.1	22.4	0.9
Cashew nuts	193.7	13.6	206.4	11.2	230.3	7.9	220.0	8.4
Fruits and nut	18.3	1.3	154.7	8.4	159.3	5.5	84.2	3.2
Sugar	0.9	0.1	126.5	6.9	264.1	9.0	255.2	9.7
Oil seeds	1.3	0.1	0.7	—	2.0	0.1	3.1	0.1
Veg. oils	825.1	57.8	743.9	40.3	1803.9	61.8	1842.5	70.2
Total Agri. imports	1428.0	100.0	1846.7	100.0	2918.8	100.0	2624.1	100.0
Total country import	39132.9		41484.5		42388.7		47212.1	
Percent of Agri. to total import	3.7		4.5		6.9		5.6	

* Negligible

in production. Pulses are a typical example, where there is zero import duty. High tariff walls were raised this year for many agricultural and allied products, such as rice, wheat, millets, sugar, milk powder, apple, chicken, edible oils etc. to ally the fears of large scale dumping of such products in Indian market in view of liberalisation of import policy in respect of many such products. Current tariff rate for import of some agricultural products are listed in Table 1.17.

Table 1.17 Import Tariff Rate on Selected Agricultural Commodities, 2000-01

Item	*Tariff (per cent (Basic + Surcharge)*	*Item*	*Tariff (per cent (Basic + Surcharge)*
Foodgrains		**Edible Oil**	
Wheat	50	RBD Palmolein	71.6
Rice in husk	60	Other refined oil	50.8
Polished rice	70	Crude palm oil (for vanaspati)	25
Millets	50	Crude palm oil (for uses other than vanaspati)	55
Pulses	0	Crude coconut oil	45
Fruits		Other vegetable crude oil	35
Apple	50		
Peas & quinces	35	**Other Products**	
Other fruits	25	Spices	58.5
		Sugar	60 per cent + Rs. 850 as CVO
Nuts			
Arecanut	100	Chicken meat	100
Cashewnuts (shelled)	40		

Export Import Policy 2001-02

The focus of the Government's exam policy announced on the 31st March 2001 by the Commerce Minister is on formulating a medium-term export strategy to boost exports so as to achieve 1% share in global trade, up from around 0.7% at present. Exports have been targeted to touch $ 75 billion by 2004-05 from around $ 40 billion at present. For this, exports need to grow by about 18% a year. Against this background, several measures have been announced to give a boost to exports and position Indian producers and exporters to take advantage of liberalisation in world trade as well as make India an attractive destination for foreign investment. The Government had also focused attention on complying with WTO requirements for removal of Quantitative Restrictions (QRs) by April 1,2001, while at the same time giving industry some support in adjusting to the new environment.

Quantitative Restrictions Removed

Quantitative Restrictions on 715 items have been removed. Out of these, 342 are textile products, 147 are agricultural products including alcoholic beverages and 226 are other manufactured products including automobiles. Also, 58 items are those which are reserved for small-scale sector. To guard against any surge in imports, a Standing Group has been set up to monitor imports of 300 sensitive items including cars, poultry, dairy and meat products, fruits, coffee, tea, spices, grains, edible oils, toys, stationery, etc. and take safeguard measures including imposition of duties. To ensure that highly subsidised farm goods do not enter the country, import of vital agricultural and energy items including wheat, rice, maize, petroleum, diesel and aviation turbine fuel and urea will be allowed only through the designated state trading enterprises as permitted under Article XVII of WTO. The nominated State enterprises will conduct the imports of these commodities solely as per commercial considerations. As a further safeguard, imports of all primary products of plant and animal origin will be allowed only after assessing their bio-security implications and will be subjected to permits to be issued by Agriculture Ministry. In addition, import of all food products will be subjected to compliance of all the provisions of Food Adulteration Act.

In view of internal security concerns, import of 59 items has been banned and import of 518 items is restricted broadly covering sectors like defence, communication, live animals, drugs and chemicals. Further, no import of textile material using prohibited dyes like azo is to be allowed. While free import of second hand capital goods upto 10 years old have been allowed, stiff non-tariff barriers like ban on left-hand drive cars and than on vehicles over three years has been imposed to discourage second hand cars from flooding the domestic market.

Agricultural Export Zones

To give a fillip to export of agricultural products, particularly fruits and vegetables, the Export Import Policy 2001-2 has announced the setting up of Agricultural Export Zones (AEZs) on the lines of Special Economic Zones (SEZs). State governments will have to identify products specific agricultural export zones for development of export of specific products from a geographically contiguous area. Facilities offered by the AEZs would include pre/post harvest treatment and operations, plant protection, processing, packaging, storage and related research and development. The Export Promotion Capital Goods (EPCG) scheme has been extended to agriculture and will cover common infrastructural facilities in AEZs such as sorting, grading, polishing, packaging, cold storage, transport equipment/refrigerated vans, heat treatment plant, x-ray screening facility, etc. The facility of export house/trading house/star trading house/super-star trading house has been extended to agricultural exports on achieving one-third of the threshold limit prescribed for exporters of goods.

Special Economic Zones

Developers in Special Economic Zones are allowed duty-free import/procurement from Domestic Tariff Area for development of integrated infrastructure for exports. Items reserved for SSI do not require any licence for setting up units in SEZ. To facilitate greater flexibility and to attract capital intensive units into SEZs, amortisation of value of imported capital goods is being spread over a period of 8 years instead of 5 years at present. By way of incentive, units in SEZs have been allowed to bring back export proceeds in 365 days instead of 180 days. These units have also been allowed to retain 100 per cent of their proceeds in EEFC account. Subcontracting of part of production abroad has also been permitted.

Export Oriented Units/Export Processing Zones

EOU/EPZ units now have to account for duty-free goods in overall terms and not consignment-wise, which is expected to facilitate ease in operation. EOU/EPZ Units have been allowed to achieve minimum export performance of 3 times the value of capital goods cover over 5 years instead of 5 times the value of capital goods. Subcontracting of production process abroad has also been permitted. At present, subcontracting is permissible only within the country.

Appendix 1.1

Parameters of Indian Economy

Key indicators	*1997-98*	*1998-99*	*1999-00*	*2000-01*	*2001-02*	*1997-98*	*1998-99*	*1999-00*	*2001-01*	*2001-02*
	Absolute Values					% change over previous period				
Gross national product (Rs thousand crore)										
At current prices	1376.8	1583.1	1740.2P	1878.4Q	2060.6A	11.9	15.0	c	7.9Q	9.7A
At 1993-94 prices	1005.6	1070.5	1136.9P	1181.5Q	1245.5A	4.8	6.4	6.2P	3.9Q	5.4A
Gross domestic product (Rs thousand crore)										
At current prices	1390.0	1598.1	1755.6P	1895.8Q	2080.3A	11.8	15.0	9.9P	8.0Q	9.7A
At 1993-94 prices	1016.3	1082.5	1148.5P	1193.9Q	1258.8A	4.8	6.5	6.1P	4.0Q	5.4A
Agriculture and allied sectors (Rs crore) (at 1993-94 prices)	269383	286094	289842	289194	305643	-2.4	6.2	1.3	-0.2	5.7
Index of agricultural production (1)	165.3	177.9	176.2P	164.6P	175.9P	-6.1	7.6	-0.9P	-6.6P	6.9P
Index of industrial production (2)	139.5	145.2	154.9	162.7	163.3**	6.7	4.1	6.7	5.0	2.3**
Wholesale price index (3)	134.6	141.7	150.9	159.2	160.7*	4.5	5.3	6.5	4.9	1.3*
CPI for industrial workers	380.0	414	434	445	469@	8.3	8.9	4.8	2.5	5.2@
Money supply (M3) (5) (Rs thousand crore)	821.3	981	1124.2	1311.6	1458.4(6)	18.0	19.4	14.6	16.7	11.2(6)
Imports at current prices										
(Rs crore)	154176	178332	215236	230873	181753**	11.0	15.7	20.7	7.3	4.5**
(US $ million)	41484	42389	49671	50536	38362**	6.0	2.2	17.2	1.7	0.3**
Exports at current prices										
(Rs crore)	130101	139752	159561	203571	154445**	9.5	7.4	14.2	27.6	5.1**
(US $ million)	35006	33218	36822	44560	32572**	4.6	-5.1	10.8	21.0	0.6**
Foreign currency assets (7)										
(Rs crore)	102507	125412	152924	184482	226195(8)	27.5	22.3	21.9	20.8	22.6(8)
(US $ million)	25975	29522	35058	39554	46561(8)	16.1	13.7	18.8	12.7	17.7(8)
Exchange rate (Rs/US $ (9)	37.16	42.07	43.33	45.68	47.49(10)	-4.5	-11.7	-2.9	-5.1	-3.8(10)

Note: Gross national product and Gross domestic product figures are at factor cost (base 1993-94)

Q-Quick estimates, A-Advance estimates, P-Provisional.

*As on 19.1.2002 (provisional) @December 2001 **April–December 2001

1. Index of agricultural production (of 46 crops including plantations) with base triennium ending 1981-82 = 100.
2. Index of industrial production, base 1993-94 = 100.
3. Index (with base 1993-94 = 100) at the end of fiscal year.
4. Index (with base 1982 = 100) at the end of fiscal year.
5. Outstanding at the end of financial year.
6. As on January 12, 2001.
7. Outstanding at the end of fiscal year.
8. At the end of January, 2000-01.
9. % change indicates the rate of appreciation/depreciation (—) of the Rupee vis-a-vis the US dollar.
10. Average for April-January, 2000-01.

Appendix 1.2

The Big Picture in Black and White

Items	*1990-91*	*1991-92*	*1998-99*	*1999-00*	*2000-01*	*2001-02*
1. Growth rates (%)						
GDP at constant factor cost	5.6	1.3	6.5	6.1P	4.00	5.4A
Industrial production (IIP)	8.2	0.6	4.1	6.7	5.0	2.3c
of which, Electricity	7.8	8.5	6.5	7.3	4.0	2.7c
Agriculture production	3.8	-2.0	7.6	-0.9	-6.6P	6.9P
Foodgrains production	3.1	-4.5	5.9	3.0	-6.6P	6.8P
Exports (BOP in terms of US $)	9.0	-1.1	-3.9	9.5	19.6	0.6b
Imports (BOP in terms of US $)	14.4	-24.5	-7.1	16.5	7.0	0.3b
of which POL	60.0	-11.7	-21.6	97.1	24.1	-14.6b
2. Foodgrains prodn. (million tonnes)	176.4	168.4	203.6	209.8	195.9	209.2P
3. Electricity generated (million Kwh)	264.3	287.0	448.5	480.7	499.6	383.2c
4. Average exchange rate (Rs/US $)	17.94	24.65	42.07	43.33	45.68	47.49d
5. Growth rate of money supply (M3)	15.1	19.3	19.4	14.6	16.7	11.2e
6. Average rate of inflation (%)						
in terms of WPI	12.1	13.6	5.9	3.3	7.1	4.4f
in terms of CPI	13.6	13.9	13.1	3.4	3.7	4.2g
7. As % of GDP at current market prices:						
Gross domestic savings (GDS)	23.1	22.0	21.7	23.2	23.4	
Gross domestic investment (GDI)	26.3	22.5	22.7	24.3	24.0	
Central Government expenditure	17.3	16.2	14.7	15.4	15.3PU	16.4BE
Central Government receipts	15.3	15.2	14.7	15.4	15.3PU	16.4BE
Gross fiscal deficit of Central Govt.	6.6	4.7	5.1	5.4	5.5PU	5.1BE
Exports fob (BOP)	5.8	6.9	8.3	8.4	9.8	
Imports cif (BOP)	8.8	7.9	11.5	12.4	13.0	
Trade Balance	-3.0	-1.0	-3.2	-4.0	-3.1	
Net invisibles	-0.1	0.7	2.2	3.0	2.6	
Current account balance	-3.1	-0.3	-1.0	-1.1	-0.5	
Total capital flows	2.7	1.7	1.9	2.4	1.8	
Total foreign investment net (BOP)	0.03	0.05	0.6	1.2	1.0	
Foreign direct investment (FDI) net	0.03	0.05	0.6	0.5	0.4	
Portfolio investment	Negl.	Negl.	-0.0	0.7	0.6	
8. Parameters for external debt:						
External debt/GDP ratio (%)	28.7	38.7	23.6	22.2	22.3	21.0h
Debt service ratio (%)	35.3	30.2	18.0	16.2	17.1	
Debt/exports ratio	454	467	283	262	222	
Short term debt to total debt ratio (%)	10.2	8.3	4.4	4.0	3.5	2.8h
9. Foreign exch. reserves (US$ Bln)	5.8	9.2	32.5	38.0	42.3	49.5*
Imports cover of foreign exch. reserves (in no. of months of imports)	2.5	5.3	8.2	8.2	8.6	9.6

Q Quick estimate A Advance estimate P Provisional estimate PU Provisional and unaudited (as reported by Controller General of Accounts, Department of Expenditure) RE Revised estimate BE Budget estimate E Expected Negl negligible

a. During April-December 2000 b. During April-December 2000 (DGCL & S data)
c. During April-December 2000 d. Average for April-January 2000-01
e. Annual growth rate as on 12 January 2001 f. As on January 27, 2001
g. For December 2000. h. At the end of September 2000. *At the end of January 2000.

CHAPTER 2

Agricultural Development —An Overview

As the bed rock of India's economy, agriculture and allied activities have remained the focal point of the country's planned economic development. In fact, with two-thirds of our rural workforce deriving their livelihood from agriculture and allied activities, the performance of this sector still holds the key to improvements in real incomes and living standards of the bulk of India' population. Despite phenomenal diversification of the country's economy, this sector even now constitutes the single largest contributor to the Gross Domestic Product (GDP), accounting for almost 29 per cent of the total. Thus, there can be no sustained growth of the Indian economy without broad-based progress of our agriculture. This is also the experience of most of the fast growing countries of East Asia.

The sector produces 51 major crops, provides raw material to the country's agro-based industries and fetches nearly one-sixth of the total export earnings. India has in addition the added advantage of a rich endowment of nature. Her most abundant natural resource is her diverse agro-climatic conditions, perennial rivers, tropical location, diverse climate, large arable land (second largest) suitable fertile soil qualities, abundant sunlight, spread of monsoon rains, comparative advantage in the global markets and a receptive and resurgent farming community. As against world share of arable to total land area of only 11 per cent, India is bestowed with 51 per cent. Our climate, being moderate, enables us to grow two to three crops a year; whereas in most parts of the world, due to severe winters, only one crop can be grown a year. India also has more irrigated land than any other country.

These resources if complemented with suitable technology can create wonders for the Indian economy. Present need is to focus upon the quality of agricultural production so that a niche is created for Indian agricultural products in the domestic and foreign markets. Areas where climate is favourable and resources are available to produce exportable produces should be identified and encouraged to produce quality products. These pockets should be developed on the pattern of export promotion parks where production should be targeted at the overseas markets only. Basmati rice producing areas is one of such examples.

At the same time it has to be accepted that: India has only 2% of the world's land, 4% of its fresh water resources but carries 16% of the world's population and 10% of its cattle. India has geographical area of 329 million hectares of which 47% cultivated, 23% under forest, 7% under non-agricultural uses, remaining 23% falls under the categories of barren and un-culturable land, culturable wasteland, permanent pastures and fallow lands. An estimated 150 million hect of degraded land suffers from water and wind erosion. Per capita availability of land declined from 0.89 hectare in the early 1950s to 0.37 hectare in the mid 1990s and is expected to reduce further to 0.19 hectare by 2020. India produces more than 200 million tonnes of foodgrain from 142 million hectares of cultivated land. Irrigated areas account for 37% of crop-land and contribute 55% of foodgrain production whereas rainfed areas account for 63% of cultivated land but contribute 45% of foodgrain production.

PRE-INDEPENDENCE SCENARIO

Agriculture in India till Independence was traditional with a very slow growth rate having little application of science and technology. In a study on "Growth and Instability in Indian Agriculture', Sen (1967)* observed that "during the first 24 years of the century foodgrains production increased at an average annual (linear) rate of 0.3 per cent. The next 24 years, however, presented a completely different picture. During this period, foodgrains production showed a declining trend of 0.02 per cent per annum (linear) on the average, in spite of the fact that droughts turned out to be relatively moderate and less frequent". The National Commission on Agriculture (1976) in their study on progress of agricultural development also observed that during the period 1931-47, production and productivity of both foodgrains and non foodgrains exhibited mostly a declining trend.

During the period 1931-47, besides irrigation, improved seeds and agricultural education were the other technological factors which had started making some impact on the agricultural economy of the country. In spite of increased imports, fertilizer use remained limited to plantations and commercial crops which alone could fetch remunerative prices. Other factors like types of crops grown and manner of farming remained traditional. Agricultural implements used were

---

* Sen, S.R. (1967): "Growth and Instability in Indian Agriculture" in Agricultural Situation in India, January, 1967, Directorate of Economics and Statistics, Ministry of Food and Agriculture, Government of India, New Delhi.

largely conventional and whatever new types of iron ploughs were publicised were not widely accepted by the farmers. Apart from being expensive and strenuous to bullocks, these were unsuitable for small fragmented holdings and less effective in uprooting weeds and, at the same time, were prone to expose and dry out comparatively more of the under-soil moisture. Moreover, there was lack of repairing facilities.

The improved seed technology was mainly confined to cash crops though the Imperial Institute of Agricultural Research had initiated work of multiplication and dissemination of improved varieties right from its establishment. Research was conducted with the object of introducing new crops, improving indigenous types and producing new and better varieties with regard to rice, wheat, gram, sugarcane, cotton, jute, tobacco and oilseeds. Though it is now difficult to evaluate the impact of improved seeds on yield rates of individual crops, during the period substantial progress was achieved in bringing additional areas under improved varieties of commercial crops.

Grow More Food (GMF) Campaign

The Grow More Food (GMF) campaign launched in 1942 marked the beginning of a sustained national endeavour at increasing agricultural production and improving agriculture. Its main objective was to achieve immediate increase in food production through extension of area under cultivation, including diversion of acreage from cash crops like cotton, extension of irrigation and use of inputs like improved seeds, manures and fertilizers. From 1943, in the wake of increasing scarcities and the Bengal famine, the Government of India began assuming wider responsibilities in regard to food production, a field which for over two decades was the primary concern of provincial governments. It began to direct the GMF campaign and also sought to bring about greater involvement of provincial governments in the drive, by offering them special assistance. The Foodgrains Policy Committee and the Famine Enquiry Commission, appointed during this period, not only endorsed the campaign, but also gave suggestions for improving agriculture (NCA, 1976)*.

Statement of Agriculture and Food Policy in India

A major development in the immediate pre-Independence period was the first ever elaboration in January 1946, of an all India policy in agriculture known as `Statement of Agriculture and Food Policy in India.' The ten objectives of the policy included: increase in production of foodgrains and protective foods; improvement in methods of agricultural production and marketing; stimulating production of raw materials for industry and exports, securing remunerative price for the producer and fair wages to the agricultural labour; ensuring fair distribution of the food produced and promoting nutritional research and education (NCA, 1976)*.

Post-Independence Policy Framework and Development—Initial Phase

Despite these developments, agricultural performance remained at a low key and together with the problems created by the Second World War, the food situation steadily deteriorated. The partition of the country in 1947 and the growing population aggravated the critical food situation. The government, therefore, felt necessary to give urgent attention to agriculture so as to alleviate widespread hunger and malnutrition and facilitate the nation's general economic progress. The Grow More Food (GMF) campaign, which was launched earlier in 1942 in order to accelerate food production, was, therefore, placed on a planned basis from 1947-48 for a period of five years.

The Foodgrains Policy Committee appointed in 1947 under the Chairmanship of Mr Purshotamdas Thakurdas recommended greater attention to minor irrigation, development of local manurial resources, distribution of improved seeds, and land reclamation. The Report also impressed the need for planning production of fertilisers. A greater reliance on the use of science and technology for faster growth in agriculture was emphasized. The impact of GMF was minimal as there was no real breakthrough in any crop and the increase in foodgrains production was very modest. In view of the persisting stagnation in agricultural production, a committee was appointed in 1952 (V.T. Krishnamachari Committee) to review the working of GMF campaign. The committee felt that the lack of success of the programme was mainly due to its failure to arouse enthusiasm in the countryside. Its important recommendations related to:

(a) the setting up of countrywide extension service organisation;
(b) the acceleration of minor irrigation programme; and
(c) the provision of adequate credit and quality seed, and development of local manurial resources.

FIFTY YEARS OF INDIAN AGRICULTURE: AN APPRAISAL

The quantum of plan outlay, its financing and the targets set for the agricultural sector were all decided through the planning process at the state and central levels. The first three Five-Year Plans concentrated on growth with some institutional changes. The intermediaries in agriculture, like Zamindars and Jagirdars, were abolished within a few years after independence and the actual tillers, accounting for about 40 per cent of the cultivated area, became the owners. This

* NCA (1076): Report of the National Commission on Agriculture, 1976, Ministry of Agriculture and Irrigation, Government of India, New Delhi.

provided a major incentive to the growth of agriculture in large parts of the country. In the mid-sixties, a new technology in the form of high-yielding varieties (HYVs) was introduced for cereals. Apart from the new technology, public investment in agriculture particularly in irrigation, was stepped up significantly. The public sector played an important role in promoting agricultural research and education. Large investments were made for the development of research system under the aegis of the Indian Council of Agricultural Research and the State Agricultural Universities. Simultaneously, a well designed extension network was created for disseminating new technologies to the cultivators. The administered price policy has provided incentives to the farmers. In short, successive Five-year Plans have aimed at improving the infrastructure through irrigation, stepping up the use of fertilizers and improved varieties of seeds and effecting institutional changes, supply of credit through the banking system, ensuring remunerative prices for agricultural commodities, etc. There has been a significant increase in the use of modern inputs.

The agricultural development strategy followed since independence particularly since the mid-sixties, has paid rich dividends. In terms of growth, the performance has been quite impressive in the post-independence period as compared to the pre-independence period. The all crop growth of around 2.7 per cent per annum in the post-independence period (during 1949-98) was much higher than the negligible growth rate of around 0.3 per cent per annum in the first half of this century. It shows that the long-term growth rate of agriculture during the period 1949-50 to 1998-99 has been around 2.7 per cent per annum (Table 2.1). The growth rates for sub-periods show that agriculture recorded much higher growth during 1980s and 1990s than in the earlier decades though there was, some deceleration in 1990's decade (Tables 2.2 and 2.3). The production of foodgrains increased from 51 m.t. in 1950-51 to a record level of about 209 m.t. in 1999-00. The country has been able to meet its food needs in spite of about 2 per cent per annum growth in population. Commendable progress has been made in increasing the production of commercial crops like cotton, oilseeds, sugarcane, besides livestock products, poultry, fisheries, fruits and vegetables. Within the agriculture sector, animal husbandry and fisheries have shown a much impressive growth (Table 2.4).

The green revolution has transformed agriculture from subsistence to production-intensive farming. Over the first five decades, the gross cropped area has gone up by almost a third, production has quadrupled, yield tripled and coverage under irrigation doubled. A point for elation for India has been the increase in food production by 4 times from 51 million tonnes in 1950-51 to over 208 million tonnes during 1999-2000. Crop-wise, there were 17 times increase in potato production, 11 times in wheat, 5 times each in oilseed and sugarcane,

Table 2.1 All India Compound Growth-Rates of Area, Production and Yield of Principal Crops Since 1949–50.

(Base: T.E. 1981–82 = 100) (% Per Annum)

Crop	1949–50 to 1998–99*			1949–50 to 1964–65			1967–68 to 1998–99*		
	A	P	Y	A	P	Y	A	P	Y
1	2	3	4	5	6	7	5	6	7
Rice	0.77	2.67	1.89	1.21	3.50	2.25	0.63	2.84	2.26
Wheat	2.19	5.42	3.16	2.69	3.98	1.27	1.50	4.54	2.99
Jowar	–0.79	0.74	1.54	0.99	2.51	1.49	–1.55	0.24	1.81
Bajra	–0.19	1.66	1.86	1.08	2.34	1.24	–0.89	1.03	1.94
Maize	1.13	2.40	1.25	2.67	3.88	1.18	0.10	1.90	1.80
Ragi	–0.45	1.17	1.63	0.84	3.08	2.22	–1.12	0.66	1.81
Small millets	–2.26	–2.06	0.21	–0.30	–0.20	0.09	–3.97	–3.31	0.68
Barley	–3.26	–1.42	1.90	–0.64	–0.28	0.36	–4.82	–2.42	2.53
Coarse cereals	–0.60	1.05	1.55	0.90	2.25	1.23	–1.40	0.57	1.93
Total cereals	0.46	2.89	2.04	1.25	3.21	1.77	0.00	2.85	2.37
Gram	–0.58	0.13	0.72	1.64	2.66	1.00	–0.39	0.32	0.72
Tur	0.96	0.83	–0.12	0.57	–1.34	–1.90	1.34	1.38	0.04
Other pulses	0.46	0.92	0.46	2.06	1.28	–0.77	0.17	1.38	1.21
Total pulses	0.16	0.58	0.46	1.72	1.41	–0.18	0.15	0.95	0.76
Total foodgrains	0.40	2.50	1.76	1.35	2.82	1.36	0.03	2.59	2.15
Sugarcane	1.83	3.08	1.22	3.28	4.26	0.95	1.76	3.14	1.36
Groundnut	0.95	1.84	0.88	4.01	4.34	0.31	0.37	1.70	1.33
Sesamum	–0.29	0.92	1.21	0.14	–0.32	–0.46	–0.75	1.43	2.19
R & M	2.21	4.30	2.05	2.97	3.35	0.37	2.68	5.32	2.58
Sunflower†							12.81	12.07	–0.65
Soyabean†							22.20	24.14	1.58
Nine oilseeds	1.46	2.85	1.22	2.53	3.12	0.00	1.84	3.76	1.82
Total oilseeds	1.25	2.80	1.16	2.67	3.20	0.30	1.43	3.62	1.71
Cotton	0.31	2.56	2.25	2.47	4.55	2.04	0.26	2.82	2.56
Jute	0.48	1.70	1.21	3.00	3.50	0.49	0.30	2.24	1.93
Mesta	–0.29	0.34	0.63	6.21	7.97	1.66	–2.03	–0.78	1.28
Jute & mesta	0.29	1.48	1.12	3.88	4.31	0.70	–0.30	1.75	1.86
Total fibres	0.28	2.40	2.09	2.71	4.56	1.88	0.15	2.66	2.46
Potato	3.65	5.79	2.06	4.38	4.28	–0.11	3.34	5.76	2.34
Tobacco	0.28	1.95	1.66	1.66	2.79	1.10	–0.23	1.79	2.02
Non Foodgrains	1.28	3.00	1.38	2.44	3.74	0.89	1.43	3.36	1.73
All Crops	0.61	2.68	1.61	1.58	3.15	1.21	0.38	2.88	1.98

* — Provisional for Non Foodgrains and All Crops
† — Growth Rates for the Period from 1970-71
Nine oilseeds include groundnut, castorseed, seasamum, rapessed & mustard linseed, nigerseed, safflower sunflower & soyabean.
Total oilseeds include nine oilseeds, cottonseed and coconut.
A — Growth rates of area P — Growth rates of production
Y — Growth rates of yield

Table 2.2 All India Compound Growth-Rates of Area, Production and Yield of Principal Crops During Decades of Eighties and Nineties

(Base: T.E. 1981–82 = 100) (% Per annum)

Crops	1980–81 to 1998–99*			Eighties 1979–80 to 1989–90			Nineties 1989–90 to 1998–99*		
	A	P	Y	A	P	Y	A	P	Y
1	2	3	4	5	6	7	5	6	7
Rice	0.56	3.01	2.43	0.45	4.29	3.82	0.49	1.70	1.21
Wheat	0.90	3.56	2.64	0.57	4.24	3.65	1.64	3.64	1.96
Jowar	–2.77	–1.25	1.56	–0.97	–0.02	0.96	–3.85	–3.74	0.10
Bajra	–1.12	1.87	3.02	–0.61	1.43	2.06	–1.42	1.65	3.11
Maize	0.33	2.72	2.39	–0.07	2.66	2.74	0.66	2.11	1.44
Ragi	–2.47	–0.37	2.16	–1.28	–0.36	0.93	–3.18	–0.76	2.49
Small millets	–5.55	–4.63	0.97	–4.19	–2.77	1.49	–5.84	–6.05	–0.22
Barley	–4.50	–1.66	2.97	–5.82	–2.21	3.83	–2.58	–0.24	2.40
Coarse cereals	–2.01	0.45	2.29	–1.19	0.74	1.84	–2.36	–0.48	1.63
Total cereals	–0.27	2.76	2.49	–0.16	3.63	3.43	–0.17	1.94	1.52
Gram	0.13	1.43	1.29	–1.08	0.87	1.97	2.38	4.47	2.03
Tur	0.99	0.46	–0.52	2.43	3.54	1.08	–0.69	–0.53	0.16
Other pulses	–0.50	1.06	1.57	0.23	4.19	3.95	–1.53	–1.85	–0.32
Total pulses	–0.08	1.13	1.04	0.15	2.78	2.63	–0.22	0.75	0.65
Total foodgrains	–0.23	2.56	2.32	–0.11	3.54	3.33	–0.18	1.80	1.42
Sugarcane	2.07	3.48	1.39	1.89	3.73	1.81	1.81	2.90	1.08
Groundnut	0.52	2.40	1.88	1.41	3.31	1.88	–2.00	0.99	3.05
Sesamum	–1.55	0.99	2.59	–0.56	4.59	5.18	–4.77	–4.07	0.73
R & M	3.80	6.41	2.51	2.24	8.84	6.46	2.49	2.25	–0.24
Nine oilseeds	2.75	5.17	2.25	2.45	5.75	2.93	1.27	3.06	1.93
Total oilseeds	2.30	5.18	2.25	1.45	5.45	2.73	1.71	3.18	1.62
Cotton	0.90	3.78	2.86	–1.32	2.19	3.56	2.71	2.22	–0.47
Jute	–0.24	1.94	2.19	–1.97	1.25	3.29	1.99	2.55	0.55
Mesta	–3.60	–2.04	1.61	–4.48	–4.25	0.24	–2.82	–2.30	0.53
Jute & mesta	–1.03	1.38	2.17	–2.69	0.28	2.80	0.97	1.98	0.67
Total fibres	0.62	3.45	2.77	–1.53	1.96	3.49	2.48	2.57	–0.34
Potato	3.11	4.59	1.44	3.03	5.56	2.46	3.51	4.60	1.05
Tobacco	–0.19	1.57	1.76	–2.22	–0.34	1.92	1.04	1.48	0.44
Non Foodgrains	1.95	4.16	2.04	1.21	4.02	2.47	1.67	3.17	1.28
All Crops	0.33	3.16	2.18	0.21	3.72	2.99	0.33	2.35	1.34

* — Provisional for Non Foodgrains and All Crops

Nine oilseeds include groundnut, castorseed, seasamum, rapessed & mustard linseed, nigerseed, safflower sunflower & soyabean.

Total oilseeds include nine oilseeds, cottonseed and coconut.

A — Growth rates of area P — Growth rates of production

Y — Growth rates of yield

Table 2.3 Average Annual Growth Rates in Agriculture and Allied Sectors

Period	Agriculture	Animal Husbandry	Forestry	Fishing	Agriculture and allied (total)
1950-51 to 1966-67	1.90	1.02	1.85	4.73	1.77
1966-67 to 1980-81	3.72	2.33	0.13	3.16	3.01
1980-81 to 1996-97	3.85	7.97	-0.67	5.67	3.91
1990-91 to 1996-97	2.16	7.32	-0.94	6.50	2.90

SOURCE: Computed from CSO, "National Accounts Statistics", Various Issues.

Table 2.4 Production of Major Crops, Milk and Fish 1950-51 to 1998-99

Crops	1950-51	1970-71	1980-81	1990-91	1998-99
			Million tonnes		
Foodgrains	50.82	108.42	129.59	179:39	203.00
Rice	20.58	42.22	53.63	74.29	85.99
Wheat	6.46	23.83	36.31	55.14	70.78
Coarse Cereals	15.38	30.55	29.02	32.70	31.46
Pulses	8.41	11.82	10.63	14.26	14.81
Sugarcane	57.05	126.37	154.25	241.05	295.73
Cotton (m.bales)	3.04	4.76	7.01	9.84	12.18
Nine Oilseeds	5.16	9.63	9.37	18.61	25.21
Milk	17.0	21.2*	31.6	53.9	74.70*
Fish	0.75	1.76	2.44	3.84	5.26*

* Anticipated

SOURCE: Agricultural Statistics at a Glance, 2000

4 times each in rice and cotton. India today has become the largest producer of pulses, groundnut, jute, milk and vegetables and the second largest producer of wheat, rice, sugarcane and fruits. Targets and achievements of agriculture in the Ninth Plan have been given in detail in Table 2.5.

Table 2.5 Physical Targets and Achievements of Agriculture and Allied Sector

Part-A: Production and Targets of Crops

(In million tonnes/bales for cotton, jute and mesta)

Crop	*1996-97*	*Ninth plan Target*	*1997-98*	*1998-99*	*1999-2000*		*2000-01*		*Production ever achieved in*
					Target	*Likely Achievement*	*Target*	*Highest Quantity*	*Year*
1	2	3	4	5	6	7	8	9	10
Rice	81.74	99.00	82.53	85.99	86.00**	88.25	90.00	88.55	1999-2000
Wheat	69.35	83.00	66.35	70.78	74.00*	74.25	74.25	74.25	1998-99
C. Cereals	34.10	35.50	30.40	31.46	34.50	30.35	33.00	36.59	1992-93
Pulses	14.25	16.50	12.98	14.81	15.50	13.05	15.00	14.81	1998-99
Foodgrains	199.44	234.00	192.26	203.04	210.00*	205.11	212.00	205.91	1998-99
Oilseeds	24.38	30.00	21.32	25.21	28.00	21.18	28.00	25.21	1998-99
Sugarcane	277.56	336.00	279.54	295.73	305.00	309.31	325.00	309.31	1998-99
Cotton	14.23	15.70	10.85	12.18	15.00	11.99	14.50	14.23	1996-97
Jute & mesta	11.13	Not fixed	11.02	9.70	11.00	10.57	10.00	12.65	1985-86

*Revised

Table 2.5 ***Physical Targets and Achievements of Agriculture and Allied Sector*** *(Contd.)*

Part-B: Production of fruits & vegetables and plantation crops

(In million/tonnes/bales for cotton, jute and mesta)

Crop	*1996-97*	*Ninth plan Target*	*1997-98*	*1998-99*	*1999-2000*		*2000-01*		*Production ever achieved in*
					Target	*Likely Achievement*	*Target*	*Highest Quantity*	*Year*
1	2	3	4	5	6	7	8	9	10
Fruits & Vegetables (Million tonnes)	141.00	179.00	112.88	122.00	—	—	—	113.10	1996-97
Tea (Million kg)	775.00	1000.00	838.00	850.00	905.00	816.00	950.00	850.00	1998-99
Coffee (Lakh tonnes)	2.05	3.00	2.28	2.65	2.60	2.82	2.80	2.82	1999-2000
Rubber (Lakh tonnes)	5.49	7.17	5.84	6.05	6.61	6.22	6.95	6.22	1999-2000

@ 141.10 MT indicated in the ninth plan document

Table 2.5 ***Physical Targets and Achievements of Agriculture and Allied Sector*** **(Contd.)**

Part-C: Animal husbandry, dairying & fishery

(In million tones/bales for cotton, jute and mesta)

Crop	*1996-97*	*Ninth plan Target*	*1997-98*	*1998-99*	*1999-2000*		*2000-01*		*Production ever achieved in Year*
					Target	*Likely Achieve-ment*	*Target*	*Highest Quantity*	
1	2	3	4	5	6	7	8	9	10
Milk (Million Tonnes)	69.10	96.49	70.80	74.70	84.18	78.10	90.13	78.10	1998-99
Egg (Billion No.)	27.50	35.00	28.57	30.14	31.50	31.32	32.42	31.32	1998-99
Fish (Lakh Tonnes)	53.48	70.40	53.90	52.62	63.00	58.00	66.60	58.00	1997-98

Since the driving force for agricultural development was the food crisis, the focus of all the efforts came to be placed more on the areas which already had better infrastructure in terms of irrigation systems and roads etc. in order to overcome the crisis quickly. Therefore, it was no coincidence that the Green Revolution took its roots in Punjab first and then spread to Haryana and part of Western Uttar Pradesh. A few other districts and regions in the country, where the conditions were similarly conducive also took advantage of the Green Revolution. Thus, regions such as Punjab, Haryana, Western Uttar Pradesh, etc. have benefitted more, during the initial phase of the Green Revolution, than others. This is partly explained by agroclimatic factors, and partly by earlier introduction of high yielding varieties and better irrigation.

Green Revolution thus helped in eradicating poverty in a way that no other development activity has done. Poverty in Punjab in 1993-94 was just 12 per cent while at all India level it was 36 per cent. This has however, resulted in accentuating regional disparities in the immediate post-Green Revolution period. A district level analysis of the growth rates between the early sixties and the early eighties shows that out of 281 districts covered, 17 reported an absolute decline in output; 82 districts recorded a growth rate of less than 1.5 per cent a year, while 23 had more than 5 per cent per annum. An important feature of the 1980s and the 1990s, however, is that there has been much more equitable spread of agricultural growth. After performing poorly during the early years of the Green Revolution, many of the States, where poverty is widespread namely Assam, Bihar, Orissa, Madhya Pradesh and West Bengal, have shown significant growth in the 1980s. Oilseeds have also gained in the dry belt of Rajasthan, Madhya Pradesh, Karnataka and Maharashtra. An interesting development during this period was that agricultural growth had spread to all the regions of India. Apart from the eastern region, States like Madhya Pradesh and Rajasthan also recorded higher growth during this period. Thus, there seems to have been a reduction in the regional disparities in output growth during the 1980s and 90s.

INDIAN AGRICULTURE AT CROSS ROADS

Malthusian predictions of 1798 appeared in its stark reality when India was declared as a `basket case' and a sinking ship by the international community during mid sixties. Living from ship to mouth, the sustained cooperation between ICAR and CIMMYT supplemented by research of Indian scientists brought about a sea change in the Indian food economy and India today has emerged as the second largest wheat producer of the world. Indian agriculture has at the same time moved from food scarcity to food surpluses.

As discussed earlier, during the last 50 years, agricultural production has increased manyfold. Agricultural research, supplemented with modern inputs carried out by the Indian Council of Agricultural

Research and the state agricultural universities, has played a pivotal role, particularly after the Green Revolution, in increasing productivity of crops, which has so far kept pace, with the population growth.

This euphoria on the food front has, however, not been without accompanying problems. We are acutely aware today, as never before in the past, that there are both costs and benefits attached to the intensification of agriculture to feed a population of over one billion and growing. The natural resource base, namely land and water, which sustains the production process, is under considerable stress. Per capita and availability has halved since independence and will decline further in the next quarter century. Of the total geographical area, about 50 per cent suffers from varying degrees of degradation. Unless great efforts are undertaken, there will be continuing decline in biodiversity, which is the source of genetic material needed to make further advances in plant and animal breeding. There could also be accelerated global climate change. The impact of all these factors on our land resources compels us to focus on the issue of sustainable production.

The green revolution areas of Punjab, Haryana and Western U.P. have started showing signs of fatigue. We may go into the problems faced by Punjab agriculture. The water resource there is being over-exploited because of the adoption of high water requiring cropping sequences. Water table in Central districts of the State is declining at 23 cm per annum, whereas, the Western districts are facing an acute problem of water logging. The water table has risen by 4 to 5 metres within a decade's time. If the process of declining water table continues for the next 15 years, state would have to spend Rs. 2000 crore on submersible pumps for replacing 2.5 lakh centrifugal pumps. In view of such a constraint, there is a need to adopt technologies related to ground water recharge and crop related practices having no adverse effect on water resources.

Punjab soils are primarily light textured, poor in organic carbon and nutrient resources. The nutrient reserves of soil are being exploited at a much faster rate than its replenishment due to extremely high cropping intensity (almost 200 per cent) and extensive adoption of rice-wheat cropping system. The organic content of soil has gone down from 0.5 to 0.2 per cent. Micro-nutrient's deficiency on large scale is affecting the crop as well as animal health adversely. Accumulation of salt on the soil surface in the waterlogged southwestern zone where underground water is brackish is a matter of serious concern. Therefore, there is an urgent need to sustain the soil-health through integrated nutrient management (using chemical fertilizers in conjunction with organic manures and incorporation of crop residues). It has been estimated that 59 lakh tonnes of organic waste containing 2.6 lakh tonnes of nutrients are burnt with paddy straw every season (1997-98), in addition to creating pollution problems of the environment. Likewise, press mud-an industrial waste from sugar factories can be put to use for reclaiming/improving alkaline soils. Thus, for ecologically sustainable agriculture, there is an urgent need to substitute chemical fertilisers with biowastes to maintain productivity level in future.

After attaining an exemplary rise in production, Punjab agriculture has come to a stage beyond which sustaining the growth rate is an arduous task. Being mainly the agricultural economy, the overall development of the state has slowed down. During 1993-94, the per capita real income was Rs. 4,025 at 1980-81 prices which increased to Rs. 4,627 in 1998-99 showing a growth of 15.0 per cent against a comparative figure of 26.51 per cent (at 1993-94 prices) for the country. The average annual growth rate in the state agriculture, including livestock, has declined from 5.44 per cent in the Sixth Plan to 3.32 per cent in Eighth Plan which is projected to fall further to 2.38 per cent in the Ninth Plan. This is much lower as compared to other sectors of the economy.

Decelerating Growth

Our soil resources in the country continue to undergo increasing stresses due to population pressure, loss of vegetative cover, soil degradation, pollution, and climatic changes. The vagaries of nature, with floods in one part of the country and drought in the other, and unseasonal and erratic rains, adversely affect crop production. Thus looking into our resource and targets to be achieved for crop production there need to be a comprehensive policy on development and adoption of low input sustainable agriculture (LISA) technologies.

Growth of Indian agriculture (Table 2.3) is showing clear signs of deceleration. Having touched the highest levels (3.72%) during the eighties, the nineties are likely to be around 2.3 per cent even when the all time bumper crop of 1998-99 is taken into account. This is when we had good favourable monsoon over a decade in a row and vagaries of Southwest monsoon did not have adverse impact on food production as they did during the eighties. What is most disturbing in this scenario is the declining trend in productivity. This is true not only for foodgrains, but also for all crops. Pulses and cotton have also shown a negative growth. The continued increase in the livestock and fisheries sub sectors is, however, quite encouraging.

Waste Land Problem

Our record in tackling problems of denudation and soil erosion has unfortunately been most unsatisfactory and wasteful. Although soil conservation schemes for agricultural lands have been on the scene for nearly half a century, they have failed to make any significant dent on the problem on account of disregarding the "complete mini-watershed" principle. As a result, excessive runoff from denuded forest lands that are almost invariably situated in the higher reaches of watersheds has caused great damage to the terraces and bunds on agricultural fields, particularly because such bunds are not correctly aligned along contour lines but built along field boundaries. This basic flaw is common to all the other schemes which aim essentially at soil and water conservation and explains why they too have not succeeded in their objectives. The position is not very much different with regard to waterlogging and salinization. It appears that we have just not taken any notice of these issues. As the Eighth Plan document admits, there has so far not been even a systematic survey of the extent and location of lands that are affected by this malady. The Ninth Plan also appreciates that the deterioration in land and water resources has been in the form of land degradation, water logging and decline in water table. There is a greater need to have an integrated approach in the management of agricultural nutrients, chemicals and in taking effective measures to deal with the overall pollution problems.

The present scenario in wastelands development is depressing in the extreme because while there is just no talk of wastelands that are suffering from waterlogging and salinisation, even the responsibility for attending to denuded wastelands has been split between two Ministries and there is yet no institutional arrangement for bringing them together so that they may follow the "complete mini-watershed" approach on the ground. It is necessary to remember in this connection that since forest wastelands and non-forest wastelands are inextricably juxtaposed in most situations, neither of these can be tackled alone in a cost-effective manner under the existing administrative arrangements.

This by no means is the end of the story. For even if we were to correct this anomaly by once again creating a unified agency for dealing with both forest and non-forest wastelands, and even if we were also to place responsibility for the reclamation of waterlogged and saline lands squarely on such an agency, the case for treating "wastelands development" as a separate subject by itself, would still be untenable. For such an approach would necessarily push the problem of over 96 odd million hectare of degraded agricultural lands further into the background, where indeed they are already languishing. This would be a great tragedy because contrary to popular belief schemes of the Department of Agriculture for the conservation of soil and water on eroding agricultural lands are not at all doing well because they are being implemented in violation of the "complete mini-watershed" principle.

Better Land Management

Per capita availability of land had declined from 0.89 hectare in the early fifties to 0.37 hectare in the mid nineties due to population increase. The shortage of land is compounded by the increase of waste land, which is estimated to be 63.8 million hectares. We are losing around 15 million hectares of land due to spread of urbanization and the demand for more land for housing, industries and communication. There is then hardly any possibility, in such a situation to provide 0.5 hectare of arable land per capita which was the minimum required for ensuring food and other essential needs of an individual. Future of food security thus lies in conserving prime land for agriculture and restoring the biological potential of degraded lands. Emphasising on the need for effective community-led land-care movement, the people should be in the forefront to manage land and water resources and the scientists must provide leadership in the movement.

While doing so, we ought to be mindful of the soil health. An effective community-led land care movement, people should be in the forefront to manage land and water resources and scientists must provide leadership in the movement. At the same time, the vital role of women who are the worst victim of land degradation must be acknowledged. Green Revolution can be converted into an evergreen revolution if there is a paradigm shift in our research and development strategy leading to a change from a purely commodity-centred approach to an integrated natural resource management. Therefore, the scientific and agricultural experts will have to join with the farmers and the common people in a popular movement for land protection. While there is a global concern for land care, greater political and public support in this area is needed. Land resource management is a challenging task as it will have to take care of the twin needs of increasing food production and improving land resources. There is the need for according high priority for development of rainfed areas and a common approach to watershed development. The fragile ecosystem poses serious implications for the mankind and there is a need for sound land and water management. It is heartening to note that India had demonstrated that it was possible to reverse the trend of land degradation through people centred efforts.*

Our Land is one of our most valuable assets. It continues to feed our growing population. However, there is increasing evidence that the land's capacity to go on producing enough food for the nation may be under threat—rising biotic pressures, expansion of agriculture into fragile ecosystems, over-exploitation of groundwater, water logging resulting in the salinisation of soil. Overuse of chemicals and practice of slash-and-burn agriculture are leading to declining soil health. Farmlands are being made vulnerable due to loss of topsoil and small hills have been transformed into wide gullies and non-reclaimable ravines. Soil erosion due to wind and water, waterlogging, salinity, alkalinity, mining and improper farming practices are well known causes of soil degradation. It has been said about soils that "a

---

* *The Hindu*, November 10, 2000.

handful of good soil is a miracle. Treated well by man it will support life almost indefinitely. Abuse it, the soil will collapse and die taking man with it".

According to available estimates, of the 175 mha of degraded and wastelands that the country possesses, around 150 mha suffer from erosion of the topsoil and its attendant ills (such as floods and gully formation, etc.) and around 25 mha from wind erosion. Over 5.3 billion tonnes of top soil is lost every year due to soil erosion. Nature takes about a thousand years to form one cm. of soil. The average soil loss is estimated to be over 16 tonnes/hectares/year which translate into approximately 1 mm each year or 1 cm every decade. Soil loss varies from less than 1 tonne/hectare/year in dense forests to more than 80 tonnes/hectare/year in the Shivalik Hills. For every tonne of foodgrain, about 105 kg of nutrients are removed from the soil; a cereal crop absorbs 35-46 kg of NPK to produce a tonne of grain; leguminous crop absorbs 210 kg NPK to produce 1 tonne of grain and legumes fix upto 450 kg of Nitrogen/hectare/year.

There is no doubt that lands subject to erosion constitute the biggest single threat to country's economy. For not only do such lands suffer an increasing loss of productivity because of the progressive loss of the fertile topsoil but they also contribute to the loss of a great deal of priceless sweet water by way excessive runoff along denuded slopes. This runoff loaded as it is with soil also causes a great deal of damage by contributing to the causation of floods and the premature siltation of river beds, tanks and reservoirs—before it reaches the sea. And since a large part of this water could have been, under better conditions of land management, retained either as soil moisture (so vital for rainfed agricultural lands) or as ground water (which is the mainstay of the country's irrigation infrastructure today), its loss is also a major reason for droughts. Floods and droughts are indeed two sides of the same coin of poor land management and both can be moderated very substantially by preventing excessive soil erosion.

Considering that prevention is better than cure, and that wastelands have gone out of production in any case, the protection of erosion-prone agricultural lands against further deterioration needs very high priority. This means that we should start worrying a little less about wastelands, but a little more about degraded lands, which if they are not saved in time may also get slowly converted into wastelands. We cannot also continue to be complacent with regard to the dangers of depletion and deterioration faced by lands that do not belong to either of these categories and are believed to be in good health. Such lands are around 89 mha (264 -175 mha) in extent and comprise of around 50 mha of good agricultural lands and around 39 of good forests. Finally together we can care for land :

- By educating, informing and sensitizing all stakeholders about various aspects of this precious resource and its sustainable use.

- By nourishing the land through conservation of rain water, recharging of ground water and judicious water use.
- By anchoring soil to the earth through tree plantation, afforestation and enhanced green cover.
- By enriching soil fertility through planting of leguminous crops and adoption of suitable crop rotations that support diversification.
- By nurturing soil health through recycling organic wastes and adoption of Integrated Plant Nutrient Management (IPNM) techniques.
- By protecting land from overuse of chemical pesticides through adoption of Integrated Pest Management (IPM) practices.
- By saving land from overgrazing through adoption of suitable animal husbandry policy and "Social" and other fencing.
- By adoption of resource conservation technologies such as zero-tillage, reduced tillage, surface seeding, bed-planting, use of drip and sprinkler irrigation and agronomic practices that promote precision agriculture, save water, energy and improve factor productivity.
- By creating suitable incentives to conserve land such as security of land tenure, productive land conservation techniques, people's participation, charges and sanctions.
- By empowering local communities to make and implement decisions in order to tap knowledge, enthusiasm and energy and creating forums for negotiation and conflict resolution.
- By adopting the integrated watershed approach for rainfed farming which promotes need-based soil conservation measures in arable and non-arable lands.

Rainfed Farming

Rainfed agriculture, a dominant sector of agricultural economy, is practised over 64% of crop land and contributes about 40% of food grains production in the country. Bulk of pulses and oilseeds are produced under rainfed conditions. Rainfed farming accounts for 25.7% of agricultural GDP and 9% of total GDP in the country. This sector supports 42.2% of the country's production including meat, milk, hides and skins, wool, etc. which are largely produced in rainfed areas. Rainfed areas contribute 36% of the agricultural export and 10.26% of the total exports of the country.

These areas are under heavy human and livestock pressure and subject to the process of ecological degradation. The restoration of ecological balance on such fragile ecological endowments holds the key to the environmental health of the country. Development of rainfed areas is thus important from economical, social and environmental points of view.

In the case of rainfed areas, hilly regions, etc. it has been accepted that a watershed approach, which is a natural hydrological unit, for planning for development is essential. Allied to this is need for adopting a Farming System approach to enhance incomes of farmers from the alternative use of land pattern. The process of rainfed area development on watershed basis has to be based on a holistic view for comprehensive and integrated development.

The earliest experiments in watershed management in India were conducted in the semi-arid tropics under the aegis of ICRISAT. Between 1975 and 1988, fourteen cropping systems were evaluated along with a range of management practices. The Indian Council for Agricultural Research also took up forty-six model watersheds in the dryland areas of the country in 1982.

During the seventies and eighties the thrust of policy shifted to the improvement and stabilisation of productivity in rainfed areas. It was understood that, in these areas, the main focus of development strategy should be on minimizing risk through appropriate land management systems which ensured greater retention of soil moisture for increased production. The emphasis was therefore shifted to the area development approach taking the watershed[1] as the unit of development. The components include appropriate cropping systems, dryland horticulture, fodder and economically viable plantations in an integrated manner.

Development of rainfed agriculture figures as one of the high priority area in the Twenty Point Programme (T.P.P.) of 1982 and new T.P.P. of 1986. Four pilot projects were operationalised during 1984 with World Bank assistance to provide an integrated approach. A vigorous National Watershed Development Project for Rainfed Areas (NWDPRA) was launched in the Seventh Five Year Plan and restructured during Eighth Plan to achieve the twin objectives of sustainable production bio-mass and restroration of ecological balance in the vast rainfed areas in the country.

The programme is being implemented in sixteen states and extends to ninety-nine districts. Around 2,328 watersheds are receiving treatment under this programme.[2] The idea of an integrated treatment of the watershed was also behind the centrally sponsored schemes aimed at reducing the inflow of sediment into the river valley projects and flood prone rivers. Two such schemes are currently in operation,

---

1 GOI (1994): Ministry of Rural Areas and Employment, Guidelines for Watershed Development which give details of various programmes related to watershed and soil conservation.

2 Vaidyanathan (1991): Integrated Watershed Development some Major Issues, Foundation Day Lecture, Society for Promotion of Watershed Development for a review on the integrated watershed development programmes in India. The review includes the evolution of the concept, people's participation, distributional aspects in the light of Indian experience.

one in the catchments of River Valley Projects (RVP) and the second as an integrated watershed management scheme in the catchments of Flood Prone Rivers FPR) in about 900 priority watershed of 35 catchments spread over in India[3].

In an integrated watershed development programme, all principal practices, viz. soil and water conservation, improved farming systems, dryland horticulture, pasture land development and forestry need to be taken up simultaneously. In the implementation of these practices, two phases can be identified. The first one involves fairly long-term public and private investment. This should be followed by a phase of efficient management of resources and technologies on a sustainable basis. Both these aspects of investment and management of watershed practices are influenced by several factors. Once these practices are identified, the impact of these watershed measures and the factors influencing the adoption are most significant in economic analysis. Therefore, analysis needs to be focussed on the impact of technologies, costs, benefits and distributional aspects.

Watershed management practices should aim at achieving the twin objectives of restoration of ecological balance and promotion of diversified sustainable farming systems through synergistic combination of annual crops, agro-forestry, dryland horticulture, livestock management, household production systems, etc. both in arable and non-arable areas. The holistic approach of treating arable-land, non-arable land and drainage-lines on the principles and practices of watershed management are to be pursued. Local initiative, self-help culture and participation of the watershed community as partner in the project planning and implementation and not merely as beneficiary, is the central theme of the strategy and approach.

SUSTAINABLE DEVELOPMENT

Probably the first comprehensive definition of sustainable agriculture was put forth by the US Farm Bill, 1990. It has defined sustainable agriculture "as an integrated system of plant and animal production practices having a site specific application that will, over the long term, satisfy human food and fibre needs, enhance environmental quality and conservation of natural resources base, upon which the agricultural economy depends, make the most efficient use of non-renewable resources and on-farm resources; and integrate, where appropriate, natural biological cycles and controls, sustain the economic viability of farm operations; and enhance the quality of life of farmers and society as a whole".

Sustainable agriculture has been recognized as agriculture that combines modern technological innovations with proven resource

[3] Joshi, R.K. and Bantalian (MCS) 1997) Vertical Watershed Research in the Semi-Arid Tropics: Directions for Impact Assessment, Arthvijuana Vol. 39 (3) pp. 362, 373.

conservation and food and fibre production practices to protect environmental quality, maintain and enhance profitability, preserve rural communities, and produce a safe and adequate supply of food for current and future generations. The sustainable agriculture entails management of agricultural activities to protect air, soil and water quality and to conserve biodiversity, thereby increasing long-term productivity and profitability, as well as enhancing human health and well being. Production of a safe, high quality and affordable supply of food and fibre in a manner that protects and conserves natural resources. Natural resource conservation, profitability, productivity and human health are all interrelated aspects of sustainable agriculture.

Of the total geographical area of 328.8 million hectares of the country, approximately 142 million hectares are arable lands of which about 55 million hectares are irrigated and the remaining rainfed. The management of these agricultural lands can affect the quality of ecosystems and the conditions of natural resources over a significant portion of the country's land base. The farmers should, therefore, be encouraged to control land degradation, use environmentally sound pest and nutrient management techniques and take other actions that would preserve the health of ecosystems and conserve natural resources, particularly soil and water. If these two resources are not properly used and conserved, we will be faced not in the too distant future with serious problems which may be difficult or very expensive to solve later. With the intensification of agriculture and an increased use of chemical fertilizers and pesticides, not only the ground water is polluted, the soil health is also affected, particularly due to depletion of organic matter, a main source of nutrients and fabric of soil structure. In canal-irrigated areas, the most pervasive damage has occurred from waterlogging and salinization.

Hence, natural resource management has become a critical issue, because sustainable management of water and soils, combined with sustainable agricultural development, is the only hope for providing food, feed, fuel and fibre for the present generation, while assuring that future generations have equal access to the same resources in order to ensure their own survival.

A key consideration in approaches to achieve sustainability in agriculture is to give serious thought to possible impacts of technological advancements in short as well as long term perspective and their cross sectoral linkages. If the technology does not proceed or match the new situations, the consequences can be disastrous to the state's economy. The options for achieving sustainability are never confined to technological innovations. Revival or redevelopment of the old practices abandoned as a result of technological or socioeconomic or political forces in the past, with appropriate scientific and institutional inputs, is also considered to be an equally effective option of mitigating many of the present problems.

For sustainability of agriculture, it is essential to achieve optimal production with minimal external inputs and enhanced use of on-farm resources, maintain productivity, reduce the level of production risk, protect the potential of natural resources, prevent degradation of soil and water quality and satisfy human needs. Besides it should give adequate economic returns and have minimal adverse environmental impacts. The Ninth Plan does talk about environmental sustainability, but the problem does not go beyond raising the issue, and lacks concrete steps.

CAPITAL FORMATION IN INDIAN AGRICULTURE

There is continuing concern about the falling share of public investment in agriculture. This has happened mainly because a large proportion of public expenditure has been going into current expenditure in the form of increased level of subsidy for food, irrigation, fertilizer, electricity, credit and other agricultural inputs rather than creation of assets. Annual investment in agriculture was Rs. 13523 crore in 1993-94, one third of which was public investment. In 1999-2000 it rose to Rs. 18656 crore (38 per cent increase over 1993-94) but the share of public investment decline to 25 per cent.

Investment in agriculture is estimated at 1.5 per cent of GDP in 1999-2000 as against the public sector stagnation (0.71% rate of growth) in the nineties. It was the private sector (7.6% annual) growth which has saved the situation. Official estimates put private sector investment in agriculture towards the end of the 1990s to be more than 50 per cent higher, as compared to the early 1990s. During the seven year period 1993-94 to 1999-2000 agriculture investment has ranged between a low of 1.4 per cent to a high of 1.6 per cent of GDP (Table 2.6).

***Table 2.6** Gross Capital Formation in Agriculture (At 1993-94 Prices)*

(Rs. crore)

Year	*Total*	*Public*	*Private*	*Per cent share*		*Investment in agriculture as*	
				Public	*Private*	*Per cent of GDP*	*Per cent of current Ex.*
1993-94	13523	4467	9056	33.0	67.0	1.6	3.4
1994-95	14969	4947	10022	33.0	67.0	1.6	3.3
1995-96	15690	4848	10842	30.9	69.1	1.6	2.8
1996-97	16176	4668	11508	28.9	71.1	1.5	2.3
1997-98	15953	3979	11974	24.9	75.1	1.4	1.7
1998-99	16384	3846	12538	23.5	76.5	1.4	1.4
1999-2000*	18656	4668	13988	25.0	75.0	1.5	1.4

* Quick Estimates

** This does not include forestry, logging and fishing.

Definitions/Concepts of terms used in Table 2.6:

(i) Gross Fixed Capital Formation:
Gross fixed Capital formation represents the gross value of fixed assets such as buildings roads, bridges and other construction works, machinery and equipment etc., acquired or from own account production of such assets during the year. The type of assets in the public agriculture sector comprises of mainly buildings, construction works and machinery and equipment created for irrigation.

(ii) Change in inventories:
Change in inventories represents the value of net additions in raw materials, works in progress and finished products during the year.

(iii) Gross Capital Formation:
Gross capital formation is the total of gross fixed capital formation and change in inventories.

(iv) Departmental Commercial Undertakings (DCU)
Departmental enterprises are unincorporated enterprises owned, controlled and run directly by the Government. These are mainly engaged in furnishing the kinds of goods and services which are often produced by business establishments but do not hold or manage financial assets and liabilities apart from their working balances and business accounts, payable and receivable.

(v) Non-Departmental Commercial Undertakings (NDCU)
Non-departmental enterprises comprise government companies registered under Companies Act 1956 and having 51% or more share of government and public corporations set up in the Central/State Government Act wholly, or mainly, owned and/or controlled by the public authorities excluding housing boards, municipal corporations and improvement trusts.

Some of the factors for slower growth in the investment/capital formation in agriculture could perhaps be ascribed to some of the following factors:

(a) Large part of the allocation in public sector is going out in the form of subsidies;
(b) Growing recurring expenditure on maintenance of existing assets thus draining out the resources from investment;
(c) Rising time and cost over-runs of ongoing projects;
(d) Relatively lower allocations for irrigation and Agricultural Research;
(e) Inadequate credit support and credit infrastructure in rural areas.

With the burden on productivity—driven growth in the future, this worrisome trend must be reversed. Private investment in agriculture must also be stimulated further though appropriate policies. Considering that nearly 70 per cent of India still lives in villages, agricultural growth will continue to be the engine of broad-based economic growth and development as well as of natural resource conservation, leave alone food security and poverty alleviation. Accelerated investment are needed to facilitate agricultural and rural development through:

- Productivity increasing varieties of crops, breeds of livestock, strains of microbes and efficient packages of technologies, particularly those for land and water management, for obviating biotic, socioeconomic and environmental constraints;
- Yield increasing and environmental-friendly production and post-harvest and value-addition technologies;
- Reliable and timely availability of quality inputs at reasonable prices, institutional and credit supports, especially for small and resource-poor farmers, and support to land and water resources development.
- Effective and credible technology, procurement, assessment and transfer and extension system involving appropriate linkages and partnerships; again with an emphasis on reaching the small farmers;
- Improved institutional and credit support and increased rural employment opportunities, including those through creating agriculture-based rural agro-processing and agro-industries, improved rural infrastructures, including access to information, and effective markets, farm to market roads and related infrastructure;
- Particular attention to the needs and participation of women farmers; and
- Primary education, health care, clean drinking water, safe sanitation, adequate nutrition, particularly for children (including through midday meal at schools) and women.

This will need to be supported through appropriate policies that do not discriminate against agriculture and the rural poor. Given the increasing role of small farmers in food security and poverty alleviation, development efforts must be geared to meet the needs and potential of such farmers through their active participation in the growth process. There is the need to facilitate and support community level action by private voluntary organizations, including farmers groups aimed at improving food security, reducing poverty, and assuring sustainability in the management of natural resources. In addition, government should enhance efforts to ensure good nutrition and access to sufficient food for all through primary health care and education for all.

Modern biotechnology tools, genetic engineering, as well as conventional breeding methods are all expected to play important roles in the generation of higher yielding, past and stress resistant varieties of rice, wheat, maize and other cereal crops. The availability of genetic innovations in developing countries will depend on continued high levels of investments in agricultural research, both at the international and the national levels. Free and unhindered access to germplasm to breeders is absolutely crucial to the rapid dissemination and adoption of improved germplasm. This free movement and the dissemination of modern biotechnology innovations to developing countries are hampered by increased patent protection and private sector investments. There is an urgent need to address this problem of free access to technology in the future.

Increased attention will also have to be given to development of sustainable system that protect the natural resource base. Recent evidence of resource degradation and declining productivity in some intensively cropped areas is of particular concern. Also population driven intensification of agriculture without the use of external inputs, is leading to a serious problem of maintaining soil fertility. In addition to investments in research, infrastructure investments, particularly in irrigation, transport and market infrastructure development are equally important for sustaining the productivity and profitability of food crop production. It is also necessary to mobilize the best of science and development efforts (including traditional knowledge and modern scientific approach) through partnerships involving national and international research institutions, NGOs, farmer's organizations and private sector in order to tackle the present and future problems of food security and production.

INDIAN AGRICULTURE—1999-2000

Robust growth in foodgrains production, despite below normal rainfall in some regions, characterised 1999-2000, yielding a record foodgrains output of 208.9 million tonnes which included 89.5 million tonnes of rice—a gain of 3.5 million tonnes over the preceding year's rice output and, 75.6 million tonnes of wheat which was 4.3 million tonnes more than the previous year. Commercial crops too did fairly well except oilseeds and cotton. Production of sugarcane which continued its high growth path reached a new high of 299.2 million tonnes compared to 288.7 million tonnes in 1998-99. Jute and mesta improved to 10.5 million tonnes, compared to 9.8 million tonnes achieved in 1998-99. Output of cotton at 11.6 million bales (170 kg each) was lower than 12.3 million bales achieved in 1998-99 but higher than the 10.9 million bales achieved in 1997-98. There was substantial fall in production of oilseeds in 1999-2000. Oilseeds output of 20.9 million tonnes was significantly lower than the 24.7 million tonnes produced in 1988-99. Bulk of the shortfall was due to large decline in groundnut production in Gujarat, adversely affected by weather conditions.

Whereas lower rainfall in 1999 may not have caused much decline in crop production due to residual moisture, deficient rainfall in 71 districts for the second year in succession in 2000, is bound to result in lowering this year's output in kharif foodgrains and oilseeds and possibly too in rabi 2000-1. Consequently agriculture together with forestry and fisheries is expected to grow only by 0.9 per cent as compared to 0.7 per cent in 1999-2000. Yet growth in crop agriculture (46 crops) is likely to show a 3.5 per cent decline because of lower foodgrains and oilseeds production.

Monsoon 2000

The Southwest Monsoon (June September) normally brings 80 per cent of annual rainfall to the country and covers almost the entire country. After the withdrawal of the Southwest Monsoon from the country, rainfall is mainly confined to (a) South Peninsula particularly Tamilnadu, which comes under the influence of the Northeast Monsoon during October-December and (b) Northwest India which receives winter rains during October-March in association with the passage of extra-tropical systems called western disturbances. There are no large-scale weather systems, that can bring rain over other parts of the country, except generating some local thunderstorm activity in the summer season of April-May.

The Southwest Monsoon advanced over Kerala on its normal date, 1 June. Initially the monsoon current was active due to the formation of low pressure area in the west-central Bay of Bengal and its northwestward movement over the central parts of the country. The monsoon flow was weak from 10 June onwards and it strengthened again on 23 June. The Monsoon covered the entire country by 2 July, about a fortnight earlier than the normal date. During the entire season of four months, the country as a whole had an average rainfall of 83.4 cms, which is 92 per cent of the long period average (LPA) (Table 2.7 and Fig. 2.1). This statistically, the country experienced a normal monsoon, this being defined as +/- 10 per cent of LPA, yet, at the end of the monsoon season, the following 7 out of 35 meteorological subdivisions of the country had received deficient rainfall:

In more disaggregated terms, 142 out of 424 meteorological districts of the country (34 per cent) received deficient rainfall, i.e. – 20 per cent or less (Fig. 2.2). States with large number of rainfall-deficient districts as shown in Table 2.7A.

It is important to note that there were 71 districts which received deficient monsoon rainfall not only in 2000 but also in 1999, that is, for two successive years. Further, there were 17 districts which received less rainfall for three successive years 1998, 1999 and 2000. South Peninsula comes under the influence of northeast monsoon during October–December and Northwest India receives winter rains during October-March. The normal rainfall over South Peninsula during the northeast monsoon season (Oct.–Dec.) is 313 mm. But in 2000 less rainfall was received which was – 25 per cent of the normal rainfall. The normal rainfall during the winter season of October–March over Northwest India is 136 mm. Rainfall in the first three months of

Table 2.7 South-West Monsoon Performance (1 June-30 September)

Year	*Excess/ Normal rainfall (No. of meterological subdivision)*	*Deficient/ Scanty/No. rainfall*	*Normal/ Excess rainfall (percentage of districts)*	*Per cent of Normal rainfall received (All India)*
1991	27	8	68	91
1992	32	3	65	93
1996	32	3	82	103
1997	32	3	81	102
1998	33	2	81	106
1999	28	7	67	96
2000	28	7	66	92

@ Total number of Meteorological subdivision is 35.

Meterological subdivisions	*Per cent*
Saurashtra and Kutch	– 44
West Madhya Pradesh	– 35
Gujarat Region	– 31
Andaman and Nicobar Island	– 31
East Rajasthan	– 30
East Madhya Pradesh	– 28
West Rajasthan	– 32

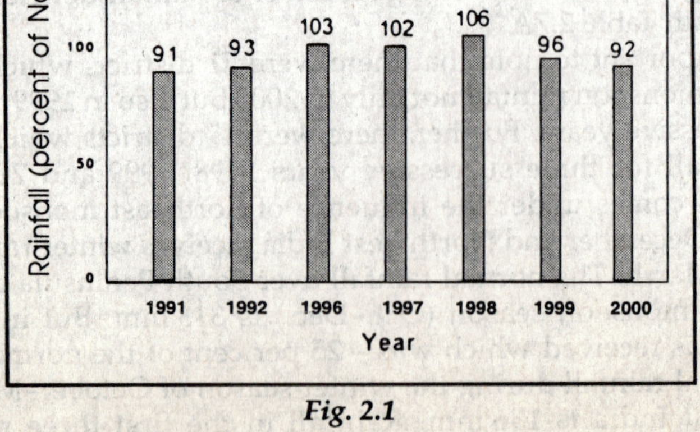

Fig. 2.1

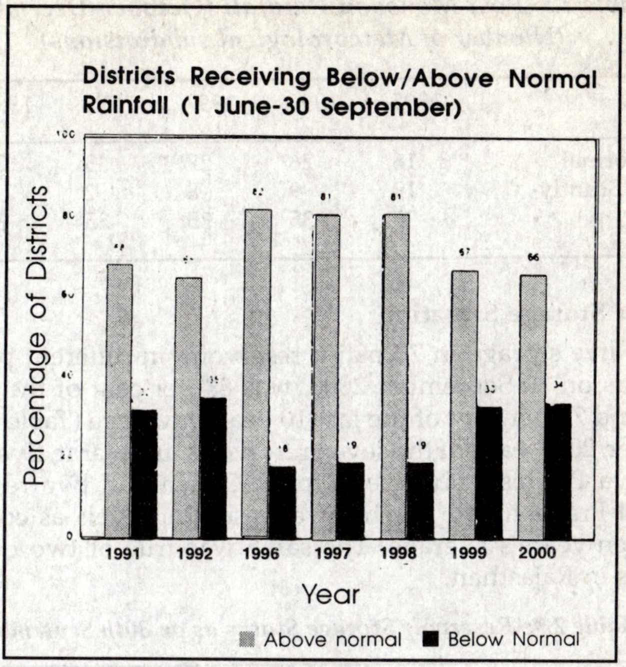

Fig. 2.2

Table 2.7A

State	*No. of districts*	*State*	*No. of districts*
Madhya Pradesh	32	Orissa	6
Rajasthan	26	Punjab	6
Gujarat	16	Tamil Nadu	5
Uttar Pradesh	9	Chhatisgarh	4
Haryana	8	Himachal Pradesh	4
Kerala	7		

October–December accounts for 33 per cent of the season's normal and, rainfall in the latter three months of January-March is 67 per cent of season's normal. During October–December 2000 period departure of rainfall from the normal was – 82 per cent over Northwest India.

For the country as a whole the cumulative rainfall during post monsoon season 2000 (Oct.–Dec.) was excess or normal in 4 out of 35 meteorological subdivisions as compared to 26 subdivisions in 1999 (Table 2.8). It is a not a satisfactory situation and the country may face severe water shortage in summer months of 2001.

Table 2.8 Post Monsoon Rainfall (October–December)
(Number of Meteorological subdivisions)

	1995	1996	1997	1998	1999	2000
Excess/Normal	16	26	27	33	26	4
Deficient/Scantly	19	9	8	2	9	31
Total	35	35	35	35	35	35

Reservoir Storage Situation

The total live storage in 70 major reservoirs in different parts of the country, as on 30 September 2000, was 83 per cent of the last year's storage and 79 per cent of the last 10 year's average (Table 2.9). As on November, 2000, each of the seven reservoirs in Gujarat, five reservoirs in Madhya Pradesh, six reservoirs in Orissa and two reservoirs in Himachal Pradesh had much lower reservoir levels as compared to the last ten years's average. The same was true of two out of three reservoirs in Rajasthan.

Table 2.9: Reservoir Storage Status as on 30th September

	1999	2000
1. Reservoirs (number)	70	70
2. Designed live capacity at full reservoir level (TMC)	130.6	130.6
3. Total live storage (TMC)	97.6	81.4
4. Average of last 10 years (TMC)	104.9	103.2
5. Current year storage as per cent of the design storage	75	62
6. Per cent of this years live capacity to last year	92	83
7. Per cent of this year's capacity to average of last 10 years	93	79

Agriculture and allied sector is anticipated to grow by about 0.9 per cent in 2000-01, which is marginally better than 0.7 per cent growth in the preceding year. Adverse climatic conditions have dampened considerably the growth prospects of crops, which is expected to decline by 3.5 per cent mainly because of 4.7 per cent decline in production of foodgrains (Table 2.10).

Trend of growth in agricultural should, however, be seen over a large time span in order to even out annual seasonal effects on growth. The country's performance in agriculture during the last two decades has been reasonably satisfactory. The average annual growth recorded in agriculture and allied sector (agriculture, forestry and fishing) during

Table 2.10 *Growth in Agriculture*

(Per cent)

	1998-99	1999-2000	2000-2001
Agriculture and Allied (GDP at 1993-94 prices)	7.1	0.7	0.9
Agricultural Production (Index of agricultural production with base triennium ending (1981-82 = 100)	7.7	– 0.7	– 3.5
Foodgrains production	5.8	2.7	– 4.7

the post reform years 1992-93 to 1999-2000 was 3.6 per cent compared to 3.9 per cent in the period 1980-81 to 1991-92 (at 1993-1994 prices). It is important to search for indications pointing toward structural change in the agri-output mix. Even if growth in foodgrains, the most dominant segment of crop agriculture, declerated from 2.9 per cent to 2 per cent in the post reform period, (which is still higher than population growth of 1.6 per cent), there has been high growth maintained in wheat (3.6 per cent) and even rice (2.2 per cent) leading perhaps to the problem of the excess stock of foodgrains (Table 2.11). Decline in coarse cereals (– 1.6 per cent) conformed to the trend of no growth even before the

Table 2.11 *Pre-reform and Post-reform Growth in Agriculture (Annual Average Growth Rates at 1993-94 Prices)*

(Per cent)

Crop	1980-81 to 1991-92	1992-93 to 1999-2000
Agriculture and Allied	3.9	3.6
Agriculture (all crop. animal husbandry, dairying)	4.2	3.7
Forestry	– 0.1	0.8
Fishing	5.4	5.5
Annual Compound Growth of Crop Agriculture (Base: Triennium ending 1981-82)		
Crop agriculture	3.4	2.2
Foodgrains	2.9	2.0
Cereals	3.1	2.1
Rice	3.7	2.2
Wheat	3.6	3.6
Coarse cereals	0.0	– 1.6
Pulses	1.4	0.8
Non foodgrains	4.3	2.4

reforms, indicating producers' and consumers' preference for higher value foodgrains. All crops (46 crops) including plantation crops have registered 2.2 per cent annual growth in the post-reform period compared to 3.4 per cent in eighties. This deceleration is obviously due to decline in coarse cereals production and lack of any growth in pulses production. Annual growth in rice and wheat has been fairly robust.

Foodgrain Area and Production

In the 10 year period 1990-2000, foodgrains area has ranged between 123 million ha. to 130 million ha., the inter-year variation being influenced by weather conditions. The country has thus reached a plateau in so far as area devoted to foodgrains production is concerned. Any increase in foodgrains production in the country has therefore, to come through increase in productivity. The trend in respect of area, production and productivity of foodgrains is given in Table 2.12.

Table 2.12 Foodgrains Area, Production and Productivity

Year	*Area (million hectares)*	*Production (million tonnes)*	*Productivity (Kg./ha.)*
1950-51	87.3	50.8	522
1960-61	115.6	82.0	710
1970-71	124.3	108.4	872
1980-81	126.7	129.6	1023
1990-91	1278	176.4	1380
1997-98	123.8	192.3	1552
1998-99	129.6	203.5	1571
1999-2000*	123.1	208.9	1697

*Anticipated.

Within foodgrains, rice with 42 to 45 million ha. area (about one third of foodgrains area), and wheat with 25 to 27 million ha. area (about one fifth of foodgrains area) have gained at the cost of coarse cereal area, which is now 29 million ha. as compared with 40 million ha. in the 1980s. The area under pulses has remained stagnant at about 21 to 23 million ha. for over thirty years.

CROP PROSPECTS—2000-01

Foodgrains

The Ministry of Agriculture puts the kharif foodgrains production for the year 2000-01 at 102.7 million tonnes compared to last year's production of 104.9 million tonnes (Table 2.13). The shortfall in production by 2.2 million tonnes, is primarily due to drought con-

Table 2.13 Trends in Agricultural Production

Crop	*Agricultural season*	*2001-02† (advance estimates)*	*Targets 2001-02*	*2000-2001* (advance estimates)*	*1999-2000*	*1998-99*	*1997-98*	*1996-97*	*1995-96*	*1994-95*	*1993-94*	*1992-93*	*1991-92*	*1990-91*
(1)	(2)	(3)	(4)	(5)	(6)	(7)	(8)	(9)	(10)	(11)	(12)	(13)	(14)	(15)
1. Foodgrains production													*(Million*	*tonnes)*
Rice	Kharif	76.42	77.98	74.41	76.71	72.72	72.53	71.32	67.88	72.6	70.72	65.24	66.37	66.32
	Rabi		14.02	11.89	12.77	13.36	10.01	10.41	9.1	9.21	9.58	7.62	8.31	7.97
	Total		92.0	86.3	89.48	86.08	82.54	81.73	76.98	81.81	80.3	72.86	74.68	74.29
Wheat	Rabi		78.0	68.46	75.57	71.29	66.35	69.35	62.10	65.77	59.84	57.21	55.69	55.14
Jowar	Kharif	3.89	6.15	4.66	4.82	5.28	4.96	6.99	5.66	5.87	7.28	9.38	5.71	8.33
	Rabi		3.35	2.75	4.04	3.13	2.57	3.95	3.67	3.10	4.13	3.43	2.39	3.35
	Total		9.5	7.41	8.86	8.41	7.53	10.94	9.33	8.97	11.41	12.81	8.1	11.68
Bajra	Kharif	7.53	6.95	6.39	5.66	6.95	7.64	7.87	5.38	7.16	4.97	8.88	4.67	6.89
Maize	Kharif	10.13	10.0	9.85	9.73	9.54	9.43	9.18	8.34	7.64	8.53	8.94	6.96	8.96
	Rabi		2.0	1.99	1.74	1.61	1.39	1.59	1.19	1.24	1.07	1.05	1.1	
	Total		12.0	11.84	11.47	11.15	10.82	10.77	9.53	8.88	9.6	9.99	8.06	8.96
Ragi	Kharif	1.73	2.4	2.47	2.38	2.61	2.09	2.34	2.5	2.34	2.6	2.53	2.58	2.34
Small millets	Kharif	0.64	0.65	0.65	0.64	0.67	0.64	0.73	0.78	0.8	0.92	0.87	0.88	1.19
Barley	Rabi		1.5	1.49	1.46	1.54	1.68	1.46	1.51	1.73	1.31	1.51	1.7	1.64
Coarse cereals	Kharif		25.15	24.02	23.23	25.05	24.76	27.11	22.66	23.81	24.30	30.60	20.80	27.71
	Rabi		6.85	6.23	7.24	6.28	5.64	7.0	6.37	6.07	6.51	5.99	5.19	4.99
	Total		33.0	30.25	30.47	31.33	30.4	34.11	29.03	29.88	30.81	36.59	25.99	32.7
Cereals	Kharif	100.34	104.13	98.43	99.94	97.77	97.29	98.43	90.54	96.41	95.02	95.84	87.17	94.03
	Rabi		98.87	86.58	95.58	90.93	82.0	86.76	77.57	81.05	75.93	70.82	69.19	68.1
	Total		203.0	185.01	195.52	188.7	179.29	185.19	168.11	177.46	170.95	166.66	156.36	162.13

Table 2.13 Trends in Agricultural Production (Contd.)

Crop (1)	Agricultural season (2)	2001-02† (advance estimates) (3)	Targets 2001-02 (4)	2000-2001* (advance estimates) (5)	1999-2000 (6)	1998-99 (7)	1997-98 (8)	1996-97 (9)	1995-96 (10)	1994-95 (11)	1993-94 (12)	1992-93 (13)	1991-92 (14)	1990-91 (15)
Tur	Kharif	2.3	2.9	2.85	2.79	2.71	1.85	2.66	2.31	2.14	2.69	2.33	2.13	2.41
Other kharif pulses	Kharif	2.95	3.1	2.32	2.12	2.43	2.44	2.83	2.27	2.52	2.69	3.3	2.29	3.00
Gram	Rabi		8.0	3.39	5.08	6.8	6.13	5.57	4.98	6.44	4.98	4.42	4.12	5.36
Other rabi pulses	Rabi		3.0	2.99	3.36	2.97	2.55	3.19	2.75	2.94	2.95	2.77	3.48	3.49
Total pulses	Kharif	5.25	6.0	4.68	4.91	5.14	4.29	5.49	4.58	4.66	5.38	5.63	4.42	5.41
	Rabi		9.0	6.38	8.44	9.77	8.68	8.76	7.73	9.38	7.93	7.19	7.6	8.85
	Total		15.0	11.06	13.35	14.91	12.97	14.25	12.31	14.04	13.31	12.82	12.02	14.26
Total foodgrains	Kharif	105.59	110.13	103.11	104.85	102.91	101.58	103.92	95.12	101.07	100.4	101.47	91.59	99.44
	Rabi		107.87	92.96	104.02	100.7	90.68	95.52	85.3	90.43	83.86	78.01	76.79	76.95
	Total		218.0	196.07	208.87	203.61	192.26	199.44	180.42	191.5	184.26	179.48	168.38	176.39
2. Oilseeds and other Commercial Crops											*(Lakh tonnes except cotton and jute)*			
Groundnut	Kharif	52.9	70.0	46.7	38.8	69.1	59.0	69.4	60.5	60.6	57.1	66.6	49.9	51.2
	Rabi		23.0	17.4	14.3	20.7	14.7	17.0	15.3	20.0	21.2	19.0	21.0	23.9
	Total		93.0	64.1	53.1	89.8	73.7	86.4	75.8	80.6	78.3	85.6	70.9	75.1
Castorseed	Kharif	7.0	10.0	9.0	7.8	8.4	8.3	9.0	7.8	8.5	6.3	6.3	5.8	7.2
Sesamum	Kharif	6.6	8.0	5.4	5.1	5.3	5.7	6.4	5.3	5.9	5.6	7.6	7.1	8.4
Nigerseed	Kharif	0.7	2.0	1.0	1.5	1.4	1.4	1.5	1.9	1.9	2.0	1.6	1.8	1.9
Rapeseed and mustard	Rabi		75.0	40.9	59.6	56.6	47.0	66.6	60.0	57.6	53.3	48.0	58.7	52.3
Linseed	Rabi		8.0	2.4	2.9	2.7	2.4	3.1	2.9	3.2	3.3	2.8	2.9	3.3
Safflower	Rabi		4.0	1.7	2.8	2.4	1.2	4.5	3.8	4.2	5.2	3.5	2.0	3.2

Table 2.13 Trends in Agricultural Production (Contd.)

Crop	Agricultural season	2001-02† (advance estimates)	Targets 2001-02	2000-2001* (advance estimates)	1999-2000	1998-99	1997-98	1996-97	1995-96	1994-95	1993-94	1992-93	1991-92	1990-91
(1)	(2)	(3)	(4)	(5)	(6)	(7)	(8)	(9)	(10)	(11)	(12)	(13)	(14)	(15)
Sunflower	Kharif	1.3	5.0	2.8	2.1	2.4	2.4	3.9	4.5	3.3	5.0	4.3	3.6	3.3
	Rabi		10.0	3.8	5.9	7.1	6.5	8.6	8.1	8.9	8.5	7.5	8.3	5.4
	Total		15.0	6.6	8.0	9.5	8.9	12.5	12.6	12.2	13.5	11.8	11.9	8.7
Soyabean	Kharif	57.9	70.0	50.9	67.9	71.4	64.6	53.8	50.9	39.3	47.5	33.9	24.9	26.0
Total: nine oilseeds	Kharif	125.4	165.0	115.8	123.2	158.0	141.4	144.0	130.9	119.5	123.5	120.3	93.1	98.0
	Rabi		115.0	66.2	85.5	89.5	71.8	99.8	90.1	93.9	91.5	80.8	92.9	88.1
	Total		280.0	182.0	208.7	247.5	213.8	243.8	221	213.4	215.0	201.1	186.0	186.1
Cotton #	Total	123.0	145.0	99.9	116.4	122.9	108.5	142.3	128.6	118.9	107.4	114.0	97.1	98.4
Jute #	Total	80.7	97.5	92.5	94.2	88.4	99.6	99.6	76.7	80.0	73.5	75.0	89.4	79.2
Mesta ##	Total	14.1	12.5	11.2	11.1	9.7	10.6	11.7	11.3	10.8	10.7	10.9	13.5	13.1
Jute and meata##	Total	94.7	110.0	103.7	105.3	98.1	110.2	111.3	88.0	90.8	84.2	85.9	102.9	92.3
Sugar cane (cane)	Total	2799.6	3250.0	3003.2	2992.3	2887.2	2795.4	2775.6	2811	2755.4	2296.6	2280.3	2540.0	2410.5

Lakh basis of 170 kgs each ## Lakh bales of 180 kgs each * Fourth advance estimates as on 29.06.2001
† First advance estimates as on 28.09.2001
Blacks mean advance estimates are yet to be made.
Source: Agriculture Statistics Division, Directorate of Economics and Statistics, Department of Agriculture and Cooperation, GOI (as on 28.09.2001).

ditions prevailing in 71 districts not only in 1999 but also in 2000, that is, for two successive years. Production of kharif rice, estimated at 74.1 million tonnes, would be lower by about 2.6 million tonnes compared to last year's record production of 76.7 million tonnes. Kharif pulses, estimated at 5.5 million tonnes, is somewhat better than last year's production of 4.9 million tonnes. Production of kharif coarse cereals, despite more area coverage, is estimated at 23.1 million tonnes marginally lower than last year, due mainly to lower productivity on account of deficient rainfall in some areas.

Rabi crop prospects were also not satisfactory. As already stated earlier, the post-monsoon rainfall has been inadequate. Consequently, area sown under rabi crops has been lower this year. Preliminary estimates indicate that rabi foodgrains (where wheat dominates) may be at best reach 96.3 million tonnes which represents a sharp decline of 7.7 million tonnes over last year rabi foodgrains output of 104 million tonnes. Expected wheat production of 70 million tonnes would be 5.6 million tonnes lower compared to last year. Whereas Punjab and Haryana may reap a normal wheat crop because of assured irrigation, decline in wheat production would be mainly in M.P., Rajasthan, Gujarat and U.P. Total foodgrains production in 2000-01 is thus estimated at 196.07 million tonnes compared to 208.9 million tonnes in the preceding year. This represents a fall of nearly 10 million tonnes (4.7 per cent drop). The effect of this large decline is not worrisome as the country sits on a very large public food stock of over 43 million tonnes.

Commercial Crops

Amongst major commercial crops; cotton jute/mesta, and sugarcane are kharif crops whereas oilseeds are produced both during kharif and rabi seasons. The latest estimate for the current year points to an improvement in production of two of these crops, that is, sugarcane and cotton; whereas it predicts a fall in the other two, that is, oilseeds and, jute/mesta (Table 2.13).

Sugarcane is likely to reach a new peak of 300.6 million tonnes in the current year compared to 299.2 million tonnes achieved last year. The current year's expected cotton output of 13.2 million bales is an improvement over last year's 11.6 million bales, despite shrinkage in area.

The decline in output of oilseeds has continued for the second successive year. The current year's oilseed output at 18.6 million tonnes, is lower by 2.3 million tonnes compared to 20.9 million tonnes achieved in 1999-2000. Soyabean output would be lower by 1.6 million tonnes compared to 6.8 million tonnes achieved last year. Repeseed/mustard output too would be lower by 1.7 million tonnes to reach 4.3 million tonnes compared to last year's output of 6 million tonnes. Production of jute and mesta has been fluctuating between 8 and 10 million bales. During the current year, production of jute and mesta is likely to be 9.9 million bales marginally less than last year's 10.5 million bales.

UNION BUDGET 2001-02 PROPOSALS

Agriculture and Rural Development

- Interest rate charged by National Bank for Agricultural Rural Development (NABARD) on lending from RIDF to States reduced from 11.5% to 10.5%. The corpus of RIDF VII increased from Rs. 45 billion to Rs. 50 billion next year.
- Banks to accelerate Kisan Credit Card programme and cover all eligible agricultural farmers within the next three years. Banks also to provide a personal insurance package to the KCC holders, as is often done with other credit cards, to cover them against accidental death or permanent disability, upto maximum amount of Rs. 50,000 and Rs. 25,000 respectively. The premium burden to be shared by the card issuing institutions.
- Nabard to link 100,000 additional Self Help Groups during 2001-02, which would help in providing access to credit to an additional 2 million families. Sharecroppers and tenant farmers to become eligible for this scheme and special attention to be given to SC/ST groups.
- Nabard capital gains tax exemption bonus to continue.
- The resources from the Watershed Development Fund set up in Nabard to be used to promote people's participation and also enable water users' associations to implement, operate and maintain irrigation schemes.
- Coverage of credit-linked subsidy scheme for construction of cold stores for perishable commodities scheme extended to cover rural godowns. Nabard to reduce its rate of interest for funding the storage of crops from 10% to 8.5%.
- Scheme for setting up Agriclinics and Agribusiness Centres by agricultural graduates to be launched with Nabard support. Loans on attractive terms for setting up these centres to be provided by banks with refinance from Nabard.
- Increase rural road connectivity and rural electrification.
- Enlarged role to the State Governments in both procurement and distribution of foodgrains for PDS in their respective states.
- Review of the operation of the Essential Commodities Act, 1955.
- Agriculture and Rural Development Budget (2002-03) is at Appendix 2.1.

Putting Agriculture on A Political Agenda*

There is then the question of political commitment on the subject. Success of All Programmes Lies in Political (Government) Marketing, which does not mean to politicize the issue but bring it on the agenda of the Government. We have seen its success in the field of industrialization in the 1960's and 70's and currently it is all about infrastructure, power, communications, roads and bridges. Agriculture

---

* B.K. Taimni, Food Security in 21st Century, 2001.

has never been on the agenda except in Punjab, Haryana and Western UP because it helps form or fall the government. The second Green Revolution referred to earlier cannot sustain unless followed by masses and masses follow the lead of revolution for the ultimate agenda is the same for leaders and the followers.

We also see the importance of groundnut and cotton in Gujarat, sugarcane and cotton in Maharashtra. In the case of the latter State, aim of the powers-that-be is rarely to ensure increase in productivity but it is to control the powerful lobbies be it sugar, (not so much sugarcane production), cotton trade (not so much cotton) or groundnut oil (not so much groundnut production); the production regime is relegated to secondary levels. Be that it may, what is seen is that unless it is on the agenda of the government, agriculture will continue to get high, strident and loud noises but no actual support, focus or attention as required. Rice and wheat in Punjab and Haryana and Sugarcane in Western UP would never have reached where they are today but for the total cohesive and focused, let us say 'one track' approach for production and marketing of these commodities. The states having potential will also call for and need a similar approach. *Bring agriculture on the political agenda of the governments-it shall never fail.*

Currently, of the about 190 million hectares of gross cropped area, about 145 million hectares is sown in kharif and only about 45 million hectares in rabi. We have more than 60 million hectares of area under irrigation. We have so seen that the productivity levels of wheat, paddy/rice, oil seeds, pulses are consistently much higher during rabi i.e. under controlled conditions. *One of the short-term strategy for development could be to increase area under rabi, both under irrigated and rainfed conditions.* It results in better and controlled water use, better fertilizer use efficiency and better use of machine and manpower as also less of plant pests and diseases. If that is so, then logically, the approach and 'shift' needs to be further exploited to get the best from the area under plough on a sustainable basis.

Ministry of Water Resources of Government of India had earlier estimated the total area which could be brought under irrigation is about 113 million hectares which has now been revised to 139 million hectares. According to available figures, irrigation potential has already been created to irrigate about 92 million hectares by the end of 8th Five Year Plan thus leaving about 47 million hectares of creating potential. We are adding about one million hectares of irrigation every year and on this basis, it will take us another 47 years to realize the full potential. The question is can we wait. Answer is a clear 'No'. There are over 300 projects (131 major and 176 medium) which are at different stages of implementation. A three-pronged strategy is required in this regard. Firstly, take up repair and maintenance of the irrigation works and simultaneously start charging for the services at least to meet the maintenance costs.

Secondly and definitely, provide for completion of the ongoing works during the coming Plan even if sacrifices have to be made in certain other sectors, including exploring the possibility of involving private sector even at the stage on 'Build-Operate and Transfer' or 'Build, Own and Operate' principle assuring them a certain return on the capital/collection of irrigation revenue. Thirdly, go whole-hog for exploitation of ground water exploitation so that in the next five years we use that much water for irrigation as can and is allocated by the Ground Water Organization for this purpose. *There is no escape* from realizing our irrigation potential to the maximum at the earliest and then play a role by becoming the largest provider for employment, export earner and providing food security. *A single point agenda, cutting across party lines needs to be drawn up in this regard if we have to become intrinsically strong economically and then paving the way for accelerated industrial development*. The agenda should include efficient use of water, considering water as a scarce but critical input. It is the purchasing power generated by agriculture which will help generate demand and it is the rising demand for future market that everyone is after.

CONCLUSION

The discussion so far shows that despite commendable achievements, there have been some failures and causes for concern regarding Indian agriculture. First, India has become not only self sufficient in foodgrains but has accumulated unmanageable surpluses of over 62 million tonnes (end of October, 2001) major part of which is lying in the open without appropriate storage facilities. The country has been priced out both in the national and international markets making disposal of foodgrains difficult. Secondly, land reforms in the form of redistribution of land in favour of the poor and tenancy reforms are largely failures, except in the States of Kerala and West Bengal, where some achievements have been made. Thirdly, the demographic pressures have been quite high on agricultural sector as shown by the large number of workers dependent on agriculture. As a result, the rate of growth of labour productivity has been very low. There has also been a widening of disparities between agriculture and non-agriculture. The demographic pressures have also led to parcelisation of land holdings. Fourthly, the input subsidies have increased significantly since the mid-70s. This has led to inefficient use of land and water resources. Fifthly, the growth of infrastructure has not been satisfactory. The growth rate of investment in agriculture rose only for a decade following the Green Revolution and later it declined significantly in both public and private sectors. There has been an absolute decline in public capital formation during the 1980s. It further declined in the early 1990s. Lastly, regarding land and water resources, there are problems such as land degradation, chemicalization of agriculture, water logging and ground water depletion. There is also, the problem of severe moisture stress in dryland areas.

Appendix 2.1

GREEN REVOLUTION

During the early sixties, the country was going through a food crisis not known and experienced in post-independent India. The country imported 25.4 million tonnes of foodgrains between 1961 and 1965 and 19 million tonnes in just two years, 1966 and 1967. The import of foodgrains was about 10 per cent of the indigenous production and the population of the country was 480 million. The international community put India in the category of 'non salvageable'—a country that one should not try to salvage because it would probably sink the life boat for the rest of mankind. It was not surprising that Lal Bahadur Shastri (the then Prime Minister) gave a call to the countrymen to miss a meal in a week.

Two important decisions were taken by the then Agriculture Minister (C. Subramanian) for achieving self-sufficiency in food grains. These were (i) introduce science and technology in agriculture, and (ii) establish a pricing policy to motivate farmers for enhancing production. He constituted a panel of scientists from the Indian Agricultural Research Institute (IARI), New Delhi led by Dr. B.P. Pal to advise him on scientific aspects. Dr. Ralph Cummings of the Rockefeller Foundation, with the support of the Ford Foundation had been attempting to introduce new high yielding wheat varieties from Mexico. Seeds of wheat varieties were distributed to IARI, Pantnagar and Ludhiana that gave yield of 5000 to 6000 kg per hectare, and yet there was no progresss in the propagation of these new varieties.

The results though encouraging, met criticism from various quarters both politicians like communists (American seeds), bureaucrats and even scientists. But the Agriculture Minister with the support of the then Prime Minister took a bold decision and converted his 5 acre bungalow lawns and playgrounds to a demonstration farm with high yielding varieties of seeds and once it proved to be a success, he obtained instant approval from his cabinet colleagues for the new agricultural policy. It so happened that the Agricultural Minister (CS) visited Manila to attend an FAO regional conference, which took him to the International Rice Research Institute. He was given small quantities of seed of 12 new varieties including Taichung Native 1, and Taichung Native 3. This material brought in 1965 was not only suitable for cultivation, but also as parental lines for developing high yielding varieties to meet consumer needs in India. Thus with his new policy, we took advantage of both wheat and rice technology unlike many other countries where only one of these could be successfully attempted. Accordingly, the change was to be brought in North, East and South. Subramanian took a deliberate decision to introduce high yielding wheat varieties in Punjab (Punjab and Haryana of today) and parts of western U.P. while recognizing that the climate and soil of Bihar were good for introduction. But he had a lot of confidence in farmers of Punjab who indeed lived up to this expectations.

Having decided to introduce new technology, there were several decisions to be taken (i) to gain confidence that the technology would be successful in wheat growing regions, (ii) if it was indeed successful then to spread to as large area as possible to do away with PL-480 supplies. In a meeting of scientists. M.S. Swaminathan, then head of the Botany Division, IARI, suggested organization of 1000 demonstration plots of two hectare each in farmers' fields. On the question of failure of demonstrations, farmers were promised compensation if they lost. Thus began the ambitious programme of producing 25 million tonnes of wheat, unparalleled in the history of agriculture anywhere in the world. 23,000 tonnes of seed was imported from Mexico for distribution in the 1966-67 crop season. Dr. Borlaug later said that while CIMMYT evolved the new seed, the decision of India to import 18,000 tonnes (23,000 tonnes in all) of this seed set a chain reaction not only in India but also elsewhere. This was the birth of new agricultural production programme that popularly came to be known as 'Green Revolution"—a term coined by Dr. William Gaud of USA in 1968.

The new policy had to decide whether we go in the same way of traditional agriculture or break away from that to one of scientific and modern agriculture. This is the issue, the fertilizer and non-fertilizer (cow dung), the plant protection, non-plant protection. Some of us had been saying that we have been carrying on this agriculture for 2000 years and our peasants know everything in the world with reference to traditional agriculture but modern scientific agriculture is not known to every one of us. We had to learn many new things. Therefore, the policy decision with reference to the question was that we are not going to stick to traditional agriculture.

The seeds of Green Revolution were sown much earlier when there was a significant scientific breakthrough in five major food crops in the preceding five to six years starting with hybrid maize or hybrid corn in 1961. And four double-cross hybrids were released under a programme jointly organized by the Indian Council of Agricultural Research and the Rockefeller Foundation. The introduction of first hybrid sorghum was in 1963. In 1964 we had identified, from the material sent by Dr. Borlaug, two wheat varieties—Lerma Rojo and Sonora 64. Then came the work of the Punjab Agricultural University on hybrid millet. Finally, dwarf varieties of rice like IR8 were introduced from Taiwan through IRRI. Scientists felt that there was significant breakthrough in all these crops. Compared to the actual yields in the farmer's fields, the potential yields of these varieties were high, two-to-three times as much as are harvested. This position was verified in the farmer's field through a national demonstration programme in 1965.

No one could have anticipated in those early days the miracle for which C. Subramaniam laid only the foundation but also a road map for self-sufficiency in food in the country. On the floor of the Parliament he said, "Therefore if this House and the country want that we should reach self-sufficiency, as far as I am concerned, as far as this Government is concerned, I want to give this pledge that we shall do everything possible to become self-sufficient and to see that we get rid of our dependence on imported food grains as early as possible." The pledge was fulfilled when the country, between 1976 and 1980, did not import any grains despite a severe drought of 1979 that resulted in decreased production by 22 million tonnes over the previous year. It has been more than fulfilled today when the country has a stock of over 60 million tonnes of foodgrains which are threatening to cross 70-75 million tonnes at the end of current Kharif (2001).

Several important decisions were needed for sustaining the change. The first was the reorganization of agricultural research in the country. The Indian Council of Agricultural Research was reorganized following the vision of Homi Bhabha called "Growing Science". The Director General was to be the Secretary to the Government of India and thus agricultural research and education were taken out of the Department of Agriculture. It was emphasized that time has come to realize that agricultural sciences cannot function in isolation. It has to interact with other scientific disciplines. Mathematics has its own impact on agricultural sciences, physics has its own and of course so does biology. Therefore, in the fora in which we have been participating in the last few years, we have been suggesting that there is no question of isolating agricultural universities. There should be greater interaction with the general universities and with research in other disciplines. The organizations that were established in the short period are National seed Corporations, State Farm Corporation of India, Agriculture Price Commission and many others. An important organization which earned a name for itself is the National Dairy Development Board.

Ever Green Revolution

Deceleration of the impact of green revolution has been discussed in this study elsewhere. It has to be realized that genetic homogeneity enhances genetic vulnerability to pests and diseases. Excessive use of mineral fertilizers and chemical pesticides have caused soil degradation, ground water pollution and the spread of pests resistant to pesticides in several green revolution areas. There are also the added issues concerning increasing demand and shrinking land and water resources, improved purchasing power and increased urbanization lead to higher per capita foodgrain requirements due to an increased consumption of animal products, increasing damage to the ecological foundations of agriculture, such as land, water, forests, biodiversity and the atmosphere and distinct possibilities for adverse changes in climate and sea level, no dramatic technological breakthroughs on the horizon which can help to halt the fatigue of the green revolution.

Consequently, the per person world grain harvest declined from 415 kg in 1985 to 360 kg in 1996. It would, therefore, be useful to examine how science can be mobilized for ending the technological stagnation by raising further the ceiling to biological productivity without associated ecological harm. It will be appropriate to refer to the emerging scientific progress on the farms as evergreen revolution, to emphasize that it is sustainable overtime since it is rooted in the principles of ecology, economics, social and gender equity and employment generation. If the green revolution is to yield sustained benefits, it has to become evergreen. The transition from a green to an evergreen revolution can be achieved by shifting the focus from a purely commodity-centred approach to a farming systems one. The biophysical endowments of an area will have to be taken into consideration while tailoring technologies for a given ecosystem. Appropriate crop rotations will have to be devised. Since irrigated farms in the tropics offer scope for multiple cropping, the introduction of stem-nodulating legumes like Sesbania rostrata in the rotation becomes feasible.

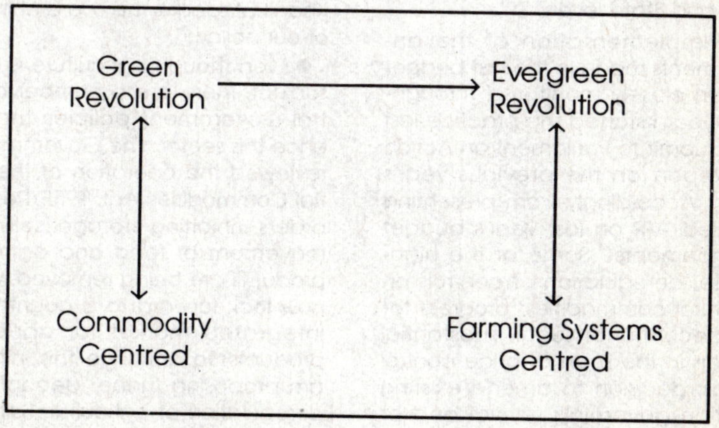

Appendix 2.2

UNION BUDGET 2002-03
AGRICULTURE AND RURAL DEVELOPMENT

BUDGET STRATEGY

● In my last budget I had laid out a comprehensive agenda of the second generation economic reforms. I had also deepened tax reforms aimed at providing a modern tax regime. My aim this year is to consolidate and implement these policies at all levels. I propose to take this process further at the State level through a strategy of reform linked public funding.

● The broad strategy of the budget, therefore, is to:

◗ Continue the emphasis on agriculture and food economy reforms.

◗ Enhance public and private investment in infrastructure.

◗ Strengthen the financial sector and capital markets.

◗ Deepen structural reforms and regenerate industrial growth.

◗ Provide social security to the poor.

◗ Consolidate tax reforms and continue fiscal adjustment at both the Central and State levels.

● The implementation of the announcements made in the last budget has been closely monitored throughout the year. I started the practice last year to submit to Parliament an Action Taken.Report on the previous year's budget. Accordingly, I am presenting a detailed ATR on last year's budget announcements. Some of the highlights are: deregulation of controls on agricultural commodities; progress towards decontrol of sugar; substantial reduction in the span of price control of drugs; decision to amend existing legislation governing revival and or winding up of companies, along with abolition of SICA; substantial progress in privatization; progress in the implementation of Expenditure Reforms Commission's recommendations and announcement of VRS for surplus government employees.

● These decisions demonstrate the resolve of this Government to carry forward the process of economic reforms, and to ensure that the benefits reach the common man. This will require improved implementation and governance. We shall put in place measures to effect improvement in these areas with the objective of eliminating poverty and improving the quality of life of our citizens.

Deregulation

● Having achieved great success with the Green Revolution and then the White Revolution, the country is now ready for its third revolution of agricultural diversification and food processing. This requires policy changes, a renewed thrust on agricultural research and extension, and a new climate that encourages much greater investment in both the public and private sectors. Removal of the remaining regulatory and procedural rigidities that still exist and improved rural infrastructure is essential for this new revolution. Freedom to the farmer, Kisan Ki Azaadi is the overarching goal of our policy.

● Even though agriculture is a State subject, there are a number of Central Government policies that influence this sector. The Government has reviewed the operation of the Essential Commodities Act, 1955. Restrictive orders inhibiting storage, selling and movement of food and agricultural products are being removed. We can now look forward to a country- wide integrated market for agricultural products. To continue this initiative, I am proposing further decontrol and deregulation of agriculture along the following lines:

◗ Amendment of the Milk and Milk Products Control Order (MMPO) to remove restrictions on new milk processing capacity, while continuing to regulate health and safety conditions.

◗ Removal of small scale industry reservations related to various agricultural equipment items.

- Decanalization of the export of agricultural commodities and phasing out of remaining export controls.

- Expansion of futures and forward trading to cover all agricultural commodities.

- A multiplicity of regulations for food standards under the Prevention of Food Adulteration Act, the Food Products Order, the Meat Products Order, the Bureau of Industrial Standards and the MMPO, affect the food and food processing sectors. They need to be modernised and converged. The Prime Minister has decided to set up a Group of Ministers (GOM) to propose legislative and other changes for preparing a modem integrated food law and related regulations.

- This process of providing freedom to the farmers needs to be carried forward by State Governments. Amendment of the Agricultural Produce Marketing Acts to enable farmers to sell directly to potential processors would help them to receive better prices and to access potential new markets. In addition, the remaining State control orders which are acting as barriers to inter-State trade need to be lifted. I am proposing that additional allocations in respect of centrally sponsored schemes would be linked to decontrol deregulation of the agricultural sector by the States.

- The 2000-01 budget had announced a credit-linked Subsidy Scheme for construction of cold storages. Sanction has already been given for the creation of 21 lakh tonnes capacity in cold storages, much higher than the target of 12 lakh tonnes. The rural godown scheme announced last year has also become operational. With the removal of various control orders much greater investment would be forthcoming under both these schemes. Accordingly, I propose to allocate Rs 70 crore to each of these subsidy-linked credit schemes in 2002-3.

Agricultural Credit

- As Finance Minister I feel particularly responsible for the flow of adequate credit to the agriculture sector. I am glad to report that the total credit flow to the agriculture sector through institutional channels is expected to reach the targeted level of Rs 64,000 crore this year. It is expected to increase to Rs 75,000 crore in 2002-2003. I propose the following steps to further improve the delivery of agricultural credit:

- The funds for RIDF VIII will be enhanced from Rs 5000 crore to Rs 5500 crore next year, while the rate of interest will be reduced from 10.5 per cent to 8.5 per cent. Henceforth it will be fixed at the prevailing bank rate plus 2 per cent. Assistance to the States from RIDF will be linked to reforms in the agriculture and rural sectors.

- Kisan Credit Cards introduced in 1998-99, have been a resounding success and have helped our farmers considerably in their access to agricultural credit. An additional 63 lakh KCCs have been issued up to December 31, 2001 taking the total to 2.07 crore. The personal insurance package linked to KCCs has also been operationalised.

- Similarly, the scheme of micro-credit through Self-Help Groups is progressing well. The target of one lakh additional self-help groups during the current year is expected to be achieved taking the total so far to more than 3.5 lakh covering more than 70 lakh families, making it the largest micro credit programme hi the world. I am raising the target to 1.25 lakh for 2002-03.

- A one-time settlement scheme for small loan accounts with outstanding principal balance upto Rs 25,000 as on March 31, 1998 is already in operation. A special OTS scheme for small and marginal farmers will be announced by RBI to cover loans upto Rs 50,000.

Crop Insurance

- The National Agriculture Insurance Scheme is already in operation. To subserve the needs of farmers better and to move towards a sustainable actuarial regime, I propose to set up a new Corporation for Agriculture Insurance to be promoted by the existing public sector general insurance companies.

Irrigation

● I propose to increase the allocation for the Accelerated Irrigation Benefit Progranme (AIBP) from Rs 2000 crore this year to Rs 2800 crore in 2002-03. This will assist the States to accelerate the completion of unfinished medium and maor irrigation projects, and also to undertake reforms by revising user charges and setting up of water users associations.

Agriculture Extension and Research

● The accelerated diversification and modernization of agriculture will require a new approach to research and extension services. I therefore propose to enhance the allocation for 2002-03 for agriculture research to Rs 775 crore from Rs 684 crore in the current year. A full review of the governance of agricultural research is also proposed so that the system can serve the new needs creatively.

Linkages between research and extension will be strengthened to improve quality and effectiveness of research and extension systems. The extension system will be revitalised and broad-based through Krishi Vigyan Kendras (KVKs), NGOs, farmers organisations, cooperatives, the corporate sector and agri-business clinics. KVKs will be designated as nodal agencies for quality certification including organic products, bio-fertilizers, and bio-pesticides. The supply of inputs, agro-processing and trade through such co-operatives/ companies will be encouraged through the availability of credit with the help of NABARD.

The Companies (Second Amendment) Bill 2001, already introduced in Parliament will enable the conversion of existing producer cooperative businesses into companies.

Agricultural Exports

● Promotion of agricultural exports is important for creating conditions for providing remunerative prices to farm produce. For this purpose Agri Export zones are being promoted in different States and 15 such zones have been approved so far. APEDA will catalyse development of infrastructure and flow of credit to the units in these Agri Export zones.

RURAL DEVELOPMENT

Rural Roads

● The Pradhan Mantri Gram Sadak Yojana (PMGSY) initiated to provide connectivity through all weather roads to all our villages is making considerable headway. A further allocation of Rs 2,500 crore for the year 2002-03 is being made over and above Rs 5,000 crore provided so far. Depending on the accelerated implementation of these works I intend to find additional resources including those from multilateral sources in the course of the year.

Rural Electrification

● During my last budget speech I had announced a package of initiatives for electrification of 80,000 villages that have no access to electricity. Considering the fact that SEBs find it difficult to service debt, the Government proposes to introduce a new interest subsidy scheme called the Accelerated Rural Electrification Programme. An outlay of Rs 164 crore has been provided for this scheme in 2002-03.

Rural Employment

● The Sampoorna Grameen Rozgar Yojana (SGRY) announced by the Prime Minister in his Independence Day speech of 2001 was launched on September 25, 2001 by merging the ongoing Employment Assurance Scheme (EAS) and the Jawahar Gram Samridhi Yojana (JGSY). Since the launch of the scheme, release of 30.6 lakh tonnes of food grains to States has already been authorised, out of the 50 lakh tonnes allocated. This scheme will be continued next year. I urge upon all the States to come forward to take full advantage of the free food grains being offered under this scheme.

● Lok Nayak Shri Jai Prakash Narayan always had a special concern for the disadvantaged. In his birth centenary year I propose to launch the Jai Prakash Rozgar Guarantee Yojana (JPRGY) to provide employment guarantee to the unemployed in the most distressed districts of the country. A Task Force headed by my colleague, the Minister of Rural Development, will be set up to design and implement a massive programme for employment generation in these districts. KVIC, DC (SSI), and other agencies will be fully involved in the implementation of this scheme.

● The promotion of rural industrialisation would be helped greatly through capacity building and technology upgradation in Khadi and Village Industries. To help in this effort I propose to upgrade the Wardha Institute started by Mahatma Gandhi in 1935 as a national institute to be called Mahatma Gandhi Institute for Rural Industrialisation.

● The diversification of agriculture will not succeed without appropriate infrastructure for marketing. For this purpose, rural local bodies, cooperatives and NG0s will be assisted to set up rural produce marketing centres and subcentres at the district and block levels and to upgrade village *haats* under a special scheme of the Swaran Jayanti Gram Swarozgar Yojna (SJGSY).

● Some parts of our country have been particularly afflicted with natural calamities. Additional allocation of Rs 480 crore was provided under the Indira Awas Yojana for the affected States. Houses constructed by the poor under the Indira Awas Yojana (IAY) in such disaster prone areas YAN henceforth be provided insurance cover through a Master Policy.

Management of the Food Economy

● I had drawn attention last year to the severe policy and fiscal difficulties arising from the growing mismatch between the unprecedented level of procurement of wheat and rice by FCI and the much lower PDS and buffer stock needs in the last few years. The current situation of open-ended procurement by FCI at a high price and disposal at a heavily subsidised price is not sustainable. The concept of decentralised procurement has not yet found favour with the States. The report of the High Level Committee on Long Term Grain Policy is expected to be submitted shortly. We shall formulate a more durable approach for better management of our food economy after considering this report.

● A number of steps have been taken by the Government to reduce the high food grain stocks that are posing serious problems of storage and disposal. These measures include: increased allocations for BPL families; launching of a major food for work programme under the SGRY, allocation of 30 lakh tonnes of free food grains to States for relief works in areas affected by natural calamities; open market sales of 30 lakh tonnes this year compared to 5.5 lakh tonnes in 2000-2001; and enhanced incentives for export of food grains.

CHAPTER 3

Agricultural Development Strategy

Fifty four years after independence and fifty one years since we set out with the First Five Year Plan "to translate ... the goals of social and economic policy prescribed in the Directive Principles of the Constitution., into a national programme based upon the assessment of needs and resources", it is clearly a time to take stock of how far we have come towards attaining these goals, and record the achievements and the shortcomings, so that we may better chart the course of the nation's future development. The Development Strategy can be based on this analysis. India's development strategy, like that of most other developing countries, has evolved over successive plan periods, reflecting the growing strength of our economy.

It is a cause of legitimate national pride that over this period a stagnant and dependent economy has been modernized and made more self-reliant. A modest rate of growth of per capita income has been maintained despite the growth of population. Agricultural output has risen throughout this period, though slowly. While the production of foodgrains has increased to levels where we have attained not only self-sufficiency but also exportable surpluses. However, in two key cash crops, oilseeds and occasionally cotton, we continue to rely to a significant degree on imports. Though the area under irrigation has more than doubled in the period of planning, we are far short of developing the full potential. Yields generally have grown slowly, despite the dramatic increase in the productivity of wheat in the sixties. This has proved to be a constraint on the pace of general economic development, and fluctuations in agricultural output have often led to unplanned cutbacks in public investment and bouts of inflation, both of which had a depressing effect on growth.

The main features of India's agricultural development since Independence are too well known and need no detailed description. It suffices to highlight that during the last fifty years the country has achieved and sustained historically unprecedented growth of output, averaging somewhat under 3 per cent per year as against less than 1 per cent per annum during the first half of the century. According to Alan Hestan (1983) (`National Income' in Dharma Kumar (ed), Cambridge Economic History of India, Vol. 2, Cambridge University Press), the increase in agricultural output was 32 per cent between 1900 and 1947. On the other hand, Dr. S.R. Sen observed in his article entitled "Growth and Instability in Indian Agriculture" (Agricultural Situation in India, January 1967) that "during the first 24 years of the century foodgrains production increased at an average annual (linear) rate of 0.3 per cent.. The next 24 years, however presented completely different picture. During this period, foodgrains production showed a declining trend of 0.02 per cent per annum (linear) on the average, in spite of the fact that droughts turned out to be relatively moderate and less frequent". Needless to say, during the plan period output growth has been well ahead of population. That this has happened despite reaching the limit of expansion of cultivated land is significant. Expansion of cultivated area has virtually come to a stop in recent years. Growth in yields per hectare of cultivated area has become increasingly important and is now the predominant source of growth.

Over the years, the country has experienced considerable changes in the agrarian structure. The most striking trend has been the progressive decline in the average size of land holdings due to demographic pressure, and subdivision and fragmentation of holdings. The steep decline in the incidence of tenancy is another distinct feature of the agrarian structure. This tendency gets reinforced by technological progress. In so far as it increases the returns to the farmers, the owners have incentive to shift from tenancy to self-cultivation. The tenancy-ceiling law prevents farmers from adopting large-scale technologies. Abolition of tenancy in states like Karnataka prevented tenants from leasing in sufficient land to create large operational holdings. Further, fragmentation of holdings with each successive generation has made the ceiling even less relevant.

A major achievement has been the diversification and expansion of India's industrial capability with the public sector playing a leading role. The country is self-sufficient in all consumer goods and in basic commodities like steel and cement, while the capacity of other industries like fertilisers is rapidly expanding. The growth of capital goods production has been particularly impressive, and India can now sustain the likely growth of most of her industries, whether textiles, food processing or cement or chemical, metallurgical and engineering industries, power or transport, by the domestic production of the capital goods needed with only marginal imports. However, this pace of industrialization has not been brought cheaply. The concentration of economic power has increased, in the sense that, within the corporate sector, the assets of bigger corporations have increased more rapidly.

The expansion of large-scale industries has failed to absorb a significant proportion of the increment to the labour force, and led in some cases to a loss of income for the rural poor engaged in cottage industries like textiles, leather, pottery, etc.

The development of productive capacity has also been marked in the area of energy sources. The output of India's primary fuel source-coal, has been expanded more than threefold and much of the industry has been modernized. The intensive search for oil and gas, launched in the late fifties, has achieved notable success both on and off shore. An efficient complex of refineries, pipelines, storage and distribution has been developed and the country is moving into the petrochemicals age. A large infrastructure has been built to sustain this subcontinental economy: the network of irrigation storage works and canals, hydro and thermal power generation, regional power grids, a largely electrified and dieselised railway system, national and State highways on which a rapidly growing road transport fleet can operate and a telecommunication system covering most urban centres and linking India with the world. Expansion and improvement of the transport network, especially rural roads, has made it easier and cheaper for farmers to access inputs and market their produce.

The development of agriculture and modern industry has stimulated the growth of banking, insurance and commerce, and matching expansion and modernization of ports, shipping and internal and external air services. However, the major beneficiaries especially of the banking system, have been the wealthier section of the population, both in urban and rural areas, and the vast majority have barely been touched.

India's foreign trade has expanded rapidly in recent years, the commodity composition of our exports having changed with emphasis on manufactures and mineral ores. Of late, the inflow of remittances has also been very high. Because of these factors and the substantial measure of import substitution that has been attained, our foreign exchange situation has improved to a stage where it is not a major constraint on development. However, the successes in import substitution and export promotion were achieved in some cases at an unduly high cost.

The pattern of industrial development that has emerged obviously reflects the structure of effective demand, which is determined by the distribution of incomes. An unduly large share of resources is thus absorbed in production which relates directly or indirectly to maintaining or improving the living standards of the higher income groups. The demand of this relatively small class, not only for a few visible items of conspicuous consumption but for the outlay on high quality housing and urban amenities, aviation and superior travel facilities, telephone services, and so on, sustain a large part of the existing industrial structure. This means that the further expansion of industry is limited by the narrowness of the market. As a result, further import substitution of consumer goods or capital goods cannot, at the current level of demand, afford any great impetus for continued industrial growth. In fact, of late there has been a slow down in the manufacturing sector due to excessive buildup of capacities in the private sector during 1994-97 which was clearly not sustainable on the basis of normal growth in domestic demand and general slow-down in world trade.

Significant results have been achieved in agricultural research, and Indian scientists and technologists are working in many areas on the frontiers of today's knowledge, as in the development of nuclear power and the use of space technology for communications and resource development. For further industrial and scientific advance, with growing competence in adaptive research and development, we need only a selective import of technology. It is not clear, however, that all the areas of research have the social and economic relevance that would justify the application of our limited resources to these fields. Small and cottage industries and other rural activities have not received the research and development support that they required. The expansion of output of scientists, engineers and technicians has been rapid since the late fifties; supply has actually outstripped the domestic demand for some categories of trained personnel.

Much of the benefits from infrastructure have accrued largely to the relatively affluent. Our pattern of investment, particularly in the provision of social infrastructure, has been based in favour of urban area. Thus, though the output of doctors is numerically adequate and the urban well-to-do have reasonable hospitals to go to, the rural areas continue to be poorly served in respect of access to medical services. Many areas of the country remain backward and regional disparities in agricultural development have increased. Many segment of the population, like the scheduled castes and tribes, have not shared fully the benefits of growth.

The average life expectancy of the Indian people rose from 32 years in the forties to around 46 years in the sixties and 62 years now owing to the extinction of smallpox and reduction of the incidence of malaria and cholera as well as a marked fall in infant mortality. However, the level of malnutrition is still very high and not enough has been done by way of protected water supply and sanitation in rural areas to provide protection against water-borne diseases.

The enrolment of students at the elementary level has risen from 32 per cent to 92 per cent and at secondary level from 5 per cent to 58 per cent of the relevant age-groups in the period of planning. But we have still to attain the goal of universal primary education which the Constitution had enjoined should be done within ten years. The number of dropouts is very high indeed, reflecting economic pressures and the rural poor's view of the relevance of the education given to their children. The degree of adult illiteracy continues to be massive; the present estimate being that over 200 million of the adult population is unlettered. The enrolment at the stage of higher education, which rose from 416,000 a year in 1950-51 to over 3 million currently, has led to a high degree of wastage and the growing unemployment of graduates.

This assessment of India's economic development over half a century of planning had indicated some fundamental failures and it is on account of these that the need has arisen for a re-appraisal of the development strategy. We must face the fact that the most important objectives of planning have not been achieved, the most cherished goals seem to be almost as distant today as when we set out on the road to planned development. These aims-implicit in all our plans, but more explicitly stated in the later formulations of our development strategy-are universally accepted by the Indian people: they are the achievement of full employment, the eradication of poverty and the creation of a more equal society.

STRATEGIES ADOPTED

Pre-Independence Period

In view of its importance in the national economy, the government has been framing policies from time to time for agriculture as a whole as well as for individual crops according to the exigencies of the situation. A systematic policy framework in agriculture initiated by the government dates back towards the second half of the eighteenth century (1871) when the British Government felt the need for establishing the Department of Revenue, Agriculture and Commerce and then a separate Department of Revenue and Agriculture in 1880-81. Later on, the first serious step to frame a policy of agricultural research suited to the condition of India was initiated towards the last decade of the previous century.

The most important landmark in the agricultural policy framework was the appointment of Royal Commission on Agriculture in 1926 which submitted its report in 1928 and made detailed suggestions and recommendations in various fields like agricultural research, crop production, animal husbandry, fisheries, etc. The Commission's report is still considered as a reference volume on agricultural policy.

The Grow More Food (GMF) campaign launched in 1942 marked the beginning of a sustained national endeavour at increasing agricultural production. Another major development in the immediate pre-independence period was the first ever elaboration in January, 1946 of an All India Policy in Agriculture known as "Statement on Agriculture and Food Policy in India"

Post Independence Period

Meeting the domestic food requirements has been the foremost social priority before the country since independence. Hence major thrust was given in food production beginning with First Five Year Plan, particularly during mid-sixties. A clear policy framework coupled with sound planning and implementation backed by generous research and development investments, ensured sustained production of foodgrains and other agricultural commodities. Indeed, it is generally recognized that the post-independence period growth owes much to a conscious and proactive policy of government for promoting agricultural development. The main elements of it once again is well known. Massive public investments in canal systems and rural electrification have resulted in a near trebling of irrigated area in the past five decades. In fact, increase in the availability of irrigation facility had brought about a perceptible change in the cropping pattern among the cereal crops at the macro level. Among the commercial crops, there was substantial increase in area under irrigation in case of oilseeds and sugarcane. A major fall out of significant increase in irrigation facility has, in fact, benefited only a few crops and the growth in agricultural output has been lopsided. The cropping pattern in the dryland areas has remained, by and large, static with poor growth in productivity.

Strategies in Need

Despite impressive development in agriculture following adoption of various strategies, all has not gone well with this development. In fact, there are many dimensions in which performance has lagged behind expectations. Agricultural growth has not been as regionally balanced as it should have been. Despite five decades of planning, the vast majority of the rural inhabitants still rely, directly or indirectly, on agriculture, forestry, or fishing for the livelihoods, a dependence that places enormous pressure on natural resources. The continuing degradation of these resources could well cause social conflict over remaining resources and discontent about the widening gap between urban and rural quality of life.

There has been no worthwhile land reform and rural labour has become increasingly proletarianised. The new technology is alleged to be against wage labour and there are apprehensions of growing underemployment and decline in real wages. The problem of regional disparities and the growing disparities between rainfed and irrigated agriculture are matters of serious concern.

High growth rate in agriculture in the long run can be sustained only by broadening the regional base of agriculture. This will have to be achieved through devoting greater amount of resources to rain-fed areas, ensuring more intensive and efficient utilization of irrigation facilities and continuous flow of improved technologies and farm practices. To complete the economic transformation in rural India requires further growth, but growth that is more equitable and environmentally sustainable than it has been in the past. Meeting this challenge will warrant more efficient application of resources for agricultural growth, public sector investment, rural poverty reduction and natural resource protection. Agricultural output must continue to grow. Slower agricultural growth could jeopardize food security and increase child malnutrition, cause significant new unemployment and poverty and reduce non-agricultural growth.

True, the country is now not only self-sufficient in cereal production but also has exportable surplus. The excellent record of the agricultural research system, applying science to farming and developing new technologies, of agricultural extension systems in helping farmers learn how to use those technologies, of farm input supply systems, in providing irrigation, water, seeds, fertilizers, credit, and other inputs to farmers in a timely fashion, improvement of marketing infrastructure and government policies, ensuring continuous effective demand to encourage production; and of an agricultural education system providing trained people to do all of these are heroic success stories. However, sustaining such a rate of agricultural growth would require much larger use of inputs, particularly land, irrigation, fertilizers, pesticides, high yielding variety seeds, etc.

But there are second general problems. Irrigation was an ideal way to overcome drought in rain dependent agricultural areas, but it has brought its own problems. These include salinization and water logging where drainage has not been adequate, new water borne diseases in formerly dry areas. This calls for a scientific `Water Resource Planning' which aims at not only in optimizing the utilization and management of water resources but also making the planners aware of environment and social security consideration. Modernization of canal water delivery system and command area development to raise the irrigation efficiency is the need of the hour. It may be pointed out that in many regions in the country the efficiency continues to be around 40 per cent or even less as compared to 75 per cent in Israel.

Full utilization of the potential created also involves another important problem. All our big dams and water storage tanks are silting at an alarmingly high rate due to indiscriminate felling of forests in the catchment areas, threatening to reduce the total life span of all of them drastically. Our costly and irreplaceable reservoirs, which represent not only valuable irrigation potential but very often hydel power and flood control potential also, must be saved from the threat of premature siltation. Huge wastage of water and water logging of vast cultivable areas caused by the seepage from badly managed canals are no less a serious problem.

We must aim at reducing the present volume of water used for irrigation, through increase of conveyance, distribution and application efficiencies, at the same time conserving the quality of water use efficiency. For improved water use efficiency we should adopt better on-farm management and command area management programmes which should cover rational overall system of management. Needless to say, cropping intensity crucially depends on the availability as well as the quality of irrigation facility. Hence, our irrigation strategy should aim at not only of augmenting irrigation facility but also use of existing facilities.

Further, mineral fertilizers helped immensely increasing yield of cereal and other commercial crops – beyond what natural soil fertility could provide. But again, some soils are being contaminated with excessive quantities of nitrates and other chemicals which endanger the drinking water supplies on which human life depends. And every time a new plant variety is developed which is resistant to a particular insect on disease pest, a new variation of that pest evolves to attack the new plant. We are now face to face with the challenge of ensuring sustainable system of agriculture which tries to balance the concern of both improved productivity and production from our basic assets, namely the land and so managing these resources that the soil health and water quality remains unimpaired. Without these measures not only would we find it difficult to sustain even present level of yields, but much less production in the coming years. The use of biofertilizers will have to be intensified through evolution of improved strains, organizing a more efficient production and distribution system.

Availability of land is expected to emerge as a major constraint on agricultural growth in India. Increase in yield is expected to be the primary contributor to the enhanced agricultural production. So long, the yield growth rate has largely been based on increasingly more intensive use of inputs, particularly chemical fertilizers and pesticide and the ill-effects of high level use of these inputs are already evident in the country's agriculture. Under the present yield-coefficient with respect to chemical fertilizer use, achieving a higher growth rate in yield in future could result in an unsustainably high level of fertilizer-intensity. Concerted efforts will therefore need to be made to increase the yield coefficient with respect to both fertilizer use and irrigation. This alone will not be sufficient and increased attention will have to be paid on replacing chemical fertilizer with bio-fertilizers and the production of bio-fertilizers will have to be encouraged in right earnest immediately.

The scientific management of soil and optimum use of available precipitation, necessitate the diversification of traditional cropping system to high value generating enterprises such as animal husbandry, dryland horticulture, pasture land development, agro-forestry from the point of view of both improving income level of the small farmers as well as optimum use of land and water resources in the hilly terrains and rainfed/dryland areas.

It has been pointed out that India has achieved self-sufficiency in cereal production. However, there has been no proper breakthrough in the productivity of pulses and oilseeds. Due to prevailing food crisis after independence, the thrust of the country's research programme was mainly to attain improvement in the productivity of food crops. Once the high yielding varieties of wheat and rice were brought out, irrigated areas were brought mainly under these two crops. Further, our oil seeds policy has also been responsible for shrinkage in area under the crop. Low import duty on oils, higher cost of production and sick condition of the crushing units have resulted in an unprecedented crisis in the mustard industry with sharp decline in area. For instance, Rajasthan has been the major producer of mustard as the crop required less water, but with better monsoon in 2001-2002 crop year and higher prices for wheat and gram, the scenario was changing. Farmers also often do not get good quality seeds from the market effecting productivity.

Area under oilseeds in the country has shrunk, with farmers complaining of unremunerative prices. Often it is suggested to revise the tariff value upwards to discourage imports of edible oil. But perhaps the answer does not lie in erecting high tariff walls or in mounting purchase operations at artificially high prices by agencies such as NAFED, on par with the operations of the FCI in wheat and rice which have become millstone around the central government's neck. It must be sought in improving the productivity of oilseeds cultivation and reducing costs of production as well as diversification into non-traditional oilseeds.

In addition to various issues discussed above, Indian Agriculture today is also plagued by:

1. Managing Food Mountains.
2. Depleting Water Resources leading to second generation environmental programs.
3. Absence of adequate private investment in agriculture and
4. Tardy growth of organic farming and branding of organic products.

MANAGING FOOD MOUNTAINS

Three important initiatives have been taken recently for dealing with the mounting grain stocks in a socially and environmentally meaningful manner. First, the initiation of the Sampoorna Gramin Rozgar Yojana with foodgrains for organizing food-for-work programmes. Second, a million tonnes of foodgrains have been offered to Afghanistan, through the World Food Programme, the largest assistance of this kind given by any nation to the people in deep distress. Third, the Government has decided to launch a Grain Bank Scheme (GBS) in tribal areas, with an initial allocation of one million tonnes of foodgrains and Rs. 66 crores in cash for meeting the transportation costs.

In the current demand recession when other sources of demand such as government expenditure, exports, consumption and investment are all faltering, it looks like agriculture is coming to the rescue. Since it still accounts for about a third of the output and two-thirds of employment, forecasts of 9 per cent growth imply a revival in aggregate growth to above 6 per cent. Over the past decades double digit agricultural growth in any year has stimulated industrial output in that and the next year. Low agricultural growth in the past two years is partially responsible for the slowdown in industrial growth.

More money in the hands of so many more people will increase sales, but industry has to focus on the rural and semi-urban consumer to make full use of the opportunity. Already, in anticipation of monsoon largesse there is a boom in sales of CTVs in non-metropolitan areas.

The Food Mountains: Given the huge accumulation of foodgrains stocks, will the rise in output translate into a rise in agricultural incomes? Will prices crash? At Indian per capita income levels and price elasticity of demand, farmers benefit from stable prices more than from rising prices. Since demand for food products falls as incomes rise, most countries begin support programmes to moderate the fall in agricultural incomes after food falls to less than half the budget share. In India, because of the farm lobby, this type of support began much earlier at the cost of much more essential infrastructure. There is evidence that stable agricultural prices lower inflation, poverty and raise demand for both industrial and food products. Although the increase in agricultural price was lower in the eighties compared to the nineties, agricultural income, production, and price relative to manufacturing improved more in the eighties. India's agricultural price policy needs to be reformed to keep agricultural prices stable (correcting for cost of production), not to keep raising them. Farmers only need to be protected against sharp fluctuations in crop prices. The supply response is better at stable prices and agricultural incomes still improve (Table 3.1).

Table 3.1 Price Policy and its Consequences

Rate of Growth in	*80s*	*90s*
WPI primary articles	7.1	9
WPI foodgrains	7.2	11.2
Index nos. of agricultural production	4.2	1.7
Agricultural GDP at (1993-94 prices)	3.8	3.1
Wheat procurement price	8.4	14.3
Index nos. of wheat production	4.7	3.7
Agricultural price terms of trade (range)	+ 8	+ 7

The distinction between the procurement and support price was lost from seventies, and the support price at which farmers could make assured sales, approached the market price. In the nineties it had overtaken the latter, and by the end of the nineties domestic prices exceeded world prices. An indication that prices were set too high is the steady increase in foodgrain stocks with the government. The average level rose from 10.1 million tonnes in the seventies to 13.8 in the eighties and 17.4 in the nineties. In June 2001 it was 46 and crossed 60 million tonnes by June 2001. Before liberalization the farm lobby had argued that agriculture was discriminated against because world prices were higher than domestic and they were not allowed to export. Now when export is feasible grain prices are not competitive. Stable domestic prices would make our products more competitive and help the farmer find new markets.

Relative agricultural prices depend on what is happening to non-agricultural prices, Since the wage –price spiral does not kick in when food prices are stable, non-food prices rise less and terms of trade turn in agriculture's favour. This explains the surprising last row of the Table, which shows the maximum variation in the ratio of agricultural to non-agricultural prices over the decade. Thus ironically the farmer can buy more in real terms when he raises his price less. Manufacturing prices are also falling with increased competition and fall in protection. If these indirect systematic effects are understood such a policy change may become acceptable.

DELINKING MSP FROM PROCUREMENT

The proposal is being considered to reduce the Government's role to fixing an MSP and doing away with the procurement which has become unmanageable and was costing the public exchequer around Rs. 21,000 crores annually. This envisages sale of their produce by the farmers at open market price and the differential, if any with MSP. The system would be linked with the National Agriculture Insurance Scheme compulsory for all farmers and loanees records to be maintained. To safeguard the interest of farmers, average production of each farmer, his family's consumption and surplus would be recorded and after taking the market, his MSP into account, payments will be made. As far as the requirements of the PDS and buffer stock were concerned, those would be met at the state level through open tender. Existing surplus over and above the buffer stocks would gradually be disbursed through various centrally sponsored schemes. This supposed to be a better system as farmers nationwide could benefit unlike the present one where 80 percent of the procurement was from the three states of Punjab, Haryana and Andhra Pradesh.

Current high stock of 62.5 million tonnes, expected procurement of 20 million tonnes paddy in 2001-02 season and the low projected offtake would lead to an unprecedented stock pile up. Procurement from Punjab was nearly 58 per cent whereas it produced 20 per cent of the total wheat output in the country. Similarly Haryana's output was 12 per cent of the total but procurement was 27 per cent. However, the situation was reverse in States such as Madhya Pradesh where production was 11.8 per cent, but procurement a measly 2.1 per cent. In Bihar there was no procurement at all though its share was six per cent in production. Uttar Pradesh produced 33 per cent but procurement was 9.4 per cent. As for rice, Punjab's share in the country's output was a mere nine per cent yet the procurement was 40 per cent of the total in the country. As far as Andhra Pradesh, Bihar, U.P. and West Bengal were concerned, the corresponding figures were 13.3 and 31; 8.0 and 0.11; 13.5 and 8.0 and 15.5 and 2.0 per cent respectively.

Does the implementation of this policy mean automatically that the Centre will save its large subsidy bill, estimated at around Rs. 21,000 crores a year? Not necessarily. The Government's commitment to the farmers in terms of MSP will continue to operate in the sense that the Government (Centre or States?) will compensate the farmer for the shortfall of the market price received in relation to the MSP announced. Given the certainty that market price will vary among the diverse regions in the country, a policy of actual cash disbursement to the farmers will entail enormous administrative hassles. Yet the Government point that the system of MSP and procurement based on it, at present, benefits largely the producers in Punjab, Haryana and Andhra pradesh, accounting for 80 per cent of procurement of foodgrains in the country, and that the alternative proposed, would benefit every farmer in the country, indeed specious given the fact that the MSP and marketable surplus with the farmers are necessarily correlated.

Buffer stocks for food security and PDS for consumer protection from the inequities of the market will evidently continue but under the responsibility of the States. That, over a period, the FCI will have to be downsized and that the determination of the MSP will itself be taken outside the purview of the political establishment are the necessary ingredients of the new food policy adumbrated.

Problem of Flour Millers

Flour millers have demanded rationalization of government's open market sale scheme prices for wheat so as to bring them in line with market prices to improve offtake from FCI. The Roller Four Mills Federation has also asked for zero tax on basic cereals like wheat under value-added tax regime and removal of the commodity from the purview of Essential Commodities Act. Many flour mills have closed down, others are having a capacity utilization of a mere 55 per cent as the prices offered by the government were beyond the reach of the industry. It is a paradoxical situation that mills were operating at much below capacity at a time when government stocks were rising and sizeable quantity was likely to become unfit for human consumption. Prevailing system of categorizing procured wheat as of fair average quality (FAQ) by FCI also failed to meet the requirement of the millers.

Classification in different categories based on quality parameters should take place simultaneously with the procurement operations. Improper pricing and segregation has led to less purchase by millers and government stocks have swelled by 11.3 million tonnes to 38.72 mt. in August 2001 from 27.59 mt. an year ago.

In the wake of arguments and criticism from several states on the first-ever National Agricultural Policy evolved by the government, the BJP President, set up a seven-member committee headed by Mr.Bhairon Singh Shekhawat to examine and suggest specific policy measures to effectively implement the policy. The report recommends 23 specific measures. Some are routine, some already known. The main problem is a paradox-stockpile of 60 million tonnes of foodgrains and 30 crore poor people unfed, undernourished and unable to buy two square meals. The second issue relates to wheat, paddy and sugarcane being produced continuously more than the demand, while edible oils and pulses are being imported regularly at a very high price in terms of foreign exchange.

The report says "need is for rationalization of the buffer stock. It should be kept in reserve for use in times of scarcity and famine. It pegs this stock at 30 million tonnes. Ideal would be 20 million tonnes with the new stock being added with the new crop coming in and the old stock disposed of." And why not use foodgrain stock for "mutual exchange" with crisis-ridden countries in time of scarcity at the international level? On remunerative or the minimum support price, the report stresses that it should be such in respect of oilseeds, pulses and coarse grains as to remunerate farmers habitually growing wheat and paddy. To do so, impose the minimum rates of import duty on these commodities within the World Trade Organization regime in order to stop their imports. Also discontinue any type of subsidies and concessions to vegetable oil mills or any government or private agencies.

Remove all restrictions on the sugar industry. India is burdened with 10 million tonnes of sugar after meeting all requirements. Value addition is limited and process of modernization and diversification has failed. It is possible to produce 27 valuable chemicals from molasses by introducing the updated technology. It is an irony that while there exist no controls on import of Vodka and wine products, processing from potatoes, grapes, molasses, coarse grains and other agricultural products is still licensed. All these restrictions should go. Even the outdated "milk products order" must be scrapped to free the Indian dairy and milk processing from shackles.

There should be free movement of all foodgrains and agricultural commodities. It dis-favours continuation of restrictions on granting loans against agricultural commodities, their storage and processing and future trading. Amend the Essential Commodities Act, 1955, to achieve the objectives of allowing free trade. The report mentions about the harmful side effects of excessive use of chemicals-fertilizers to plant protection – so very essential when need was to have high production to meet food scarcity in mix-sixties. That meant intensive irrigation. Time has now changed. Soil has lost fertility. There is toxicity. Ecology and environment are threatened with pollution. Out of 23 micro-nutrients, 16 elements, including iron, zinc, manganese, sulphur, ferrum, nitrogen, phosphate and potash, are lacking in the soil. Even quality of fertilizers is poor. The result is that to obtain 1 kg of produce, quantity of fertilizer required now is up by two and a half to three times against earlier days.

A group of scientists at the Indian Council of Agricultural Research revealed in 1998 that the Indian farmers spent Rs. 1,72,000 crore annually on three agricultural inputs alone: chemical fertilizers, pesticides and seeds. This resulted rise in cost of production. While production increased, there was no corresponding increase in agricultural output proportionate to inputs. And, of course, farmers income also did not increase. Therefore, it was time to revert to compost, farmyard manure, making use of agricultural wastes, village garbage and city sullage. Promotion of worm-culture can give good results. Need was for financial and institutional framework and promoting food processing industry.

The report wants the minimum support price (MSP) to take care of both the producer and the consumer. This means, striking a scientific balance rather than keeping MSP unrealistically high because it curtailed the government's supporting role since it could not extend to the consumers due to high issue price. The report recommends removal of export restrictions, promoting agro-based industry and cultivation of medicinal plants, protection of indigenous cattle and higher investment in water management. For the latter, it demands an allocation of Rs. 1 lakh crore under a national plan for irrigation, rainwater collection and water management in the next Five-year plan.

Among other things, it suggests diversification of agriculture, promoting horticulture, leasing land and consolidating small holdings as a prerequisite for economics of agricultural operations. It recommends leasing of government waste land to the private sector for agricultural research and development, protection of agriculture under the WTO and a broad-based consultative process by including the Ministries of Agriculture, Commerce, Food, Science, Technology and Finance. It favours an "integrated" system of agriculture to reduce cost of production and compensate farmers. It will protect environment and take care of farm residues. Rationalization of fertilizer subsidies and development of agricultural infrastructure, including setting up of agricultural export zones, has also been suggested.

Consultative Committee

The consultative committee members of the Finance Ministry have suggested that the producer subsidy given to farmers, currently routed through the Food Corporation of India and its procurement prices, should be transferred directly to the farmers instead as direct income support. This is a form of subsidy in vogue in the US and much of Europe. Currently, the government extends support to the farmers in the form of input subsidy and support prices. But are deemed inefficient by experts, whose theoretical positions stand more than vindicated by the current state of affairs where high support has resulted in reduced consumption and accumulation of huge grain stocks – expected to be closed to 80 million tonnes of grain with the government by the time the on-going procurement of rice is completed (by only 2002).

Income supplements are considered to be the ideal forms of subsidy. They are considered to be trade non-distorting as well, meaning that such subsidy leaves product prices undisturbed so that they reflect the actual cost of production. When inputs are subsidized or support prices are offered, these impact the price of produce and distort trade. It is on this ground that the World Trade Organization (WTO) has mandated reduction in agricultural subsidies barring income support.

However, India would have practical problems in switching to income support from product subsides. In developed countries, farmers are relatively small and easily identifiable group – around 2 per cent of the population in countries like the US and UK. In India, in contrast, two thirds of the population live on agriculture, including a large army of marginal farmers. Distributing direct incomes support to all of them would be an administrative task that would overwhelm the most efficient administrative machinery in the world. What it would do to the creaking, leaking mass of babus and red tape that goes by the name of administration in this country is anyone's guess.

CROP DIVERSIFICATION

India inherited a stagnant agriculture at the time of independence in 1947, hence the primary task of the Government of India in the initial years of the post-independence period was to initiate a growth process in this sector. The major problem which the country faced was acute food shortage. As such expansion of food production was the primary focus of the agricultural planning process. In fact, the focus mirrored a universal drive to raise agricultural growth rates and attain a greater degree of self-sufficiency. In the mid-sixties, a new technology in the form of high-yielding varieties (HYVs) was introduced for cereals. Apart from the new technology, public investment in agriculture particularly in irrigation was stepped up significantly. Large investments were made for the development of research system under the aegis of the Indian Council of Agricultural Research (ICAR) and the State Agricultural Universities (SAUs).

Simultaneously a well designed extension network was created for disseminating new technologies to the farmers. The administered price policy has provided incentives to the farmers. Successive Five-year Plans aimed at improving infrastructure through irrigation, stepping up the use of fertilizers, improved varieties of seeds, implements and machinery and supply of credit. As a result, there has been a significant increase in the use of modern inputs leading to higher productivity and production, particularly of rice and wheat. The production of foodgrains increased from 50.8 million tonnes in 1950-51 to 209 million tonnes in 1999-2000. the country is now proud of achieving self sufficiency in foodgrains and maintains a buffer-stock of over 60 million tonnes.

It is intriguing (and even paradoxical) to perceive that it is the process of accelerated economic growth that leads to pollution and natural resource degradation, but only through economic growth can environmental protection and natural resource conservation be sustainably maintained. The question, therefore, is to grow or not to grow, but how the process of economic growth can be carefully planned and how relevant policy measures be rationally designed so that economic growth would meet the challenge of conserving the natural resource base protecting the environment, be technically appropriate; economically viable and socially acceptable.

While making announcements about increasing the productivity levels in dry areas and thus improving the living standards of farmers in those regions, not much has been done with regard to soil and water conservation practices. We have been talking about these schemes right from the First Plan. One would imagine the fate of future agriculture where the farmer is having no access to proper seed, with water table going down, soil degradation taking place at a rapid speed. We will now have to adopt policies to implement these programmes on a war footing. To enhance productivity and promote crop diversification, funds had to be pumped in for creation of infrastructure such as roads, cold storage, refrigerated transportation and marketing networks. The corporate sector has to play a big role in providing these physical and knowledge infrastructure.

The Case of Punjab

Having made its major contribution towards the goal of food self sufficiency for the country, Punjab agriculture today is at cross roads. It is showing signs of fatigue. Punjab which is considered as one of the most prosperous State is plagued by a number of basic problems. It is quite low on the human development scale. Total workers (6.27 million) constitute 30% of the population. Of these those engaged in agriculture and allied activity are 3.96 million (63%). Here again as many as 1.54 million (39%) are agricultural labourers and only 0.5 million are engaged in the allied sectors - livestock etc. The share of agriculture in the NDP has, come down to 43.4% at current prices.

The Green Revolution in Punjab and Haryana has achieved its objective but with some negative externalities. Apart from storage blues, long honeymooning with such a limited crop pattern where it is now paddy that dominates the earlier diversified kharif scenario, has become the source of much worry. Excessively water hungry, its excessive cultivation in otherwise poor rain blessed areas has resulted in excessive drawing of underground water resulting in waterlogging in some areas, high disturbances of underground watertables in others.

In fact such a situation has resulted in considerable environment damage. Waterlogged areas have also been inaccessible to farmers and thus added to their suffering and losses where several farming under heavy debt have been forced to take the extreme step when cases of suicides have occurred. On the other hand, areas where underground water balance has been disturbed due to excessive discharge of water and its slow replenishment are turning into danger spots with high contamination of underground water due to liberal use of chemicals which is posing danger to both human beings as well as animals.

The misery does not end here. Considerable post-paddy harvesting period now witnesses low clouds of smog hanging allround the rural areas. Its harmful consequences affect children and old people and those who suffer from respiration problems. This smog results from reckless burning of leftovers in the paddy fields which have to be soon made ready for the sowing of wheat crop. In fact, with fields yet wet, their operations resulting fast multiplication of mosquitoes encouraging spread of malaria in surrounding areas. Lately both Punjab and Haryana have witnessed unusual rise in malarial cases.

Thus, it is the excessive cultivation of paddy on soils, otherwise not conducive to such cultivation which lately has turned out to be a big villain disturbing the environment balance as well as sending adverse signals to the health of rural areas. A serious cost benefit exercise of economic gains as against social fallouts from paddy cultivation would without hesitation suggest immediate slow down of this mad race, which though has brought good income to farmers who failed to find alternative equally paying crops. But then we have reached a situation where there is no alternative to putting firm foot against further growth of paddy cultivation and stop all those experiments which promise raising two short crops of paddy in place of one. This would help farmers raise three crops a year, but then at what cost? Already the existing two-crop pattern is proving harmful. Thus such madness should not be encouraged further.

Rather we should seriously concentrate on developing both early maturing as well as high-yielding varieties of alternative environment friendly and less water demanding crops which in fact had figure prominently before high paddy cultivation took over the farmers. Here, our farm universities both Punjab Agricultural University (PAU) and Haryana Agricultural University (HAU) have earned global recognition for their good work done in promoting green revolution. Now they should seriously get down in extending their research capability to work out the same magic in alternative crops like oilseed, pulses, sugarcane, cotton, maize, fodder and others which suit the soil and environment of this area. A similar revolution in these areas can certainly figure out from their persistent efforts.

Now country is no doubt self-sufficient in foodgrains, but still we have to depend upon the imports for the pulses, edible oil and sometimes even sugar. There is no justification in producing surplus substandard foodgrains on one hand and importing others. This anomaly in the cropping pattern of Punjab and Haryana needs change and diversification into low volume and high value crop alternatives. Dominance of the paddy-wheat rotation in these states is the root cause of the present crisis. It must be diluted as production of these crops has been increasing steadily in other states and their dependence upon Punjab and Haryana to meet their foodgrain demand, is reducing year after year due to the spread of latest agricultural technologies in these states. At least 10 to 20 per cent area under this rotation in Punjab and Haryana must be shifted to the other crops such as oilseeds, pulses, vegetables and horticultural crops keeping in view the market conditions, environmental issues and above all the interests of the farmers. These crops have been ignored by the farmers of these states due to higher risks in their production, labour intensive nature and unfavourable market prices. Diversification of farming systems in these states will not be an easier task and will require major initiative on the part of their state governments to remove these bottlenecks before suggesting the farmers to change the existing cropping pattern. The present minimum support price mechanism is also biased towards paddy-wheat rotation and must be reshaped to encourage agricultural diversification in these states. This will also help us in reducing our dependence upon the imports of the agricultural goods, particularly edible oil and pulses. Shift in area from paddy-wheat rotation to pulses will improve soil health as their production require lesser irrigations, and chemical fertilizers due to their nitrogen fixing properties.

It is heartening that PAU is already on the job. It has prepared meticulous plan for slashing down area under paddy cultivation to 1.6 million hectares from its present level of 2.6 million hectares. It works to reducing to 60 percent from its current level and they think that it can be achieved in two to three years. Even though it is an ambitious plan, particularly considering the past experience, it should nonetheless be taken seriously by the government for only by this aggressive policy approach we can save the current situation from worsening further. The government should provide special incentive for encouraging research into these areas which should gradually fill our farm operations to restore the health of rural areas which, as observed earlier, are under high pressure.

Crop diversification is not a new talk. A shift of 10% rice area to horticulture is the policy being followed by Punjab for long, but achievement is poor. This needs to be re-examined. Here below, we are putting together some of the views of scientists in this regard and giving an idea of some success stories also.

Possibilities of Diversification

The scientists say that in the flood-prone areas the choice of crops would depend on the depth and duration of water stagnation in the fields. According to them, the farmers in these areas in the kharif season could grow dhaincha and jowar, jowar and castor, jowar and paddy or sugarcane. However, if the flood water recedes before September, then from the first week to the end of September farmers can grow maize and cowpea, toria, or Chinese cabbage for fodder and lobia sarson. In case the flood water remains there beyond September, then from the end of September to mid- October the crops like barseem, rapeseed, multicut oats (OS6 and OS7 varieties) and sugarcane (CoH99, CoH92 and Co7717) should be grown.

Under similar conditions, the scientists add, from mid-October to mid-November, autumn sugarcane, raya (Varuna RH 30), barseem (muskan) and oats should be preferred. From mid-November to mid-December, wheat varieties like KRL 1-4 and WH 157 (for moderate saline condition), UP 2338, PBW 343, WH 147, WH 542 and WH 533 (for normal sowing) can be grown. On the other hand, in the declining water-table areas, the scientists advise to follow rain water conservation practices for recharging soil profile and ground water-table. They also suggest restriction on boring of extra deep tubewells. Besides, they say, the farmers should alternately grow less water-consuming crops. In this regard, the scientists have suggested reduction in the rice growing area by at least 15 per cent because paddy consumes more water than any other crop.

There is also the talk of more emphasis on dairying, poultry, fisheries and horticulture. Products of these being perishable, there would be a need for improvement of infrastructure facilities, create efficient marketing, improve crop production technology, and extension services. There is a need for an additional thrust on agro processing and agro industries. There is also a talk of rice wine in this context.

Problems in Haryana

The steep rise in the crime in Haryana is often attributed to the crisis in the agrarian economy and the growing unemployment among the youth. The Green Revolution has reached its plateau and most of the landholdings are too small to be economical. The land cannot absorb the youth and there has been no concerted plan to industrialize the state. In Haryana there is not one industrial unit that employs 5000 or more workers. The five largest public sector companies in Bangalore in Karnataka alone employed 81,000 workers in 1991. There has been no attempt to set up some big industrial units in the state that could generate large-scale employment. Rather, Haryana politicians treat the industries as milch cows to generate cash for them and as such no big industrialist is interested in this state though it has a lot of potential to attract industries. Nor is there any attempt to make small-scale farming viable.

The number of unemployed persons on the live registers in Haryana increased from 36,522 in 1966, to 8,11,359 in 1999. The majority of the unemployed youth comes from the dominant agrarian communities. Any kind of lowly work is considered below their dignity. Moreover, they have become aware of better lifestyle, thanks to TV and the proximity to Delhi. There is a rare possibility of matrimonial alliance for rural unemployed youth. The sexual frustration coupled with unemployment makes them a fit material for crime. All this is true. However, this does not explain the thing fully. This kind of analysis underplays the role of culture.

Haryana has been historically deficient in matter of reform movements. The Arya Samaj is the only reform movement seen by the state. However, the backward-looking tradition of gurukuls became more prominent here than its progressive tradition of DAV institutions that played a significant role in the spread of modern education in the Punjab region. The Indian cultural renaissance, however, half-baked it was, hardly ever touched Haryana. All these factors have a profound impact on agricultural development which must be kept in mind.

Story of the Eastern Region*.

In the eighties, Indian agriculture was doing well, particularly in the eastern states. Rice growth improved, as compared to wheat. Also, diversification was setting in. Mustard, pulses and potatoes were growing faster. New market centres were coming up. Earlier, desolate roads, for example, the link between Dum Dum and Kalyani were now full of loaded trucks taking farm produce to the urban centres. But how the kisan in eastern India is now doing, particularly the poor. A recent book published by the World Food Programme shows that between 1980-83 and 1990-93 all states grew by 3.4 percent annual and between 1990-93 and 1996-99 by 2.83 per cent, but the eastern region which was growing at 3.63 per cent in the eighties grew only by 1.25 per cent in the nineties.

Agricultural growth in West Bengal in the nineties is half of what it was in the eighties. In Assam it has gone down from 2.42 to 1.31 per cent annually and in Orissa from a positive growth rate of 2.92 to a

* Prof Y.K. Alag, *Indian Express*, Nov. 2001.

negative rate of minus 5.14 per cent in the nineties. The story in the Northeast is the same. This has meant a slow-down in the reduction of poverty and a lower rate of employment growth in the farm and non-farm sectors in eastern India. Eastern India is no longer on the path of growth and structural change. The kisan is taking the brunt of the impact of this slowdown. It was tubewells and the new rice varieties which made the difference. Shorter duration crops and higher rice yields meant that the farmer could spare land for a cash crop. Small changes happening to a large number of people end up making waves. Areas with deficits of 5 million tonnes became surplus.

The stagnation of the last few years is man-made and, therefore, must be reversed. It was a mixture of policy initiatives and the functioning of markets which made the difference. Floods and water logging, runoff and water scarcity and drainage were seen as holistic problems. Raising embankments, drainage, dug wells, tube wells, tank deepening were identified and targeted in different sub-regions. An enthusiastic scientist worked out for an NGO that in an area of three districts in the lower Gangetic region if every village tank was deepened, around 8 per cent of the peak flood would be stored, rather than causing damage and could then be used in the summer, when in many years there was a drought. HYV kharif paddy and rabi maize, early maturing rice allowing a second mustard crop, diversification to groundnut, mung and arhar in kharif and gram and peas in rabi were seen happening in different sub-regions. Sesamum, potato and mustard were emerging as high value crops. Fish, duck and lamb were possible in some areas and a major programme for mango, banana and citrus was considered.

Variants of this programme were targeted in West Bengal, Orissa and parts of Bihar. A programme, similar in nature but different in content, was developed for the Assam valley. It was a mistake to discontinue the shallow tubewell programme in the eastern region from 1990. The nineties saw a sharp fall in expansion of minor irrigation as a source of growth in the eastern region.

Once the World Bank-sponsored fish farmers development agencies were over, growth stagnated. The East Asian meltdown cut short the nascent attempts at deep-water fishing. Sea water aquaculture got into some well deserved hassles. Forests were anyway not growing. One of the strange ironies of agricultural research in India has been that while the east was a target of the hybrid paddy programme, it is not at all a beneficiary. Chinsura was an associate centre of Dr. Siddiqui's group. CNHR 3 variety was released for Boro paddy, with a yield of 8.10 tonnes per hectare, the highest of all the varieties. But it was not marketed. The tubewell irrigation programme has now again seen the light of the day and one prays that it will be adequately funded. Forest and fish have a great future in this part of the country. The east needs policy champions of the political economy of rural growth. Farmers' organizations have to take things in their own hand. The state has to support them. India cannot develop with the populous east stagnating.

Some Healthy Signs

There is already some move towards diversification which is visible. But it was not enough. In kharif season (2000-01), there has been a significant decline in the area under several crops. The fall has been more dramatic in the case of foodgrains. In terms of absolute numbers, the highest decline has been in Kharif rice. Most of this shift has happened in Punjab where farmers have switched in large numbers to cotton. This was expected. The government is sitting on a 62 million tonnes food mountain and has absolutely no idea what to do with it. The farmers have realized that given this problem of plenty, the government would not be a willing buyer for the next couple of seasons. Unfortunately, this is not likely to ease the problem of enormous surplus. For in spite of decrease in area under cultivation, the foodgrain production is expected to touch 210 million tonnes in 2001-02, a seven per cent increase over the last year. With this bumper crop, food stocks are projected to touch 75 million tonnes (Table 3.2).

Table 3.2 Progress of Area under Kharif Crops (Lakh Hectares)

	September 2000	*September 2001*	*% of normal*	*% change*
Foodgrains	706.36	684.65	93.0	-3.1
Rice Kharif	366.36	350.04	86.9	-4.5
Coarse Cereals	235.00	229.61	99.4	-2.3
Bajra	90.00	88.10	94.7	-2.1
Jowar Kharif	47.30	44.30	88.6	-6.3
Maize Kharif	60.00	61.00	107.0	1.7
Other Cereals	37.70	36.21	116.8	-4.0
Kharif Pulses	105.80	105.70	102.9	-0.1
Kharif Oilseeds	151.0	142.00	91.0	-6.0
Sugarcane	42.50	42.70	104.1	0.5
Jute/mesta	8.20	8.20	94.3	0.0
Cotton	76.40	81.60	89.7	6.8

Contrary to popular belief, food for work programmes are not a solution to the problem. Such programmes have elicited poor response from most parts of the country. The only possible explanation for this is that starvation is not as common as believed. This highlights the need for a complete rethink on the question of food security. True, the Indian population is nowhere near stabilizing. However, at the same time, per capita consumption of cereals is also going down. This is expected. As economic development takes place, there is a shift to other food products away from cereals. But even today, the rural per capita consumption of 154 kg per year is about 30 kg. more than the urban consumption. Therefore, one would expect rural per capita consumption to fall to urban levels as development takes place. Hence, the overall cereal consumption is not likely to go up with population increase. The government's procurement policy needs to reconcile this and ensure that it leads to optimum production of foodgrain.

Consumption Pattern Shifts

Besides these second generation problems of environmental and other issues, need for further diversification also arises because of shifts in the consumption pattern and behavioural changes. The composition of agricultural production in India has been changing over the years, though some would argue that it's not as fast as changes in food consumption. Fruits, vegetables and milk products now account for 34.5 per cent of the value of agricultural output (crops and livestock), marginally more than the share of foodgrains. The share of these new economy sectors in agriculture has gone up steadily from 25 per cent in 1980 and 29 per cent in 1990.

On the other hand, the share of foodgrains has fallen from 36.5 per cent in 1980 to 32 per cent in 1990; and further to 30 per cent in 1998-99, before moving up in 1999-2000. These trends reveal that agriculturists have responded to changing consumption habits by diversifying their activities. But the pace of changing composition of output has been somewhat slower than that of consumption (Table 3.3). The share of cereals and pulses in the real consumption expenditure on food has fallen faster- from 34 per cent in 1990 to 27 per cent in 2000.

Table 3.3 Changes in the Composition of Agriculture Output

	Shares in output				*CAGR (Real)*	
	1980-81	*1990-91*	*1998-99*	*1999-00*	*1980-90*	*1990-99*
Cereals	31.3	26.9	26.1	30.1	3.2	2.2
Pulses	5.2	5.1	3.9	3.4	2.8	- 0.4
Oilseeds	7.2	10.2	7.4	5.4	6.5	1.6
Sugars	6.6	5.2	5.6	5.8	4.1	2.3
Fibres	3.1	3.0	2.7	2.2	3.5	2.3
Fruits & Vegetables	14.0	13.9	19.5	17.7	2.7	5.6
Others & By-products	15.2	12.6	11.5	11.0	1.0	2.6
All Crops	82.7	76.9	76.7	75.7	3.1	2.7
Milk	11.3	15.1	15.8	16.9	5.5	4.2
Other Livestock	6.0	7.9	7.5	7.4	3.8	3.3
Overall Agriculture	100.0	100.0	100.0	100.0	3.5	3.0

The production of fruits and vegetables grew at an average annual rate of 5.6 per cent during the 1990s, more than double the growth rate in the previous decade. This becomes all the more impressive when all other categories have witnessed a deceleration during the 1990s; production of pulses has actually declined. This changing composition of agricultural output also has some implication for the analysts who track agricultural GDP as an important demand indicator. Very often, in the absence of adequate data on other crops, analysts base their expectations of growth in agricultural GDP on the available estimates of foodgrains production. But with the changing composition, that could be misleading.

In 1999-2000, forestry and fishing comprised about 8 per cent of the value addition in the agriculture and allied activities sector. Of the value of output in remaining activities, livestock accounted for one-fourth and crops for about 75 per cent. Within the crops too, cereals and pulses together contribute close to 40 per cent of the value of output.

Thus, when one extrapolates the trends in foodgrains production to the entire agricultural sector, and sometimes the entire rural demand, one runs a huge risk of misinterpreting the trends! For instance, foodgrains production increased by 2.7 per cent in 1999-2000 and declined by 6 per cent in 2000-2001, but in both these years, agricultural GDP was nearly stagnant. Again, in the first quarter of the current year, agricultural GDP accelerated to 2.3 per cent, despite a drop in rabi foodgrains production.

Agriculture Needs a Serious Focus

When RBI Governor Bimal Jalan was presenting the busy season credit policy, he stated that if not for agriculture even the 5.5 per cent to 6 per cent expected rate of growth would not have been possible. It's not that agriculture was having a wonderful run, but in this present fiscal with the foodgrain production expected to jump to over 7 per cent growth there is still some hope left of the growth in GDP not sinking below the 5 per cent levels.

Even after 10 years of reforms there is still the general impression that agriculture in India operates amidst a number of restraints and controls and that farmers do not receive the benefits of free trade as compared to the other sectors of the economy. The National Agriculture Policy which aims at freeing agriculture and targeting above 4 per cent growth levels. This growth is to be achieved through a combination of measures including structural, institutional agronomics and tax reforms. The policy of focuses on the privatization of agriculture and price protection of farmers in view of the post quantitative restrictions regime. The new policy on agriculture in addition to providing a backdrop on the external requirement focuses more on the internal issues and domestic policy measure that would provide the required thrust.

But this is all in the backdrop of some concerning factors. The agricultural sector, excluding forestry and fishing, has exhibited a decline in its contribution to GDP over the last two decades from a share of 45 per cent in overall GDP in the 1970s, the existing share is a little over 28 per cent. However, notwithstanding the fall in GDP share, agriculture still provides employment to approximately three out of every five employed person in the country. To increase the level of income of this populace under agriculture, not only it is important to increase growth in agriculture but also assert a prime priority to this sector.

The decade of reforms (i.e. from June 1991 onwards) witnessed lot of volatility in the agricultural sector. During this decade while most of the major sectors recorded positive growth rates, agricultural production was varied, recording negative growth in three years. The net sown area has remained almost constant over the past decade though the cropping intensity, which is defined as ratio of gross cropped area to net sown area, has increased from 128.1 million hectares in 1989-90 to 132.7 million hectares in 1996-97. The cropping pattern also shifted in the last three decades. From the 1970s the area under non food crops grew at a faster pace than that under non foodgrains. This trend continued both in the 1980s and in the 1990s. Though in the post eighties, the area under non food crops expanded at an increasing rate.

The reforms period has drawn a major focus on the industry side of development. Hence there were revolutionary changes adopted in the industry side, while agriculture still continues to be dependent on good monsoons. Such a neglect can be observed for example through the growth in fertilizer consumption. Between 1979-80 to 1989-90 the fertilizer consumption per hectare increased from 30.99 kg/hectare to 63.47kg./hectare, a growth of 104 per cent. In the following decade between 1989-90 to 1999-00 the fertilizer consumption per hectare increased from 63.47 kg/hectare to 95.33 kg/hectare, a growth of 50 per cent. What we have missed out is that without a simultaneous growth in both industry and agriculture, the growth path would remain sluggish.

The new policy is a step forward for it realizes that apart from traditional agriculture, agri based industry, fishing, aquaculture, horticulture, sericulture, etc. should now be given a serious focus. These sectors hold tremendous potential in the export markets. Value of fish exports for example increased from Rs. 893 crore in 1990-91 to Rs. 5116 crore in 1999-00, a jump of 472 per cent in one decade. The green revolution, the yellow revolution (in oil seeds), the white revolution (in milk), the blue revolution (in fish) and the golden revolution (horticulture) are certainly our testimony to research and growth. Yet, the potential of agriculture still remains to be fully tapped.

Private Investment in Agriculture

It has been observed that in recent years public investment in agriculture has shrunken and private investment has also shown no perceptible increase (Table 3.4). Private investment in agriculture can take off only when complementary public investment in the farm sector takes place. Instead of merely bemoaning the steady decline in public investment in agriculture, policy-makers must take bold step to move away from the current strategy and divert resources currently wasted in inefficient and opaque subsidies to investment in farm infrastructure, including R and D, water management, rural roads, rural electrification and cold chains. Such investment would also create off-farm incomes and jobs for rural households, eroding poverty and increasing the market for agricultural produce. Agro-processing industry, which serves as a natural link between industry and agriculture, must be given every encouragement to expand agriculture market and generate off-farm employment.

There are small countries like Portugal where they have succeeded to reduce the role of public sector in agricultural development only to research and administration. A time has now come in India where we have to think seriously about the role of private/cooperative sector responsible directly to the farmer and the farmer organizations. This would include seed multiplication, extension and veterinary services including artificial insemination. To start with a plan should be prepared for resorting to the cooperative movement in three basic values: democratic functioning, professional management and financial discipline.

In order to create a further growth momentum in agriculture and accelerating the export growth of agricultural products (processed and unprocessed) an integrated strategy is urgently called for. This may cover areas like organic farming, branding of organic products for export purposes and corporate farming.

BRANDING OF ORGANIC PRODUCTS

Organic agriculture aims at the development of viable and sustainable agriculture. Organic food is produced by following a system of farm management practices that seek to nurture ecosystem which achieve sustainable productivity and provide weed and pest-control through diverse mix of mutually dependent life farms, recycling plant and animal residues, crop selection and rotation, water management, tillage and cultivation. Chemicals are being replaced with effective micro-organism, commonly known as E.M. There is an urgent need to initiate research on E.M. under laboratory conditions. Agricultural universities should prepare projects on priority basis to test the efficacy of this wonder formulation. Successful application will give a new direction to Indian agriculture. In addition, it will promote sustainability and help in preserving the environment.

Recent years have witnessed a growing awareness among corporates about the financial power of the brands they own. There are two reasons

Table 3.4 Gross Capital Formation in Agriculture and Allied Sector (at 1993-94 prices)

(Rs. in crores)

Year	Gross domestic capital formation			Gross capital formation in agriculture			Percentage		
	Total Unadjusted*	Public Sector	Private Sector	Total	Public Sector	Private Sector	Col. 5 as % of Col. 2	Col. 6 as % of Col. 3	Col. 7 as % of Col. 4
(1)	(2)	(3)	(4)	(5)	(6)	(7)	(8)	(9)	(10)
1993-94	181133	70834	110299	15249	4918	10331	8.42	8.94	9.37
1994-95	229878	80680	149199	16785	5368	11417	7.30	6.65	7.65
1995-96	284557	75470	209087	17689	5319	12370	6.22	7.05	5.92
1996-97	252555	73098	179457	18326	5149	13177	7.26	7.04	7.34
1997-98	261541	72476	189065	18305	4504	13801	7.00	6.21	7.30
1998-99	240672	76147	164525	18964	4423	14541	7.88	5.81	8.84
1999-2000†	268527	90634	177893	21388	5212	16176	7.96	5.75	9.09

† Quick estimates.

* GCF unadjusted by industry of use.

SOURCE: Central Statistical Organisation, New Delhi.

for this phenomenon. First, there has been mounting evidence to support the hypothesis that consumers are becoming increasingly brand conscious not just in relation to products of conspicuous consumption, but also about commonplace commodities such as various types of fruits and vegetables which were, for a long time, sold as unbranded goods. This trend is likely to get accentuated with the growing importance of e-commerce where most consumer purchase decisions will be brand driven. The second reason has been growing investor interest in companies with strong brand portfolios.

Export marketing of agricultural and horticultural products is expected to get tougher and difficult in the new millennium. It will demand thinking in unconventional ways about new kinds of distributional channels, media strategies, distinctive brand positioning and may even developing a new language for brand development. In fact, the rising stress of the future will be those manufacturers that have very clearly positioned brands. The customers also will become more open to buying into well constructed, motivating brand positioning. The implication of this is that brand owners who, for several reasons, have reduced the amount of time they spend thinking about their brands, should re-order their priorities.

Branding should be the foundation of any export business. Branding is all about securing the future of our exporting business establishment, its products and services by building relationship and loyalty. While brand evolution dictates that the fittest shall survive, a brand will need much more than a strong identity to see it through the "Brandage". In today's global market, segmented brand valuation helps in determining the relative values of a brand in different geographical areas. This sets the basis for determining the advertising and sales promotion budgets for different geographical areas.

The concept of organic farming is slowly catching up with the Indian farmers. However, area under organic farming at the moment is very miniscule as the process is labour-intensive and very difficult. While there are no exact figures for the area under organic farming as the concept practised is still not at organized level, it is estimated that not more than a couple of hundred hectares is under organic farming. Among the food crops, it is mainly the vegetables and fruits that are widely grown under organic farming. The corporates are, however, better equipped compared to individual farmers in taking up organic farming. Apart from the advantage of having big land holdings, they can also ensure and maintain quality. They are also in a better position to promote the concept.

Demand is gradually increasing for organic products abroad, and the country may brand these products, cut out a niche by maintaining their quality. In India, the corporate sector has, of late, been showing interest in farming. This sector may be encouraged to take up organic farming. This may be possible through contract farming.

CONTRACT FARMING FOR EXPORTS

Introducing contract or corporatisation of farming by private sector companies will help solve some of the basic problems with regard to quality production, processing and exports. Experiments in this regard in the past have shown success. Many multinationals and private individuals have made inroads into selected areas and specialized fields through a system of contract farming as for tomato (Brooke Bond Pvt. Ltd. and Nijjar Agro), chillies, garlic and ginger in the case of Pepsi Foods Limited, and mentha in the case of Indo US Mint Pvt. Ltd., The trend of the corporate sector playing an increasingly active role in the agricultural sector has given rise to what is known as "Corporatisation of Agriculture".

It is considered that large scale corporate cultivation will lead to better allocative efficiency, induce higher private investment in exportable varieties and result in higher output, income and exports. This would lead to high multiplier effect, which would help spur India's wealth creation, especially in the rural heartland of the country. The development of corporate integrated agriculture will require investment by industry, often working in tandem with the government. The industry will invest in agriculture through contract/lease farming and also in the upstream elements of food chain agriculture, procurement and storage. They will give farmers access to high yielding seeds and plant breeds. In addition, they will provide credit, fertilisers and pesticides and other inputs to raise yields. They will help develop storage and transport infrastructure, ensuring that farm produce is stored properly and transported to the markets and customers in good time. They will add value to the farm produce by processing the surplus. This will ensure that the farmers' increased yields find a market.

The corporate may enter into a contract with farmer to purchase his produce at predetermined price. Further, the corporate may market the produce in the domestic and export market. The corporate may also do the entire spade work on behalf of farmers for credit and financing needs. This model indicates a basic structure on which the corporatisation of agriculture would be feasible and will become a growing phenomenon in coming years. The philosophy of this system is an integrated approach, i.e. laboratory-land- factory-market. The objective is to organise production of adequate quantities of produce for the processing unit. Farmers are identified in compact blocks assigned contracts for areas and quantities at an agreed price and served for critical inputs such as seed or nursery. It is necessary that the government make suitable amendments in land ceiling laws so that the processing industry may own land for meeting its requirements of horticultural products. In fact, contract farming needs to be implemented with greater thrust and efficacy.

McDonald in Gujarat

Fast food chain McDonald's India and french fry giant McCain Foods have joined hands with 30-odd farmers in Gujarat' Banaskantha and Kheda districts to cultivate and procure process-grade potatoes for making McDonald's world-class french fries and potato wedges. The alliance is the result of McDonald's need for a particular variety of potato which has a certain length, high solids and low moisture content. After several years of search, the company finally zeroed in on the Dessa and Kheda, both traditionally potato-growing areas. Around three years ago, the company roped in its supplier McCain Foods to implement the project.

The farmers had so far been using age-old techniques and low-quality seeds. The MNC demonstrated how to achieve better yields at a lower cost. The McCain team introduced the farmers to the use of sprinkler and drip irrigation systems, saving 40 per cent water use. 20 per cent fertilizer use and a rise of 12 per cent in yield. Farmers were also shown the results of pre-sowing seed treatment to maximize sprouting in the field. Besides, the McCain team also modified a traditional potato cold-store with air circulation and humidifier system. They also demonstrated CIPE-controlled, high-temperature method for storing potato. The yield went up by around 30 per cent." "Besides, the farmers realised that if they grew this variety, there is an assured market."

The potato price is negotiated in advance; it was Rs 5,000 for a tonne. However, most farmers prefer to commit only part of their land for the project, so that they can sell their remaining crop at the prevailing market price. Encouraged by the results, both McDonald's and McCain want to rope in more farmers. They wants the number of member farmers to grow to 500 to 1,000 over the next few years. This is possible as the marketing for value-added potato products is growing rapidly. "In India, not even one per cent of the total potato crop is converted into value-added products at, present.

Mahindra Agri-services

Another approach to the problem is like the one of Mahindra Shubh Labh Services Ltd. (MSSL), a stunning success story of Vadipettai village (Madura). The Vihar helps farmers choose the right seed and fertilizers and provides expert advice on farming. Interactive kiosks, called `spokes', attached to the Vihar enable farmers to buy quality agri-products online. The purchase is delivered at the farmer's doorstep, saving him time and money.

The aim is to make MSSL an enabled agri-services and consultancy provider. It also rents out transplanters, rotovators, reapers and post-harvest machinery to the farmers. The technical support package costs 10 per cent of the increase in productivity. Trained personnel from the

Vihar (all graduates in agriculture – related subjects) visit the farms 15 to 20 times during a crop cycle. Registered farmers can access weather, field and market information from the Vihar's Web site.

MSSL plans to tackle deficiencies in the farm sector, such as low consumption of quality inputs, lack of mechanization, scarcity of farm finance and low awareness of scientific farm practices. It also plans to establish franchises, utilizing the goodwill of its tractor dealers. "Where needed they will tie up with leading regional players in the business". The company has entered into distributorship and retail agreements with fertilizer manufacturers like SPIC and Madras Fertilizers and agro-chemical companies like Aventis, Bayer and Rallis. It operates in six taluks in Tamil Nadu and has 750 acres under consultancy services.

MSSL recently opened Vihars at Nalgonda in Andhra Pradesh and Alwar and Kota in Rajasthan. A franchise outlet is being planned at Kumbakonam, a major paddy belt of Tamil Nadu. They plan to open Vihars throughout the country, each one functioning as a hub, linked via satellite to other centres. Over the next two years, they intend to reach 180 districts. If things work to plan MSSL will then generate business worth Rs. 70 crore to Rs. 80 crore from consultancy and marketing. *ShubhLabh* all the way!

CONCLUSION

An Important development strategy, which needs immediate adoption is that each of the holdings may be looked as an `Economic Unit' on the parallel of small scale/tiny industry. What it calls for a commercialization of agriculture. Each unit is rendered advice directly or indirectly about the cropping pattern and also arranges for the supply of inputs and then `insure' not the loan but the minimum of output in terms of cost. Coverage under this dispensation should be not for everyone but all those who adopt the `package' and the cropping pattern as advised by the Extension Agent based on the output, generated and given by Zonal Research Stations or its substations.

In order to do so on a sustained basis and making the farming sector an important instrument of change, viability of holding is they key to success. Current paradox in the agriculture sector is marked by lower investments in farming sector, nonuse or lower use of inputs, non adoption of higher productivity, increased cropping intensity modern agriculture technology and large number of unviable farm units. If this be the case then the first item on agenda should be to look at making each holding a viable unit, not necessarily by engaging them in producing food crops but perhaps putting them into producing high value crop or taking up allied activities like animal husbandry, fisheries, horticultural crops which brings us to the practical question of use of extension services for preparing a `farm plan' for each unit. There is a need to treat each holding as a production unit and the land holder an entrepreneur, i.e., subsistence agriculture for a very large number of farmers giving place to commercial agriculture.

Commercialization of agriculture has made great strides in States like Gujarat, Maharashtra, Karnataka and to some extent in Andhra Pradesh, Punjab and Haryana. Commercialisation cannot be deemed to mean treating each unit a production unit keeping in view its efficiency but also to mean that a unit should take up production of that crop where it has a natural advantage on account of soil and agricultural conditions. The State of Madhya Pradesh is the latest example which experimented with soyabean and the result is for any one to see. This natural advantage is bound to play a lead role in changing our cropping pattern once almost free supply of inputs-water and power, and subsidized inputs like fertilizers get phased out over the next decade or so and the state comes to give the farmers only market support; sugarcane is a case import. Productivity levels will determine its production regime and not the props being given at present.

Modern Technology could also usher in what is called urban agriculture wherein people having some open spaces can start pisciculture, floriculture, growing vegetables and the like in their backyards/ balconies. Of the total arable land, less than half is plain, rest is featured either by being upland or low land marking flow irrigation a difficult proposition. A massive induction of drip and sprinkler irrigation is envisaged to meet their specific requirement.

The state cannot afford to be pusillanimous at this stage. Perhaps that time is passed when ideology reined in such an effort. It is the imperatives of `Economics of Agriculture' which must govern and guide and, they call for a change in our approach, to widen and strengthen the "Targeted – assisted Group". Sunken in ideological divide the faithful may permit their fancy to magnify the importance of their pursuit but it is time that they shed their fancy and address the realities. The challenges is to produce over 300 million tonnes of foodgrains and host of other crops before the end of quarter of this Century to meet their requirements of our industry, oil seeds to meet the rising demand for edible oil, fast rising demand for fruits and vegetables and fodder for the cattle.

There has been no time in the history of mankind when the human ingenuity and self interest has not risen to meet the challenge. This country has the wherewithal even at the current levels of available technology to be not only self-sufficient, but also become a net exporter of agro-commodities on a sustained basis, provided we `Will' to do so – both at political and administrative level. The solution lies within us – it is to make Agriculture `farmer centred' and not measure achievements only in terms of cold faceless `production' statistics. If this hypothesis is found acceptable, based on the known parameters like soil, water, socioeconomic strengths and weaknesses, States' role can then be redefined to suggest a viable proposition in respect of cropping system/pattern, providing infrastructural support in the form of irrigation, power, rural roads and developed markets, credit arrangements/tie-up, advice/extension of appropriate updated technology and marketing support or tie-up to ensure viability to the farm unit-market will take care of the rest.

If such a scenario has to be developed, one can envision downsizing of agri-bureaucratic administration as well as doing away with `Subsidy-regime' over time, say, over the next ten years. This must be agreed to by all political parties at National level to transcend it beyond the narrow meaning of political economy. This approach shall be the outcome of comprehension the whole subject aposteriori – what is required is Economic Engineering! Obviously, this will call for apostasy and depositing some of the till recently held views to `intellectual archeological museum'. The enlightened leadership has held this to be pandemic fact that no one can stop events from happening – even the most powerful may not succeed in that regard, but they can certainly make an honest attempt to influence the direction of the events and its concomitant result – for the common good. The people who succeed are called MEN OF DESTINY OR HISTORY.

CHAPTER 4

Agriculture and the Plans

On the initiative of All India Congress, a National Planning Committee was created towards the end of 1938. This committee consisted of 15 members, to whom were attached representatives of the growing body of each province, and of those princely states which agreed to take part in this work. Among the members were well-known industrialists, financiers, economists, professors and scientists as well as representatives of the Trade Union Congress and of the Village Industry Association. The non-Congress Provincial Governments like Bengal and Punjab cooperated with this committee. Hardheaded businessmen were there, as well as people who are called idealist and doctrinaire; socialists and near communists were also included.[1]

Agricultural planning of a rudimentary type was introduced in India during the Second World War when the country faced food shortages. This was in the shape of the Bombay Plan, worked out by a group of businessmen connected in the main with the Tata Enterprises. The plan which envisaged an outlay of Rs. 100 billions, fixed targets to double the net output of agriculture and quadruple the industrial output within 15 years. This plan gave preference to industry over agriculture. It was widely discussed, enthusiastically received, vehemently criticized, rejected and approved, but nothing practical followed. This, however, succeeded in giving recognition to the idea of a planned economy. Since a number of experts preparing this plan were members of the National Planning Committee, it was not surprising that the aims of this plan were very close to those agreed upon by the former on the National Planning Committee.

We might also mention here in passing the 'People's Plan' and the 'Gandhian Plan'. The former originated as a result of the tendencies of

---

[1] Jawaharlal Nehru, The Discovery of India, Third Edition, 1951, p. 372.

certain social groups towards different kinds of state capitalism. The Committee was formed on the initiative of Mr. H.N. Ray by the Indian Federation of Labour after Independence. The Gandhian Plan aimed at creating a self-sufficient village economy.[2]

It was in 1950 that the principal meeting of the Consultative Committee of the Colombo Plan took place. The Government of India had already decided in March 1950 to set up the Planning Commission. The first task of the Commission was to work out a quick Six Year Plan which could be used along with the Colombo Plan. The idea for the Colombo Plan came from the United Kingdom. The founder members of this plan were Australia, Canada, Ceylon (now Sri Lanka), India, New Zealand, Pakistan and the United Kingdom. The financial aim of the plan was to ensure the coordination of technical aid from member countries to South and South-East Asia. The plan was only of minor importance to the economic development of India, from the point of view of technical and financial assistance. Of the 38 million rupees of financial aid received by India during the First Five Year Plan, less than Rs. 5 million came from aid under the Colombo Plan. The proportion was even smaller during the Second Plan.

The Colombo Plan was prepared by the Planning Commission by August 1950 and included a number of projects prepared by various administrative bodies. It was only when this task was finished that the Commission got down to its true work, which was to draw up a development plan based on socially and economically justified priorities.

In July 1951, the Commission had prepared a draft of the plan which was to be effective from April 1951 to March 31, 1956. It was certainly a remarkable feat to prepare an economic plan, however generalized, for a country as large and complex as India. After the main projects had been examined by the Central Ministries, the state governments and the representatives of the principal industries, many problems were discussed in the press, and the Commission drew up the final version of the First Five Year Plan. This was submitted to the Government on December 7, 1952, and ratified by Parliament early in 1953.

REVIEW OF PREVIOUS FIVE YEAR PLANS

Plan Objectives

The Grow More Food campaign started as early as 1942 had miserably failed to deliver the goods. At the time of the formulation of the First Five Year Plan the Planning Commission rightly pointed out that the

[2] For details refer to S.C. Dube, India's Changing Villages, 1958 c.f. Dr. Gyan Chand, Provincial Development Programme, 1950, for composite treatment of the development programme undertaken before the creation of the Planning Commission.

conception of priorities over a period had to be dynamic. The emphasis as between different sectors shifts as development in those taken up initially prepares the ground for development in others. With this broad principle before them, the Commission gave top priority to agriculture including irrigation. It was opined that without substantial increase in the production of food and raw materials needed for industry, it would be impossible to sustain a high tempo of industrial development. It was thought necessary on economic as well as other grounds, first of all to strengthen the economy at the base and to create conditions of sufficiency and even plenitude in respect of food and raw materials. The results of the First Five Year Plan were encouraging, though in retrospective appears that the bulk of the increase was due to good weather conditions and statistical improvements. These comfortable situation on the agriculture front induced the Planning Commission to shift the emphasis towards industrialization at the time of formulating the Second Five Year Plan.

The objective of the Second Five Year Plan was stated to be "rapid industrialisation with particular emphasis on the development of basic and heavy industry". There was no specific mention of development in agriculture, although the approach of balanced growth was not given up. It was stated that balanced pattern of industrialisation required well-recognised effort to utilise labour for increasing the supplies of much-needed consumer goods in a manner which economized the use of capital. Though in the last year of the Second Plan foodgrains production nearly reached the revised plan target, in the preceding year, shortages were experienced resulting in a substantial increase in foodgrains prices.

The Third Plan, therefore, restored the primacy of agriculture in its development programme. The achievement of self-sufficiency in foodgrains and increased agricultural production to meet the requirements of industry and export, found place in the principal objectives of the Third Plan. It was stated that in the scheme of development, the first priority necessarily belonged to agriculture. As a matter of fact, there appears to be a degree of ambivalence regarding the relative importance of agriculture and industry. On the one hand, it was stated: "The development of agriculture based on utilization of manpower resources of the countryside and the maximum use of local resources holds the key to the rapid development of the country." On the other, it was also stated: "There is no doubt that industry has a leading role in securing rapid economic advance." This was sought to be reconciled by the following statement: "The growth of agriculture and the development of human resources alike hinge upon the advance made by industry, Not only does industry provide the new tools, but it begins to change the mental outlook of the peasant."

The draft Fourth Five Year Plan submitted in August 1966 reaffirmed the objectives enunciated in the earlier plans and included such policy programmes which would help in the attainment of economic self-reliance with adequate growth rate so as to accelerate the progress towards a socialistic society. The main objectives were:

(i) To ensure the achievement of self-reliance as early as possible, highest priority will be given to all such schemes of agricultural and industrial production as are designed to promote exports and replace imports;

(ii) To ensure price stability, effective steps will be taken to check all inflationary factors and avoid deficit financing;

(iii) To enlarge the income of the rural population, as well as for augmenting the supplies of food articles and agricultural raw materials, all possible efforts will be made to maximise agricultural production;

(iv) To enable this objective to be realised, production of such goods as fertilisers, insecticides, agricultural implements, including pumps, diesel engines, tractors, etc., will be given the highest priority in the programme for industrial development.

(v) To enlarge the supplies of essential mass consumption goods on which additional income will be spent, production of articles like textiles, sugar, drugs, kerosene, paper, etc., will be stepped up;

(vi) To ensure continued growth in the metals, machinery, chemical, mining, power and transport industries, which are important for self-reliance, schemes in hand will be completed with the maximum possible expedition and such new schemes will be undertaken as are essential for keeping up the momentum of economic growth already built up and for meeting the basic needs of the country during the Fifth Plan Period; and

(vii) To limit the growth of population and ensuring better standard of living for the people, all necessary resources will be provided to enable the family planning programme to be implemented on a massive and country wide scale.

Growth with stability remained the objective of the perspective as well as the new Fourth Plan. It essentially meant the supply of consumer goods should increase commensurate with the expansion of demand for these goods after allowing for the specified level of investment. What was sought to be ensured was stability in the price level of essential consumer goods taken as a whole, the criterion of "essentiality" being the importance of the particular goods or class of goods in the consumption of the people. Reasonable changes in relative prices were to be permitted to provide for flexibility in the economy and imbalances between the pattern of supply and demand to adjust themselves.

The Fourth Five Year Plan thus had two main objectives to fulfil in so far as the agriculture sector was concerned. It aimed at providing the conditions necessary for sustained increase of about 5 per cent per annum over a decade. The second objective was to enable as large a section of the rural population as possible including agricultural labourers to participate in development and share its benefits. Accordingly the priority programmes of development in agriculture was broadly distributed into two categories, namely, those which aim at maximising production and others that remedy imbalance. The creation of conditions necessary for 5 percent growth in agriculture was basic to the approach of the Fourth Plan. The crucial position of agriculture and extreme urgency for achieving rapid growth in production were brought home more than ever before the experience of the few years of plan holiday during 1965-66 and 1966-67. It was realised that the pace of development in the agricultural sector set a limit to the growth of industry, exports, and of the economy as a whole. This constituted a major condition for achieving economic and social stability and improving the level of living and nutrition for the mass of the people. The success of the Fourth Plan was, therefore, to be judged, above all, by performance in agriculture. The main plank of the agricultural development programme depended on the New Strategy of Production discussed elsewhere in detail.

The two bad years of the Fourth Five Year Plan brought home the weakness of the agriculture sector and its contribution towards ameliorating the economic conditions of the poorer section of the population. The Fifth Five Year Plan accordingly put before itself removal of poverty and attainment of economic self-reliance as the two major tasks, which the country must accomplish. The country must, at the same time, firmly move forward towards consolidation of the democratic political order, prevention of concentration of economic power, reduction of disparity in incomes and wealth, attainment of balanced regional development and spread of the institutions, values and attitudes of a free and just society. The establishment of a fully democratic and socialistic society has been accepted as the only means for the realisation of these goals. This has become the basic premise of the Fifth Five Year Plan which had to take the country to another major step forward along the chosen course.

The launching of the Sixth Five Year Plan synchronised with the beginning of a new decade during which the major goal was to be realised on an economic and social order based on principles of socialism, secularism and self reliance. The major objectives of that period were to improve the quality of life of the people in general with the reduction of poverty and unemployment as well as active involvement of all section of people towards the development. The improvement of skills, productivity and earnings of rural people achieved through the national programme for Training Rural Youth for Self-Employment (TRYSEM), National Rural Employment Programme (NREP) etc. In agriculture sector main thrusts were given in foodgrain production as well as other agricultural production especially on oilseeds production.

The Seventh Plan sought to emphasise policies and programmes which would accelerate the growth in foodgrains production, increase employment opportunities and raise productivity. The central element in the development strategy of the Seventh Plan was the generation of productive employment. This was aimed at achieving through increase in cropping intensity making it possible by increased availability of irrigation facilities, extension of new agricultural technologies to low productivity regions and to small farmers, through measures which would make the rural development programmes more effective in the creation of productive assets, through the expansion of labour intensive construction activities for providing housing, urban amenities, roads and rural infrastructure, through the expansion of primary education and basic health facilities and through changes in the pattern of industrial growth. With this emphasis on the generation of productive employment, the Seventh Plan aimed at a significant reduction in the incidence of poverty and an improvement in the quality of life for the poor in the villages and towns.

In the Eighth plan, the strategy, aim and thrust were mainly on consolidating the gains from the base built over the years in agricultural production; sustaining the improvements in productivity and production to meet the increasing demands of the growing population; enlarging the incomes of farmers and realizing the country's potential by stepping up agricultural export.

PLAN OBJECTIVES

Self-Reliance

The objective of self-reliance to be realised within a definite time-schedule, was formulated explicitly for the first time in the Third Plan and is being continued till today. This as articulated in our plans has several dimensions of which the most important ones are a reduction in the dependence on foreign aid, diversification of domestic production and a consequential reduction in imports for certain critical commodities and the promotion of exports to enable us to pay for imports from our own resources.

The possibility of foreign exchange becoming a constraint in promoting development has been recognized in our plans. The First Plan pointed out that in the early stages of development a deterioration in the balance of payments was inevitable as the increase in the rate of investment would necessitate imports of machinery and other producer goods which, to start with, could not be met from domestic supplies. These balance of payments problems could be met by the use of reserves (if an excess of such reserves was available), inflows of external finance and, in the longer term, by adjustments in the pattern of foreign trade via import substitution and export promotion. Each of these methods has played a role in the management of the balance of payments during the planning era.

In the first two plans the balance of payments gap was financed to a large extent by a drawing down of the sterling balance accumulated in the pre-independence period. Imports financed by net aid was only 4.9 per cent in the First Plan but rose to 26.9 per cent in the Second Plan. The very rapid reduction in reserves led to a foreign exchange crisis in 1957-58 after which the dependence on external assistance increased substantially. Imports financed by net aid rose to 37.5 per cent in the Third Plan and the Annual Plan period (1966-67 to 1968-69). Thereafter there had been a steady decline and in the Fifth Plan, net aid financed was 12.8 per cent of imports.

The inflow of external assistance carries with it a debt service obligation in subsequent years which has to be discharged from foreign exchange earnings. The burden of debt service as a percentage of exports rose from less than 1 per cent in the First Plan to a peak of 27 per cent in the Fourth Plan; thereafter, because of the rapid rise in export earnings, the percentage declined to 15.4 in 1978-79. The dependence on external assistance has to be judged against the objectives specified in the plans. The need to reduce dependence on external assistance was articulated for the first time in the Third Plan. The Fourth Plan specified the objective as the reduction of net aid by half over the plan period and its speedy elimination thereafter.

In 8th Plan the projected amount of net inflow of budgetary resources from abroad were Rs. 28,700 crores in the form of external loans and grants but India had received only Rs. 19,234 crores. The proportion of repayments which constituted about 45% of gross external borrowings in the initial year, increased to about 73% by the terminal year of the 8th Plan. The flow of grants registered only a modest increase from Rs. 919 crore to Rs. 1199 crore during this period. Hence the erosion experienced in net external borrowings could not be made good by the small increase in the external grants. On the other hand at the end of 8th Plan foreign direct investment increased to $ 3.2 billion as compared to 0.1 billion during 1990-91. It happened mainly due to the new economic policy where thrust was given on Globalisation and Privatisation.

The management of foreign trade during the planning era has been dominated, by the drive for self-reliance and import substitution in critical areas. Some data in this regard are presented in Table 4.1. These data show both the increase in import dependence with the acceleration of growth and the subsequent decline as domestic production was built up. A particularly noteworthy feature of the drive for import substitution has been the development of machinery manufacture within the country. Today the bulk of the equipment required for industrial and infrastructural development is produced within the

Table 4.1 Cumulative Export, Import, over the Five Year Plans and their Rate of Change

(US $ million)

Plan	Export		Import	
	Rs. Crore	*% Change*	*Rs. Crore*	*% Change*
1st Five Year Plan (1951-56)	6324	—	7679	—
2nd Five Year Plan (1956-61)	6338	00.22	10180	32.5
3rd Five Year Plan (1961-66)	7871	24.10	12968	27.4
ANNUAL PLANS (1966-69)	5002	—	8092	—
4th Five Year Plan (1969-74)	11809	50.03	10988	–15.26
5th Five Year Plan (1974-79)	27886	136.14	32758	198.12
ANNUAL PLAN (1979-80)	7947	—	11321	—
6th Five Year Plan (1980-85)	45584	63.46	75553	130.63
7th Five Year Plan (1985-90)	61320	34.52	89666	18.67
ANNUAL PLAN (1990-92)	36008	—	43486	—
8th Five Year Plan (1992-97)	132372	115.80	149653	66.90
9th Five Year Plan (1997-99) (First 2 years)	68665	—	83342	—

* The volume of export increased from US$ 1016 million in 1949-50 to US $ 33659 million in 1998-99
* The trade balance reduced from US $ 276 million to US $ 8199 million in the same period.

NB: The rate of change taken into account of five year plans only.
Data base: Economic survey, 1999-2000, Government of India.

country. In fact, self-reliance in this sector goes further. We have also built up capacity for project consultancy, design engineering and project implementation to a level at which we are in a position to export these services. In many ways this is one of the most fruitful consequences of the drive for self-reliance.

Though the volume of import is still very high over the volume of export but India is now able to concentrate on non-agricultural import due to lesser volume of agricultural import following self sufficiency in many sectors under agriculture. The reduction of tariff cost for import will facilitate technologically advanced modern machinery and equipment import for more rapid development of industrial sector which will lead India towards a self dependent nation in near future.

Performance of the economy with regard to export promotion is indicated in Table 4.2. In the first three plan periods export growth was very low. To a certain extent this could be attributed to the lack of coherent domestic policies since even in traditional exports our share in world exports declined. But it must be noted that this was not a period of rapid growth in exports from developing countries and

Table 4.2 Average Annual Expenditure Per Rural Labour Household in Different Item Groups

All Households		All India			
Sl. No.	Item groups	Average annual expenditure per household (Rs)		Percentage to total consumption expenditure	
		1983	1987-88	1983	1987-88
(1)	(2)	(3)	(4)	(5)	(6)
A.	AGRICULTURAL LABOUR HOUSEHOLDS				
1.	Food	3295	4483	68.6	67.10
2.	Clothing, Bedding & Footwear	347	402	7.2	6.02
3.	Fuel & Light	392	590	8.2	8.83
4.	Stimulants & Intoxicants	179	274	3.7	4.10
5.	House Rent	—	7	—	0.10
6.	Services & Miscellaneous	587	925	12.2	13.86
7.	Total Consumption Expenditure	4800	6681	100.0	100.0
B.	RURAL LABOUR HOUSE-HOLDS				
1.	Food	3425	4674	68.2	66.25
2.	Clothing, Bedding & Footwear	365	439	7.3	6.22
3.	Fuel & Light	403	604	8.0	8.56
4.	Stimulants & Intoxicants	191	293	3.8	4.15
5.	House Rent	—	15	—	0.21
6.	Services & Miscellaneous	640	1030	12.7	14.60
7.	Total Consumption Expenditure	5024	7055	100.0	

SOURCE: Rural Labour Enquiry Report, 43rd of NSS, 1987-88
Author's SOURCE: Basic Rural Statistics, 1996.

India's export growth rate was comparable to that of other developing countries. The real difference between India and other countries was evident after 1965 when, right up to the middle of the Fourth Plan, we could not profit from the boom in world trade. Export growth since 1971 has been much more impressive and during the Fifth Plan India's exports grew nearly as rapidly as those of the countries classified as fast growing exporters of manufactures. One further feature of the growth in exports over this later period has been the diversification in terms of commodities and foreign markets and from that period up to 1997-98 India has been keeping a steady percentage share of world export. In the year 1970 India exported US $ 2031 million and in the year 1997-98 it has reached to US$ 33470 million which was 7% of world export.

The objective of self-reliance articulated our desire to ensure a more equal relationship with the world economy and to reduce our vulnerability to international pressures and disturbances. This has been achieved to a substantial extent. One example of this is our ability to cope with shortfalls in food production. Presently on the beginning of 9th Plan we are exporting a significant amount of rice (US$ 989.6 of rice exported in 1997 which was 12.6% of total rice export of the world) and have achieved self sufficiency in foodgrain production. In the year 1998-99 we produced 203.0 million tonnes of foodgrains and crossed the target of producing 200 million tonnes. The drought of the mid-sixties necessitated substantial imports of foodgrains and that too on concessional terms, the drought of the early seventies required imports but there after imports were from the open market and did not come in the form of food aid. The latest drought of 1979, however, could be managed without further foodgrain imports. Another example of the success of self-reliance lies in the fact that the tempo of investment in critical sectors like power was maintained in the Fifth Plan despite the balance of payments burden of the oil price increase because of the limited dependence on imports for equipment supplies. In fact it could be said that the most significant achievement of the planning period has been the fact that the Indian economy today has achieved a greater degree of resilience to cope with disturbances in the international economy.

Improvement in our capacity to weather international shocks has to be seen in the context of the very rapid deterioration in recent years in the international environment within which we have to function. The prices that we pay for our imports of petroleum products, fertilisers, machinery and other products have increased much more rapidly during the latter half of the seventies than the value of our exports. In the 8th plan the thrust was given on export potentiality and India has achieved a significant position in export. The import payment over export receipt was near about US$ 6799 million during the year 1997-98. At the same time it is true that during this period the growth in export earnings and remittances helped not merely to pay for the much higher import bill but to accumulate a substantial volume of foreign exchange reserves. Apart from international inflation we have also had to cope with sudden shortages in availability of critical items, and growing protectionism in developed countries.

Social Justice

The objective of social justice as articulated in the plans have two major dimensions. The first dimension is an improvement in the living standards of the poorest groups in society and the second is a reduction in inequalities in asset distribution. For about three decades, a variety of instruments ranging from direct attacks on poverty and asset inequality to more indirect fiscal measures, had been used to pursue these ends. An assessment of the extent to which these ends have been attained is given in what follows.

There has been an improvement in the quality of life over the planning period. The percentage share of annual expenditure of rural people on food article is gradually decreasing and vice versa in non food articles (exception in clothing, bedding, etc. which are basic necessities among the non-food articles).

Trends in the level and distribution of private consumption expenditure do not reflect the improvements in living standards brought about by public expenditure on social services. In the field of health, the programme to control communicable diseases particularly smallpox and malaria and the gradual extension of health care facilities to rural areas through rural hospitals, primary health centres and dispensaries has led to a significant improvement in the expectation of life at birth from 32 in 1951 to 46 for men and 45 for women in 1971. This age rose to 62.36 for male and 63.99 for female in the year 1999-2000. Infant mortality rate goes down to 74 from 129 on an average in all over India.

In education, enrolment in elementary education has shown the growth of 46% during 1996. At this level of enrolment it is clear that a very substantial proportion of elementary school students must be from the disadvantaged groups in society though the rate of enrolment for these groups remains well below the average. The access of the poor to secondary and higher education has also improved with the extension of scholarships for weaker sections and better geographical spread of institutions. Though the number of higher educational institutes and private institutes is increasing with a faster rate but the literacy percentage is too low as compared to other developed and many developing countries. It is also true that the illiteracy percentage reduced to 48.79% in 1991 from 65.5% in 1971 but better planning and more emphasis in this regard are needed to tackle the problem. Simultaneously the quality of schooling also needs substantial improvement. Besides these two major social services, public expenditure has provided water supply and other municipal services in urban slums and in villages, house sites for the poor in rural areas and supplementary nutrition for vulnerable mothers and children, all of which benefit the poor but do not necessarily show up in the data on consumption expenditure.

An individual obtains an income from the ownership of assets and from employment. The limited impact of the Plans on the wellbeing of the poorer section of the population is a consequence of our inability to restructure the distribution of assets and to provide sufficient employment opportunity for a growing work force. Rural assets and liabilities are also a concerned matter for social justice. The bulk of the assets of these 'poor' households consist only of their huts, some household goods and some livestock. But the main factor which is responsible for maintaining the quality of life is the area of cultivable land holding in rural areas. The principal productive asset in rural areas is land which was distributed as follows in the year 1990-91 (Table 4.3).

Table 4.3 Operational Holdings and Area Operated by Size of Holdings (All India)

Size class (ha.)	*Number (lakhs)*				*Area Operated (lakh ha.)*			
	1960-61	*70-71*	*80-81*	*90-91*	*60-61*	*70-71*	*80-81*	*90-91*
Below 1.0	199	357	501	621	88	146	197	246
1.0-2.0	109	134	161	200	160	193	232	287
2.0-4.0	92	107	124	139	262	300	347	384
4.0-10.0	66	79	81	76	401	482	485	450
10.0 and above	23	28	22	17	404	501	377	289
TOTAL	489	705	889	1053	1314	1621	1638	1656

SOURCE: Ministry of Agriculture, Department of Agriculture and Cooperation, Government of India.

Small and marginal farmers who constitute over 70 per cent of the landholders operate barely 24 per cent of the land. The very substantial improvement in agricultural productivity brought about by irrigation and the new seed-fertilizers technology improve directly the earning power of agricultural land and only indirectly that of agricultural labour. Hence agricultural growth by itself may not solve the problem of poverty. It is, therefore, necessary to adopt positive measures combining a mix of employment generation, diversification of occupations, land reforms, reorientation of the credit systems and massive public investment in rural infrastructure so as to ensure that the fruits of economic progress are more equitably distributed in rural areas.

The programme of land reforms instituted right at the beginning of the planning period was meant to redistribute this primary resource. The first phase of this programme which involved the abolition of zamindari and intermediary tenures has been, to a large extent, successfully implemented. The later phases of land reform involved elements like tenancy reforms, protection of sharecropper, land ceiling and land consolidation. The pace of implementation of these measures particularly of ceiling legislation has been slow and full of loopholes so that their impact on the structure of landholdings has been minimal. The land reform programme is by no means complete, but has to be pursued further if we are to tackle effectively the problem of poverty and inequality.

Trends in the ownership of assets in urban areas are less fully known. The principal instruments used to influence the distribution of assets other than land are essentially fiscal in character e.g., progressive taxation of income and wealth and the preferential treatment of poorer sections in the provision of credit. The extent to which progressive taxation has helped to check inequalities has been limited by tax evasion which creates further problem of black money and conspicuous consumption. The one direct measure to control the distribution of assets in urban areas, viz., the Urban Land Ceiling Act has faced major difficulties in implementation. In an indirect way the growth of the public sector in industry and the nationalization of almost the entire financial system have probably helped to restrict the number of people at the very top of the income distribution.

The limited success in redistributing assets may not have mattered as much for poverty reduction had employment increased at a faster rate. Such a growth in employment would have increased incomes both by reducing idle time and by exerting an upward pressure on wages. However, the pace of generation of employment opportunities seems to have lagged behind the growth in the labour force.

Thus the Rural Labour Enquiry has shown that between 1964-65 and 1974-75, the number of days for which employment was available for rural labourers declined by 10 per cent for men, 7.5 per cent for women and 5 per cent for children. The data on average earnings from these enquiries when corrected for inflation also show a decline. In urban areas the figures for the number of persons on the live register provide some indication of the trend. These figures show an increase from 1.6 million in 1960 to 12.7 million in 1978, an increase that is attributable partly to changes in coverage but which nevertheless reflects a substantial deterioration in the availability of employment. Direct data on unemployment from the National Sample Survey are unfortunately not comparable over time. However, the latest available data for 1993-94 person-day unemployment over the period of nearly 20 years is given in Table 4.4.

The statistics have shown that the rate of unemployment has reduced to same extent but comparatively better in case of female labour. But the major problem of rural farmers are seasonal unemployment which compels them to migrate during the off season. But often they have to return back with empty hand. The economic planning should give

Table 4.4 Unemployment by Daily Status

(Percentage of labour force)

Year	Rural		Urban	
	Male	*Female*	*Male*	*Female*
1972-73	6.8	11.2	8.0	13.7
1977-78	7.1	9.2	9.4	14.5
1983	7.5	9.0	9.2	11.0
1987-88	4.6	6.7	8.8	12.0
1993-94	5.6	5.6	6.7	10.4

SOURCE: Manpower Yearbook 1997, Institute of Applied Manpower Research.

emphasis on this particular aspect. The farm and non farm base cottage industry and small scale agricultural product based industry may provide work during off season and also would provide profitable and sustainable rural business for the peasants and artisans. Some of these industries have a significant export potentiality. So, development of this side of business may also provide self employment opportunity for educated unemployed people.

The search for social justice has one further dimension that has been articulated in our plans; the desire to reduce regional imbalances. At independence we inherited an economy where industry and modern agriculture had developed only in a few pockets. The deliberate policy of industrial dispersal that we have followed has led to the development of some new industrial centres situated away from the older centres situated like Bombay, Calcutta and Ahmedabad, but the degree of success achieved is limited since even in 1971 around 27.5 per cent of the employment in manufacturing was concentrated in 9 towns. In agriculture the lack of diffusion of the new seed-fertiliser technology has probably accentuated regional imbalances and in 1977-78 the value of agricultural output per head of rural population ranged between Rs. 888 in Rajasthan and Rs. 3,361 in Punjab. These imbalances in the pace of agricultural and industrial advances are reflected in the large differences between the states in the percentage of population below the national poverty line. The data for 1993-94 given in Table 4.5 show a range from 12 per cent in Punjab to 4.9 per cent in Orissa. The geographical spread of industry and modern agriculture is undoubtedly better now than at the start of the planning era but it is clear that we have a long way to go in this task of reducing regional imbalances.

A simple summary assessment is not possible about the extent to which plan objectives with regard to social justice have been attained. There are no specific quantified targets against which performances can be compared since what the plan indicates is a direction of

Table 4.5 Number and Percentage of Population Below Poverty Line by States, 1987-88 and 1993-94

State/Union Territory	*Combined for both rural and urban areas*			
	1987-88		*1993-94*	
	No. of persons (Lakhs)	*Percentage of persons*	*No. of persons (Lakhs)*	*Percentage of persons*
1. Andhra Pradesh	160.43	25.86	153.97	22.19
2. Arunachal Pradesh	2.83	36.22	3.73	39.35
3. Assam	75.75	36.21	96.36	40.86
4. Bihar	420.93	52.13	493.35	54.96
5. Delhi	10.25	12.41	15.51	14.69
6. Goa	2.96	24.52	1.91	14.92
7. Gujarat	122.36	31.54	105.19	24.21
8. Haryana	25.37	16.64	43.88	25.05
9. Himachal Pradesh	7.52	15.45	15.86	28.44
10. Jammu & Kashmir	16.95	23.82	20.92	25.17
11. Karnataka	158.61	37.53	156.46	33.16
12. Kerala	88.48	31.79	76.41	25.43
13. Madhya Pradesh	264.30	43.07	298.52	42.52
14. Maharashtra	296.27	40.41	305.22	36.86
15. Manipur	5.29	31.35	6.80	33.78
16. Meghalaya	5.48	33.92	7.38	37.92
17. Mizoram	1.70	27.52	1.94	25.66
18. Nagaland	3.66	34.43	5.05	37.92
19. Orissa	165.93	55.58	160.60	48.56
20. Punjab	25.17	13.20	25.11	11.77
21. Rajasthan	142.90	35.15	128.50	27.41
22. Sikkim	1.36	36.06	1.84	41.43
23. Tamil Nadu	231.07	43.39	202.10	35.03
24. Tripura	8.84	35.3	11.79	39.01
25. Uttar Pradesh	536.53	41.46	604.46	40.85
26. West Bengal	283.61	44.72	254.56	35.66
27. Andaman & Nicobar Islands	1.09	43.89	1.06	34.47
28. Chandigarh	0.84	14.67	0.80	11.35
29. Dadra & Nagar Haveli	0.79	67.11	0.77	50.84
30. Daman & Diu	—	—	0.18	15.80
31. Lakshadweep	0.17	34.95	0.14	25.04
32. Pondicherry	3.05	41.46	3.31	37.40
All India	3,070.49	38.86	3203.68	35.97

SOURCE: Planning Commission, Govt. of India,
Author's SOURCE: Manpower Profile India, Year Book 1997.

movement, not a specific goal. The evidence presented above suggests that the most that can be claimed is that there has been no perverse movement, no worsening of inequalities or in the incidence of poverty. In fact, in some respects a certain degree of progress has been achieved. But, on balance, the pace of movement is much slower than what is acceptable or possible within the framework of the plans and a greater degree of redistributive justice has to be built into our development effort.

The 9th Five Year Plan and Agriculture

The Ninth Five Year Plan, launched in the 50th year of India's Independence, will take the country into the new millennium. Time has now come to redouble our efforts at development especially in the social and economic spheres, so that the country will realize its full economic potential and poorest and the weakest will be able to shape their destiny in unfettered manner. Some specific areas from within the broad objectives of the plan as laid down by the NDC (National Development Council) have been selected for special focus. For these areas, Special Action Plans (SAPs) have been evolved in order to provide actionable, time-bound targets with adequate resources, among which agriculture is the one of the priority sectors. The basic objective of the 9th Five Year Plan is to achieve 'growth with social justice, and equity'. To make it successful a special emphasis on all round human development, with stress on social sectors and a thrust on eradication of poverty is needed and for which higher rates of growth of output and employment are called for.

Agriculture provides livelihood to the largest number of people and rapid growth in this sector is the best guarantee of achieving a broad based growth of income levels and employment especially in rural areas. Our development strategy must focus on this sector which requires a unique combination of private effort and public support. Agriculture has not benefited as much as it should have from policies of economic liberalization because agricultural products continue to suffer from too many restrictions and impediments which prevent farmers from marketing their produce at attractive prices. The phased reduction in the high levels of protection given to industry, and the opening up of export market for agricultural products, will help to shift the terms of trade in favour of agriculture and this should help to raise rural incomes. But broad based agricultural development also requires substantial investments in economic infrastructure especially irrigation, rural roads and creation of organized markets.

These are other areas where the States must play a leading role. Agricultural research is another area where the role of the States will continue to be important. In the Ninth Plan, a target to achieve a growth rate of 4.5% per annum in agricultural output has been set up in order to make a significant impact on overall growth and poverty. The specific objectives of the overall Ninth Plan as approved by the National Development Council are as follows:-

(i) Priority to agriculture and rural development with a view to generating adequate productive employment and eradication of poverty;

(ii) Accelerating the growth rate of the economy with stable prices;

(iii) Ensuring food and nutritional security for all, particularly the vulnerable sections of society;

(iv) Providing the basic minimum services of safe drinking water, primary health care facilities, universal primary education, shelter, and connectivity to all in a time bound manner;

(v) Containing the growth rate of population;

(vi) Ensuring environmental sustainability of the development process through social mobilization and participation of people at all levels.

(vii) Empowerment of women and socially disadvantaged groups such as Scheduled Castes, Scheduled Tribes and other Backward Classes and Minorities as agents of socioeconomic change and development;

(viii) Promoting and developing people's participatory institutions like Panchayati Raj Institutions, Cooperatives and self-help groups;

(ix) Strengthening efforts to build self-reliance.

The Development Strategy

India's development strategy, like that of most other developing countries, has evolved over successive Plan periods, reflecting the growing strength of our economy, structural transformation taking place in the domestic economy and also developments in the world economy. In the early stages of development planning, government was viewed as the principal actor in development, exercising strict control over private investment, ensuring a dominant role for the public sector in all important industries. Trade policy tended to be inward oriented focusing on industrial development through import substitution which was encouraged through a tight control over imports and maintenance of high tariffs. The limitation of this strategy became evident by the end of the 1970s and early 1980s when it became clear that these policies reduced efficiency and competitiveness and growth was much lower than targeted. While government was over-active in industry, it was under-active in many areas, especially relating to social development and this was reflected in a very slow pace of improvement in critical social indicators.

There is no doubt that the process of reforms which has yielded many good results, must continue and be strengthened. The reforms involve a major re-orientation of the role of state which must play most important role in development process in future.

The strategies are also on the infrastructural development as the top priorities, along with developing marketing efficiency, market infrastructure, proper input supply in proper time.

Availability of land has emerged as one of the most important constraints on agricultural growth. As the potential of further expansion of net sown area is nil and even may have the possibility of decline, there is the need for augmenting cropping intensity. Consequential to this the need, high input use is also required. The projected area, yield and associated input requirements commensurate with 4.5% growth in value of agricultural output are given in the (Table 4.6).

Preparations for 10th Plan-Stress on Basic Needs at Grassroots

The Planning Commission has begun preparing the Tenth Five Year Plan with the focus on "back to the basics". Its thrust will be on rural development by tackling basic needs of villagers at the grassroots with the aim of checking influx of rural population to urban centres. The plan aims to educate the people, to make them aware of their rights and responsibilities, and introduce elements of accountability and transparency. The plan will aim to be time-bound, cost-effective, economically competitive, pragmatic and practical.

The Plan envisages growth with equity and sustainability. Some of the social targets to be achieved during the tenth Plan would be to reduce the rate of decadal population growth between 2001 and 2011 to 16.2 per cent. Literacy rate would also be increased to 75 per cent within the plan period. The next plan would ensure all children in schools by 2003 and all children to complete five years of schooling by 2007. Reduction of gender gaps in literacy and wage rates by at least 50 per cent by 2007 was also one of the objectives.

The next Plan envisages high economic growth but at the same time it has also been noticed that social development need not follow economic growth. As the economic and social development of human wellbeing was considered to be a national priority, the approach paper to the Tenth Plan outlines that the wellbeing of an individual was not just limited to consumption of food, but also access to basic social services, especially in education, health, availability of drinking water and basic sanitation.

Past experience has shown that despite best of efforts the targets were not achieved. Distortions intervened even before the implementation of plans. Therefore, a change in approach, in terms of concept, planning, monitoring, methodology of implementation had to be made in the next Five Year Plan. It will be bigger in size than the Ninth Plan that ends in 2001-02. Steps are required to avoid pitfalls due to political or bureaucratic hurdles in the way of effective implementation of Plan. In fact, for the success of any scheme under the Plan, the ruling political parties shall have to rise above party line,

Table 4.6 Projected Area, Yield and Input use in Agriculture for the Ninth Plan

Item	1996-97	2001-02
1. Net Sown Area (million hectares)	142.00	142.00
2. Gross Sown Area (million hectares)	190.50	203.00
3. Area under Foodgrains (million hectares)	124.51	126.00
4. Area under Non-Foodgrains (million hectares)	65.99	77.00
5. Cropping-intensity (%)	134.20	143.00
6. Annual Growth in Value of Output of Crops* (%):		
a) All Crops	2.77	3.82
b) Foodgrains	2.67	3.05
c) Non-Foodgrains	2.88	4.44
7. Annual Growth in Area* (%):		
a) Gross Sown Area	0.54	1.28
b) Area Under Foodgrains	–0.23	0.24
c) Area Under Non-Foodgrains	2.37	3.13
8. Yield Level (1996-97 prices) (Rs./hectare)	15326	17688
9. Annual Growth in Yield* (%):		
a) Total Agricultural Crops	2.24	2.91
b) Foodgrains	2.98	2.60
c) Non-Foodgrains	0.37	2.72
10. Fertilizer Consumption (million hectares)	14.31	20.00
11. Fertilizer Intensity (kg./hectare)	75.12	98.52
12. Gross Irrigated Area† (million hectares)	76.25	91.50
13. Percentage of Gross Area Under Irrigation (%)	40.00	45.07

* Base year growth rate relates to growth rate between 1980-94. Terminal year growth rate relates to target annual growth rate in the ninth plan

† Gross irrigated area as per land-use statistics.

taking community interests into consideration for equitable socioeconomic development. Key to India becoming a superpower lies in development of villages taking the block as a unit. Today, technological advances and intelligence development are of a high order, requiring different strokes to do planning. These strokes would take into account the population increase, shrinking resources of water, need for its conservation and poverty alleviation. Education and health for all would require new independent monitoring and scrutiny system. It depends on the feedback from the ministries concerned. Alongside planning, it would have to introduce an element of policing to crosscheck claims of states on utilization of funds.

There are lessons to be learnt from the past for proper appraisal of the future to bring about systematic changes within given system constraints and certain parameters set by the National Development Council. This calls for competitive plans and planning. Future planning has to begin from the block level, going up in the form of pyramid. The constitution now provides for (as per the 73rd and 74th Amendments) "empowerment" of the grassroots democratic institutions, municipalities and panchayat. When the government gives power to the people at the village level it also transfers transparency. The people must question and assert without confrontation and demand what is due to them. This can happen if there is widespread literacy and awakening. The Tenth Plan proposes to precisely do this by giving an opportunity to the people. The next Plan is expected to be "people-friendly, need-based and region-specific" and reflect the "collective will" of the people.

Despite "sacred" intentions and spending Rs. 10,000 crore annually on rural development, the "soft" democratic states itself were responsible in providing little benefit to the targeted population. Therefore, the village economy has to be made self-sufficient by providing basic facilities for development. The domestic service sector, which thrives in urban slums, will also be part of the planning process. Should it be allowed to exist merely as a vote-bank?

Rural Development

Despite good achievements on the growth front, India faces significant challenges in the poverty alleviation programmes and needs to take some difficult political decisions. Concerted policy action is needed to lift the country's 250 million poor—increasingly concentrated in the poorer States—out of poverty. Various Union Ministries spend roughly Rs. 350 billion annually on programmes that are meant to achieve poverty alleviation. These funds, if directly transferred to the poor, could buy for poor households 3 kg. of foodgrain every day from the market at the rate of Rs. 7.50 per kg and thus wipe out all poverty.

If poverty still persists, the obvious conclusion is that the availability of funds can at best be a necessary but not sufficient condition to tackle poverty and backwardness. The focus must be shifted from maximising the quantity of development funding to maximising of development outcomes and effectiveness of public service delivery. The Planning Commission has now recommended for the Tenth Plan new policies in sectors vital for poverty alleviation, such as agriculture, watershed development, food policy, antipoverty schemes and tribal development. The suggested changes would make an immense impact on poverty reduction, which would hopefully drop to 10 per cent by the end of the 10th Plan. Institutional weaknesses, lack of monitoring and governance issues had exacerbated the lack of funds. For instance not only are the teacher-pupil ratios very low, teachers' absenteeism is common. Numbers shown as working in rural employment programmes or attending school appear to be much less in surveys than in official statistics.

These are serious problems in both formulation and implementation of most poverty alleviation programmes, except the scheme for old-age pension. The problems range from sub-critical investment to unviable projects, lack of institutional capability in designing and executing projects, illiterate and unskilled beneficiaries, indifferent delivery of credit by banks, and poor targeting. A disturbing feature of the much talked about Integrated Rural Development Project in several States has been the rising indebtedness of the beneficiaries. There is still under-emphasis on activities which require no fixed assets, such as a large number of trading, service and even simple processing activities. In some cases, nonexistent training centres and nonpayment of stipend were discovered.

The Planning Commission has suggested that during the 10th Five Year Plan period the Integrated Rural Development Project be made a micro-finance programme to be run by banks with no subsidy on the lines of the Rashtriya Mahila Kosh for women. The funds to the gram sabhas should be given only when the people contribute 25 per cent. Similarly, the employment programmes should be replaced by food-for-work programme to be run only in areas of extreme distress. The focus should also shift to strengthening of the economy of the marginal and small farmers, forest gatherers, artisans and unskilled workers, etc.. The poor should not merely benefit from growth generated elsewhere, but they should contribute to growth. The priority should also shift from the safety net programmes to asset creation.

CONCLUSION

In the eighties, the economy was faced with a formidable task of maintaining and accelerating the tempo of economic growth following a sharp deterioration in the international environment. The ever rising prices and highly uncertain supply of imported energy can disrupt the implementation of development plans. Nevertheless, the fact that the economy now enjoys the advantages of a high savings rate, a developed skill base and a substantial degree of self-reliance providing a valuable cushion to absorb external shocks. However, we need to learn certain important lessons from our past experience.

With regard to growth and modernisation, the first lesson is that we must mobilise resources to maintain and increase the tempo of investment and protect the size of the Plan both against inflation and external disturbances. The second is the paramount need to improve efficiency in key infrastructural and industrial sectors. The third is that we must reduce the variability of the growth rate and ensure that weather abnormalities and inflation do not lead to undue cutbacks in public or private investment.

The fourth is the need to extend the agricultural revolution to all areas and farming systems and in particular to ensure that the incomes of the poor are raised in the process of agricultural development. The fifth is the need to ensure a vigorous expansion in exports and a rapid increase in domestic production of oil, steel, fertilisers and vegetable oils so as to restrain growth of imports in order to maintain viability of our external payments. Sixth, we must develop effective domestic substitutes for imported energy so that our dependence on imported oil is contained within reasonable limits. Finally, there is an urgent need to revitalise the family planning programme so as to bring about a substantial decline in the birth rate through the voluntary adoption of the small family norm. Success on all these points is essential if the overall rate of growth is to be raised, as it must be well above the levels reached in the past.

As far as self-reliance is concerned the economy today is in a stronger position than at the start of the planning era. Dependence on external finance has been substantially reduced and in many areas of production, a high degree of import substitution achieved. But there are many unfinished tasks in this area, particularly in the field of energy and technology. The world economy is in a much more disturbed state since the mid-seventies than at any time in the past three decades and there is an atmosphere of confrontation rather than cooperation in international economic relations. In this situation the objective of self-reliance needs to be pursued with continuous vigour. However, self-reliance can no longer take the form of indiscriminate import substitution. There is a continuous need to replace imports in critical areas where there are sudden and sharp changes in prices and availability. But, as the complexity of the economy grows, import requirements will also increase and in order to finance these, export earnings will have to be stepped up substantially. In the eighties, export promotion is as much a part of the drive for self-reliance as efficient import substitution.

With regard to social justice, what we have achieved is far short of what we aimed at. After three decades of planned development large segments of the population have yet to share the benefits of progress or participate in the process of development. Since the Fourth Plan, several programmes for assisting backward areas and weaker sections have been in force. Yet, judging by the statistics on asset distribution, employment and consumption the impact seems to be limited. What is needed is a more effective implementation of asset transfer measures such as land reforms, more equitable distribution of credit and a coordinated effort that enables the poor to join the mainstream of economic activity and provides them with an opportunity for advancement. This will require firstly, an improvement in their productivity and earning power in their existing activity, secondly, supplementary employment in new activities to use up any spare labour time and thirdly, training, credit and support systems to assist them in both their existing and new activities.

Growth, modernization, self-reliance and social justice are not independent objectives. They are linked in such a way that success with respect to any one makes it easier to achieve the others. The sustained growth of the past fifty years and the very considerable diversification of our economic structure that has taken place during this period are the positive national assets for launching a more direct attack on poverty and underdevelopment. However, the enormity of the task should not be underestimated, particularly in view of a sharp deterioration in the external environment. The nation will have to mobilise all its latent energies for a more vigorous pursuit of cherished national objectives of accelerated growth, greater social justice and a modern self-reliant economy.

Annexure 4.1

Public Sector Outlay by Major Heads of Development—Ninth Five Year Plan

(Rs. crore at 1996-97 prices)

Sl. No.	*Sectors*	*Centre*	*%*	*States/ UTs*	*%*	*Total*	*%*
1.	Agriculture and Allied	13017	2.6	23641	6.4	36658	4.2
2.	Rural Development	46077	9.1	28865	7.8	74942	8.6
3.	Special Programme		—	3790	1	3790	0.4
4.	Irrigation and Flood Control	2546	0.5	55189	14.9	57735	6.6
5.	Energy	150746	29.8	71227	19.3	221973	25.4
6.	Industry & Mineral	57677	11.4	14007	3.8	71684	8.2
7.	Transport	85149	16.9	39039	10.6	124188	14.2
8.	Communication	48759	9.7	32	0.006	48791	5.6
9.	Science, Technology & Environment	23217	4.6	3126	0.8	26343	3
10.	General Economic Services	6946	1.4	8623	2.3	15569	1.8
11.	Social Services	70165	13.9	110766	29.9	180931	20.7
12.	General Services	862	0.2	11534	3.1	12396	1.4
13.	TOTAL	505161	100	369839	100	875000	100

Note: Figures for the States/UTs are likely to undergo inter-sectoral changes as many States are yet to communicate the revised figures on the basis of Working Group recommendations.

Annexure 4.2

All India Pattern of Outlay and Expenditure in Public Sector (Plan wise)

Five year Plan		*Agriculture & allied activities*		*Total*		*% of agriculture & allied ativities to total*	
		Plan outlay	*Actual expen-diture*	*Plan outlay*	*Actual expen-diture*	*Plan outlay*	*Actual expen-diture*
First Plan	(1951-56)	354	290	2378	1960	14.9	14.8
Second Plan	(1956-61)	510	549	4500	4672	11.3	11.8
Third Plan	(1961-66)	1086	1089	7500	8577	14.5	12.7
Annual Plans	(1966-69)	1037	1107	6665	6625	15.6	16.7
Fourth Plan	(1996-74)	2728	2320	15902	15779	17.2	14.2
Fifth Plan	(1974-79)	4766	4865	39322	39426	12.1	12.3
Annual Plan	(1979-80)	1815	1966	12601	12176	14.4	16.4
Sixth Plan	(1980-85)	12539	15201	97500	109292	12.9	13.9
Seventh Plan	(1985-90)	22233	31509	180000	218730	12.4	14.4
Annual Plan	(1990-92)	19200	17602	137034	64844	14.1	14.3
Eighth Plan	(1992-97)	63642	—	434100	—	14.7	—
Ninth Plan	(1997-2002)	115390	N.A.	875000	N.A.	13.2	N.A.

(N.A. -Not available)

SOURCE: Agricultural Statistics at a Glance, Ministry of Agriculture, Government of India, 1999.

CHAPTER 5

Agriculture Policy

An agricultural policy has to take into consideration the ground situation and framed accordingly. It would then be possible to highlight the competitive advantages that India enjoys in so far as agricultural development is concerned. Its climate is its biggest blessing, conducive to the cultivation of two or even three crops annually, and making it a congenial home to every economic plant species grown in the world-ranging from temperate orchard crops like apples to tropical mangoes. It already has the largest acreage of irrigated land in the world with 40 per cent of the potential still to be tapped. The country's abundant human resource encompassing all categories skilled, unskilled, technical, scientific and managerial is its other most precious asset.

According to available estimates the country has exploited only 20 percent of its agricultural potential; whereas arable land is a mere 11 per cent of the total land area taking the world as a whole, it constitutes as much as 52 percent of India's total, the per capita availability being two-and-a-half times that of China. It is another matter which is also an index of the gap between possibility and performance, that China, with approximately the same cultivable area (140 million hectares) as India but with less per capita availability and much less area under irrigation (47 million hectares as against India's 60 million) produces 392 million tonnes of foodgrains when the latter is struggling around 200 million tonnes.

Even then India is the world's largest producer of tea, cotton and sugar, and among the top three for foodgrains, groundnut, coffee, eggs and milk. No other country produces such a wide range of annual and perennial oilseeds; it alone cultivates all the four major species of cotton. In sericulture, it produces mulberry, tasar, moga and seric silks, with possibilities of producing new blend; its seacoast extending to some 8,000 km is a repository of as yet inadequately fathomed marine wealth. There is a shining example of a 70 acre waterspread, the largest in Asia in Chaengalpattu (Tamil Nadu), where fish production has touched 60 tonnes an acre as against the national average of two tonnes.

No other country grows such a wide range of vegetables, fruits and flowers than India which is the second largest producer of fruits after Brazil and the U.S., but processes only 0.1 percent of it as against Brazil's 70 per cent, and lets an estimated Rs. 3,000 crores worth of fruits and vegetables to get spoilt. The Netherlands with a population of less than 15 million and an area one-hundredth the size of India corners 64 per cent of the world's market for cut flowers, 61 percent for eggs, 57 percent for fresh tomatoes and 36 percent for potatoes. The way tiny Switzerland capitalizes on its dairy and animal husbandry is legendary. India is yet to realize the magical and vast properties of its herbs in their plentitude. Many of our experts may not be aware that Chinese cucumber roots contain a substance that promises to control AIDS; that the extract from rosy periwinkle in Madagascar is effective in the treatment of childhood leukaemia.

THE PROBLEM

It is really a matter of pride that Indian Agriculture has today achieved a respectable place in the world. It is able to feed the increasing population at more than self-sufficiency level. No doubt this is an achievement for which the country and more so the farmer as well as our researchers can be proud of. But during the course of these five decades of development we have now come to a situation when the agricultural scene does not seem to be very bright. It has brought in its wake uneven development, in both research and production across regions and crops. The green revolution which was, in any case, confined to regions of assured irrigation has also reached a plateau.

While around 47 percent of the geographical area in the country is under agriculture, the forest area has shrunk from over 33 percent in 1947 to about 21 percent now. Hardly four percent of the geographical area is under pastures and grasses. Over 90 million hectares of farm land in the country suffers from second generation problems like soil erosion, degradation and compaction, water logging, salinity, acidity and alkalinity. Increasingly agriculture is becoming dependent on the exploitation of ground water. We are now facing complications which would possibly need drastic measures.

The need for a policy aimed at rectifying these distortions, therefore, cannot be overemphasised. While the country has had an industrial policy resolution since 1956, there had only been occasional official pronouncements on agriculture, emphasizing its importance as a source of food and industrial raw material. The lone formal statement on "agriculture and food policy" that existed till the other day was made prior to Independence in 1946. The then Government had declared: "The all-India policy is to promote the welfare of the people and to secure a progressive improvement in their standard of living. This includes the responsibility of providing enough food for all, sufficient in quantity and of requisite quality". However, the first ever

National Agricultural Policy was announced on 28th July, 2000. The details of the policy will be discussed later.

Policy Frame

The economists were of the view that our future agriculture policy should take a proper note of the prevailing ground situation. Some of the urgent issues which the new policy should aim at were envisaged as:

1. Developing an honourable as well as respectable farming community.
2. Evolving cost effective technologies.
3. Creating a healthier as well as export oriented agriculture.
4. Managing land and water resources.
5. Branding organic products.

A RESPECTABLE FARMING COMMUNITY*

While the share of agriculture and allied sectors in GDP has come down from say around 60 percent at the time of independence to about 25 percent as today, number of persons depending on agriculture has more or less remained around 60 percent with only some marginal changes (Table 5.1). In absolute terms, the number of persons eking out a precarious living from agriculture has doubled from 290 to about 580

Table 5.1 Relative Income of Agricultural Workers (Including Both Cultivators and Labourers)

	Share (%) Agriculture in			*Ratio per worker income in agriculture to non-agriculture sector at*	
	SDP at 1980-81 prices	*SDP at current prices*	*Work force*	*1980-81 prices*	*Current prices*
1960-61	45.9	43.0	69.5	0.37	0.33
1970-71	39.7	42.4	69.8	0.28	0.31
1980-81	34.7	34.7	66.5	0.27	0.27
1990-91	29.5	29.8	64.9	0.23	0.23
1999-2000*	25.2†	27.1	59.0‡	NA	NA

* Provisional, † At 1993-94Prices, ‡ 1991 census data

SOURCE: Calculated from National Accounts Statistics, CSO, and Population Census.

* For more detailed discussion, read Chapter 20: Indian Farmer in the New Millennium.

million. The quality of life in villages has not improved to the desired extent. The intense pressure on land has resulted in cultivation of even marginal lands, causing further degradation of this vital natural resource.

There are 107 million operational holdings in the country, every fourth family in the world being Indian. But as many as 78 percent of them have only 32 percent of the land with them (top 2 percent having 20 percent) leads to further skewed income distribution within the agriculture sector. (Tables 5.2 and 5.3). It is a question mark where our policies so far adopted would lead us in the coming decades. The present land policy under which people are being compelled to reduce the size of holdings further (while the need is to put a ceiling on the minimum size) would, if at all, mean redistributing poverty by making even marginally viable holdings non-viable and unsustainable. Is it necessary for us to keep all the 70 percent of the work force wedded to land which under no circumstances can support it. We must take a cue

Table 5.2 Distribution of Operational Holdings-All India

No. of Holdings: '000' Number
Area '000' hectares
Average size : Hectare

Category of holdings	*No. of operational holdings*		*Area operated*		*Average size of operational holdings*	
	1985-86	*1990-91*	*1985-86*	*1990-91*	*1985-86*	*1990-91*
(1)	*(2)*	*(3)*	*(4)*	*(5)*	*(6)*	*(7)*
Marginal (Less than 1 hectares)	56147 (57.8)	63389 (59.4)	22042 (13.4)	24894 (15.0)	0.34	0.39
Small (1.0 to 2.0 hectares)	17922 (18.4)	20092 (18.8)	25708 (15.6)	28827 (17.4)	1.43	1.43
Semi-Medium (2.0 to 4.0 hectares)	13252 (13.6)	13923 (13.1)	36666 (22.3)	38375 (23.2)	2.77	2.76
Medium (4.0 to 10.0 hectares)	7916 (8.2)	7580 (7.1)	47144 (28.6)	44752 (27.0)	5.96	5.90
Large (10.0 hectares and above)	1918 (2.0)	1654 (1.6)	33002 (20.1)	28659	17.21	17.33
All Holdings	97155 (100.0)	106637 (100.0)	164562 (100.0)	165507 (100.0)	1.69	1.57

Note: Figures in parentheses indicate the percentage of respective column total.

SOURCE: Agricultural Census Division, Ministry of Agriculture, New Delhi.

Author's SOURCE: Bansil P.C., Agricultural Statistical Compendium Volume I.

Table 5.3 Agriculture Workers in India (Defined in Terms of Main Activity)

Census	Cultivators (million)	Agrl. labour (million)	Percentage to cultivators	All main workers agriculture labour
1971	78.3	47.5	43.4	26.3
1981	92.5	55.5	37.8	22.7
1991	110.6	74.6	38.8	26.1

SOURCE: Census of India for respective years

from the experience of developed countries that a growing economy must lead to a decline in the population depending on agriculture.

After all these decades of populism, let us now have a close look at the ground situation. No useful purpose will be served by beating the dead horse. Let us admit that we have failed to implement the various components of the land policy. If at all, it has only created irritants and impediments in the efficient maintenance and utilization of land resources. The whole issue needs to be re-examined. Public policy will no doubt provide incentives for small/marginal farmers towards a cooperative effort in areas such as land development, nutrient supply and improved post harvest and marketing technology. We might also think of corporatisation of agriculture, of requiring corporations to assume more social, economic and environmental responsibilities in agricultural development.

The corporate sector is usually considered as representing big business. This is really not correct. Agriculture provides the largest avenue for self employment in the country and is an excellent example of small and decentralized enterprises. There is much scope for the growth of a dynamic services sector in rural areas. Improvement of agricultural productivity under small farm conditions can be achieved only through a process of decentralized production supported by a few key centralized services in areas such as water and pest management and post-harvest technology. It is in fostering a new management revolution in small farms that the corporate sector can perform a meaningful role. This will not, however, be enough. People will have to be shifted from agriculture on the pattern of our neighbouring countries, viz. Thailand and Indonesia.

We have to frame our policies so that the small and marginal land holders and landless labourers are encouraged to get into occupations other than agriculture in the rural area itself without moving to the cities. The steps taken in this direction in the past show more or less a complete failure of our rural development programmes where a multiple number of schemes quite often working at cross roads, are being implemented in rural India. Starting from the Community Development Programmes of early fifties, we have sunk under these programmes billions and billions of rupees without any visible impact on the rural economy or even in any pocket of the country. (Table 5.4). If poverty could be removed by an investment of Rs. 5-7 thousand per family with a high degree of leakages, India could have possibly been on the top of the world in this respect. What is required now is to introduce appropriate technology in the rural programmes to attract non viable farmers towards non-farm activities. At the same time, there will be a need for a complete reorientation of poverty alleviation programmes. This will mean a shift from individual to area approach to enable us to plug various leakages. Available skills in rural areas are not capable to adopt modern technologies in any of the rural activity. We need to have a clear policy to introduce an integrated programmes to cover:

1. Micro level assessment of human and natural resource base.
2. Provide appropriate training facilities so as to exploit the full potential of all the available resources, and
3. Introduce appropriate technologies directed to generate off farm employment and additional income.

Even smaller countries like Korea, Indonesia and Thailand have implemented such programmes with success. There is no reason that

Table 5.4 Structure of Rural Poverty (As in 1983)

Household (hh) type	*Percentage share in all rural hhs.*	*Incidence of poverty within each hh type*	*Percentage share in a rural hhs below poverty line*	*Percentage share of each hh-type in the total une-mployed persons days*
1. Self-employed Agriculture (Cultivators)	40.7	24.1	32.0	16.3
2. Self-employed in non- agricultural operations	11.7	26.9	10.3	8.5
3. Agriculture labour hhs	30.7	45.5	45.6	59.5
4. Other labour hhs	6.6	27.9	6.0	10.2
5. Other rural hhs.	10.3	18.3	6.1	5.4
6. All rural hhs	100.0	30.6	100.0	100.0

SOURCE: Dev et al, 1991: 58 Agricultural Policy in India, Context Issues and Instruments. H.V. Nadherni, Department of Economic Analysis and Policy, Reserve Bank of India, Bombay, February 10, 1993.

India will not succeed. The future, therefore, lies in an optimum blend of technologies, old and new which can lead to a new paradigm of rural development based on the principles of ecological sustainability, economic viability and social equity. The corporate sector can take a lead in such technology blending.

EVOLVING COST EFFECTIVE TECHNOLOGIES

The present situation in the country on the food front is quite precarious. Our unit cost of production of various agricultural commodities at the farmer level is increasing. This results in substantial increases in the procurement price by the Government which in turn involves higher issue prices and still higher open market prices. The net result is that both the farmer as well as the consumer are unhappy. Our future agricultural policy has to be cost effective and aim at reducing unit costs so that a healthy situation is created in the Indian Economy. There are plenty of examples within the country itself which if examined carefully and implemented over larger areas would help us to solve this problem.

Further, populist and 'catch vote' policies of the Government are responsible for jacking up MSP which has now really become Procurement Price. In the mid-1960s, there used to be two prices, namely, procurement price and minimum support price (MSP), the latter coming into operation as guaranteed floor price when bountiful production occurred. However, with the obliteration of the distinction between MSP and procurement prices for quite some years now, support operations for cereals are undertaken at the higher levels of procurement prices which are also annually increased. The terms of reference of the then Agricultural Prices Commission were also modified to keep in view the terms of trade while recommending the price policy. Further, according to the change in methodology for estimating the cost of production suggested by a committee of the Ministry of Agriculture, cost C was calculated by including 10 per cent of cost C_2 on account of managerial function performed by farmers. It has been observed that the average ratio of recommended MSP for wheat to cost C_2 has been around 1:2 over the last 15 years. Over and above this, when government gives a bonus, the ratio crosses 1:3. Since management and risk factors are already covered, the bonus inclusive price is high and it also affects the intercrop price parities; throughout the nineties, real purchase price of wheat had been increasing significantly.

The net result is that public sector stocks of foodgrains have crossed all time high levels threatening to touch 70-75 million tonnes. This has lead to a huge fiscal burden which in 1999-2000 was of the order of Rs. 13000 crores. Of this, the subsidy element was Rs. 6000 crores as the cost of holding the stocks. This is not all. We have been priced out in the world market for rice, wheat, sugar and cotton. There is no taker of these surpluses even at heavily subsidized prices. If so, the need to reduce costs becomes all the more imperative.

Even a cursory analysis of cost of production data indicates that there does exist considerable scope for reducing the cost of production. For example, in Andhra Pradesh during 1983-84 the cost of production of paddy on 15 percent of holdings having least cost, averaged not more than Rs. 106-148 per quintal whereas for the entire sample, it averaged at Rs. 141-153 quintal. To the extent, this difference in the cost of production was on account of difference in the pattern and level of use of inputs and the agronomical practices followed. It is indicative of the potential which exists for reducing the unit cost or production. The situation may not be much different in the case of other crops in other areas. Such studies should be undertaken which should come up with specific recommendations.

It is doubtful if the extension machinery in the country is even aware of these issues. The question of their advising the farmer as to how efficiency of input use could be raised so as to reduce the unit cost of production, would not then arise. Even otherwise we have not yet been able to realize more than 35 percent of the potential of known technology. According to an IARI study when full potential of known technology is used it should help reduce the costs.

Expenditure on plant protection chemicals used to form the single most important item in most of the States till the late seventies and in many States farmers were applying more than the necessary doses. However, as a result of propagation of integrated pest management, based on the threshold level of pest infestation, number of sprays for cotton crop got reduced substantially and as a result, the unit cost of production of cotton also came down in many States.

An analysis of the pattern of input in the case of different commodities further indicates that there exists a large scope for their more efficient use. Report of the Commission for Agricultural Costs and Prices on Price Policy for Kharif crops for the year 1985-86 highlighted that it is possible to obtain much larger incremental levels of output within the framework of available technology through a more efficient use of inputs. It was pointed out that the synergistic effect of a balanced use of different inputs which is missing at the micro level, if realized is bound to lead to additional production at reduced unit costs.

Strip Tillage Tillage is one of the major crop production operations and is an important contributor to the total cost of production. It is estimated that tillage and sowing almost consumes 25 per cent of the total operational energy in wheat production. Tillage operation is mainly physical soil manipulation achieved by harrow, cultivator, plough and other implements to make a fine seed bed for proper germination along with other benefits like better aeration, moisture conservation, friability, biomass incorporation and weed control.

Earlier heavy tillage was emphasised by the farmers and farm scientists for successful farming of wheat after paddy. It resulted in speedy mechanisation of tillage and sowing operations in the wheat crop and the number of agricultural tractors equipped with costly implement has already reached about 24 lakh at the all-India level.

The rising cost of crop production, depletion of fossil fuels, timeliness of sowing operation, non-availability of longer duration for crop growth and soil health problems have forced the scientists and engineers to optimise the requirement of field preparation by adopting precision farming. It was thought that wheat cultivation expenditure can be reduced by reducing tillage. The possibilities of controlling weed with the help of herbicides and weedicides also encouraged the researchers to closely investigate the tillage operation in the light of the minimum tillage research findings all over the world. In view of this fact the work was started on minimum/optimum tillage to establish the effect on crop raising parameters and yield. The engineers and scientists at Punjab Agricultural University, Ludhiana, have successfully demonstrated that wheat can be grown after pady without any prior field preparation. To adopt precision farming and take advantage of both tillage and no tillage a strip till drill has been developed. The successful development of this machine achieved the goal of cost reduction and timely sowing in the wheat crop. This results in saving energy and time in the range of 60-70 per cent in comparison to traditional sowing where five to seven operations are required, depending upon the soil conditions. Its use also increases yield due to timely sowing and lower weed population. Punjab Agricultural University has already recommended this machine for the farmers of Punjab.

Technology is available in the country by which we can increase 10-12 qtls. yield per hectare without any additional investment. Again bidirectional sowing of wheat in Punjab can give an increase of 5 qtls. yield per hectare. Timely sowing can increase the yield to the extent of 3.75 qtls. per hectare every week over the late sown. Two-three qtls. of Raya crop per hectare can be taken by sowing 9th row alternatively in wheat. Similarly application of one-fourth of required dose of nitrogen at first irrigation before the preparatory tillage has given more than 3% increase in wheat yield. Various other methods also exist by which yield in other crops can be increased without additional investment.

If Indian agriculture becomes a 'professional avocation', it would also strive to optimize gains from technological developments and promote production patterns where the country has comparative advantage. Such a move should help increase the export of farm commodities, traditional as well as non-tradition, both of primary produce and the value added processed products.

Under the peculiar conditions of Indian Agriculture which continues to be subjected to vagaries of nature and is faced with a high internal demand, export policy of agricultural products has been based on available surpluses at a point of time. While continuity of business is very essential in marketing and export our policies in this respect have been ad hoc and we have never had a regular export policy so far. The new slogan of fixing high targets for agricultural exports would imply a complete re-orientation of our thinking in this respect. The new export policy would thus involve the following:

1. Agricultural export commodities will have to be independent of those being grown for domestic consumption and a continued supply of the specified commodity must be ensured.
2. Emphasis has to be on special and value added products which must be grown and processed primarily for export.
3. While there are weak links in Agricultural research in general, no thinking has yet started for research on commodities intended for export or processing. The product must be of uniform size with a much longer shelf life. No wonder then that a major part of the horticultural produce is being wasted.

CREATING EXPORT POTENTIAL

Durum wheat is already in production in Punjab, Madhya Pradesh, Haryana, Uttar Pradesh and Maharashtra. It is being grown in about 10 percent area in Punjab. This has a very high export potential because of its industrial consumption and being disease free. It has a much better baking quality, but does not make good *chapaties* on the pan. It is not liked in Northern India as people mainly eat chapaties here. Gujarati people have preference for this wheat. Government does not have separate stocking arrangements for this type of wheat. Once a decision is taken to procure and stock this variety of wheat separately, this can exclusively be used for export purposes.

Rice of Basmati 370 variety has super aroma. This is being cultivated mostly in India. The production of this rice which is known for its long grain, fragrance and aroma constitutes about 2 percent of the total production of rice in India. Commercial production of Basmati has been confined to Punjab, Haryana and U.P. No other variety matches the quality of super aroma of Basmati in the world. The only other country which produces basmati rice is Pakistan, but quality is poorer than India. Traori rice grown in District Karnal (Haryana) is also of a very superior quality. A recent study completed by Techno Economic Research Institute, New Delhi under ICAR sponsorship has recommended a special Basmati Development Corporation primarily for export. Thus, where aroma is the requirement, we can exploit the export potential of this variety and can make the production programme exclusively for export. We can compete in the world market by supplying rice of other varieties as well where aroma is not required but have other characteristics of basmati. We can produce this rice much cheaper than most of the competing countries. Similar programmes can also be prepared for extra long linted cotton, HPS groundnut, vegetables, fruits, tobacco, jute, etc. The whole process of production right from seed production to end with export, must be organized in a chain tie-up system.

The Indian Oil Produce and Exporters Association (IOPEA), the export promotion and monitoring agency designated by the Ministry of Commerce, have identified new markets for HPS groundnut which include Indonesia, Philippines, Malaysia and other countries in the Far East. India can also pose a major challenge for the main suppliers of peanut in the world market - US, China and Argentina by developing bold size kernels (40/50 kernels per ounce). There is an urgent need to improve the quality of edible peanuts in India, which should be of bold size and have less fat content.

India also produces various kinds of fruits like mango, banana, papaya, pomegranate , apple, ber, etc. Indian Alphonso mango has got international demand. A few varieties of banana like 'Basrai', 'Grand Nain', and 'Williums' have high export potentialities. To achieve the full potential of agricultural/horticultural commodities, there is a need to establish independent development corporations in each case. They will be responsible for full development of the commodity right from the point of providing quality seed to prospective growers, guiding them about management practices, providing them with necessary inputs, procuring the final products at reasonable prices, processing the same, packing them in appropriate and attractive packs and will have regular contracts with foreign buyers. It would also be the responsibility of these corporations to keep in reserve sufficient foreign exchange funds which can be utilized not only to import technology or machinery etc. if required, but also to import low value substitutes of comparable commodities in those years when there is expected to be a shortage at home due to natural factors. This would, for example, mean that if oilseed production has suffered in a particular year, the corporation will arrange to bridge the gap by importing palm oil or soyabean oil which are cheaper in the world market.

Speciality Items

There are other non-traditional export items like flowers, marine products, meat and poultry products etc. If adequate emphasis is laid on effective management and a proper mechanism is evolved to remove the constraints (marketing infrastructure, transportation and above all fiscal) exports could be increased substantially within a short period.

World consumption of flowers is valued at more than $ 25 billion. Holland has more than 68 percent of the world trade. India could grow and occupy an honourable place in the international market. Going by the recent report prepared by Netherlands, India's potential is between 29 and 34 thousand hectares in traditional flowers and 10 thousand hectares in modern flowers. For the former, Tamil Nadu and

Karnataka are the leading producers. On the other hand, floriculture in the north has remained more or less neglected. The potential for growing floriculture in Northern India should be fully explored.

Processed food exports is another thrust area so far ignored. Though India is the second largest producer of fruits and vegetables in the world, only one percent of the produce is processed. In the developed world, 60-70 percent of the perishables are processed. The Government has given liberal incentives to processing units. Licensing has been abolished in most areas and this activity has been included in the high priority list for grant of automatic approvals for direct foreign investment up to 51 percent. Blanket permission has also been given to the industry for hiring foreign technicians.

Export Oriented Research

These are only a few examples of perishable commodities which are being already grown in the country. The only problem is that we have not till recently paid any attention to the processing industry. With the new found emphasis in this area, as discussed above, we have to go a step further. The quality of various fruits and vegetables needed for processing or direct export need special attention with regard to not only their physical appearance but also intrinsic qualities. Nobody has so far thought of undertaking research in this area. There is an urgent need to initiate research on horticultural crops to meet the requirements of export in the fresh form (uniform size and long shelf-life, etc.) and processing industry. Special grading, packing, transportation and marketing techniques will need to be developed for the purpose. It would not be out of context to mention here that the whole of North Eastern Region has an untapped potential for growing and processing high value horticultural crops which can be grown without any competition with either foodgrains or cash crops being grown in the region.

HEALTHY AGRICULTURE

It may be mentioned that judicious exploitation of flora and agricultural practices for food, fodder, fibre and medicines has been the hall mark of man's effort for a long time. But wasteful practices like the jhum cultivation in the north-eastern parts of our country, population pressure, increased urbanization, indiscriminate use of fertilizers and pesticides, floods, droughts increased carbon dioxide in the atmosphere have damaged our ecosystem, and thus loss of genetic resources, This has, of late, created increased awareness in conservation of biological diversity and genetic resources in food security, sustainable agriculture and rural development, environment management and international trade in commodities.

Basic policy must then aim to promote environment friendly agricultural development, so as to make it sustainable. There are certain otherwise highly productive areas of Punjab and Haryana in the country where land and soil degradation has already taken place and environmental pollution is visible. Environment friendly production functions will have to be implemented to establish a healthy and strong agriculture base.

Conservation of natural resources figure prominently in the process of sustainable development. Taking into consideration other elements of the definition, sustainable development should be conceived as a comprehensive national development approach where the criteria of efficiency, equity and sustainability are carefully integrated within a coherent and operational framework. In this approach, efficiency implies the optimum use of national resources; equity calls for the reduction in the variance in income `distribution and introducing measures for poverty alleviation; and sustainability aims at the conservation of the natural resources base for use by future generations.

For these criteria to be fully integrated in the process of economic development, it is our view that environmental protection and sustainability dimensions should be carefully integrated into agricultural planning and policy analysis; thus translating these concepts into strategies and operational actions. A recent issue of the Journal, Choice, being brought out by the American Agricultural Economic Association gives ten commandments for Farm Policy and the most important of them is that we will leave behind for posterity our lands if not better at least in the same quality as we inherited. Failing this, our fruitful lands shall become sterile stony ground and wasting gullies. Our descendants will decrease and live in poverty or perish from the face of the earth.

It is intriguing (and even paradoxical) to perceive that it is the process of accelerated economic growth that leads to pollution and natural resource degradation, but only through economic growth can environmental protection and natural resource conservation be sustainably maintained. The question, therefore, is to grow or not to grow, but how the process of economic growth can be carefully planned and how relevant policy measures be rationally designed so that economic growth would meet the challenge of conserving the natural resource base protecting the environment, be technically appropriate; economically viable and socially acceptable.

While making announcements about increasing the productivity levels in dry areas and thus improving the living standards of farmers in those regions, not much has been done with regard to soil and water conservation practices. We have been talking about these schemes right from the First Plan Period. We will now have to adopt policies to implement these programmes on a war footing.

High yielding varieties were introduced in mid-sixties and it was perfectly alright for the public sector organizations like the Seed Development Corporations in the country to take up the responsibilities to supply certified seed to the farmer. After a lapse of nearly 25 years, it is quite evident that the public sector has miserably failed to perform its responsibility in this area. A study conducted by the Techno-Economic Research Institute in a progressive district like Karnal in Haryana shows that the supply of certified seed by the public sector both for rice and wheat is hardly 4-5 per cent. Another study conducted by the Government of Haryana says that the farmers are utilizing only 15% good quality seed.

One would imagine the fate of future agriculture where the farmer is having no access to proper seed, with water table going down, soil degradation taking place at a rapid speed and on the top of all this the so called T & V (Touch and Vanish in the rural parlance) the prevalent extension system, is ineffective. There are small countries like Portugal where they have succeeded to reduce the role of public sector in agricultural development only to research and administration. A time has now come in India where we have to think seriously about the role of private/cooperative sector responsible directly to the farmer and the farmer organizations. This would include seed multiplication, extension and veterinary services including artificial insemination. To start with a plan should be prepared for resorting to the cooperative movement it three basic values: democratic functioning, professional management and financial discipline.

For the development of a healthy agriculture Dr. Swaminathan, has highlighted a six point programme, which is relevant to the present situation.*

1. We must change our mindset with reference to farming. While agriculture may be a food producing machine in industrialised countries, it is the very backbone of our live hood and ecological security systems, as well as our national sovereignty. Opportunities for assured and remunerative marketing hold the key to increasing the productivity of small farm and animal holdings. Post-harvest technology hence needs priority attention.

2. A second thrust area relates to enlarging the space for economically viable self-employment in the on-farm rural sectors for educated youth. The Government must desist from expanding its own staff if initiatives such as agri-clinics and agri-business centres to be run by self-employed agricultural, veterinary, commerce, fisheries and home science graduates, are to be economically viable. There is a need for a New Deal for the Self-Employed through appropriate infrastructure and public policies including venture capital for small scale enterprises.

3. There are a large number of Technology Missions in operation now. Unfortunately, several of these commodity-centred missions are

* Dr. M.S. Swaminathan, Food for Peace and Development; Hindu, January 10, 2002.

not having the desired impact, as is clear from the increasing import of pulses and oilseeds, although these very crops can be the catalysts of agrarian prosperity in dry farming areas. It would be useful to link the various crop-centred missions horizontally with the water harvesting and watershed management programmes in the form of a National Mission for Farmers' Wellbeing. The goals of such an integrated mission should be to assist rural families in increasing productivity and income per unit of water and land and to link producers with markets.

4. There is a growing gap between academic know-how and field level do-how. Farm families need integrated and timely advice on both production and post-harvest operations. There is also need for proactive advice on land use so that there is a proper match between production and market demand. A mechanism has to be developed to enable all the principal national and State scientific agencies to provide both dynamic and generic information to rural and tribal families in every part of the country. An Inter-Agency Action Council for Rural Technologies is an urgent need. Such a Council could provide a single window service to farmers as well as the youth operating agri-clinics and agri-business centres through a computer and internet-aided virtual college system.

5. Even if we are able to accelerate the pace of creation of livelihoods/ jobs in rural and peri-urban areas, the problem of chronic hunger will still haunt families without assets such as land or livestock. This is where recently launched schemes such as the Sampoorna Gramin Rozgar Yojana, grain banks for tribal areas and Annapoorna could make an important contribution, if implemented with the total involvement of community organisations. It is also necessary to launch a Nagarpalika Rozgar Yojana for undertaking bio-environmental management of mosquitoes, harvesting rain water and recycling solid and liquid wastes. Another urgent need is a Food for Ecodevelopment programme in the Himalayan, Western and Eastern Ghats regions as well as in coastal areas and islands, for the restoration of hydrologic and biodiversity "hot spots" and for the rehabilitation of mangrove wetlands.

6. Above all, there is an immediate need for a "Food for Healthy Children" programme to help overcome maternal and foetal undernutrition as well as malnutrition in infants in the 0-2 age group, when over 80 per cent of brain formation is completed. All these programmes can be knit in the form of a well-planned Food for Peace and Sustainable Development movement, involving a total allocation of 15 million tonnes of foodgrains during 2002 (this includes the quantities already approved for different programmes).

INDIAN AGRICULTURE: A CRISIS

Indian agriculture is at cross roads today. Although there is a deceleration in agricultural productivity over the last few years, public sector stocks of foodgrains are threatening to pierce the sky. There is no taker of the grain—both within or outside the country even at the highly subsidized BPL prices of Rs. 415 and Rs. 565 per quintal for wheat and rice respectively. Economic price (procurement plus ancillary as well as storage) works out to be nearly double at Rs. 830 and Rs. 1130 per quintal for wheat and rice respectively during 2000-01. State managed prices of sugarcane are being artificially jacked up leading to huge payment of arrears and accumulated stocks. At the same time the story of oilseeds presents another dismal picture and cotton is facing further complications. We have discussed the issue relating to mounting stocks of foodgrains elsewhere in this study. Basic problems faced by oilseeds, cotton and sugarcane are discussed here. The future agriculture policy has to address itself to all these questions which are very serious in nature.

Oilseeds

In response to the protests against bringing edible oils under OGL, the customs duty has been hiked four times in the past 18 months (2000-01), with the latest increase announced in 2001-2 budget. But all this does not seem to have had the desired effect, thanks to the steadily declining international prices. Edible oil imports touched the highest ever monthly figure of 6.5 lakh tonnes in August 2001 and imports in the full year 2000-01 (November-October) are expected to set a record of 5 million tonnes, compared to 4.5 million tonnes last year. Imports now provide 45 per cent of the country's edible oils requirements, Domestic oilseeds production this year, on the other hand, is feared to be the lowest in a decade, the crop having suffered from drought in major producing states, especially Gujarat. India is now the world's biggest importer of edible oils, which have emerged as the second largest item in the country's import bill after petroleum products.

Palm oil products now account for 61 percent of total edible oil imports and soft oils, such as soyabean, sunflower and rapeseed, make up the rest. Low import duty on edible oils, higher cost of production and sick condition of the crushing units have resulted in an unprecedented crisis in the mustard oil industry with a fall in cultivated area by 38 per cent. A comprehensive survey conducted by the Mustard Research and Promotion Consortium (MRCP) in Punjab, Haryana, U.P and Rajasthan shows a fall in mustard acreage to 43 lakh hectare (ha) from 70 la ha in the last four years.

Stocks of mustard are piling up, there are few buyers as many crushing units have shut down due to unremunerative prices and unless remedical (2002) steps are taken the production in rabi season could fall below 40 lakh tonnes. Major reason, for shifting to other crops was the large inventory of 14 lakh tonnes from previous year's output including eight lakh tonnes in Rajasthan alone. While the cost of production was around Rs. 30 per kg., mustard oil was selling at Rs. 29 per kg. forcing crushers to close down units. All 26 units in Hisar had stopped production.

Demand had fallen as crude palm oil and RBD palmolein were selling cheaply at Rs. 20 and Rs. 22 per kg respectively. Things came full circle when cheaper imported oils led to less demand for indigenous ones like mustard, putting pressure on the crushing units which in turn affected the farmers who shifted to other crops resulting in fall in putput and more imports. During the sowing season when the farmer decides on crops to be sown it is critical that the prices are remunerative, but at present they were hovering around Rs. 1250 per quintal, little above the minimum support price of Rs. 1200 per quintal. Transportation and cultivation expenses were Rs. 340 per quintals. Meanwhile the market rate of gram was Rs 1650-1700 per quintal and growing costs were lesser at Rs. 280 per quintal.

Rajasthan had been the major producer of mustard as the crop required less water but with better monsoon during 2001 and higher prices for wheat and gram the scenario was changing. Situation had aggravated with the crushing units going into the red. Of the 30 units in Khairthal in Alwar district 15 had shut down. Particularly affected was western Rajasthan including Kota. Farmers were also not getting good quality seeds from the market effecting productivity which was below 1000 kg per ha against a potential of 1700 kg per ha. The potential could only be realised if fertilisers, insecticides and pesticides were applied in a particular proportion but most farmers could not afford their purchase. Cultivated areas under salty water, lack of irrigation and obsolete crushing technology had also been detrimental to the farmers' interests.

According to one estimate, domestic demand for vegetable oils is set to rise to 19 mn tonnes by 2009-2010 from 10.2 mn tonnes in 1999-2000. On the other hand, annual oilseeds production has declined to around 18 million tonnes in 2000-01 from 25 mn tonnes three years ago. The domestic oil extraction industry has suffered as a consequence, with average capacity utilization coming down to some 40 percent. Area under oilseeds has shrunk, with farmers complaining of unremunerative prices. The country's heavy dependence on edible oil imports has again been manifested in the just-concluded oil year 2001-01 (Nov-Oct). When imports rose by 7.5 per cent to 4.83 million tonnes from the last year's level of nearly 4.50 million tonnes.

Import increased despite hike in import tariffs on four occasions in the year. However, the oil extraction units took solace from the fact that imports did not rise beyond the predicted level of five million tonnes. Expectedly, due to a 20 per cent duty differential between crude palm oil (CPO) and RBD palmolein, CPO import in the year spurted by 69.5 per cent to 14 lakh tonnes from 8.3 lakh tonnes in the last oil year. Against this RBD palmolein import, slapped with about 95 per cent duty, fell 32 per cent 15 lakh tonnes from the previous year's level of 22 lakh-tonnes.

Edible oil imports, though declined in September and October following the imposition of tarriff values or base import price on palm products in August, hefty imports in the preceding months took the overall ceding months took the overall import up by 7.5 per cent in the year. But the answer does not lie in erecting high tariff walls or in mounting purchase operations at artificially high prices by agencies such as Nafed, on par with the operations of the FCI in wheat and rice which have become a millstone around the central government's neck. It must be sought in improving the productivity of oilseeds cultivation and reducing costs of production as well as in encouraging diversification into non-traditional oilseeds.

Cotton

The position regarding cotton is also not very comfortable. Cotton crisis deepens further with prices crashing to new recent lows even before the new crop arrivals start picking up. The Cotton Corporation of India has geared up to support prices. Cotton prices crashed by 5 to 8 per cent in (Nov. 2001) and are expected to decline further as the new crop arrivals gather momentum. The prevailing prices are 10 to 15 per cent lower when compared with the prices same time a year ago, but the chances of a further fall in value can not be ruled out if the international prices of comparable varieties are any indications. From the earlier level of Rs. 1,830 per *maund*, the prices have fallen this year (2001-02) to Rs. 1,480 in Punjab and a little lower in Haryana. Demand is there, but not at the price expected. Indian agriculture has landed in serious crisis because of being inefficient and uncompetitive by global standards. Cheaper imports have made the domestic cotton unviable and unwanted. Some 20 lakh bales have been imported into the country this season. Of these three lakh bales have moved into Punjab. Top mills are rejecting the costly Indian cotton and importing it cheaper from the USA, Australia, Israel, Greece, Uzbekistan, Syria and Africa.

Smaller spinning, ginning and processing mills are on the verge of closure due to a high lumpsum power tariff, though most are working at almost half the capacity levels, faced with poor supplies. Punjab cotton has gone beyond millers' reach also by a 4 per cent cess—2 per cent market fee and 2 per cent levy for rural development. Such a cess also exists in Haryana, Rajasthan and Madhya Pradesh, but it is lower there. Given the unchecked supply of substandard and spurious pesticides, fertilisers and seeds to farmers, there seems to be a nexus at work. Farmers had to repeatedly spray (some time 20-22 against normal 4-5) their cotton crop to fight the pest attack, but often without success, losing not just the crop but also the manual and financial investment.

Prices of J-34, M.P. H-4 and Gujarat Sankar-6 are currently ruling 8 to 15 per cent above support levels. But rule out the possibility of these prices coming down to MSP level considering the scenario in the domestic and international markets. The country is expected to produce around 160 lakh bales of cotton this season (2001-02) against 140 bales last season and industry may import around 20 lakh bales, if not more, considering the price advantage along with quality and other facilities the foreign cotton offers.

Succumbing to the pressure from the cotton grower's and trader's lobby, and ignoring a huge burden of Rs 3,000 crore, the Maharashtra government decided to go ahead with the cotton procurement. As per the chief minister's own admission, the scheme is currently reeling under a shortfall of Rs 2,700 crore. Considering the falling rates and a slump in the textile industry, we expect a loss of around Rs. 1,500 crore even this year. This will put the overall burden on the state at Rs 4,200 crore.

The minimum support price fixed by the centre for the year 2001 is Rs. 1,800 per quintal for the season, whereas the state will be paying Rs. 2,300 per quintal. The state government has even written to the Centre asking it to hike an import duty on cotton. The state wants the Centre to increase the import duty to 50 per cent from the current five per cent. Despite the fall in prices the Centre has allowed cotton imports which further had a negative impact on the local market. Over 22 lakh bales have been imported recently at Rs. 1,500 per quintal, a rate which is much lower than the local rate.

Sugar

Sugar is also facing more or less the same problem. The industry in India is loaded with excessive stocks (Table 5.5) that have distorted the financial parameters of the mills. The industry is reported to have

Table 5.5 Supply and Demand of Sugar 1989-90–200-01

(In million tonnes)

	1989-90	*1995-96*	*1996-97*	*1997-98*	*1998-99*	*1999-00*	*2000-01*
Opening stock (on October 1)	1.229	5.598	7.902	6.522	5,404	8.891	10.010
Production (October-September)	10.958	16.452	12.905	12.855	15.541	18.200	18.500
Imports	9.242	—	—	0.935	1.003	0.404	—
Total supply	12.459	22.050	20.807	20.312	21.948	25.495	28.510
Offtake							
Internal consumption	10.215	13.127	13.866	14.839	15.035	15.419	15.800
Exports	0.023	1.021	0.419	0.069	0.022	0.066	1.000
Closing stock (on September 30)	2.141* (0.08)	7.902	6.522	5.404* (0.235)	6.881* (0.225)	10.010	11.710

recommended to the government to create buffer stocks of roughly two million tonnes, but this proposal has not found favour with the central ministry of Finance. It appears that the government does not know how to tackle surpluses. However, it has acquired skills to push the distress signal (through imports) when sugar shortage raises its head. In the current situation, the industry is being forced to carry stocks and face the financial burden of interest payments.

Thanks to the highly remunerative prices being paid to sugarcane growers, our country has continued to produce increasing quantities of sugar year after year. Output in the sugar year 2000-01 (October-September), touched the all-time peak at 18.5 million tonnes. It was almost double the production in 1993-94 at 9.8 million tonnes. A study of long-term consumption trends indicates that the domestic market needs a rise of no more than three per cent a year. Understandably, the current stocks of sugar with the mills are exerting a crippling burden on their financial status. At the time of the beginning of the new sugar year 2001-02 (i.e. October 1, 2001), the stocks were estimated at 11.5 million tonnes—more than 62 per cent of the output in 2000-01.

The mills have no option but to seek credit from the banks to pay for sugarcane purchases, which in nine cases out of ten the banks are not able to provide fully. Consequently, arrears in payments take place. The mills also seek credit from the market at excessive rates of interest, which tends to inflate their costs. Since the sugarcane arrears can be recovered by the sugarcane suppliers as arrears of land revenue, the mills are forced to borrow at excessive rates even from non-banking sources to avoid this humiliating situation.

It is a pity that a decade after the initiation of economic reforms, the sugar industry is being governed by rules and regulations framed in the hoary past. In order to satisfy its vote bank, the government of every party in every state has tended to fix higher remunerative prices for sugarcane. The price fixed for sugarcane by the central authority is invariably enhanced by every state not for any economic reasons but out of sheer political considerations. The government decided to reduce the quantum of levy sugar from 30 to 15 per cent with effect from February 1, 2001. According to Shanta Kumar, central minister for Consumer Affairs and Public Distribution, the sale of sugar through the Public Distribution System (PDS) would be restricted to only the below-poverty line (BPL) population. It was certainly a concession to the sugar mills because the quantum of sugar procured by the government for PDS at concessional rate was halved. However, the subsidy by the sugar industry to the BPL would amount to no less than Rs. 400 crore a year. And this is no a small burden.

The glut in the sugar market has however resulted in severe competition with the result that mills are reported to be in a financial mess due to the market price ruling at below-cost level. From the consumer's point of view, competition is healthy and welcome but if the mills are not able to recover the cost of production, they might be forced to pull down the shutters. The central question is to keep in good humour not only the sugarcane grower and the sugar consumer but the sugar mills as well.

For the sugar sector, the year 2001 was literally a mixed bag—half empty, half full—as a lot has been done but still more remains to be done. First the half-full part, illustrated by lifting of quantitative ceiling on exports, doing away with registration cum allocation export certificates, go-ahead for futures trading, switching over to quarterly domestic release quota, clearance for export subsidies and concessions, amongst others. The bag was half empty because cane pricing structure needs reform, post-decontrol levy mechanism has to be devised, large-scale manufacture and cogeneration of power is yet to become a reality, cane price arrears are substantial and raw sugar exports nil.

Being a "political economy", factors other than economic ensure that cane price is divorced from reality and the government referred the matter to the Commission on Agricultural Costs and Prices. The Commission began working on a suitable formula which takes into account profit sharing with farmers and sales price realisation but it will remain a contentious issue, as fixing the final price is state government's discretion. However, millers and farmers are striking individual deals in Maharashtra and Tamil Nadu where, in a season of lower output of 168 million tonnes, farmers are likely to benefit.

MANAGING LAND AND WATER RESOURCES

Population pressure on the land, agricultural intensification and inappropriate farming practices, and waste disposal from a rapidly growing livestock sector, all pose significant threats to the rural environment. But water scarcity and quality are probably the most severe challenges facing developing Asia and will reach crisis levels in India in the next decade or two. Water is becoming scarce not only because of growing demand from agriculture, industry, and households but because the potential for expanding the water supply is diminishing. Deteriorating water quality will further aggravate water shortages. Policies that can improve water management include removal of subsidies and taxes that encourage misuse of resources and establishment of secured property rights. Water users will need to have greater power to make their own decisions regarding water use, and markets will need to send correct signals about the real value of water.

The situation in south Asia is no better. In western, northwestern and peninsular India, where in recent times, over a million irrigation wells have got added every year, groundwater withdrawal exceeds annual recharge in vast areas that are growing every year. Where this process has been rapid, the consequences are serious and visible. In Punjab, Haryana and western Rajasthan, the main consequence has been salinity; in north Gujarat and southern Rajasthan, it is fluoride contamination of ground water; in hard-rock southern India, it is declining well-yields and increasing pumping costs arising from competitive deepening of wells. In West Bengal, the consequence is arsenic contamination . In coastal areas, the most serious consequence of intensified pumping of groundwater for irrigation is saline ingress into coastal aquifers. All these problems will impair the region's capacity to feed its growing population. According to David Seckler, IWMI's director general, a quarter of India's harvest may well be at risk from groundwater depletion.

Besides depletion, waterlogging and the pollution of aquifers through human activity is another major groundwater challenge. Water logged areas in India are estimated at 6 m ha; 12 major irrigation projects with a design command of 11 m ha had 2 m ha water logged, and 1 more m ha salinised. An Irrigation Commission set up by the government of India placed canal irrigated areas suffering from waterlogging and salinization at 6 m in early 1970s; these have increased substantially since then. An earlier programme of public tubewells in water logged areas on the Satluj—Yamuna canal in north India to pump water for irrigation or to augment canal supplies seemed promising but have proved institutionally unsustainable. In many arid and semi-arid areas, however, salinity comes with waterlogging which complicates matters. Desalination of brackish water though cheaper than desalinising sea water yet to become a mainstream option. Farmers in west Haryana and Punjab have evolved home-grown formula for blending saline ground water with good quality canal irrigation; these seem to be effective but need close examination.

Aquifer pollution, from both point and non-point sources, is becoming extensive worldwide. In North Arcot district in Tamil Nadu, coconut water contained 0.2 per cent of residual chromium derived from chrome-tanning process-based tanneries that contaminated the groundwater. In the west Indian state of Gujarat, groundwater by textile processing and the rapidly growing chemical industry earned such notoriety that, in 1998, acting suo moto, the state's high court ordered an entire industrial estate-housing over 1,200 manufacturing units, 70 per cent of its chemical closed, pending the establishment of waste water treatment and disposal system.

If underdeveloped ground water in the Ganga basin presents an opportunity for the poor, groundwater depletion and contamination elsewhere holds out a big threat for them. Depletion has far-reaching social as well as environmental dimensions, and leave longlasting aftereffects on all, but, often, on poor more than on the rich. In south Asia, when muscle-driven traditional water lifts went out of business with the onslaught of tubewells, it was the poor who got hit the hardest. New siting and licensing policies reinforce the rights of the early tubewell owners and exclude the late comers, who typically are the poor.

Responses to Groundwater Depletion

By far the most serious groundwater challenge facing the world, then is not in developing the resource but in its sustainable management. As problems of groundwater depletion—and its deleterious consequences—have surfaced in different parts of the world, a variety of responses have been forged to mitigate or even reverse these. The standard reasoning is that even with 800,000 big and small dams around the world, the reservoirs can capture and store no more than a fifth of the rainwater, the bulk of the remainder still running off to the seas. India, which has built more than its share of the world's dams, 1,150 cubic km of its rainwater precipitation still runs off to the seas annually in the form of 'rejected recharge'. If a fraction of this could be stored underground by reducing the velocity of the run off and providing time for recharge, groundwater supplies could be enhanced significantly. But this presumes active aquifer management where planned drawing down of the water table in the pre-monsoon dry months is an important element of the strategy for enhancing recharge from monsoon rainwater as well as from irrigation return flows. In the developing world, however, such active aquifer management is still a far cry. In what is being done, several approaches stand out.

Recharge with Rainwater

Long distance transport of large quantities of water is often problematic besides being expensive. In many parts of the world, especially in south Asia, increasing stress is being placed on in situ rainwater harvesting and recharge. In the monsoon region, this approach seems particularly important because, as in India, the bulk of the year's rainfall is received in some 100 hours of heavy downpour; providing little time for recharging the groundwater. Moreover the relationship between the recharge area, recharge rate and the extent of sustainable groundwater irrigation is now becoming increasingly important.

Some of the water-scarce regions of Asia have age-old traditions and structures for rainwater harvesting which have fallen in to disuse and are now attracting renewed attention. And in south India—where the three states of Karnataka, Andhra Pradesh and Tamil Nadu—have over 2,000,000 tanks, a strategy that has been widely recommended is of transforming these into recharge tanks by filling them up with canal water. In the Kurnool irrigation system of Andhra Pradesh, nine percolation and seven check dams constructed in an experimental recharge project increased the duration of spring flow from 75 days to 207 days; and post-monsoon water table rose by 2.5 m. India's Central Groundwater Board too has been carrying out recharge experiments at several sites. Tarun Bharat Sangh and Pradan, two local NGOs in the Alwar district of western Rajasthan—whose work IWMI has been studying—have helped local communities to rehabilitate centuries old tanks (known locally as *johads* or *paals*) with dramatic impact on groundwater recharge and revival of dried-up springs and rivulets in a 6,500 sq. km area.

In India's western region, hit hardest by groundwater depletion, however, people have figured out that they have no time for experiments or for governmental action. Catalysed by spiritual Hindu organizations such as the 'Swadhyaya Pariwar' and Swaminaryana Sampradaya'—and supported by numerous local NGOs people have spontaneously created a massive well-recharge movement based on the principle: water on your roof, stays on your roof; water on your field stays on your field; and water in your village, stays in your village'. Some 3,00,000 wells—open and bore have been modified by the people to divert rain water to them; and thousands of ponds, check dams and other rain water harvesting and recharge structures have been constructed by the people on the self-help principle and kept the rain water gushing one into the Arabian sea. While IWMI plans systematic studies of the impact of the movement and the popular science of well-recharge that has emerged as a result of farmers' experiments, indicative evidence available suggests that for regions critically affected by ground water depletion, only mass popular action on regional scale may be adequate to meet the challenge of depletion.

Another example is the silent revolution sweeping through Nagpur's countryside: A water harvest of 390 TMC (million cubic meters). And while the traditional Kolhapuri-type (KT) or cement weirs would have cost approximately Rs 50 lakh to achieve similar results, Nagpur's experiment comes at virtually no cost. They have constructed 222 Vanrai-type bandharas (weirs) in just 21 days. This is believed to have delayed water scarcity in many villages by at least three months, villages that used to feel the water pinch from January. Today they can be least assured of a comfortable water position until April.

A timely intervention considering the KT or cement weirs requires Rs. 50 lakh to harvest 390 TMC water. The project would have taken more than a year to take off along with the additional annual Zila Pradesh (ZP), budget touching up to Rs seven crore. Moreover, the KT and cement weirs are difficultt to maintain. Due to high silting and theft of needle plugs, they often go defunct. And there is clear evidence: Of the 1,000 such weirs in the district, less than 100 are functioning. The other relieving aspect is the elimination of problems arising out of lack of coordination among various concerned state government departments which normally act in a compartmentalised way.

India has begun to take rain-water harvesting and groundwater recharge seriously at all levels. These are at the heart of its massive Integrated Watershed Development Programme which provides public resources to local communities for treatment of watershed catchment areas and for constructing rainwater harvesting and recharge structures. Trends during the 1990s also suggest a progressive shift of budgetary allocations from irrigation development of water harvesting and recharge. One indication of the seriousness assigned to an issue by Indian leadership is the message delivered to the citizens on Republic Day, January 26, 2000 when the nation's prime minister and the water resources minister went to the people with a full-page story espousing the benefits and critically of groundwater recharge.*

Water Harvesting in Haryana

Residents of water-scarce areas of Haryana will soon participate in the mission-mode approach (involving an integrated approach by 13 departments. adopted by the Haryana Government for conservation and optimum management of water when tubewell operators of the Haryana State Minor Irrigation and Tubewells Corporation will visit every village to prepare action plans for water harvesting. The idea is to convert the mission into the mass movement as a result of the holistic approach. According to an official spokes-person, the water conservation mission constituted by the Haryana Government has directed HMITC to undertake a massive exercise of preparation of physical village-wise inventories of water harvesting structures, mapping of entire village and preparation of action plans with the people's participation in every village of selected 46 development blocks. These 46 blocks are categorised as 'DARK' because of their critical conditions regarding availability and extraction of groundwater.

Various financial institutions have already been prohibited from financing projects involving exploitation of ground water in these areas. Out of 46 blocks, one block each of Panchkula. Faridabad, Sirsa, Sonipat, two blocks each of Ambala, Hisar, Jind, Kaithal, Yamunagar and Rohtak, three blocks each of Bhiwani and Panipat, four blocks each of Gurgaon and Kurukshetra, five blocks each of Mahendergarh and Rewari and six blocks of Karnal have been categorized as 'DARK'. The tubewell operators of the Minor Irrigation and Tubewell Corporation (MITC), who possess adequate knowledge of water table and awareness for conservation of water, would be used as resource person in the entire programme. The methodology would be based on physical survey of the area by the investigators and group discussions with members of the community. A four page long questionnaire has been prepared in Hindi to enable the investigators to collect authentic data from the concerned villages. They will also use the visit to increase awareness of villagers for the need of conservation of water as also propagation of best practices for optimum management of water.

Action Plans would be prepared for each of these development blocks covering a total of 18000 sq. kms of area for water conservation.

* Please refer to Tusher Shah et al, Global Ground Water Siltation, EPW Vol. XXXVI, No. 43 for more details.

These would be prepared in three months and indicate the number and kind of structures proposed to be created and their cost. The existing depressions, which are being used for harvesting water or those not still used would be identified. The MITC plans to first launch a pilot project based on the Action Plan to arrest the further decline of ground water and life support system. It would involve the stake holders to seek their physical support to terms of labour in the project. The project would help in saving electricity, revival and reactivation of defunct tubewells and other ground water structures.

Vegetative Treatment of the Catchment

Vegetative cover on the free catchment of a basin have proved to be a problem as well as an aid to ground water recharge. For example, some 10 m ha of land in South Africa are infested by an alien weed-Acacia spp (especially mearnsii, and saligna and longifolia), pinus spp, eucalyptus spp. prospis spp (Guy Preston, pers. Comm.) that uses up 3.3 b cu m more water almost 7 per cent of the country's total run-off than the indigenous plants it replaced; the weed infestation is considered to be a major threat to groundwater recharge. And a special long-term programme by the South African government's department of water affairs and forestry, called 'Working for Water' to remove the alien weed, employs some 42,000 people at its peak every year, but will take 20 years or more to complete the job. In contrast, there is a growing worldwide movement to promote the cultivation of vetiver grass hedgerows as a powerful way of reducing the velocity of rainwater run-off re-charging groundwater. The vetiver network, supported by the World Bank, Danish government and several global NGOs claims that rainwater run-off is reduced by 70 per cent when vetiver hedgerows are planted across the slope by slowing down and spreading out runoff over larger areas but also because the strong roots of this grass can penetrate hard pans and improve infiltration. The network claims Indian evidence showing that where such hedgerows are planted, water levels in wells are higher, springs do not dry up or run longer into the dry seasons Hence, in our agricultural policy framework, this technology should also receive proper attention.

Demand Management

There are potentially powerful indirect demand—management strategies that are not even part of the academic discussion in the developing world. These offer important trade-offs that need closer scrutiny. For example, it has been suggested that Indian Punjab's groundwater depletion problems could be easier to resolve if its export of 'virtual' groundwater in the form of rice could be reduced or; on the other hand, IWMI researchers have argued that using rain-water for rice cultivation may be an efficient way of recharging the aquifers, especially because evaporation from rice fields is limited and, after intensive working of soils, paddy fields provide ideal sites for recharge. Water-saving irrigation research—such as for rice in China—can help reduce ground water use; but it needs to be examined if these technologies would work as well in dry areas.

BRANDING OF ORGANIC PRODUCTS

Organic agriculture aims at the development of viable and sustainable agriculture. Organic food is produced by following a system of farm management practices that seek to nurture ecosystem which achieve sustainable productivity and provide weed and pest-control through diverse mix of mutually dependent life forms, recycling plant and animal residues, crop selection and rotation, water management, tillage and cultivation. Chemicals are being replaced with effective microorganism, commonly known as E.M. There is an urgent need to initiate research on E.M. under laboratory conditions. Agricultural universities should prepare projects on priority basis to test the efficacy of this wonder formulation. Successful application will give a new direction to Indian agriculture. In addition, it will promote sustainability and help in preserving the environment.

Recent years have witnessed a growing awareness among corporates about the financial power of the brands they own. There are two reasons for this phenomenon. First, there has been mounting evidence to support the hypothesis that consumers are becoming increasingly brand conscious not just in relation to products of conspicuous consumption, but also about commonplace commodities such as various types of fruits and vegetables which were, for a long time, sold as unbranded goods. This trend is likely to get accentuated with the growing importance of e-commerce where most consumer purchase decisions will be brand driven. The second reason has been growing investor interest in companies with strong brand portfolios.

Export marketing of agricultural and horticultural products is expected to get tougher and difficult in the new millennium. It will demand thinking in unconventional ways about new kinds of distributional channels, media strategies, distinctive brand positioning may even developing a new language for brand development. In fact, the rising stress of the future will be those manufacturers that have very clearly positioned brands. The customers also will become more open to buying to well constructed, motivating brand positioning. The implication of this is that brand owners who, for several reasons, have reduced the amount of time they spend thinking about their brands, should reorder their priorities.

Branding should be the foundation of any export business. Branding is all about securing the future of our exporting business establishment, its products and services by building relationship and loyalty. While brand evolution dictates that the fittest shall survive, a brand will need much more than a strong identity to see it through the "Brandage". In today's global market, segmented brand valuation helps in determining the relative values of a brand in different geographical areas. This sets basis for determining the advertising and sales promotion budgets for different geographical areas.

The concept of organic farming is slowly catching up with the Indian farmers. However, area under organic farming at the moment is very miniscule as the process is labour-intensive and very difficult. While there are no exact figures for the area under organic farming as the concept practised is still not at organized level, it is estimated that not more than a couple of hundred hectares is under organic farming. Among the food crops, it is mainly the vegetables and fruits that are widely grown under organic farming. The corporates are, however, better equipped compared to individual farmers in taking up organic farming. Apart from the advantage of having big land holdings, they can also ensure and maintain quality. They are also in a better position to promote the concept.

Demand is gradually increasing for organic products abroad, and the country may brand these products, cut out a niche by maintaining their quality. In India, the corporate sector has, of late, been showing interest in farming. This sector may be encouraged to take up organic farming. This may be possible through contract farming.

Contract Farming for Exports

Introducing contract or corporatisation of farming by private sector companies will help solve some of the basic problems with regard to quality production, processing and exports. Experiments in this regard in the past have shown success. Many multinationals and private individuals have made inroads into selected areas and specialized fields through a system of contract farming as for tomato (Brooke Bond Pvt. Ltd. and Nijjar Agro), chillies, garlic and ginger in the case of Pepsi Foods Limited, and mentha in the case of Indo US Mint Pvt. Ltd., The trend of the corporate sector playing an increasingly active role in the agricultural sector has given rise to what is known as "Corporatisation of Agriculture".

It is considered that large scale corporate cultivation will lead to better allocative efficiency, induce higher private investment in exportable varieties and result in higher output, income and exports. This would lead to high multiplier effect, which would help spur India's wealth creation, especially in the rural heartland of the country. The development of corporate integrated agriculture will require investment by industry, often working in tandem with the government. The industry will invest in agriculture through contract/lease farming and also in the upstream elements of food chain agriculture, procurement and storage. They will give farmers access to high yielding seeds and plant breeds. In addition, they will provide credit, fertilisers and pesticides and other inputs to raise yields. They will help develop storage and transport infrastructure, ensuring that farm produce is stored properly and transported to the markets and customers in good time. They will add value to the farm produce by processing the surplus. This will ensure that the farmers' increased yields find a market.

The corporate may enter into a contract with farmer to purchase his produce at predetermined price. Further, the corporate may market the produce in the domestic and export market. The corporate may also do the entire spade work on behalf of farmers for credit and financing needs. This model indicates a basic structure on which the corporatisation of agriculture would be feasible and will become a growing phenomenon in coming years. The philosophy of this system is an integrated approach i.e. laboratory—land-factory-market. The objective is to organise production of adequate quantities of produce for the processing unit. Farmers are identified in compact blocks assigned contracts for areas and quantities at an agreed price and served for critical inputs such as seed or nursery. It is necessary that the government make suitable amendments in land ceiling laws so that the processing industry may own land for meeting its requirements of agricultural products. In fact, contract farming needs to be implemented with greater thrust and efficacy.

The Union agriculture ministry has now formally permitted two Gurgaon-based. British food-processing MNCs. Nestle India and Glaxo Smithkline Beecham to tie-up with Nabard for extending the concept of "contract farming" in the dairy sector, beginning with select dairy animal breeders of Punjab and Haryana. This will be somewhat different from the contract farming model, started by Pepsi. Hindustan Lever and United Breweries in the two states, which insist that farmers must adopt milch animals as part of a "package of services". Under the scheme, the farmers will be assisted to raise soft-loans from the apex cooperative banks and others in the region under Nabard's re-financing scheme. The MNCs would recruit competent veterinary staff to regularly check the health of the animals purchased under the scheme supply subsidised cattlefeed and arrange free veterinary aid at the doorsteps of the dairy-farmers.

The entire "surplus" milk produced in the dairy-units, set up under the scheme, will be "contracted" to be purchased by the two MNCs from the doorsteps of the farmers at competitive market rates. Union agriculture minister Ajit Singh, however, feels that "as in the case of farm products, there is need to fix a minimum support price (MSP) for milk to be procured by the two MNCs under "contract farming" operations. The MSP, to be computed by a competent authority, should be applicable even for the cooperative and private dairy plants who procure milk to process the same to manufacture ghee, butter, cheese, ice-cream etc. Modalities to enforce the MSP for milk during various seasons would be worked out by the ICAR scientists.

Summing Up

We have discussed so far the major issues relating to improving the conditions of agriculture as well as the farmer and a policy framework for exports. There are other areas like agricultural investments and a new approach to micro-level Agricultural Policies dealing with the management of crop and livestock husbandry. These are equally important, but need independent discussions.

While research on agriculture, as in any other field, is a continuing process, our policies must aim at making full use of what is already available. This in other world would mean that Agricultural Policies for transferring the available technology in all its micro-level contents have to emphasise such issues. This applies primarily to crops like pulses, oilseed and coarse cereals which are growing under dry farming conditions. These crops have not shown any improvements in the past, but the results of National Demonstrations etc., clearly bring out that there is still a sufficient gap between farmer level yields and research findings. Our Agricultural Policy must lay proper emphasis on this aspect to exploit fully such potential to narrow this gap.

Finally, the National Agricultural Policy must keep in view the fact that despite allround growth and achievements, Indian agriculture is faced with multiple concerns and challenges. Productivity has plateaued in the green revolution areas responding less and less to agro-inputs as compared to other areas, lopsided development, various structural bottlenecks, declining investment and capital formation resulting in unimpressive infrastructural development, growing income disparity, continued resources degradation, and recently declining of prices and sluggish off-take of foodgrains, are some of the most disturbing trends that affect rural populace.

Other supportive policies are required. The monsoon can only give us a break; we need to build on it to realize our potential. Food stocks can be used to start massive food for work programmes to improve rural infrastructure and water management. In the longer-term, both information and bio-technology can be harnessed. Low cost computers and local area network based community centres can provide employment, improve information and compensate for missing markets. A local net would help him contact a buyer. The Gyandoot project in Dhar, MP, and the Lokmitra in HP has already made a beginning. The farmer must be given more freedom along with better information. Good marketing facilities would lower the spread between retail and farm gate prices, and give both the farmer and the consumer a better deal. Exports of agricultural products have shown more fluctuations than growth, but are quite significant at between 15 and 20 per cent of India's total exports. With supportive policies there are possibilities of sustained rise. In general, policies need to improve supply in agriculture and demand in industry. As we wait for manna from heaven it would be well to remember that even the heavens only help those who help themselves.

National Agricultural Policy

The first ever national Agriculture Policy was announced on 28th July, 2000. The formulation of agriculture Policy had been under consideration of the Government for the last few years as a comprehensive National Agriculture Policy was absolutely essential to build on the inherent strength of the agriculture and allied sectors to address the constraints and to make optimal use of resources and opportunities emerging as a result of advancement in science and technology and emerging of a new economic regime.

The National agriculture Policy seeks to actualize vast untapped growth potential of Indian agriculture, strengthen rural infrastructure to support faster agricultural development, promote value addition, accelerate the growth of agro business, create employment in rural areas, secure a fair standard of living for the farmers and agricultural workers and their families, discourage migration to urban areas and face the challenges arising out of economic liberalization and globalization over the next two decades it aims to attain.

- A growth rate excess of 4 per cent per annum in the agriculture sector;
- Growth that is based on efficient use of resources and conserves our soil, water and bio-diversity;
- Growth with equity, i.e., growth which is widespread across regions and farmers;
- Growth that is demand driven and caters to domestic markets and maximizes benefits from exports of agricultural products in the face of the challenges arising from economic liberalization and globalization;
- Growth that is sustainable technologically, environmentally and economically;

Nine pronged strategy has been devised to meet the challenges of enhancing production and strengthening rural economies while taking care to promote technically sound, economically viable, environmentally non-degrading and socially acceptable use of country's natural resources land and water in particular.

The unutilized wastelands will be put to use for agriculture and afforestation besides reclamation of degraded lands. Integrated and holistic development of rainfed areas, conjunctive use of surface and ground water, on farm water management, sensitization of farming community with environmental concerns will be given priority. Survey and evaluation of genetic resources and safe conservation of both indigenous and exogenously introduced genetic variability in crop plants, animals and their wild relatives will receive particular attention.

The use of bio-technologies will be promoted for evolving plants which consume less water, and are drought resistant, pest resistant, contain more nutrition, give higher yields and are environmentally safe. Conservation of bio-resource through their ex situ preservation in Gene Banks, as also in situ conservation in their natural habitats through bio-diversity parks, etc. will receive a high priority to prevent their extinction.

A regionally differentiated strategy for development of horticulture, floriculture, roots and tubers, plantation crops, aromatic and medicinal plants, bee keeping and sericulture shall be adopted. Livestock breeding dairying, poultry, aquaculture shall be promoted through generation and dissemination of appropriate technologies. Research and extension linkages will be broad based and strengthened to improve effective use of new technologies. Adequate and timely supply of quality inputs such as seed, fertilizers, plant protection chemicals, bio pesticides, agricultural machinery and credit at reasonable rates to farmers will be the endeavour of the Government.

Agriculture in India has suffered for want of infrastructural facilities, The National Agriculture Policy gives emphasis on stepping up public investment for narrowing regional imbalances, accelerating development of supportive infrastructure for agriculture and rural development particularly rural connectivity. A conducive climate will be created through a favourable price and trade regime to promote farmers' own investments as also investments by industries producing inputs for agriculture and agro based industries. High priority is also given to rural electrification, development of market infrastructure and setting up of agro processing units to reduce wastage, particularly, of horticulture produce, and to enhance value addition with the objective to create off-farm employment in rural areas. To safeguard the interest of farmers, National Agriculture Insurance Scheme covering all farmers and all crops throughout the country with built in provisions for insulating farmers from financial distress caused by natural disasters and making agriculture financially viable will be made more farmer specific and effective. Endeavour will be made to provide a package insurance policy for the farmers, right from sowing of the crops to post-harvest operations, including market fluctuations in the prices of agricultural produce.

Indian agriculture is characterized by predominance of small and marginal farmers. Institutional reforms will be so pursued as to channelize their energies for achieving greater productivity and production. The approach to rural development and land reforms will focus on the following areas:

- Consolidation of holdings all over the country on the pattern of north western States.
- Redistribution of ceiling surplus lands and waste lands among the landless farmers, unemployed youth with initial start up capital;

- Tenancy reforms to recognize the rights of the tenants and share croppers;
- Development of lease markets for increasing the size of the holdings by making legal provisions for giving private lands on lease for cultivation and agri business;
- Updating and improvement of land records, computerization and issue of land pass book to the farmers; and
- Recognition of women's rights on land.

People's participation through Panchayati Raj Institutions, Voluntary Groups, Social Activities and Community Leaders shall be adequately encouraged for implementation of programmes. Progressive institutionalization of rural and farm credit for providing timely adequate credit to farmers will be continued. Cooperative sector shall be strengthened by:

- Structural reforms for promoting greater efficiency and viability by freeing them from excessive bureaucratic control and political interference;
- Creation of infrastructure and human resource development;
- Improvement in financial viability and organizational sustainability of cooperatives.
- Democratization of management and increased professionalism in their operation; and
- Creating a viable interface with other grass root organizations.

Sophisticated techniques including latest information technology, remote sensing technology, etc. will be used for compilation and dissemination of information in the process of planing and policy making.

CONCLUSION

The National Agricultural Policy as announced gives broad indications about what would be the growth rate of agriculture over the two decades, how this is to be achieved and also emphasizes the need for infrastructure development and institutional reforms. No doubt, the policy enunciations are laudable, yet these do not cover many vital issues like the strategy for development of a few selected crops for export purposes, expansion of floriculture, diversification of agriculture, etc. which we have discussed earlier. The future of agriculture is largely dependent upon the technological improvements. A massive application of science and technology alone can enable Indian agriculture to face the serious challenges of food security, and ensure a place for Indian agricultural products globally by the enhancement of value addition process. National Agriculture Policy should have given emphasis on harvesting the power of science and technology for improvement of productivity and also for amelioration of the living condition of the poor. It is rather difficult to obtain incremental production from the conventional Green Revolution areas. For the second Green Revolution, it is necessary for making the gray areas green. Hence, major support for rainfed areas, especially in the eastern and arid peninsular India would be necessary. In the context of present lopsided production pattern—mountains of foodgrains and increasing imports of oils as well as pulses—it is high time that a 'cropping map' of the country is redrawn. This should define crops and agricultural practices best suited to various regions. This regional specialisation will help reducing competition among states and lead to a healthy growth of agriculture in the country.

In fact, farming efficiency cannot increase just because farmers are inclined in that direction. They must have access to technology and irrigation and resources to deploy what can technically be accessed. For this, a number of things are necessary. At one level, protection received by industry must go down sharply, so as to improve terms of trade, historically distorted against agriculture by import-substituting industrialization strategies—further in favour of agriculture. This is necessary to make it viable to invest in agriculture. Private investment in agriculture can take off only when complementary public investment in the farm sector takes place. Unfortunately, there is no mention about it in the Policy.

A policy reform which evolves little enthusiasm among farmers or the political class, relates to subsidies. The main agricultural inputs, namely, water, electricity, fertilizers and credit—are all being supplied to farmers at prices which do not cover the costs incurred in providing them. The magnitude of uncovered costs on these inputs has been rising at a much faster rate than public investment in this sector. Not only is this fiscally unsustainable but under-pricing of inputs is a major cause of indiscriminate and wasteful use of these inputs raising the costs of production and contributing to degradation of land, pollution of water sources, and over-exploitation of groundwater. Policies to arrest and reverse runaway increase in these loses are therefore necessary for fiscal stability, and to ensure efficient and sustainable use of production resources.

Needless to say, in order to achieve a growth rate of 4 per cent in agriculture as envisaged in the Policy, focus must be laid on raising productivity by stepping up public investment, by accelerating the evolution and adoption of cost reducing technologies, and by removing restrictions on agricultural trade, marketing and processing within the country. All this required to be achieved through major reforms in governance and institutions.

Meeting the Challenges of the Future

Further growth momentum is needed to complete the economic transformation of rural India. But such growth should be more equitable and environmentally sustainable than it has been in the past. Meeting this challenge will warrant careful consideration of the mistakes we committed in the attainment of the desired rate of growth. The agricultural growth must help in wiping out rural poverty and protection of natural resources, besides encouraging increased public sector investment. Because the poor live mostly in rural areas and generally depend on the farm sector for their income, growth that stems from agricultural productivity and that raises the income of small and marginal farmers as also the landless labourers is of paramount importance. However, agricultural growth alone will perhaps not be able to eradicate rural poverty. Policy makers must reach the poor directly by investing in health, nutrition and education. In the case of particularly vulnerable or marginalised groups, policy makers may use income transfers or safety nets to help relieve short-term stress. For the poor to participate in growth, tillers must be the owners of land, agricultural research must be focused on the problems of small as well as large farmers, new technologies must be scale-neutral and profitable for all farm sizes, there must exist efficient input, credit and product markets which benefit all farmers, the labour force must find non-farm activities in their villages during lean season and policies must not discriminate against agriculture in general and small farms in particular.

CHAPTER 6

Economics of Farm Size

Agricultural holding normally implies the management unit, i.e. the area of land held for cultivation as a single unit by an individual, joint family or more than one farmer on a joint basis. The land may be owned, taken on lease or may be partly owned and partly rented. The term agricultural holding has also been used to mean the total area of land owned by an individual or a joint family whether cultivated by the family or rented out. The former definition is based on the facts of cultivation and management while the latter is based on the right of ownership. The term "operational holding" is used for the management unit to distinguish it from the ownership holding. An operational holding does not mean that every bit of land is cultivated all the time, it includes fallow land and may also have some area which is not under cultivation. In fact, it refers to the total land area held under single management for the purpose of cultivation. It excludes any land leased to another person. One may have a single or a number of operational holdings if each of them constitutes a separate unit of management. An operational holding may be held and operated by an individual or jointly by a number of farmers.

The distribution of total land in a community or nation in terms of operational holdings and ownership holdings may be very different. The concept of ownership holding has its uses, particularly in feudal systems and in the landlord-tenant system. It indicates whether land ownership is concentrated in a few hands or is evenly distributed. The information over a period of time can show whether there is a tendency towards further concentration or else of dispersion of ownership in fewer hands or among a greater number. A comparison of distribution of the size of ownership holding and operational holding will show the difference between the two and the extent of leasing. Such information is necessary for the policy decision on agrarian relations. In a socialistic democratic country, if land ownership is concentrated in a few hands, legislation may be introduced to reduce the inequality in distribution and make the distribution of land among the people more equitable. With the abolition of the zamindari system and a statutory provision to make title of ownership and right of cultivation inseparable as in UP, the difference between ownership holding and operational holding is gradually narrowing and may disappear.

The concept of an operational holding is important from the point of view of agricultural organization and economics of production. The size of an operational holding together with basic information on type of farming, intensity of cultivation, and agricultural features in a region can help in finding out the level of income and living of the farmer, employment requirements of hired labour, and utilization of farming equipment. All such information is essential for a proper understanding of the agricultural economy of any region.

The land records maintained currently in India do not provide directly the information on the number of holdings held individually or jointly by the farmers, either on ownership or cultivation bases. Each field has a separate survey number. The tenurial titles and the name of the person actually tilling are recorded by fields. A farmer may have one or more fields. Just by consolidating the information on fields farmer-wise the data on the size of holding and its distribution can be built up. Absence of such basic information in the land records underlines the ancillary character of the land record system to the revenue administration. There has been lack of emphasis on collection of data useful for policy-making and for an understanding of the agriculture economy. Table 6.1 gives the average size of holding in India and some other countries of the world.

Table 6.1 Average Size of Holdings in Some Selected Countries

Country	*Year*	*Hectares*
Australia	1970	1993
U.S.A.	1969	158
U.K.	1970	55
Belgium	1970	8.4
Yugoslavia	1970	5.0
India	1990	1.55
Japan	1970	1.0

SOURCE: FAO Production Year Book, 1971, Agriculture Statistics at a Glance 2001.

The size of holding gives an indication of the broad magnitude of the problem of pressure of population on land and the average unit of cultivation in terms of acreage. But it would be erroneous to infer from it productivity, income, and level of living of farmers in different parts of the world, because there are considerable variations in soil, climate, type of farming, intensity of cultivation etc. Although the average holding in Japan is only 1 hectare which is less than the average size of farms in India, a Japanese farmer has a much higher level of living because of a very intensive system of farming practised by him and additional earnings per household from employment in industries.

TRENDS IN OPERATIONAL HOLDINGS

Data on operational holdings are being collected regularly by the NSSO since its eighth round (1954-55). So far, five such holding surveys, including the 48th one, have been conducted. The results of these surveys form a useful series of data spanning a long period of time. The estimates of different rounds are on the whole comparable, except for those of the 8th round, which due to differences in definitions, are not strictly comparable with the other rounds.

The definition of operational holdings has undergone only a marginal change since the 17th round (1960-61) with respect to the coverage of "operated land." In the 37th round (1981-82), the definition of operated land was extended to include land encroached or occupied on squatter basis, which is referred to as "otherwise possessed" land in the 48th round. It is seen from Table 6.2 that the percentage shares of such land in the operated area were only 1.7% and 1.0% in 1981-82 and 1991-92 respectively. This means the results of the four surveys since the 17th round remain comparable in spite of the change in definition (Table 6.2).

Size of Operational Holdings

Any significant change in agrarian structure should have some impact on the size distribution in the land holdings. The Agricultural Census has adopted five size-classes. The NSSO has also adopted these size classes in their 48th round survey on Operational Land Holdings in India. These are as follows:

Marginal	:	less than 1.01 ha.
Small	:	1.01-2.00 ha
Semi medium	:	2.01 - 4.00 ha.
Medium	:	4.01 - 10.00
Large	:	larger than 10.00 ha.

A number of agricultural censuses of operational holdings were conducted from 1970-71 onwards. The basic unit for study in these censuses has been the 'operational holdings' as distinct from the `ownership holdings'. Data provided in Table 6.3 indicate that the number of holdings increased from 71 million in 1970-71 to 107 million in 1990-91 recording an increase of almost 51 per cent. On the other

Table 6.2 Estimates of Certain Key Characteristics of Operational Holdings in Rural India from Land Holdings Surveys of NSS. 1960-61 to 1991-92

Sl. No.	Item	1960-61 (17th)	1970-71 (26th)	1981-82 (37th)	1991-92 (48th)
1.	Number of operational holdings (millions)	50.77	57.07	71.04	93.45
	1.1 percentage increase	—	12.4%	24.5%	31.5%
2.	Area operated (mha.)	133.48	125.68	118.57	125.10
3.	Average area operated (ha.)	2.63	2.20	1.67	1.34
4.	Percentage of joint holdings	4.22	0.60	0.62	0.08
5.	Number of parcels per holding	5.7	n.a.	4.0	2.7
6.	Percentage of operational holdings with partly or wholly				
	(a) owned land	94.86	95.64	92.91	96.15
	(b) Leased-in land	23.52	24.68	15.20	10.99
7.	In area operated, p.c share of				
	(a) area owned	89.30	89.43	91.08	90.44
	(b) area leased in	10.70	10.57	7.18	8.52
	(c) area otherwise possessed	—	—	1.74	1.04
8.	No. of sample villages	3,486	4,547	3,692	4,231
9.	No. of sample households	53,138	35,947	29,089	33,289

1. Source of estimates of 17th, 26th and 37th rounds : NSS Report Nos. 144, *Servekshana* Issue No. 16 & 36, and 48th round-Sarvekshana Issue No. 70.
2. Estimates for item 7 are based only on area reporting the type of possession.

hand, the area operated increased only marginally from 162 million hectares to 167 million hectares, i.e. by 1.8 percent. There was more marginalization of holdings as would be evident from the fact, the number of marginal holdings increased from 36 million in 1970-71 to 63 million in 1990-91 constituting about 59.4 percent of the total operational holdings as against 51 percent in 1970-71. However, the total operational area in this category increased to 25 million hectares or 15 percent of the total area in 1990-91 as against 9 percent in 1970-71. The increase in area operated just compensated the increase in the number of holdings. This highlights the fact that this category of land holders generally continued to live below the poverty line since the average size of marginal holding of 0.39 hectare of area is too meagre to eke out a living. There is growing pauperization of the Indian peasantry as indicated by the data swelling the ranks of marginal farmers or nearly landless labourers (Table 6.3).

Small Holdings This category consists of holding size between 1 and 4 hectares. In 1970-71 the number of holdings, in the category was 24 million with an operated area of 49 million hectares. But in 1990-91 the number swelled to 34 million with an operated area of 67.2 million hectares. They accounted for 32 per cent of the total operational

Table 6.3 Distribution of Operational Holdings—All India

No. of Holdings : In million
Operated Area : In million hectares
Average Size : Hectare

Category of holdings	No. of operational holdings		Area operated		Average size of operational holdings	
	1970-71	1990-91	1970-71	1990-91	1970-71	1990-91
Marginal Holding	36	63.4	15	24.9	0.42	0.39
(Less than 1 hectare)	(51)	(59.5)	(9)	(15)		
Small Holding	24	34.0	49	67.2	2.0	1.98
(1.0 to 4.0 hectares)	(34)	(32)	(30)	(41)		
Medium Holding	8	7.6	48	44.7	6.0	5.89
(4.0 to 10.0 hectares)	(11)	(7)	(30)	(27)		
Large Holding	3	1.6	50	28.7	16.67	17.93
(10 hectares & above)	(4)	(1.5)	(31)	(17)		
All Holding	71	106.6	162	165.5	2.28	1.55
	(100)	(100)	(100)	(100)		

Note 1 : (a) Figures in parentheses indicate the percentage of respective column total. (b) For the sake of brevity, the size classes small and semi-medium have been merged into one class.

2. For more details on the subject refer to *Sarvekshna*, 84th Issue, July–Sept. 2000.

SOURCE: Agricultural statistics at a Glance (1995 and 2001), Directorate of Economics & Statistics, Ministry of Agriculture & Cooperation, Ministry of Agriculture, Government of India.

holdings and 41 per cent of the total operated area as against 34 and 30 percent respectively in 1970-71. Thus, in two decades, there was a small increase in this category both in absolute and relative sense, (i.e. in terms of number of holdings and area operated under them). The average size of small holdings is around 2 hectares only.

Medium Holdings This group consists of holdings in the range of 4 to 10 hectares. In 1970-71, there were less than 8 million holdings in this category accounting for 11 per cent of total operational holdings and these holdings covered 48 million hectares i.e. 30 per cent of the total operational area. But in 1990-91 their respective positions were 7.6 million holdings and 44.7 million hectares of operated area constituting 7 and 27 per cent respectively of the total. The average size of the operational holdings in this category had declined marginally from 6 hectares to 5.89 hectares.

Large Holdings This group comprises holdings of the size of 10 hectares and above. In 1990-91 there were nearly 1.6 million holdings with an operated area of 28.7 million hectares constituting 1.5 and 17 per cent respectively of the total. There were decline over the two decades both in number of holdings and operated area prevalent in 1970-71 when these were 3 million (4 per cent) and 50 million hectares (31 per cent) respectively. In point of fact, there was sharpest decline in the total operated area in this category during the 20 year period. However, due to decline in the number of operated holdings also, the average size of operated holdings increased marginally from 16.67 hectares in 1970-71 to 17.93 hectares in 1990-91.

Table 6.3 reveals the following facts very clearly;

(i) The number of marginal and small holdings had increased from 60 million to 97 million between 1970-71 and 1990-91, i.e. from 85 per cent to 92 per cent of land holdings;

(ii) During the period under review, i.e. 1971-91 marginal and small holdings accounted for 64 and 92 million hectares respectively; that is to say these holdings accounted for 56 per cent of the total area in 1990-91 as against only 39 per cent in 1970-71;

(iii) On the other hand, there was a decline both in number (from 15 per cent to 8 per cent) as well as in area (from 61 per cent to 44 per cent) with respect to medium and large holdings;

(iv) In fact, there was not much change in the number of medium holdings which was about 8 million in both the years. The area under this category also remained by and large the same, viz. 48 million hectares in 1970-71 and 45 million hectares in 1990-91;

(v) The major change during the period took place in case of large holdings whose number declined from 3 million to 1.6 million and the area from 50 million hectares to 29 million hectares between the period from 1970-71 to 1990-91.

Hence, it can be inferred that there is a gradual but positive shift in favour of small and marginal holdings and the concentration of land with very large landowners coming down.

State Comparison

Table 6.4 gives the percentage distribution of operational holdings and percentage of area operated in different categories of holdings in 15 major states for 1991-92, 1981-82 and 1970-71, as obtained from the Land Holding Surveys of NSS 48th, 37th and 26th rounds respectively. The general feature emerging from the table is that the distribution of operational holdings continued to be highly unequal in all the major states.

In all the major states, the pressure of population growth on the limited land base is reflected in the progressive downward shift in the distribution of operational holdings over the two decades. It is observed that, in general, there was a rise in the percentage of marginal holdings and a decline in the percentage of holdings in the semi-medium

Table 6.4 Changes in Percentage Distribution of Operational Holdings and Area Operated by Size Categories in 15 Major States

State	Year	Marginal		Small		Semi-medium		Medium		Large	
		Number	Area	Number	Area	Number	Area	Number	Area	Number	Area
Andhra Pradesh	91-92	59.27	17.54	21.38	23.34	13.16	26.23	5.38	23.49	0.81	9.40
	70-71	47.29	9.28	19.14	11.74	18.23	21.91	11.87	31.32	3.47	25.75
Assam	91-92	70.78	34.24	19.99	31.22	7.53	22.92	1.51	9.07	0.19	2.55
	70-71	52.40	21.64	30.23	34.90	14.30	30.54	2.99	12.20	0.08	0.072
Bihar	91-92	76.76	29.01	13.68	25.14	6.86	23.69	2.48	18.24	0.22	3.92
	70-71	58.86	18.14	23.32	26.22	12.85	28.92	4.52	21.01	0.45	5.71
Gujarat	91-92	47.90	8.49	19.86	13.79	17.69	24.92	12.06	35.02	2.49	17.78
	70-71	27.19	3.90	20.70	8.55	22.24	17.41	21.64	35.95	8.23	34.19
Haryana	91-92	50.73	5.32	13.50	8.81	20.32	25.54	11.49	29.38	3.96	30.95
	70-71	17.48	2.53	17.54	6.54	28.30	19.86	31.06	49.24	5.62	21.83
Karnataka	91-92	49.71	9.56	20.26	15.41	17.98	25.21	9.77	30.78	2.28	19.04
	70-71	28.76	5.10	22.81	10.69	25.44	22.97	17.59	34.29	5.40	26.95
Kerala	91-92	91.58	53.27	5.94	23.36	1.99	14.93	0.48	8.08	0.01	0.36
	70-71	86.21	40.05	8.90	24.75	3.66	20.08	1.13	12.26	0.10	2.86
Madhya Pradesh	91-92	38.71	6.70	24.43	15.56	20.90	25.47	13.49	35.92	2.47	16.35
	70-71	26.11	3.42	20.29	8.86	25.77	21.15	21.64	37.99	61.19	28.58
Maharashtra	91-92	43.59	6.66	18.92	11.77	20.38	24.67	14.07	36.59	3.04	20.31
	70-71	23.71	3.06	21.74	8.38	23.44	17.59	22.44	35.29	8.67	35.68

Table 6.4 Changes in Percentage Distribution of Operational Holdings and Area Operated by Size Categories in 15 Major States (Contd.)

State	Year	Marginal		Small		Semi-medium		Medium		Large	
		Number	Area	Number	Area	Number	Area	Number	Area	Number	Area
Orissa	91-92	59.99	22.09	24.34	30.16	12.02	27.87	3.36	16.20	0.29	3.68
	70-71	54.52	18.60	25.78	27.32	13.90	27.06	5.25	21.56	0.55	5.46
Punjab	91-92	63.22	6.20	11.42	10.74	13.85	26.72	9.82	40.55	1.69	15.79
	70-71	11.71	1.46	19.06	7.09	32.70	24.28	30.51	45.05	6.02	22.12
Rajasthan	91-92	39.34	5.56	19.88	9.36	18.46	17.25	15.23	30.16	7.09	37.67
	70-71	31.00	2.01	16.40	5.79	21.30	14.19	21.77	33.23	9.53	44.78
Tamil	91-92	77.17	28.94	14.14	28.06	6.62	24.72	1.80	13.22	0.27	5.06
Nadu	70-71	60.06	21.93	21.26	22.73	13.17	27.32	4.93	21.72	0.58	6.30
Uttar	91-92	68.01	24.96	18.52	26.31	9.85	26.30	3.33	18.18	0.29	4.25
Pradesh	70-71	49.78	15.64	26.92	25.30	16.45	29.76	6.20	23.33	0.65	5.97
West	91-92	80.69	39.98	13.43	30.69	5.00	22.06	0.88	7.27	0.00	0.00
Bengal	70-71	61.21	24.80	22.80	28.92	12.94	31.06	2.98	14.58	0.07	0.64
India	91-92	62.79	15.60	17.79	18.70	11.99	24.13	6.10	26.37	1.33	15.20
	70-71	45.77	9.21	22.38	14.80	17.66	22.52	11.11	30.49	3.08	22.98

SOURCE: Sarvekshana Issue No. 70, National Sample Survey Organisation, Department of Statistics, Ministry of Planning and Programme Implementation, Government of India.

category. Only in respect of small holdings could some amount of inter-state variation both in magnitude and direction, be observed during the period. Contrary to the general declining trend, the percentage of small holders in Madhya Pradesh underwent a steady rise since 1970-71. In Punjab and Haryana, too, the proportion of small holders registered a rise during the eighties, after having declined sharply in the preceding decade.

Less than half the rural labour households in the country have land and, of those who do, only about 13 per cent own land over one hectare. An inter-state comparison shows very disparate results. States where over 50 per cent of rural labour households own land—that is, which are clearly above the national average—include Madhya Pradesh, Orissa, Rajasthan and Uttar Pradesh. Interestingly, these are among the poorer states in terms of per capita income. On the other hand, the wealthier states of Punjab and Haryana have abysmally low proportions of rural labour households owning land: at 6 per cent and 12 per cent respectively.

A look at the average size of cultivated land in the above mentioned states shows that for a majority of these states, the size of holding has declined, from the late 1980s to the mid-1990s. In Madhya Pradesh and Rajasthan, the average size declined from 0.52 hectare to 0.44 hectare and 1.19 hectare to 0.79 hectare respectively. However, these two states still had among the highest proportions of households with land above one hectare compared to other major states in the country. This was around 22 per cent for Madhya Pradesh and 25 per cent for Rajasthan.

A fall in average landholding size accompanied by the rise in the number of operational holdings can be explained by numerous factors. According to the findings of a study commissioned by the Ministry of Agriculture, this can be attributed to a "re-peasantisation of the landless holdings", made possible by redistributive efforts of land reforms and changes in land tenure structure with ownership rights being conferred on tenants, thereby adding to the number of operational holdings. This is in addition to the usual reasons for subdivision of landholdings such as breaking up of joint family units, notional transfer with a view to obtaining government subsidy assistance, subdivision of holdings arising from parental transfer, subdivision of holdings occurring from family partitioning and so on. Although this means that a larger number of households have land, they are largely small or marginal, bringing into fore the question of their viability.

Among the scheduled castes and tribes, land inequalities are typically lower in the case of the latter, although this again varies according to different states. This is probably attributable to the region of inhabitation (like mountainous regions) and informal customs with regard to land and common property resources. The proportion of scheduled tribe rural households having land over one hectare in all such households having cultivable land at the all-India level was around 16 per cent in 1993-94. The state of Maharashtra showed a huge proportion, around 50 per cent, of such households owning land over one hectare. Interestingly, at the other end is Kerala, where almost the entire scheduled tribe rural population with cultivable land had a tiny holding size of 0.01-0.02 hectares.

Size Distribution of Operational Holdings—Unchanging Nature

It is observed from the last four Land Holding Surveys of NSS that the nature of size distribution of operational holdings has by and large, remained unchanged over the three decades, notwithstanding the progressively downward shift in the distribution. Table 6.5 shows the cumulative distribution of operational holdings and area operated by size class. The data are presented for the 12 size classes which could be formed maintaining comparability of the result of the four surveys conducted by NSS.

Table 6.5 Cumulative Percentage Distribution of Operational Holdings and Area Operated by Size Class in Different Land Holding Surveys of NSS

Size-class of operational holdings (ha.)	*1960-61 (17th round)*		*1970-71 (26th round)*		*1981-82th round)*		*1991-92 (48th round)*	
	Holdings	*Area*	*Holdings*	*Area*	*Holdings*	*Area*	*Holdings*	*Area*
Below 0.21	8.55	0.32	11.78	0.47	23.14	0.74	27.84	1.18
Below 0.41	17.13	1.27	21.25	1.69	33.05	2.43	37.70	3.32
Below 1.01	39.07	6.86	45.77	9.21	56.01	11.51	62.79	15.60
Below 2.01	61.69	19.18	68.15	24.01	75.33	28.10	80.58	34.30
Below 3.01	74.53	30.91	79.92	37.19	84.99	42.18	88.92	49.13
Below 4.01	81.49	39.88	85.81	46.53	89.56	51.65	92.57	58.43
Below 5.01	86.54	48.13	90.01	55.12	93.03	60.92	95.15	66.93
Below 6.01	89.44	54.08	92.28	60.82	94.82	66.85	96.35	71.84
Below 8.01	93.19	63.66	95.24	70.16	97.01	75.87	97.84	79.36
Below 10.01	95.48	71.05	96.92	77.02	98.12	81.80	98.67	84.80
Below 12.01	96.79	76.35	97.89	81.86	98.70	85.63	99.10	88.26
Below 20.01	98.97	88.40	99.43	92.34	99.69	94.57	99.80	95.83
All	100.00	100.00	100.00	100.00	100.00	100.00	100.00	100.00

Definitions of Various Types of Holdings

Size of a holdings in agriculture being very important, various concepts and definitions for a holding have been evolved for different purposes.

Economic holding: Keatings defines an economic holding as one "which allows a man the chance of producing sufficient to support himself and his family, in reasonable comfort after paying his necessary expenses." According to him, in Deccan, an ideal economic holding would consist of forty acres of fair land in one block with at least one good irrigation-well, and a house situated on the holding. This desirable area would vary greatly in different parts according to circumstances. In the Surat district, three acres of good garden land can support a family in comfort, while in the dry part of the Deccan with poor soil, thirty acres might not suffice. Between the ideal economic holding and uneconomic holding there are many gradations.

The UP Banking Enquiry Committee takes into consideration the standard of comfort of the farmers, and since this varies, the committee concludes that, " the point at which a holding becomes uneconomic, is not fixed but movable. Nothing more is possible than to work out a complete set of average typical economic circumstances and to fix a point in relation to them". The committee further points out that "it is scarcely an exaggeration to say that there are as many economic holdings as there are cultivators. An economic holding, in a world, is an economist's abstraction. It is an amalgam of average distribution of soil, average cropping, average out-turn and prices, with an average tenant paying an average rent, possessing an average family, and incurring average expenditure yet some of these averages involve hopeless impossibilities."

In all the definitions, emphasis is mainly on a certain minimum income from the holding for the maintenance of the farmer and his family. While some workers have placed this income as basic minimum for maintenance, others have allowed for some margin over the basic minimum to provide some expenditure on comforts and call such a holding as a model holding. Stanley Jevons also held similar views. According to him, a model holding was about 30 acres in U.P. The return from a holding and therefore, the economic size based on such a criterion will depend on: (a) fertility of soil; (b) intensity of cultivation; (c) crops raised, method of cultivation, and the organisation of agriculture; (d) costs and returns; and (e) living costs.

Another term "work unit" lays stress on the areas of land commanded by a pair of average bullocks which is the most common draught unit in the current agricultural technology in the country. Because of differences in the quality of work animals and soil, the work unit also differs from region to region in India. A majority of holdings fail to fulfil any of the criteria, whether of income for mere maintenance, or of work unit for employment of an average pair of draught cattle, or labour resources of an average family. The supply of land is short on any of these considerations. Confronted with a situation like this, the Agrarian Reforms Committee coined new terms such as "basic holding" and "optimum holding:" and the Planning Commission introduced the term "family holding."

Basic Holding The Congress Agrarian Committee (1950) while agreeing with the view that an economic holding should afford a reasonable standard of living, provide full employment to a normal sized family, and be in relation to the factors of agrarian economy of the region, recommended smaller holdings than an economic holding on sociological rather than economic considerations. The Committee gave the name of basic holding to this size of holding. It suggested such a unit for individual cultivation with the assistance of the multipurpose cooperative organization in all other respects.

Optimum Holding The Agrarian Committee favoured an upper limit to the size of an individual's holding on the ground that an average Indian farmer has neither the means nor the capacity to have a very large size of holding. In the opinion of the Committee, mechanized capitalist farming led to exploitation and was socially an evil. Hence they suggested the concept of "optimum holding" not in the economic but social sense. It refers to the size not exceeding three times the size of an economic holding. Exception could be made in the case of a charitable institution.

Family Holding The Planning Commission in its First Five Year Plan introduced the concept of "family holding." Family holding is looked at from two angles, viz., (1) as an operational unit, and (2) an area of land which can yield a certain average income. The commission defined the "family holding" as an area equivalent, according to local conditions and under existing conditions of techniques, either to a plough unit or to a work unit for a family of average size using a pair of bullocks.

Factors Responsible for Small Holdings

Subdivision It refers to the division of land among heirs on the death of the owner or during his lifetime due to distribution of his property among his sons and daughters. Formerly, among Hindus, only sons inherited the property but now under the Hindu Code Bill, daughters will also inherit it. This further accentuates the evils of subdivision. The division is not confined merely to the total area of land but each heir claims a share in each individual field. This leads to fragmentation, i.e. scattered fields not contiguous with each other. It may not be quite an easy thing to analyse the reasons for this tendency on the part of people in India. The predominating factor for subdivision, besides the laws of inheritance, is the pressure of population due to the absence of employment opportunities in non-agricultural occupations.

Disintegration of Joint Family System With the growth of individualism, the number of joint families is on the decline. The number of subdivisions and partitions has, therefore, increased. Lack of economic development: It is common to ascribe the small size of holdings to the evil of subdivision, defective inheritance, and succession laws. The real issue, however, is the lack of economic development in the country. Population has multiplied but during all this period there has been no corresponding economic growth. On the other hand under alien rule, the situation deteriorated. India was developed as a market for British manufactured goods. This led to the decline of whatever industries India had. Persons employed in cottage industries had to fall back on farming as a profession which was already overcrowded. The pressure on land increased, agriculture in India had to absorb the unemployed and provide some security for them. This accounts for the large backlog of disguised unemployment in the agricultural sector. Obviously, with no other walks of life open as a choice to a farmer's son he had perforce to fall back on agriculture and insisted on his share in land. But to consider it as an evil of subdivision is not true. The other social and economic forces, e.g., lack of literacy, a large number of local languages, inadequate transport and communication facilities, extremely poor level of income also favours the concentration of people in agriculture.

Remedial Measures

These can be grouped under two heads-preventive and curative. The former relates to all those measures which prevent further deterioration of the situation. The object of curative measures is to remedy the evil of subdivision. The preventive measures adopted so far are primarily legislative. The main aim of such legislation is that no holding should be transferred or partitioned in such a way as to aggravate the problem of the uneconomic size of holdings. They have not proved very effective. There is hardly anything to prevent a cosharer from subdividing the lands informally. The utility of legislative measures for the prevention of subdivision is, therefore, very doubtful.

Egypt passed the Five Fedden Law to make holdings "impartable" beyond a specified size. The land is nominally divided amongst heirs but it is left in the hands of one to cultivate it on behalf of the others or may be handed over to trustees to manage for all. The Royal Commission[1] opined that Belgium custom, whereby one heir buys out the rest through the agency of mortage bonds, if adopted, would check both the evils of subdivision and fragmentation, although they felt that this would not find favour with the people. Firstly, there is difficulty in finding funds for this purpose. Secondly, the heirs receiving the money which in most cases will not be large in amount, can be hardly used it profitably for earning a living because of lack of alternative means of livelihood; even if advances are somehow arranged, it would be rather difficult to realize such loans from a small holder who has hardly any surplus income after meeting his living expenses.

The problem of dealing effectively with these evils was also considered by the Famine Inquiry Commission[2] which put forward

---

[1] Royal Commission Report, p. 138.

[2] Final Report of Famine Inquiry Commission: 1954, p. 258.

the suggestion that subdivision could be checked by bringing additional land under cultivation and by an increase in industrial employments. They recommended no change in the law of inheritance. However, one of the members of the Commission, Sir M.B. Nanavati, advocated the formation and maintenance of impartable holdings and suitable modification of the law of inheritance. He defines a medium holding as an area which is normally capable of yielding in terms of cereals not less than two tonnes or more than five tonnes. Professor K.T. Shah[3] considers that unless and until land owning or holding is wholly nationalized and cultivation reconditioned as a public enterprise, eliminating the profit motive, e.g. under a system of collective or cooperative farming, there is little hope of the great problem of excessive and successive fragmentation of cultivated land as its dispersal in minute strips all over the place, being solved.

The Punjab Land Revenue Committee had recommended that every holding should be subject to a minimum charge of one rupee a harvest or two rupees a year, so as to set a premium on joint holding. Thus the various remedial measures may be summarised as follows:

(a) Prohibition of partition of holding below a certain size.
(b) Compulsory acquisition of petty and uneconomic holding and their distribution to those whose holdings would thereby be made economic.
(c) The Egyptian system whereby land is nominally divided amongst heirs, but it is actually left in the hands of one to cultivate on behalf of all the members or handed to trustees to manage for all.
(d) Joint farming of the inheritance without partition.

None of these measures has, however, any chance of success in India unless the pressure on land is relieved. Cooperative and collective farming are the other obvious remedies. In both cases it has to be appreciated that any size of farm can provide employment and living to a limited number of persons and not beyond that number. In India, this stage has passed long ago and the number depending on land far exceeds the number for which land can provide a reasonable standard of living.

No-doubt, agricultural developmental programmes can raise productivity considerably and thereby add to the farming income, yet in many areas the size of holdings has been reduced so low that, without a real change in the occupational distribution of the population, the problem of subdivision cannot be adequately dealt with. All efforts in reclaiming land, extending cultivation to new land, intensification of cultivation, changes in land-use in order to give larger calories or

[3] *Ibid*, p. 261.

more money per unit of land, financial assistance to make holdings economic are, however, commendable. Nonetheless, it has to be constantly borne in mind that the evil of subdivision is of a larger magnitude and calls for a higher rate of economic growth supported with effective propaganda and measures to bring down the rate of increase in the population.

ACTIVATION OF LAND LEASE MARKETS

At the core of a multitude of issues in Indian agriculture is the institution of land, its relation to labour and its distribution among the agrarian population. While the Green Revolution introduced land saving technologies such as high-yielding varieties, increased fertiliser use and irrigation, agriculture as it stands today needs to urgently take a re-look at the distributional problem especially in the context of globalisation.

Two schools of thought prevail with regard to land reforms. One of them root for relaxation of land ceilings, the idea being augmentation of technology-related economies of scale, promotion of farm entrepreneurship and economic viability. Relaxation of ceilings, however, come with a number of repercussions, which need to be carefully weighed before any policy in this regard is formulated. For instance, the era of 'corporate farming' can widen already existing inequalities and lead to higher marginalisation. Besides, there have been a number of studies that question whether ceiling relaxation actually increases scale economies in the Indian context.

A way out suggested by researchers to encourage corporate farming, which has, on the other hand, positive effects such as providing forward linkages and giving a boost to non-farm income generation, is the relaxation of ceiling for the land lease market and wastelands. However, this again needs to be done in a manner that it does not accentuate inequities or introduce further distortions. It can be argued that relaxation of ceiling for wastelands should go hand in hand with a specification that these lands are used for high-value agricultural products such as horticulture. This should also be accompanied by a policy that enables a transfer of benefits gained from corporate farming to the rural poor of that area, since the option of distributing the wastelands to the poor is closed once they are taken up by the corporates (Table 6.6).

Another important issue regarding land distribution is the increasing rate of fragmentation and subdivision of holdings, leading to non-viability. According to the Rural Labour Enquiry for 1993-94, the average size of cultivated land by rural labour households at an all-India level had declined from 0.32 hectare in 1987-88 to 0.23 hectare in 1993-94 with almost every state witnessing a fall compared to the previous survey. Again a revival of the land lease market would largely

Table 6.6 Ceiling Limits on Land Holdings: Major States

(In hectares)

State	*Irrigated with two crops*	*Irrigated with one crop*	*Dryland*
AP	4.05-7.28	6.07-10.93	14.16-21.85
Bihar	6.07-7.28	10.12	12.14-18.21
Gujarat	4.05-7.29	6.07-10.93	8.09-21.85
Haryana	7.25	10.9	21.8
Karnataka	4.05-8.10	10.12-12.14	21.85
Kerala	4.86-6.07	4.86-6.07	4.86-6.07
MP	7.28	10.93	21.85
Maharashtra	7.28	10.93	21.85
Orissa	4.05	6.07	12.14-18.21
Punjab	7	11	20.50
Rajasthan	7.28	10.93	21.85-70.82
Tamil Nadu	4.86	12.14	24.28
UP	7.3	10.95	18.25
West Bengal	5	5	7

help to solve this problem without getting into difficult-to-implement legislation such as imposition of floor limits.

Tenancy Status of Operational Holdings

According to NSS surveys, during the thirty years from 1960-61 to 1990-91, land tenure status of operational holdings underwent significant changes. Table 6.2 given earlier reveals that the percentage of holdings with partly or wholly owned operated area increased from 95% in 1960-61 to 96% in 1991-92, whereas, that of holdings operating on partly or wholly leased in land (i.e. tenant holdings) declined sharply from 24% to 11% during the some period. This trend, indicating a continuous shift from tenant cultivation to self cultivation, has been a characteristic feature of Indian agriculture in the post-Independence period. Table 6.6A gives the estimates of the 1991-92 survey of the NSS indicating extent of tenancy in rural India. The number of tenant holdings i.e. holdings with wholly or partly leased-in land was about 10 million, reporting an area of about 10 million hectares of tenanted land. Thus, on an average, a tenant holding had a hectare of leased-in land in its possession during 1991-92.

Though the measures of land reform undertaken since Independence appear to have deterred the growth of exploitative tenancy, there is still a high proportion of tenanted land in total operated area. What is most remarkable about tenancy in rural India is the significantly high proportion of total tenanted land operated by a small proportion of holdings.

Table 6.6A A Few Important Indicators of Land Tenure Status in 1991-92

Sl. No.	Item	Estimate
1.	No. of tenant holdings (mill.)	10.27 (10.99%)
2.	Total operated area leased in (mha.)	10.36 (8.28%)
3.	Area leased in per tenant holding (ha.)	1.01
4.	No. of holdings with otherwise possessed land (mill.)	3.87 (4.14%)
5.	Total otherwise possessed operated area (mha.)	1.26 (1.01%)
6.	Otherwise possessed area per holding with otherwise possessed land (ha.)	0.33

Note: (i) "tenant holding" stands for operational holding with wholly or partly leased- in area. (ii) figures in brackets indicate the percentage of the number of holdings or of total operated area.

SOURCE: Sarvekshana, 70th Issue.

Table 6.7 shows the incidence of tenancy by broad size class of operational holdings in 1991-92. The percentage of tenant holdings shows, largely, a rising tendency with the holding size. In the lowest class i.e. holdings below 0.20 hectares constituting 28% of the operational holdings, the percentage is much smaller than in the rest of the classes. The percentage of tenanted land (area leased-in) in operated area, on the other hand, falls as one passes from size class

Table 6.7 Percentage of Tenant Holdings and Area Leased in by Broad Size-Class in 1991-92

Broad size class (ha.)	*% of tenant holdings*	*% of area leased in*	*% dist. of area leased in*
Less than 0.20	6.4	6.98	1.0
0.21 - 0.50	11.6	9.04	4.7
0.51- 1.00	12.4	8.70	10.6
Marginal	9.3	8.7	16.3
Small	14.9	8.53	19.3
Semi-medium	12.2	7.41	21.6
Medium	13.1	6.90	22.0
Large	16.7	11.37	20.9
Over 1.00	13.8	8.2	83.7
All sizes	11.0	8.28	100.0

SOURCE: Sarvekshana, 70th Issue.

0.21-0.50 to size class 4.01-10.00. But in the topmost size (over 10.00 ha.) it is significantly higher (11.4%) than in the rest of the classes.

Fragmentation

Usually each heir claims a share in each of the individual field. This leads to fragmentation, i.e. scattered fields not contiguous to each other. Fragmented holding has been a chronic problem in Indian agriculture. In fact, the subject is important enough to have a chapter by itself even it be too short. It has been established that small farmers having a hectare of land with irrigation facilities can become a surplus producer. But if his holdings are scattered over 4 or 5 places, he cannot organize his farming sufficiently closely and cannot also supervise and protect his crop. The estimates available from three NSS Land Holding Surveys show that the number of parcels per holding has decreased from 5.7 in 1960-61 to 2.7 in 1991-92 (*Sarvekshana*, 70th Issue), (Tables 6.8 and 6.9).

The evil of fragmentation is widespread throughout the country. It was observed in 1916 that in Bombay Presidency in general, and in Konkan in particular, fields measuring less than half an acre were subdivided into more than 20 separately owned plots[4]. The position has only worsened during these years. In the village of Pimpla Saudagar, it was found that 56 owners owned between 729 plots of which 463 were less than 0.4 hectare each and 121 less than 0.1 hectare each. In Ratnagir, the size of individual plots is sometimes as small as 0.00625 of an acre. In Punjab too some fields have been found which were a mile long and a few yards wide, and others so small that it was not possible to cultivate them. In Bairampore (Punjab) it was found that 34.4 percent of the cultivators had over 25 fragments each.

The NSS during their Eighth Round investigated into the nature and extent of the parcelization of holdings and collected information about the number of fragments constituting on operational holdings (Table 6.8) . For the purpose of the survey, a distinct and exclusive piece of land, not connected to any other piece of land, was defined as a fragment. With an operational holding, fragments were thus compact pieces of land physically detached from one another.

A holding on an average consisted of five fragments, the number of fragments varying from three in South Zone to seven in North. Again, there is a clear indication of increase in the average number of fragments with an increase in the size of holdings in all the population zones. Summary results are given in Table 6.10.

There is, however, some justification for fragmentation of a holding. As stated by Moomaw, on the basis of his interview with farmers, "scattered land means less risk of crop failure. With land scattered in

[4] Statement of objects of the draft bill for consolidation of holdings, 1916.

Table 6.8 Land Holdings—Rural Sector

Population zone	North	East	South	West	Central	North-West	All-India
Total number of operational holdings ('000 nos.)	11052 (10467)	16185 (15649)	13030 (11409)	5789 (4482)	9662 (8113)	6062 (4892)	61780 (55012)
Total area operated ('000 acres)	41171	54307	43192	49284	88287	58870	335711
Average size (acres)	3.73 (3.93)	3.36 (3.47)	3.31 (3.79)	8.82 (11.13)	9.14 (10.88)	9.71 (12.03)	5.43 (6.10)
Percentage of							
(i) holdings below average size	66.15 (65.95)	66.37 (66.09)	72.11 (71.00)	70.03 (68.12)	70.40 (69.41)	70.42 (69.40)	72.72 (72.03)
(ii) area under such holdings	19.48	16.83	13.71	15.61	15.28	18.76	17.06
Percentage of holdings	(21.13)	(17.69)	(16.36)	(21.63)	(19.42)	(24.20)	(19.55)
(i) entirely owned	72.80	60.21	53.26	61.69	52.82	59.77	60.15
(ii) entirely leased in	5.83	18.53	24.92	16.96	16.61	17.52	16.94
(iii) mixed	21.37	21.26	21.82	21.35	30.57	22.71	22.91
Percentage of							
(i) Agricultural to total holdings	76.53	77.03	65.48	67.59	67.63	73.39	71.79
(ii) Area under agricultural holdings to total operated area	99.24	98.88	99.63	99.91	99.48	99.76	99.49
Average size of							
(i) agricultural holdings (acres)	4.83	4.31	5.04	12.74	13.44	13.20	7.53
(ii) non-agricultural holdings (acres)	0.12	0.16	0.04	0.02	0.15	0.09	0.10

Table 6.8 *Land Holdings—Rural Sector* (Contd.)

Population zone	*North*	*East*	*South*	*West*	*Central*	*North-West*	*All-India*
Percentage of							
(i) Agricultural holdings below average size	67.45	65.89	71.06	67.37	68.47	69.54	72.29
(ii) Area under such holdings	28.94	25.79	24.05	25.68	25.49	27.47	25.48
Area under agricultural holdings ('000 acres)	40,857	53,700	48,003	49,840	87.832	58,731	333,993
Total area irrigated ('000 acres)	13897	8297	10467	2598	4651	9593	49503
Population zone	North	East	South	West	Central	North-West	All-India
Percentage of area irrigated by							
(i) Canal	35.19	25.62	32.17	18.48	28.06	39.85	32.31
(ii) Tank	10.67	25.94	33.18	2.85	38.66	2.21	18.57
(iii) Well	45.90	4.71	22.09	72.40	27.87	41.78	32.86
(iv) Other sources	7.75	43.17	11.14	5.81	5.20	15.95	15.86
(v) Unspecified	0.49	0.56	1.42	0.46	0.21	0.21	0.61

Note: Figures in brackets have been obtained by excluding holdings of sizes less than 0.005 acre.
SOURCE: NSS Survey 8th Round.

Table 6.9 ***Distribution of Number and Area of Holdings in India by Irrigation Status, in Major Size Classes for All Social Groups, 1990-91***

(Number in thousand/Area in thousand ha.)

S.l. No.	*Major size classes No. of Holdings*	*Wholly irrigated Net sown area*	*Partly irrigated No. of Holdings*	*Wholly unirrigated Net sown area*	*Net irrigated area*	*No. of Holdings*	*Net sown area*
1. Marginal	19707 (69.20)	7386 (25.49)	10245 (48.49)	4461 (11.54)	2071 (12.38)	31810 (58.40)	9866 (13.6)
2. Small	4672 (16.41)	6212 (21.44)	4475 (21.18)	5952 (15.39)	2873 (17.17)	10482 (19.24)	13307 (18.28)
3. Semi-medium	2727 (9.58)	6814 (23.52)	3550 (16.80)	8995 (23.26)	4157 (24.84)	7384 (13.56)	17611 (24.20)
4. Medium	1194 (4.19)	6140 (21.19)	2342 (11.08)	12292 (31.79)	5145 (30.75)	3890 (7.14)	19534 (26.84)
5. Large	177 (0.62)	2418 (8.35)	518 (2.45)	6967 18.02)	2487 (14.86)	900 (1.65)	12458 (17.12)
All size Classes All size Classes	28477 (100.0)	28971 (100.0)	21130 (100.0)	38666 (100.0)	16733 (100.0)	54466 (100.0)	72775 (100.0)

Note: 1. Totals may not tally due to rounding off.
2. Figures in parentheses indicate Percentage Distribution

SOURCE: All-India Reports on Agricultural Census 1990-91 D.A.C.

Author's SOURCE: Indian Agricultural in Brief, 27 Edition, Directorate of Economics & Statistics, Department of Agriculture & Cooperation Government of India.

Table 6.10 Average Number of Fragments Per Reporting Holding by Size-Classes and by Zones

Holding size (acres)	Average number of fragments per reporting holding						
	North India	East India	South India	West India	Central India	North west India	All India
1. 0.00	1.00	1.00	1.00	1.00	1.00	1.00	1.00
2. 0.01-2.49	4.04	3.51	1.94	2.36	1.69	2.81	2.89
3. 2.50-4-99	8.43	9.14	4.81	4.10	3.95	5.84	7.02
4. 5.00-7.49	10.76	10.83	6.06	4.79	4.84	7.41	8.19
5. 7.50-9.99	11.97	13.66	6.91	5.36	5.66	7.18	8.82
6. 10.00-14.99	14.82	15.79	6.95	5.46	5.65	7.14	9.21
7. 15.00-19.99	17.11	18.81	8.35	6.34	5.84	7.43	9.46
8. 20.00 and above	23.43	25.67	10.81	7.22	7.17	7.28	9.88
9. All sizes	7.02	6.89	3.22	3.72	3.64	4.86	5.09

different places one field may suffer from flood, frost or drought while fields in other localities might escape." Again, a farmer can have different kinds of soils to enable him to have a more diversified cropping pattern.

Disadvantages

Fragmentation of holding seriously impedes agricultural progress. It interferes with the full utilization of land. Time is wasted and extra expenses are involved in moving workers, animals, and implements from one field to another and in transporting seed, manure, etc., to the field and the harvested produce from the field to the threshing floor, barn, and the store house. Supervision is rendered more difficult, depredation of animals and birds are harder to control; expenses on fences, water supply, building, threshing floors, etc. are often much greater; the implementation of any comprehensive drainage or other schemes of improvement is almost impossible. There is difficulty in reaching fields, especially when crops are standing. More money and manpower are required for watching crops.

It entails waste of land in boundaries, hedges, and pathways. It has been calculated that in Punjab nine per cent of land is wasted as it is in fragments too small for cultivation. As much as another ten per cent is lost to cultivation in boundaries maintained for the demarcation of holdings. Finally, prevalence of subdivision and fragmentation is a hindrance in the use of improved agricultural practices, such as better seeds, manure, use of superior agricultural machinery, construction of wells, fencing of land, protection of crops from pests and improvement of drainage systems. Moreover, quarrels over boundaries of small plots lead to litigation. Thus, small and scattered farms are clearly an impediment for the efficient organization of agriculture. As a result, the cost of production becomes very high as compared to large farms.

Consolidation of Holdings

Consolidation of holdings means the substitution by exchange of fields of the farmers in any area in such a way as to make the holdings held by each of them more compact. On consolidation, the number of fragments in the holding is reduced. The fields are made contiguous with each other. After consolidation, all the fields of a farmer may lie in one compact block or the holding may comprise more than one block. Consolidation measures aim at giving every farmer a compact area equivalent in value, and as far as possible in area to area held by him previously. It may also be defined as the amalgamation and redistribution of fields constituting individual holdings or estates so as to reduce the number of fragments in the holdings.

To bring about an improvement in agriculture, this measure was advocated as early as 1880. However, the problem of fragmentation and the need to deal with it attracted attention more widely only in 1920. Consolidation of holdings has a number of advantages. It saves both time and labour, supervision and management of land become easy and efficient. Operational efficiency is promoted. There is much greater scope for irrigation and conservation practices. Consolidation provides an opportunity for replanning the entire village community. It encourages adoption of modern farming practices. The other advantages of the consolidation measures are:

(1) Agricultural operations are carried out on the entire area of the holding at the most favourable time. In the scattered field system, agricultural operations in the outlying fields are often not done in time.
(2) Distribution of the farm among different crops is easier, economical, and more efficient in the sense of water utilization.
(3) Damage in the form of grazing by stray cattle is minimised
(4) Chances of thefts during harvests are minimised.
(5) Disputes on account of encroachments are kept to a minimum.
(6) Manure is conserved and more intensive cultivation is possible.
(7) Much of the land, which otherwise goes waste due to field alignments, comes under cultivation. Agricultural production has been observed to increase by 5 to 10 per cent in a village after consolidation.

It is said that the virtues of consolidation should not be emphasised too much. The present system enables a farmer to have different kinds of soils and grow a variety of crops. In India, where there is both human and animal unemployment, there is not much point in stressing waste of energy and time in moving from plot to plot. There may be some truth in such arguments but they in no way minimise the importance of consolidation. Most of these arguments are invalidated by the adoption of a correct procedure in consolidation which ensures the allotment of fields to the farmer on the basis of variations in soil, topography, location, etc., to enable him to grow the major crops of the area. Even when labour supply may not be fully employed, no one would suggest its misuse. Another important aspect of the labour-use is that in spite of its abundance during slack periods it is in short supply during the peak periods of farming operations. It is most important to economise every unit of human and animal labour during this period.

Social advantages of consolidation are numerous. It enables development of village communication, planning of the village *abadi* and provision of social amenities and works of common utility. It becomes possible to develop inter-village, intra-village, and inter-tehsil roads, thus enabling the farmer to carry fodder to homes and markets in carts instead of as headloads. Consolidation of fragmented agricultural land holdings forms an integral part of the Land Reform Policy, and the Five Year Plans have accordingly been laying stress on its implementation. Though many states had enacted legislation , but not much progress could be made except in the states of Uttar Pradesh, Haryana and Punjab. In other states, work was continued for some years and lost momentum thereafter. In the state of Uttar Pradesh, even now annually about 9000 to 10,000 villages are being put under this activity. So far, an area of 1633,47 lakh acres has been consolidated all over the country. The latest position is show in Table 6.11.

Consolidation of the fragments, however, does not solve the problem of small holdings; only it makes the operation of the existing holdings more economic. The problem of small holdings can be tackled at two different ends. Firstly, further division of small holdings can be prohibited. Legislation for this has been enacted in several states, but for a variety of reasons-mainly the inheritance laws and lack of alternative occupation for descendants who are denied the share-implementation of the legislation is not effective. At the other end, small holdings may be pooled together for the purposes of joint cultivation. The pooling together has certain distinct advantages; economy in the use of bullock power, improved creditworthiness, capital formation through joint labour, etc. It, however, does not alter the adverse man-land ratio. With the increase in the size of the cultivation unit, there would be economy in the use of labour and disguised unemployment will become open and apparent. In spite of repeated policy decisions to encourage cooperative joint farming, efforts in this direction have not yet yielded demonstrable results.

Legislation on Consolidation of Holdings

The legislation on consolidation of holdings in India has passed through three stages since its inception. In the first stage it was wholly

Table 6.11 Consolidation of Land Holdings—Statement Position as on September, 2000

(Area in lakh acres)

S.No.	States/Uts	Area consolidated
1.	Andhra Pradesh	8.18*
2.	Bihar	96.05*
3.	Gujarat	69.88
4.	Haryana	104.38
5.	Himachal Pradesh	29.91
6.	Jammu & Kashmir	1.37*
7.	Karnataka	26.76**
8.	Madhya Pradesh	95.53
9.	Maharashtra	526.50†
10.	Orissa	26.74
11.	Punjab	121.81
12.	Rajasthan	42.30‡
13.	Uttar Pradesh	481.63
14.	Delhi	2.33
	Total	1633.47

* Scheme has been discontinued (w.e.f. July, 92 in Bihar).
** Consolidation of holdings Act, 1966 has been repeated in 1991.
‡ Scheme discontinued from 1965.
† Implementation of the schemes stopped w.e.f. 1.4.93.

SOURCE: Annual Report 2000-2001, Government of India, Ministry of Rural Development.

permissive and was aimed at facilitating transfer and exchange mainly through the offer of some concessions and also the help of trained staff. The initiative to consolidate the small and scattered holdings was left to farmers themselves. Cooperative societies were encouraged to take up consolidation work with the help of the staff under the cooperative department on a voluntary basis. As no commendable progress was made through these legislations, an element of compulsion had to be introduced in the second stage. The Central Provinces Consolidation of Holdings Act, 1928, for example, authorised the consolidation officers to confirm and implement a scheme of redistribution of holdings, when not less than one-half on the permanent land holders holding not less than two-thirds of the occupied areas, agreed to it. Such a scheme would then become compulsory and binding on all permanent right holders in the village. Similarly, if two -thirds of the tenure holders in a village apply for consolidation, the application would be considered as one made on behalf of all the tenure holders in the village. The Uttar Pradesh Consolidation of Holdings Act, 1953, provided for the compulsory consolidation on the initiative of the state.

The enactment of Bombay Prevention of Fragmentation and Consolidation of Holdings act, 1947, marked the beginning of the third stage in the consolidation legislation in the country, This act provides for a greater element of compulsion in the enforcement of a scheme of consolidation in any given area regardless of the willingness or otherwise of the land holders of the locality. But at each stage of the consolidation programme objections from the people affected are given due consideration by the consolidation officer. Though the timings of the three stages were different in various states, at present compulsory consolidation is accepted as the common policy objective in most states.

The broad framework of the consolidation programme has been the same for all the states, but within it there are many minor differences in the methods and the procedures and the administrative setup as well as in regard to the recovery of the cost of consolidation. A noteworthy feature of the consolidation programme of Punjab and Haryana is that the object of consolidation in these states is not merely to consolidate small and scattered holdings into compact blocks, but also of replanning of the entire village land. It seeks to coordinate all-round developmental activities in the villages reserving sites for schools, playground, Panchayat ghar, etc. Circular roads round the village and roads linking different villages are also laid. Thus, it may be said that in Punjab and Haryana consolidation truly forms a part of a comprehensive plan of rational layout of land surface. In Maharashtra state, part of former Bombay State, incentives are provided in the form of various concessions to agriculturists whose lands are consolidated to enlist their cooperation and participation. To enable the poor agriculturists to pay compensation that may become due from them on account of consolidation work, *taccavi* loans are advanced to them.

A National Level Committee has been constituted under the chairmanship of Secretary (RD) to evaluate progress of consolidation of land holdings and to look into matters pertaining to updation of survey data/record of rights and maps through technological upgradation. A subcommittee has also been constituted under the Chairmanship of Director General , NIRD to assist the National Level Committee (NLC). The Committee will also draw up a plan of action for consolidation of holdings and identify the main features of a new Centrally Sponsored Scheme on Consolidation of Land Holdings.

Administrative Staff College of India (ASCI), Hyderabad , has been assigned a study of land consolidation and Computerisation of Land Records in ten States and to document the efforts made on Consolidation and Computerization in various States. ASCI has carried out the "spot study" on progress of Land Consolidation and Computerisation of Land Records in ten States. However, the report of ASCI is still awaited.

Consolidation Problems and Prospects

In the operation of the consolidation programme during last three or four-decades, several problems of practical importance have been noticed. These problems relate to the land records and administrative procedures. Preparing the proper revenue records for the whole country is a stupendous task. But its absence has delayed the consolidation programmes to such an extent that instances are not lacking when as many as 10 to 15 years were taken to finish the consolidation work in some villages. Special legislative measures have been taken to expedite completion of land records. New administrative wings have been set up in some states with a view to quickening the pace of administrative procedures.

The sentimental attachment of the cultivators to their ancestral land has rendered the exchange of lands very difficult in many cases. There is also the psychological tendency of assessing the value of one's own land at a higher rate than that of others. These types of attachments of the peasants of their lands retard the pace of the implementation of consolidation schemes. Recent thinking in the Planning Commission is that consolidation of holdings must be made compulsory under law. Prior to consolidation the entire land in each village should be topographically surveyed and levelled to receive water wherever it is available, and irrigation channels and drains be constructed for the entire village. If there exists a potential for additional minor irrigation (ground or surface) works, these should be constructed, and in dry villages without any potential for water distribution, land levelling and contour bunding for soil and moisture conservation be effected. The laying of feeder roads will also be tied to the land development programme. The developed land should be so distributed among the owners that each one of them has his holdings in one or at the most two pieces.

The maintenance and operation of the works constructed as part of the integrated programme may be the joint responsibility of the state and the Panchayats. Compulsory consolidation works must be effected in millions of hectares of land which are envisaged to receive irrigation benefits from the major, medium and minor irrigation schemes. Size distribution of holdings according to irrigation status in the country is shown in Table 6.11.

Agricultural Census

The Department of Agriculture and Cooperation in the Ministry of Agriculture, Government of India organizes quniquennial Agricultural Census in the country keeping in view the data needs of the Department and the requirements of World Agricultural Census conducted by the F.A.O. The census is followed by an input survey. So far, the Department has completed five Agricultural Censuses and is in the process of completing the sixth Census with reference year 1995-96. Seventh Agricultural census with reference year 2000-2001 (Agricultural year) will also be started soon.

The number of operational holdings according to the size classes as per 1970-71 census (first census) and 1990-91 census have already been indicated earlier in Table 16.3. The Census of operational holdings provides the key indicators of the structure of agricultural sector of the country which include data on number and area of operational holdings, dispersal of holdings, tenancy particulars, land utilization, irrigation status, number of pumpsets, wells and tubewells and cropping pattern etc. The Input Survey, which follows the Census operations, brings out detailed countrywide information like pattern of use of inputs like manures, pesticides fertilisers, live stock, agricultural credit, etc, in the country.

CHAPTER 7

Crop Varieties Improvement Programme

INTRODUCTION

The principal difficulty of Indian agriculture is the continued exposure of vast areas in different parts of the country to the vagaries of weather reflected by natural calamities like droughts, floods, furious cyclones, untimely and erratic rains causing serious setbacks to production from time to time and leading to threat in food availability in our country. Such a situation enforced Government to build up a permanent bulwark against it and it was necessary to ensure a rate of growth corresponding to the requirements of the growing population for food. Keeping these in view a new strategy for agricultural development was put into action from 1966-67.

The adoption of the new strategy can be called a significant landmark in the history of agricultural development in India. It stressed increased use of science and technology for raising agricultural productivity. The principal ingredients of the new strategy were:

(i) Cultivation of new high yielding varieties of seed,

(ii) Development of multiple cropping, i.e., bringing additional area under crop production in the irrigated and assured rainfall areas.

(iii) Development of irrigation for intensive cultivation.

(iv) Soil and water management measures.

(v) Using a package of practices including high yielding seeds, optimum quantities of fertilizers and pest control measures.

(vi) Emphasis on research and its application.

(vii) Farmer's training and education.

(viii) Development of the infrastructure of credit, marketing, distribution system for supply of inputs etc.

The late sixties and early seventies were the years of Green Revolution. The subsequent years could be considered the years of sustaining this evolution and stabilization of production. The policy taken by government had brought an immediate result in both production and productivity to high levels. The implementation of the high yielding variety programme (HYVP), which revolutionised Indian agriculture, continued to be the main strategy of increasing foodgrain production since its inception. The coverage of area under the programme increased from 1.86 million ha. in 1966-67 to 76.4 million ha in 1997-98 ha. From that period (1966-67) a continuous and sustainable growth has been attained in foodgrain production. Today India is self sufficient in foodgrain production (202 million tonnes during 1999-2000 as compared to 50.82 million tonnes in 1950-51); exporting a considerable amount of agricultural commodities (total foodgrain export including pulses Rs. 3643.13 crores in 1998-99 and having a significant amount of buffer stock, so much so that on July 2001 end, public sector stocks of foodgrains had crossed an all time high of 60.0 million tonnes.

Among the different improvements, the high yielding varieties programmer (HYVP) received maximum credit for growth in agriculture. Research work of Geneticists and Plant Breeding Scientists since the mid sixties has brought revolutionary changes in the growth of agriculture. Government and ICAR are still keenly interested on varietal development towards attaining a better place in world agriculture. The Varietal Improvement Research has two phases, one for increasing productivity along with quality and second is breeding for pest and disease resistance varieties. India has achieved a significant and commanding position in developing technology in both these aspects.

MODE OF RESEARCH AND DEVELOPMENT IN HIGH YIELDING VARIETIES

Prior to fifties, varietal improvement had been largely through pureline selection. Hybrid breeding has helped in overcoming yield barriers, accelerating the increase in productivity on a long-term basis and in obtaining quantum jump initially and recurrently. The mode of research primarily rested on breaking the yield barrier. High yielding of crops was the primary need for our much needed food production. Plant breeders were engaged in this context of varietal development for several years like identification of HY (High Yielding) races, restoration of plant genetic resources, developing the hybrid varieties to grow tolerance and resistance against different yield-reducing problems, viz. lodging, susceptibility to pest and diseases, water logging, problems related with soil etc. The superiority of hybrids is established not only in plant parts of economic importance but also in other agronomic traits and a range of industrial and nutritional qualitative traits that add to the value of the produce. The rapidly rising population in the developing world led to serious food shortages. In contrast, developed world witnessed surpluses in food and other crops due to early modernization of their agriculture with emphasis on vertical growth through hybrid breeding as well as developing HY varieties.

The successes achieved particularly in food security through improvement and identification of HYV e.g. cereal crops like rice and maize in China, maize in Republic of Korea and sorghum and pearl millet in India, make a strong case for adopting hybrid research as a universal approach. The success of hybrids in vegetable crops like tomato, brinjal, onion, etc, is again indicative of the need for a pro-hybrid policy. Besides, popularization of a diversity of hybrids is equally helpful in economic and social development of agriculture in the developing countries. Hybrid varieties provide an in-built mechanism for quality seed production, which in itself pays for higher cost of buying hybrid seed, and helps in generating employment through their specialized seed-production programmes. Thus, hybrid varieties have geared up the growth of seed industry, and consequently, because of in-built protection to a great extent even without plant variety protection provisions in many countries, private investment has gone up in hybrid research and development, and the private seed industry in the hybrid sector has developed with a far greater pace than in crops where inbred varieties continue to rule. The developments of HYV research in India in different crops are as under:

CEREAL CROPS

Rice

Research to improve rice (*Oryza sativa* L.) production was initiated in India almost a century back. It was, however, only after independence that the country started witnessing landmark achievements in basic and applied research. Institutional infrastructure and sectoral linkages that facilitated organised and result-oriented research to achieve the singular goal of self-sufficiency included establishment of the Central Rice Research Institute (CRRI) at Cuttack in 1946, the All-India Co-ordinated Rice Improvement Project (AICRIP) at Hyderabad in 1965, creation of State Agricultural Universities, most of which with strong rice research programmes. Partnership with the International Rice Research Institute, IRRI, Phillippines since its inception in 1960, and establishment of the International Rice Commission by the FAO, Rome in 1947 also assisted to a great extent. Most importantly it was the political freedom that enabled the countries leadership to appreciate the importance of rice to our food security and create a favourable policy environment for accelerated research and development. The impact of these developments is visible from sustained self-sufficiently in rice and foodgrains as a whole, sizeable excess for buffer stocking and export, and accessibility at prices affordable by all sections of the society.

India has been one of the few countries to resort to recombination breeding since the twenties. The approach along with pureline selection and introduction resulted in as many as 500 improved varieties for varied ecologies, seasons and situations. The improvement had been in terms of quality and resistance to biotic and abiotic stresses, rather than yield increase. The first serious research effort to break the yield barrier of tropical rice was through inter-varietial (indica/japonica) hybridization programme sponsored by the FAO in 1952. The ambitious 10 year programme launched to combine the fertilizer responsibilities of japonica rice, and adaptability and quality of Indica rice, however, failed to give the desired results.

This was immediately changed by a separate breeding research for which India was much indebted to the international Rice Research Institute (IRRI), Phillippines, for providing with semi-dwarf, high yielding varieties of rice. The importance of non-lodging habit combined with earliness and photosensitivity could be realised only after crossing between first semi-dwarf indica variety Taichung (Native)1, and tropical japonica varieties, Tainanan 3 and Taichung 65 from Taiwan. Although T (N) 1 has the distinction of being the first to break the yield barrier in tropical rice IR 8, the miracle yielder developed by the IRRI and introduced in India in the mid-sixties was the forerunner to rice revolution. Closely following the release of IR 8, the first Indian dwarf variety Jaya with as high yield performance as the former was developed and released.

Later, hybrid rice research in India received real impetus with the sanction of a special project on hybrids in December 1989, and the efforts were further strengthened with the onset of the UNDP-funded project on `Development and Use of Hybrid Rice-technology'. Since then, emphasis has been on identification of stable male-sterile lines well-adapted to Indian situations, and multilocation testing for their yield performance.

Experiments on optimization of seed-production technology revealed possibility of raising hybrid seed yield beyond 2 tonnes/ha. The success, however, appeared to vary with hybrid, location and season even under optimum package of seed production. Proper synchronization of male and female parental lines is being worked out but supplementary treatment of gibberellic acid with rope pulling has been found effective in increasing seed yields irrespective of location. Different centres are mandated to develop parent lines and hybrids for different purposes. For example, the CRRI, Cuttack for rainfed lowlands; the IARI, New Delhi, and the PAU, for `basmati' quality rice.

Improvement of rice crop has not only occurred in the quantity of production but also in quality of produce. Quality means its fine-grained types, red rice, aromatic rice, early maturing varieties etc. Comprising over 120 cooperating centres representing nearly all rice-growing regions of the country, the AICRIP through its 3 tier system of evaluation identified dwarf –statured, high- yielding varieties of short and medium duration for irrigated areas during the first phase. They included 17 centrally released and 73 state released varieties till 1979. Among them, medium-maturing Sona, Jayanthi and IR 20; medium early Padma and Ratna; and early Pusa 2.21, Saket 4 and Annapurrna etc. are important. Also, during this period long duration varieties like Jagannath and IR 5 were released for rainfed lowland conditions. The effort continued during the second and third phases as well leading to the identification of several promising varieties. Quality improvement largely from consumer angle was confined to fine grain white rice free of abdominal white, aromatic rice to replace traditional varieties and red rice for Kerala consumers. Among them, fine-grained types like Pusa 4-1-11, red rice like Annapurna and TKM 9 are important. As for aromatic rice, concerted effort continued for over 20 years to develop a high –yielding basmati quality rice. Through convergent breeding ultimately the IARI could come out with the World's first high-yielding dwarf variety Pusa Basmati 1. Pusa Basmati 1 yields 50-60% higher than the highly prized traditional Basmati varieties like Basmati 370 and Taroai Basmati.

One of the major yield-destabilizing factors in rice is pest-disease syndrome which accounts for 25-30% of yield loss. The pest problem has assumed serious proportion because of favourable host environment facilitated by the spread of high-yielding varieties. Genetic homogeneity due to contiguously vast area planted to few varieties, double and triple cropping of rice in resource-rich areas and high input management , in the absence of resistant varieties have made the pest-disease problem increasingly serious and complex. Appearance of new diseases and insect pests like Bacterial Leaf Blight (BLB), Rice Tungro Virus (RTV), Grassy Stunt Virus (GSV), Sheath Blight, Brown Plant Hopper (BPH) and Green Leaf Hopper (GLH) , Leaf folder and hispa in addition to the traditional ones like blast, steam-borer and gall midge, new strains with increased virulence/ viruliference, and the phenomenon of pest resurgence and pesticide resistance have compounded the problem and made pest management more and more expensive and difficult.

Various researches on High Yielding Varieties are being carried out for new pest and disease resistant varieties. Varieties like Phalguna, Ruchi Lalat Samalie, Rajendradhan 202, IET 10831 Vijram, Nandi, HKR-120, PR10, IET 9994, IR-64 are important HY rice which are some of the pest and disease resistant.

Wheat

Wheat (*Triticum aestivum*) is the second most important crop after rice in India. The last 52 years have witnessed unprecedented growth in production and productivity of wheat. The decade ending 1975 witnessed a boom in wheat production and productivity, which, in conjunction with near similar breakthrough in rice, was termed as Green Revolution. Since Lyallpur, the headquaters of Wheat Research in Punjab had gone to Pakistan, a research centre was established at Jalandhar in 1947. From 1947 onwards the country underwent transformation in its research on crop improvement after facing the severe black rust epidemic of 1946-47. This epidemic devastated vast areas of wheat crop in central and peninsular India and led the ICAR direct the mode of wheat research to develop wheat varieties resistant to hill bunts and Karnal bunt. Planned breeding programmes of the IARI resulted in the development and release of a number of improved varieties, which were high resistant to rusts and these varieties helped in raising the productivity significantly.

The varieties which were widely adopted and cultivated were NP 770, NP 809, NP 824, NP 828, NP 830, NP 846, C 253, C 281, C 285, HY11, HY 38 and HY 277. But these varieties made a little bit disappointment in productivity. It was in Japan that the genes of 'Norin' wheat variety having semi-dwarf, non-lodging plants were first discovered, 'Norin-10' was identified as the first strain which combined the desired characteristics of short plant height, lodging resistance. The first exposure of India to semi-dwarf wheat having 'Norin 10' genes was through the N.E. Borlaug's International Nurseries planted at the IARI in 1961-62. The lines were impressive with short-erect stature, high tillering and large heads. Then IARI immediately requested Rockefeller Foundation for seeds of dwarf wheat and to visit India. After visit of the scientists and visit of Dr. Borlaug, India had important assortment of materials which included 100 kg of seeds of each 4 lines, viz Sonora 63, Sonora 64, Mayo 64 and Lerma Rojo 64A.

Testing and working with the semi-dwarf line marked the beginning of an era comprising of accelerated advancement in wheat production and productivity. The variety improvement research led to the identification of several selections, such as, S 227, S 307, and S 308 and S 331, which performed very well. After the All India coordinated trials, the above mentioned four lines were released in 1967 under the popular names of Kalyansona, Safed Lerma, Sonalika and Chhoti Lerma respectively. Of these 4 varieties, Kalyansona became highly popular for a long time. It had remarkable adaptability being suitable for cultivation in practically all the wheat-growing regions of India and under varying input uses.

Since the Green Revolution era, researches on HYV of wheat as well as hybrid varieties, have been going on with jet speed. The Research and Development on wheat variety do not rest only upon the high yielding but also on the quality of produce for different preparation, colour and size of grain etc.

Strong gluten varieties were found most suitable for bread and for expression of high loaf volume, attractive brownish crust, silky and small granular structure of crumbs. Popular varieties such as Hi 977, Ni 5439, HW 657 and DWR 39 make excellent `chappaties'. Varieties like Sujata, Mukta, Lok-1, WH 291, Kundan and Raj 3077 also belonged to this group. Weak gluten varieties suited most for biscuits and cookies. Sonalika, HD 2285, PBW 175 belonged to this class of quality trait.

The developed Indian varieties now have a great demand in several countries. True to her tradition to help neighbours and friends, India extended the benefits of the research achievements by supplying the required seeds of High Yielding Varieties to Afganistan, Bangladesh, Nepal, Bhutan, Pakistan, Myanmar, Indonesia, Sri Lanka, Thailand, Lebanon, Sudan, Syria, Saudi Arabia, South Korea, Algeria Ethiopia, Mongolia, Oman, Vietnam, Yemen and China.

Maize

Globally, maize (*Zea mays*) is the second most important cereal grain after wheat, if we take into consideration the statistics of dehusked edible rice instead of rice husk. It has a great worldwide significance as human food, animal feed and as a source of large number of industrial products. .

No comprehensive research efforts for maize improvement were made at the national level prior to 1950. A number of locally grown varieties were adopted by the state Departments of Agriculture. Basically, work during mid forties and early fifties involved mass selection of local varieties like KT 41 in Uttar Pradesh, Basi in Rajasthan, Pusa Yellow-2 in Bihar, etc.,

In early fifties, the Government of India imported a number of commercial maize hybrids, mainly from USA and Caribbean region. The introduced varieties were US 13, Texas 26, Dixie 18 and NC 27, etc. which showed marked yield superiority ranging from 30 to 50% over local types. But these hybrids could also not become popular because of their dent grain type and very late maturity.

Observing failure of imported Hybrids as direct introduction and the suggestion of visiting scientists of Rockefellar Foundation (RF) in India in 1953, led to set up All India Coordinated Maize Project in 1957. With the rendered assistance of RF with scientific personnel, equipment and germplasm, breeding on yield improvement was started. The scientists thought best to go on double cross hybrids. In 1961 the first set of 4 double-cross hybrids, viz Ganga 1, Ganga 101, Ranjit and Decan, were released for commercial cultivation.

Though these varieties improved the yield up to 30-40% but these were very susceptible to prevailing leaf and stalk diseases and stem-borer. To fight these deseases the researchers developed several new hybrids like Ganga Safed 2, Hi-Starch, Ganga 5, and these were released during 1963-68. Ganga 11, another double-cross hybrid, although was released much later after this phase (in 1988), was widely accepted by farmers throughout the country because of its excellent qualities and possibility to grow in both rainy (Kharif) and winter (rabi) seasons. In 1967, 6 composite varieties, viz, Amber, Jawahar, Kisan, Vikram, Sona and Vijay, were released for commercial cultivation for the first time in the world.

During 1971 intra-population improvement programme at the national level was initiated in 10 elite composite varieties and MCU 508 was released for the cultivation across the country. Along with the other varieties, MCU 314, a yellow-seeded composite variety and G 25 a yellow seeded early maturing variety, two important varieties for cultivation in Rabi Season were also released.

Presently, in the nineties Hybrid Research Programme of the ICAR given to maize mainly included (i) developing high yielding hybrids of full season maturity, (ii) developing early maturity hybrids (iii) developing HYV maizes for cultivation in Rabi season.

Millets

Unlike other cereal crops, millets have not yet received due focus on varietal improvement though a large number of people are dependent on millets for their food intake in the country. But presently hybridisations as well as local selection have helped in improving the yield significantly. BD 763, a dual-purpose hybrid for grain and fodder of good quality, and widely diverse hybrids like MBH 110 and CM 46, based on African and 5054 AI male steriles, were released in 1982. New hybrids MH-34, MH 36, MH 60 MH 62 and MH 65, in final stages of testing, recorded 3.3 to 14.3 per cent more grain yield than the standard BH 104.

WCC 75 was recommended for general cultivation in place of the most popular hybrid, BJ 104 (19.0 q/ha). These seeds of WCC 75 do not require to be produced afresh every year, unlike the seeds of hybrids.

Certain new pearl millet populations equalled the hybrids in performance and some even excelled them. MP 15 (19.4 q/ha) and MP 31 (19.5q/ha) recorded 2.3 per cent more grain yield than BJ 104.

OILSEEDS AND PULSES

Groundnut

The groundnut (*Arachis hypogea*) , king of vegetable oilseeds in India, occupies a prominent position in the national edible oil economy. It was introduced in the country in the sixteenth century. The groundnut crop falls into 4 categories, viz. Spanish, valeneia, virgina bunch and virgina runner. In India groundnut breeding was first taken up in the erstwhile composite states of Mysore, Madhya Pradesh, Mumbai (Maharashtra), U.P., and Punjab.

Based on introductions and selections from indigenous and exotic germplasms, a number of promising strains were developed in various states, like TMV series 1,2,3,4 from Tamil Nadu, HG 1 & 3 from Karnataka, PG1 from Punjab and T 23 & 24 from Uttar Pradesh. Under the All India co-ordinated Research Project on Oilseeds since 1967 a number of improved High Yielding Varieties have been released like Kaushal, UF 70-703, M 145 and 197, GGii, M 37, Kissan, Jawan, CO2, Dh 8, etc. Among the later improved varieties during nineties, which are pest and disease resistant, are ICGS 11, ICGS 44, Girnar 1, Tirupati 2 and 3 etc. High Yielding Varieties recently released for rabi/summer cultivation are RSHYI, TAG 24, ICGS 1, etc. There are also a few varieties released for bold kernels like M13, Somnath, BAU 13, etc.

Rapeseed – Mustard

Oilseeds Brassicae, commonly referred to as rapeseed-mustard in India, comes next in importance to groundnut. Unlike other crops, rapeseed-mustard includes varieties having wide spectrum of mating system ranging from total cross-pollination to pre-dominant self pollination. Among the recommended released varieties of rapeseed-mustard some important varieties are as under:

Toria: BR 23, M27, T9, TS 29, Panchali, Rant 17, TH 68, etc.
Brown Sarson : BS2, BS 70, Pusa Kalyani, KBSI, etc.
Yellow Sarson: Benoy (B9), Subinnoy, Jhumka, Randays 89-115
Mustard: Prakash, Shekhar, Seeta, Pusa Bold, Vardam, Rohini, Pusa jaikisan, Laxmi (RH 8812), etc.

Sunflower

Variety improvement in India on sunflower (*Helianthus annuus*) started in 1972. But immense research was started by a special project on 'Promotion of Research and Development Efforts on Hybrids in Selected Crops – Sunflower' during 1989. Over 1000 hybrids were developed and as many as 15-20 hybrids superior to presently grown hybrids were identified. A few important hybrids are KBSH 1, PSFH 67 and PKVSH 27 with a high oil content. Other important hybrids are MSFH-1, MSFH 8, MSFH 10, and Jwalamukhi (PSCL 11025), etc.

Pulses

India is a major pulse growing country in the world sharing 35-36% of area and 27-28% of production. Among the pulses, gram and pigeon pea are most important in the country.

Chickpea

India is the largest producer of chickpea in the world. Systematic research work on chickpea was started under the ambit of All-India Coordinated Pulses Improvement Project. The first variety of chickpea, chaffa having medium-size grain and early maturity was developed in 1948. Other varieties developed from 1947 to 1960 were CO1, RS 10, RS 11, C235, Annegri, etc. In later years, hybrid varieties developed were C 214, G 130, B 108, H 208, Pusa 329, Gourav, Haryana Chana 1, Bheena, etc. having the quality of high yield, desired colour and different pest and disease resistance. KPG59, BG 372, PBG1, BG 256, and KWR 108 are most promising late sown chickpea varieties and DDR17, KMPR 385, LFP 224 are very popular High Yielding Varieties.

Pigeon Pea

Released early varieties with wider adaptability still in vogue are T7, T17 and C11 of Pigeon Pea. Some important varieties released later are – Pusa 74, Sharada, Pusa Ageti (S5) for early maturity; C28, G51, RG37, RG 72 etc. for medium maturity; Pusa JA 3, HY 3C, etc. for late maturity, Mukhta, Bahar, Sharad, GAUT 82-53 etc. are for different pest and disease resistence.

Other Pulses

Some important varieties of other pulses are as under:

Urad Bean: Pragati, Jawahar Urad 2, Basant Bahar, Birsa URDI, etc.
Mung Bean: Basanti, TARMI, TARMI 8, MLI, ML 613, PDM 84-178, JM 721, etc.
Pea: Alakar (DMR 7) Shikha (KFP 103), Apporva (DDR 13), Uttara (HFP 8909)
Lentil: Pant L 4, Priya (DPL 15), Pusa Vaibhava (lens 4147), Shivalik (Pant L 234)
Cow Pea: Rambha, Pusa Safed (V 120), Cow Pea 88, etc.
Rajma: HPR 62, Jwala (HPR 62), VL Rajma 1963, etc.

COMMERCIAL CROPS

Cotton

Cotton (*Gossypium species*) has been in cultivation in India since time immemorial. However, work on improvement of production and quality of cotton began only in the second half of eighteenth century when British East India Company attempted to introduce American Cotton (*G. hirustum*) into India for supply of raw material to England. Systematic cotton improvement was launched by several states much later through Indian Central Cotton Committee (ICCC) in 1921. The launching of All India Coordinated Cotton Improvement Project (AICCIP) by the ICAR in 1967 brought the entire cotton research under one umbrella. The commonly known short-staple (fibre length less than 199 mm) cotton varieties of *G. arboreium* (known as `Bengals') are Mollisoni, G 27, R41. But crossing between different *arboreium* races improved the better yield producing and early maturity type cotton varieties like LD131, LD 230, L327 and RG 8.

Medium staple varieties, viz. LSS, 320 F and H14 were predominant in the fifties and sixties. Later improved high yielding varieties were F 414, H 777, SH 131, LH 1134, HS 6 in north zone, Indore 2, A 51-9 (narmada), L 147, Deviraj (170 CO2) in central and southern zone as well as in western zone having better fibre length and better ginning quality. Varieties released later (1982) like Reba B 50, Laxmi and AC 122 developed by CSIR were pest resistant and high yielding. Other varieties like Sujata Suvin, DHY 286, Badnawar 12 of long type, and MCU and Varalaxmi among extra long type are important high yielding varieties of cotton.

Tobacco

Tobacco was introduced by Portuguese in India in 1502. Efforts to conduct research in tobacco underwent in different regional stations early in this century. Organised and systematic tobacco research commenced in India with the establishment of the Central Tobacco Research Institute (CTRI), Rajamundry, Andhra Pradesh in 1947. Different regional cotton research centres were established during the fist half of the fifties. Among the earlier varieties, main variety was Harison special, a high yielding variety. Later improved superior flue-cured virginia variety, Goutham was developed and it was one of the most cultivated varieties. Among others, fine – cured varieties Bharya (1989), GT 5(1989), bidi tobacco variety menekashri, chewing tobacco varieties are important and now being widely cultivated. Very high yielding and first hybrid variety was Gujarat Tobacco Hybrid 1 (GTH1).

Sugarcane

Sugarcane cultivation is pre-Vedic and historical in commercial significance and social context especially in rural India. To carry out research on sugarcane, ICAR has two central institutes, Sugarcane Breeding Institute (SBI) Coimbatore, and Indian Institute of Sugarcane Research (IISR), Lucknow. The first successful intergenic hybrid was made in 1916 between *Saccharum officinarum* with *Narenga porphyocana*. The first hybrid variety for commercial cultivation was Co 205 and was released in 1926. The varietal improvement programme persuaded by the SBI, Coimbatore, over the past 84 years have kept pace with the changing requirements. Since then the institutes are engaged in improving varieties through hybridization, local selection and Mutation Breeding. Mutagen varieties like Co 449 and Co 997 were developed which were red rot resistant.

Varieties which came into prominence during the decade 1957-1966 included Co 62174, Co 62175, Co 6304, and 6415. The varieties developed in the following decades are mainly Co 6806, Co 7527, Co 7508, Co 7804, Co 8011, Co 8013, and Co 8362. Besides these, there are also some short-duration varieties such as Co 8338, Co 8339, Co 8340 and Co 8341. All India Coordinated Research Project on Sugarcane also developed a few very high quality and HY Variety for different zones for commercial cultivation. Among them CoC 671, CoJ 69 Co LK 8102, BO 91, BO100, etc. are important. A brief description of the new high yielding varieties is given in Table 7.1.

EMERGING PROBLEMS AND TECHNOLOGY DEVELOPED WITH THE VARIETY IMPROVEMENT

As HYV programme has changed the production scenario in respect of volume and quality as well as mode of cultivation practice, it also has brought several severe problems like occurrence of new pest and diseases; exploitation of soil nutrients; misuse of inorganic chemicals in the form of pesticides, herbicides, fertilisers; and socioeconomic inter regional and intra regional imbalances. So some mechanisms have been adopted to fight back these problems evolved from HYVP. These mechanisms are as under:

New Production Technology—Multiple Cropping

Varieties of crops that are not bound by the constraints of seasons and the recent soil and crop management techniques like minimum tillage, application of agro-chemicals like herbicides, insecticides and fertilisers have made it possible to grow several crops of cereals, legumes and vegetables in a year. Several systems of multiple cropping such as sequential planting, relay cropping, mixed cropping and intercropping emerged.

Multiple cropping is a unique asset of the tropics and subtropics and is an effective instrument for increasing the income of small holdings, reducing unemployment and underemployment on the farm, achieving stability of production in both irrigated and unirrigated lands, and improving human nutrition and animal husbandry. However unless the multiple cropping sequences are scientifically designed, the long term productivity of the soil may be affected through a buildup of soil borne pathogens and defects in solid structure and nutrient status.

The important scientific principles upon which such rotations are based are first, the crops grown in succession should not have the same diseases and pests. Secondly, there should be a leguminous crop in the rotation so that biological nitrogen fixation is promoted; and thirdly, the crops grown one after another should have different rooting patterns so that one crop takes nutrients from the upper layer of the soil, while the other taps the lower area. Above all, such rotations naturally will have to be developed according to the marketability and profitability of the crops grown since in the ultimate analysis, it is only the net return and not total yield which determines the response of the farmer to new practices. An example of a profitable rotation in Delhi, Punjab, Haryana, and Western U.P. region is potato during

Table 7.1 A Synoptic View of a Few Popular High Yielding Varieties Recently Released

Variety	*Area of adoption, recommended*	*Salient features*
Rice		
V1 dhan 81*	Transplanted areas of hills in UP, HP, Meghalaya	Yield potential 4-5 tonnes/ha, grains long bold, duration 120 days.
Neeraja*	WB, UP	Duration 120 days, tolerent to sheath rot and sheath rust.
Pro Agro 103*	AP and eastern states	Yield 6t/ha. Resistant to blast and BP Commercial Hybrid, Yield 5t/ha.
APHR-1**	All rice growing states	Resistant to rice tungro virus
Jaya**	Eastern India	Cultivated in deep water ecology
Jalamagna**	Coastal region of eastern and southern India	Adopted to flood
Madhukar**	Northern Region	High yielding export quality aromatic rice
Pusa Basmati 1**	All over India except hill and deep water area.	Very popular, matures in 140-145 days, yield range 6-7 tonnes/ha.
IR-8*		
Pankaj**	Suitable for long duration cropping	High tillering capacity, matures late, yield 5t/ha.
IR20**	WB, Bihar, Orissa, as kharif crop	Yield 6t/ha. Matures in 145 days
Wheat		
UP 26**	UP, Bihar, Assam, WB and Orissa	HYV, single dwarf, resistant to rust
Janak (HD-1982)**	UP, Bihar, WB, Assam	Double dwarf, medium maturity, suitable for late sowing
Arjuna (HD2009)**	Karnal bunt free area of Punjab, Haryana, Rajasthan and Western UP	Double dwarf, high resistant of rust, highly susceptible to Karnal bunt, grains soft, small, and amber
Sonalika**	North Eastern, North Western and Peninsular zone	Very popular, suitable for late sowing resistant to rust single dwarf
Kalyan Sona**	Adopted all over India	A double dwarf, HYV in past but now becomes susceptible to all rusts

***Table 7.1 A Synoptic View of a Few Popular High Yielding Varieties Recently Released* (Contd.)**

Variety	*Area of adoption, recommended*	*Salient features*
PBW 435*	North Eastern plains and UP, Bihar, WB	Suitable for irrigated late sown area
NIDW 15 (D)*	Peninsular region	Suitable for Rainfed, timely sown region
Maize		
D 931*	UP, Haryana, Punjab	Grains orange yellow, early maturity
Prakash (JH 3189)*	Across the country	Cultivated in both irrigated and rainfed area, early maturity
Vijay**	Punjab, Haryana, Bihar, UP	Tall plant, early maturity, yield 5t/ha
Amber**	Hilly regions up to an altitude of 1800 metres	Tall plants, vigorous growth, yield 6t/ha.
Jawahar**	Indo Gangetic plain	Matures in 100-105 days, grain yield 4.5-5t/ha.
Millets		
Sorghum		
CSH 1**	Southern region	First dwarf, tall plant, yield 2.5-3 tonnes/ha
Swarna**	Gujarat, Maharashtra, Karnataka, UP	First HYV, Yield 3,5-4 tonnes/ha.
BAJRA		
BJ 104**	Gujarat, Maharashtra, Karnataka, UP, Rajasthan, Haryana	Early maturity within 85 days, attractive ears, bold grains, yield 3.5-4t/ha.
BK 560-230**	All over India	Early maturity, tall plants, tolerant to Downey mildew, Yield 3.5-4t/ha

* Recently released variety, ** Popular variety.

October to December, wheat during late December to middle of April, moong between middle of April and middle of June and hybrid or composite maize during July to early October. Various permutations of crops could be grown in the different parts of our country depending upon the climate and needs of the region. The primary requisite for initiating such new cropping patterns is the breeding of photo-insensitive varieties of crops which are capable of quick maturity.

Proper Fertiliser Management

World experience has shown that the efficient use of fertilizers can step up production manifold. This is important where land for cultivation per family is limited to a small acreage. An intelligent and sufficient application of the proper types of fertilizers is of strategic importance in our campaign to increase agricultural production. The stage of agricultural production is often judged by the amount of chemical fertilizers used per hectare. Needless to say, besides high yielding varieties, chemical fertilizers played a key role in India's green revolution. The breakthrough for the use of chemical fertilizers came with the arrival of high yielding varieties of wheat and rice. However, use of organic fertilizers was not dispensed with. For example, the farmers in Punjab and Haryana use chemical fertilizers for raising the wheat crop in winter; for the monsoon crop they use farmyard manure and green manure. Very sensibly, the Government of India adopted the practical policy of encouraging the use of both chemical fertilizers and organic manures.

Consumption of chemical fertilizers has increased phenomenally over the years as would be evident from Fig. 7.1. Fertiliser consumption is highest in Punjab, followed by Andhra Pradesh and Tamil Nadu. In these three states, it was above 150 kgs per hectare in 1999-2000 when the total consumption at the national level reached its peak at 18.1 million tonnes. If one considers 150 kg as the optimal per hectare nutrient consumption, states like Madhya Pradesh, Assam, Orissa and Himachal Pradesh lag far behind to catch up with the optimal dose. Gujarat and Maharasthra, in spite of producing the bulk of cotton and oilseeds of the country still refrain from higher application of fertilizer. During 1999-2000, per hectare fertilizer consumption in Gujarat was 91 kg and 88.8 kg in Maharashtra. However, India's fertilizer industry expects that country's per hectare consumption may improve in 2001-02

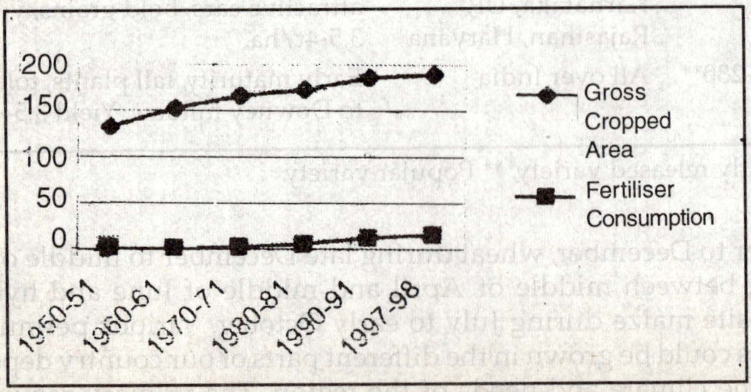

Fig. 7.1 Gross Cropped Area in Million Hectares with Fertilizer consumption in Million Tonnes.

over 2000-01 (87 kg) and 1999-2000 (95 kg) as some laggards state have been trying to gradually improve the application of fertilizers.

Although average per hectare consumption of fertilizers in India is comparatively lower than that of many other developed and developing countries, yet indiscriminate and excess use of chemical fertilizers have caused soil degradation, ground water pollution and other hazards. Though the per hectare consumption of fertilizer in Netherland is almost 550 kgs as against India's less than 100 kgs, the residual toxicity in India is much higher than the standard level. This has led to warnings of impending food crisis in this millennium. In order to mitigate the ill effects of the use of fertilizers and to sustain benefits of green revolution, it is necessary to shift the focus from a purely commodity centred approach to a farming systems one. The biophysical endowments of an area need to be taken into consideration while tailoring technologies for a given system. For maintaining soil fertility and soil quality, use of farmyard manure, other organic manure, cultivation of leguminous crops like Dhaincha (*Seasbania acuilia*) for symbiotic nitrogen fixation, rhizobium and Azola cultivation for green manure are foremost necessity.

Collective Management Technology for Small Farmers

The majority of agricultural holdings in our country are small. The national goal is also to eliminate large holdings. Hence, the most urgent need of our agricultural system is the generation of cooperative endeavour on the part of entire village communities in the adoption of modern technology. The small farms afford an excellent opportunity for intensive agriculture and for the exploitation of the natural endowments of tropical and subtropical farming and mixed farming. The technology now being developed is such that it is difficult for a small farmer to adopt it efficiently in isolation particularly in crops which do not pose serious pest or water management problems. Therefore, fertiliser use has caught up with these crops. On the other hand, in crops like rice, the efficient transfer of new technology involves scientific water management and pest control. Unless efficient water management and pest and weed control techniques are applied in cooperative endeavour , fertiliser use will not catch up as desired.

Development of Irrigation For Intensive Cultivation

In the development of canal irrigation in the past, one of the main considerations was protection against drought. Moreover, our farms were mainly dependent on rain-fed cultivation. To increase crop area under HY varieties and cropping intensity, irrigation to a large extent, was immediately needed. It was felt that through ground water exploitation specially developing tubewell irrigation in the command of irrigation projects, it should be possible to produce two or more crops. It was also suggested that the tempo of exploitation of ground water facilities should be accelerated. Presently, India has the highest percentage of irrigated area being almost 40 percent of the net area sown.

Now net irrigated area was 55.05 million ha. which in 38.5% of total net cropped area in India (1996-97) This percentage is highest in the world. But the programme of groundwater investigations needs to be intensified for the development of groundwater irrigation on a rational basis.

Water use and Management

An important element in the new strategy for agricultural development is the scientific management of irrigation water and its integrated use with other production inputs and services.

The optimum utilization of water available from irrigation projects involves study of various factors including soil and climatic conditions and water requirements of various crops at different stages of their growth in addition to drainage and other needs. The centrally sponsored Scheme of Integrated Watershed Management in the catchments of Flood Prone Rivers (FPR) is being implemented in about 252 watersheds in 10 catchments spread over 8 states. The scheme is being implemented with the objective of reducing peak rates or run off by increasing in-site conservation of water and ground water recharge. This may be achieved by increasing the time of concentration helping in reducing flood hazards and by measures of soil and water conservation such as contour/graded bunding, drainage line treatment, horticulture, plantation, afforestation, etc. for minimising land degradation in "very high" and "high" watersheds.

Evaluation of the sprinkler irrigation in order to find out its economics under Indian conditions was undertaken. A study was also undertaken to find the effects of loose sands and sand storms on the functioning of the canal system in the Rajasthan Canal area and to determine remedial steps to avoid silting of the system. Technical literature in the form of bulletins having a bearing on soil survey and land classification, soil-water-plant relationships, lining of channels, irrigation of various crops, irrigation methods, estimating water requirements of various crops, etc., were issued by the Water Management Division of the Department for the use of State Governments, universities, research institutes, cultivators and extension workers.

Social Implications

There are a few social implications emerging from the operation of the new technology. It has been said that inter-and intra-regional disparities have widened, and one would not dispute such observations on the face of it. After all, whether it is the Japanese method of rice cultivation, or IADP or programme of HYVP now, the initiative is always taken by the better off classes of the society. Because of their affluence, they can afford to take risks and thus reap the benefit of the new technology if it proves a success. They are liable to lose also if it fails. It is normal that in the first few years of the introduction of the HYVP the bigger farmers would have taken the lead. The new practices are, however, spreading widely and with the help of the special schemes of the Government (discussed elsewhere) to help the weaker sections of the population there is no reason to believe that cultivators of smaller holdings will remain behind. A look at the productivity levels in Tamil Nadu, Andhra Pradesh or even Karnataka where rice yields during 1998-99 were higher than that of Haryana will be of interest to all students of agricultural economics. Productivity levels achieved by Tamil Nadu in rice are higher than even in Punjab. While Punjab and Haryana agriculture is showing signs of fatigue, other laggards are coming up.

EVALUATION

To achieve the twin national objectives of poverty alleviation and welfare of the disadvantaged and weaker sections of the society, it has now become imperative to increase agricultural productivity, profitability, and sustainability through judicious and more integrated use of natural resources as well as proper field application of research achievements. The HYV Programme has actually changed the motto of agriculture from way of life to agri-business, from insufficiency of foodgrains to self sufficiency and even export. The researches are still going on to attain better position in world agriculture and reduce agricultural import. Evolution of plant genetic resources and their conservation have been the main thrust of our efforts in order to maintain our bio-diversity and broadening the genetic base by having improved varieties to increase productivity.

Though HYV Programme has proficiently developed our agricultural economy, in some cases it has not paid up to the desired level. This has mainly happened because of single disciplinary approach and gap between on-farm and off-farm research and very poor technology transfer system. Before HYVP, farmers used to go to cultivation practice with low input and low output basis. HYVP changed the system with more input and more output basis. But due to incomplete information and technology, farmers are now faced with the operation of the Law of Diminishing Returns whereby output is not commensurate with input

ICAR now has taken different steps in NATP Project for multidisciplinary approach of research and technology dissemination. An example of the strategy is like- a release of HYV would comprise complete package of practices with different aspects with different agro-ecological regions along with the variety.

Appendix 7.1

Area Under HYVP of Different Cereal Crops

(In `000 hectares)

Year	Paddy	Wheat	Maize	Total*
1966-67	888	541	207	1886
1971-72	7,412	7,861	437	18173
1976-77	13,337	14,522	1,063	33,560
1981-82	19,687	16,751	1,598	46,491
1986-87	24,026	19,192	2,186	56,174
1991-92	27,953	20,545	2,786	64,174
1996-97(a)	33,399	23,726	3,764	76,428**
1997-98(T)	32,200	23,000	3,600	76,000
1998-99 (T)	33,000	24,000	3,600	78,350

SOURCE: Fertilizer Statistics (1998-99), Fertiliser Association of India.
(a) Anticipated (T) = Target
* Includes All coarse cereal

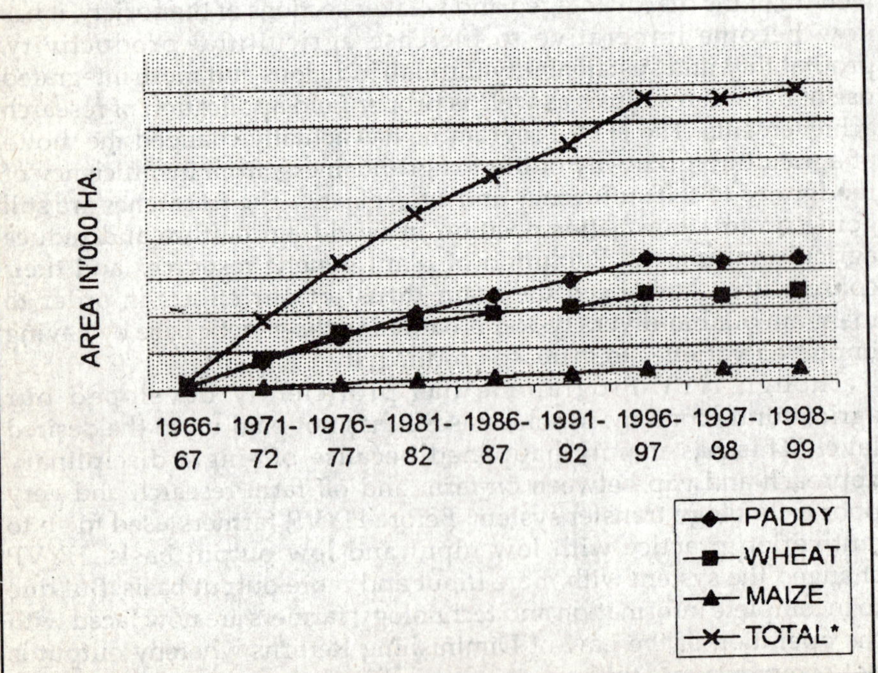

Fig. 7.2 Area under High Yielding Varieties.

CHAPTER 8

Irrigation

Agricultural growth is a prerequisite for the economic and social development of the country. Agriculture contributes 28% of GNP, about 60% of employment and is the primary source of livelihood in rural areas which account for 72% of India's population and 80% of its poor. Irrigated agriculture, contributes nearly 56% of agricultural output. Addressing the irrigation sector's current performance problems will thus be a central element of future strategy for agricultural development. India has now reached nearly the ceiling of available land suitable for cultivation. Between 1970-71 to 1999-2000, net sown area remained virtually unchanged (from 140.27 to 142.10 m.ha.). The increase in irrigation intensity has contributed to the growth in the overall cropping intensity (including rainfed crops) which increased from 111.07% in 1950-51 to 132.7 in 1996-97. The nature of irrigation development in northwest areas has had much to do with its impact on cropping intensity. Expansion of tube wells and availability of surface water from storage type irrigation projects has enabled the production of rabi and summer crops. Supplemental irrigation is available via run-of-the river irrigation schemes as the snow melts. In the 1950s and 1960s, extension in cultivated area contributed substantially to increase in our foodgrain production. From mid-sixties onwards, expansion of irrigation as well as introduction of high yielding varieties of rice, wheat and other crops brought the country's foodgrain production to a satisfactory level. Further step up in foodgrain production, would mainly depend on the availability and performance efficiency of irrigation.

NEED FOR IRRIGATION

Human effort to fight nature's niggardliness in the supply of water to agriculture takes the form of irrigation in the first attempt. Major function of irrigation is to mitigate the impact of irregular, uneven and inadequate rainfall with wide fluctuations from year to year.

Since the lay of mountain ranges affects significantly the distribution of rainfall, windward slopes receive heavy rainfall while the areas situated on the leeward are very dry. For example, south of 18°N parallel, the west coastal lowlands and the Western Ghats at most of the places, have a rainfall over 250 cm. but a narrow strip of land east of the Western Ghats receives only 38 to 65 cm of rainfall in monsoon season. Southern Tamil Nadu which is situated to the east of the Cardamom Hills also receives very little rainfall. Pudukottai, for example, receives only 5.5 cm of rainfall during June to September. Excluding the Western Ghats and West coast lowlands, rainfall decreases, in general, from east to west. The number of rainy months and the amount of rainfall are of considerable importance, because they determine the agricultural possibilities of a particular area (Table 8.1).

Table 8.1 Rainfall Pattern in India

Town	*Highest rainfall (annual) (c.m.)*	*Lowest rainfall (annual) (c.m.)*
Shillong	241.5	158.9
Kolkata	158.9	115.6
Allahabad	102.7	90.5
New Delhi	71.4	56.2
Srinagar	66.4	19.1
Bikaner	30.5	26.3
Jabalpur	144.8	128.9
Nagpur	112.7	98.3
Malegaon	58.0	45.7
Ahmedabad	82.3	79.2
Nagappattinam	133.7	20.0
Mangalore	346.7	288.4

Salient Feature of Monsoon Rainy Season

June to September is the main rainy season of India. As high as four-fifths of her annual rainfall is received during this season. These rains are of great importance for the agricultural prosperity of India as the successful cultivation of about three-fourths of the cultivated land depends on the adequacy of these rains. Hence, this is the period of major agricultural activity. Rice, jowar, bajra, jute, sugarcane, cotton, groundnut, etc. are raised in this season. Even tea and coffee cultivation is possible largely due to these rains. However, the dates of the onset and the withdrawal of the monsoon rainy season depart from the normal occasionally. Even when the date of onset of monsoon is normal, monthly and seasonal amount of rainfall deviated widely from the normal. Some months receive exceptionally heavy rainfall in certain years while the others are abnormally dry (Table 8.2).

Table 8.2 Variation in Actual and Mean Rainfall

Town	*Month*	*Mean rainfall in the month*	*Actual rainfall in the month with year (Wettest)*	*rainfall in the month with year (Wettest)*	*Mean annual rainfall*
Hissar (Hissar)	August	11.39.cm.	53.85 cm in 1926	1.97 cm. in 1957	44.60 cm.
Kolkata	September	28.97 cm.	115.70 cm. in 1900	5.61 cm. in 1938	158.18 cm.
Bombay	July	70.95 cm.	149.98 cm in 1907	10.79 cm. in 1918	209.92 cm.
Nagpur	September	18.05 cm.	62.71 cm. in 1891	5.18 cm. in 1899	112.73 cm.
Allahabad	August	33.31.cm.	91.47 cm. in 1953	5.33 cm in 1883	102.73 cm.

SOURCE: A Geography of India by Gopal Singh, pp. 29-30

The rainfall in most of the areas except North Eastern and coastal regions is erratic with occasional long dry spells turning agriculture into a gamble. Supplementary irrigation is therefore essential even for kharif while for Rabi a substantial supply is needed for assured and higher production. Use of ground water can be helpful in areas where it is available, hence the need for an assessment of water resources. Normally there is a five year rainfall cycle. It is, however, interesting to note that India has witnessed normal monsoon since 1988 (Table 8.3).

Water Resources

Although India possesses about 17 per cent of global population, its water resources are just 4 per cent of the total average annual runoff in the rivers of the world. As in 1987, per capita average runoff in India has come down from 5277 cu.mt. in 1955 to 1970 cu.mt. now (1999) as against 36,690 cu.mt. per year in Brazil, 17,500 cu.mt. per year in Russia, 6,500 cu.mt. per year in Japan and 6,200 cu.mt. in USA. The distribution of rainfall in the country is also highly uneven with 100 mm. In Western Rajasthan to over 11,000 mm. At Cherrapunji in Meghalaya. Further, variability of rainfall from season to season is also very high. The compounding effect of such factors is the uneven water availability from basin to basin. India has been divided into 20 river basins with as high as annual per capita runoff of 18,417 cu.mt. in the Brahmaputra basin and as low as 411 cu.mt. in east-flowing rivers from Pennar to Kanyakumari in south and 631 cu.mt. in west-flowing rivers of Kutch and Saurashtra including Lumi in the west of India. According to the Central Water Commission's estimate, total average annual runoff of the river system of the country is around 1869 cubic kilometres.

Table 8.3 Monsoon Track Record

Year	Rainfall as % of long period average*		Arrival date in Delhi
	Actual	Forecast	
1988	119	113	30 June
1989	101	102	1 July
1990	106	101	1 July
1991	91	94	14 July
1992	93	92	11 July
1993	100	103	27 June
1994	110	92	25 June
1995	100	97	11 July
1996	103	96	23 June
1997	102	92	9 July
1998	105	99	17 June
1999	96	108	28 June
2000**	—	99	29 June

* average annual rainfall over 70 years; ** anticipated

Water Stress

India's total annual renewable fresh water resources are estimated at 2085 BCM. However, the annual average water availability (AWA) in terms of utilizable water resources within the limitations of physiographic conditions, sociopolitical environment, legal and constitutional constraints and the technology of development as available is estimated at 1086 BCM, comprising 690 BCM of surface water and 395.6 BCM of ground water. Accordingly, at the beginning of the century, India's per capita water availability was 4555 cubic metres (cu.m.) per year. Thereafter, due to exponential population growth, particularly since 1960s, the per capita water availability decreased from 3008 cu.m. in 1951 to 1981 cu.m. in 1971 to 1283 cu.m. in the year 1991. As estimated, India's population by the year 2010, 2025 and 2050 will be 1189 millions, 1392 millions and 1640 millions respectively. Accordingly, the per capita water availability (AWA) will be 913 cu.m. 780 cu.m. and 662 cu.m. by the year 2010, 2025 and 2050 respectively. Water scarcity has been defined according to "supply-side" approach in the pioneering study by Falkenmark, Lundquist and Widstrand. For this purpose, ranking has been done according to per capita amount of "Annual Water Resources" (AWR). They define 1700 cu.m. per capita per year as the level of water supply above which shortage will be local and rare. Below 1000 cu.m. per capita per year, water supply will hamper health, economic development and human wellbeing. At less than 500 cu.m. per capita per year, water availability is a primary constraint to life. In fact, India is likely to experience "water stress" from the year 2007 onwards. A number of studies conducted in India and abroad have also drawn the similar conclusions.

Water Use

Directly or indirectly, quantum of consumption of water is related to population, demand for food, production of non-food agricultural and industrial items, consumption of energy, level of quality of life and ecological need of a nation, availability of water, in turn , determines suitable technology for adoption in these sectors. Water requirement for agricultural and domestic needs including drinking cooking, sanitation, etc. together constitutes bulk of total water consumption. However, due to competing sectoral water demands, particularly from energy and industrial sectors in next 5 decades, the share of irrigation in total water use would come down from 83.3% in the year 1990 to 72.8% in 2025 and further to 64.7% by the year 2050 (Table 8.4).

Table 8.4 Water Use in the Year

Purpose	1990 BCM	1990 % of total	2000 BCM	2000 % of total	2025 BCM	2025 % of total	2050 BCM	2050 % of total
Domestic	25	4.5	44	6.6	77	6.2	93	5.6
Irrigation	460	83.3	520	78.5	909	72.8	1072	64.7
Energy	19	3.5	27	4.1	70	5.6	212	12.8
Industries	15	2.7	30	4.5	120	9.6	199	12.0
Others	33	6.0	41	6.2	72	5.8	80	4.8
TOTAL	552	100.0	662	100.0	1248	100.0	1656	100.0

SOURCE: Draft of Basic Document on the Assessment of Availability and Requirement of Water for Diverse Users in the Country; Ministry of Water Resources, GOI, New Delhi, 1997. Revised in October 1998.

Therefore, if we want to have an optimistic long-term view of our water resources availability, we ought to adopt a two-pronged strategy comprising on the one hand, optimization of water use efficiency and water conservation including rainwater harvesting besides effective control of our population growth and augmenting the utilizable water availability through inter-basic transfer of surplus waters on the other. Keeping such a scenario in view, the National Perspective for Water Resources Development envisaging inter-basin transfer of water assumes a great significance. Long distance inter-basin transfer of water is not a new concept but has been in practice in India for over five centuries. The Western Yamuna canal and the Agra canal built in Mughal times are examples, water was carried from the Himalayas to the districts of Punjab, Uttar Pradesh and Rajasthan. The Kurnool-Cuddappah canal and the Periyar-Vaigai canal are other examples of inter water transfers executed in India in the 19th century. In the present century. Indira Gandhi Canal Project is another example of inter basin transfer of water from the Himalayas to the desert of Rajasthan.

SOURCES OF IRRIGATION WATER

There are two main sources of irrigation water; surface water and groundwater. Source-wise irrigated area is shown in Table 8.5.

Surface Water

Surface water is provided by the flowing waters of rivers or from the still waters of tanks, ponds, lakes or artificial reservoirs. Irrigation from rivers is mainly through canals drawn from dams constructed across the rivers, and is mainly seasonal, i.e., during the flood season. When the dam is high enough to form a large reservoir, the water is available throughout the year. The possibilities of diverting the normal flow of rivers into irrigation aims at impounding the surplus river-flow during the monsoon for use during the dry weather. Tanks which form an important source of irrigation are mostly rainfed. They depend for their replenishment on the surrounding drainage areas and watershed. As runoff waters from the drainage areas carry large quantities of sediment, tank sites are usually selected in watershed that are protected by vegetation. Where this is not possible, suitable soil conservation practices are adopted to remove as much sediment from runoff waters as possible.

The Water from these sources is carried to the fields by flow due to gravity and is, therefore, cheap. It is diverted to the land to be irrigated through a system of canals, branch canals, distributaries and minors. From the distributaries and minors, water is given to farmers or a group of farmers through small structures known as outlets. From the outlets, water is carried in small channels called watercourses to the field. On a typical water distribution system, the quantity of water that finally reaches the field is about 55 per cent of the water that enters the canal. The loss which is mainly due to absorption, percolation, seepage and evaporation is of the order of 15 per cent in main canals, 10 per cent in distributaries and 20 per cent in watercourses.

Groundwater

The subterranean water is tapped by digging or drilling wells. Wells may be shallow (30 to 40 feet) or deep (86 to 100 feet or more). In either case, it is necessary to lift the water before it can be used for irrigation. This makes the groundwater more costly than surface water. It is generally free of turbidity and bacterial pollution.

Table 8.5 Irrigated Area by Source

(Million hectares)

Year	*Canals*		*Tanks*	*Wells*		*Other sources*	*Total net irrigated*
	Govern-ment	*Pri-vate*		*Tube-wells*	*Other wells*		
1950-51	7.2	1.1	3.6	—	6.0	3.0	20.9
	(34.4)	(5.3)	(17.2)	—	(28.7)	(14.4)	(100.0)
1960-61	9.2	1.2	4.6	0.2	7.2	2.4	24.8
	(37.1)	(4.8)	(18.5)	0.8	(29.0)	(9.7)	(100.0)
1970-71	12.0	0.9	4.1	4.5	7.4	2.3	31.2
	(38.5)	(2.9)	(13.1)	(14.4)	(23.7)	(7.4)	(100.0)
1980-81	14.5	0.8	3.2	9.5	8.2	2.6	38.8
	(37.4)	(2.1)	(8.2)	(24.5)	(21.1)	(6.7)	(100.0)
1983-84	16.3	0.5	3.5	10.9	8.5	2.2	41.9
	(38.9)	(1.2)	(8.4)	(26.0)	(20.3)	(5.2)	(100.0)
1984-85	15.8	0.5	3.0	11.6	8.8	2.4	42.1
	(37.5)	(1.2)	(7.1)	(27.6)	(20.9)	(5.7)	(100.0)
1985-86	15.7	0.5	2.8	11.9	8.5	2.5	41.9
	(37.5)	(1.2)	(6.7)	(23.4)	(20.2)	(6.0)	(100.0)
1986-87	16.0	0.5	2.7	12.3	8.5	2.6	42.6
	(37.6)	(1.2)	(6.3)	(28.9)	(19.9)	(6.1)	(100.0)
1987-88	15.4	0.5	2.5	13.2	8.5	2.8	42.9
	(35.9)	(1.2)	(5.8)	(30.8)	(19.8)	(6.5)	(100.0)
1988-89	16.5	0.5	3.0	13.7	9.2	2.8	45.8
	(36.2)	(1.1)	(6.6)	(29.9)	(20.1)	(6.1)	(100.0)
1989-90	16.5	0.5	2.9	14.1	9.4	3.1	46.2
	(34.5)	(1.1)	(6.3)	(30.5)	(20.3)	(6.5)	(100.0)
1990-91	16.5	0.5	3.3	14.3	10.1	3.2	47.8
	(34.5)	(1.1)	(6.9)	(29.9)	(21.1)	(6.4)	(100.0)
1991-92	16.8	0.5	3.3	15.2	10.9	3.2	49.9
	(33.7)	(1.0)	(6.8)	(30.5)	(21.8)	(6.4)	(100.0)
1992-93	16.5	0.5	3.2	15.8	11.1	3.2	50.3
	(32.8)	(1.0)	(6.4)	(31.4)	(22.1)	(6.3)	(100.0)
1993-94	16.6	0.5	3.2	16.4	11.4	3.4	51.5
	(32.2)	(1.0)	(6.2)	(31.9)	(22.1)	(6.6)	(100.0)
1994-95	16.8	0.5	3.3	17.2	11.7	3.5	53.0
	(31.7)	(0.9)	(6.2)	(32.5)	(22.1)	(6.6)	(100.0)
1995-96	16.6	0.6	3.1	17.9	11.9	3.5	53.5
	(31.0)	(1.1)	(5.8)	(33.4)	(22.2)	(6.5)	(100.0)
1996-97	16.8	0.5	3.3	18.4	12.4	3.6	55.0
	(30.5)	(0.9)	(6.0)	(33.5)	(22.5)	(6.6)	(100.0)
1997-98	16.6	0.5	3.1	18.4	12.5	3.5	54.6
	(30.4)	(0.9)	(5.7)	(33.7)	(22.9)	(6.4)	(100.0)

P: Provisional

Note: Figures in brackets, indicate percentage to total net irrigated area.

SOURCE: Land Utilisation Statistics, Directorate of Economics and Statistics.

Minor Irrigation/Groundwater Irrigation

The Grow More Food Campaign launched in 1943, and finally integrated with the First Plan, emphasised the importance of irrigation. After a review of irrigation performance carried out by the Union and State Governments before the commencement of the First Plan, the programme was given a compact area-approach with a big tubewell component. The Grow More Food Enquiry Committee recommended in 1952 that priority should be given to new minor irrigation schemes, and to the repairing of existing works. A lot of changes have taken place since then. Present classification of major/minor irrigation schemes is as follows.

1. Up to the early Fifth Plan period:
   - Minor Projects — Costing up to Rs. 25 lakhs in plain areas; Costing up to Rs. 30 lakhs in hilly areas
   - Medium Projects — Costing above Rs. 25 lakhs and up to Rs.5 crores
   - Major Projects — Costing above Rs. 5 crores.
2. Later Fifth Plan period:
   - Minor Projects — Costing up to Rs. 25 lakhs in plain areas; Costing up to Rs. 30 lakhs in hilly areas
   - Medium Projects — With culturable command area (CCA) up to 10,000 hectares
   - Major Projects — With CCA more than 10,000 hectares
3. Present Position.
   - Minor Projects — With CCA up to 2,000 hectares
   - Medium Projects — With CCA above 2,000 hectares up to 10,000 hectares
   - Major Projects — With CCA more than 10,000 hectares

The Minor Irrigation Projects comprise wells, tubewells, bhandaras, tanks, etc.

As a predominantly private investment activity (to the extent of 90%) the pace of groundwater development is determined primarily by financial returns accruing to the individual farmers making the investment. Over time, however, the role of Government has expanded through the provision of infrastructure (e.g. rural electrification, subsidy programmes for small farmers, and institutional support in the form of technical groundwater services, long-term credit for financing investments and extension).

As per 1986-87 Minor Irrigation Census, 95 lakh wells, 0.64 lakh deep tubewells and 4.75 lakh shallow tubewells were dug: 4.22 lakh surface works completed and the number of pumpsets energized rose from 0.2 million in 1950-51 to 11.2 million by 1989-90. The second census of minor irrigation works was initiated in September, 1994. Upto January, 1998, 21 States/UTs had completed the census. The field work has also been completed in four other States/UTs and computerization of the data is in progress. The field work in the remaining four States is in progress. Out of a total allocation of Rs. 10.50 crore, an amount of Rs. 7.26 crore has been released to the different States/UTs/NIC for conducting the census.

While the irrigation potential created through major irrigation projects has recorded about a four fold increase, the irrigation potential created through ground water schemes, which mostly executed and managed by the farmers themselves has recorded about seven-fold increase. Among the most important 11 States, from the point of view of irrigation, (Andhra Pradesh, Bihar, Gujarat, Haryana, Karnataka, Madhya Pradesh, Maharashtra, Punjab, Rajasthan, Tamil Nadu and Uttar Pradesh) ground water dominates over other sources in all except Haryana. In Gujarat, Bihar, Himachal Pradesh, Punjab, Tamil Nadu and West Bengal, the share of ground water in overall irrigation is over 60 per cent. State-wise data on ground water resource and its irrigation potential are indicated in the statement at Annexure 8.1.

While groundwater irrigation occurs in most areas of India, both the pace and type of investment has varied considerably between regions and states. The spread of dwarf wheat varieties in the mid-1960s, and later, of high-yielding rice varieties in Punjab, Haryana, Western Uttar Pradesh and in the alluvial areas of Andhra Pradesh and Tamil Nadu in the south, was accompanied by rapid growth in private tubewell development. This growth has continued during the 1970s, although at a somewhat reduced pace, due to the approaching saturation of tubewells in the areas mentioned above. Other areas of India, particularly eastern Uttar Pradesh, Bihar, West Bengal, Orissa, and Assam have the aquifer and agroclimatic conditions to exploit the same high-yielding technology. Although HYV cereals are spreading to these areas, tubewell growth has been much slower due to higher rainfall and hence less dramatic benefits from irrigation. Smaller and more fragmented holdings, weaker credit and other support services are also responsible for tardy growth.

Until the mid-1960s, the main forces accelerating tubewell development were of a cost-reducing nature. Expansion and technical progress in the domestic pumpset and well construction industries brought cheaper and lower capacity equipment on to the market, enabling more small farmers to capture the benefits of private irrigation. Additional stimuli were provided by the spread of cheap power through rural electrification, and rapid progress in land consolidation in northwestern states, together with the emergence of waterlogging problems caused by widespread surface irrigation.

After the mid-1960s, the main engine of growth was the greatly enhanced profits from newly available high-yielding wheat and rice varieties under conditions of high fertilization and good water management. At the same time, institutional credit for minor irrigation began to grow rapidly. Funds for refinance to, and on lending by State Cooperative Land Development Banks, and later commercial banks, were increasing with refinance facility from NABARD. These facts portray the rapid growth in public expenditures and institutional finance for minor irrigation from the First Plan onwards but particularly since 1960s.

One determinant in the growth of groundwater irrigation has been the spread of electricity to rural areas. In the 1960s, the Government's rural electrification programme gave increasing priority to the supply of power for agricultural purposes. With the establishment in 1979-80 of the Rural Electrification Corporation (REC) to provide special finance, growth in pumpset connections was given additional impetus. Now about 90 per cent of the villages are electrified and the scope remains considerable to intensify connection beyond the current level.

NEED FOR RE-EXAMINATION

Notwithstanding the revised assessment there appears to be a need for the re-examination of the underground water resources. The Indo-Gangetic plains, for example, are estimated to be several thousand feet deep. The entire plains are thus capable for being covered by conventional wells or tubewells for irrigation purposes. The total cropped area of Punjab, Haryana, U.P. and Bihar is around 60 million hectares. There are large coastal areas of Andhra Pradesh and Tamil Nadu and huge areas of Madhya Pradesh, Maharashtra and Gujarat which can also be irrigated with the help of underground water. The available figures may thus turn out to be gross underestimate when a careful study is made. In order to step up agricultural production through better irrigation facilities, it is necessary to compile complete data of irrigation potential for the entire country. This can be done after the necessary field studies, keeping in mind the availability of water and the suitability of soils.

The second task is to prepare adequate basin plans which each state should prepare for phased implementation. The hydrological data of each river basin has to be systematically compiled and analysed for a correct appraisal of the water potential. Later, a duly authorized central agency could be instituted to integrate the various state plans into a single strong unit. All the same, such a plan would not be quite feasible because of inadequate guidelines for equitable distribution of water resources. For this reason, a national committee setting out the priority for the use of water for different purposes should be established.

In order to fill in the gaps in our knowledge of technical processes connected with irrigation engineering, the Union Government is reportedly considering the establishment of a Institute for Hydrological Research. Planning and construction of irrigation schemes are entrusted to the Planning Department while the responsibility for the development of agriculture rests with the Revenue Department,

Community Development Department, Panchayats etc. Unfortunately, so far there has been little coordination among these departments.

HISTORY OF IRRIGATION DEVELOPMENT

Perhaps, the earliest irrigation started on the river Nile, and there are indication of irrigation as early as 5000 B.C. There is evidence of masonry works having been constructed across the Nile in about the year 4000 B.C. Construction of minor irrigation works in India dates back to the ancient times when agriculture had just started and the farmers used to dig wells and lift water from rivers or ponds for irrigation purposes. Total responsibility for construction, maintenance and usage etc. was that of the village community. From the numerous references available the use of artificial irrigation in India can be traced to as early a period as 4000 millennium B.C.

Historical records bear testimony to the existence of a number of old irrigation works in different parts of India. The character of these works was largely conditioned by the physiographical features of the area in which they were located. In the arid and semi-arid plains of north India, perennial rivers like the Indus and the Ganga made it relatively easy to divert flood flows through inundation channels. In the Peninsula, where the rainfall is low, the practice of trapping storm water in large tanks for domestic and agricultural purposes was widespread. In areas where a high ground water table permitted lift irrigation, wells were a common feature.

Down the history lane, perhaps, the first organized effort for perennial irrigation started with the construction of Grand Anicut by the Cholas as early as second century to provide water for irrigation from Cauvery river. Impounding of water, construction of tanks and earthern dams continued till about the middle ages when Tughlaq dynasty was recognized as the greatest builders of canals. British started with upkeep and repairs of existing system and with experience, ventured into new irrigation projects on Ganges, Krishna and Godavari deltas and few others.

In the Vedas, the earliest sacred books of the Aryans, mention is made of wells, canals and dams. In the Rigveda, four types of waters are mentioned, viz. water which comes from the sky or rainwater; those which flow in rivers and streams; those which are obtained by digging; and those which ooze out from springs. Rigveda mentions the term `*avata*' which signifies a `well'. In the lexicon of Nighantu as many as fourteen types of wells are mentioned. In another place reference is made to a (dried up) reservoir in which a dry bucket is lying. Another passage mentions `*kulya*' an artificial river or canal, reaching a lake. In Yajurveda also, mention is made of canals and dams. They are termed as kulya and *sarasi* respectively. Sarasi denotes a big reservoir of water as well as lake. Some of the dams, tanks and canals which came into existence before the 11th century can still be seen even today.

Pre-Independence

Irrigation was developed in the pre-independence period for the purpose of stabilizing output in agriculture. The role of Government was to provide water upto outlets from the distributaries and minors, after which the conveyance to fields and application was often the responsibility of farmers. The system was not developed in totality and irrigation was often not considered as essential for `modernization' of agriculture. The technology of diversion canals also could not provide assured supplies. Irrigation departments often had bureaucratic cadres of officers, not motivated, seeing irrigation as an essential element in helping poor farmers.

A definite irrigation policy laying a criterion for investment on irrigation works which also provided a policy frame for fixation of water rates was introduced in 1854 with the setting up of the Public Works Department and instituting separate funds for irrigation works. Prior to 1854, all the irrigation works taken up were financed from the general revenue and no separate account for revenue and expenditure was kept. After 1954, two categories of irrigation works came into existence-major and minor.

Minor irrigation works, which were undertaken in principle more for the sake of making revenue from existing cultivation continued to be financed out of general revenue. This criterion evolved over the years was formalized in 1876. Later, the Indian Irrigation Commission (1903) recognized the importance of small irrigation works and assessed that they were responsible for more than half the irrigated area in the country. The importance of minor irrigation was later stressed by the Royal Commission on agriculture (1928).

The drive for minor irrigation works, however, started under the Grow More Food Campaign, launched in 1943, when financial assistance began to be extended by the Government for these works. The programme was integrated on all India basis, and intensified with the initiation of the first Five Year Plan, when greater emphasis was laid on the programme and additional finances were made available for expanding it. Although irrigation practice in the country can be traced to the prehistoric period, substantial development took place only during the 20th century. The pace has further been accelerated during the era of development planning. Irrigated area in the country increased from about less than a million hectares in 1800 to about 5 million hectares in 1900, 16 million hectares in 1925 and 22.6 million hectares in pre-plan period.

Post-Independence

Major issues facing the country at that time were to get away from the throes of partition and rehabilitation of migrants. This called for the development process in agriculture sector, which was quasi developed at that time, and needed a jump-start not only to pave the foundation for development but also provide food security to over 330 million people. The challenges were enormous. By then, it had been realized that the risk involved in dependence only in the 'gamble-of-monsoon' is not worth it. Hence, a permanent and lasting solution had to be found for sustained agriculture, which was not possible without perennial irrigation. Hence, the foundation of 'Modern Temples' of India in the form of multi purpose irrigation projects was laid.

After partition in 1947, India was left with 83 per cent of the population of undivided India and 84 per cent of net land area but only 69 per cent of irrigated area, amounting to 19.4 million hectares. Over half of all area irrigated by government canals in undivided India was located in Pakistan. As many agriculturally surplus areas ended up in Pakistan, the need to accelerate the rate of irrigation development was acutely felt after Independence. Several large river development projects, such as Bhakra-Nangal, the Damodar Valley and the Hirakud schemes were begun between 1947 and the start of the First Plan. With the beginning of planning in 1951, many more irrigation projects were started throughout the country. Each plan period saw successive increases in the number of projects initiated, while public support for the development of private irrigation was progressively increased through investment in essential infrastructural and institutional services. As a result, India now has the largest and most ambitious irrigation programme in the world (Tables 8.6 and 8.7).

Irrigation Potential

No systematic study of the irrigation potential of the country has so far been made. The few estimates that have been prepared suffer from all the limitations imposed by the lack of adequate information. In the fifties, the Central Water and Power Commission (CW & PC) made an attempt to assess the irrigation potential of different river basins on the basis of information furnished by the states, and their own examination of toposheets. Detailed surveys of large parts of the country were, however, missing and the study was limited and incomplete in scope.

Since then some states have made attempts to estimate their irrigation potential. Others have had techno-economic surveys made by the National Council of Applied Economic Research. The Council's estimate of the irrigation potentials of various states was based on available materials and discussions with state officers. The Planning Commission, as part of its data collection activities, also attempted to work out the irrigation potential of the country. Taking into account the various figures and estimates available, the Planning Commission assessed in 1963 that the ultimate irrigation potential of India for major and medium irrigation works was of the order of 45 million hectares.

Table 8.6 Region-wise Status of Irrigation Development in India

Sl. No.	Region	Geographical area in (1000 sq. km.)	Total population (1991 census in mill. ha.)	Total cultivable area (in mill. ha.)	Cultivable area as % of geographical area	Total ultimate irrigation potential (U.I.P) in million ha.			U.I.P. as% of geographical area	U.I.P. as% of total cultivable area	per '000 population in ha.
						Major & medium	Minor & surface	Total			
(1)	(2)	(3)	(4)	(5)	(6)	(7)	(8)	(9)	(10)	(11)	(12)
1.	Eastern	425.4	186.5	25.0	58.74	12.4	16.7	29.1	68.49	116.60	156.22
2.	North-Eastern	255.1	31.5	6.3	24.85	1.2	3.0	4.2	16.65	66.97	134.59
3.	Northern	1009.1	232.8	56.4	55.87	21.6	26.3	47.8	47.38	84.81	205.44
4.	Southern	635.8	196.4	39.5	62.18	10.0	15.4	25.4	40.02	64.37	129.53
5.	Western	950.9	187.6	56.5	59.42	13.2	19.9	33.1	34.81	58.58	176.46
Total		3276.3	834.8	183.7	261.06	58.4	81.3	139.6			
6.	U.Ts	11.0	11.4	0.2	18.96	0.09	0.04	0.1			
Grand Total		3287.3	846.2	183.9	280.02	58.49	81.34	139.7			

Eastern — Orissa, West Bengal, Bihar, Sikkim
North Eastern — Arunachal Pradesh, Assam, Manipur, Meghalaya, Mizoram, Nagaland, Tripura
Northern — Haryana, Himachal pradesh, J & K, Punjab, Rajasthan, Uttar Pradesh.
Southern — Andhra Pradesh, Karnataka, Kerala, Tamil Nadu.
Western — Goa, Gujarat, Maharashtra, Madhya Pradesh
UT's — Andaman & Nicobar, Delhi, Dadra & Nagar haveli, Daman & Diu, Pondicherry, Chandigarh, Lakshadweep.

Author's Source: Ninth Five Year Plan 1997-2002, Volume -II, Thematic Issues and Sectoral Programmes, Government of India, Planning Commission.

Table 8.7 Development of Irrigation Potential (Cumulative) Through Plan Periods

(In million ha.)

Plan	*Major/Medium irrigation*		*Minor irrigation*		*Total irrigation*		*Gross irrigated Area as Utl. Statistics*
	Pot	*Utl.*	*Pot*	*Utl.*	*Pot*	*Utl.*	
Pre Plan	9.70	9.70	12.90	12.90	22.60	22.60	22.56
First (1951-56)	12.20	10.98	14.06	14.06	25.04	25.04	25.64
Second (1956-61)-GW	14.33	13.05	14.75 (8.28)*	17.75 (8.28)	29.08	27.80	27.98
Third (1961-66)	16.57	15.17	17.00	17.00	33.57	32.17	30.90
Annual (1966-69)	18.10	16.75	19.00 (12.50)	19.00 (12.50)	37.10	35.75	35.48
Fourth (1969-74)	20.70	18.69	23.50 (16.44)	23.50 (16.44)	44.20	42.19	40.28
Fifth (1974-78)	24.72	21.16	27.30 (19.80)	27.30 (19.80)	52.02	48.46	46.08
Annual (1978-80)	26.61	22.64	30.00 (22.00)	30.00 (22.00)	56.61	52.64	49.21
Sixth (1980-85)	27.70	23.57	37.52 (27.82)	35.25 (26.24)	65.22	58.82	54.53
Seventh (1985-90)	29.92	25.47	46.61 (35.62)	43.12 (33.15)	76.53	68.59	61.85
Annual (1990-92)	30.74	26.32	50.35 (38.89)	46.54 (36.25)	81.09	72.86	65.68
Eighth (1992-97)	32.96	28.44	56.60	52.31	89.56	80.75	70.64

* Component of ground water (GW)

SOURCE: Ministry of Water Resources and Reports of Working Groups and Ninth Five Year Plan proposals of various states.

About the same time, the Ministry of Food and Agriculture (Department of Agriculture) also made an assessment of the minor irrigation potentialities of the country both from surface and groundwater resources. Its studies indicated that an area of 30 million hectares could be irrigated with minor irrigation schemes. But subsequently, when the Fourth Five Year Plan was formulated, the Working Group on Minor Irrigation and Rural Electrification revised this figure to 36 million hectares, comprising 14 million hectares from surface water resources and 22 million hectares from groundwater.

The Irrigation Commission has now made detailed projections of both water availability and scope for planned exploitation. It appears that the total groundwater recharge available for utilisation may be of the order of 26.75 million hectare metres per annum, in contrast to the current utilisation of about 10 million hectare-metres. Major, medium and minor irrigation works have gradually expanded the irrigated area. The states which still have less than 19 per cent of the net cultivated area with irrigation facilities are Madhya Pradesh, Maharashtra, Karnataka, Gujarat and Rajasthan. The Irrigation Commission has made a broad assessment of the irrigation potential in the different states. Upto the end of 8th Plan, it was estimated as 113.5 million hect. This has now been revised to 139.7 million hect. Total increase is in minor irrigation (from 55.0 to 81.4 million hect.)

An analysis of the data collected shows that India annually receives 370 million hectare metres of rainfall. Out of this, 170 units are wasted through the rivers, 120 units are lost by evaporation and 80 units enter the soil as seepage. From the 80 units 43 units are held by the soil as moisture and 37 units go as deep percolation. But only 26.3 units (out of 37) are available for groundwater recharge. Thus a staggeringly low 7.2 per cent of the annual rainfall replenishes the groundwater reservoirs which feed the open wells and tubewells of India.

One acre-inch of rainfall has been calculated to be equal to 27,154 US gallons. This would permit 100 pumps for small irrigation at the rate of 5,000 gallons per hour each to pump 545 hours. As explained above, as much as 93 per cent of the water has been calculated in tests conducted in various types of soils to be lost. There is therefore justification for extensive groundwater surveys, the outcome of which might give us a better picture of the geological structure of the area, but the achievements in terms of water may be negligible or uneconomical when one takes into consideration the cost of imported rigs for exploration, for drilling, compiling data, the salaries of the skilled workers, the processing of the technical information and then finally arriving at a more or less indefinite conclusion after years of research.

UTILIZATION

Although the real ground position about irrigated area is the one given in Table 8.7 according to Land Use Statistics (LUS), the Planning Commission also publishes data regarding potential created and utilized which is rather misleading. For a proper understanding of the issue, there are two types of data available which throw light on the subject. The Planning Commission estimates creation and utilization of irrigation potential (both major and minor) on the basis of certain norms. Real ground situation (as already mentioned) with regard to utilization is, however, available from Land Use Statistics (LUS) (Directorate of Economics & Statistics). There is always a time lag of 3-4 years in this case. The latest available information relates to the year 1996-97.

Upto the year 1996-97 (Table 8.7A) potential created was 89.56 million hectares and utilized as 80.75 million hectares, leaving a gap

Table 8.7A Statewise Irrigation Potential and Utilisation, 1994-95

('000 ha.)

Sl. No.	State	Irrigation potential created			Utilisation			Gross irrigated area	changes (7-8)
		Major & medium	Minor	Total	Major & medium	Minor	Total		
	(1)	(2)	(3)	(4)	(5)	(6)	(7)	(8)	(9)
1.	Andhra Pradesh	3113	2948	6061	2894	2722	5616	5185	–431
2.	Arunachal Pradesh	—	75	75	—	66	66	37	–29
3.	Assam	204	611	815	134	502	636	572	–64
4.	Bihar	2826	5389	8215	2397	4774	7171	4403	–2768
5.	Goa	14	20	34	13	17	30	36	6
6.	Gujarat	1321	1964	3285	1158	1835	2993	3655	662
7.	Haryana	2065	1555	3620	1829	1512	3341	4592	1251
8.	Himachal Pradesh	9	147	156	5	126	131	171	40
9.	Jammu & Kashmir	173	374	547	146	359	505	430	–75
10.	Karnataka	1557	1484	3041	1319	1444	2763	2923	160
11.	Kerala	503	570	1073	454	533	987	506	–481
12.	Madhya Pradesh	2157	2717	4874	1529	2447	3976	6071	2095
13.	Maharashtra	2175	2552	4727	1150	2287	3437	3149	–288
14.	Manipur	70	56	126	61	46	107	75	–32
15.	Meghalaya	—	49	49	—	42	42	45	3
16.	Mizoram	—	12	12	—	10	10	8	–2
17.	Nagaland	—	67	67	—	57	57	65	8
18.	Orissa	1458	1337	2795	1379	1165	2544	2510	–34
19.	Punjab	2455	3382	5837	2395	3326	5721	7319	1598
20.	Rajasthan	2170	2427	4597	1914	2345	4259	5815	1556
21.	Sikkim	—	24	24	—	18	18	16	–2
22.	Tamil Nadu	1552	2155	3707	1546	2152	3698	3588	–110
23.	Tripura	2	97	99	2	89	91	60	–31
24.	Uttar Pradesh	6976	21678	28654	5948	19760	25708	16823	–8885
25.	West Bengal	1432	3015	4447	1341	2493	3834	2491	–1343
	Total States	32232	54705	86937	27614	50127	77741	70545	–7196
	Total Uts	17	85	102	9	80	89	94	5
	Grand Total	32249	54790	87039	27623	50207	77830	70639	-7119

of 8.8 million hectares as unutilized according to Planning Commission. Actual utilization of gross irrigated area during 1996-97, as released by LUS was 73.3 million hectares, giving an addition of another 7.5 million hect. to the unutilized component. This is not, however, the end of the story. To have a clearer picture of the ground situation, it is necessary to examine the position at the State level.

There are a number of states where the claimed utilization is much less than the actual numbers as given in LUS Table 8.7A. Major states in this category are U.P. (8.9 million hectares), Bihar (2.1 million) and West Bengal (1.3 million). When we add up all these negatives in column 9 (Table 8.7A), we come to a staggering figure of 14.6 million hectares as the difference between utilized according to Planning Commission and LUS. This would mean that the unutilized potential for these 15 states only is of the order of (61.4 – 39.9) = 21.5 million hect. A study of this nature at the all India level has no meaning because under utilization of 15 states cannot be neutralised by over utilization in other states - Madhya Pradesh (2.1 mh.) Punjab (1.6 mh), Rajasthan (1.6 ml.) Haryana (1.3 mh.) and Gujarat (0.7mh.). An unfortunate part of the story is that this gap instead of going down is increasing year after year. A similar exercise for 1984-85 showed that the unutilized potential was 16.3 million hect. Over utilization in these states is really creating another problem. The case of Punjab is rather interesting where gross irrigated area under LUS is 7319 thousand hectares as against the ultimate potential of 5667 thousand hectares. Similarly in Tamil Nadu potential created was more than the ultimate for major irrigation. Same is the position for minor irrigation in U.P. It would be of interest to point out that additional targets were provided for even these states in the Eighth plan and the same is the position for the Ninth plan. The main issue is whether or not such an over-exploitation, if real, is sustainable. According to available information the position is rather serious in a state like Punjab where 52.5 percent of the Blocks have reported over exploitation of ground water resources.

The case of U.P. will be all the more interesting. Ultimate irrigation potential for minor irrigation is 18.0 million hectares, potential created is 21.7 million hectares and utilized is 19.8 million hectares. As against all these, total gross irrigated area according to LUS is only 16.8 million hectares. One would wonder, what do we do with this type of data. Distribution of gross irrigated area as between major and minor irrigation is not available to enable us to go deep into the issue.

Ninth Plan

The plan is committed to make a thrust in this direction through a "Special Action Plan" and overall strategy of irrigation development and management during the Ninth Plan have the following core ingredients.

(a) To improve water use efficiency by progressive reduction in conveyance and application losses.

(b) To bridge the gap between the potential created and its utilization by strengthening the Command Area Development Programme (CADP), institutional reforms and promoting farmers' involvement in irrigation management.

(c) To complete all the ongoing projects, particularly those which were started during pre-Plan period as a time bound programme to yield benefits from the investments already made.

(d) To restore and modernize the old irrigation systems which were executed during the pre-Independence period and 25 years ago.

(e) To introduce rational pricing of irrigation water based initially on O & M cost and then to encourage higher level of water use efficiency.

(f) To make concrete steps towards comprehensive and integrated development of natural water resources, taking into account the possibility of inter-river-basin transfer of surplus water.

(g) To promote adaptive research and development to ensure more cost effective and efficient execution and management of irrigation systems.

(h) To promote 'Particularly Irrigation Management (PIM)' with full involvement of the water user community , which will be at the centre stage of the implementation of above strategies of the Ninth Plan.

(i) To encourage and implement the conjunctive use of ground and surface waters towards optimal utilization of water resource and to have its development environmentally sustainable as well, and

(j) To accelerate the development and utilization of ground water, particularly in the eastern region on sound technical, environmental and economic considerations along with proper regulatory mechanisms.

Investment

Along with plan outlays-mainly for public tubewells and minor surface irrigation-and private expenditures, institutional credit is an integral part of total investment expenditure on minor-irrigation (Table 8.8). Up to the end of Eighth Plan a total investment of Rs. 91943.4 crore (Rs. 231386.59 crore at 1996-97 prices) had been made. Nearly one third of this represents the share of minor irrigation and flood control. Total investment proposed in the Ninth Plan is Rs. 58163.75 crore (Table 8.9).

Micro Irrigation

The two most important micro-irrigation methods are: drip irrigation and sprinkler irrigation. These two systems were originally developed for arid and semi-arid regions of the world. The drip system uses only

Table 8.8 Magnitude and Composition of Investment Through Plan Periods in Irrigation and Flood Control sectors.

(Rs. crore)

Plans	Major & medium irrign.	Minor irrigation: Public sector	Minor irrigation: Institutional finance	Minor irrigation: Total	C.A.D.	Flood Control	Total at current prices
First	376.24	65.62	Neg.	65.62		13.21	455.07
(1951-56)	(7803.42)	(1360.99)		(1360.99)	—	(273.98)	(9438.39)
Second	380	142.23	19.35	161.58		48.06	589.64
(1956-61)-	(6013.98)	(2250.97)	(306.24)	(2557.21)	—	(760.61)	(9331.80)
Third	576	327	115.37	443.10		82.09	1101.19
(1961-66)	(6674.84)	(3797.82)	(1336.94)	(5134.76)	—	(551.28)	(12760.88)
Annual	429.81	326.19	234.74	560.93		41.96	1032.70
(1966-69)	(3943.90)	(2993.10)	(2153.96)	(5147.06)	—	(585.02)	(9475.98)
Fourth	1242.30	512.28	661.06	1173.34		162.04	2577.48
(1969-74)	(7976.41)	(3289.18)	(4243.45)	(7532.63)	—	(1040.40)	(16549.18)
Fifth	2516.18	630.83	778.76	1409.58		298.61	4224.36
(1974-78)	(12519.42)	(3138.74)	(3874.67)	(7013.41)	—	(1485.75)	(21018.59)
Annual	2078.58	501.50	480.40	981.90	362.96*	329.96	3753.40
(1978-80)	(7949.67)	(1918.02)	(1837.32)	(3755.34)	(1388.16)	(1261.95)	(14355.15)
Sixth	7368.83	1979.26	1437.56	3416.82	743.05	786.85	1215.55
(1980-85)	(19625.50)	(5271.39)	(3826.67)	(5100.06)	(1978.97)	(2095.63)	(32800.16)
Seventh	1107.29	3118.35	3060.95	6179.30	1447.50	941.58	19675.67
(1985-90)	(21207.15)	(5953.87)	(5844.27)	(11798.14)	(2762.85)	(1797.76)	(37566.77)
Annual	5459.15	1680.48	1349.59	3030.07	619.45	460.64	9569.31
(1990-92)	(8125.60)	(2501.29)	(2008.78)	(4510.07)	(922.01)	(685.64)	(14243.32)
Eighth	21071.87	6408.36	5331.00	11739.39	2145.92	1691.68	36648.83
(1992-97)	(31057.63)	(9445.22)	(7857.31)	(1730.52)	(3162.85)	(2493.35.)	(54016.36)
Total	52606.25	15692.83	13468.77	29161.60	5418.88	4856.67	91943.40
	(132389.93)	(39492.89)	(33895.77)	(73388.66)	(13385.66)	(12222.39)	(231386.59)
Ninth	42974.23			9369.84	2887.19	2932.49	5863.75
(1997-02)†							

SOURCE: Reports of the working groups of Ninth Five Year Plan.

* Upto 3/80, *Note*: Figures within brackets above indicate the expenditure at constant prices at 1996-97.

† Agreed Outlay.

30-50% of the water used by conventional flood irrigation methods while sprinkler systems use about 70 per cent. A farmer can irrigate about 2 to 3 times the farm land with the water saved by micro-irrigation systems. Over the last three decades, however, these technologies have come to be valued in the world over for water conservation, as well as for their contribution to increasing yield levels.

Table 8.9 Irrigation, Command Area Development and Flood Control

		Ninth Five plan 1997-02				
S.l. No.	*Name of States & UTs*	*Agreed outlay*				*(Rs. in core)*
		Major & medium Irrig.	*Minor irrigation*	*CAD*	*Flood control*	*Total*
1.	Andhra Pradesh	5027.16	775.73	76.50	127.41	6006.80
2.	Arunachal Pradesh	2.30	202.48	5.65	69.52	279.95
3.	Assam	135.12	429.99	25.07	120.24	710.42
4.	Bihar	1450.00	725.00	125.00	400.00	2700.00
5.	Goa	237.02	27.31	7.31	6.46	278.10
6.	Gujarat	7358.00	963.55	50.00	10.00	8381.55
7.	Haryana	1372.43	172.13	68.22	60.41	1673.19
8.	Himachal Pradesh	35.00	196.55	7.30	20.00	258.85
9.	Jammu & Kashmir‡	173.85	148.20	22.32	80.75	425.12
10.	Karnataka	5500.00	500.00	12.00	50.00	6170.00
11.	Kerala	650.00	250.00	40.00	88.00	1028.00
12.	Madhya Pradesh	1915.76	782.90	18.69	4.67	2722.02
13.	Maharashtra	8969.08	1568.56	388.46	2.70	10928.80
14.	Manipur	222.00	44.00	18.60	36.00	320.60
15.	Meghalaya	15.00	60.00	5.00	18.00	98.00
16.	Mizoram	0.40	17.52	0.19	0.00	18.11
17.	Nagaland	9.85	40.28	1.50	5.37	57.00
18.	Orissa	3084.76	267.32	16.50	20.00	3388.58
19.	Punjab	238.25	252.82	384.47	409.70	1285.24
20.	Rajasthan	1855.54	196.30	422.86	51.16	2525.86
21.	Sikkim	0.00	10.00	1.00	30.00	41.00
22.	Tamil Nadu	1000.00	357.65	90.00	0.00	1447.65
23.	Tripura	60.55	105.36	0.10	28.00	194.01
24.	Uttar Pradesh	2600.12	490.00	120.00	80.00	3290.12
25.	West Bengal	710.93	347.86	16.33	328.45	1403.57
	Total States	42623.12	8931.51	2013.07	2046.84	55632.54
26.	A & N Islands	0.00	5.77	0.00	4.23	10.00
27.	Chandigarh	0.00	1.20	0.00	0.00	1.20
28.	D & N Haveli	4.50	7.00	0.74	0.00	12.24
29.	Daman & Diu	1.60	1.02	0.30	2.19	5.11
30.	Delhi	0.00	13.03	0.00	120.00	133.03
31.	Lakshadweep	0.00	0.00	0.00	17.36	17.36

Table 8.9 Irrigation, Command Area Development and Flood Control (Contd.)

Ninth Five plan 1997-02

S.l. No.	Name of States & UTs	Agreed outlay				(Rs. in crore)
		Major & medium Irrig.	Minor irrigation	CAD	Flood control	Total
32.	Pondicherry	0.00	17.50	0.00	21.50	39.00
	Total UTs.	6.10	45.52	1.04	165.28	217.94
	Total States & Uts.	42629.22	8977.03	2032.11	2212.12	55850.48
	Central Sector	330.12*	385.00	860.00	716.13†	2291.25
	Grand Total	42959.34	9362.03‡	2892.11	2928.25	58141.73

* The figure of Rs. 330.12 crore under the Major & medium component includes a total of Rs. 37.79. Crore for R & D and Rs. 75. Crore for Sectt. Eco. Services.
† Figure Rs.716.13 includes Rs. 110.00 crore for Farakka Barrage Project under Transport Sector. ‡ The Outlays indicated are based on Ninth Plan Outlay of Rs. 9500 Crore.

The drip system can be used, for all row crops other than bunch crops like rice, jute, wheat, millets, etc. The system is cost-efficient primarily in plantation/cash crops such as sugarcane, coconut, spices, cotton, rubber, tea & Coffee and horticultural crops such as grapes, bananas, mangoes and other fruits, flowers and vegetables. The sprinkler system is more popular amongst closely spaced bunch crops such as cereals, pulses and oilseeds.

Keeping in mind the threat to one of the most valuable natural resources, water management in agriculture assumes even greater significance than ever before. Water being the most important ingredient of modern agriculture, "water management techniques" become important for controlled irrigation and also to avoid problems related to excessive watering, and to preserve water and control the declining water-table. Micro-irrigation is the phenomenon, which is practised the world-over to meet the objective of controlled irrigation. It is the universal term for drip, trickle or micro-spray irrigation systems. It is a growing technology that has the potential to maximize crop productivity, conserve soil and water while protecting the environment. With a declining water-table due to the excessive use of ground level water, it stands as a perfect case for the adoption of water management techniques at the earliest.

At present the topic remains confined to conferences or as part of armour of experts who are yet to agree with each other on the significance, scope and model of irrigation techniques in the Indian context. On account of poor information dissemination and the prevalent confusion amongst experts and the government agencies, irrigation companies have inflicted upon themselves an advisory role to the farmers, which could be a dangerous trend. For example, the citrus farmers are strangely caught in a debate vis-à-vis micro sprinkler and drip irrigation in the absence of proper guidance and authentic R & D to determine which system is beneficial for different crops.

The Government of India offers a subsidy of 35 per cent for putting up micro-irrigation system, but increases to 50 per cent for women and the Scheduled Castes. There is an upper limit of Rs. 15000 and Rs. 25000, respectively, on both the schemes. The government has fixed the upper ceiling of 10 acres for one beneficiary family. In fact most farmers are going in for the micro-irrigation system without seeking the benefits of the subsidies as there are official bottlenecks, absurd rules and corruption involved at all levels to seek subsidy. Another important factor going against farmers not seeking subsidies is because the Central Government is offering subsidy only to those irrigation companies that manufacture plastic pipes also. This rule is ridiculous. For example, company makes the best PVC pipes, but is not an irrigation company, meaning that there would be no subsidy available if a farmer were to use this company's pipes. It means that a farmer can never have good quality PVC pipes in his farm. This leads to his (farmer's) buying an overpriced irrigation model because big companies usually tie up with very up-market irrigation multinationals. Or he has to do with poor quality sprinklers, drippers and PVC pipes because cheaper material is available from small time irrigation companies who manufacture low-quality pipes and have no expertise in irrigation management techniques. The main aim of this policy remains to sell pipes rather than irrigation technology. A farmer should be allowed to purchase his own superior quality sprinklers, drippers, PVC pipes and get his design made from wherever he feels like.

Deficit Irrigation

For an efficient and optimum utilization of water resources, a new system-Deficit Irrigation has been evolved. The very name `deficit irrigation' means less than normal supply of water for irrigation. In fact, deficit irrigation is usually practised during drought conditions. However, it is still not used as a concept in the process of irrigation planning. Apart from efficiently operating and maintaining the canal system, the aspects that need consideration for developing the concept of deficit irrigation are:

- Proper estimation of irrigation requirement for different crops for the entire maturity period and match them with supplies to identify the deficit;

- Understanding yield response of crops to supply of water at different stages of crop growth;
- Ensuring timely supply of required quantity of water;
- Ensuring judicious use of water; and
- Obtaining response of users to professional advice from time to time.

National Water Development Agency

Established in July, 1982 as a registered society under the Ministry of Water Resources, the National Water Development Agency (NWDA) aims to promote scientific development for optimum utilization of water resources in the country for preparing feasibility reports for inter-basin transfer of water from surplus to deficit areas as envisaged in the National Perspective for Water Resources Development. The Agency is headed by a Director General. The Society with the Union Minister of Water Resources as the president meets at least once in a year. The Governing Body of NWDA, with the secretary, Ministry of Water Resources as its Chairman, meets at least twice in a year. The National Perspective Plan for transfer of water from surplus areas to water short areas, has two components, namely, Peninsular Rivers Development Component and Himalayan Rivers Development component.

Peninsular Component

The peninsular rivers are divided into the following four parts:

(i) Inter linking of the Mahanadi-Godavari-Krishna-Pennar-Cavery;
(ii) interlinking of the west flowing rivers north of Mumbai and south of Tapi;
(iii) interlinking of the ken with Chambal; and
(iv) diversion of the west flowing rivers of Kerala to the east.

This will cover 17 transfer links. The Peninsular region has been divided into 137 basins/sub-basins for the purpose of undertaking studies relating to the availability of surface and ground water resources; level of reasonable utilization likely to be achieved in the foreseeable future; determination of the order of surpluses/deficits; possible reservoir sites; toposheet studies of the links, etc. The NWDA is undertaking studies for all water transfer links identified in the National Perspectives. The Agency has also taken up studies relating to Himalayan Rivers Development on the same lines as those of Peninsular Rivers Development.

Identification of Action Areas

The Ministry of Water Resources has identified the integrated management and development of water resources, the optimal use of developed resources and the preservation and augmentation of the transfer of water resources from surplus regions to water deficit areas, as the key action points. The long-term vision of the Ministry aimed at optimum sustainable development, maintenance of quality and efficient use of water resources to meet the growing demands in the 21st century.

This would require intervention at various levels like systematic policy focus, bridging the knowledge gap to enable educated decision-making, administrative initiatives, enactment of suitable legal instruments and facilitation of sufficient flow of funds for water resources development. It would require active involvement of all stakeholders and a mass awareness campaign and the application of modern technology and research. India would have to fulfil the food and fibre requirement of projected population of 1200 million by 2015 and 1600 million by 2050. The country would have to make safe drinking water available for all, safeguard existing water sources from pollution and over exploitation, maximise hydro power generation and navigation, maintain ecological balance and take care of the people against water-related natural disasters like food and drought.

New Irrigation Projects Unlikely—Problems of Spillover

Irrigation projects in the country are marked by spillovers from as early as the first plan period with the situation reaching a stage where there is no scope for any fresh project in the next two plan periods.

Consider these data: Spillover cost of 162 major irrigation projects amounted to Rs. 1,36,133 crore in the beginning of the ninth plan. And this is much higher than the fixed plan outlay of Rs. 42,974 crore. Work has been going on in some 43 projects since pre-fifth plan periods and the need for funds to complete these amounts to Rs. 70,000 crore in the 10th plan and Rs. 1,10,000 crore in the 11th plan. In a move to check spillovers, the commission has decided to relax investment clearance guidelines by allowing states to accord approvals to major projects. Now the panel would intervene only if the projects have interstate ramifications. The plan panel has asked states to take into account the committed liabilities of ongoing schemes with respect to available resources. The panel has also proposed that the resources should not be so thinly spread over a number of schemes resulting in time and cost overruns.

The step is seen to expedite implementation by removing procedural hurdles. The plan panel move assumes significance as the irrigation sector is way behind achieving its targets. Things have reached such a crucial stage that the government will be left with little option but to abandon some projects by way of prioritizing the key ones. It has been found that the plan funds would not be adequate to finance ongoing projects so the possibility of new projects is minimal. Some steps have been taken in the last few years to hasten the completion of some projects (Table 8.10). For instance, the accelerated irrigation benefit

Table 8.10

(In Rs. crore)

	Cummulative expenditure till 8th plan	*9th plan outlay*
Andhra (4)	2,019.63	1,127
Bihar (1)	255	512.24
Goa (1)	108.49	50
Gujarat (4)	501.39	51.4
Haryana(2)	70.57	55.81
Karnataka (5)	3,274.39	1,694
Kerala (3)	700.36	240
MP (7)	697.63	156.03
Maharahstra (7)	2.082.4	1,116
Orissa 92)	302.23	NA
Rajasthan(3)	650.49	217.14
UP (2)	1,028.33	281.57
West Bengal (2)	253.40	24.03

Figures mentioned within bracket next to states indicate the number of projects.

programme was launched in 1996-97 to complete some projects. However, the measure could not alter the picture drastically.

Of the pre-fifth plan projects, 11 works are nearing completion. Of the 43 projects, 19 have been targeted to be completed within the 9th plan period and another 10 projects do not appear to be making it within this plan. The National Commission for Integrated Water Resources Development Plan has suggested a priority criteria that includes selection on weightage points like stage of construction, efficiency of remaining part of the projects in creating residual benefits, projects addressing regional imbalances, projects with no change in scope and multipurpose projects.

Role of Private Sector

Large-scale private sector participation in irrigation projects across the country may not form part of the Union Government's second generation of economic reforms. The Planning Commission, which is studying various aspects of involving the private sector in infrastructure development, has found that attracting such investments in irrigation may not be feasible. On the contrary, the Planning Commission feels that the best possibility of involving the private sector could be in ongoing schemes which are 'lingering on' for want of adequate allocations to complete the projects. In such schemes, the private investor is unlikely to face many problems since the requisite clearances, rehabilitation and resettlement (R&R) problems would have been sorted out and land acquisition and development of project infrastructure would have already taken place.

Also, in such schemes, the residual work may be a small proportion of the total cost of the project and the private sector could look forward to immediate result while the Government would be able to utilise its 'sunk' investments in the stuck-up projects more productively. The Planning Commission came to the view that attracting large-scale private investment in new irrigation projects may not be feasible because, apart from the massive investments, such projects involve extensive land acquisition, R&R of a significant number of project-affected persons, and servicing of a large number of cultivators, a majority of whom are small and marginal farmers. Also, irrigation projects involve technically sound design and operational and maintenance inputs which may not be readily available with the private sector.

Besides, the private sector investor would have to deal with irrigators not used to treating irrigation as a commercial service. This process would involve employing large trained manpower to distribute water to extensively spread out fields with open channels where distribution controls would be very difficult to put in place. Apart from all these, the irrigation projects involve very large investments and low returns. No private investor would come forward unless the returns are reasonable and commensurate with the risks involved. The Commission also found that in new irrigation projects, where the entire funding has to be provided by the private sector, such involvement could be considered feasible only in case of relatively small projects where the investment range would be Rs 50 crores to Rs 200 crores. Any investment above Rs. 200 crores and up to Rs. 500 crores would have to be broken down into different components while private sector participation in projects requiring investments exceeding Rs. 500 crores are unlikely to materialise, the Planning Commission has concluded.

The Rural Development Ministry's bid to reform villagers through a 'build, operate and maintain' strategy in water schemes has found few takers. Of the 63 districts in the country where the Ministry's sector reform programme is in operation, just five or six districts have identified projects for water supply and built them so far. Villages in these districts are supposed to identify their water or sanitation needs and set up schemes with the money sent a year ago by the Ministry. A total of Rs. 40 crore is being given to each district under the scheme. So far, the highest expenditure has been Rs. 9 crore in Vellore and Rs. 6 crore in Coimbatore.

Five other districts, Khammam, Srinagar, Bhatinda, Dimapur (Nagaland) and Perambulur, have reported spending Rs. 1-2 crore. Of the Rs. 498.31 crore released so far, Rs. 51.41 crore has been spent in the 27 districts which have reported expenditure. There is no news from the 36 of the 63 districts. But in about 20 other districts, villages are, according to figures available, beginning to respond as district level societies set up by the Ministry are flooding them with Information, Education and Communication (IEC).

The new approach is about letting a community decide what it needs and give it the money for the same. It is a total shift in approach and needs an attitudinal change. So the slow start is not surprising. Apart from the fact that the schemes would be selected by the villagers, the Centre would provide only 90 per cent of the funds for any project. The rest has to be raised by the community. The object is to only make people regard their projects as assets rather than as government property. It is one scheme which is completely operated at the community level. There are no middle men. Besides, water is a state subject. The states should take advantage of the Central assistance.

IRRIGATION POLICIES

The importance for an irrigation policy was stressed as far back as in 1929. The J.C. Kumarappa Committee observed the need for a policy to optimally conserve and utilize water resources at the village level. The apex body of the National Water Resources Council (NWRC) on the water resources sector was formed with the objective of laying down the national water policy and reviewing its implementation from time to time. The first meeting of the council was held in October 1985 and other in September 1987 where in a draft water policy document was considered and adopted unanimously. There has been no action to operationalize the guiding principles described in the policy, nor any mechanism in place for implementation despite years of experience in water resources development.

While there was a broad consensus on most of the clauses of the draft policy guidelines, serious objections of some states to the provisions made in the modified daft still remained unresolved. The modified draft was made after incorporating suggestions from the states. While the guidelines have no legal binding, these would help both the tribunals and the states in narrowing down the differences of opinion. The objections are mainly on account of inclusion of ground water for assessment, overriding national interest vis-à-vis existing agreements between states, water transfer to drought areas and non-sharing of hydro-power generated enroute. Besides progress in implementation of national water policy, the agenda for the meet include consideration and approval of Water Information Bill, policy note on setting up river basin organizations, national policy for resettlement and rehabilitation and overall policy guidelines for water management and pricing of water for industrial purposes.

Controversies being faced by the water resources sector and Union Government's stand on various issues figures in the policy discussions as also on approach to organizational and procedural changes in the irrigation sector and irrigation management policy. Another major item on the agenda included modification in water allocation priorities. The national water policy has laid down priorities for allocation in which drinking water has the precedence followed by irrigation, hydropower, navigation and industrial and other uses.

The National Water Policy (NWP) was adopted by the National Water Resources Council, headed by the Prime Minister in its meeting held on 09-09-1987. The NWP recognizes water to be prime natural resource, a basic human need and a precious national asset. Therefore, planning and development of water resources need to be governed by a national perspective. The intention of the NWP was to mark the territory in broad terms, so as to establish the need for a National Water Policy, and to give a broad outline of what the policy document needs to cover. The formulation of NWP is not a one time exercise but is to be kept constantly under review, thereby including within its purview more and more issues and areas of concern as they emerge. The Principal elements of the policy are:-

- Water is a precious national resource and its development should be governed by the national perspectives;
- The available resources, both surface and ground water, should be made utilizable to the maximum extent;
- Planning for water resources to be on the basis of the hydrological unit such as a drainage basin or sub-basin. Appropriate organizations should be established for the planned development and management of the river basins as a whole;
- Water should be made available to areas where there is a shortage by transfer from other areas including transfers from one river basin to another, after taking into account the requirements of the basins;
- Project planning for development of water resource should, as far as possible, be for multiple benefits based on integrated and multidisciplinary approach having regard to human and ecological aspects and special needs of disadvantaged sections of the society.
- In the allocation of water, ordinarily first priority should be for drinking water, with irrigation, hydropower, industrial and other uses following in that order;
- The ground water potential should be periodically reassessed and its exploitation regulated with reference to recharge possibilities and consideration of social equity;
- Due care should be taken right from the project planning state to promote conjunctive use of surface and groundwater;
- Maintenance, modernization and safety of structures should be ensured through proper organizational arrangements;
- There should be close integration of water use and land use policies and distribution of water should be with due regard to equity and social justice;
- Efficiency of utilization should be improved in all the diverse uses of water and conservation consciousness promoted through education, regulation, incentives and disincentives;

- Water rates should be such as to foster the motivation for economy in water use and should adequately cover the annual maintenance and operational charges and a part of the fixed cost;
- Farmers should be progressively involved in the management of irrigation system;
- There should be a Master Plan for flood control and management for each flood prone basin. In flood control and management, the strategy should be to reduce the intensity of floods by sound watershed management and provision of adequate flood cushion in water storage projects wherever feasible to facilitate better flood management of each flood prone basin;
- Land erosion by sea or river should be minimized by suitable cost-effective measures. Indiscriminate occupation of, and economic activity in coastal areas and flood prone zones should be regulated.
- Needs of drought-prone areas should be given priority in the planning of projects for development of water resources. These areas should be made less vulnerable through soil moisture conservation measures, water harvesting practices, the minimization of evaporation losses, the development of ground water potential and transfer of surface water from surplus areas wherever feasible and appropriate. Pastures, forestry or other modes of development which are relatively less water demanding should be encouraged;
- A national information system on water resources should be established with a network of data banks and data bases integrating and strengthening the existing Central and State level agencies;
- Training and research efforts should be intensified as an integral part of water resources development programmes.

EPILOGUE

Though there has been tremendous achievement in creating irrigation potential since Independence, irrigation projects in the country are, however, marked by spillovers from as early as the first plan period with the situation reaching a stage where there is no scope for any fresh projects in the next 10 years or so. At the beginning of the ninth plan it was estimated that spillover cost of 162 major irrigation projects amounted to Rs. 1,36,133 crore which was much higher than the fixed plan outlay of Rs. 42,974 crore. Work has been going on in some 43 projects since pre-fifth plan periods and the Planning Commission estimates that there will a need for funds of Rs. 70,000 crore in the tenth plan and Rs. 1,10,000 crore in the eleventh plan to complete these projects. However, in a move to check spillovers, the Commission has decided to relax investment clearance guidelines by allowing states to accord approvals to major projects. There will be intervention from the plan panel only if the projects have interstate ramifications. The plan panel has also rightly proposed that the resources should not be so thinly spread over a number of schemes resulting in time and cost overruns.

It has been found that plan funds would not be adequate to finance ongoing projects. Hence, the possibility of initiating any new project at the present juncture is minimal. However, some steps have been taken in the last few years to hasten the completion of some projects. For instance, the accelerated irrigation benefit programme was launched in 1996-97 to complete some of the incomplete projects. However, the measure could not alter the picture substantially.

Of the pre-fifth plan projects, 11 works are nearing completion. And, of the 43 projects, 19 have been targeted to be completed within 9th plan period. The National Commission for Integrated Water Resources Development Plan has suggested a priority criteria that includes selection on weightage points like stage of construction, efficiency of remaining part of the project in creating residual benefits, projects addressing regional imbalances, projects with no change in scope and multipurpose projects.

Annexure 8.1

Ground Water Resource and Irrigation Potential of India

Sl. No.	States/Uts	Total repleni-shable ground water resources (m.ha.m/Yr)	Provision domestic, industrial & other uses (m.ha.m/Yr)	Available ground water on resources for irrigation in net terms (m.ha.m/Yr)	Utilizable ground water on resources for irrigation in net terms (m.ha.m/Yr)	Gross draft estimated on prorata basis (m.ha.m/Yr)	Net draft (m.ha.m/Yr)	Balance ground water resources for future use in net terms (m.ha.m/Yr)	Level of ground water develop-ment (%)	Weighted Average delta (m)	Utilizable irrigation potential for develop-ment (m.ha.)
1	2	3	4	5	6	7	8	9	10	11	12
1.	Andhra Pradesh	3.52916	0.52938	2.99978	20.69981	1.01318	0.70922	2.29056	23.64	0.047-.472	3.96008
2.	Arunachal Pradesh	0.14385	0.02158	0.12227	0.11005	-	-	0.12227	-	-	0.01800
3.	Assam	2.47192	0.37079	2.10113	1.89102	0.13455	0.09418	2.00695	4.48	1.283	0.90000
4.	Bihar	3.35213	0.50282	2.84931	2.56439	0.78108	0.54676	2.30255	19.19	0.40-0.65	4.94763
5.	Goa	0.02182	0.00327	0.01855	0.01670	0.00219	0.00154	0.01701	8.30	0.870	0.02928
6.	Gujarat	2.03767	0.30565	1.73202	1.55881	1.02431	0.71702	1.01500	41.45	0.45-0.714	2.75590
7.	Haryana	0.85276	0.12792	0.72484	0.65236	0.86853	0.60798	0.11686	83.88	0.385-0.6	1.46170
8.	Himachal Pradesh	0.03660	0.00731	0.02929	0.02637	0.00757	0.00530	0.02399	18.10	0.385	0.06850
9.	Jammu & Kashmir	0.44257	0.06639	0.37618	0.33858	0.00713	0.00500	0.37118	1.33	0.385-0.6	0.70795
10.	Karnataka	1.61857	0.24279	1.37578	1.23821	0.61443	0.43010	0.94568	31.26	0.18-0.74	2.57281
11.	Kerala	0.79003	0.13135	0.65868	0.59281	0.14374	0.10062	0.55806	15.28	0.53-0.83	0. 87925
12.	Madhya Pradesh	5.08892	0.76332	4.32560	3.89298	1.01866	0.71312	3.61248	16.49	0.400	9.73249

Annexure 8.1 *(Contd)*

1	2	3	4	5	6	7	8	9	10	11	12
13.	Maharashtra	3.78673	1.23972	2.54701	2.29231	1.10576	0.77403	1.77298	30.39	0.43-1.28	3.65197
14.	Manipur	0.31540	0.04730	0.268810	0.24129	Neg.	Neg.	0.26810	Neg.	0.650	0.36300
15.	Meghalaya	0.05397	0.00810	0.04587	0.04128	0.00260	0.00182	0.04405	Neg.	0.650	0.0351
16.	Mizoram	Not Assessed									
17.	Nagaland	-0.07240	0.01090	0.06150	0.5535	Neg.	Neg.	0.06150	Neg.	-	-
18.	Orissa	2.00014	0.30002	1.70012	1.53009	0.20447	0.14313	1.55699	8.42	0.34-0.44	4.20258
19.	Punjab	1.86550	0.18652	1.67898	1.51109	2.25109	1.57576	0.10322	93.85	0.518	2.91715
20.	Rajasthan	1.27076	0.19945	1.07131	0.96418	0.77483	0.54238	0.52893	50-63	0.457-0.6	1.77783
21.	Sikkim	Not Assessed									
22.	Tamil Nadu	2.63912	0.39586	2.24326	2.01892	1.93683	1.35578	0.87848	60.44	0.37-0.93	2.83205
23.	Tripura	0.06634	0.00995	0.05639	0.05076	0.02692	0.01885	0.03754	33.43	0.630	0.08056
24.	Uttar Pradesh	8.38210	1.25743	7.12467	6.41233	3.83364	2.68354	4.44113	37.67	0.20-0.50	16.79896
25.	West Bengal	2.30923	0.34642	1.96281	1.76653	0.67794	0.47452	1.48829	24.18	0.33-0.75	3.31794
	Total States	43.14769	7.07414	36.07355	3246621	16.42936	11.50055	24.57300	31.88		-64.04513
	Union Territories										
1.	A & N Islands	Not Assessed									
2	Chandigargh	0.002966	-	-		0.00351	0.002454	0.000512	-	-	-
3.	D & N Haveli	0.004220	0.000633	0.003587	0.00323	0.00065	0.000457	0.003130	12.74	0.640	0.00504
4.	Daman & Diu	0.001300	0.000200	0.001100	0.00099	0.00129	0.000900	0.000200	-	-	-
5	NCT Delhi	0.029154	0.017832	-	-	0.01684	0.011800	-	-	-	-
6.	Lakshadweep	0.000243	-	-	-	0.00022	0.000155	0.000088	63.79	-	-
7.	Pondicherry	0.002877	0.000432	0.002445	0.00220	0.00085	0.000595	0.001850	24.34	-	-
	Total UTs	0.040760	0.019197	0.007132	0.00642	0.02336	0.016362	0.005780	-	-	0.00504
	Grand Total	43.18850	7.093337	36.080682	32.47264	16.45272	11.516912	24.57878	31.92	-	64.05017

SOURCE: Annual report- 1990-2000, Government of India , Ministry of Water Resources.

Annexure 8.2

Major and Medium Irrigation State-Wise Creation and Utilisation of Irrigation Potential at the End of VIII Plan (1992-97)

(In thousand hectares)

Sl. No.	Name of state	Potential created upto the end of VIII plan (1992-97)*	Potential utilized upto the end of VIII plan (1992-97)*
1.	Andhra Pradesh	3045.10	2883.80
2.	Arunachal Pradesh	—	—
3.	Assam	196.67	138.17
4.	Bihar	2802.50	2324.20
5.	Goa	13.02	12.07
6.	Gujarat	1350.00	1200.00
7.	Haryana	2078.79	1833.62
8.	Himachal Pradesh	10.55	5.59
9.	Jammu & Kashmir	173.70	147.57
10.	Karnataka	1666.02	1471.70
11.	Kerala	513.31	464.31
12.	Madhya Pradesh	2317.60	1620.95
13.	Maharashtra	2313.00	1287.70
14.	Manipur	63.00	52.00
15.	Meghalaya	—	—
16.	Mizoram	—	—
17.	Nagaland	—	—
18.	Orissa	1557.75	1442.66
19.	Punjab	2512.85	2452.34
20.	Rajasthan	2273.88	2088.39
21.	Sikkim	—	—
22.	Tamil Nadu	1545.51	1545.49
23.	Tripura	2.30	2.30
24.	Uttar Pradesh	7059.00	6126.00
25.	West Bengal	1444.08	1332.52
	Total States	32938.63	28431.38
	TOTAL - UT	18.51	9.29
	Grand Total	32957.14	28440.67

* Provisional

SOURCE: Planning Commission

Annexure 8.3

Statewise Details of Targets for Creation and Utilization of Irrigation Potential Through Major, Medium and Minor Irrigation Projects During IX Plan

(In thousand ha.)

Sl. No.	Name of State	Creation of Potential			Utilization of Potential		
		Major & medium	Minor	Total	Major & medium	Minor	Total
1.	Andhra Pradesh	579.13	28.90	608.03	506.28	28.70	534.98
2.	Arunachal Pradesh	0.00	23.00	23.00	0.00	23.00	23.00
3.	Assam	6.50	12.84	19.34	4.00	12.00	16.00
4.	Bihar	492.00	205.25	697.25	518.00	190.00	708.00
5.	Goa	16.22	3.02	19.24	12.00	1.68	13.68
6.	Gujarat	1867.00	70.10	1937.10	1892.00	50.00	1942.80
7.	Haryana	197.71	80.64	278.35	211.21	80.64	291.85
8.	Himachal Pradesh	3.00	6.00	9.00	1.50	6.00	7.50
9.	Jammu & Kashmir	29.00	21.00	50.90	40.10	15.00	55.10
10.	Karnataka	1109.88	155.00	1264.88	887.90	155.00	1042.90
11.	Kerala	373.12	50.18	423.30	373.12	50.18	423.30
12.	Madhya Pradesh	384.75	150.00	534.75	195.11	67.00	262.11
13.	Maharashtra	1755.00	528.00	2283.00	1700.00	400.00	2100.00
14.	Manipur	50.38	15.00	65.38	42.33	12.00	54.33
15.	Meghalaya	3.88	8.82	12.70	3.88	6.62	10.50
16.	Mizoram	0.00	1.85	1.85	0.00	1.85	1.85
17.	Nagaland	4.50	14.30	18.80	4.50	12.00	16.50
18.	Orissa	915.39	89.60	1004.99	819.27	101.07	920.34
19.	Punjab	126.25	241.61	367.86	126.25	241.61	367.86
20.	Rajasthan	469.26	39.94	508.70	394.92	25.67	420.59
21.	Sikkim	0.00	4.50	4.50	0.00	4.00	4.00
22.	Tamil Nadu	4.80	11.57	16.37	3.80	7.38	11.18
23.	Tripura	22.92	16.00	38.92	11.05	16.00	27.05
24.	Uttar Pradesh	1000.00	5000.00	6000.00	600.00	3000.00	3600.00
25.	West Bengal	395.00	450.00	845.00	355.00	400.00	755.00
	Total States	9806.59	7226.62	17033.21	8702.22	4908.20	13610.42
	TOTAL - UT	5.20	17.11	22.31	3.00	16.91	19.91
	Grand Total	9811.79	7243.73	17055.52	8705.22	4925.11	13630.33

SOURCE: Annual Report 1999 - 2000, Government of India, Ministry of Water Resources.

Annexure 8.4

Tehri Dam Project

Bhagirathi will now flow for the development of India. After closing the T3 and T4 tunnels of the long awaited, multidimensional, World's 5th and Asia's largest project, water storage has commenced in the reservoir from 5th December, 2001, by March, 2003 one unit of the project will start producing 250 MW of electricity, by August, 2003, all the four units would start production of 1000 MW of electricity, the nation will gain Rs. 2000 crore per annum, Uttaranchal stands to get 12% of the total electricity produced, free of cost, the Tehri Rehabilitation Directorate of the Government of Uttaranchal is fully committed to the task of rehabilitation, package in the region beyond submergence is being worked out. In the first phase of rehabilitation, 3251 urban families and 2583 rural families have been rehabilitated. In the second phase, 2604 families from the villages in full submergence and 3663 families from the villages in partial submergence will be rehabilitated.

Benefits from the Project

Electricity Production Increase of 2400 MW in the installed power capacity of Northern Zone. (1000 MW after completion of 1st phase). Availability of 6500 million units of power annually, after the completion of the complex (3568 million units after the completion of first phase).

Irrigation Permanent irrigation of presently irrigated 6.04 lakh hectare land and irrigation facility to additional 2.7 lakh hectare land. The dam will provide water for irrigation during dry seasons also.

Drinking Water 40 lakh residents of Delhi will get 162 million gallons (300 cusecs) of drinking water. Various towns and villages of Uttar Pradesh will get 108 million gallons (200 cusecs) of drinking waters.

Employment As earlier, even today and in future also local manpower will get employment.

Flood Control During monsoon, extra water can be stored to save Uttar Pradesh, Bihar and West Bengal from flood.

Other Benefits It includes combined growth of Garhwal area, construction of New Tehri Town with all basic and modern facilities like developed communication, education, health, tourism, transport and development of non-polluting industries, fisheries, afforestation, etc.

Tehri Project—At a Glance

- Tehri Dam and Hydro Power Project (HPP): 1000 MW.
- Tehri Pump Storage Plant (PSP): 1000 MW.

- Koteshwar Dam and HPP: 400 MW.
- 800 KV/400 KV Assolated Transmission System for evacuation of power (being implemented by Power Grid Corporation).
- 260.5 m high Earth and Rockfill Dam (India's highest Dam) at Tehri with a Chute and two Shaft Spillways.
- 4 Nos. Diversion Tunnel, 11 m dia each. Total length: 603 km.
- Water Conductor System comprising of 2 nos. 8 m dia each head race. Tunnels, pressure shafts, expansion chambers and tail Rce turrets, etc.
- 1000 MW underground power house having four convention Turbine Generator Gets of 250 MW each.
- Being constructed by "Tehri Hydro Development Corporation"

Tehri—Status on Rehabilitation

- Central Government's order received for transfer of 550 acres and 400 acres of forest land in Pashulok (Rishikesh) and Pathri (Haridwar) respectively.
- Efforts are on to procure additional 3260 acres of forest land in Pathri (Haridwar).
- Proposal to acquire 2500 acres of land in Dehradun for rehabilitation purposes.

Power—Schemes of Uttaranchal

- Uttaranchal Power Corporation Limited for transmission and distribution of power and Uttaranchal Jal Vidut Nigam Limited for generation of power have been set up.
- All assets and properties concerned with Uttaranchal Power Corporation have been transferred to the Corporation from April 1, 2001.
- All assets and properties concerned with Uttaranchal Jal Vidyut Nigam Limited have been transferred to the Corporation from Nov. 2001.
- Committed for electrification of each and every village by 2007 and each and every house by 2012.
- Central Government's sanction received for setting up of a grid for Uttaranchal, independent of Uttar Pradesh.
- Uttaranchal Jal Vidyut Nigam has commenced work on Maneri-Bhali II (304 MW).
- Early decision to be taken on Lakhward Vyasi (420 MW) and Kishau Dam (600 MW) projects.
- State Government policy regarding SHP units of upto 5 MW capacity announced.

CHAPTER 9

Land Policy and Agricultural Development

An ideal land system should aim at ensuring the most productive use of land without any damage to it and loss of its fertility in the long run. This means that the tiller of the land should enjoy full security over the piece of land held by him provided he assumes responsibility for its proper maintenance and cultivation. The system of taxes and rent, if the land is not owned, should assure reasonable reward for his labour and expenses. There should be necessary incentives and sanctions for investment on improvements in land. Keeping this in mind, the role of land reforms in India as an instrument of social justice, rather than incentive to production, is brought into sharp focus.

AGRARIAN STRUCTURE

One of the main causes of slow progress in agricultural development is said to be the existing agrarian structure which needed radical changes. While the rural economy is faced with the problem of underemployment, and unemployment, productivity of labour is very low. According to Agriculture Labour Enquiry Report on Intensive Survey, male agriculture workers can find only on an average 190 days' work a year and the women 120 days a year. Same is true of farmers. An enquiry made in West Bengal showed that the farmer in that region did productive work for only four months of the year (on the basis of 8 hours working day) and that also not for agricultural work alone. The situation is much the same throughout India, except where irrigation development allows for two or three crops a year.

Malnutrition and poor living conditions of the peasant have created a vicious circle from which the country is finding it difficult to get out. The undeveloped nature of the economy is due to the underfeeding of its workers. If the social structure of Indian economy was different, it would have been of enormous advantage. The immense reserve of unemployed and underemployed labour could be systematically employed in land improvement, irrigation, drainage works, rural forestation, and to combat soil erosion and thus increase productive forces to a great extent. The example of China where huge masses of unemployed labour have been utilised for such purposes is an example before us. Once agricultural production goes up, the living standards and food standards of the agricultural workers will automatically improve, thus raising their productivity.

Agricultural production is also affected by defective means of production: soil exhaustion through lack of fertilisation, weakened draught cattle which can only do light work, inefficient or badly used agricultural machinery. The great majority of small farmers have too small incomes to live on. According to National Sample Survey (NSS) about 52 per cent of smallest holders occupy only 6 per cent of the land under cultivation, whereas 10 per cent of the biggest occupy more than 40 per cent of the land under cultivation. The land available is also unevenly distributed. Added to this, the underemployment of industry keeps 80 per cent of India's population in the village-in some regions as much as 90 per cent- heavily in debt. Productive investment is evidently at a minimum and the productivity of most farms is bound to remain low.

If part of the land available were grouped into large holdings, this would certainly allow the richer proprietors to use the surplus profits for increasing productivity. Some farmers were doing so at the time of Independence, but the practice was by no means widespread. The use of fairly large profits mainly for consumption was, however, widely practised. Moreover, savings out of income were mainly used to buy land (which was usually then let to tenant-farmers or crop sharers) and to serve as commercial or lending capital. We know little about productive accumulation in the past. The few inquiries carried out shortly before Independence or shortly afterwards show that there was very little productive accumulation.

According to the NSS, the total value of all implements (including carts and wagons) was something like Rs. 69 per holding. The total sum of capital employed in agriculture and stockbreeding (excluding plantations) was estimated to be Rs. 26,500 million in 1949-50, or precisely, about Rs. 25,000 million excluding capital for state irrigation works. This is equivalent to about Rs.90 per acre, cattle representing Rs.74 and agricultural implements less than Rs. 10. The figures include loss of value through wear.

The productive agricultural accumulation totals about Rs. 1,500 millions a year in gross investments, and about 2.8 per cent of the net income from agriculture. The low rate of capital formation is significant. It explains why there is almost no rise in agricultural production, and shows to what extent the agrarian structure hampers development of productive forces in agriculture. The resistance is so great that there is a falling-off of investment out of capital inherited by owners of small and medium-sized farms. Each year, the latter are forced to sell a part of their lands to the big land owners, liquidate a part of their other possessions, and go deeper and deeper into debt.

LAND REFORMS AND PRODUCTION

There is a general belief that the existing pattern of land ownership is a hindrance to agricultural production. The available empirical data, however, do not go to support this. According to the 8th round of the NSS report only 20 per cent of the cultivated area was under tenancy. This was reduced to 12 per cent according to the 16th round. Tenancy will not thus appear to be a big problem in this respect. Even otherwise, under the reform package in the 1990s, raising the land ceiling and liberalisation of the lease market, which may be called `reverse tenancy' emerged as a policy option for agriculture. In the pursuit of green revolution also the demand for land reforms has faded away at least to some extent from the policy agenda.

Recent field studies in UP, Maharashtra and elsewhere, revealed that many accepted idea about the economics of land reform were no longer tenable. Between 1952-53 and 1966-67, for instance, the output of cereals rose at the annual compound rate of 4.16 per cent in Punjab, 3.56 per cent in Tamil Nadu and 2.91 per cent in Andhra Pradesh as against only 1.28 per cent in Maharashtra and 1.33 per cent in Gujarat. It is well known that the former three states have been laggards in carrying out effective land reforms compared to the other two. There is no reason to believe that the advent of Green Revolution has altered the picture radically. For, the new strategy is neutral to the scale of farming. It may be that in certain districts like Ludhiana in Punjab and Thanjavur in Tamil Nadu the big farmers, with 10 acres or more of land, have been able to raise yields higher and faster than their smaller neighbours. But that is hardly because suitable technologies to achieve similar results, with proportionately lower investment, in small farm units are not available. The average size of farms in Japan is only 0.84 hectare compared to nearly 2 hectares in India. Yet the average output per acre of both wheat and rice there, is about as good if not better than in some of the best managed large farms in the country.

Again a "tenant" is not generally properly defined. For this purpose it is essential to know as to who leases in and who leases out land. All those who lease out are not land lords-even the petty landlords owning an acre or a half lease out their land, mainly due to their poor resources position. Village artisans and agricultural labourers who possess tiny plots of lands also lease out. There are interesting cases like that of sugar cane, grape or vegetable cultivators in Maharashtra earning over Rs. 10,000 per annum but cultivating only the leased in land and remaining thereby as mere tenants. The petty small holder who has leased out an acre of land is thus a "landlord" under our normally expected definition.

The extent of poor tenancy—where no land is owned by the tenant—is very small, only 4.2 per cent of the land is under poor tenancy and 7.7 per cent of the rural household are poor tenants. Mixed tenancy is a little unevenly distributed among the states, varying from 6 per cent in UP to about 40 per cent in Kashmir. Of the land owning rural households, about 84 per cent do not lease out land, 13 percent lease out partially and 0.8 per cent fully. It is also worth noting that all the land leased in by the rural households does not equal the total land leased out because a part of its is leased out by non-rural households. It must also be conceded that even otherwise the absentee landlordism of the extreme type which prevailed in the earlier days has been completely eradicated. Vague and ambiguous though the definition of personal cultivation continues to be, it has been successful in one particular aspect. The landlord has now to reside in the village and closely supervise the farm operations. If so, "land to the tillers" is a slogan which would appear to be only political but slogan is almost rendered redundant.

Even the idea of size of holdings standing in the way of agricultural development is not really tenable. Nearly 65 per cent of the total cultivated land in the country is cultivated in units of 2.5 hectares or more. On the basis of the size of ownership holdings it is difficult to fix a standard to measure the excessiveness of the ownership, as it ignores the qualitative differences in land. If the criteria of gross value of crops grown is taken, we find according to Rural Credit Follow up Survey Report that the value of the crops of first 10 per cent farmers in most of the districts is less than Rs.5,000 per year. They cannot, therefore, be termed as big cultivators. Not more than 6 to 7 per cent of the area is cultivated in the 40 hectare size unit and major portion of this would be under plantation crops.

Land reforms in India have altered the agrarian structure in two ways. At the one end, a number of large holdings have come into existence where the erstwhile absentee landlords have taken to personal cultivation. Farming under them has all the characteristics of commercial farming. They have availed of all the financial and material assistance offered by the state for agricultural development. At the other end, there are the old landless tenants and the sharecroppers who have now come to possess some tiny plots of land. But they have failed to show any progress in their farm practices. Their poor resources position has rendered them almost helpless. There is however, a remarkable change in their attitudes. Their misplaced pride in ownership of land has lured them to indulge in some wasteful social expenditures in order to "act" like landlords. No improvement in the farm production could be expected from this class of farmers.

In between these two groups, the middle peasantry is functioning in a muddle of transitory tenurial relationship. Concealed and insecure tenancies are very common among this section of the farm population.

It is thus beyond the scope and competence of any statistical analysis to assess the impact of land reforms on the productive efficiency of these farmers.

Pre-Independence Legislation

During the pre-Independence era, some piecemeal attempts were made for eliminating some of the worst features of the existing land tenure relations. Thus, the Government of Bombay enacted in 1938 a law creating a class of protected tenants who could not be evicted except for nonpayment of rent and some such specific reasons. Rents were also reduced. In Bihar, all rent enhancements between 1911 and 1913 were cancelled and illegal evictions by the zamindars were made a penal offence. In Uttar Pradesh, a moratorium was declared on all arrears of rent and debts, and ejectment of tenants were prohibited. When the UP Tenancy Act of 1939 came into force, permanent and heritable occupancy rights were given to seven million tenants over an area of 65 million hectares.

Land Pattern on the Eve of Independence

Various interests in land on the eve of independence can be divided into four classes:

(i) Cultivating holders;
(ii) intermediaries-non-cultivating holders;
(iii) tenants-at-will; and
(v) agricultural labourers.

Cultivating holders can be classified into two categories-owners and tenants. If the owner cultivates the land himself, there is no other person holding interest in his land above or below him and between him and the state.

As against this, tenant holders do not have any ownership rights in land. They may more appropriately be described as "occupancy tenants" to distinguish them from the "tenants-at-will." They have no direct relation with the state, but there is a chain of intermediaries in between. Land tilled by them may have any number of interests above them.

Intermediaries are either the non-cultivating occupancy tenants. In the zamindari areas, all those interests above the "occupancy tenant" and below (if he himself was a non-cultivator) can be termed as intermediaries. In the ryotwari areas, owner holders, not cultivating the land themselves, are intermediaries. They pay a fixed revenue to the state and receive higher rents. As in the case of Bengal, there could be as many as 15 to 20 intermediaries between the state and the actual tenant or the tiller of the soil.

A tenant-at-will cultivates the land and bears its cost of cultivation. He may or may not have any security of tenure. The land tilled by him can have any number of interests above him. His rights on the land also differed from region to region. Invariably his interest is not permanent and heritable. But there are examples like those of Bihar, where even the under ryot, the man at the bottom, can also acquire occupancy rights by a continuous possession of land for twelve years. Agricultural labourers constitute the mass of unemployed and underemployed landless population in the villages. Very few of them are able to secure permanent employment. Some cultivate small parcels of land may even own the plots but their major source of living is the wages earned. This class is always exerting great pressure to obtain land for cultivation.

Post-Independence Era

Before Independence there prevailed in India a feudal land system whereby the tiller of the soil was deprived, in a majority of cases, of the well-known 3 F's-fact rents, fixity to tenures, and free sale. He had, therefore, little incentive to improve his agricultural methods.

Land reform measures have been introduced throughout the country after independence. They have been directed mainly towards eliminating intermediaries, securing fixity of tenures, and fixing fair rents. The ultimate aim is to work a cooperative system of land management in which the entire land, and entire resources of the village will be so managed and developed as to increase and diversify production and provide fuller employment to all the people working on the land.

In spite of all that has been done so far, the progress made with particular reference to measures for ensuring security of tenures of tenants and sharecropper is not encouraging. The government itself is gravely concerned over the tardy progress in this respect. Besides a hindrance to agricultural development, recent analysis indicates that the root cause for the growing social tensions and violations in certain parts of the country is due to this very factor. Many clashes between landlords and tenants could be traced to large-scale evictions of tenants following the introduction of land reforms and resumption of cultivating rights by the land owners.

Legislation for security of tenure has been passed in most of the states. While in some states like UP, no resumption was permitted to landlords and tenants have substantial rights in respect of their entire holding, in other states, such as Gujarat, Orissa, Maharashtra, Kerala, Madhya Pradesh, Rajasthan, Manipur and Tripura, landlords were permitted to resume land for personal cultivation within a specified period of time in certain cases; in respect of the remaining area, the tenants got substantial rights.

In Punjab and Haryana, the landlord's right of resumption is subject to the condition that the tenant is given alternative land up to the prescribed limit for cultivation. In other states, the tenants and sharecroppers have only interim protection.

The Central Government and the Planning Commission are now of the view that the existing tenancies should be made non-resumable and penalties must be provided for "wrongful evictions". This will require amending legislation.

Some of the other related problems are the lack of land records in some states like Kerala, high rents, and delay in the settlement of landless labourers on waste lands. The problem of landless agricultural workers looms large because they constitute nearly a fourth of the country's total population.

It has also been observed that, with the ushering in of the Green Revolution, the benefits of increased production and productivity, have not percolated to lower levels. According to the report of the Evaluation Committee on the Intensive Agricultural Development Programme, headed by Dr.S.R. Sen, there had been no substantial increase in the wage level in areas where the programme had been in operation except where the demand for labour had been higher than the supply. The Sen Committee found that while there were substantial gains for the tenants in areas like Ludhiana in Punjab, the same was not the case in Thanjavur in Tamil Nadu or Burdwan in West Bengal.

PLANNING ERA

Agrarian change may be said to comprise two systems of change interacting upon one another:

(1) Changes in the legal framework under which land is held and operated;

(2) Changes in the situation of small and marginal farmers and of landless labour and others dependent on agriculture.

The successes and failures in efforts since Independence in creating new productive capacities and infrastructures and establishing institutional networks are reflected in the present rural situation-in the conditions of affluence and poverty, in the tensions and conflicts of rural society, and in the relative advance of some sections of the rural population and some regions and the relative backwardness of others. The historical social background and the basic economic and resource opportunities differ greatly from one area or region to another. Therefore, beyond general trends, the total agrarian problem of each region has to be understood and resolved on its own terms, as much through overall policy and planning as through the mobilization of local and regional, social and political forces and leadership. National or state policies can at best provide a total setting, which may be favourable or unfavourable to the directions of agrarian change called for in the conditions of each distinct area or region. It is also apparent that political, social, economic and technological factors bearing on rural life continually influence one another. Singly and in combination, they determine the state of socioeconomic and production relations in rural society; in turn, these latter influence decisively the working of politics, administration and the institutional structures created in the processes of national development and planning.

Legal Framework for Land

Before Independence, the national movement had defined its approach to land and the tiller mainly in the context of Zamindari conditions. Little attention had been given to tenurial and other changes required in ryotwari areas. The Congress Agrarian Reforms Committee (Chairman, Mr. J.C.Kumarappa) elaborated the approach to land in several directions, including introduction of the idea of ceilings and suggestions on the organisation of agriculture. The Committee's Report (1949) had considerable influence in giving shape to land policy as formulated in part in the First Five Year Plan and, more completely, in the Second Plan.

Under the Constitution, `land' is a state subject but, through planning and a broad national consensus on land policy, it became possible for the Centre to propose and, to an extent, pursue the lines along which land reform legislation should be enacted in all states. Variations between states from time to time have reflected both the differing conditions, the pull of diverse social and political influences at work in each state and, in some measure, also weaknesses on the side of the Centre.

From the Third Plan onward, every Plan document has drawn pointed attention to the failures in implementation of land reform legislation and to the wide chasm between declared policy and action on the ground. The deficiencies observed have been carefully presented by the National Commission on Agriculture (NCA) in Part XV of its Report (Agrarian Reforms).

Land Reforms

The National Government, since Independence, has been continuing to play its advisory and coordinating role in the field of land reforms as the subject is under exclusive legislative and administrative jurisdiction of the states as per our constitution. Even then, agrarian reforms remained as a central issue of the National Agenda for rural reconstruction ensuring social justice to actual tillers as well as landless rural poor and thus for creating sustainable basic for the overall growth of industrial and tertiary sector of our economy. Generating access to land by the landless rural poor is also considered as an important programme for poverty alleviation.

The Land Reforms Division has, therefore, been playing a crucial role of evolving a national consensus at various fora for initiating effective land reforms which include abolition of zamindari and all intermediaries since the beginning of fifties, introduction of a family ceiling in the mid fifties, reduction of the ceiling limit and monitoring of the progress of the distribution of ceiling surplus land as part of the 20-Point Programme of the Government since 1972.

The main components of the land reform policy are abolition of intermediary tenures, distribution of ceiling surplus as well as existing surplus land, tenancy reform, consolidation of holdings, providing access to the poor on common lands and wastelands and rights to women. However, for the successful implementation of land reforms, updating of the land records both by traditional methods and through computerization, is considered an essential prerequisite.

Abolition of Intermediary Tenures

The movement for abolition of zamindari had already gained strength by the late thirties. Most of the legislation was enacted before the First Plan, although its implementation took several years. At Independence, about 57 per cent of agricultural land in British India was under statutory landlordship; including the princely states, the proportion would be even higher. Legislative provisions have been made in many states of the country for conferment of ownership rights on tenants or allowing cultivating tenants to acquire ownership rights on payment of compensation. Some of the States have acquired ownership of land from landowners and transferred it to tenants. Subtenancies are generally prohibited all over the country except in certain cases, viz. widows, members of armed forces, minors, unmarried women, persons suffering from disabilities, etc.

The programme for conferment of ownership rights to tenants or otherwise protecting the rights of tenants/sharecroppers from eviction-at-will is not getting adequate attention from the State Governments. Till date (January 2000) 124.22 lakh tenants have got their rights protected over an area of 156.30 lakh acres. Cumulative figure showing total number of tenants and sharecroppers who have received ownership rights or protection from eviction-at-will as reported by the States/UTs is given at Table 9.1.

Tenancy Reforms

The declared national policy is to make a tiller of land its owner. Tenancy laws of most states have, therefore abolished tenancies. However, tenancy reforms have not been implemented properly with the result that insecure and clandestine tenancy exists on a large scale in many areas of the country. It is often argued, therefore, that the existing realities should be recognized and tenancy should be legally permitted as this would enable a number of small and marginal farmers to lease in land from others who are unable to cultivate it and thereby improve their income. But this may lead to a number of adverse consequences which are as follows:

(i) Reversing the national policy of making the tiller of the land as owner;

Table 9.1 Number of Tenants Conferred Ownership Rights (or Rights Protected) and Area Accrued to them

Sl. No.	*States*	*No of tenants (in lakhs)*	*Area accrued (lakh acres)*
1.	Andhra Pradesh	1.07	5.95
2.	Arunachal Pradesh	System not prevalent	
3.	Assam	29.08	31.75
4.	Bihar	NR	NR
5.	Gujarat	12.76	25.92
6.	Goa	NR	NR
7.	Haryana	Nil	Nil
8.	Himachal Pradesh	4.01	NR
9.	Jammu and Kashmir	6.10	NR
10.	Karnataka	6.05	26.32
11.	Kerala	29.42	14.50
12.	Madhya Pradesh	Tenancy not prevalent	
13.	Maharashtra	14.92	42.90
14.	Manipur	NR	NR
15.	Meghalaya	Nil	Nil
16.	Mizoram	Nil	Nil
17.	Nagaland	NR	NR
18.	Orissa	1.65	0.98
19.	Punjab	NR	NR
20.	Rajasthan	0.18	NR
21.	Sikkim	NR	NR
22.	Tamil Nadu	4.98	6.95
23.	Tripura	0.14	0.39
24.	Uttar Pradesh	NR	NR
25.	West Bengal	14.60	NR
	Union Territories		
26.	A.N. Islands	Nil	Nil
27.	Chandigarh	NR	NR
28.	D & N Haveli	0.26	0.64
29.	Delhi	NR	NR
30.	Daman and Diu	NR	NR
31.	Lakshadweep	Neg	Neg
32.	Pondicherry	Neg	Neg
	All India	124.22	156.30

Tenancy is not prevalent in Haryana
NR- Not reported.
SOURCE: Ministry of Rural Development Annual Report, 1999-2000.

(ii) Opening up the floodgates for creation of tenants and sub-tenants;
(iii) The land owners may not allow such tenancies to be entered into land records in the absence of which tenants would continue to be insecured and would have no access to credit and other facilities for improving their earnings from the land;
(iv) Tenants would continue to have weak bargaining capacity vis-a-vis land owners as is the case at present; and
(v) There may be land concentration and marginalization of the poor peasantry, more particularly, if lands are leased out to corporate sector.

In view of the above, it is of prime importance to reiterate the commitment to vigorously enforce the land reforms laws in their true spirit.

The goal of making tiller of the land its owner, has not been fully realized as rights of the tillers are still not adequately protected in many parts of the country. The incidence of oral and insecure tenancy is widely prevalent which leads to low investment and low productivity and severely impedes the growth process in rural areas besides being a major unsettling factor in agrarian relations. Large lands are also being left fallow due to `absentee landlordism' because the land owners are neither prepared to lease them out nor they are in a position to cultivate them even with hired labour. It is, therefore, necessary that steps should be taken to eliminate absentee landlordism by plugging the loopholes in legal provisions concerning definitions of `personal cultivation', tightening the implementation machinery and providing for speedy adjudication of disputes in revenue courts. Rights and interests of tenants or share croppers need to be recorded and various other measures for protection of tenants against displacement, eviction, extraction of excess rent, and other forms of exploitation need to be enforced.

Protection of Tribal Land

Despite the commitment that the tribal lands must remain with the tribals,, alienation of the tribals from their land continues on a large scale due to various loopholes and administrative lapses. It is therefore necessary that legal provisions are made for their restoration, not only in the notified scheduled tribe areas but also in the tribal lands in other areas. Also, the regulation of resale of the tribal lands, should be made as stringent as possible. Even in the case of acquisition of lands of the tribals by the Government for the public purposes, it should be restricted to a minimum. Encroachment of land belonging to tribals should not be permitted.

Regulation on Rents

The explicit intention to bring down the rents paid by tenants from the customary level of one-half or one-third of the produce to one-fourth or one-fifth has been invariably defeated on account of the economic weakness of tenants which has deeply accentuated by pressure of population on land and lack of alternative employment opportunities.

Ceilings on Land Holdings

The First Plan accepted the idea of ceilings in principle, but there was a degree of caution and hesitation because of lack of data. A firm view came with the Second Plan and much of the legislation in the states was enacted before the end of the decade of the fifties. Before legislation was enacted and its implementation could begin, through subdivisions and benami transfers, a considerable amount of surplus land was lost. The ceilings initially fixed were somewhat on the high side. They were reduced, applied on a family basis rather than to individuals, and provisions otherwise tightened up only after the national guidelines framed in 1972 in consultation with the Chief Ministers of States. The date for retrospective effect was then fixed as 24 January, 1971. Statewise details of implementation of ceiling Laws is as in Table 9.2. Distribution of *Bhudan* and Government waste land is as in Tables 9.3 and 9.4.

With the introduction of the Land Ceilings Act in 1972, the ceiling on land holdings was introduced in almost all the states, though the ceiling limit varied depending on the quality of land. The ceiling surplus land was to be distributed among the landless poor. In this way, land ceiling was considered an important instrument for reducing disparities in the ownership of land and as a way of increased productivity through greater utilisation of labour. However, in practice, the extent of land declared surplus was very limited. The total area declared surplus is estimated at less than 2 per cent of the total cultivated area. Further, distribution of surplus land has been limited in several states because of institutional and legal rigidities. There are other reasons too, which have led to the poor performance with regard to land ceiling. Most importantly, the ceiling surplus land continued to exist in a concealed way particularly in areas which have been covered by irrigation in the post-1972 era. Also, in order to circumvent the ceiling laws, benami transfers are effected which need to be identified. There is clearly a need to detect the land falling within the ceiling limits and redistribute it. But detection and distribution of ceiling surplus land require tremendous political and administrative will.

It has to be admitted that benefits which have actually accrued so far from the extensive legislation which has been enacted have been meagre. The legislation enacted in India had followed a middle course, seeking basically to reduce disparities in land and to provide protection for tenants. It is still a moot question whether more radical concepts could have been proposed and accepted in the fifties and the extent to which they might have succeeded better. Due to defective land records and considerable collusion and laxity in administration, in substantial

Table 9.2 State-wise Details of Implementation of Ceiling Laws (September 1999)

Sl. No.	*State/UTs*	*Area (in acres)*			
		Declared Surplus	*Taken possession of*	*Distributed to individuals*	*Total number of beneficiaries*
1.	Andhra Pradesh	792762	640218	580007	533590
2.	Assam	612500	575337	483951	444997
3.	Bihar	415447	389303	308549	380161
4.	Gujarat	229062	159540	116658	32016
5.	Haryana	107434	102488	101615	29109
6.	Himachal Pradesh	316556	304895	4374	6365
7.	Jammu & Kashmir	455575	450000	450000	450000
8.	Karnataka	268478	161834	119484	32560
9.	Kerala	139056	96180	65957	154161
10.	Madhya Pradesh	298929	263711	188563	73870
11.	Maharashtra	752731	692361	652606	141366
12.	Manipur	1830	1685	1682	1258
13.	Orissa	177996	166902	155864	137711
14.	Punjab	223115	105801	104199	28570
15.	Rajasthan	609315	566612	460064	80678
16.	Tamil Nadu	198680	184800	172954	137533
17.	Tripura	1955	1944	1598	1424
18.	Uttar Pradesh	373614	341141	257895	292838
19.	West Bengal	1363131	1274467	1034273	2501533
20.	Dadra & Nagar Haveli	9406	9305	6851	3353
21.	Delhi	1132	394	394	654
22.	Pondicherry	2326	1185	1046	1427
	Total:	7351030	6490103	5268584	5465174

SOURCE: Ministry of Rural Development Annual Report, 1999-2000.

degree, even the gains expected were not realised. This is the bare truth, and responsibility has to be widely shared.

The causes which have frustrated effective action in the past, being in nature political, social, economic and administrative, still persist. Whatever their imperfections, the main policy initiatives have come from the national level. However, legislation and implementation lie in the states where, by and large, landed interests have been influential beyond the letter of the law. Moreover, there have been no organised

Table 9.3 Distribution of Bhoodan Land (up to September 1999)
(Area in lakh acres)

Sl. No.	*States*	*Area*			*Period of reporting*
		Donated	*Distributed*	*Balance*	
1.	Andhra Pradesh	2.52	1.10	1.42	12/98
2.	Assam	0.01	0.01	Nil	9/97
3.	Bihar	21.98	7.23	13.95	9/97
4.	Gujarat	0.34	0.27	0.07	
5.	Haryana	0.02	0.02	Nil	9/98
6.	Himachal Pradesh	Neg.	Neg.	Neg.	
7.	J & K	Neg.	Neg.	Neg.	
8.	Karnataka	0.11	0.05	0.06	
9.	Kerala	0.02	0.02	Nil	9/97
10.	Madhya Pradesh	1.72	1.41	0.31	12/97
11.	Maharashtra	1.04	0.27	0.77	9/98
12.	Orissa	6.39	5.80	0.59	12/98
13.	Punjab	0.05	0.01	0.04†	9.98
14.	Rajasthan	1.15	1.14	0.01	3/98
15.	Tamil Nadu	0.24	0.21	0.03	11/92
16.	Uttar Pradesh	4.37	4.21	0.16	3/97
17.	West Bengal	Neg.	Neg.	Neg.	
	Total	39.96	21.75	17.41	

† Area not taken possession.

SOURCE: Annual report 1999-2000, Government of India, Ministry of Rural Development

movements or pressures strong enough to ensure effective enforcement of the laws.

Remedial Action

A considerable part of the damage done is now beyond repair, but it is essential that, even at this late stage, as much as possible of the ground lost should be regained through concerted action at the national and state levels supported perhaps by reaffirmed consensus at the political level. It should be possible to implement the following measures with general support from almost all sections of political opinion. Several of these suggestions have been already made by the National Commission on Agriculture.

(i) In each state, adequate machinery should be established, separate from the ordinary revenue administration, for enforcing land reform legislation at the district level and below. Resources for helping tenants who gain occupancy or ownership rights and allottees of surplus lands to become viable should also be administered through this machinery.

Table 9.4 Distribution of Government Wastelands as on September, 1999

Sl. No.	Name of States/UT.	Area Distributed in Lakh acres	Period of Reporting
1.	Andhra Pradesh	42.02	3/97
2.	Assam	5.89	3/97
3.	Bihar	13.21	7/97
4.	Gujarat	13.81	9/91
5.	Haryana	0.00	3/98
6.	Himachal Pradesh	0.17	
7.	Karnataka	13.72	10/94
8.	Kerala	4.57	3/92
9.	Madhya Pradesh	0.79	12/97
10.	Maharashtra	10.23	
11.	Manipur	0.32	
12.	Punjab	1.10	(Land since transferred) to forest department)
13.	Orissa	7.26	3/97
14.	Tamil Nadu	2.07	
15.	Tripura	1.32	
16.	Uttar Pradesh	24.89	6/97
17.	West Bengal	4.32	12/90
18.	Goa	0.05	3/92
19.	Mizoram	0.74	
20.	Rajasthan	0.93	
21.	Delhi	0.06	12/94
	Total	147.47	

SOURCE: Annual report 1999-2000, Government of India, Ministry of Rural Development.

(ii) Barring certain limited categories of owners (widows, orphans, serving defence personnel etc.), the right of `personal resumption' of land held by tenants should be ended and `voluntary surrenders' should no longer be legally admissible.

(iii) Existing tenants of lands, other than those specifically exempted, should be declared owners of lands cultivated by them. The present owners of the lands may be compensated through bonds issued by state governments with such support as may be required from the Centre and the Reserve Bank of India.

(iv) Benami transfers of land should be identified and cancelled. Since the basis of ceilings legislation was altered in 1972 and a specific date (24 January 1971) fixed for giving retrospective effect, it would be administratively difficult to go further back.

(v) For enforcing land reform legislation, there should be land tribunals at the district level and (for a final appeal) at the state level. At the same time, as proposed by the National Commission on Agriculture, there should be `popular supervisory committees' at district, tahsil/block and panchayat levels, including representatives of beneficiaries and independent persons and responsible officials to oversee implementation.

(vi) For several years, efforts have been under way to complete the records of ownership, tenancy etc., and gaps which still exist should be filled with the utmost speed by the proposed land reforms machinery in each state.

The remedial action proposed above is intended to secure the legal framework for holding and operating land once and for all. It is essentially in the nature of necessary cleansing operation to be undertaken deliberately throughout the country. As this task is accomplished, the stage will be set for undertaking the more important and hitherto largely neglected tasks of strengthening the organisation of agriculture at the base, turning deficit into viable economic units, solving the basic problems of landless labour (the vast majority among them belonging to scheduled castes and tribes and other backward classes) and bringing about fundamental changes in the economic structure and pattern of occupations within each rural region. In the limited sense of creating a new set of man-land relations through legislation, land reform was always conceived as the first phase of more far-reaching agrarian change and reorganization. Because the first phase has been spread over too long a period and has got heavily bogged down in the various processes of legislation and implementation, the country has still to embark earnestly on the second and, in developmental terms, the more vital phase of agrarian and agricultural reconstruction. It is unfortunate that for many years even plan documents have failed to emphasize the need for restructuring the agricultural economy. In the fifties, food aid from abroad reduced the sense of urgency in relation to the tasks of basic reconstruction. In the sixties the onset of high-yielding varieties had the same effect. In the seventies, after the oil crisis, planners had largely focused on short-term exigencies, and the essential social and structural changes needed had received little attention. The same situation is still persisting and the land reform has remained as neglected subject in the country.

Consolidation of Land Holdings

Consolidation of Agricultural Holdings forms an integral part of land reforms policy and Five Year Plans have accordingly been laying stress on the importance of its implementation. This operation is considered necessary for planned development of villages and achieving efficiency and economy in agriculture. In pursuance of this strategy, a number of states have enacted legislation for carrying out consolidation of holdings. However, of late, the programme of consolidation of agricultural land holdings has virtually stopped in most of the states due to certain genuine problems in the process of consolidation including proper valuation of lands, fear of eviction of small and marginal farmers who are tenants, inadequate availability of staff and lack of updated land records. So far, only an area of 1583.45 lakh acres has been consolidated in the country. The position as available from 14 States/UTs indicating the area covered under the programme and the year of suspension of the programme is given Table 9.5

Table 9.5 Consolidation of Land Holdings—State-wise

(Area in lakh acres)

Sl.	*States/UTs*	*Area Consolidated*	*Period of Reporting*
1.	Andhra Pradesh	8.18*	1/92
2.	Bihar	96.05*	5/99
3.	Gujarat	69.88	6/99
4.	Haryana	104.38	5/99
5.	Himachal Pradesh	29.91	8/99
6.	Jammu & Kashmir	1.37*	3/73
7.	Karnataka	26.76**	
8.	Madhya Pradesh	95.53	
9.	Maharashtra	526.50†	1/93
10.	Orissa	26.74	6/99
11.	Punjab	103.74	8/99
12.	Rajasthan	42.30‡	
13.	Uttar Pradesh	481.63	5/99
14.	Delhi	2.33	9/92
	Total	1615.30	As on 10/99

* Scheme has been discontinued (w.e.f. July, 92 in Bihar)
** Consolidation of holding Act, 1966 has been repeated in 1991
† Implementation of the scheme stopped w.e.f. 1.4.93
‡ Scheme discontinued from 1965
SOURCE: Annual Report, 1999-2000, Ministry of Rural Development

Small and Marginal Farmers and Landless Labourers

There has been impressive progress in the development of institutions and services designed to support agriculture. These include:

(a) Extension services and block administration;
(b) Credit provided by commercial banks;
(c) Credit provided by cooperative institutions;
(d) Agricultural research;
(e) Marketing and processing services.

By and large, the benefits of these institutions and services have been availed of more fully in areas which have irrigation and assured rainfall. Even in these areas, farmers with viable holdings have been able to derive much larger benefits than those with small and marginal holdings or cultivating land as tenants. Landless labourers have yet to be reached except through rural works programmes. Therefore, beyond enforcement of land reform legislation, the central issue in agrarian change is to find ways to strengthen the economy of small and marginal farmers and tenant cultivators and to bring landless labourers into the mainstream of development. The agricultural census of 1990-91 shows a marked deterioration in the numbers of small and marginal holdings compared even to as recent an event as the census of 1985-86 (Table 9.6).

In states under heavy population pressure, the average holding, already small, has become even more uneconomic to operate. Both in consequences of population growth and effects of land reform, the numbers of small and marginal holdings may go on increasing. Through expansion of irrigation and increase in area under high yielding varieties, under favourable conditions, a somewhat larger proportion of small holdings may become viable. But the vast majority of small holdings and most marginal holdings will continue to be deficit units. This is part of the explanation for the increase in area leased in

Table 9.6 Distribution of Operational Holdings—All India

No. of holdings: '000' Number
Area, '000' ha.
Average size: Hectare.

Category of Holdings	*No of operational Holding*		*Area operated*		*Size of operational holdings*	
	1985-86	*1990-91*	*1985-86*	*1990-91*	*1985-86*	*1990-91*
1	2	3	4	5	6	7
Marginal	56147	63389	22042	24894	0.39	0.39
(Less than 1 ha.)	(57.8)	(59.4)	(13.4)	(15.0)		
Small	17922	20092	25708	28827	1.43	1.43
(1.0 to 2.0 ha.)	(18.4)	(18.8)	(15.6)	(17.4)		
Semi-medium	13252	13923	36666	38375	2.77	2.76
(2.0 to 4.0 ha)	(13.6)	(13.1)	(22.3)	(23.2)		
Medium	7916	7580	47144	44752	5.96	5.9
(4.0 to 10.0 ha.)	(8.2)	(7.1)	(28.6)	(27.0)		
Large	1918	1654	33002	28659	17.21	17.33
(10.0 ha. and above)	(2.0)	(1.6)	(20.1)	(17.3)		
All holdings	97155	106637	164562	165507	1.69	1.57
	(100.0)	(100.0	(100.0)	(100.0)		

Note: Figures in brackets indicate the percentage of respective column to total percentages are on the basis of absolute values.

SOURCE: Agricultural Census Division, Ministry of Agriculture.

by relatively larger farmers from small and marginal farmers. This has been noted as one of the consequences of the `green revolution'. Together, in 1990-91, small and marginal holdings accounted for 78 per cent of the number of holdings and 32.2 per cent of the area. Position regarding statewise number, area operated and average size of operational holdings is shown in Tables 9.7, 9.8 and 9.9.

Clearly, even among cultivators, there is intense poverty in the bottom rungs; at the same time, there is a high degree of concentration of land with medium and large holdings. No conceivable land reform legislation will materially alter this situation. The problem can only be dealt with by reorganisation of agriculture as an industry. Within the existing pattern of organisation, here and there additional relief or support can be given but, except in some favoured areas, there can be no solution either to the problem of inequitable distribution of services or to the problem of poverty for the bulk of the cultivators.

However soundly conceived from some angles, the development strategy followed in India has thrown over increasing numbers on to agriculture. The labour reserve within agriculture has increased steadily. The competition for available work between labour available within the cultivator's family and landless labour seeking wage employment is certainly becoming more intense in most regions in the country. Therefore, all claims by central or state authorities, based on the amount of credit or other assets given to individual households, about decline in number below the poverty line must be taken with extreme caution. Within the rural community, marginal farmers, tenant cultivators, rural artisans and landless labourers form one great mass of poverty, one great continuum, with shades of difference between one subgroup and another, depending upon the total economic circumstances of each region and factors like caste and tribe.

Accentuating political and social factors apart, in the rural situation as it has developed and is now developing, there is reason to expect that tensions will go on increasing. Within the traditional mould of castes and sub-castes, these tensions all too easily take the form of inter-caste conflicts resorting to violence. The forces at work being of a fundamental nature, the rural problem must also be seen and dealt within fundamental terms.

The problem of landless labour, of the mass of small and marginal farmers, and of tenant cultivators and rural artisans, though also requiring specific action directed to the conditions of each group, have to be seen and dealt with as a whole.

One striking trend is the progressive decline in the average size of land holdings due to demographic pressure, and subdivision and fragmentation of holdings. Other salient features of the agrarian structure are:

(a) The extent of landlessness and inequality in land ownership have not changed much; (b) the proportion of households not operating

Table 9.7 State-wise Number of Operational Holdings by Major Size-groups (1990-91)

(No. in '000)

State	Marginal	Small	Semi-medium	Medium	Large	All holdings
1	2	3	4	5	6	7
Andhra Pradesh	5211	1972	1345	644	118	9290
Arunachal Pradesh	16	17	30	26	5	94
Assam	1521	560	343	95	5	2523
Bihar	10193	1438	945	351	39	12966
Goa	58	7	4	2	1	72
Gujarat	924	915	890	669	118	3517
Haryana	622	304	336	222	46	1530
Himachal Pradesh	532	166	94	36	6	834
Jammu & Kashmir	902	197	98	20	1	1217
Karnataka	2262	1586	1163	636	129	5776
Kerala	5016	280	98	21	3	5418
Madhya Pradesh	3136	1917	1738	1287	323	8401
Maharashtra	3275	2728	2126	1171	171	9470
Manipur	69	49	21	3	Neg	142
Meghalaya	59	51	46	13	1	171
Mizoram	29	23	9	1	Neg	61
Nagaland	13	21	26	47	33	142
Orissa	2118	1035	594	186	15	3948
Punjab	296	204	289	261	67	1117
Rajasthan	1517	1019	1061	1017	493	5107
Sikkim	26	11	9	5	1	52
Tamil Nadu	5848	1275	618	228	31	7999
Tripura	217	69	28	4	Neg	318
Uttar Pradesh	14819	3118	1543	548	45	20074
West Bengal	4639	1107	457	79	1	6284
A & N Island	2	2	3	2	Neg	10
Chandigarh	1	Neg	Neg	Neg	Neg	2
D & N Haveli	6	4	2	1	Neg	13
Daman & Diu	3	Neg	Neg	Neg	Neg	4
Delhi	26	8	5	3	Neg	42
Lakshdweep	6	Nrg	Neg	Neg	Neg	6
Pondicherry	26	5	3	1	Neg	35
All-India	63389	20092	13923	7580	1654	106637

Neg = Negligible

Totals may not tally exactly due to rounding off.

SOURCE: Agricultural census, 1990-91

Table 9.8 State-wise Area Operated by Major Size-groups (1990-91)

(Area in '000' ha.)

State/UTs	*Marginal*	*Small*	*Semi-medium*	*Medium*	*Large*	*All holdings*
1	*2*	*3*	*4*	*5*	*6*	*7*
Andhra Pradesh	2369	2827	3640	3777	1848	14460
Arunachal Pradesh	10	26	84	147	82	350
Assam	607	784	918	492	404	3205
Bihar	3591	1954	2576	1982	640	10743
Goa	19	11	9	9	19	67
Gujarat	489	1343	2515	4005	1941	10292
Haryana	295	463	944	1300	709	3711
Himachal Pradesh	215	235	258	205	97	1010
Jammu & Kashmir	347	272	264	108	23	1014
Karnataka	1072	2308	3200	3771	1971	12321
Kerala	865	383	255	114	178	1796
Madhya Pradesh	1409	2783	4838	7772	5309	22111
Maharashtra	1618	3983	5880	6856	2588	20925
Manipur	38	67	54	71	1	175
Mizoram	18	36	25	4	Neg	84
Meghalaya	32	68	117	71	13	302
Nagaland	9	30	76	298	556	968
Orissa	1045	1426	1561	1012	252	5296
Punjab	164	328	842	1622	1077	4033
Rajasthan	725	1469	3021	6334	9422	20971
Sikkim	11	19	27	31	22	111
Tamil Nadu	2118	1794	1687	1301	574	7474
Tripura	87	106	77	18	20	308
Uttar Pradesh	5653	4391	4206	3042	694	17986
West Bengal	2064	1694	1269	426	203	5656
A & N Island	1	3	8	9	5	27
Chandigarh	1	Neg	1	1	Neg	3
D & N Haveli	3	5	5	5	3	22
Daman & Diu	1	1	Neg	Neg	Neg	3
Delhi	7	8	12	16	5	49
Lakshdweep	2	Neg	Neg	Neg	Neg	3
Pondicherry	9	7	7	6	4	33
All-India	24894	28827	38375	44752	28659	165507

Neg = Negligible

Totals may not tally exactly due to rounding off.

SOURCE: Agricultural census, 1990-91

Table 9.9 State-wise Average size of Operational Holdings by Major Size-groups (1990-91)

(In hectare)

State	Marginal	Small	Semi-medium	Medium	Large	All holdings
1	2	3	4	5	6	7
Andhra Pradesh	0.45	1.43	2.71	5.86	15.66	1.56
Arunachal Pradesh	0.63	1.53	2.80	5.65	16.40	3.71
Assam	0.40	1.40	2.68	5.18	80.80	1.27
Bihar	0.35	1.36	2.73	5.65	16.41	0.83
Goa	0.33	1.38	2.25	4.50	19.00	0.93
Gujarat	0.53	1.47	2.83	5.99	16.45	2.93
Haryana	0.47	1.52	2.81	5.86	15.41	2.43
Himachal Pradesh	0.40	1.42	2.74	5.69	16.17	1.21
Jammu & Kashmir	0.39	1.38	2.69	5.40	23.09	0.83
Karnataka	0.47	1.46	2.75	5.93	15.28	2.13
Kerala	0.17	1.37	2.60	5.43	59.33	0.33
Madhya Pradesh	0.45	1.45	2.78	6.04	16.44	2.63
Maharashtra	0.49	1.46	2.77	5.86	15.13	2.21
Manipur	0.55	1.37	2.57	5.00	12.16	1.23
Meghalaya	0.54	1.33	2.54	5.46	13.00	1.77
Mizoram	0.62	1.57	2.78	4.00	150.00	1.38
Nagaland	0.69	1.43	2.92	6.34	16.85	6.82
Orissa	0.49	1.38	2.63	5.45	16.80	1.34
Punjab	0.55	1.61	2.91	6.21	16.07	3.61
Rajasthan	0.48	1.44	2.85	6.23	19.11	4.11
Sikkim	0.42	1.73	3.00	6.20	22.00	2.09
Tamil Nadu	0.36	1.41	2.73	5.72	18.52	0.93
Tripura	0.40	1.54	2.75	4.50	20.00	0.97
Uttar Pradesh	0.38	1.41	2.73	5.55	15.42	0.90
West Bengal	0.45	1.53	2.78	5.39	203.00	0.90
All-India	0.39	1.43	2.76	5.90	17.33	1.55

SOURCE: Agricultural Census Division, Ministry of Agriculture.

any land, though much higher than that not owning any land, has not changed much; (c) among those who operate same land, inequality has increased; (d) the incidence of tenancy (in terms of proportion of households leasing in land as well as the proportion of area leased in) has declined; and (e) the proportion of rural labour force dependent on wage labour, as well as the ratio of agricultural wage labour is getting increasingly casualized.

The overall index of land concentration has not changed much, implying that widespread dispossession has not taken place in the wake of progressive commercialisation and rapid technological progress as originally apprehended. Nevertheless, an operational holding has to attain a minimum size in order to be economically viable. A proliferation of small holdings at the cost of larger ones may indeed retard the growth of agriculture. In fact, the typical operational holding is getting too small to accumulate a significant surplus for reinvestment within agriculture, there is not much that can be done to arrest this downward drift of households in the land status hierarchy. The incidence of marginal holdings is already so high in Orissa, Tamil Nadu, West Bengal and Bihar that no conceivable land distribution measure (short of collectivisation) would score to bring them up above viability.

Computerisation of Land Records

The Centrally Sponsored Scheme on Computerisation of Land Records was started in 1988-89 with 100 per cent financial assistance as a pilot project in eight districts, viz. Rangareddy (A.P.), Sonitpur (Assam), Singhbhum (Bihar), Gandhinagar (Gujarat), Morena (M.P.). Wardha (Maharashtra), Mayurbhanj (Orissa), and Dungarpur (Rajasthan) with a view to removing problems inherent in manual system of maintenance and updating of land records and meeting requirements of various group of users. It was decided that efforts should be made to computerise core data contained in land records, so as to assist development planning and to make records accessible to people/ planners/administrators.

The main objectives of the Scheme are:

(i) Computerisation of ownership and plot-wise details for issue of timely and accurate copy of the record of rights to the land owners.

(ii) To achieve low cost, easily reproducible storage media for reliable preservation for long time.

(iii) To have a fast and efficient retrieval of information, both graphical and textual.

(iv) Creation of a land information system and database for Agricultural Census.

Progress During Eighth Plan

During the Eighth Five Year Plan Period, the scheme was approved as a separate Centrally Sponsored Scheme on Computerisation of Land Records. The total expenditure under the scheme was Rs. 59.42 crore by covering 299 new districts and providing additional funds for ongoing pilot projects. Thus, by the end of the Eighth Plan, 323 districts in the country were brought under the scheme with an expenditure of Rs. 64.44 crore.

The scheme is being implemented since 1994-95 in joint collaboration with the National Informatics Centre (NIC), which is responsible for supply, installation and maintenance of hardware, software and other peripherals. NIC is also providing training to revenue officials and technical support for implementation. The Ministry is providing funds to State Governments for site preparation, data entry work and miscellaneous expenditure. But so far the scheme has made little progress. Several factors like, power constraints, lack of trained manpower and bureaucratic procedures involved at various stages, are stated to be responsible for the unsatisfactory situation. In the interest of the small and marginal land holders, it is necessary that computerisation must be given a top priority. Updating of land records can be expedited even without computerisation through the involvement of Panchayat Institutions and the local revenue functionaries.

CRITICAL APPRAISAL

A report prepared by the All-India Congress Forum for socialist action (now dissolved) after a critical analysis of the action taken by the various states on implementation of land reforms comes to the conclusion that non-implementation of land reforms is primarily due to the attitude of leaders of the state governments. Halfhearted attempts of land reform, with the state government deliberately leaving loopholes in agrarian law to nullify its full implementation, have created an explosive situation in rural India. The report suggested a programme of action comprising 26 urgent measures including immediate abolition of all intermediary tenures. One-third of the Indian population lives in "absolute poverty". Over 16 crores of people (16 per cent of the total population) eke out an existence of a subhuman level with a per capita expenditure of less than Rs. 15 per month in the rural areas. Those below the poverty line have a per capita expenditure of only Rs. 13. The situation of poverty, according to the report, is a direct consequence of the failure on the agrarian front. This has brought the kisans already to the edge of an economic precipice.

The agrarian legislation according to the study is "vague and seeded" with loopholes which had led to the "ultra-reactionary" landlord and the village `arthya' entrenching themselves in agrarian life. The abolition of zamindari had not brought the needed relief to the tillers as intermediaries had falsified village records by bribing village officials and otherwise circumventing the law. In the resultant situation, after abolition of intermediaries, only 30 lakh of tillers in India could acquire ownership of over just 2.8 million hectares of land. Millions of tillers were left out and could not become owners after land reforms.

The ludicrous character of the implementation of the ceiling programme would be evident from the fact that whereas in the vast state of undivided U.P. only 2,40,534 acres of land was acquired, in the small state of Jammu and Kashmir as much as 4,50,000 acres of land was made available for redistribution.

The Centre and the Planning Commission are now of the view that the existing tenancies should be made non-resumable and penalties must be provided for "wrongful evictions". This will require amending legislation. Some of the other related problems are the lack of land records in some states like Kerala, high rents, and delay in the settlement of landless labourers on waste lands. The problem of landless agricultural workers looms large because they constitute nearly a fourth of the country's total population.

Land ceiling and redistribution of the surplus to the landless has been the burden of the reformists. Early in the sixties many states then under Congress rule did, in fact, enact laws to limit the size of personal holdings, the ceiling ranging from 8 to 12 and more "standard hectares". Against the background of some landlords owning even 400 hectares and more, these limits were quite radical indeed. But the surplus (on paper) thrown up for the entire country was barely 1.0 million odd hectares. The comparatively small surplus becomes even more insignificant, when it is noted that less than half of it has been redistributed even by 1971, a decade after the enactment of the laws. And yet, according to the Planning Commission's projection of the possible surplus for the 18 states it studied, with some of the bigger states left out, on the basis of a 12 hectares ceiling, was as much as 14.7 million hectares-almost enough as it were to give every landless family in Indian villages a hectare of land.

As for the administration that has ultimately to implement the law there is as yet no ground to believe that it has changed and in consequence the seventies would have any more abundance of surplus land for redistribution than that of the sixties. Defective land records, official corruption, political soft-pedalling at every stage in the face of pressures, not to speak of the proverbial red tape of the Revenue Department would perhaps lead to emerge another mouse from all the Himalayan labour.

Consequence of Implementation

Supposing that the implementation of the lower ceiling laws are really made more effective and speedier in enforcement, an inescapable result will be proliferation of small, uneconomic holdings, often in the hands of those not fitted to benefit by the new farm technology. The oft-cited Farm Management Studies that made the observation that the gross output per acre was actually higher in the case of small farms and that productivity per acre decreased with the size of the holding may not be valid in the case of these new farmers of very small holdings, created out of the resourceless rural labourers.

Should the ceiling exercise be aimed not merely at cutting down to size of the remnant of big landlords but also at levelling up small holdings to make them economic and viable, by restricting the redistribution of the surplus land to them, it would make better sense.

But the primary approach of the committee is that because land is scarce and is a limited resource, it must be "rationed" like all other goods in short supply and in general demand. What they do not see, in their socialistic favour, is that rationing implies something (and an equal measure) of what is rationed to everyone in need. And it is not the planners' professed objective to seize all land in the country and ration it in microscopic bits among everyone in the rural areas. Nor can they ever contemplate so calamitous a proposal, unless the aim is to plunge the country into stark famine.

It would therefore appear that even with a more competent enforcement of the ceilings, results would not be commensurate with the effort. Only a small fraction of the millions of landless can be given uneconomic holdings. And they will have to be followed up by a massive programme of aid, technical and financial, if the land taken away from a productive farmer and given to a landless labourer is tc remain productive. It cannot also be ignored that the land declared surplus is often of poor quality, "the rejects" as it were of the bigger holders forced to give up something. Hence, whatever else we hope to achieve, it cannot be either more production of food, or even minimum holdings for enough number of the landless to make a dent on rural poverty. It is also their considered finding that owner-cultivators in sizeable farms have been able to make them a profitable proposition, thanks to the new technological advances and their capacity to benefit them.

The Japanese Example

The post-war land reforms in Japan which have been claimed to be the most successful in history are often quoted in India for purposes of emulation. It must, however, be noted that the conditions in Japan were entirely different. Out of an estimated population of 80 million, 16 million (20 per cent) only were in the rural sector. Even this small population was slowly becoming smaller because of the migration of workers to industries in urban areas. In India it is the other way round; 74 per cent live in the rural areas and there has not been an appreciable shift to urban areas. Since the migration to cities had already started in a big way in Japan by 1945, the agricultural structure could withstand the shake-up.

Besides, the Japanese reforms were so drastic that a third of the total cultivated land became available as surplus and was distributed among the tenants. In India the land reforms are likely to yield only 3 percent of sown area as surplus, unless the Ceiling Acts are made retroactive from 1958 which is extremely difficult. But even then only about 10 per cent of the area is likely to be available for distribution if the ceilings are reduced drastically to about 2 to 4 hectares.

Reverting to the Japanese economy, during 1945-49 there was a hyperinflation; price of rice which was 150 yen for 150 kg in 1945 rose to 4,600 yen in 1949--a rise of more than 30 times. Therefore the tenants were able to repay the total value of land selling only 5 per cent of the annual yield. The problem of compensation disappeared. This was an exceptionally favourable situation for the tenants which is not going to have a parallel anywhere, let alone in India.

There had been a good deal of controversy about the ceiling limit to be placed on irrigated land from private and public sources as well. It was finally decided that the ceiling range for the best category of land with assured irrigation and yielding at least two crops a year will be 10 to 80 acres. Allowances will be made for the next category of land irrigated from private sources by equating 0.5 hectare of such land with 0.4 hectare with irrigation from public sources. All the same the ceiling for such land irrigated from private sources will not exceed 7.2 hectares.

The Central Land Reforms Committee as well as the Congress Committee has suggested disregarding all the transfers and petitions made after September 26,1970. It was then agreed in principle to lower the ceilings and disregard all transfers of land only after January 24,1971 (this was the date when the Congress manifesto for legislatures was issued). Mr. C. Subramaniam, the then Planning Minister, had also suggested that instead of taking into account area which would be irrigated now or in future by private tubewells it would be more appropriate to fix a lower ceiling for the entire tract where there was water potentiality. As against all this the Union Ministry of Agriculture advised all the state governments that all the private irrigation works constructed after August 15, 1972 in dry lands would not be considered while classifying land for ceiling with the sole purpose of giving a big push to the rabi production drive.

Agrarian Equality

The pattern of land ownership in India is manifestly nonegalitarian. Seventy-eight per cent of the landholders own only 24 per cent of the cultivated area, while 22 per cent own 76 per cent of the land. Over the last two decades, however, this has become somewhat less inequitable. The National Sample Survey data for 1953-54, 1961-62 and 1971-72, would show that though land reform has not brought about profound structural changes in Indian agriculture, it has not been wholly inconsequential either. The bigger holders with 15 acres or more of land accounted for 10 per cent of the land owning households and 52.5 per cent of the area in 1953-54. By 1971-72, they accounted for only 5.4 per cent of holders and 39.4 per cent of the acreage. On the other hand, small holders in the ownership range of 1 to 5 acres improved their position from 15 per cent of the acreage to 28 per cent in the same period, while their proportion of total landholders dropped somewhat from 36 per cent to 34 per cent. Medium holders also improved their share of the area from 31 per cent to 36 per cent, while their proportion dropped from 23 per cent to 17 per cent. Obviously, this means that the proportion of marginal holders increased- from 31 per cent to 44 per cent, while their share of land continued to be miniscule, 7.4 per cent in 1953-54 and 1.6 per cent in 1971-72. Thus, while the small and medium farmers have emerged as more powerful economic forces over this period, the ranks of the poorest have also been swelling.

These changes could be attributed to three sets of factors, namely, market processes, institutional changes and demographic pressures. Movements both up and down the ladder have been seen although at the bottom end of the spectrum, a greater influence of the downward movement could perhaps be discerned.

In view of the slowing of the agricultural growth in the last decade, further emphasis on egalitarian distribution of land might be questioned. But, experiences elsewhere shows that agricultural development has been accelerated, rather than slowed down, by redistribution of land. A more equitable distribution leads to greater subsistence production, even when technological changes is slow, as is the case with rice in India. Emphasis on equality alone, however, is no guarantee of higher productivity, while this can create a more conducive environment for the adoption of a superior technology, its actual adoption will depend on supportive systems, such as credit, distribution of inputs and extension. Our record on these factors is not as greatly in favour of the small farmers as are the structural changes. As recent events show, the emerging conflict is between the medium and small holders, not on economic and political fronts. If the structural changes in the distribution of assets are to lead to a more egalitarian distribution of incomes as well as power, greater emphasis on the supportive systems is called for.

Need of Change in Policy

There are two main instruments of land reform, viz. tenancy legislation and land ceilings. These two instruments have very different effect depending on the conditions on the ground. A number of state governments have now been considering amendment of the guidelines on land reforms. They observed that protecting tenancy per se sometimes implied protecting large tenants just as attacking all those who leased out land also implied attacking small farmers who had leased out land because they did not have the resources to cultivate. Further, in predominantly small-farmer agriculture, the ceilings were ineffective as very few farmers owned land that could be considered surplus.

The tenancy-ceiling package also prevented farmers from adopting some large-scale technologies. The ceiling prevented them from owning large enough farms to do so and the abolition of tenancy in the state like Karnataka prevented tenants from leasing in sufficient land to create large operational holdings.

In these situation the need for new guidelines has become paramount. These guidelines could be to ensure that the opportunities to develop the rural economy are enhanced in a way that benefits all sections of rural society, particularly the poor. Among the measures required would be a recognition that modern tenancy could be a means of increasing the scale of agricultural operations without adversely affecting equity, the large tenant farms in dryland areas can be given incentives to invest in watershed management, drip irrigation or even tank irrigation, these farmers would then be able to offset any decline in public investment in agriculture. Since the objectives would vary from region to region, the guidelines need to be flexible enough to allow states to adopt them to local conditions.

CHAPTER 10

Agricultural Finance

Agriculture is a science, a craft, and a business. Land itself is, or course, absolutely immobile, and capital sunk in land tends to assume more permanent or fixed form than in manufactures, and the supply of capital by way of either addition or subtraction is consequently less elastic than in other industries. Agricultural credit extended to farmers is of three types: short-term to purchase seeds, manure, fodder, etc., medium term to purchase cattle and implements and long term finance for making permanent improvements in land for reclamation and for constructing wells and buildings. To meet the credit needs of the farmer, the Government of India established a separate department of agricultural credit in the Reserve Bank of India as early as in 1935.

The agricultural credit system includes commercial and private agencies and government-owned institutions. But the real difficulty is that the cultivators are poor and illiterate and, in most cases, unable to offer adequate security. Agriculture cannot develop unless credit facilities are available to the peasantry in areas which are not viable. The supply of credit to such areas will be highly effective in rehabilitating the agriculturists. The need for such credit has become all the more important in the context of new strategy and the introduction of high yield raising technologies. No doubt there are various agencies to finance the farmers, but in India the role of cooperatives cannot be overemphasised.

THE NEED FOR AN INSTITUTIONAL CREDIT AGENCY

For progressive agriculture adequate agricultural credit facility is most essential. It is a fact that the credit requirements in agriculture cannot be met by private individual resources alone even when the money lender is not fettered by any legal restrictions in his credit operations. Moreover, profit being the sole guiding consideration of the private agency, credit from the money lender cannot be canalised to uses which are socially most desirable nor can it be made available to farmers who are not creditworthy under strict banking rules. The returns from capital investment on certain types of agricultural improvements are so low that these improvements can only be taken up if credit is made available at exceptionally low rates of interest and for a long term. As the agriculturists need credit at specially favourable terms, an effective control over its use becomes a social obligation. That is why the public and expert opinions always favour an institutional agency for agricultural credit. Institutional credit system has actually been developed with liberal state assistance in most countries of the world during the twentieth century.

Another strong point in support of the institutional system is that agricultural credit is no more interpreted in the narrow sense of mere granting of loans. It has a much broader connotation now and combines in itself both technical guidance and planning of the farm business. The farmer is not only to be helped with a loan but he has also to be given the necessary guidance to make the most effective use of it so that he may maximise his earnings from the land. The view that the agricultural improvement and banking are two quite different activities and should be handled separately, is slowly losing ground. It is increasingly felt that, if the farmer who is taught the improved methods of farming, is not provided with the means for carrying them out, no useful purpose will be served by merely expanding the agricultural extension services. Therefore, the credit services and the agriculture extension service in other countries work in close collaboration. There can be no doubt that to dispense with this type of credit among the farmers and also for its recovery there cannot be a more suitable organization than that of village cooperatives. The idea of cooperation, particularly in agriculture, is inherently sound. If life has been lacking in agricultural cooperatives so far, it is mainly due to the poor management for which lack of proper internal leadership is chiefly responsible. This fact and the absence of a well defined cooperative loan policy together explain the paradox of funds lying idle with cooperatives and agriculture suffering for want of finance.

However, for improving the management through either the development of internal leadership or official assistance, the situation is now more favourable than ever before. Under various schemes such as community projects, national extension blocks, and reorientation of education with greater agricultural bias as in U.P., the services of a very large number of trained village and group level workers have become available for proper guidance and even actual management of the village cooperatives. The old controversy of officials *vs.* non-officials, more of a legacy of alien rule, has now to be shelved and in the early stages of their growth it is highly desirable that the village cooperatives take full advantage of the services of trained workers whether officials or non-officials. In real life, there is no 'free lunch', more so in a market economy where one has to rely on personal income or loans to meet one's demand for finance. Along with the evolution of market economy, evolved the system of savings and investment/loan/credit. History of economic development runs coterminus with the investments made both by the government and the private sector in productive assets.

Even though the development process is a post independence phenomenon, one of the few exceptions to this hypothesis is the credit facilities for agricultural sector. Introducing credit cooperatives in its institutionalized form as we understand today, were the culmination of a series of steps taken by the then government during the last three decades of 19th century to combat usury rural indebtedness and alienation of land, all of which were eating into the vitals of an already stagnant rural economy. The earlier steps comprised providing state loans known as 'Taccavi', legislative steps for debt relief, curbing usury and alienation of land. These proved to be mere sops.

By then, alternative methods for providing rural credit through 'self-help' and 'mutual-help' working so successfully in many parts of Europe, caught the eye of policy makers of the country and steps were taken to replicate the model with suitable modifications to adapt to our country's needs. After careful studies by sending officers abroad the broad consensus was to introduce Raiffessein type of cooperative society. It was felt that this would need legislative support as a sequel to which, would Cooperative Credit Societies Act, 1904 was passed resulting in the emergence of cooperative credit system as the premier source of rural credit—which tradition is kept even till date. Winding its ways through several hiccups like the great depression of thirties and adopting modifications as a result of several studies and recommendations of committees, rural/farm credit through cooperatives continued its journey forward till independence.

A firm basis was laid for further progress in this sector by the report/ recommendations of Rural Banking Enquiry Committee (1950) and All India Rural Credit Survey Committee 1969. These Committees found several inadequacies in the system, mainly that credit given was far short of requirements; it was untargeted and not related to specific productive purpose materializing in the annual harvest; and mainly it failed to reach the right people. The Committee recommended state partnership, effective integration of credit with marketing and processing and management of credit system through adequately trained personnel. Along with the cooperative credit institution, State Bank of India also was asked to supplement the efforts of the cooperatives in meeting the rural credit requirements. This got a fillip with the nationalisation of 14 major private banks and later by Regional Rural Banks and NABARD. Today, commercial banks with an extensive network of their rural/semi-urban branches, are major players in rural credit.

Credit Agencies

Decades ago the main agencies which supplied credit to the agriculturists primarily were big landlords and money lenders. In fact, the non-institutional private creditors dominated rural credit. Institutional agencies like cooperatives and commercial banks played insignificant role in providing much needed credit for increasing agricultural production. Lately, it was realized that timely and adequate credit to the farmers was very crucial input for modernizing Indian agriculture. Consequently, the policy on agricultural credit continues to be one of providing adequate and timely credit to farmers through institutional agencies like cooperatives, commercial banks and regional rural banks to support agriculture and allied activities. The main objective of the policy is to enable the farmers specially the small and marginal farmers and other weaker sections to adopt modern technology and improved agricultural practices for increasing production and productivity.

There is generally a three-tier structure of cooperative in most of the states for the delivery of short and medium term credit to farmers. This consists of the State Cooperative Banks (SCBs) at the apex level, the District Central Cooperative Banks (DCCBs) at the District level and Primary Agricultural Credit Societies (PACS) at base level. Investment credit is provided to the farmers by Land Development Banks (LDBs) The National Bank for Agriculture and Rural Development (NABARD) is the nodal institution which provides refinance for agricultural credit. The network of the multi-agency system meant for agricultural credit is as Table 10.1.

Table 10.1 Agricultural Credit Agencies

(As on 31-3-1998)

Sl. No.	*Name of the Institution*	*Number*
1.	State Cooperative Banks (SCBs)	28
2.	District Central Cooperative Banks (DCCBs)	367
3.	Primary Agricultural Credit Societies (PACS)	92,000
4.	State Land Development Banks (SLDBs) / Agricultural & Rural Development Banks (ARDBs)	2585
5.	Regional Rural Banks (RRBs)	196 (with 14191 branches)
6.	Commercial Banks (CBs)	46,691 (Branches)

Government also provides financial assistance by way of loans to farmers under (i) Improvement Loans Act of 1883, and (ii) Agriculturists Loans Act, 1884. These loans are known as taccavi loans. The former authorizes the grant of long-term loans for permanent improvement of land. The loan is generally given for periods extending up to 25 years on the security of landed property. It is repayable in equal annual instalments. Under the latter act, short and medium term loans are given for current agricultural needs. These loans are repayable after the harvest. Loans granted under the two acts form a small proportion of the total loans. The system of taccavi loans, beside being inadequate, suffers from many defects. For instance, the method of distribution and collection is defective and very rigid. Delays in granting loans, extreme strictness in realisation, and administrative inelasticity have made these loans very unpopular and rather ineffective in serving the need of the farmers.

Rural Credit Cooperative Institutions (RCCIs)

The Rural Credit Cooperative Institutions (RCCIs), one of the strong arms of Rural Financial Institutions (RFIs), have made significant strides in delivering credit for agriculture and rural development. Beginning with the first decade of the twentieth century, the cooperative movement has taken deep-roots and culminated in a massive rural cooperative institutional structure. Today, cooperatives form the major component of the rural credit system in India. Of the total credit disbursed (including short-term, medium-term and long-term) disbursed during the year 1998-99, the share of cooperatives was almost 45 per cent. The share of commercial and regional rural banks (RRBs), the other two institutional players in the rural credit market together was 55 per cent. In other words, cooperatives still constitute a dominant segment of the rural credit market. However, it would be pertinent here to study the genesis of the cooperative credit societies and their growth. The idea of using cooperatives in India as a means of combating rural indebtedness and supplying credit was first suggested by Sir Frederick Nicholson in 1897. He pleaded forcefully for the introduction of cooperative credit societies in India.

For this purpose, the first Cooperative Credit Societies Act was introduced in 1904 on the recommendation of the Law Committee appointed by the Government of India under the chairmanship of Edward Law. The cooperative movement in India was the sequel to the move against private money lenders, notorious for charging exorbitant rates of interest and oppressive practices forcing the peasant borrowers into perpetual state of indebtedness.

As it was felt that the cooperative credit societies Act, 1904 prevented the formation of other non-credit societies, in 1912, another legislation was enacted to enable formation of non-credit cooperatives of producers and consumers and central organizations like cooperative unions, central cooperative banks (CCBs), etc. In 1919, the responsibility for cooperative legislation was transferred to states/provinces which gave adequate stimulus to provincial states to enact independent cooperative legislation. By the 1920s, the cooperative credit system emerged as the premier institutional agency in the country for the provision of agricultural credit. But there was a serious set back in the growth of this agency in the 1930s with the onset of economic depression and also there was mounting overdues. The recovery of the economy in 1940s, however, resuscitated the cooperative institutions. Efforts were made to develop rural credit cooperative institutions as the exclusive institutional agency for providing rural credit.

Maclagan Committee (1915) urged a separate institutional structure for providing long-term loans to the farmers. However, it was in 1926 that the idea of organising Land Mortgage Banks (LMBs) was finalised and was later endorsed by the Royal Commission on Agriculture in India (1928) as well as the Indian Central Banking Enquiry Committee (1931). On the eve of independence there were five central land mortgage banks (CLMBs) operating through 284 primary LMBs (PLMBs).

All-India Rural Credit Survey Committee (RCSC), 1954

Despite all these efforts for about half a century, at the beginning of the plan era i.e. 1951-52, the rural cooperative credit societies provided only 3.3 per cent of the total credit requirements. In order to find out the reasons for the slow progress of this institutional agency and suggest remedial measures, at the instance of the government of India, the Reserve Bank of India set up the All-India Rural Credit Survey Committee (RCSC) with a committee of directions. The Reserve Bank of India pointed out that the cooperative credit movement was inadequate in three important respects. Firstly, there were large parts of the country which were not covered. Secondly, even in those areas where the cooperative system was extended there were large sections of agriculturists, particularly medium and small cultivators, who were not its members. Thirdly, even those who were members of cooperative societies, met the bulk of their credit requirements from sources other than cooperatives.

Analysing the cause of these inadequacies of cooperative credit, the All India Rural Credit Survey Report (1954) stated that functional, structural or administrative defects, existence of small-sized primary societies on the basis of one society for one village, generally with unlimited liability, predominance of single purpose societies as distinguished from multipurpose societies, lack of education, inadequacy of training, deficiency in roads, storage and other vital economic requirements and official sponsorship of the cooperative movement, were responsible for the tardy growth of credit cooperative societies. The more fundamental causes of the failure were economic and socioeconomic and were related to certain basic weaknesses in the rural structure. The most fundamental of these causes of the failure of the cooperative movement was the competition, virtual opposition, which the cooperative credit and other types of societies had to face from the relatively powerful private agencies. The ubiquity of these private agencies, their widespread network from village to town, and in particular, the financial strength which they derived from connection with some of the most powerful elements in the urban economy, were all important factors which placed the cooperative institutions at a relatively greater disadvantage.

Recommendations of the RCSC

The RCSC made a number of far-reaching recommendations. However, the committee's most outstanding contribution was keeping up the nation's commitment to the cooperation with its most famous verdict `cooperation has failed but it must succeed'. The committee also called for an integrated scheme of the reorganization of the system-based on three fundamental principles: (i) state partnership at different levels, (ii) coordination between credit and other economic activities specifically marketing and processing, and (iii) management of cooperatives through adequately trained and efficient personnel who were responsive to the needs of the rural population. All these efforts led to a massive expansion of the rural cooperative credit institutions (RCCIs), organized basically by government employees as state participation in cooperation at all levels was significantly emphasised.

The main lines of reorganization and development as recommended by RCSC were: (i) Reorganization and strengthening of primary cooperative societies, supplying not only agricultural credit but also rural industrial credit and also meeting, to a limited extent, the consumption needs of agricultural labourers, handicraftsman, etc., besides, those of the member cultivators. At the apex level, financial, administrative and technical strengthening of State Cooperative Banks (SCBs), and at the district level by either establishing branches of SCBs or expansion and consolidation of central banks; coordination with LMBs, and organization of new central and primary LMBs, (ii) Progressive organization, on a cooperative basis, of marketing and processing with the needed financial, administrative and technical assistance from the state, and the development of storage and warehousing through state partnered organizations, (iii) Progressive organization, on a cooperative basis, of as large a sector of economic activity as possible, e.g., farming, irrigation, transport, milk supply, livestock-breeding, cottage industries, etc., with financial, administrative and technical assistance from the state, (iv) Organization by a central committee for cooperative training, all-India, regional and statewise, of training for personnel of both cooperative departments and cooperative institutions.

Acting on the Recommendations of the RCSC, the cooperative development plan of each state contemplates the establishment or reorganization of a sound, efficient, and strong credit structure at all levels. An important principle in this reorganization is state partnership at all levels and the state contributing substantially to the share capital of the apex banks, the central cooperative banks, the large sized primary credit societies, and the central land mortgage banks. Under this scheme, state's interest in cooperative does not cease with administration, control, and assistance; it extends to partnership and powerful support. State partnership would not only increase the financial strength of the cooperatives but would also enable them to obtain by way of deposits and borrowings, from public and the Reserve Bank, a much larger amount of finance than they are now able to command, and provide vastly increased credit facilities to agriculturists.

State partnership is intended not only to strengthen cooperatives financially, but also to ensure the adoption of right policies, viz, the admission of the hitherto neglected medium and small farmers as members, the fulfilment of their credit needs and ensuring of the productive use of credit. While not interfering with the essential autonomy of cooperative institutions state's nominees, on their boards of management would endeavour to bring about a reorientation of the policies followed by cooperatives with a view to promoting agricultural production and meeting the needs of the underprivileged sections of the rural community.

The most important unit in cooperative credit to the agriculturists is the village primary society. Only if the society works efficiently and economically it can perform its due role and supply credit to all needy agriculturists in the village. For the achievement of this objective, a number of prerequisites are necessary. Some of the conditions are: (1) the area of the primary society should be such that it will ensure personal knowledge of each other among members; (2) the disbursement of loans should be speedy; (3) there should be a proper supervision to ensure effective utilization of loans; and (4) arrangements should be made for a prompt repayment of loans. With due consideration of all these factors, the Cooperative Planning Committee (1946) recommended that, as a rule, there should be one society for one village. The All India Rural Credit Survey Committee Report in 1954 did not agree with the earlier decision and pointed out that large-sized primary agricultural societies comprising about 500 members in all should be organized. This was accepted in the Second Five Year Plan.

In November 1958, the National Development Council in its resolution on cooperative policy, reversed the Second Plan decision and agreed that cooperatives should be organized on the basis of village community as the primary unit. Where, however, the villages were too small, it would be convenient to form them into larger groups with a population of about 1,000. This was accepted in the Third Five Year Plan. This problem was again examined by the Committee on Cooperative Credit which advocated the setting up of viable units of cooperatives at the village level covering a radius of 7-8 miles. The National Development Council considered these proposals and agreed that while, as a general rule, cooperatives should be organized on the basis of the village community as a primary unit, where villages are too small, the number of villages to be served by the cooperative society could be increased in the interest of viability. The aim should be to ensure viability and the essential characteristics of cooperation, namely, voluntary basis, close contact, social cohesion, and mutual obligation. However, such extension should be subject to certain maximum limits, namely, a population of 3,000 (i.e. 600 families or about 500 cultivator families) and a distance of not more than 3-4 miles from the village headquarters.

In 1993-94 there were 66,111 multipurpose cooperative and credit societies in the country with a total membership of 91,961 thousand. The societies advanced loan to the tune of Rs. 71,577,636 thousand and 50,098 number of societies undertook distribution of various agricultural inputs worth Rs. 20,501,040 thousand. Table 10.2 indicates the year-wise position from 1970-71 to 1993-94. One of the so far neglected aspect of the problem is the rehabilitation and revitalization of the primary societies. If these societies are to play their due role and supply credit to all agriculturists in the village, this aspect would need all the emphasis in the future development of cooperative credit. The Mehta Committee on Cooperative Credit, 1960 rightly remarked that a systematic programme of rectification, consolidation, and revitalization of the large number of dormant primary credit societies should be chalked out before they can be relied upon to play their part in the expansion of rural credit.

A review of the working of cooperative banks and credit societies in 1970-71, released by the Reserve Bank of India, was one more unpleasant reminder that efforts at strengthening the cooperative credit structure had to be redoubled if cooperative credit societies were to stand on their own legs and meet the credit requirements of the weaker sections of society adequately. As it became apparent that cooperative credit structure would not be able to meet the increased demand generating from the green revolution, the All-India Rural Credit Review Committee (1969), recommended an active and positive role for commercial banks in the field of agricultural credit. In July 1969, the largest 14 commercial banks were nationalized and their lending policies and procedures were oriented to meet the requirements of the priority sectors of the economy. Thus, the predominance of the cooperative movement in the supply of institutional credit between 1951-52 and 1968-69 gave way to multi-agency approach.

For several reasons, the cooperative credit structure is now almost defunct in most of the states. Limited ability to mobilize resources, low levels of recovery of the loans advanced, high transaction costs, frequent suspensions of recovery, administered interest rates and externally imposed controls, have all affected the health of the system. A number of measures have been initiated to ensure their growth and

Table 10.2 Multipurpose Cooperative and Primary Agricultural Credit Societies-All India 1970-71 to 1993-94

Year	No. of societies	Membership ('000)	Loan advanced (Rs. '000)	No. of societies undertaking distribution of inputs	Distribution operation: Value of goods distributed (Rs. '000)					
					Seeds	Fertiliser	Pesticides	Machinery/ Implements	Others	Total
1970-71	160,780	30,963	5,778,131	62,467	69,983	1,111,789	23,678	80,811		1,288,261
1971-72	157,454	32,009	6,111,751	61,556	82,231	1,313,788	35,475	14,782	94,927	1,541,112
1972-73	154,670	33,528	7,721,710	57,036	85,480	1,501,331	65,826	12,383	98,879	1,763,899
1973-74	153,808	34,956	7,579,073	51,304	125,941	1,777,619	128,797	38,938	169,810	2,241,105
1974-75	152,572	36,442	8,991,380	59,256	114,124	2,510,612	97,170	14,972	159,030	2,895,908
1975-76	134,835	39,521	10,217,764	52,436	98,657	2,703,473	95,178	17,418	181,141	3,095,867
1976-77	123,356	44,832	12,105,432	51,917	117,668	3,352,425	88,006	10,872	332,852	3,902,823
1977-78	116,125	47,860	12,704,549	43,605	136,815	4,249,990	167,097	19,054	308,661	4,881,617
1978-79	95,782	52,569	14,584,466	38,630	146,522	5,113,195	233,257	14,735	286,955	5,794,664
1979-80	94,592	54,836	16,286,734	40,722	164,569	5,649,904	213,080	20,961	452,835	6,502,339
1980-81	94,484	57,653	17,692,764[aa]	42,947	174,137	6,182,501	212,983	33,291	573,785	7,176,697
1981-82	93,889	63,171	22,233,722[a]	45,789	220,622	8,121,733	292,275	29,878	782,972	9,447,480
1982-83	92,714	64,036	24,411,201	44,707	255,067	7,757,042	530,732	42,342	826,054	9,411,237

Table 10.2 Multipurpose Cooperative and Primary Agricultural Credit Societies-All India 1970-71 to 1993-94 (Contd.)

Year	No. of societies	Membership ('000)	Loan advanced (Rs. '000)	No. of societies undertaking distribution of inputs	Distribution operation: Value of goods distributed (Rs. '000)					
					Seeds	Fertiliser	Pesticides	Machinery/ Implements	Others	Total
1983-84	92,695	67,409	26,504,390	46,585	417,769	8,704,684	306,860	47,123	854,560	10,330,996
1984-85	89,001	64,949	28,831,934	45,379	429,958	9,193,000	305,082	110,061	691,496	10,729,597
1985-86	89,041	67,362	33,190,979	43,264	473,724	9,806,255	315,514	42,654	988,929	11,627,076
1986-87	88,171	69,545	36,206,505	44,937	412,657	9,647,600	373,937	46,400	962,267	11,442,861
1987-88	86,581	74,343	46,122,351	45,685	547,939	11,925,868	332,501	75,212	1,434,447	14,314,517
1988-89	79,019	73,822	50,585,258	46,206	423,767	10,618,598	255,442	83,549	1,169,856	12,750,995
1989-90	71,417	68,339	46,852,160	37,362	662,128	11,248,645	346,306	103,778	6,887,827	19,248,684
1990-91	69,911	59,308	38,839,700	39,565	723,192	9,420,344	719,583	100,293	1,422,934	12,386,346
1991-92	66,507	66,226	47,951,268	41,216	490,469	11,091,246	912,931	206,787	3,381,565	16,082,998
1992-93	65,833	90,887	52,924,978	35,373	599,249	12,646,436	579,622	82,134	3,677,067	17,584,508
1993-94	66,111	91,961	71,577,636	50,098	495,088	15,746,672	594,305	91,096	3,573,879	20,501,040

[a] Break up of Rs.65,123,000 not available, [aa] Break up of Rs. 36,006,000 not available.

SOURCE: Various issues of Statistical Statements relating to the Cooperative Movement in India," Reserve Bank of India, Mumbai & NABARD.

development and also make them strong, viable, self reliant, dynamic and democratic. However, these institutions have remained underdeveloped. The impact of the externally imposed policy measures such as waiver of loans, prevailing accumulated losses, imbalances, the insistence upon the adherence to prudential norms and the stipulation of minimum involvement, etc. have left the cooperative credit structure in a very poor state.

Structure of Cooperative Banking in India

The structure of cooperative banking is federal in character. It consists of primary societies at village level, cooperative banks at district level, and state cooperative banks at the apex. Though the organisation has credit as well as non-credit functions both in agricultural as well as non-agricultural spheres, non-credit side has not made much progress. In fact, cooperative movement in India was started with the object of organizing and developing a special agency for providing credit for agriculture. Horace Plunkett,[1] for instance, while referring to cooperative societies says, "These societies are so predominant for the purpose of credit that comparatively little attention has been given to other cooperative objects and functions needed to bring the movement into the cooperative category. It would not have been otherwise, since indebtedness and its relief is necessarily the primary purpose in view." This has been a great weakness of agricultural cooperatives from the very inception and it predominates the whole cooperative scene even now. It has not only limited the usefulness of cooperation, but also failed to foster to the cooperative spirit among the members. To most of them it was just a lending institution and nothing more. V.L. Mehta[2] has rightly observed that cooperative credit is only one aspect of a vast movement which promotes the voluntary association of individuals having common economic needs.

Two distinct types of cooperative financing banks have come up in this country. One provides short term and medium term credit and the other long term credit. The former consists of the state cooperative banks at the apex, i.e. at the state level, and central banks as intermediaries between the apex and the primary societies. The central cooperative banks form an important link in the chain as they help in balancing the deficits and surpluses in the resources of their constituents. Besides, they tap local savings for financing local production and provide the channel at the district level for the funds to flow from the state cooperative bank, the money market and the Reserve Bank of India. The banks lead support to the primaries. At the

---

[1] Horace Plunkett, quoted from the Introduction given in E.M. Hough's Book Cooperative Movement in India, 1959, p. xxxiii.

[2] V.L. Mehta, Cooperative Finance, Bombay, 1930, p. 2.

base are the primary cooperative societies which cater to the needs of the members who may be drawn from one or more villages. In certain states, grain banks also serve as primary credit societies.

The long term credit structure consists of the central land mortgage banks and primary banks. By 1959-60 central land mortgage banks existed in all the states except Jammu and Kashmir. In Madhya Pradesh the state cooperative bank functions as a central land mortgage bank through a separate land mortgage banking department. While the set up at the apex level is the same except in Madhya Pradesh, where there is considerable diversity in the organisation below that level. In Andhra Pradesh, Tamil Nadu and Karnataka the units of operation at the taluka level are the primary land mortgage banks. They are affiliated to the apex bank and they advance loans to individual agriculturists out of the funds provided by the central land mortgage bank. In Saurashtra and Orissa, there are no primary banks. The Central Land Mortgage Bank operates through its branches in Orissa and also through its agencies. The Mumbai State Land Mortgage Bank works through affiliated primaries, branches of its own, and central banks acting as agents.

The Committee of Direction of the All-India Rural Credit Survey made several recommendations for the development of land mortgage bank. The Committee suggested that before organising primary land mortgage banks, enquiry into the conditions of each area such as the volume of business available, number of persons willing to form such banks, and the nature of holdings, tenures, and facilities for irrigation should be conducted. As regards the strengthening of the resources of these banks, the Committee suggested that while subject to a minimum of 51 per cent, government contribution should be such as to help establish an adequate number of central land mortgage banks whose financial structure enables them to borrow and lend adequately. The Committee further pointed out that these banks should change their loan policy with a view to increasing agricultural production. The Reserve Bank is expected to assist these banks by making long term loans to state governments for the purpose of subscribing directly or indirectly, to the share capital of cooperative credit institutions including land mortgage banks. The Reserve Bank can also provide long term accommodation to land mortgage banks (a) by way of direct loans; and (b) by purchase of the whole or part of "special development debentures" of the land mortgage banks.

Flow of Credit

There has been substantial improvement in the flow of institutional credit. The flow of institutional credit for agriculture and allied activities has increased from Rs. 22032 crore in the year 1995-96 to Rs. 41,764 crore in the year 1999-2000. The total credit flow from all agencies is expected to go up to Rs. 60,842 crore by 2002. Agency-wise disbursement of Agricultural Credit during 1995-96 to 1999-2000 and projections for 2000-2001 is shown in Table 10.3.

Table 10.3 Flow of Institutional Credit to Agriculture

(In thousand)

Agency	*1995-96*	*1996-97*	*1997-98*	*1998-9*	*1999-2000 Estimated*	*2000-2001 Projection*
Cooperative						
Short-term	8331	9328	10895	12320	15024	17698
Medium- /Long-term	2148	2616	3190	3596	4069	5108
Sub-Total	10479	11944	14085	15916	19093	22806
Commercial/Regional Rural Banks						
Short-term	6194	7670	9745	11313	12215	13285
Medium/Long term	5359	6797	8126	9668	10456	15369
Sub-Total	11553	14467	17871	20981	22671	28654
Grand Total	22032	26411	31956	36897	4176	51460

SOURCE: Annual Report-2000-2001, Department of Agriculture and Cooperation, Govt. of India.

Mounting Overdues of RCCLs

The poor recovery of loans, coupled with high transaction cost and lower level of loan business, results in losses in large amount and thus, low financial viability. Mounting overdues is one of the important weaknesses of the RCCIs. Table 10.4 indicates increasing trend from year to year of the overdues of PACS, DCCBS and SCBS. It was only Rs. 6 crore in 1950-51 in respect of PACS which went up to Rs. 44 crore in 1960-61, Rs. 1085 crore in 1980-81 and Rs. 3635 crore in 1994-95.

On the road of growth of cooperative movement, the spirit of 'cooperative' was lost as the institutions and the agenda were hijacked by officialdom and their political masters in spite of clear warning from the visionary Prime Minister, Nehru, who, in 1961, said ... "I think it (cooperative movement) is basic thing for our agriculture–for our industry and still more, for our attitude to life–national and international. It is not a government directed show, although it is government assisted. There are to be no big bosses of the government sitting in big offices with big (number) chaprasis outside, directing and controlling the whole thing. In cooperation, there has to be a feeling that any ordinary peasant can walk in unafraid of the big boss." How his worst apprehensions came true. It is not the concern of this chapter to detail the history of cooperative movement but the fact remains

Table 10.4 Overdues of Different Agencies of Short-term Credit

(Rs. crore)

	PACS		DCCB		SCB	
Year	*Amount*	*Per cent to outstanding*	*Amount to outstanding*	*Per cent to outstanding*	*Amount*	*Per cent*
1950-51	6	20.7	3	8.8	2	11.1
1951-52	9	26.5	5	13.2	3	15.0
1952-53	10	26.3	6	15.4	3	15.0
1953-54	12	28.6	7	16.7	3	13.0
1954-55	15	30.6	8	17.4	4	16.7
1955-56	15	25.4	8	13.8	4	11.4
1956-57	17	23.9	9	9.6	4	8.0
1957-58	23	21.5	12	11.9	6	8.0
1958-59	27	20.0	9	6.9	6	5.9
1959-60	38	21.3	24	13.6	6	4.6
1960-61	44	20.2	27	12.3	7	4.2
1961-62	63	26.6	41	15.8	8	4.1
1962-63	77	26.3	52	18.0	7	3.3
1963-64	77	22.4	54	15.9	7	2.9
1964-65	96	25.9	66	16.9	7	2.5
1965-66	125	29.3	87	19.9	9	2.9
1966-67	160	33.5	124	24.8	17	5.2
1967-68	171	32.0	136	24.8	18	5.0
1968-69	214	34.6	173	27.0	23	5.0
1969-70	268	37.7	215	29.1	28	5.5
1970-71	322	41.1	274	33.7	38	7.3
1971-72	377	43.9	319	35.9	38	6.9
1972-73	368	37.6	310	30.2	42	6.6
1973-74	443	42.0	376	32.3	63	8.9
1974-75	503	42.7	434	32.2	44	4.8
1975-76	561	43.2	460	32.2	43	4.8
1976-77	683	42.7	596	33.2	58	5.3
1977-78	809	45.0	754	35.7	96	7.2
1978-79	927	45.2	835	35.9	127	8.9
1979-80	1088	45.8	969	37.0	175	11.6
1980-81	1085	41.4	940	31.5	162	8.8
1981-82	1248	42.1	1110	29.7	164	6.6
1982-83	1417	43.8	1329	30.3	180	6.2
1983-84	1574	45.0	1567	32.3	178	5.9
1984-85	1630	41.0	1463	28.3	244	7.7
1985-86	1806	41.8	1696	28.5	292	7.8
1986-87	1896	40.9	1883	26.2	366	9.1
1987-88	2132	40.5	2044	23.2	401	8.5
1988-89	2405	38.5	2321	23.0	611	10.4
1989-90	2874	38.9	3528	30.2	933	13.7
1990-91	3139	45.6	3155	26.1	717	9.2
1991-92	2875	38.1	3402	24.5	540	7.0
1992-93	3256	40.1	4211	26.4	533	5.1
1993-94	3160	26.1	4550	27.0	807	8.0
1994-95	3635	27.5	5099	25.1	1140	8.2

SOURCE: RBI/NABARD: Statistical Statements Relating to Cooperative Movement in India, Mumbai (various issues).

that the apprehension of the late Prime Minister which came true had an egregious effect on the whole cooperative credit regime directly affecting the Agricultural production regime.

Modern technology is a reasonably high cost technology and the post green revolution era had a price tag, which could not come from the savings of the farming community. Green revolution came on the shoulders of high yielding varieties of seeds, higher dosages of fertilizers, use of machines and implements and high cost pesticides/ weedicides/herbicides. All the need for inputs was accompanied with the need of another input i.e., credit. The system, in spite of a large number of inadequacies, rose to meet the challenge and ushered us in an era of near self-sufficiency and, at times, turned us as exporter of grains much to the chagrin of some of the major players in the world market.

Even though certain section of the people, for a variety of reasons, resort to cash purchases of inputs, still a very large percentage of farmers depend upon the credit line for purchase of inputs, land improvement and for creation of durable assets. This ratio could roughly be placed at 70:30. This co-relationship of credit with productivity, is the need for credit on trend line basis, more so by the resource poor farmers zeroes in the need to elevate the subject of credit to the level of say fertilizer use—not in isolation, but as an integral part of agricultural development process.

In the institutional credit, CCS dominates the rural financial system with about 92,327 PACs and 2,960 units of Agricultural Rural Development Banks (ARDBs). The coverage of villages by PACs/ ARDBs is about 99.7% with a membership of 94 million, and 19.37 million respectively. Though CCS has formidable presence in terms of its geographical coverage, it suffers from so many limitations.

Having stated all this, the obverse side is that the total membership of the credit societies (PACS) is coming down in macro terms and the percentage of borrowing membership to the total membership is showing a disturbing stagnating trend from 45.2 in 1975-76 to 27.3 in 1985-86 to 48.85 in 1996-97. Further disturbing feature is that there are number of large states where their percentage is lower than the national average. The reason could be stagnation of cooperative credit structure and large number of defaulters, thus making them ineligible borrowers. Loans issued per hectare of gross cropped area makes a dismal reading (in rupees) (Table 10.5).

One of the key factors influencing our credit system is large growing overdues creating liquidity problem for banks to finance in future and making many banks sick. Against the total loans issued by PACS' which showed an increase overdues from Rs. 1023 crores in 1975-76 to Rs. 3140 crores in 1985-86 and Rs. 9754 crores in 1996-97, the overdues were Rs. 560.5 crores in 1975-76 and Rs. 180.6 crores in 1985-86 and Rs. 5096 in 1996-97, thus affecting the number of profit making PACS' which

Table 10.5 Loans Issued Per Hectare of Gross Cropped Area (GCA)

(Rs in lakhs)

State	*1975-76*	*1985-86*	*1994-95*	*1996-97*
Haryana	7.65	364.31	1828	3582.99
Himachal Pradesh	5.95	156.95	385	401.97
Punjab	10.74	524.30	1255	1437.97
Rajasthan	3.16	82.57	189	190.75
Assam	NA	10.03	24	NA
Bihar	2.14	31.63	98	50.19
Orissa	2.16	60.58	179	213.23
West Bengal	2.71	93.54	320	325.55
Madhya Pradesh	3.07	119.64	778	368.62
Uttar Pradesh	3.79	107.88	397	312.06
Gujarat	12.72	280.66	640.00	704.58
Maharashtra	8.04	173.92	613	722.10
Andhra Pradesh	5.48	173.09	1238	704.75
Tamil Nadu	14.8	363.31	3008	3055.49

(Data after this period is not available)

came down from 58.1 percent in 1975-76 to 56.5 per cent in 1985-86 and 42.92 per cent in 1995-96, thus further restricting the access to credit by a very large number of farmers.

Estimation of Credit

Main problem in agriculture credit appears to be that firstly, the total credit requirements are not estimated/projected properly. One reason cited for this is perhaps the general practice presently followed in many places relating to the fixing the 'scales of finance'; scales of finance which should be based on realistic and current prices are shockingly fixed on ad hoc basis taking into account the availability of resources with District Cooperative Credit Banks rather than the requirement of crops in question. The actual disbursements to borrowers are generally below the scale of finance sanctioned resulting in under financing, thus forcing the borrower to work in sub-optimal environment obviously resulting in lower productivity levels affecting his repaying capacity. Related question is updating the norms of financing which are really not fixed in a scientific basis in many places. The pity is that RRB's and commercial banks follow the same norms of financing as defined by the cooperative system. More or similar trends are discernible in medium/long term loans on all counts.

While short term loans affect the productivity and production levels during the season itself, medium/long term loans result in improvements which help sustain higher levels of production on the one hand and also reflect on the gross capital formation on the other. The problem is too much bureaucratization, Government interference and meddling in sensitive areas like financing and recovery in the form of stay or laxity in recoveries and at times loans *'mafi'* (remission) create an adverse climate for recoveries in future.

Cleansing of Balance Sheets

Lot many recommendations have emanated from as many Committees set up by NABARD, RBI and others. Emphasis is on better deposits by PACS, better recoveries, advancing loan for productive purposes as well as in part for consumption purposes—separately, so that the two are not mixed up, improvement in management, better role by the 'Lead Bank' for purposes of working out the credit requirements and preparation of credit plans and now the most strident noises are made about cleansing the balance sheets of the cooperative credit structure. It is all right to make the suggestion as otherwise there shall not be enough resources to lend but no word is heard as to what measures shall be taken to ensure non-recurrence of the past and history not repeating itself.

The need to meet the credit requirements of all, to use and apply modern means of technology and innovative both for short term and long term need no emphasis. Without monetary inputs there can be no technological and physical inputs but may be the system needs a fresh look and restructuring. Farmer is looking for credit, state supports the need it is only the intermediate level of bloated managerial bureaucracy and high level of state interference with little professional commitment or competence which are coming in the ways to let the two ends meet.

Issues

(a) An approach worth considering is to make a beginning with estimation of total credit requirement with a continued process of updating of 'norms of finance'. Again the credit requirement should not be looked at institutional credit only but should also include credit from informal sources as well, and simultaneously addressing the question of the number of borrowers—a declining trend which should be a cause of concern to the planners. Need is to bring larger numbers within the fold especially the small and marginal farmers.

(b) The system is known to address itself to the question of cleansing the balance sheets of CCS's but the question dealing with the defaulters also needs to be looked into. The reasons for default need to be gone into. This can be very revealing. Recommendations or action points must emerge to bring the hitherto defaulter back in the 'credit' fold if the motto set for equity with justice is to be attained.

(c) Having addressed the question of appropriate assessment of credit requirement and wider coverage of farmers, the next issue to be addressed could be allocation to the three players namely commercial banks (CBs), cooperative credit structure and RRBs.

(d) Most intriguing aspect of 'credit' planning and performance is that firstly we plan for far below of our requirements and than we see a wide gap between supply and demand (for the IX Plan period estimated demand for the first year of the plan on 'trend' basis, is placed at Rs. 105290 crore and supply is Rs. 72316 crore; for the last year of Plan corresponding figures are 196240 crores and Rs. 14072 crore showing a whopping gap of Rs. 32974 in the first year and Rs. 55518 crore in the last year and hoping that the gap will somehow be met by mobilization of funds, private investments and for non-banking sector). The past experience shows that this proposal begs the question. During the VII Plan credit flow figures in absolute terms came up to 89.3 per cent of the estimates of the working group, which further went down to 86.9 per cent during the VIII Plan.

(e) If the key lies in almost doubling of cooperative credit to help us attain the proposed 4.5% growth in agriculture during the IX Plan period, and the major bottlenecks are flow and recycling of liquidity, spoiled so far by the 'system in place' then, perhaps, the recommendation of Rural Banking Enquiry Committee to involve the States in this sector should be reviewed in the light of its past performance and more so when demand is being made from several quarters on cleansing the balance sheet without in any way attacking the reasons which landed the system into such a situation. May be a time has come to jettison it from the control of states. States have no control over commercial banks and they were lending up to 40% and they were not poorer but not having state at their back. Why cannot we think of NABARD as it exists, as an Apex bank and the whole of the cooperative credit structure (state, district and society level) coming under one roof (Nabard), run professionally all the way downwards. They will be in a better position to reuse resources by deposit mobilisation, raising money from the market, transfer resources from one region to another and also resort to better recovery methods. They will have the wherewithal and the teeth to perform the assigned role more capably, competently, and professionally free from 'officialization' and 'politicization' of the important sector.

Increasing crop productivity and cropping intensity are the function of application of inputs and 'credit' is one input which facilitates use of other inputs. No other input does that. A time has come to grab this opportunity when economy is opening up in the liberalization mood, to lend credit management a professional face from end to end to achieve the desired objectives of equity with justice, higher share in

GDP and keep higher investment in agriculture by contribution to gross capital formation.

STATE BANK OF INDIA

The State Bank of India has been responsive to the need of the agricultural sector in keeping with the spirit of the times. The role conceived for the Bank by the Rural Credit Survey Committee in its integrated scheme of rural credit was that of being responsive to the needs of the cooperative institutions connected with credit and, especially, marketing and processing.

Keeping this in view, the Bank has been financing marketing and processing cooperative societies and has also been extending remittance facilities and short term accommodation to the cooperative central financing institutions to stimulate and assist them in their operations. With the passage of time, it has extended the scope of its assistance to wider field, viz., cooperative sugar factories, land mortgage bank, industrial cooperatives, and wholesale consumer stores.

Special Activities

Advances to farmers directly are granted for all agricultural operations right from sowing to harvesting of crops, processing, preservation, storage, transportation, and marketing of agricultural produce. The objective that the Bank has placed before it is that its financial assistance should result in increased agricultural production and not merely be used for substitution of any existing credit channels. Special farming activities, such as animal husbandry, dairy farming, pisciculture, piggery, poultry farming, horticulture, and fruit cultivation are also eligible for the Bank's finance. The Bank also finances agro-industries corporations to enable them to purchase tractors, power-tillers, pump sets, etc., and extend hire-purchase facilities to farmers for the purchase of agricultural machinery and equipment, custom service units, and the storage and distribution of agricultural inputs, such as fertilisers, pesticides, and seeds.

The factors governing the eligibility for agricultural advances are primarily the progressiveness of the farmers and the economic viability of their schemes, as worked out on the basis of anticipated expenditure and income. The usual methods of credit evaluation, such as purpose of advance, integrity of the borrowers, yield prospects, and protection are duly taken into consideration, but more than ordinary emphasis is placed on proper utilisation of the advances. Agricultural credit cells have been created at the Bank's local head offices and at the head offices of the subsidiaries as also in certain strategic locations. These cells have been placed in charge of appropriate officers who coordinate the work of agricultural finance in their respective circles and subsidiaries.

Arrangements for the training of staff have also been made with the agricultural universities and with the Bankers Training College of the Reserve Bank of India. Officials from the agricultural department of various state governments have also been taken on a deputation basis for assisting the Bank in the implementation of its various schemes.

Commercial Banks

Success of the green revolution technologies in late sixties brought new hopes for Indian agriculture. However, it was realized that the gigantic financial cost of ensuring complete modernization of India's agriculture, would have a very little chance of being realised unless there was some dramatic change in banking tradition and the rural credit system. The total short term credit needs by the end of 1973-74 was estimated at Rs. 1,600 crores and no single institution could possibly finance this huge amount. The Fourth Plan envisaged that though the cooperatives would continue to be the principal agency for agricultural credit, and would have to be strengthened for the purpose, the approach would be to ensure that agricultural production was not inhibited by the weakness of the cooperatives. The policy aimed at institutionalising agricultural credit to the maximum extent possible and reducing the direct loaning by the Government to the minimum.

Till that period, the commercial banks had played only a minor role in agricultural finance. The reform of agricultural finance meant a new role for the commercial banks in India and a coordination of facilities to rural areas with the cooperative banks. Under the scheme of social control which was approved by the Parliament and received the assent of the President in January 1969, two main steps were envisaged: (1) The creation of National Credit Council to formulate and integrate credit policies and (2) A change in the composition of Board of Directors of every bank. The National Credit Council was set up at the all India level in January 1968. By January 1969, the banking companies had also reconstituted their board of directors in such a way that a majority of persons of the boards had a special knowledge or experience in agriculture, rural economy, small-scale industries, cooperation, banking, finance, etc., which would be useful for the efficient conduct of banking operations and directing credit along new channels.

National Credit Council started functioning as a forum where the relative claims for credit of different sectors were being discussed and priorities assessed. The Council was expected to assist the government and the Reserve Bank of India in the task of allocating credit among the different sectors in conformity with the objectives of planning and social control over banks. Credit budgeting, and credit planning are jointly undertaken by the Reserve Bank of India and the National Credit Council, to help coordinate and synchronise the banking programme with national policies. In fact, the establishment of a National Credit

Council makes it possible to carry budgeting and planning to the official end-point of ensuring allocation of credit along proper channels.

Bank Nationalisation

The major fourteen commercial banks were nationalised in July 1969 with a view to giving a purposeful direction to resources commanded by them and to wean these resources from monopolistic business houses. These banks were merely an overgrowth of agency houses, subserving a colonial economy till recently (before socialisation) and were engaged only in safe banking business. No sericus effort had been made by these banks to help agriculturist or agro-based industries. The sense of involvement even from the Reserve Bank of India came only after the Gorawala Committee Report (Rural Credit Survey). Although the nationalised State Bank of India (the earlier Imperial Bank) did make some efforts to move away from its earlier policies, the bank advances continued to be given predominantly for trade and commerce.

With the Green Revolution in agriculture during 1967-68, there arose the need for an increasing quantum of credit for procurement and distribution of various inputs. The existing setup of cooperative credit structure, with the primary agricultural societies as its base was unable to absorb all the credit, provided to it. One of the main problems is that of overdues. The requirements of the agricultural sector were so large and diverse that both commercial banks and cooperative banks could play a mutually complimentary role without getting into conflict with each other. Some of the other advantages of nationalisation of banks as pointed out by the then Prime Minister were:

(a) Banks would better serve farmers in promoting agricultural production and rural development generally.
(b) Use of bank credit for speculative and other unproductive purposes would be curbed.
(c) Control of big industrial groups on major banks would end.
(d) The right atmosphere would be created for development of adequate professional management in the banking field.

It was made clear that the 14 nationalized banks would continue to be scheduled banks and the power of the Reserve Bank of India in relation to them would not only remain but even become more significant and purposeful. There was no intention to set up a central monolithic agency to run all the banks. The identity and initiative of the nationalised banks would be preserved and autonomy of each bank would be assured. The board of directors would have well defined powers. The government's directions will only be in the matter of policies and general issues. No policy direction would be given on specific loans to specific parties. With a view to overcoming the problems and catering to the need of the unbanked rural areas, a system of "lead bank scheme" was introduced. All the districts in the country had been allocated to one or the other of the nationalised banks for a comprehensive survey of the district concerned. The survey covers problems like:

(1) Resources and potential for banking development in the districts;
(2) The number of industrial and commercial units and other establishments and farms which do not have banking accounts and depend mainly on moneylenders,
(3) Increasing their own resources through the creation of surpluses from additional production financed from the banking system;
(4) Marketing facilities for agricultural produce, industrial produce, storage and warehousing space, and the linking of credit and servicing of equipment ; and
(5) To examine the possibilities of primary lending agencies and maintain contact with government and quasi-government agencies.

Over the years there has been phenomenal increase in bank credit. Immediately prior to nationalisation, the total agricultural advances of the scheduled commercial banks were only Rs. 188 crore. But in 1999-2000, the advances in agricultural sector were to the tune of Rs. 4747 crore. In the priority sector viz. agriculture, small-scale industry and other priority sectors, the total advances were as high as 717216 crore in 1999-2000 comprising nearly 29.3 per cent of the total bank credit covering all sectors.

National Bank for Agriculture and Rural Development (NABARD)

Though rural financial institutions have played a leading role in the provision of rural credit, the rural sector, especially the agricultural sector is still in need of more credit. The National Bank for Agriculture and Rural Development (NABARD), which is the apex organisation in the field of rural credit, has taken several initiatives in this regard. Notable developments in recent years are the introduction of Kisan Credit Card (KCC) and the linkage of Self Help Groups (SHGs) with banks. Cooperative banks, Regional Rural Banks, and Commercial Banks together issued about 59 lakh KCCs till the end of March 2000. These agencies were asked to redouble their promotional efforts so as to issue an additional 75 lakh KCCs by March 2001. During April-October, 2000, the public sector banks issued 11.54 lakh cards involving a sanctioned amount of Rs. 2969.7 crore. The sanctioned amount worked out to Rs. 25,744 per card issued by public sector banks during April- October 2000. In order to enable NABARD to leverage its capital funds for raising more resources, its capital base has been progressively increased from Rs. 500 crore in 1996-97 to Rs. 5,000 crore. Besides share capital contribution, Reserve Bank of India has been providing to NABARD a General Line of Credit (GLC) to enable it to meet the short-term credit requirements of cooperatives and Regional Rural Banks (RRBs).

Credit for Weaker Sections

Small and marginal farmers who constitute over 70 per cent of the farming population have little input mobilising power and risk taking capacity. Hence credit is a key input in achieving a rapid diffusion of benefits from new technology. It is also essential for promoting self-employment and in the creation of productive assets. The success of Integrated Rural Development Programme will mainly hinge on the preparation of viable schemes for those identified for assistance and the provision of investment credit therefore on an assured basis. While over the years there has undoubtedly been an impressive step-up in credit availability to the weaker sections, its disposal among various strata of the rural poor has been extremely disparate. Among them the main beneficiaries have been the small and marginal farmers, the former distinctly more than the latter. The least to benefit have been the landless and the rural artisans, who as a category account for as much as one-fourth of the rural work force. The policy of stipulating a minimum percentage for the entire target group of weaker sections has done little to prevent glaring intra-group distortions. Experience shows that bracketing those who have some resource (land) with those who have none, generally tends to operate to the disadvantage of the latter. It, therefore, appears necessary that the strategy of credit deployment should be so oriented as to equitably serve the needs of each category. This will call for more effective credit planning and prescription of separate targets of credit for the subgroup of the landless and the artisans, along with arrangements for the formulation of economically viable projects for them.

While attempting to do this, it needs to be stressed that the credit delivery systems, of both cooperative and commercial banks, will require considerable toning up. Simplification of procedures, systematic identification of the most needy among the target group and preparation of appropriate investment projects for them and reorientation from security-based lending to project-based lending are some of the important aspects of an improved delivery system. Credit-cum-input supply melas or other effective credit and input delivery systems will have to be adopted on a large scale before the onset of kharif and rabi sowing. Full support will need to be given by the extension agency in building up the awareness and motivation of the rural poor in respect of their production and investment needs. It is also proposed to devise suitable credit insurance schemes for insulating weaker sections from total loss due to factors beyond their control. Alongside, fullest emphasis will be given to recovery disciplines, pressures which have lately developed in some parts of the country for general writing off of overdues can only be viewed with extreme concern, for the consequences of this will be disastrous for the credit system as a whole.

Although the lead bank is to assume a big role in the banking development and credit in the concerned districts, it is not expected to have a monopoly of banking business in that district. The bank will act as a consortium leader and after identifying underbanked areas and areas suffering from credit gaps, it would invoke the cooperation of other banks operating in the district. The progress of the lead bank scheme so far is, to say the least, appalling. Quite a few banks seem to have shown little respect to the scheme in that not many branches have been opened in their lead districts. There are instances that in a number of states the lead bank has opened only one office in its lead district. The problems of the lead bank scheme are two-fold. There is the basic inconsistency in the scheme of allotting a district to a bank so that it can "lead" and coordinate the branch expansion with other banks coming to the district. Secondly, they have been operating without any sense of purpose.

Kisan Credit Card Scheme

The Kisan Credit Cards Scheme, introduced in 1998-99, is an innovative mechanism for facilitating short-term credit to farmers. The scheme has gained popularity and its implementation has been taken up by 27 Commercial Banks, 334 Central Cooperative Banks and 187 Regional Rural Banks. The progress in issue of Kisan Credit Cards and credit sanction up to December 2000 is listed in Table 10.6.

Present Position

The cooperative credit movement was started to get the farmers out of the clutches of the moneylenders. The system was encouraged to take over the credit requirements of the farmer and enable him to get credit, in time, at fair rates of interest. In the thirties, the agrarian situation was so bad that debt relief measures were also undertaken to save the agriculturists from utter ruin. Various steps were taken to give new life to a languishing cooperative system like consolidation of existing societies by developing their resources, close supervision and scrutiny of their loan operations, assistance to apex cooperative banks for financing rehabilitated societies, etc.

In recent years, there has been a significant increase in institutionalisation of rural credit and cooperatives are an integral part of the country's agricultural system. The cooperatives have played a major role in disbursement of agricultural credit. Cooperative credit system and refinancing institutions are the two major channels for providing agricultural credit. Short term advances by credit cooperatives accounted for about 55 per cent of the total disbursal, while commercial banks and Regional Rural Banks accounted for 39 and 6 per cent respectively in the year 1996-97. In investment credit, cooperatives accounted for about 35 per cent, commercial banks and Regional Rural

Table 10.6 Number of Kisan Cards Issued and Amount Sanctioned

(Rs. in crore)

Agency	*1998-99*		*1999-2000*		*2000-01 (up to 31 December, 2000)*		*Cumulative Progress (up to 31 December, 2000)* †	
	Cards issued (lakh No.)	*Amount sanctioned*	*Cards issued (lakh No.)*	*Amount sanctioned*	*Cards issued (lakh No.)*	*Amount sanctioned*	*Cards issued (lakh No.)*	*Amount sanctioned*
Coop Banks	1.55	826	38.50	4432	31.97	7573	71.02	128.31
RRBs	0.06	11	1.80	416	4.06	965	5.92	1381
Comm. Banks*	6.24	1477	13.68	2548	11.56	2985	31.48	7010
Total	7.85	2314	53.98	7396	47.59	11512	108.42	21222

*Data available upto 31 October 2000. † Provisional

Banks for about 58 per cent and 7 per cent respectively. Presently about 45 per cent of the total credit requirement is met from the institutional sources.

Efforts to strengthen agricultural credit agencies were given top priority in the Eighth Plan. The Working Group set up by the Planning Commission had given projections/targets for the Seventh and the Eighth Plans. In absolute terms, aggregate short-term agricultural credit was Rs. 6201 crore and Rs. 19,678 crore (estimated) as against the Working Group targets of Rs. 8040 crore and Rs. 21,647 crore during the terminal years of the Seventh and the Eighth Plans respectively. However, the performance of all the banks including cooperatives in short term agricultural credit declined from 89.3 per cent during the Seventh Plan to 86.9 per cent during the Eighth Plan. The target for advances to agricultural sector under the scheme of priority sector lending (fixed at 18% of net bank credit) declined from 17 per cent in 1988-89 to 14.3 per cent in 1995-96. Thus, the credit situation during the Eighth Plan was somewhat better than that of the Seventh Plan. The credit flow, growth rate and percentage share of various agencies during the Eighth Five Year Plan is shown in the following Table 10.7.

Table 10.7 Credit Flow, Growth Rate and % Share of Various Agencies During the Eighth Five Year Plan

(Rs. in crore)

Particulars/ Agency	*92-93*	*Share%*	*93-94*	*Share%*	*94-95*	*95-96*	*Share%*	*96-97*	*Share%*
A. Production (ST) credit Cooperative Banks	7170	71	7839	70	7250	8331	57	9750	55
RRBs	489	5	732	6	688	849	6	1144	6
Commercial Banks	2432	24	2700	24	@	5345	37	6797	39
Sub Total(A)	10091	100	11271	100	7938@	14525	100	17691	100
Growth Rate	(+43%)		(+12%)					(+22%)	
B. ML/LT Credit									
Cooperative Banks	2208	43	2278	43	2156	2148	29	2729	25
RRBs	342	7	245	5	395	532	7	777	7
Commercial Banks	2528	50	2700	52	8255@	4827	64	7456	68
Sub Total(B)	5978	100	5223	100	10806@	7507	100	10962	100
Growth Rate	(+23%)		(+3%)					(+46%)	
Grand Total (A+B) Growth Rate	15169 (+35%)		16494 (+9%)		18744 (+14%)	22032 (+18%)		28653 (+30%)	

SOURCE: Draft Ninth Five Year Plan 1997-2002 Vol. II

Ninth Plan Targets

Needless to say that credit is an important input for increasing growth in agriculture. For achieving a growth rate of 4.5 per cent in Agriculture output, the rate of growth in agricultural credit should be higher than that of the previous plan periods. A strong, viable and professional system of credit disbursal is essential for meeting the emerging credit demands adequately and timely. Credit support needs to be increased for traditional sectors like minor irrigation, farm mechanisation, rainfed farming, wasteland/forestry, dairy and other animal husbandry activities and also for crop production. In addition, the emerging scenario provides vast scope for diversification of activities under horticulture, as well as agro-processing storage and the use of advanced technologies like tissue culture, drip irrigation, green house, etc. All these activities need more credit during the Ninth Plan. Accordingly, a target of Rs. 1,49,400 crore as short-term credit and Rs. 80,350 crore as investment credit has been set for the Ninth Plan. The likely resource gap is expected to be met by banks through mobilisation of additional resources from the market and borrowings from NABARD and other financial institutions. Rural credit system is being restructured to double the flow of credit to agriculture and allied sectors particularly to small and marginal farmers. The initiatives proposed to be taken by NABARD to enhance the credit flow are as follows:

(i) Progressively increasing the quantum of refinance to cooperatives and RRBs. Commercial banks are expected to increase their ground-level credit substantially from their own resources, NABARD will continue to provide refinance facility to commercial banks because of weak cooperative credit structure and RRBs in the States of Bihar, Orissa and North Eastern Region.

(ii) The State Level Agricultural Development Finance Corporation recently established by NABARD will give a further boost to the flow of ground-level credit.

(iii) For increasing the out-reach of credit to small and marginal farmers, the encouragement towards linking of self-help with formal banking system as a supplementary credit delivery system through NABARD will be continued with greater vigour.

(iv) The new local area banks (LABs) being established are expected to increase the credit flow to agricultural and allied sectors.

(v) Financial assistance is being provided by NABARD under RIDF for irrigation, watershed development, rural roads/bridges etc. to State Governments which would generate demand for credit for agriculture sector.

(vi) The short-term limit sanctioned by NABARD during 1996-97 (Rs. 6997 crore) for production credit, tribal development, oilseeds to the small and marginal farmers have supplemented resources of cooperative banks and RRBs.

(vii) For reducing the regional imbalances, particularly in the North-Eastern region, NABARD has been extending the following concessions in the refinance facilities,

(a) NABARD has extended refinance facilities for all purpose to commercial banks in this region.

(b) NABARD has been providing refinance to all financing agencies at 90% of their ground level credit (as against 50-70% applicable to the rest of the country).

(c) The eligibility norm relating to minimum recovery level for drawing unrestricted re-finance from NABARD has been fixed at 50% for NE region (as against 60% stipulated for the other parts of the country).

(d) Sanctioning credit limits for seasonal agricultural operations by waiving overdues and minimum involvement criteria.

(e) NABARD has introduced several refinance schemes under the non-farm sector. The share of total refinance availed of by the NE region has shown as increasing trend from 1993-94 to 1996-97.

(viii) NABARD will develop appropriate operational and policy initiatives to support the Agricultural Credit System, particularly its information and communication system.

(ix) NABARD and RBI would take necessary initiatives to rehabilitate weak and uneconomic primary level cooperative societies.

(x) Special attention to the training needs of all rural financial institutions would be given by the NABARD and RBI with the support of training institutes. Skill development through HRD systems for cooperatives and RRBs, imparting trainer's training for the facility to improve the contents and quality of courses, etc. would continue.

(xi) To strengthen the cooperatives, NABARD has set up a Cooperative Development Fund with a corpus of Rs. 10 crore. The Fund is providing assistance to the cooperatives for HRD, MIS, mobilisation efforts, etc. The scope of the funding is being widened further.

(xii) To improve the resource base of NABARD for promoting enhancement of credit flow with its own resources, some of the measures required are; contribution to its share capital, allowing floatation of tax-free bonds as also resumption of Govt. of India contribution to its NRC (LTO) fund etc.

(xiii) Need for setting up a fund at NABARD for institutional development at national level for recapitalisation of co-operatives.

The estimation of year-wise credit flow during the Ninth Five Plan is given in Table 10.8.

Table 10.8 Estimate of Credit Flow in Ninth Five Year Plan

(Rs. in crore)

Year	Production Credit	Investment Credit	Total	Growth Rate (%)
Ninth Plan*				
1997-98	22500	10875	33375	16.48
1998-99	25650	12995	38645	15.79
1999-2000	29250	15530	44780	15.88
2000-01	33500	18608	52108	16.36
2001-02	38500	22342	60842	16.76

* (As estimated in the Working Group Report)
Total Ground Level Credit in 2000-01 will be 137% of the flow of credit achieved in 1995-96.

CHAPTER 11

Agricultural Subsidies

INTRODUCTION

It may very well be appreciated that subsidies in general are intended to introduce a new product and encourage its consumption. Once people concerned are able to realise its benefits, they are to be withdrawn slowly. In India, however, food subsidies - both consumer and input have become a part of the system and taken the role of welfare activity. The basic objective of these subsidies should actually be to provide help to the target group of poorer sections by supplying foodgrains at subsidised prices and encouraging the farming community in general to increase the production of foodgrains and other cash crops badly needed by the economy.

Introduction of the concept of subsidization, started with the state's interests to promote and give an initial fillip to a given sector and is prevailing even today, be it agriculture, industry, exports or service sector. Where economies have reached a certain level of achievement, there the focus and the shape it takes shifts; agricultural sector is one sector where subsidies continue till date—the form and shape it takes varies from country to country. Richer the country, higher the levels of subsidy without any corresponding equation with the number of families or its place in their GDP.

We were quite late to start on this front. With the advent of Independence and era of food security, efforts were made to increase consumption of fertilizers, agricultural, machinery, exploit irrigation potential to increase agricultural production. For good reasons in the spatial context especially in view of the fact that about 80% of landholders were small and marginal resource poor subsidy on certain key inputs became one of the elements of strategy to increase agricultural production. Green revolution in mid-60s brought in high-cost inputs like high yielding varieties of seed, higher use of fertilizers, farm machinery, irrigation and its conjunctive use which meant power —the farmer could not afford all these—hence, state stepped in, by way of making these inputs available at subsidized prices to help boost the use and spread of technologies associated with Green Revolution. The problem with these initiatives is that they tend to become habit forming, and over time, largely led by political compulsions, silently but stridently reflecting the politico-economic nexus on account of a large number of people (read voters) involved, they have come to stay as quasi permanent if not permanent feature. The richest economies in the world, USA, Europe, Japan even when the agriculture sector plays a relatively smaller role in the whole economy, they have not been able to unshackle themselves from these subsidies.

In India, however, subsidies, both hidden and explicit, are today as ubiquitous as the omnipresent and arguably, as arbitrary in their operation as any act of Providence. This is not to say that subsidies are, per se, a bad thing. A well-crafted and precisely targeted subsidy can work wonders in correcting an imbalance or inequity that the free market by itself might not remedy. This is especially true for public goods like defence and policing but also for primary education, public health, sanitation and public transportation. But when subsidies are used to cushion the affluent or appease politically important sectors, they cease to have any welfare-enhancing effect. If anything, such subsidies, have a negative impact, first, because they introduce distortions and second, because other categories of public expenditure that might be more deserving must be scaled down to keep the budget deficit with acceptable bounds. In India, unfortunately, the subsidy bill is so huge that even after pruning allocations under crucial budgetary heads such as public investment, the fiscal deficit has reached unmanageable proportions. To bring about some semblance of sanity, therefore, the government will have to close the deficit from both ends: mobilising additional tax revenues and cutting unnecessary expenditure, especially on non-merit subsidies.

The subsidy trap is suicidal because it makes governments believe they are doing enough for the farmers. It fools the farmers, keeps the entire agricultural input industry still within the licence-quota-subsidy vortex and is in the process destroying our farm economy and the environment. Just how big a disaster this is causing is evident the moment one visits a farm input shop. Half-literate shop owners push the most dangerous pesticides and unnecessary fertilizers down the farmer's throat and the farmer is tempted to buy since it all looks so cheap because of the subsidies. He soaks his soil with poison which eventually reaches our kitchens. How many of us realise that the Indian farmer uses three or four times more pesticides than the international norm? Some of the strong pesticides last at least 45 days once absorbed by a plant. Yet, our farmers continue to soak their cauliflowers, brinjal and tomato with it even in the week of plucking. We eat some of the most poisonous vegetables and fruits in the world.

Because the farmer gets these inputs cheap, he overuses them. Because the government invests everything in subsidies, it has nothing left for research or development - many of our premier agriculture universities can hardly pay salaries now. If the government only gets out of the way completely and leaves the farmer to face the market challenges, he would perhaps be better off. And our foods less poisoned. It works exactly the same way for electricity. Punjab claims to provide free power to the farmer. Consequently one can see the quality of the basic power infrastructure - tilted poles, hanging wires, exposed fuses etc. Most farmers spend more by way of bribes and repair to get free power than they would pay for reliable, quality power. Also, because power is free, and they don't know which four or six hours of the day it will be available for, they tend to keep the tubewell motor on round the clock. The result is too much power consumed, too much water pumped out, too such subsidy and, therefore, too much deficit in the budget.

Subsidies were needed in the 1950s when the nation - building process had just started; but now there is a strong view that they should be done away with in a phased manner and they run counter to our free-market orientation. They are now being used as political bait to lure voters. The basic purpose of subsidies has been lost. The poor have not benefited from them. Instead, the exchequer has ended up subsidising middlemen and the rich. The system has to be made more transparent and efficient so that subsidies benefit the intended targets, and are not misused. There is now a demand for rationalising these subsidies so that the burden of adjustment is borne equally by the recipients - manufactures and farmers.

Agriculture is said to have preferential treatment in the form of subsidised/free power for the pumps, cheaper credit, lower prices of fertilizers, minimal water rates, low rates of land revenue, subsidised supply of agricultural machinery, constant upward revision of procurement prices and to cap them all, no income tax on agricultural income. Of these various subsidies we have examined here in detail the subsidies on fertilizers, power and irrigation. Agricultural credit, seeds and machinery also carry subsidies, but they have been left out of the scope of this paper primarily because their quantification was difficult. Because of the present system of Minimum Support Pricing (MSP) and Public Distribution System (PDS) commitments, food subsidies are affected to a large extent by the changes in various input subsidies. This chapter has, therefore, been divided into five parts - part one gives an overview of various subsidies, parts two to four examine in detail the present ground situation with regard to the major three subsidies-fertilizers, irrigation, and power and the last part provides a perspective view of these subsidies.

AN OVERVIEW

Subsidy on Foodgrains—A Rationale

With the introduction of new programmes of structural adjustment and fiscal tightening in India in 1991, reduction in subsidies, including food subsidies has been the buzzword for policy makers. Bearing in mind the improved supply situation, a section of the economists are of the view that it is appropriate to phase out current procurement operation and supply to the PDS. The emphasis in fact, is on leissez faire economy-which sans public interference in any form. On the other hand, those who oppose withdrawal of both production and consumption subsidies, are of the view that food subsidies in India affect millions of consumers and producers and is of immense importance in a country where chronic hunger and malnutrition which majority of the population suffer from, and their withdrawal will cause a sharp decline in foodgrains production and further pauperisation of millions of people. It would be the negation of the broad objective of food policy in India which is to make available food to the people at reasonable prices and providing remunerative prices to cultivators. The other objectives like supplying food at subsidised prices to the undernourished, controlling inflationary pressures, stabilising prices for consumers and producers, reducing fluctuations in food availability, and achieving self-sufficiency in foodgrains production may also be jeopardised.

Volume of Food Subsidy

A study conducted by Swaminathan (EPW, December 25-31, 1999) on food subsidy reveals that the nominal food subsidy as a proportion of GDP, over the 30 years period from 1966-67 to 1997-98 was rising rapidly, particularly after the 1980s, and it took a big jump in 1993-94. At constant prices, the increase is more subdued. The expenditure on the food subsidy, at constant prices, rose in the mid- 1980s and then remained unchanged until about 1989-90. It dipped between 1990-91 and 1992-93 and rose in 1993-94. The food subsidy fell slightly in the following years but was higher than in the 1980s. However, the food subsidy as a share of GDP appears to have remained more or less unchanged over the last 20 years, peaking at about 0.63 per cent in 1985-86 and 0.64 per cent in 1993-94 indicating that the burden of food subsidy has not risen.

However, the food subsidy as defined in the government budget includes the entire operational deficit of the state-owned FCI. The four major items of food that are handled by the FCI are rice (and paddy), wheat, imported edible oils and sugar. Now the total central food subsidy included the subsidy in sugar and this is likely to vary in different years. Thus, the subsidy for foodgrains alone is lower than the budgeted food subsidy.

Production Subsidy

Subsidies are provided by the government for all the major inputs like fertilizers, water, pesticides, power for irrigation, credit and even for agricultural machineries. During 1996-97 per hectare consumption of fertilizer was 76.75 kg. (estimated) which included all crops. Assuming that 75% of the consumption of fertilizers was for foodgrains production, the subsidy provided for fertilizers may be apportioned accordingly. During the year total power consumption for agriculture was 84331 million kwh. It is difficult to assume how much power was consumed for foodgrains production. Similar problem arises with pesticides consumption. The cost of production of each of the foodgrains is calculated on the basis of the actual price paid for the purchased inputs without deducting the subsidy element. For fixing the procurement price, the cost of production per quintal is the major consideration.

Thus domestic subsidies fall into two categories:

(a) "non-product specific subsidies" given for all crops which in our case are subsidies given for fertilizers, water, electricity, seed and credit; and

(b) "product specific subsidies" given for specific crops, which in our case is the minimum support price or procurement price given for about twenty four agricultural commodities.

As per WTO agreement, a country whose product specific and non-product specific AMS (Aggregate Measure of Support) does not exceed 10 per cent of the total value of agricultural product in the case of developing countries (5% for developed countries), is not subject to any reduction commitments. Hence, our country has no obligation in reducing agricultural subsidies, as according to the Ministry of commerce, it is less than 10 per cent of AMS. However, to reduce the fiscal deficit, reduction or withdrawal of subsidy has become essential.

The Magnitude

Not bothering immediately about the definitional and procedural issues concerning various subsidies and issues discussed above, it would be sufficient to say that the present amount of various types of food and agricultural subsidies calculate to around Rs. 500 billion* at present or say over 13 percent of agricultural GDP. Added to this another 100 billion as food subsidies, it is the sheer magnitude of these subsidies which has raised alarm bells. In addition, serious concerns have been voiced against the impact of these subsidies on the efficiency in resource use and environmental degradation in general. Despite various attempts made from time to time to reduce these subsidies, populist policies proved to be overbearing and they have grown at about 12 percent compound rate over the last 2 decades. Today political

---

* This consists of fartilisers (Rs. 133.7 billion), power (Rs. 255.8 billion) irrigation (25.5 billion) and credit (34.8 billion) plus an estimated amount of Rs. 45 billion for the remaining heads—seeds, machinery, pesticides and diesel for agriculture etc. Food subsidy budgetted for 2002-03 is Rs. 21,200 crore as against Rs. 17,612 crores in 2001-02.

leadership also appears to be concerned over the increase in expenditure, particularly the untargetted flow of funds.

There is a general agreement that growth cannot be sustained without a reallocation of funds towards public infrastructure. Incidentally, the World Bank's report on poverty in India has also noted that high allocation of funds for implicit and explicit subsidies are a constraint on the development of not only infrastructure, but also research in agriculture.

IRRIGATION

Pricing water well below its economic value is prevalent throughout the world, resulting in misallocation and inefficient use. Farmers in both industrial and developing countries often pay little for their publicly supplied irrigation water and so have few incentives to refrain from growing water intensive crops or to conserve water. This has invariably led to gross misallocations, whereby agriculture, which absorbs the lions' share of available water, often includes low-value uses compared with high-value domestic and industrial uses.

Water charges, on an average, in India are very low typically amounting to 2-3 per cent of the harvests value in most states where they have no influence on farmers' management decision. The cost of irrigation water on the basis of investment, on an average, works out to 91 paise per thousand litres against which at prevailing water charges, the highest water rates for rice and sugarcane are only 1.2 paise and 11.6 paise per thousand litres respectively. Most of the states have not revised their irrigation water rates for the last 15-20 years. On an average, gross revenue collection per hectare of irrigated command is found to be about Rs. 68 against the estimated expenses of Rs.217 per hectare and thereby resulting in financial loss of Rs. 149 per hectare per year.

Irrigation is one of the key inputs for crop production in as much as the productivity impact of better seeds, fertilizers and other inputs is critically dependent on the way water is used. It is therefore both legitimate and necessary to address the pricing of this input as one of the first steps and an integral component in the process of rationalizing the totality of the price structure, and raising the efficiency of water use.

The Vaidhyanathan Committee (1992) on Pricing of Irrigation Water calculated that in order to cover the cost of operations and maintenance (O & M) charges, the increase in revenue in various states should range from 1.5 times in Punjab and Orissa to over 14 times in West Bengal. The underpricing of water adversely affects the availability of resources for the management of irrigation systems. Inadequate allocation for maintenance and repairs is a direct consequence of the poor financial position of the states, and is responsible for the low, and possibly deteriorating quality of service. This means that the potential increases in productivity which new technology makes possible cannot be realised in full.

A revision in the level and structure of water rates is thus necessary in the interest of both efficiency and equity. The said committee was of the view that the revision should be such as to achieve full cost recovery in due course and in the process promote saving, create disincentives for waste and thereby enable the service area to be expanded and a more reliable service assumed. The Committee recommended that rates should be based on O & M norms and capital charges (interest and depreciation) and the rates should be revised once in five years.

The World Bank has also called for hiking water and power tariffs in the agriculture sector to optimize returns on projects funded by it. The states which are reluctant to revise water rates will sooner or later realise the adverse impact of under pricing on availability of water. Under pricing has not fulfilled the socialist goal of ensuring equity in resource use and distorted the distribution pattern in the agricultural sector. The relatively well off farmers merrily lift water in excess of their requirement by using powerful pumpsets. This depletes the water table faster and makes it difficult for small farmers who cannot afford to hire or own pumpsets. If the trend continues, agricultural growth will be severely affected.

In the light of what is discussed above, there is hardly any justification that water supplies should continue as at present. In terms of a realistic strategy, a few points merit attention. There can be different bases for pricing water; it would be charged on the basis of crops and area irrigated; it could also be charged on the basis of volume of water used. In most states in India, water is charged on the basis of crops and area. This does not always imply a link between the volume of water used and what you pay for it. Raising the price of water, keeping the rate structure intact, will not have a major impact on securing efficiency objectives. For pricing to have a significant effect on water use decisions, it has to be linked to the volume of water used.

Volumetric pricing is, therefore a more viable option. However, it is laden with what economists call high transaction costs; the costs of information, contracting and enforcement. It is difficult to monitor how much water each of several individual farmer uses. It is difficult to collect this information and to ensure that every farmer pays his due. Further, volumetric pricing also has certain technical requirements. It requires the installation of measuring devices such as the V-notch, the parhsall flume and the standing wave flume. Thus, the introduction of volumetric pricing to individual farmers is constrained by high transaction costs, the large spread of irrigation systems and technical requirements that such a system imposes.

Another important distinction is between cost recovery and irrigation financing. Under a system of cost recovery, which is currently in vogue in most states, what is realised by way of irrigation fees goes into the state exchequer. With no link between the resources and the expenditure, there is no incentive to improve either the recovery, or the quality of service. Under a system of irrigation financing, on the other hand, these accruals are used for improving the quality of irrigation services. We therefore, need to move from the current system of cost recovery to a system of irrigation financing.

The other myth that is now wearing out is that the farmer is unable to or reluctant to pay more for water. In places with access to both surface and ground water, farmers pay as much as ten times more for ground water. This is largely because ground water enables them greater control over irrigation. Thus, farmers would be willing to pay more for water if it is matched by productivity increases brought about through improvements in the quality of irrigation services.

This brings us to the political acceptability of water price hikes. In Maharashtra and Andhra Pradesh, recent proposals to raise irrigation prices found acceptance. In these states, there have been efforts at forming water users associations. These are groups of farmers usually below the outlet that take water from the irrigation department on a volumetric basis. It is then distributed among farmers. There develops a mutual contract wherein the irrigation department agrees to provide certain supply of water to farmers who agree to pay for it collectively. The formation of water users associations, thus, provides a forum for dual accountability between the two sides. It also makes volumetric pricing of water possible and acceptable and serves as the base for further price revisions upwards. The current process of reform in Andhra Pradesh establishes that upward price revisions are possible, but only when part of an overall reform strategy aimed at creating accountability of the irrigation departments, empowering users, putting in place improvements in the infrastructure and improving the quality of irrigation services, is accompanied.

Improvement in Water Use Efficiency

Improvement in Water Use Efficiency is also important because of the need for its conservation. Despite whatever we do, water problems are likely to become acute in the country in the coming two decades. If so, water use efficiency has to be the cornerstone of future irrigation policy. Water use efficiency is presently estimated to be only 38 to 40% for canal irrigation and about 60% for ground water irrigation schemes. On the basis of 1991 Census, per capita water availability per year in India was estimated at 2214 cubic meters against the global average of 9231 cubic metres and 3020 M3, 3962 M3 and 4792M3 per year respectively for countries like Afghanistan, Pakistan and Sudan. In 1990, India was ranked at the 42nd position among 100 countries by per capita water availability. In the total water use in 1990, the share of agriculture was 83%, followed by domestic use (4.5%), industrial use (2.5%) and energy (1.8%). The remaining 8 per cent was for other uses including environmental requirements. The projected total water demand by the year 2025 is around 1050 cubic kilometres against the country's utilizable water resources of 1140 cubic kilometres. The share of agriculture in total water demand by the year 2025 would be about 74 to 75 per cent. Thus, almost the entire utilizable water resources of the country would be required to be put to use by the year 2025 A.D.

Irrigation, being the major water user, its share in the total demand is bound to decrease from the present 83% to 74% due to more pressing and competing demands from other sectors by 2025 A.D. and, as such, the question of improving the present level of water use efficiency in general and for irrigation in particular assumes a great significance in perspective water resource planning. It is estimated that a 10% increase in the present level of water use efficiency in irrigation projects, an additional 14m.ha area can be brought under irrigation from the existing irrigation capacities which would involve a very moderate investment as compared to the investment that would be required for creating equivalent potential through new schemes. Thus, there is a need to improve the water use efficiency in most of the existing irrigation projects through modernization, renovation and upgradation to realise optimum benefits on the one hand and mitigate the consequential side effects like waterlogging etc. on the other.

A corollary of the issue allied is the water use management which means optimisation of available water for maximising crop production in a given area. In most of the Northern States, for example, it is observed from the data collected under a survey on methodological investigation into high yielding variety programme taken up by the Indian Agricultural Statistics Research Institute that the frequency of irrigation for the wheat crop is quite high ranging from five to seven. The situation is similar for paddy and maize in some of the States. A recent study by the Water Technology Centre of the Indian Agricultural Research Institute (IARI) says that mismanagement of irrigation leads to water logging and saline conditions not conducive to crop growth. Excess water interferes with field preparation, sowing, plant growth, yield and quality and harvesting operations.

About six million hectares or 15 per cent of the area under paddy is reported to suffer due to waterlogged conditions in the different parts of the country. Serious problems of waterlogging have been reported in some irrigation projects like Chambal in Rajasthan and Madhya Pradesh, Tawa in Madhya Pradesh, Pune and Jayakwadi in Maharashtra, Tungabhadra and Malaprabha in Karnataka, and Gandak and Kosi in Bihar. At a number of places, the problem of excess water has led to salinity problems aggravating the situation.

It may be mentioned that, although paddy requires large quantities of water for good growth, prolonged water logged conditions are not good for it. Certain stages of growth like early flowering have been reported to be more susceptible to waterlogged conditions than other stages of crop growth. For instance, flooding in the third month of transplanting which coincide with flowering stage reduces the yield by about 42 per cent. Similarly, yields get reduced by 20 to 24 per cent when flooding takes place at too early or too late stages.

Thus, there appears to be a considerable wastage of water by way of over irrigating crops without taking into account the actual requirements of each crop. To study the scope and extent of saving water by reducing the number of irrigations without seriously affecting the crop yield, results of an experiment of production potential at different research stations were examined and are presented in (Table 11.1).

Table 11.1 ***Production Levels (Q/ha) for Wheat and Gram for Alternative use of Irrigation***

State	*Crop*	*Number of Irrigations*	*Yield Q/ha.*	*Enhanced or Reduced Number of Irrigations*	*yield Q/ha*
Rajasthan	Wheat	6	33.5	3	31.7
	Gram	0	11.3	2	22.4
Uttar Pradesh	Wheat	4	36.6	3	32.2
	Gram	0	15.9	2	18.7
Maharashtra	Wheat	4	28.0	2	17.1
	Gram	0	8.5	2	20.9
Punjab	Wheat	4	63.0	2	56.4
	Lentil	0	9.9	2	17.5

SOURCE: D Singh, Presidential Address, Indian Agricultural Statistics Research Institute, 1981.

It will be observed that in Rajasthan the number of irrigations on wheat could be reduced from 6 to 3 without affecting the crop yield significantly. Similar results were also observed in Uttar Pradesh and Punjab. Obviously, the water so saved by reducing the number of irrigations on wheat crop can be profitably utilised for cultivation of other crops like gram and jowar. It is thus clear that for a given amount of water, there is a need for formulation of proper irrigation schedule so as to maximise the area irrigated under different crops which in turn will bring in the highest total production.

We have now to go much beyond the simple engineering concept of water utilization which merely represents the area of surface to which water has been applied or spread, and does not take into account the needs of the crops grown in respect of the quantity and timing of the irrigation. We should not really be content even with 100 per cent utilization of potential in this sense, but should aim at making the optimum use of water by adopting cropping patterns and irrigation practices based on a careful study of water requirements of crops in the particular soil and climatic conditions of any given area.

Use of Modern Techniques to Economise Water Use

There are basically three irrigation methods (each with many variations), gravity, sprinkler or drip. Gravity irrigation depends on topography. The water source must be higher than the surface, and the field contours determine the irrigation possibilities. A sprinkler system operates by water being expelled through a narrow nozzle at high velocity, resulting in spray. The system is widely used in Israel, Australia and U.S.A. Coffee growers in India and some states like Haryana and Rajasthan have also adopted it to some extent. The aim of the sprinkler system is to distribute the drops equally over a given area. In a drip system, water is distributed to designated points on the soil without passing through the atmosphere.

The Coefficient of Uniformity

A key to evaluating all systems is the coefficient of uniformity, or the CU. This is a calculated figure that represents the uniformity of water distribution over an area. According to some experts, the higher the CU, the greater the uniformity and the more effective the irrigation. Drip methods typically have CUs of about 90, sprinklers around 80 and gravity methods from 50 to 75. The impact of different CU levels on crop yields can be significant, as indicated in (Table 11.2).

It is obvious that high CUs are important for irrigation to result in high crop yields. In the case of maize, for example, increasing the CU from 70 to 80 results in an 18 per cent increase in yield.

Table 11.2 Crop Sensitivity to Water Distribution

	Yield (Kgs./ha.)		
CU	*Banana*	*Potatoes*	*Maize*
60	23.4	26.6	4.2
62	25.4	28.8	4.5
64	27.2	31.0	4.8
66	28.9	32.9	5.2
68	30.6	34.9	5.4
70	32.1	36.6	5.7
72	33.6	38.2	6.0
74	34.9	39.7	6.2
76	36.1	41.2	6.4
78	37.3	42.5	6.6
80	38.3	43.7	6.8

SOURCE: Rain Bird International.

In the conventional method of furrow irrigation, for example, only a quarter of each 100 cubic metres of moisture reaches the roots of cotton. Subsoil irrigation represents tubes buried in the soil to a definite depth. Through the openings in the tubes, water moisten the root layer. One variety of this method is droplet irrigation, where a special dropping bottle is installed near each plant from the polythene irrigating main line. The whole of the water coming by small doses is assimilated by the roots. Nine years of experimentation in the erstwhile USSR has shown that the yield of raw cotton was 41.3 metric centners per hectare in the case of furrow irrigation against 50.5 metric centners in the case of subsoil irrigation with the distance of 60 centimetres between the tubes. The loss of irrigation water per metric centner of raw cotton was thus reduced thereby 33 per cent.

Trickle or Drip System

Some new irrigation techniques economizing the usage of water direct the quantity of optimum water right at the root zone of plants through an elaborate network of pipes. The benefits are : (1) reduced labour costs, (2) economy in water usage; (3) minimum land levelling; (4) decreased tillage (5) reduced week growth (6) low fertilizer requirement and (7) high yield of crops.

The only problem with the system is its cost. This can be divided into two categories, the pump and control head, which cost around 25 per cent of the total cost and the distribution system and drippers, which account for the rest. The total cost of drip irrigation system depends on the spacing adopted for planting. For a closely spaced (IXlm), the cost is placed around Rs. 50,000 per hectare. For horticultural crops with wider spacing (6X6m) the cost is estimated to be around Rs. 12,000 per hectare. The amount of duties and levies particularly on plastics is an important element in the cost. If these are reduced by the government, cost can possibly be slashed to half. The Government of Rajasthan has introduced a subsidy on the drip irrigation system, restricted to small farmers whose total installation cost is within Rs. 20,000.

Irrigation Management

Present returns from irrigated area, being not more than half of their potentialities, agricultural scientists and water management experts have come to this conclusion that the most important issue which should now receive the highest attention is that the next 20 years should be devoted primarily to a reorganization of the management of irrigation infrastructure. According to them, the overall efficiency of the irrigation command areas can be doubled during this period if only the Government takes the important policy decision with regard to future directions of irrigation development and management in the country.

The foremost priority at this stage should be the scientific management of the resources created with so much investment and dedication. The watchward from now on has to be scientific management of irrigation rather than additions to it. Scientific management of irrigation water a relatively new concept not only in this country but in the world as a whole. The developed countries of the West do not have the kind of vast irrigation networks based on harnessing of major rivers, such as those of the Himalayas, as in this country. There are no ready models available which India can emulate. Much of the knowledge of scientific management of irrigation networks must be generated within India and must accrue from our own experience of the past fifty years.

FERTILIZER

Fertilizer subsidy during 1990-91 was Rs. 43,890 million. This is estimated to be Rs. 84560 million this year (2201-02) (Table 11.3). This was perceived to be too high and the government vowed to prune it drastically. In 1991-92, it even committed to the IMF that fertilizer subsidies would be removed in three years time. However, by 1999-2000 the payout had already more than doubled. It is interesting to observe that subsidy on indigenous fertiliser was increased to Rs. 66,000 in the 1997-98 from Rs. 47,430 million under this head in the previous year. Similar increases were made in the case of concessions on the sale of decontrolled phosphetic and potassic fertilisers. (Table 11.4). This clearly suggests the need for an in-depth study of the fundamental causes leading to growth in subsidy.

Subsidy expressed in rupees per tonne represents the amount in excess of reasonable cost of production (including a fair margin of profit)-based on prescribed efficiency norms in regard to capacity utilisation and consumption of raw materials and utilities-over net return from sales at the controlled price. This is reimbursed to producers under the retention pricing scheme (RPS). The changes in subsidy amount depend on the relative movements at reasonable cost vis-s-vis selling price.

During the 90s the ex-refinery price of naphtha increased from Rs.1,982 per tonne to about Rs 9.100 per tonne (for supplies to port based units), i.e. by Rs. 7,118 per tonne. The increase in production cost due to this alone was thus about Rs. 4,300 per tonne (based on 0.6 tonne naphtha for one tonne urea). The overall increase in cost would be much higher due to increase in conversion cost, viz., wages/salaries, other overheads, chemicals and catalysts, repairs and maintenance, cost of bags, marketing and selling expense, etc.

In sharp contrast, the selling price of urea increased from Rs 2,350 per tonne to Rs. 4,000 per tonne. Thus the hike was only Rs. 1,650 per tonne leaving an uncovered gap of Rs. 2650 per tonne towards increase in feedstock cost alone (4300-1,650). Necessarily, this was plugged by

Table 11.3 Central Subsidy on Food and Fertilizers (1976-77 to 2001-02)

(Rs. million)

Sl. No.	Year	Food	Fertilizers		
			Imported	Indigenous	Total
1.	1976-77	4.773	N.A.	N.A.	600
2.	1977-78	4,801	2,410	250	2,660
3.	1978-79	5,694	1,710	1,722	3,432
4.	1979-80	6,000	2,830	3,208	6,038
5.	1980-81	6,500	3,350	1,700	5,050
6.	1981-82	7,000	1,000	2,750	3,750
7.	1982-83	7,110	550	5,500	6,050
8.	1983-84	8,350	1,420	9,000	10,420
9.	1984-85	11,010	7,273	12,000	19,273
10.	1985-86	16,500	3,237	16,000	19,237
11.	1986-87	20,000	1,971	17,000	18,971
12.	1987-88	20,000	1,140	20,500	21,640
13.	1988-89	22,000	2,007	30,000	32,007
14.	1989-90	24,760	7,771	37,710	45,421
15.	1990-91	24,500	6,593	37,297	43,890
16.	1991-92	28,500	12,996	35,000	47,996
17.	1992-93	28,000 †	9,961	48,000	57,961
18	1993-94	55,370	7,620	38,000	45,620
19.	1994-95	51,000 †	11,660	40,750	52,410
20.	1995-96	53,770 †	19,350	43,000	62,350
21.	1996-97	60,660 †	11,630	47,430	59,080
22.	1997-98	79,000	7,220	66,000	73,220
23.	1998-99	91,000	3,330	74,730	78,060
24.	1999-2000	94,350	2,930	86,700	89,630
25.	2000-01*	121,250	10	94,800	94,810
26.	2001-02*	17,612	5,000	79,560	84,560
27.	2002-03**	212.00	—	—	—

* Revised Estimates ** Budget Estimates † Including Sugar

Note: From 1992-93 on wards the figures of subsidy on fertilizers are only on Urea.

a corresponding increase in subsidy. The scenario for units based on other feedstocks, i.e. gas, fuel oil/LSHS, etc would be broadly similar.

In view of the above, ballooning fertilizer subsidies are sustained despite steep increase in prices of feedstocks since there is a reluctance to increase the selling price of urea even by a small amount. Interestingly, the former represents a corresponding additional income in the hands of public sector units in the oil/gas sector - Indian Oil,

ONGC, GAIL, Hindustan Petroleum, Oil India, etc. This is nothing but intra-economy transfer i.e. from budget head to PSUs.

The Retention Pricing Scheme

There is no doubt that India's strides in both agriculture and fertilizer consumption were fuelled by Government policies. From a production base of almost nil in 1951-52, it has grown to 13 million tonnes of nutrients now. This has become possible on account of Government policies of intervention. Based on Marathe Formula, the retention pricing scheme (RPS) for fertilizers was introduced in November 1977. The idea was to provide a fair price to the manufacturers based on prescribed efficiency norms vis-a vis the net realisation being controlled by the Government, and at the same time making it affordable to the farmers with the Government subsidising the difference.

In this method, the normal modus operandi is to take into consideration the variable costs borne by the urea producers, which include feedstock in principal, capital costs incurred by any urea plant-like those of annual interest costs and the provision for depreciation and marketing and selling expenses etc. The annual output for any plant is fixed at 85 per cent capacity utilization for the urea plants using naptha and furnace oil as feedstock, and 90 per cent for the new plants using natural gas as their feedstock. And over and above that, besides taking into account these costs, the current specification (which have not been modified since long) allows for a 12 percent rate of return of the net worth. But the case study of 17 fertilizer units for a period between 1991 and 1996-97, which together account for more than 50 percent of market share of urea, suggests that almost half of the subsidies is owing to the rise in feed stock prices, which actually reaches the government only, through petroleum and gas distributing PSUs.

The subsidy is available on both domestic and imported fertilizers. Import subsidy is the difference between the sale price and the cost of importing fertilizers including transportation costs (inclusive of port handling) and dealer's margin. No wonder, alongwith the massive jump in nutrient production and consumption over the years, the subsidy bill also bloated. The subsidy bill which was Rs 505 crore in 1980-81 jumped up five and half times to Rs. 47,996 crore in 1991-92. With the Government embarking on reforms, it decided to go for decontrol of phosphatic (P) and potassic (K) fertilizers and allowing subsidy on urea (Tables 11.4 and 11.4A). As was expected, it proved to be a turning point. This created an imbalance in favour of consumption of cheaper (subsidized) urea. This is against the expert advice which advocates balanced use of plant nutrients in order to sustain crop productivity and soil-fertility. The present price/subsidy structure of different fertilizer nutrients has thus led to a lopsided use of the same. An ideal N.P.K. consumption ratio is 4:2:1. But as against this, 1996-97 pattern was 10:8:1. This was slightly corrected to 7.9:2.8:1 during 1997-98. This

Table 11.4 Total Concession on Sale of Decontrolled Phosphatic and Potassic Fertilizers

(Rs. million)

Year	Total Amount
1992-93	3,400‡
1993-94	5,170‡
1994-95	5,280
1995-96	5,000
1996-97	16,720
1997-98	25,960
1998-99	37,900
1999-2000	45,000
2000-1*	43,190
2001-02†	57,140

* Revised estimate † Budget estimate
‡ Assistance for fertilizer promotion.
SOURCE: Fertiliser Statistics 2000-01.

is primarily due to the decontrol of all the fertilizers other than urea since 1992. Since urea became comparatively cheaper, farmers used more of it and disturbed the balance. During November 2001, government took an interim decision to notify lower retention prices of urea for 13 factories with effect from April 2000. This will no doubt save about Rs. 800 crores in subsidies but a comprehensive long-term policy for this vital Rs. 35,000 core industry is yet to materialise (Table 11.5).

Recent Proposal

While the government has been unable to make any headway in cutting the ballooning subsidy on urea fertilisers despite setting up several committees over the past four years, it is all set to reverse the policy on even phosphatic fertilisers. The move, when implemented, will cost the exchequer around Rs. 300-400 crore. More importantly, it will open the door to a fresh set of demands for concessions, and will deal a deadly blow to the government's attempts to cut the urea subsidy of around Rs. 8,000 crore. The story began in August 1992, when Finance Minister Dr. Manmohan Singh first decided to decontrol phosphatic fertilisers like diammonium phosphate (DAP) and muriates of potash (MoP). As a part of this policy, which also went through various twists and turns, phosphatic units were given a fixed subsidy per unit of the fertiliser they produced. The subsidy rose from the initial Rs. 1,000 per tonne fixed in 1993 to Rs. 3,750 in 1997-98, and to Rs. 4,550 during February 2000, and then to Rs. 3,700 in July 2000.

Once industry had a fixed subsidy, it began making the necessary adjustments and changes in its production process. Several plants, in

Table 11.4A Rate of Concession on Decontrolled Phosphatic and Potassic Fertilizers

(Rs. per tonne)

Fertilisers	1992-93 Rabi	1993-94 to 1995-96	1996-97 April 96 to 05/07/96	1996-97 05/07/96 to 31/03/97	1997-98 01/04/97 to 30/09/97	1997-98 01/10/97 to 31/03/98	1998-99 April 98 to 30/09/98*	1998-99 w.e.f. 01/10/98**	1999-2000 w.e.f. 01/04/99†
Indigenous diammonium phosphate	1000	1000	1000	3000	3750	3500	4400	4400	4600
Imported diammonium phosphate	1000	—	—	1500	2250	2000	3400	3400	3200
Muriate of potash	1000	1000	1000	1500	2000	2000	3000	3000	3250
Single superphosphate	—	340	340	500	600	600	600	900	900
Indigenous complex fertilizers:									
15-15-15	576	576	576	1353	1723	1641	2814	2814	2970
12-32-16	962	962	962	2487	3142	2968	3827	3827	4031
23-23-0	500	500	500	1500	1875	1750	3165	3165	3370
14-35-14	994	994	994	2633	3320	3130	4071	4071	4282
28-28-0	609	609	609	1826	2283	2131	3853	3853	4026
16-20-0	435	435	435	1304	1630	1522	2477	2477	2588
20-20-0	435	435	435	1304	1630	1522	2752	2752	2876
10-26-26	999	999	999	2346	2986	2844	3777	3777	3998
17-17-17	653	653	653	1534	1953	1860	3189	3189	3366
19-19-19				1714		2079	3564	3564	3762
14-28-14									
20-10-10							3590	3590	3779

Notes: * Final rate announced on 28.12.1998

** Provisional rate pending finalisation

† Provisional rate announced on 25-5-99.

Table 11.5 Farm Subsidies and Foodgrains Productivity in Selected Countries—1991

	Country	Total farm Subsidies (US $ billn.)	Population (ailln.)	Arable land † (mill ha)	Subsidy (US$)		Subsidy value of agricultural production (at current price % (N + P2 05 + K2 0)	Kg/ha	
					Percapita	Per ha of arable land †		Fertiliser consumption	Foodgrains prodcutivity
1	2	3	4	5 = 2/3	6 = 2/4	7	8	9	
1.	EC	83.59	345.760	82.205	241.8	1016.8	49	213.0	4970
2.	USA	34.70	252.410	187.776	137.5	184.8	30	99.8	5319
3.	Japan	31.48	123.921	4.552	254.0	6915.6	66	387.3	5703
4.	Canada	7.68	27.034	45.930	284.1	167.2	45	46.8	2427
5.	Australia	1.44	17.292	46.877	83.3	30.7	15	27.3	1693
6.	New Zealand	0.13	3.380	0.410	38.5	317.1	4	934.1	4748
7.	India (1991-92)	3.02*	862.745	169.700	3.5	17.8	5	75.2*	1721

* Only food and fertiliser subsidy ** 70.3 kg/ha of gross cropped area † including land under permanent crops.

SOURCE: Compiled in FAT, New Delhi from (1) OECD Report on Farm Subsidies, OECD Secretariat, 1992. (2) 1992 % FAO Production Year Book "Vol. 46, FAO Rome.

the mid-90s, used to base their production of phosphatic fertilisers on naphtha—they would make ammonia from the naphtha route, and then go on to make phosphatic fertilisers. Now when they realised that fertiliser subsidies would generally be lowered over a period of time, these units decided to do away with the naphtha route which was an inefficient one. Instead, several firms either started using imported ammonia, or made their ammonia from natural gas—both processes were more cost-effective. All told, the industry wrote off around Rs. 200 crore while deciding to do away with the naphtha route during the mid-90s.

Now, thanks to the recommendations of the Expenditure Reforms Committee headed by former finance secretary Geethakrishnan, the government is planning a two-tier phosphatic fertiliser subsidy. One for units based on imported ammonia, and another higher one for those using naphtha. So, "never mind if you're using an inefficient technology, we'll take care of you" is the government policy. Imported ammonia costs around $160 per tonne while using naphtha takes the cost to around $250 a tonne. Clearly it doesn't make sense to use the naphtha route, and most private sector firms figured this out years ago (or are in the process of doing so). Yet, the government is going to increase the subsidy for the naphtha users.

Apart from the impact on increasing the phosphatic fertiliser subsidy, is the issue of the urea subsidy. Today, the subsidy for urea is fixed separately for each plant. Clearly this is a very inefficient system, and leads to corruption as there is no way the government can ever have fully correct details of the cost of each plant. For the last four years, the government has set up various committees, but has never had the guts to take a decision despite each report recommending the government to fix one rate of subsidy. Now, with the government introducing two subsidy rates in even the phosphatic area, the urea producers are unlikely to accept any attempts to cut their subsidies.

Basic Issues

With regard to the question of subsidies, there are three basic questions. One, who gets this subsidy: the farmer, industry, or consumers of grain? Two, what happens to the fertilizer industry if the Retention Price Scheme (RPS) is abolished? And three, what happens to fertilizer consumption and agricultural production, as one moves from administered to market pricing?

To see who gets the subsidy, we must know what the price of urea would be without controls and if imports were decanalised at zero import duty. Then, domestic urea price would be linked to import parity price. In recent years world urea prices have fluctuated between $ 90 per metric tonne and $210/mt. The long run marginal cost (LRMC) can be taken between $ 150/mt and $160/mt. Adding another $ 15 to $20/mt for freight and domestic distribution costs, we get a much higher figure than what the Indian farmer has been paying. Farmers are apparently being subsidised because urea prices are lower than world LRMC.

However, if we combine urea pricing with the pricing of output like wheat and rice, then according to import-price parity calculations it was found (of course, a few years back) that farmers were getting a raw deal. This was because the prices of their output were below corresponding import parity prices. Netting out the effect of output prices on input prices, one found that Indian farmer was not really `net subsidised'. In fact he is being `taxed' through trade and pricing policies, and the aggregate measure of support (AMS), as it is called, for Indian agriculture is actually minus 20 per cent of the value of agricultural produce. If so, who was getting the fertilizer subsidy was either for the consumer of grain or the fertilizer industry. Recently, the position has completely changed. India today is priced out in the international market for all the major agricultural commodities.

Really speaking, whatever its shape and form the subsidy has not much to do with the farmer/farming. Under the procurement policy, total produce of the farmer (whatever comes to the market) is to be purchased by the Government at fixed Minimum Support Prices (MSP). And the basic criteria to determine MSP is cost plus. This means that any increase in the cost of production of the farmer will call for an immediate increase in MSP. What really happens is that due to the strong farmer lobby, increase in the MSP is higher than the actual impact of increases in the input costs. This is what happened in June 1994, when the prices of urea were raised from Rs.6.0 to Rs. 7.22 (20.3%) and those of other fertilizers decontrolled, MSP for wheat was raised from Rs. 380 to 475 (including central bonus of Rs. 60). This meant an increase of 25 percent although the share of fertilizers in the total cost of production would workout to be much less, say 3-4% on cost A2. PDS was restructured from 1997 when under TPDS, prices for people below the poverty line were drastically reduced both for rice and wheat. This led to substantial increases in the food subsidy bill. The moral of the story is that subsidies on fertilizers or food are the two sides of the same coin.

How much of the subsidy goes to the fertilizer industry? What would happen to the urea industry if there were free imports of urea? Industry gets the subsidy because many plants have higher costs than the import price of urea. The current landed cost of concessional naphtha is in the range of Rs. 3200 to Rs. 3500 per tonne and the price to fertilizer units works out between Rs. 5500 and Rs. 5800, after including freight and sales tax elements. The landed cost on a non-concessional basis is Rs. 6684 tonne and, after adding a sales tax of 10 percent, freight charges and sales tax, the final price comes to around Rs. 9000 per tonne. Thus, the differential in price between subsidised and non-subsidised urea comes to between Rs. 3200 and Rs. 3500 per tonne. Since 0.6 tonne of naphtha is utilised to manufacture one tonne of urea, the cost differential per tonne of urea to the manufacturer comes to Rs.2000. As four million tonnes of urea is produced using naphtha as the feedstock, the extra subsidy works out to Rs. 800 crore a year.

A similar calculation will show that the differential for units that use fuel oil comes to Rs.2500 per tonne. Using the standard formula of 0.6 tonnes of oil requirement for a tonne of output, the extra cost to the producer is Rs.1500 per tonne. On an output of 2.26 million tonnes in 1997-98 the extra cost was to a whopping Rs. 600 crore. The production figures taken into account in the above calculations were based on data available from the year 1996-97. In 1997-98 , the targeted production was substantially higher and it was safe to assume that the extra burden on fertilizer units was higher by atleast Rs. 100 crore. The total yearly burden, taking fuel oil and naphtha into account, would come to Rs. 1500 crore. The Finance Ministry, however, did not bear the entire subsidy as half of it was borne by the oil pool account (for the period April-September, 1997). The incidence on the budget was calculated to roughly Rs. 750 crore in 1997-98.

If one were to price feedstocks on the basis of their opportunity cost-gas on the basis of Sankar Committee's recommendations (Rs.3,050/th.cu.m at land fall and Rs. 4,200/th.cu.m. on HBJ pipeline), and naphtha and fuel oil on import parity basis, about one-third of domestic urea production becomes economically non-viable at an import parity price of $180/mt. If the import-parity price comes down to $160/mt, 45 per cent of domestic production becomes non-viable.

Thus, roughly half to one-third of the subsidy on domestic urea production is going to support high-cost local urea producers. This remained largely hidden in the past as feedstock prices for urea industry carried high concession. But as distortions in feedstock pricing are corrected, the high costs of urea industry become glaring. The Hanumantha Rao Committee has questioned these costs, and feels that there is lot of `gold plating'. It suggests dismantling of RPS, replacing it by a flat-rate subsidy by fixing the normative referral price of urea (ex-factory) at Rs. 6,050/tonne

It suggested a method under which the RPS was to be replaced by a dual system. The system which called for fixing the exfactory normative referral prices (NRP) of urea at Rs 6050 for gas based plants. For naptha based plants, the Committee recommended Rs. 1,700/tonne extra and Rs. 1,300/tonne extra for the FO/LSHS based plants. The report invited a lot of debate. Since the system meant raising the farm-gate price of urea by almost 65 per cent (over Rs. 3660 a tonne when the report was tabled) in one shot the implementation of these recommended actions called for a real bold step.

The report recommended going for a low range marginal cost (LRMC) method, according to which subsidies on every additional tonne of urea would be lower. Because of the vested interests of those who were enjoying the benefits of RPS and inability of the Government to face the aftermaths of raising urea prices by 65 per cent, the report has been put on the back burner. The Finance Minister in his 2000-2001 budget has no doubt initiated a movement away from a system which had operated as a premium on inefficiency, on the one hand, and as an undeserved bonus for private sector companies, which had even used subsidies for dividend distribution as some kind of "other income" on the other. This is a healthy beginning to get out of the subsidy syndrome.

Future Policy

While giving a clear indication that a subsidy free regime will prevail in the coming 10-15 years, an objectives of the future fertilizer pricing policy has to lure investment to keep enlarging the fertilizer production base, imports playing only a marginal and supplementary role. The present, retention price based subsidy scheme which stems from the Marathe Formula has achieved two broad objectives: (a) ensured that the farmers got fertilizers at an affordable price; and (b) ensured India becoming a major fertilser producer, especially of nitrogen and phosphorous. This has made India immune to the blackmail of global producers. It must be realised that China and India are major players in world market and variations in their import demand has significant impact on world prices. Once the demand of these countries goes up, prices in the international market will shoot.

The focus should be on bringing down feedstock/fuel prices to reasonable levels which will automatically make indigenous production cheaper than imports. It means that fertilizer production has to be encouraged, but cost of production must be reduced by an appropriate pricing policy for feed stock/fuel prices. In order to encourage investment in fertilizer plants, the following concessions may be considered:

(i) exemption from customs, excise and other duties on capital goods (plant machinery) for setting up new plants or modernization or expansion of plants.

(ii) A ten year tax holiday for new plants.

(iii) Permission to raise money from the parallel economy (as in the case of Indira Vikas Patra). It is necessary that India continuously increase its production base, otherwise five years from now, she will become subject to the price blackmail of foreign producers.

(iv) Present restrictions on the movement of fertilizer may be removed so that all plants realise maximum profits. In fact, for the new plants being set up with these concessions, there need be no restriction about their pricing. They should sell freely at market determined prices.

(v) Budget 2002-03 has revised prices by 5 per cent. A farmer will have to pay more for each bag of urea (Rs 12), DAP (Rs. 22) and potash (Rs. 10).

POWER

In 1976, agriculture accounted for 14 percent of electricity consumption and was not subsidized at all. The average cost of production of electricity was then 18 paise per unit and the average tariff paid by the farm sector was 19 paise. By 1978, the cost had risen to 20 paise but tariff remained at 18 paisa. In the next 18 years, the cost of power generation rose to Rs. 1.328 paise per unit, but the average tariff on agriculture increased to only 24.5 paise. The share of the farm sector in electricity consumption, however, rose to 29 per cent of the total. As a result in 1995-96 the subsidy to agriculture on power supply had risen to over Rs. 13,000 crore. Latest estimates indicate that gross subsidies to the power sector in 1999-2000 had been around Rs. 33,821 crore. While agriculture accounts for a bulk of the subsidy at Rs 25,576 crore, domestic consumption accounts for Rs. 7,892.9 crore (Table 11.6).

Table 11.6 The State Power Sector

(Rs. crore)

Electricity Sale to	*Gross subsidy involved*		
	1998-99	*1999-2000 (RE)*	*2000-01 (AP)*
Agriculture *	22,537	25,577	28,217
Domestic	7,270	7,893	9,387
Interstate sales*	538	351	358
TOTAL	30,345	33,821	37,692

Note : Exclude Delhi*
RE : Revised Estimates
AP : Annual Plan Projections

Several SEBs, which have now electricity regulatory commissions, are hoping to rationalize the tariff structure in the power industry. While subsidies on agriculture and domestic consumption would not be totally withdrawn, industry experts feel that rationalisation would reduce the burden on industry which is cross-subsidising the other sectors. Also, the Regulatory Commission Act provides for subsidies only if the state government compensates the SEBs. The new Electricity Bill 2000 has made it mandatory for all SEBs to unbundle and rationalise the tariff structures.

Thus, along with uneconomic water rates, continued policy of state governments to provide subsidies to farm sector on power has made the problem further complicated. However, some of the state governments like Karnataka, Maharashtra and Haryana have already decided to increase the power tariff.

In agriculture, pumpsets are essential for farming and development of the area. They are the heart of irrigation system. Pumps provide ground water and surface water resources which are very important for irrigation. Pumps for agriculture are estimated to consume 30 per cent of total power generation in the country. The country can save more than one-third of this by having efficient pumps and pumping system.

Agricultural sector power tariff, being fixed on the basis of BHP rating of sets, also vitiates the incentive to procure the somewhat more costly-but more energy efficient-pumping sets. Nor is there any optimum use of the water for irrigation purpose and there is also friction loss through foot valves and piping.

Perhaps the most important barrier is the present electricity pricing policy of the State Electricity Boards (SEBs). Electricity prices are regulated and based on historical cost of the utility. In fact, for most of the utilities, average revenue realised per unit is actually less than the average cost of supply. The extent of subsidies for the agriculture sector is at 80 to 100 per cent, while the subsidies for the domestic sector range between 40 and 60 per cent.

Need for Different Tariff

This, however, is not the real issue. There is another aspect of the power scenario which has to be looked into. All over the world there are different tariffs for peak, normal and off-peak consumers. Normally, the tariff for off-peak consumers is less than 50 per cent of that for peak consumers. The agricultural load is not only off-peak but the power supply to it too, is limited to 8-10 hours. This load is of seasonal character and the demand goes up only in certain months. The domestic consumers are peak consumers and, therefore, the agricultural consumers should not be burdened with more than 50 per cent of the power tariff applicable to the domestic consumers. Even during off-peak time of about 18 hours a day, the agricultural sector works in shifts and hardly gets power for 8-10 hours a day during peak seasons. The power tariff for the farm sector, therefore, should be further reduced by another 50 per cent, i.e. at only 25 per cent of the domestic tariff. At present, the average domestic rate is estimated at 140 paise per unit and the average farm rate is around 35 paise per unit. The farm sector, is thus not being subsidised. All such boards which have increased the average farm rate to 50 paise per unit are, thus subsidizing the domestic sector by 15 paise per unit.

It may be of interest to note that till the end of the fifth five year plan (ending March 1979) domestic tariff in India was the highest at about 55 paise per unit, whereas the industrial tariff was only 30 per cent of this, and agricultural tariff as one-third, i.e. 18 paise per unit. All over the world the domestic tariffs are the highest and the industrial tariffs the lowest: the off-peak tariffs are still lower. This norm of international tariff formulation was completely changed in India after the Fifth Plan. While the domestic tariff has merely doubled till the end of the 8th Plan, the industrial tariff has been raised by about 25 times and the agricultural tariff about three times in several states.

It may be revealing to compare the average rates for the agricultural sector with that of LT industries. It is well known that LT industries normally get power round the clock except for some restrictions during peak time. The all-India average consumption of LT industries per KW of connected load in 1994-95 was less than 400 units. On the other hand, the average consumption of the agricultural sector which hardly gets few hours of supply even during peak months, was about 2,100 units per KW of connected load in comparison to LT industries. As there is no metering arrangement for pumping sets, it would be fair to compare the converted BHP rate of LT industries with that of the farm sector's. The average tariff of LT industries is about 250 paise per unit which on a consumption of 700 units per KW corresponds to a fixed tariff of only Rs. 1,700. On the other hand, the average BHP tariff of the agricultural sector is about Rs. 1,000 per KW of connected load and, therefore, even if for academic purposes the average tariff of the agricultural sector is raised to match the LT industries; the average tariff in majority of the Boards will still work out to only 75 paise per unit as against 50 paise at present. Therefore, it is quite obvious that there is no justification to hike the power tariff for the agricultural sector as it happens to be a off-peak consumer with limited hours of supply.

Real Agricultural Consumption

Till the end of the Fifth Plan (March 1979) the consumption in the farm sector and the LT industries was practically equal at about 800 units per KW of connected load. The SEBs cleverly manipulated figures to convince the government the necessity of heavy subsidy needed for the farm sector. In fact, the excessive T & D losses and pilferage are being transferred and shown as agricultural consumption in the absence of metering. In this way the SEBs are demanding subsidy for pilferage and high T & D losses. Rough estimates show that losses of SEBs would reach a whopping Rs. 1,70,000 crore by 2012 from Rs. 12,000 crore per annum now. Average losses due to thefts and pilferage of electricity in the country as a whole amount to over Rs. 30,000 crore annually. Outstandings of SEBs to central power utilities would reach a staggering Rs. 5,00,000 crore by 2012 from Rs. 23,000 crore now. Eighteen of the 20 SEBs have a negative rate of return, and commercial losses of SEBs had mounted four times in the last 10 years. As against this T & D losses in other countries are very low (Table 11.7).

The fact of the matter is that most of the electricity being subsidised does not go to the farmer at all. Let the following figures speak for themselves. India generated 420 billion KWH of power during 1998-

Table 11.7 Transmission and Distribution Losses of Power in Selected Countries

(In per cent)

Country	1989	1990	1991	1992	1993
Bangladesh	30.10	15.07	16.32	13.31	17.10
China	7.54	7.44	7.68	7.75	7.16
Canada	9.45	8.44	8.74	8.46	8.25
Indonesia	21.93	22.47	20.95	17.97	17.18
Denmark	5.65	5.20	6.92	6.70	6.93
Finland	5.64	5.10	5.04	5.48	5.01
France	8.25	8.19	8.28	7.64	8.02
Germany	--	5.45	5.17	4.87	5.08
Rep of Korea	5.93	5.49	5.50	5.66	5.48
Hungary	11.11	11.09	11.06	9.43	13.66
Israel	5.06	5.22	5.43	5.06	4.65
Italy	8.54	7.83	8.15	7.84	8.31
Malaysia	11.05	8.71	12.13	7.89	--
Pakistan	20.64	21.35	20.55	22.94	22.89
Poland	10.58	9.15	12.43	13.85	15.19
Switzerland	8.03	7.97	7.97	8.03	7.98
Sri Lanka	17.26	16.78	18.25	16.89	17.28
Russia	--	8.84	8.98	9.53	9.26
U.K.	8.53	8.39	8.80	7.49	7.85
U.S.A.	5.70	9.93	7.93	8.40	8.66
Thailand	10.20	10.85	11.08	10.67	8.41
* India	23.28	22.89	22.83	21.80	21.41

* For financial year

SOURCE: Lok Sabha Unstarred Question #2693, Ministry of Power.

99. According to official sources the share of agriculture in the total power sold has increased to nearly one third today. This was only 4.3 percent in 1950, which increased to 6 percent in 1960-61, to 10.2 per cent in 1998-99.

But the problem with these estimates is that there is no basis for these calculations. There being no metered supplies in the rural areas, they are just residues. There are very few micro-level studies that have attempted to estimate power consumption in agriculture by looking at how many hours the farmer has really used his irrigation pump, its horse power and so, to get to the actual consumption. The estimates so derived are less than even one-fifth of the figures being reported by official statistics in some cases. For example, in a report by Centre for Advanced Development Research, sponsored by the UP State Planning Commission, it was found that total power consumption by pumps in UP was only 1496 million units during 1993-94 as against 8924 million units reported by the UPSEB (CADR, 1995). In other words the actual consumption was just 17 per cent of what was being claimed officially. Similarly, many other studies (World Bank, 1997: p.41) also reveal that the picture is not very different i.e. what is being officially reported as going to agriculture is way above what is actually being consumed by agriculture.

Again between 1976 and 1993 the consumption of electricity by the farm sector went up from 12 billion units to 100 billion units, an increase of 8.3 times. But during this period area under irrigation increased by only 40 per cent from 25.31 million ha. to 66 m.ha. The number of electrified tubewells increased from 2.7 to 6.4 million, an increase of 140 per cent. Consumption in supplying power to tubewells cannot possibly have increased by more than 3.36 times. The rest, some 60 billion units, had therefore been swallowed by small-scale industry. Applying the same ratios to 1999, the diversion of cheap electricity is probably of the order of 85 billion units. This is being consumed by the millions of small, ramshackle factories and machine shops that are mushrooming in the rural areas all over the country.

First, that we have used official figures of power supplied, cost of power and revenue tariff from agriculture, in our estimates of power subsidy. As pointed out earlier, there are several micro level studies that indicate possible overestimation of power supplies to agriculture as per official statistics. If one were to use the figures of power consumption as estimated in these survey studies to work out the actual revenue tariff being paid by agriculture, one would literally get a shock. As per this approach, for irrigation purpose only, in western UP, the farmers are already paying Rs. 2.09 to Rs. 2.53/Kwh; in central UP the revenue tariff is even higher: between Rs 2.47 to Rs. 3.09/Kwh; and still higher in eastern UP: between Rs.2.82 to Rs. 3.53/Kwh. For all agricultural operations, and for entire UP, the revenue tariff is Rs. 1.17 to Rs. 1.46/Kwh. In Karnal (Haryana) it is 0.94/Kwh. for 7.5 HP pump, on an average. Similar situation exists in Gujarat, where the revenue tariff for different capacities of irrigation pumps turns out to be between Rs.1 and Rs. 2/Kwh (World Bank, 1997: p.44). These estimates are 5 to 10 times higher than what the official statistics would provide. This wide variation in numbers speaks of urgent need to do further research in this area before blindly recommending drastic increases in flat rate charges for power in rural areas. This also speaks of the possibility of enormous losses in transmission or simply theft, which is being shown as power supplied to agriculture in the official statistics.

Second, if one looks at the quality of power being supplied to rural areas, one would hear frequent complaints that wide fluctuations in power supplies often burn motors of irrigation pumps. Besides the extra cost that it imposes on the farmer to get his motors rewound, it leads to disruption in his irrigation schedule, as it is not always easy to get a mechanic that would repair the motor the same day. This factor compels many farmers to have stand-by diesel operated pump sets, which leads to much higher operational costs, besides the extra (avoidable) capital that he has to put in business to have some certainty in irrigating his fields. If one takes into account all these extra costs, which are imposed by unreliable and erratic power supplies in the rural sector, the cost of irrigation to farmer may not be as low as is generally perceived.

Were these users to pay domestic or industrial rates all of the State Electricity Boards' losses would disappear. If State governments want to keep giving cheap power to their farmers for their pumpsets, all they have to do is to license the 6.5 million pumpsets as they license cars today. Each farmer can then pay the market rate for power and get a rebate on the imputed consumption for irrigation per hectare per crop. That no one has even seen the discrepancy described above, let alone acted upon it, reflects the power of the small business class in the country and the abysmal incompetence of the State bureaucracies.

Transmission and Distribution

Winston Churchill once said that "a plan is nothing, planning is everything". His observation applies perfectly well to the power sector in India where the Ministry of Power (MoP) has prepared massive plan to add 40,000 MW of new installed capacity during the Ninth Plan without matching provisions for associated transmission and distribution (T & D) facilities. Apart from this, a number of mega power projects and state trading of power have also been proposed. On the other side, no study has been done from generation to utilisation of power even as the country boasts of being the leader in software. This, when all IITs and even the CEA have comprehensive software programmes for system and financial studies. It is unfortunate that even simple information of simultaneous peak demand being met in the country is not known. Rough estimates indicate that the country is meeting a gross peak demand of only 60,000 MW against installed capacity of 95,000 MW or 63 per cent against 85-90 per cent elsewhere in the world. The performance of our thermal machines is, therefore, deplorable for meeting peak demands. In fact, the availability of these machines at the peak time is only 65 per cent as MOP has very cleverly set aside about 13 per cent of the capacity towards partial unavailability which is, in fact, a part of forced outage. In earlier Plans, India had recognized the need for a balanced programme within the maximum available resources, instead of focusing alone on generation at the cost of T & D as is being done at present. It is thus obvious that power from new generation projects can not be utilized efficiently due to inadequate T & D system and losses will mount at the cost of quality of power.

The real ailment of the power sector is serious shortage of peak power in the evening time, particularly during the summer months. During the low demand period, the country is very much surplus in energy to an extent of about 30 per cent. The average technical loss exceeds 30 per cent and peak time loss 50 per cent due to poor T & D system. USAID also estimates that the current losses due to poor T & D system accounts for upto 40 to 50 per cent of the total power produced. No proper diagnosis has, however, been undertaken and the entire planning is based on adhocism. Apart from this inefficiency, the theft of electricity is increasing, resulting in heavy loss of revenues to the SEBs. It is estimated that electricity worth about Rs. 1,500 crores is "stolen" every year in the States. Over 40 per cent of the power generated is not brought into the billing process, whereas the transmission and distribution (T & D) losses are shown as only 17 to 20 per cent. Losses of the SEBs would reach a whopping Rs. 1,70,000 crore by 2012 from Rs.12,000 crore per annum now. Average losses due to thefts and pilferage of electricity in the country as a whole amounts to over Rs. 30,000 crore annually. Outstanding of SEBs to central power utilities would reach a staggering Rs.5,00,000 crore by 2012 from Rs. 23,000 crore now. 18 of the 20 SEBs have a negative rate of return, and commercial losses of SEBs had mounted four times in the last 10 years. The Power Ministers at their conference resolved that "delays in reforms only increase the financial cost of reforms". They agreed to strengthen and upgrade T & D systems and make the substation the primary unit of focus.

It is tariff and power losses which are hurting the SEBs the most. If this can be contained, they could become more viable. Billing has to improve and more revenue has to be collected. Theft syndicates must be unearthed and smashed. Central energy officials argue that if power theft is contained and the SEBs are restructured and made accountable at every point, the losses can be cut to half. About 25 per cent of the power generated was given free and another 20 per cent lost in transmission and theft. With an institutional mechanism to independently revise the power tariff, they could turn the corner in a few years, and attract private investments too.

There is a faster deterioration in the quality of power supply as the frequency even exceeds 52 Hz and the voltage profile throughout is extremely poor resulting in enormous damage to the consumer equipment. The public is not aware of the magnitude of this menace in the absence of awareness. The central planners are also unable to specify the objectives of power reforms and hesitate to quantify the same in terms of improved availability and financial gains and the likely hike in the power tariff, as they are apprehensive of public backlash.

The moot question whether the power sector will ever come forward on planned growth based on system studies and cut down the cost of power as is the objective elsewhere in the world, avoid load shedding and maintain quality power supply to consumers remains unanswered. The planners have achieved little by the reforms in power sector and are in fact responsible for worsening the situation. They are swayed by reform bills to mislead the public.

The central government has brought out an ordinance creating CERC* and SERC† with quasi-judicial powers with a proviso that revision of power rates for the farm sector should be carried out in three years. There is a general impression amongst politicians, industrialists and the public that the farm sector is highly subsidised. The truth, however, is just the opposite. In fact, this sector is subsidising the domestic consumers.

Power Reforms

Reforms are undertaken to improve efficiency and ensure accountability in the overall operation of an industry or a sector for the good of both the industry and the consumer. But far from achieving these goals, the power sector reforms in India have only done the reverse. They have neither toned up the performance of the State Electricity Boards nor brought any relief to the people. This is because of the failure to understand that reform is a dynamic process.

The net result is that:-

- The official growth rate of energy consumption in 1996-97 declined to 1 per cent against the 8 per cent projected by the Ministry of Power (MoP)
- Even though energy availability in 1996-97 increased by 4.2 per cent, around 75 per cent of this additional power was lost in either transmission or theft.
- Technical loss increased to 24.53 per cent in 1996-97 against 22.27 per cent in previous year.
- Planner have not provided any funds for the new distribution system needed for utilisation of power from private (IPP) projects. According to estimates, the investment needed for sub-transmission and distribution is of the order of Rs. 2,00,000 crore.
- There are apprehensions that all big size IPP projects may gradually withdraw due to the inability of states/SEBs to provide escrow cover.
- There has been no progress during 1997-99 in the energisation of the pumping sets and electrification of villages. The number of pumps in operation is declining.
- The country is meeting a gross peak demand of only 60,000 MW against installed capacity of 95,000 MW or 63 per cent against 85-90 per cent elsewhere in the world. The performance of our thermal machines is, therefore, deplorable for meeting peak demands.

---

* CERC = Central Electricity Regulatory Commission.
† SERC = State Electricity Regulatory Commission.

Irrational tariff structure, poor operational performance, overstaffing and huge transmission and distribution losses, which have become a euphemism for power pilferage, account for severe erosion in the financial viability of the SEBs. The culture of cross-subsidization across the so-called haves and have nots, the primacy given to sociopolitical considerations over everything else, coupled with the unwillingness and inability of the powers that be to come to grips with the simmering crises, have almost disabled the reform process initiated in the early nineties.

The situation has come to such a pass that the SEBs just cannot meet their day-to-day expenditure, leave alone muster the resources required for capacity addition. The success of India's economic reforms will be dependent, in a large measure, on the availability of power, qualitatively as well as quantitatively. At present, shortages in peak power capacity and energy are estimated at 20 per cent and 10 per cent respectively. The industrial sector which accounts for 34 per cent of total power consumption, followed by 33 per cent in the agricultural sector, has already taken to captive generation in a big way.

Given their debt-based capital structure and the poor resource position of the State governments, the SEBs have been increasingly resorting to borrowing from the market or the financial institutions, thereby adding to their interest burden, and the resultant increase in the cost of power generation and supply.

In 1991, the government allowed private sector participation in power generation. But the independent power producers (IPPs) were allowed to sell power only to the SEBs. Given the perpetual sickness of the SEBs, the IPPs were apprehensive of their bills being paid by the sole off-taker of power, and wanted the State government to give guarantee and the Central government to give counter-guarantee. The counter-guarantee route being fraught with grave financial risks was later abandoned in favour of certain workable alternatives like linking power generation with distribution, permitting direct supply by IPPs to high tension consumers, opening of an escrow account among others. All said and done, for want of clarity in government policy and a transparent mechanism, less than 1400 MW capacity has so far been operated in the private sector. It has been reported that a foreign company which entered the power market of China and India at the same time has so far commissioned two projects and constructed another three in China whereas it is yet to get financial clearance of its first project in India.

The present state of affairs has focused attention on the urgency of reforms in the energy sector. A number of States have initiated these reforms and are in the process of restructuring their Electricity Boards (SEBs). Though Orissa set the tone for reforms, other States have caught up. Rajasthan, Haryana, Andhra Pradesh, Maharashtra and Karnataka have already launched reforms.

Claims and counterclaims by employees and the Governments tend to come out with only half-truths. The problem with most of the SEBs is their finances. Because of the politics involved in power management and free or subsidised supply to vote banks, the Boards do not generate enough funds to make ends meet. So long as power generation was tilted heavily in favour of hydel sources, costs were lower and State Governments could afford to subsidise electricity to farmers, marginal consumers and even the domestic sector. But with the shift towards thermal and fuel-based power plants, the cost of generation has risen sharply. None of the States has shown the political will to pass on the costs to the consumers. They have taken the easy way out by taxing industrial or commercial consumers to cross-subsidise supply to the weaker sections.

Electoral politics has complicated the functioning of SEBs and it has become politically opportune for State Governments to provide free power to the agricultural sector, irrespective of the capacity of the farmer to pay for the energy consumed. This has led to a dramatic increase in agricultural connections and pumpsets energised in most States. But in reality, studies have shown that most of this free supply is siphoned off to industrial and commercial consumers thanks to a collusion of interests.

Sadly, only three of the SEBs in the country could keep their heads above water, while the rest have sunk under mounting losses. Loans and advances from the State Governments get converted into equity, with no chance of any returns. This while the Electricity Act envisaged a minimum three per cent return on investment in power projects. On an average, the SEBs have losses ranging from Rs. 1,500 crores to Rs. 3,000 crores. As a result, the States could not generate funds to invest in new power projects. Most SEBs could not even pay the Central power agencies such as the NTPC for the electricity bought. These agencies have threatened to even cut off supply to defaulting States, creating further problems.

It was in this dismal scenario that the Centre embarked on a thorough reform of the power sector. A Central Electricity Authority was set up and the States were asked to set up their own Regulatory Commissions (SERCs). Their role is to promote efficiency in generation, transmission and distribution of power. They are to establish norms of production and productivity, study the cost structure, establish a framework for dispute resolution, promote competition, advice the State Governments, Simultaneously, the States and their SERCs were asked to appoint a tariff regulator who could fix and revise the tariff depending on the costs and the policies of the Governments. The aim was to depoliticise the SEBs and ensure that if the States want to subsidise power, they must provide budgetary support for it every year.

Prime Minister Atal Bihari Vajpayee has now outlined a seven-point agenda to overcome problems plaguing the power sector. Increasing power through renovation of existing plants, strengthening transmission and distribution (T & D) systems to improve quality of power, unbundling T & D through corporatisation, energy audit at all levels; elimination of power theft within a specified timeframe; and strengthening of sub-transmission and distribution systems. Metering all power consumption by December 2001 and changing hydro-thermal ratios are some of the main objectives the Centre and states which would have to be followed to attain the goal of "power for all" objective by 2012.

It is becoming a model for the States to bifurcate or trifurcate their SEBs for this restructuring. Only then will they be eligible for assistance from the Power Finance Corporation or other institutions, and the private sector, Independent Power Producers (IPPs), could also enter the scene. For convenience and clear distinction, the SEBs are to be broken down into generation, transmission and distribution entities, with some States clubbing the last two into one agency. The IPPs can only sell their power to the generation corporation under a Power Purchase Agreement (PPA). State-wise tariff for electricity from 1988-89 and state-wise subsides on irrigation power, fertilizers and other inputs from 1980-81 to 1995-96 are given in Annexures 11.1 to 11.6.

PERSPECTIVE

The above discussion and the empirical facts indicate succinctly why inputs are subsidised and who actually get the benefit of subsidies. The position today is rather complicated. The commitment of the Government to PDS., procurement of foodgrains and remunerative prices to the farmer are all interrelated. Any discussion about the future of subsidies will have to take into consideration the ground situation regarding poverty, liberalised agricultural economy and the role of PDS as well as procurement prices. We shall, perhaps, not be very much wrong to assume that during the coming two decades, per capita income will atleast double at the constant 2000 prices. With the establishment of an egalitarian society, present disparities between rural/urban societies and different regions - say BIMARU states and Punjab, Haryana, Maharashtra etc. will be reduced to some extent. Some 50 million people, primarily concentrated in the Eastern region who are not having two square meals will no longer go hungry and food basket of an average citizen will get reasonably diversified.

In a scenario like this, our PDS commitments will be reduced drastically. It will not possibly be obligatory to continue the procurement of various agricultural commodities, particularly foodgrains at the present scale. If so, present regime of MSP will also have to undergo corresponding changes. Our buffer stock policy will also have to be accordingly refashioned. There may be two types of bufferstock, one a normal bufferstock and two - a contingency buffer stock and shall be the sole instrument of market intervention for price stabilization. For the operations of bufferstock we may follow the formula developed by the International Rubber Agreement, 1979 (Annexure 11.7). This would mean setting up a price range consisting of a reference price and three price levels above it and three price levels below it. The upper and lower intervention prices may be calculated as plus or minus certain percentage of the reference price. Again the upper and lower trigger action prices may be calculated as plus and minus certain percentage of reference price which would be slightly higher than the intervention prices. The upper limit may be termed as upper indicative prices and the lower limit may be termed as lower indicative prices.

We will also face a new situation under the liberalisation policy. The DGFT has already released a list, consisting of 1,429 items, to be opened up under the QR settlement with the US by April 2001. The entire group of grains, fertilizer, petroleum sectors are on the chopping block. Even coconut and coconut oil, will be on the free list. The entire range of teas and coffees too will be opened up to import competition, perhaps for the first time ever in the history of India. The government is bound to free these sectors and remove the import licensing regime. The immediate impact of proposed changes will be on the administered price system by which prices are controlled. The system must be either junked or drastically revised keeping in mind the realities of the international market. Tariff will emerge as the sole mechanism of import control.

However, the duties will move within narrow boundaries. In the case of rice, control through tariff is not possible since India has bound the rate at nil right from the early period of GATT when the country was facing food shortages. The attempts to revise the bound rates upwards have not yielded much result till now. The producers, ranging from farmers to the factories and refineries, will be forced to accept lower margins, apart from the exposure to the cold winds of the global market place. Quantitative restrictions on foreign trade will be further removed on most of the agricultural commodities to a large extent, meaning thereby competitive prices in the international market. Our pricing policy mentioned above will have to be turned to meet all the emerging challenges.

The wrong pricing policies of fertilizers, irrigation water and electricity have brought inefficiencies in the production systems and are eating up the resources which could better be used for creative production potential. In fact, continued subsidies are sending wrong signals to the farmers, distorting the age-old cropping pattern and leading to environmental degradation. We have also indicated that subsidies are acting against promotion of regional and interpersonal equity. However, it is not possible to come out of the subsidy regime in one go. They have to be phased out in such a manner that it helps in achieving a balanced growth. As for power, reforms already suggested in transmission and distribution of electricity and the organisational structure of the State Electricity Boards, if carried out earnestly, will help immensely in reducing the cost of generation and availability. Simultaneously the need for proper pricing policy keeping in view the load factors can hardly be overstated. It can be safely assumed that power meters will be installed for agriculture, as already decided. All this will take care of abysmal condition of SEB's with no subsidies involved.

Similarly, there is an urgent need for ensuring rational use of irrigation water not only to achieve the required productivity growth but also for retarding environment degradation. A judicious pricing of irrigation water will help in reversing the tendency of over use of this scarce input. Besides introducing a regular system of revising water rates at reasonable intervals, a serious attempt will have to be made to encourage the application of modern techniques of water management and conservation. This would mean providing incentives and giving training to the farmers to adopt on a large scale sprinkle, drip and mulch irrigation systems. Large parts of North and South India are already facing actuate problems of water scarcity. True, it is difficult to have water meter for individual field. Water Users' Associations or Pani Panchayats already existing in a small way will have to be established throughout the country and metered bulk supply of water will have to be given to them. These Associations will then be responsible to make payments to the Electricity Boards, but the responsibility to collect the charges from individual farmers will rest with them.

So far as subsidy on fertilizers is concerned, it is necessary to formulate a coherent pricing policy so that there is a balanced use of N,P and K. In order to phase out fertilizer subsidy, it is imperative to withstand the pressure of big farmers lobby and the industries. There must be a political will to bring reforms in agricultural subsidy. Our aim should be to achieve a balanced growth between the supply of and demand for various agricultural products, thereby helping to alleviate the serious difficulties arising from surpluses and shortages. There is at the same time need to encourage the use of organic and green manures, bio fertilizers and vermiculture. If major part of dung is being burnt today, it will be necessary to encourage village forestry and also set up Gobar Gas Plants. These issues will have to be carefully studied and every possible incentive provided to make these innovative programmes more popular. Research results have already shown that such practices are cost effective and besides improving soil structure, lead to higher productivity levels. Subsidies given in the initial stages, can certainly be withdrawn slowly, and finally removed in the coming decades.

To conclude, the subsidy policy cannot be viewed in isolation as it has its ramifications on the supply of various agricultural inputs, their judicious uses, on PDS and the output prices, besides the goal of achieving fiscal balance. In fact, withdrawal of subsidies-food, agriculture and others-is simply not an arithmetical jugglery. What is needed is that subsidy should be target and time oriented and should not be a source of just additional gains for the big farmers, industries and the suppliers. Subsidy should also not distort our limited resources allocations and cause for environmental degradation. All future policies should actually aim at creating a healthy and robust agriculture and producing a prosperous farming community.

Swaminathan Committee on Tenth Plan

An expert committee has called for redeployment of farm subsidies given for electricity and irrigation to technology transfer and development of farm resources.

It also expressed concern over the decreasing public investments in agriculture and static plan allocations to the sector which is likely to hinder a higher farm growth rate exceeding four per cent during the 10th five-year Plan. M.S. Swaminathan Committee on agriculture and allied sectors for the Tenth Plan has recommended that some of the subsidies like free electricity for ground water use and canal irrigation have adversely affected natural resources and financial health of the states. "While subsidies may be desirable to adopt improved production technologies and entrepreneurship the ones adversely affecting natural resources have to be redeployed."

These subsidies must be diverted for activities which have a direct beneficial effect on technology transfer, development on farm resources, diversification and generating employment and income for the rural poor. The report said declining investments in agriculture in the form of Gross Capital Formation (GCF) was affecting the development of infrastructure, productivity, processing and value addition.

Describing it as an area of great concern, the Swaminathan committee report said that share of agriculture in the total GCF has come down from 17.7 per cent in 1978-79 to about eight per cent in 1999-2000. Share of public sector in agriculture GCF has also dedined to 24.4 per cent in 1999-2000 (at 1980-81 prices) from 34 per cent in 1978-79 (at 1980-81 prices).

"If a higher growth rate in agriculture sector has to be achieved more investments will have to be made for development of infrastructure like irrigation, conservation and development of natural resources (water, land and biodiversity)".

Plan allocations in agriculture had remained static at around 14 per cent except the fourth plan when it was 17.2 per cent although 70-75 per cent of the population was dependent on the sector. There ought to be emphasis on the development and exploitation of non-wheat/rice crops which have potential in terms of production, industrial uses and nutritional value for human and livestock but have remained underutilised.

Nutritious millets should not be classified as "coarse cereals" since it gives the wrong impression in the mind of the consumers. India with comparatively less use of fertilisers and agrochemicals had great advantage in the international market where the demand for organically produced food was increasing. Diversion of agriculture from crop based activities to non-crop based ones should be encouraged. Based on land capability. These included tree farming, agro-forestry, dairy and fisheries.

It urged that co-operatives should be allowed to function as purely commercial bodies and decide and secure their own fate after their recapitalisation to the tune of Rs. 10,000 crore. All restrictions on the movement of foodgrains and other agricultural commodities within the country should be removed through a central act so that the farmers could get the right price for their produce and consumers benefit in terms of cost and quality.

Annexure 11.1

Input Subsidy and Input Use in Indian Agriculture

Year	Subsidy (Rs. in crores)			Total input use			Subsidy per unit		
	Fertilizer	Electricity	Canal irrigation	Fertilizer (000 tonnes)	Electrcity Million kwh)	Canal irrigation (000 ha.)	Fertilizer (Rs/kg)	Electricity (Rs/kg)	Canal irrigation (Rs/ha)
1	2	3	4	5	6	7	8	9	10
1980-81	505	334	598	5516	14489	15292	0.92	0.23	390.85
1981-82	375	401	654	6068	15201	15678	0.62	0.26	416.56
1982-83	600	630	759	6387	17817	16202	0.95	0.35	468.52
1983-84	1042	753	808	6401	18234	16828	1.64	0.40	480.95
1984-85	1927	973	1076	7710	20960	16354	2.50	0.46	656.09
1985-86	1924	1322	1146	8211	23422	15879	2.34	0.56	720.75
1986-87	1897	1845	1520	8474	29443	16027	2.24	0.63	950.00
1987-88	2164	2608	1628	8738	35267	15470	2.48	0.74	1050.50
1988-89	3201	2935	2230	8696	38878	16293	3.68	0.76	1363.10
1989-90	4542	3761	2422	11036	44056	16900	4.12	0.85	1433.14
1990-91	4389	4605	2505	12577	50321	17453	3.49	0.92	1431.43
1991-92	4800	5889	3109	12728	58557	17791	3.77	1.02	1746.63
1992-93	6136	7335	3420	12152	63328	16986	5.05	1.16	2012.76
1993-94	4400	8966	3880	12366	70699	17111	3.56	1.27	2269.01
1994-95	5241	10941	4502	13564	79301	17280	3.87	1.38	2602.31
1995-96	6235	13606	5253	13876	85732	17142	4.49	1.59	3071.92

SOURCE: Columns 2 and 5-Fertilizer Statistics (various issues). Colum 3-Annual Report of in Working of State Electricity Departments, Power and Energy Division Planning Commission. Column 4-Statements 27, 28 and 39 in the National Accounts Statistics used to estimate canal Irrigation subsidy. Column 6-CMIE, Energy, March-April 1999. Column 7-(i) Indian Agricultural Statistics and Indian Agriculture in Brief, Directorate of Economics and Statistics, Department of Agriculture and Co-operation, Ministry of Agriculture. (ii) Statistical Abstract India (Various Issues) Central Statistical Organization, Ministry of Planning and Programme Implementation, GOI, New Delhi.

Our SOURCE: Indian Agriculture Policy, S.S. Acharye and D.P. Chaudhri.

Annexure 11.2

State Average Electricity Tariff for Agriculture

(Rs/kwh)

Year	Andhra Pradesh	Bihar	Gujarat	Haryana	Karnataka	Kerala	Madhya Pradesh	Maharashtra	Orissa	Punjab	Rajasthan	Tamilnadu	Uttar Pradesh	West Bengal	Other States	All India
1988-99	0.04	0.09	0.22	0.22	0.10	0.22	0.23	0.09	0.22	0.09	0.24	0.11	0.24	0.24	0.26	0.19
1989-90	0.05	0.09	0.22	0.30	0.10	0.22	0.25	0.09	0.32	0.08	0.29	0.10	0.22	0.25	0.25	0.20
1990-91	0.03	0.08	0.15	0.23	0.07	0.25	0.15	0.15	0.17	0.09	0.25	0.00	0.19	0.20	0.25	0.12
1991-92	0.03	0.08	0.15	0.19	0.10	0.25	0.15	0.15	0.15	0.10	0.28	0.00	0.23	0.17	0.31	0.12
1992-93	0.08	0.11	0.11	0.26	0.04	0.25	0.26	0.15	0.31	0.11	0.29	0.00	0.32	0.19	0.61	0.16
1993-94	0.08	0.15	0.19	0.34	0.03	0.27	0.20	0.23	0.20	0.20	0.28	0.00	0.32	0.25	0.46	0.18
1994-95	0.08	0.15	0.27	0.50	0.03	0.22	0.06	0.24	0.30	0.27	0.33	0.00	0.41	0.27	0.50	0.22
1995-96	0.08	0.15	0.27	0.50	0.21	0.22	0.06	0.24	0.50	0.31	0.37	0.00	0.47	0.27	0.50	0.25
1995-96	0.08	0.15	0.27	0.50	0.21	0.22	0.06	0.24	0.50	0.31	0.37	0.00	0.47	0.27	0.50	0.25

SOURCE: Annual Report on the working of the State Electricity Boards and Electricity Departments, Division of Power and Energy, Planning Commission (Various Issues).

Our SOURCE: As Annexure 11.1.

Annexure 11.3

Statewise Break-up of Subsidy on Fertilizers

(Rs. in crores)

Year	Andhra Pradesh	Bihar	Gujarat	Haryana	Karnataka	Kerala	Madhya Pradesh	Maharashtra	Orissa	Punjab	Rajasthan	Tamilnadu	Uttar Pradesh	West Bengal	Other States	All India
1980-81	52.53	18.77	32.68	21.15	31.49	8.97	18.04	38.54	6.96	69.03	12.36	44.95	105.38	25.91	18.04	505.00
1981-82	40.55	12.67	24.79	15.58	23.73	5.87	8.41	32.70	5.07	50.75	8.53	31.71	78.50	15.95	20.21	375.00
1982-83	64.97	19.73	37.68	24.49	39.92	9.91	22.44	48.89	8.32	79.18	15.05	42.07	137.80	24.00	25.15	600.00
1983-84	122.85	39.46	67.84	41.22	65.82	17.57	42.57	86.77	13.92	134.07	28.38	79.33	222.05	49.87	30.27	1042.00
1984-85	229.99	89.65	118.28	79.09	138.70	30.04	87.54	136.35	26.75	245.72	48.58	163.58	378.55	95.28	58.91	1927.00
1985-86	195.89	110.52	92.87	82.06	112.65	31.10	96.40	31.10	242.21	48.75	48.75	147.36	395.52	90.22	89.78	1924.00
1986-87	197.93	115.86	88.21	91.06	124.20	33.13	130.34	143.95	33.35	244.67	54.20	147.90	368.21	109.50	14.48	1897.00
1987-88	238.23	119.73	108.89	97.06	137.47	45.08	125.15	182.30	37.45	273.95	52.97	167.28	393.48	138.21	46.81	2164.00
1988-89	392.88	224.71	183.83	147.87	202.95	62.05	198.32	256.02	62.34	323.87	88.43	222.97	619.32	184.12	31.31	3201.00
1989-90	601.52	221.45	272.88	210.08	305.86	83.24	265.03	517.10	80.49	449.57	112.29	307.04	821.39	263.46	30.63	4542.00
1991-92	596.61	227.78	276.43	240.23	341.67	84.48	305.47	426.90	73.92	469.52	166.31	316.40	848.15	284.73	91.64	4800.00
1992-93	764.35	300.89	361.98	307.46	393.79	102.49	400.35	701.75	69.17	605.32	247.88	403.38	1100.58	369.05	137.83	6136.00
1993-94	549.02	208.15	238.04	239.11	286.43	62.98	275.40	424.84	74.01	426.62	178.62	277.89	815.53	265.08	78.28	4400.00
1994-95	635.23	252.31	316.07	275.11	318.00	76.89	346.21	537.08	85.01	496.51	232.61	338.09	959.25	291.25	82.30	5241.00
1995-96	786.79	323.52	338.80	325.32	421.03	91.22	371.15	617.39	106.94	567.61	289.82	339.25	1170.52	381.04	104.70	6235.00

State-wise subsidy on fertilizer is calculated on the basis of fertilizer use by the respective state.
Our SOURCE: as Annexure 11.1.

Annexure 11.4

Statewise Subsidy on Electricity for Irrigation

(Rs. in crores)

Year	Andhra Pradesh	Bihar	Gujarat	Hary-ana	Karnat-aka	Kerala	Madhya Pradesh	Mahara-shtra	Orissa	Punjab	Rajas-than	Tamil-nadu	Uttar Pradesh	West Bengal	Other States	All India
1980-81	22.52	10.03	30.75	21.99	9.06	1.84	7.95	89.74	1.36	42.65	23.26	54.56	64.36	1.66	2.26	334.00
1981-82	26.51	13.03	34.72	30.57	11.2	2.77	10.39	49.57	1.69	49.07	27.20	65.32	74.73	1.74	2.43	401.00
1982-83	51.80	21.85	49.04	46.92	16.94	3.78	20.76	82.92	2.58	74.79	42.01	88.65	120.65	3.32	4.00	630.00
1983-84	67.19	26.58	58.97	53.73	22.05	3.88	23.00	104.93	3.06	90.40	53.97	91.35	145.28	4.17	4.34	753.00
1984-85	113.22	28.04	75.81	63.83	28.74	4.55	32.31	156.58	3.34	109.74	65.08	112.33	168.33	5.20	5.71	973.00
1985-86	152.28	45.15	97.25	77.10	65.98	5.70	43.52	206.98	4.23	156.29	82.41	159.39	210.93	6.72	8.07	1322.00
1986-87	219.38	60.78	138.04	101.76	140.17	8.21	65.23	254.22	10.46	223.76	99.51	192.87	310.42	9.09	11.09	1845.00
1987-88	307.84	84.97	285.23	160.92	184.14	10.80	83.84	329.74	13.98	313.70	135.65	230.65	435.05	17.30	15.60	2608.00
1988-89	349.53	103.65	333.30	162.91	216.81	14.04	98.44	399.05	8.53	318.58	162.99	269.81	456.13	19.40	21.82	2935.00
1989-90	467.56	124.55	440.08	217.09	304.60	18.18	89.72	524.85	14.09	442.81	179.79	276.00	620.37	15.45	25.87	3761.00
1990-91	591.17	133.88	519.79	248.18	404.58	19.03	230.98	604.35	16.75	466.35	216.61	371.56	710.05	41.55	30.38	4605.00
1991-92	726.01	165.33	701.67	355.51	458.49	22.53	342.54	845.38	27.25	557.45	300.20	453.56	627.58	65.57	39.93	5889.00
1992-93	726.00	268.00	1055.00	457.00	497.00	14.60	421.00	1031.00	20.70	687.00	348.00	643.00	1035.00	104.00	27.30	7335.00
1993-94	925.00	252.00	1206.00	540.00	668.00	16.00	756.00	1131.00	39.20	797.00	468.00	760.00	1227.00	115.00	65.80	8966.00
1995-96	1740.00	300.00	1647.00	612.00	1109.00	36.00	1416.00	2250.00	30.00	829.00	808.00	1133.00	1402.00	169.00	79.00	13606.00

Statewise subsidy on Electricity upto 1991-92 is calculated on the basis of Electricity use by the respective state. Since 1992-93 the original data on Electricity subsidy for the States is used.

Our SOURCE: As Annexure 11.1.

Annexure 11.5

Statewise Estimates of Subsidy on Canal Irrigation

(Rs. in crores)

Year	Andhra Pradesh	Bihar	Gujarat	Hary-ana	Karnat-aka	Kerala	Madhya Pradesh	Mahara-shtra	Orissa	Punjab	Rajas-than	Tamil-nadu	Uttar Pradesh	West Bengal	Other States	All India
1980-81	66.21	42.78	14.35	45.40	21.35	4.11	40.43	16.31	31.32	55.92	36.80	34.76	124.28	37.54	26.44	598.00
1981-82	73.97	49.29	17.73	49.83	24.43	4.47	45.66	17.36	33.74	55.73	39.85	37.96	134.93	40.44	28.60	654.00
1982-83	86.07	45.14	20.79	62.27	29.88	5.38	57.33	20.59	39.55	72.20	50.62	37.73	164.29	33.58	33.58	759.00
1983-84	92.06	50.51	21.53	59.32	33.09	5.21	60.68	20.68	59.42	73.99	56.02	43.25	166.71	36.24	29.29	808.00
1984-85	121.70	68.18	29.17	81.61	47.83	6.65	85.95	28.02	58.75	94.91	71.77	60.85	225.91	49.12	45.59	1076.00
1985-86	132.76	72.45	36.41	87.94	54.73	7.15	94.12	28.74	63.51	105.14	85.93	57.63	247.95	16.16	55.40	1146.00
1986-87	165.78	103.01	40.42	112.04	74.42	9.50	129.83	38.19	79.45	134.12	112.23	76.28	312.57	66.78	65.38	1520.00
1987-88	163.15	115.04	30.71	124.87	78.40	10.95	140.02	92.63	87.31	114.83	111.56	62.43	310.02	73.39	82.70	1628.00
1988-89	251.79	156.37	48.31	166.60	113.85	14.53	193.38	55.17	116.14	196.21	164.72	109.00	412.06	96.49	135.38	2330.00
1989-90	276.09	155.07	68.99	198.63	122.92	15.64	204.77	66.21	131.10	214.42	179.63	115.47	464.35	104.80	103.20	2422.00
1990-91	277.03	161.57	69.96	198.18	127.77	16.01	227.67	67.15	134.00	226.34	200.70	113.98	473.28	106.28	105.09	2505.00
1991-92	327.54	219.67	84.35	247.85	164.58	19.02	298.82	90.27	164.94	255.21	255.75	149.68	575.75	128.68	126.89	3109.00
1992-93	345.72	186.97	111.50	272.05	180.77	21.42	337.52	112.51	187.78	273.26	285.87	170.36	648.41	143.53	142.33	3420.00
1993-94	376.19	227.66	120.18	306.80	211.79	23.36	400.45	107.03	215.19	348.52	311.33	184.35	725.16	162.58	159.41	3880.00
1994-95	418.42	256.36	154.50	360.06	241.51	29.18	475.47	140.17	247.25	399.66	371.78	219.89	818.80	16.80	182.37	4502.00
1995-96	471.61	336.78	181.72	421.36	291.12	32.79	550.37	164.86	290.81	415.53	458.74	236.27	942.30	219.72	239.64	5253.00

Statewise subsidy on Canal Irrigation is calculated on the basis of net area irrigated by canals in respective states.

Our Source: As Annexure 11.1.

Annexure 11.6

Statewise Subsidy on Farm Inputs

(Rs. in crores)

Year	Andhra Pradesh	Bihar	Gujarat	Hary-ana	Karnat-aka	Kerala	Madhya Pradesh	Mahara-shtra	Orissa	Punjab	Rajas-than	Tamil-nadu	Uttar Pradesh	West Bengal	Other States	All India
1980-81	141.46	71.58	77.79	88.54	61.90	14.92	66.42	94.59	39.64	167.60	72.42	134.28	294.01	65.11	46.73	1437.00
1981-82	141.03	74.99	77.24	95.98	59.43	13.11	64.46	99.62	40.50	155.54	75.58	134.98	288.16	58.13	51.24	1430.00
1982-83	202.85	86.71	107.51	133.69	86.73	19.08	100.53	152.40	50.46	226.17	107.67	168.44	422.74	61.30	62.72	1989.00
1983-84	282.10	116.65	148.34	154.27	120.96	26.66	126.25	212.38	76.40	298.46	138.38	213.93	534.04	90.29	63.90	2603.00
1984-85	464.92	185.87	223.26	224.53	215.26	41.24	205.80	320.95	88.36	450.36	185.44	336.95	772.78	149.60	110.20	2976.00
1985-86	480.93	228.12	226.53	247.10	243.36	43.95	234.03	383.29	98.85	503.64	217.08	364.38	854.40	113.10	153.25	4392.00
1986-87	583.09	279.65	266.68	304.87	338.79	50.84	325.41	436.35	123.26	602.55	265.94	417.05	991.20	185.36	90.96	5262.00
1987-88	708.71	319.74	424.82	382.85	400.00	66.83	348.51	604.68	138.73	732.47	299.78	460.36	1138.50	228.90	145.11	6400.00
1988-89	994.19	484.73	565.44	477.39	533.62	90.62	490.15	710.25	187.00	838.65	416.14	601.78	1487.51	300.01	188.51	8366.00
1989-90	1345.17	501.07	781.94	625.78	733.38	117.06	559.62	1108.16	225.68	1106.79	471.71	698.50	1906.11	383.71	160.41	10725.00
1990-91	1434.93	504.65	836.73	651.36	823.76	120.40	742.71	113.68	218.26	1111.79	547.09	776.05	1966.95	411.25	220.83	11499.00
1991-92	1650.15	612.79	1062.48	843.59	964.74	126.03	946.83	1362.56	266.11	1282.18	722.26	919.65	2251.47	478.98	258.45	13798.00
1992-93	1836.07	755.87	1528.48	1036.51	1071.56	138.51	1158.87	1845.25	277.64	1565.58	881.75	1216.74	2783.99	618.58	307.46	16891.00
1993-94	1850.21	687.81	1564.22	1055.91	1166.22	102.33	1431.85	1662.87	328.40	1572.14	957.95	1222.24	2767.69	542.66	303.49	17246.00
1994-95	2403.64	805.68	1736.56	1125.17	1430.51	129.07	1925.25	2324.25	352.55	1677.17	1227.39	1504.98	3051.84	647.14	342.37	20684.00
1995-96	3006.40	960.30	2167.52	1358.68	1821.15	160.00	2337.52	3032.25	427.75	1812.05	1556.56	1708.51	3514.83	769.76	423.33	25094.00

SOURCE: As Annexure 11.1.

Annexure 11.7

International Natural Rubber Agreement

Starting from the first Preparatory Meeting on natural rubber in January 1977 in Geneva, at the end of its Fourth Session, on 6 October 1979, the conference established the text of the 'International RubberAgreement', 1979. Thus this agreement became the first new International Commodity Agreement successfully negotiated under the 'Integrated Programme for Commodities'. It became operational on 23 October 1980.

Main Features of the Agreement

(1) The objectives of the agreement are spelt out in article 1 as follows:

(a) To achieve a balanced growth between the supply of and demand for natural rubber, thereby helping to alleviate the serious difficulties arising from surpluses or shortages of natural rubber;

(b) To achieve stable conditions in natural rubber trade through avoiding excessive natural rubber price fluctuations, which adversely affect the long-term interests of both producers and consumers, and stabilizing these prices without distorting long-term market trends, in the interests of producers and consumers;

(c) To help to stabilize the export earnings from natural rubber of exporting members, and to increase their earnings based on expanding natural rubber export volumes at fair and remunerative prices, thereby helping to provide the necessary incentives for a dynamic and rising rate of production and the resources for accelerated economic growth and social development;

(d) To seek to ensure adequate supplies of natural rubber to meet the requirements of importing members at fair and reasonable prices and to improve the reliability and continuity of these supplies;

(e) To take feasible steps in the event of a surplus or shortage of natural rubber to mitigate the economic difficulties that members might encounter;

(f) To seek to expand international trade and to improve market access for natural rubber and processed products thereof;

(g) To improve the competitiveness of natural rubber by encouraging research and development on the problems of natural rubber;

(h) To encourage the efficient development of the natural rubber economy by seeking to facilitate and promote improvements in the processing, marketing and distribution of raw natural rubber; and

(i) To further international co-operation and consultations on natural rubber in matters affecting supply and demand, and to facilitate promotion and co-ordination of natural rubber research, assistance and other programme.

(2) In order to achieve the objectives of the agreement, an international natural rubber bufferstock of 550,000 tonnes was established. This bufferstock consists of a normal bufferstock of 400,000 tonnes and a contingency bufferstock of 150,000 tonnes and shall be the sole instrument of market intervention for price stabilization in the agreement.

(3) For the operations of the bufferstock, the agreement established a price range consisting of a reference price and three price levels above and three price levels below. The reference price that applied on the entry into force of the Agreement was set at 210 Malaysian/Singapore cents per kilogram. The upper and lower intervention prices are calculated as plus or minus 15 per cent of the reference price; the upper intervention price was therefore 242 Malaysian/Singapore cents per kilogram and the lower intervention price was 179 Malaysian/Singapore cents per kilogram. The upper and lower action prices are calculated as plus and minus 20 per cent of the reference price; these prices were therefore set at 252 and 168 Malaysian/ Singapore cents per kilogram respectively. For the first 30 months after the entry into force of the agreement, the upper and lower limits of the price range have been set at 270 and 150 Malaysian/Singapore cents per kilogram respectively. The upper limit is called 'the upper indicative prices' and the lower limit is called 'the lower indicative'.

(4) A Daily Market Indicator Price (DMIP) was established which is a composite weighted average of daily official current month prices on the Kuala Lumpur, London, New York and Singapore markets in respects of three grades, namely, RSS I, RSS 3 and TSR 20. When the 5-day average of DMIP is at the upper or lower intervention price or between them, the bufferstock manager shall not intervene in the market. When the 5-day average of DMIP is at or below the lower trigger action price, the bufferstock manager must buy rubber until the market indicator price exceeds the lower trigger action price. Similarly, when the 5-day average of DMIP is above the upper intervention price, the bufferstock manager may sell rubber to defend the upper trigger action price, but at or above the upper trigger action price he must sell rubber until the market indicator price falls below the upper trigger action price.

(5) When sales or purchases for the bufferstock reach the 400,000 tonnes level, the Council shall, by special vote, decide whether to bring the contingency bufferstock into operation at the lower or upper trigger action price; or any price between the lower trigger action price and the lower indicative price, or the upper trigger action price and the upper indicative price. Unless the Council, by special vote, decides otherwise, the contingency bufferstock shall be brought into action at a point midway between the trigger action prices and the indicative prices.

(6) Review and possibly revision of the reference price shall take place every 18 months after the entry into force of the agreement and shall be based on market trends and/or net changes in the bufferstock. In addition, the Council shall review and may, by special vote, revise the upper and lower indicative prices under the agreement every 30 months after the entry into force of the agreement or, in exceptional circumstances, at the request of a member or members holding 200 or more votes in the council.

(7) Under article 28 of the agreement, members commit themselves to financing the total costs of the international of 550,000 tonnes. The financing of both the normal and contingency stock shall be shared equally between exporting and importing categories of members. The total costs of the normal bufferstock of 400,000 tonnes are to be paid in cash. The total costs of the contingency bufferstock of 150,000 tonnes shall be financed by cash contributions and/or by cash borrowed from commercial sources by the Council upon the security of both stock warrants and government guarantees/undertakings. The agreement contains a provision which allows the International Natural Rubber Council to take full advantage of the financing facilities that will be available when the Common Fund under the Integrated Programme for Commodities becomes operational.

(8) The agreement established a 'Committee on Other Measures' to promote the development of the natural rubber economy by producing members through expanded and improved production, productivity and marketing. For this purpose, the Committee on Other Measures shall undertake economic and technical analyses in order to identify:
    (a) Natural rubber research and development programmes and projects of benefits to exporting and importing members, including scientific research in specific areas;
    (b) Programmes and projects to improve the productivity of the natural rubber industry;
    (c) Ways and means to upgrade natural rubber supplies and achieve uniformity in quality specification and presentation of natural rubber; and

(d) Methods of improving the processing, marketing and distribution of raw natural rubber.

(9) The agreement is for a period of five years, unless extended or terminated in accordance with the provisions of the Agreement.

(10) The agreement has a provision for establishment of a panel of experts from the rubber industry and trade of exporting and importing members. The panel is to provide advice and assistance to the Council and its Committees, particularly on bufferstock operations and on other measures.

The Agreement had been opened for signature from 2 January to 13 June 1980 at the Headquarters of United Nations in New York and Governments of 28 countries signed the Agreement. The agreement entered into force provisionally on 23 October 1980 and definitively on 15 April 1982.

CHAPTER 12

Agricultural Taxation

Taxation is the major source of government revenues to meet the cost of day-to-day administration and development projects of the country. Every tax has a base and the existence of a base is an essential prerequisite to government's demand on its citizens for the payment of a tax. The base may be anything like the possession of land or cattle, or the number of windows in one's house. Every tax scheme relates to the amount of payments required from taxpayers to specified objective conditions. Thus a payment may be required from a taxpayer if he satisfies the condition of earning rupees *X* of income or payment may be asked for if he satisfies the condition of possessing rupees *Y* worth of capital or *Z* hectares of land. It is the payment of the last kind, called agricultural taxation, that has been discussed in this chapter.

OBJECTIVES OF AGRICULTURAL TAXATION

The objectives of agricultural taxation can be grouped under two heads: (a) external purposes which economic, social and political policy may call upon taxation to serve, and (b) the conventional internal tests or criteria of taxation such as equity, ease of compliance, etc.

External Objectives (1) This objectives is very important in a country like India where there are visible disparities in the living standards of various section of people even in the rural areas. This disparity was sought to be reduced by the imposition of ceiling on land holdings, but if agricultural incomes from higher brackets of income are mopped up by taxation, it would serve the purpose of redistribution of incomes particularly when it is realized that agricultural land is subject neither to estate duty nor wealth tax.

(2) Since agriculture plays a major role in the economy and there is now an increasing emphasis to increase agricultural exports, agricultural taxation, particularly at the point of export, can make substantial contribution for the achievement of the broader objective before the country, which is growth stability and self-reliance.

(3) This includes various types of incentive effects of taxation. Taxes may reward desirable and penalize undesirable economic activity in agriculture. Some of the purposes of taxation may be to increase the will to work, the urge to invest, to discourage under-cultivation, to canalize agricultural resources into particular crops, to improve conditions of land tenure, to discourage land speculation and to alter the relationship between agricultural and other sectors. Agricultural taxation in India has got to take all these factors into consideration while examining the future development of agriculture.

(4) This is perhaps the most obvious and important objective of agricultural taxation in underdeveloped economies, particularly, India, which is committed to a socialist pattern of society. By mopping up the surpluses from individuals, agricultural resources can be channelled through governmental programmes for the achievement of desired objectives in the interest of the national economy.

Internal Objectives of Agricultural Taxation This refers to the conventional internal tests of criteria of taxation, namely, administrative efficiency and effectiveness, ease of compliance and impartiality of treatment.

EARLIER EFFORTS

In India till 1938, agricultural income was not taxed at all except for a brief period between 1860-1865 and between 1869-1873. It was the Indian Taxation Enquiry Committee, 1925 that set the ball rolling. It observed: "There is no historical or theoretical justification for the continued exemption from income-tax of incomes derived from agriculture." However, the Committee duly recognized that there were certain risks attending to the introduction of agricultural income-tax. It admitted "there are however administrative and political objections to the removal of the exemption at the present time". The Union Government, despite all the hurdles, did not give up its pursuit of agricultural income-tax. In 1935, it cautiously enacted the Government of India Act enabling provincial governments to levy a tax on agricultural incomes, as defined in section 2 (2) of the Indian Income-tax Act 1922. This definition which has not far been altered in any way reads:

(1) " Agricultural Incomes" means
- (a) any rent or revenue derived from land which is used for agricultural purposes and is either assessed to land revenue in India or is subject to a local rate assessed and collected by officers of the Government as such;
- (b) any income derived from such land by
  - (i) agriculture; or
  - (ii) the performance by a cultivator or receiver of rent-in-kind of any process ordinarily employed by a cultivator or

receiver of rent-in-kind to render the produce raised as received by him fit to be taken to market; or

(iii) the sale by a cultivator or receiver of rent-in-kind of the produce raised or received by him, in respect of which no process has been performed.

The assignment to states of the work relating to the levy and collection of taxes on agricultural incomes into agricultural and non-agricultural under the Income-tax Act, 1922, set a pattern that is being religiously followed even to this day. It was the State of Bihar which first availed itself of the provisions made in the Government of India Act, 1935, and this pioneered in the taxation of agricultural incomes. In the year 1938, it enacted the Bihar Agricultural Income-tax Act under which a tax at the rate of 6 pies in the Rupee on all agricultural incomes above an exemption limit of Rs. 5,000 was levied. Soon after many other states followed suit.

RAJ COMMITTEE REPORT

Various proposals for additional agricultural taxation have been made by official organizations like the Planning Commission and by the economists. These tax proposals have broadly three objectives:

(a) to secure larger investible and marketable surplus from agriculture;

(b) provide an incentive to raise agricultural output; and

(c) to introduce an element of progression in agricultural taxation so as to make it more equitable.

In order to attain the above objectives the Perspective Planning Division suggested the introduction of a progressive surcharge on land revenue, surcharge on area under commercial crops, a purchase tax on commercial crops and a tax on livestock. Some economists proposed that the land revenue rate should be raised from the present levels and that progression should be introduced. Others had suggested the removal of the regressive land tax altogether and its replacement by a progressive agricultural income tax.

The imposition of additional taxation on agriculture has always been a source of conflict between the Centre and the States. The Centre made a proposal to link or merge income tax with agricultural income tax. On the recommendation of the Chief Ministers, conference on resource mobilization, the Central Government appointed the committee on Taxation of Agricultural Wealth and Income under the chairmanship of Dr. K.N. Raj in February, 1972 to examine the question of taxation of agricultural wealth and income from all aspects. The Raj committee submitted its unanimous report in October, 1972.

The Raj Committee's major recommendations were:

(i) A progressive Agricultural Holding Tax should be imposed on agriculturists who have no other assessable income.

(ii) In the case of assesses having non-agricultural taxable income, income from agriculture should be included in the total income for the purpose of calculating income tax.
(iii) Income from livestock, fisheries, poultry, dairy farming, etc., should be subject to tax.
(iv) An integrated taxation of agricultural property through wealth tax should be introduced.
(v) Capital gains tax on transfer of agricultural lands should be imposed.

The Agricultural Holdings Tax (AHT) recommended by the Raj Committee is meant to find a way out of the constitutional and administrative difficulties bedevilling the taxation of agricultural wealth and income. Even after the land ceiling laws are fully implemented, there would be a significant number of agriculturists whose incomes would be fairly high in the context of the income levels in our country. But it has been found very difficult to bring these agricultural incomes into the taxation net. The Constitution is very clear on this point. Incomes from agriculture can be taxed only by the states. For political and other reasons the states are not willing to exploit this source of revenue to the full. This was the problem which the Committee has tried to solve through the recommendation of the agricultural holdings tax.

The Committee has come to the conclusion that the land revenue, the largest element of direct taxation of agriculture, is not amenable to the application of the principle of progression. Surcharges on land revenue have been tried. But even after that, according to the Committee, there was no perceptible progression with the result that the income-earners belonging to the higher strata of the agricultural community pay less than those in comparable strata deriving their income from non-agricultural sources. These findings led the Committee to explore alternative approaches to direct taxation of agriculture.

Any conditions prescribed for a satisfactory system of direct taxation of agriculture must take into account the differences in productivity of land depending upon the particular crops grown in a region while its incidence must fall uniformly in different parts of the country. The system must be flexible to reflect changes in productivity and prices over a period of time. It is with these conditions in mind that the agricultural holdings tax scheme has been proposed. Under the Committee's proposal the country is to be divided into a sufficiently large number of soil-climatically homogenous districts or tracts so that differences having any significant influence on productivity are taken into account. Once this map is ready, norms of output for different crops per hectare for each year are to be worked out on the basis of estimates of yield for the previous 10 years. This yield is to be converted into value of the crops by taking into account the relevant average harvest prices of preceding three years.

The rateable value of a hectare of land would be determined in terms of these norms. Every year the schedule of rateable value of lands will be prepared on this basis by the state government concerned. Provisions are to be made for costs of irrigation and development. Under the scheme the incidence of AHT would decrease progressively with the size of the holdings. In the first phase of the implementation of the scheme the present land revenue would be replaced by the AHT on all operational holdings with rateable value of Rs. 5,000 or more. In the second phase, the system will be extended to holdings below Rs. 5,000 according to the convenience of each state government.

By taking the rateable value of the holdings as a basis for the computation of tax, the Committee hopes to ensure the constitutional validity of the scheme. Under the law as it exists today, agricultural wealth can be taxed by the Centre and as the rateable value of land has the features of wealth rather than of income, there could be no constitutional challenge to the proposed scheme. As the tax is based on productivity of the soil, actual production of the crops and their prevailing prices, care has been taken to base the scheme on the income producing capacity of the wealth in the form of an agricultural land.

It is easy to introduce an element of progression in this scheme as it has been done in the case of wealth tax applicable to other forms of wealth. The difficulty arises in the highly complicated nature of computations necessary in order to arrive at the figure of the rateable value; perhaps the Indian Agricultural Research Institute has a map of India based on soil and climate productivity for different crops. If this is so, the procedure for determining the rateable value would be simplified. In any case the taxation scheme has to be based on the value of yields that could be obtained from the holdings concerned. The analogy of the computation of the value of other form of wealth could not be applied in the case of land because of the difficulty in determining the rateable value in terms of incomes.

One recommendation of the Committee which is likely to attract some criticism is the suggestion that there should be some arrangement to bring agricultural incomes under the charge of central income-tax by taking the agricultural incomes into account in determining the rate of tax applicable to no-agricultural incomes. This is rather an ingenious way of circumventing the constitutional difficulties. But the deductions that will have to be made before arriving at figures of incomes from these holdings might make the system very cumbersome.

The Committee has also recommended that there should be integrated taxation of agricultural property through wealth tax and capital gain tax. In this connection the committee has recommended that, barring the basic exemption limit which may be raised to Rs. 1.5 lakh, all other exemptions provided in the wealth tax should be done away with as far as possible. It is debatable whether such drastic change in policy would help in restoring confidence of the tax- payers on the policy pronouncements of the finance ministers. In fact a bad psychological impact could result if wealth tax exemptions earlier granted with a view to encouraging investment are withdrawn on considerations advanced by the Raj Committee.

Further, Raj Committee recommended that the definition of the capital asset be so widened as to permit taxation of capital gains from transfer of all agricultural land irrespective of their location. Gains from transaction in assets held for not more than a year should be treated as ordinary income and taxed accordingly. To mitigate the inequity involved in the taxation of capital gain derived from sale of assets held for more than a year at progressive rates, a method of prorating the long-term capital gains over a number of years, without reopening any back year's assessment, may be followed.

EXISTING STATUS OF AGRICULTURAL TAXATION

In a broad way, agricultural taxation includes taxes paid by the agriculturists directly and also those borne by them indirectly. Direct taxes on agriculture consist mainly of land revenue, cesses and surcharges on land revenue, cesses on crops and agricultural income tax. The position of land revenue and agricultural income tax in the total revenue receipts of the states is shown in Table 12.2. As consumers, they may also be paying excise duty, sales tax, import duty, the minor vehicles tax and so on. Let us briefly describe these taxes.

Land Revenue Traditionally, land revenue is the oldest of all taxes and, at present the most important tax on agricultural land. The land tax is levied and collected by State Governments. In assessing land revenue, States have followed different basis, for instance, the land tax may be on net assets, or on the value of the net produce. In some states, assessment is left to the judgement of the assessing officers. At one time the land tax assessment used to be revised periodically but this has been given up in recent years. Hence the land tax has become a crude acreage tax.

Although yield from land revenue has increased somewhat in absolute terms as seen in Table 12.1, it has to be noted that this is not due to any upward revision of land revenue rates, but various other reasons. Burden of land revenue on the cultivators has actually been diminishing while the farmer has improved his economic position considerably. A study of the position in U.P. would prove (Table 12.2) that the revenue which the cultivator was paying to the Government was less than the rent paid by him to the Zamindar who used to extract many illegal charges from the cultivator in addition to the normal rent. The increases in land revenue have been partly at the cost of the Zamindar and partly due to increase in the area under cultivation. The burden of land revenue has also fallen due to the rise in real income of the cultivator on account of increasing productivity of land and rise in the price of agricultural products. A comparison of land revenue as

Table 12.1 Revenue Receipts of States from Agricultural Income Tax and Land Revenue

Year	*Agricultural income tax*	*Land revenue*	*(Rs. crores) Total*	*% of total revenue*
1989-90	93	690	783	1.4
1990-91	198	607	805	1.2
1991-92	202	636	838	1.0
1992-93	111	617	728	0.8
1993-94	107	732	839	0.8
1994-95	98	1141	1239	1.0
1995-96	154	1326	1480	1.1
1996-97	103	1074	1177	0.8
1997-98	182	1091	1273	0.7
1998-99	241	1031	1272	0.7
1999-00 (RE)	185	1499	1684	0.8
2000-01 (BE)	197	1858	2055	0.8 P

SOURCE: EPW May 19, 2000 EPW Research Foundation.

Table 12.2 Per acre Land Revenue in U.P. Before and After Zamindari Abolition

Division	*1946-47*		*Revenue per acre 1959-60 (Rs.)*	*1959*	
	Rent per acre (Rs.)	*Revenue per acre (Rs.)*		*Revenue per acre as percentage of 1946*	*Revenue per acre as percentage of rent per acre in 1946-47*
Meerut	5.77	2.45	5.04	205.7	87.34
Agra	5.33	2.09	4.95	236.8	92.87
Rohilkhand	5.32	1.80	5.19	287.3	97.55
Allahabad	5.16	2.10	4.69	233.3	90.89
Jhansi	2.60	1.06	2.41	227.4	92.69
Varanasi	3.69	1.44	4.20	291.7	113.82
Gorakhpur	3.44	1.74	3.87	222.4	112.50
Lucknow	6.23	2.00	5.61	280.5	90.04
Faizabad	5.54	2.03	5.67	279.3	102.34
All Districts	4.88	1.87	4.67	249.7	95.69

SOURCE: A Study of Land Reforms in Uttar Pradesh by Prof. Baljit Singh and Dr. Shridhar Misra, Oxford Book Company, p. 135.

proportion of national income from agriculture (Table 12.3) would bring out that while in 1938-39 land revenue constituted 4 percent of the income originating in the agriculture sector, this has declined steadily to 0.8 per cent during 1965-66.

There have been wide variation in land revenue in different states of India. Table 12.4 provides some valuable information in the year 1959-60. There have been some changes in the land revenue structure in the recent past which have distorted the picture further. Even the

Table 12.3 Land Revenue as Proportion of National Income from Agriculture

Year	Agriculture, forestry and logging fishing, mining and quarrying (current prices)	Land revenue	Percentage
1938-39	NA	NA	4.0
1950-51	24204	48	0.2
1960-61	32793	95	0.3
1970-71	41385	113	0.3
1980-81	48536	146	0.3
1985-86	83422	353	0.4
1990-91	159786	607	0.4
1991-92	185574	636	0.3
1992-93	207634	617	0.3
1993-94	262059	732	0.3
1994-95	301332	1141	0.4
1995-96	328358	1326	0.4
1996-97	390307	1074	0.3
1997-98	420425	1091	0.3
1998-99	495005	1031	0.2
1999-00	522385	1499	0.3

SOURCE: Compiled from Report on Currency and Finance for various years.

available data indicate that there are states like Punjab, Tamil Nadu, Maharashtra and Mysore which have higher output and productivity per acre as compared to the all-India average, where land revenue rate is substantially low. This would only indicate that the present land revenue rates do not bear any relationship to output and productivity in the different parts of the country. Equity in land taxation demands that indices be given due weightage. Another tax, which falls largely (and not exclusively) on farmers is the tax on capital transactions specially known as stamps and registration fees. This is a tax on the transfer of land and buildings.

Agricultural Income Tax Agricultural income tax is levied and collected by the States. Bihar was the first to levy this tax in 1938. At present the states which have levied agricultural income tax are Assam, West Bengal, Bihar, Uttar Pradesh, Rajasthan, Madhya Pradesh, Orissa, Karnataka, Tamil Nadu and Kerala. The rates of tax have generally been lower than those applicable to the urban income tax. This tax has always occupied an insignificant role in India-a little more than 1 per cent in 1951-52 and about 0.04 per cent of the state's tax revenues in 2000-01. It is purely an historical accident which has resulted in agricultural income being outside the purview of the centre. The noted Tax Expert, N.A. Palkhiwala, had pointed out that income tax was first levied in India in 1860. It was imposed on agricultural incomes as well. When later the tax on non-agricultural income was replaced by the licence tax, agricultural income was assessed in the shape of a cess.

Table 12.4 Land Revenue Per Capita Per Acre in the States in 1959-60

States	*Agricultural population*	*Land* under cultivation (in lakh acre)*	*Per capita cultivated land*	*Land revenue (Rs. crore)*	*Per capita land revenue*	*Per acre land revenue (in Rs.)*
Andhra Pradesh	172.3	323	1.78	11.30	6.56	3.50
Assam	82.3	56	0.68	25.3	3.07	4.51
Bihar	284.9	230	0.81	83.1	2.92	3.61
Bombay	283.4	695	2.45	11.50	4.06	1.65
Kerala	52.3	45	0.86	13.0	2.49	2.89
Madhya Pradesh	195.1	405	2.08	97.2	4.98	2.40
Madras	151.8	167	1.10	49.0	3.23	2.93
Mysore	136.0	269	1.98	43.0	1.46	1.60
Orissa	113.0	161	1.48	22.4	1.98	1.39
Punjab	111.5	174	1.56	44.4	3.98	2.55
Rajasthan	127.1	373	2.93	79.4	6.25	2.13
Uttar Pradesh	491.6	420	0.85	20.91	4.25	4.98
West Bengal	197.3	130	0.66	50.4	2.55	3.88

* Area under cultivation including current fallows for 1954-55 as available from Agriculture Situation in India, February 1958.

SOURCE: Techno Economic Survey of Uttar Pradesh, National Council of Applied Economic Research, 1965, p.331.

It was the continuing existence of these cesses that was responsible for the exemption of agricultural income in the income tax act of 1886. This cess disappeared, leaving behind the anomaly of agricultural income being exempted from tax.

Present Need

Agricultural taxation now assumes special significance in the fiscal structure of an agricultural country like India which has launched big and bold development programmes and has to use her fiscal tools for economic development. Despite its strategic role in the country's economy, the agricultural sector is subject to certain peculiar conditions which must be given due consideration in any scheme of resources mobilization. They are;

(1) Majority of farm population has small land holdings and is subject to natural hazards. Land holdings statistics reveal that about a third of the household on an average own less than 0.4 hectare accounting for a little over one percent of the farm area while the top five per cent of the households own 35 per cent of the farm area. In some of-the states such as U.P. nearly 60 per cent of the households have holdings of one hectare or less. According to the National Sample Survey, 75 per cent of household belong to the size group of 2 hectares and below.

(2) There is great disparity in the distribution of income within the agricultural sector. Almost 90 per cent of the income originating in this sector belongs to well-to-do farmers. Due to heavy dependence on monsoon, the increases in agricultural production have not been evenly distributed.

(3) Savings in this sector have been meagre and too inadequate to meet its investment needs.

(4) Agricultural sector falls outside the tax jurisdiction of the central government. The Central government is therefore unable to tax agricultural land or incomes. It all depends upon the boldness of the state governments to raise resources from this sector. The state governments, on the other hand, are trying to do away with land revenue so as to win cheap popularity.

It is only agriculture which has to provide the needed surplus for the maintenance of the population employed in the industrialisation process, because workers in industry, transport, trade and various services are recruited from the land. Since creation of invisible funds is both easy and quick in this sector, agriculture has to bear the burden of development efforts relatively more. Adequate taxation of the farming sector is thus more important in the developing countries. The position in India, however, is quite different. The fiscal contribution of rural sector in real terms has been diminishing while the need for investment resources for India's economic development is tending to increase. On the other hand, the benefits accruing to this sector due to various development schemes have substantially increased during the era of planned economic development.

CASE FOR AGRICULTURAL TAXATION

On the other side, there are arguments in favour of agricultural taxation. During the process of development, agriculture has to supply the rest of the economy with larger food surplus and raw materials. Production and marketed surplus of agricultural goods have to increase to meet the requirements of the non-agricultural sector and also to supply an increasing proportion of the community's manpower. Higher price alone may not always bring about increased production and larger marketable surplus. According to Ved Gandhi: "Imposing heavier taxation on the agricultural population would force the farmers to bring forth increased market supplies."[1] Professor Kaldor argued "The taxation of agriculture has a critical role to play in the acceleration of economic development since it is only the imposition of compulsory levies in the agricultural sector itself which enlarges the supply of saving for economic development"[2].

---

[1] Ved Gandhi, Tax Burden on Indian Agriculture, p. 2.

[2] N. Kaldor, The Role of Taxation in Economic Development" quoted by Dr. E.T. Mathew in Agricultural Taxation and Economic Development p. 5.

The above argument was based on the historical experience of Japan and Soviet Russia which had successfully mobilized the agricultural surplus for industrial development through heavy land taxes and compulsory levies. Heavier agricultural taxation would help in the commercialization of agriculture which, in turn, would respond to prices and other market forces quickly. Agricultural taxation would induce farmers to go for improved technology and this would increase the labour force available for non-farm jobs. Since late sixties, the green revolution resulted an increase in agricultural productivity and agricultural income but owing to concentration of land and rural assets in a small class of rich landowners, most of the benefits of agricultural growth have gone to the small number of wealthy farmers. Low level of agricultural taxation has failed to mobilize part of this increased productivity and income for further development efforts. Indirectly, the low rates of agriculture taxation said to have further aggravated the wealth and income disparities in the rural areas of the country.

According to C.H. Hanumantha Rao, there always existed a rationale for taxing agriculture. There is a greater case now with the rise in agricultural income and the green revolution. While the upper income groups are taxed in the urban areas, but their counterparts in the agriculture sector are not being taxed. He was of the view that agricultural income should be taxed the same way as urban income. The Tax Reform Committee (Chelliah Committee) recommended that for tax purposes, agricultural income, in excess of an exemption limit of non-agricultural income-tax assessees should be clubbed with their non-agricultural income. Presently, the agricultural income of a non-agriculturist is clubbed with the rest of his income only to determine the tax rate. But his agricultural income stays outside the income tax net. Clubbing agricultural income with non-agricultural income would mean considerable improvement in horizontal equity and would also serve to plug a loophole whereby it is possible to show part of the non-agricultural income as agricultural income to avoid paying tax.

The disparity between agricultural and non-agricultural sectors will still be wider if the corporation tax levied on non-agricultural corporate incomes is also taken into account.An inadequate taxation of agriculture introduces inequity not only between the agricultural and non-agricultural sectors but also within the agricultural sector itself. The distribution pattern of operational holdings as revealed by the Agricultural Census, 1990-91 show that holdings above the size of 10 hectares numbering 1.6 per cent of the total of all operational holdings, accounted for as much as 17.3 per cent of the total area operated, whereas holdings in the size of less than two hectares numbering 78.2 per cent of all holdings comprised only 32.4 percent of the total areas operated.

Further, thanks to the large public investments made in agricultural development since the Five Year Plans began, the generally high level of agricultural prices and particularly by the profitability of commercial crops, such as tobacco, sugar and potato, the earnings of farmers with larger or even medium holdings have been going up. The green revolution is helping agriculture to move out of subsistence to commercial farming. In these circumstances, the traditional system of agricultural taxation which is generally through a low fixed flat rate of land revenue, has become "outmoded, inadequate and irrelevant" and a system of progressive taxation of agricultural income is urgently called for.

Again, the direct taxes on agriculture, viz., land revenue and agricultural income tax have almost remained static since 1950-51 - around one per cent of the income from agriculture. Agriculture has thus not contributed anything for economic development, even though the crude index of economic welfare of the agricultural sector has been rising. Further, there is a high concentration of land in the hands of a few -and the trend is increasing in recent years. The richer sections of the agriculturists are bearing a low burden because (a) they pay land tax which is a proportional tax, and (b) they may or may not pay agricultural income tax.

Finally, as Morarji Desai stated while presenting his budget proposals (for the year 1969-70) for taxation on fertilizers and power-driven pumps, "those who benefit by the substantial investments in agriculture, including research, irrigational facilities, fertilizer plants, rural electrification, credit facilities and the support prices should contribute a part of their prosperity towards the cost of development in general. This is all the more so when the benefits of improved technology cannot yet be shared by the majority of our farmers, particularly in dry regions where fertilizers and new seeds are not easy to apply. If the benefits of the new agricultural technology are to be carried progressively to a growing proportion of our farmers, the resources needed for this purpose should come at least in part from the beneficiaries of the progress".[3]

Inter-Sectoral Tax Incidence Disparity

At the beginning of the Plan era itself the question of disparity in the incidence of indirect taxation for rural and urban households was examined by the Taxation Enquiry Commission (1953-54). The Commission's findings with regard to the incidence of indirect taxes on the rural and urban households are summarised in Table 12.5.

The dimensions of taxation, direct and indirect, central and states, have been steadily rising, partly under the pressure of development expenditure and partly because of the demands of defence and civil administration. The urban sector and particularly the manufacturing and the trading sectors have had to surrender more and more of their earnings to the Government in tax payments. This process seems to

[3] Budget speech of the Finance Minister in the Parliament, February 28, 1969.

Table 12.5 Incidence of Indirect Taxes by Expenditure Level: All India (Tax as% of Total Expenditure)

Expenditure groups with monthly expenditure (Rs.)	*Urban households*	*Rural Households*	*All India*
1-50	3.3	2.2	2.4
51-100	4.4	2.3	2.7
101-150	5.1	2.7	4.1
151-300	5.1	2.8	3.3
Above 300	8.3	4.4	5.6

SOURCE: Taxation Enquiry Commission's Report, Vol. I Chapter V, "Incidence of Taxation Analysis".

have reached a stage where it is threatening to be self-defeating. It has become imperative to look for new sources - it is in this context that the taxation of agriculture is assuming great significance.

Proposals to Raise Agricultural Taxation

The draft outline of the Fourth Plan advocated revision of land revenue rates, adjustment in irrigation charges and special surcharges on commercial crops. "As for land revenue," concluded the Draft, "It will be necessary to revise the rates both for securing additional resources and for introducing elements of progression in their incidence on holdings of different sizes." Proposals were made by Dr. I.M.D. Little, Dr. A.M. Khusro and Dr. K.N. Raj for introducing an element of progression in the land revenue structure. Professor I.M.D Little suggested a progressive scale of land revenue with as many as 27 land brackets. In his scheme, land up to 2 hectares should be exempt from land revenue while the highest bracket of 12 hectares and above would be required to pay as much as Rs. 570 per annum which would be sufficient to produce disincentive effects on land holdings of 12 hectares and above. Professor Khusro suggested a scheme with a three-tier land revenue system classifying all land holdings into three brackets and Dr. K.N. Raj suggested doubling of land revenue on holdings above 2 hectares of land. The basic defect of these various proposals was that they did not take into account the differences in the growth-rate of productivity and output in the different states, which should be given considerable weight in any rational scheme of land taxation. Moreover, upward revision of basic land revenue rates is not possible in India in the present situation or in the near future because of the past settlements that the government had made with the agriculturists.

It is necessary to emphasize again that most of the state governments are incurring losses on irrigation projects. Irrigation rates should be framed in a manner that they encourage the use of water and relieve the strain on state's finances. From this view point the state governments should devise a two- tier system of irrigation rates (i) a general irrigation rates on a uniform basis payable by all cultivators, who fall within the command area, irrespective of the use of water; and (ii) specific irrigation rate on a progressive basis linked with the quantum of water used. Besides, the state governments should make improvements in their organizational setup and in the execution of projects so that their losses are minimized. The author would also like to emphasize the need for utmost economy on the part of the state governments so that the working expenses of the irrigation projects are reduced to the minimum.

CASE FOR SPECIAL TREATMENT FOR AGRICULTURE

There are two considerations which are generally advanced in favour of this theory. Land which forms the base of agriculture, is already subject to the levy of land revenue, except for small farms which have since been exempted from land revenue in certain states. Thus while in urban areas, the business premises of a businessman or factory premises of a factory-owner are not taxed as such, the owner of agricultural land has to pay land revenue no matter whether his land is brought under cultivation during a particular season or not. It is, therefore, not entirely correct to say that agriculture is exempt from tax. The landowner has to pay land revenue even if his income remains below the exemption limit for the general taxpayer. It may be that the quantum of tax that he pays in the form of land revenues is lower than the income-tax paid by the general taxpayer.

Secondly, agriculture in India has to face numerous hazards - hazards much greater than what an ordinary businessman or a factory-owner has to face in the course of his business. The vagaries of nature have a powerful influence on the growth of crops. Quite often the crops fail for want of rain—a factor beyond the control of the farmer, and the income of the farmer drops steeply. Sometimes he does not get back even the value of his inputs. Again, untimely and excessive rains can spoil his otherwise good crop. Epidemic and locust attack are some of the other curses peculiar to agriculture.

In India there is a cycle of five years of good and bad harvests. One of these years is generally good when the rains are timely and adequate and help the crop to give a good yield. Two years, however, are generally bad when the crops fail and the yield is much below the normal. The other two years are years of average production. This is why the income of a farmer, particular in a dry area, fluctuates widely from year to year. This generally does not happen in the case of a business or industrial concern. It will, therefore, be unfair to tax a farmer on the basis of his income during a year of good production when it is almost certain that his income during the subsequent years would decline substantially. Though there has been considerable improvement in the agricultural production of the country during recent years, we do not yet appear to have reached the stage when tax could be imposed on agriculture without the risk of hampering its further growth.

At the top of all this, a study of ceilings on land would show that the highest ceiling for irrigated land with two crops is 7.28 hect, although there are states like Orissa, Himachal, Tripura and Tamil Nadu where it is around 4 hect. Since 91.3 per cent of holdings during 1990-91 were marginal/small and Semi-medium, their net income will certainly fall much below the taxation exemption limit. Even from among the medium (4-10 hect.), majority of the 7.1 per cent (at least 4-5 per cent) would fall in the category of below the ceiling limit—say around 5 hect. This would mean atleast 95 per cent of the holders during 1990-91 would fall below the exemption limit. Today, 10 years later, this category would have further gone up to say 97-98 per cent, if the trend of previous 10 years is maintained.

We would then be hardly left today, with 2-3 per cent of the holders who could even theoretically be considered as eligible for taxation. This category is definitely the one which contributes a major part of its produce to procurement. MSP at present is fixed on a cost plus formula. A tax levy will mean additional cost to the farmer. The farmer lobby being strong today, Government will not be able to resist this demand. The enhanced MSP rate will obviously apply to the total procurement, operations, even from those who fall below the taxation limit. If we take into consideration the increased subsidy involved and with added collection charges, the total exercise would appear to be futile.

The collection of tax on agricultural income will itself become a gigantic task. The illiterate farmer will not be able to maintain an accurate account of his expenditure and income. The income-tax and revenue department staff will doubtlessly harass him and corrupt practices may develop. The cost of collection may work out to be disproportionately high and the government may not be able to collect any large amount of net revenue if tax is imposed on agriculture.

We would, however, have no objection to recommend that all those gentleman farmers who have major income from non-agriculture activities, but show fictitious figures of income from agriculture, should be brought under the taxation net. This will not involve any additional cost. They are already submitting their tax returns and fact of the matter is that their agriculture income component is nothing but a dubious device to convert their non-agriculture black income to white. Some of the suggestions were made by the Raj Committee (discussed in this chapter) to integrate agriculture and non-agriculture income. The whole of this question can be re-examined after taking into consideration the real ground situation as at present. In the computer age of today none of such data collection would involve any complication and the exercise in the final analysis may prove fruitful.

CHAPTER 13

Agricultural Labour Policy

INTRODUCTION

An "agricultural labour," in terms of economics, could be defined as a person who works for wages in agriculture. However, the enumeration of agricultural labourers in India presents some difficulties. This is mainly because the various agricultural classes cannot be placed into watertight division and more often than not overlap each other. A person may be farming as well as working on wages with other farmers during his spare time. What criterion should determine the enumeration of such a person into a farmer or a labourer. The successive population censuses and the Agricultural Labour Enquiries conducted in 1950-51 and 1956-57 were also faced with the problems of defining agricultural labour. There was no clear-cut categorization of agricultural labourers during the earlier censuses. While the census of 1871-72 covered only adult male workers, in 1881 all adult workers, male, and female were included. The Census Reports, 1901 to 1931 had a separate column as "unspecified labourers" who according to them were "in reality field labourers." They were also included among agricultural labourers.

The term "agricultural labourer" in 1931, and "cultivating owners" in 1951 did not differ much conceptually. But in 1931, the working dependants of cultivating owners and tenant cultivators appeared as dependent workers in the category of agricultural labourers. The 1951 census on the other hand, included among "agricultural labourers" all of them without "land and those with land" for whom the wages earned by working for others was more important than the income from land, as a means of livelihood. It excluded all those persons described as "agricultural labourers with land" whose income from land exceeded the wages earned by them. The result of all these changes in the definition and classification of agricultural labourers was that there was a sharp increase in this class in 1931 as compared with 1921 and a sharp decrease in 1951.

While the unit of enumeration in the 1951 and the previous censuses was the individual, the two agricultural labour enquiries adopted the household as their unit. Again, the labour enquiry figures relate to the families living in the villages surveyed and as such the estimate is based on the rural population only and for the villages surveyed. As between the first and the second agricultural labour enquiries, the first included among agricultural labourers those hired workers who were employed in the process of crop production for 50 per cent or more of the total number of days worked by them during the previous year. All workers in allied pursuits like dairying, horticulture, and poultry were excluded.

The second agricultural labour enquiry rectified the omission of workers in the allied occupations, but treated the households as agricultural labourer on the basis of income from wages. The change in the definition of the two enquiries obviously led to a reduction in the total number of agricultural households in the second one. It had been estimated that with agricultural wage income remaining constant, a household having a cultivated holding of 4.6 acres and above would be having an income from cultivation equal to or more than its income from agricultural labour and would, therefore, cease to be classified as an agricultural labourer, It was actually enumerated in a trial tabulation over 250 households spread in 10 villages surveyed by the National Sample Survey during its eleventh round that seven per cent of the households which would be counted as agricultural labourers according to the first enquiry, could not come under the definition of the second enquiry.

Some economists use the term agricultural labourer in the sense of total labour force in agriculture and include in it both self-employed and hired workers. Agricultural workers in India are also classified according to the nature of employment into casual and attached workers. Casual workers are engaged in peak period and attend to rush work only, while the workers attached or permanent are employed on annual or seasonal basis. According to the first agricultural labour enquiry, 90 per cent of the total agricultural labour families were casual workers and ten per cent were attached workers. The corresponding figures for the second enquiry were 73 and 27 per cent respectively.

The reason for the preponderance of casual labourers in Indian agriculture is the abundance of supply of labour on the one hand and intermittent nature of agricultural work on the other. Agriculture, according to the International Standard Industrial Classification, includes cultivation of land, rearing and maintenance of livestock, forest operations, fishing and hunting; it does not, however, include fruit growing or plantations. But according to Indian condition, all these categories are included. Workers in the agricultural sector are distributed into three main categories: (i) cultivators, (ii) agricultural labour, and (iii) workers engaged in forestry, fishing and livestock, etc. We are primarily concerned here with agricultural labour which is basically unskilled and unorganized and has little for its livelihood other than personal labour. Persons whose main source of income is wage employment will fall in this category. It consists of two sub-categories: (i) landless agricultural labour, and (ii) very small cultivators whose main source of earnings, due to their small and submarginal holdings, is wage employment. Landless labour in turn can be classified into two broad categories: (a) permanent labour attached to a cultivating household, and (b) casual labour. The second group can again be divided into three subgroups, viz., cultivators, sharecroppers and leaseholders. The first group of agricultural workers has been more or less in the position of serfs or slaves; they are also known as bonded labour. They do not normally receive wages in cash but are generally paid in kind. They have to work for their masters and cannot shift from one to another. They have to provide beggar or forced labour. In some cases, they have to offer cash and also supply fowls and goats to their masters. The problem of landless labourers is the most serious problem in the rural sector. Table 13.1 brings out the distribution of workers in the agricultural sector. State-wise classification of workers according 1991 census is shown in Table 13.2.

CHARACTERISTICS OF AGRICULTURAL LABOUR

Agricultural labour possesses certain characteristics which distinguishes it from industrial labour. Firstly, unlike industrial labour, agricultural workers are unorganized. This is primarily due to the job being scattered. Secondly, agricultural workers belong mainly to one category, i.e., unskilled. Thirdly, agricultural labour possesses migratory character. It can be drawn from distant places to the place of work during busy season. Fourthly, the employer-employee relationship is very different from that of industrial labour. Mostly one or two labourers are employed and the farmer who employs them also works with them and there is direct contact between them. In some places, labourers enjoy the status of a family member. They live and eat at farmer's house. They often belong to the same caste and community as the farmer and may be even his relatives. Fifthly, the annual earnings, particularly of the casual workers, are much smaller primarily due to low rate of wages and irregular employment. Finally, the systems of wages payment also differ. The farm worker may be paid partly in kind and partly in cash. He receives perquisites in the form of breakfast, lunch, clothes, etc. Table 13.3 would give an idea of the characteristics of Agricultural Labour Households as indicated in the Rural Labour.

Enquiry Report 1964-65. According to the Report, 21.8 per cent of the total rural households were rural labour households. However,

Table 13.1 Population and Agricultural Workers

(In millions)

Year	Total Population	Average annual exponential growth rate (%)	Rural Population	Cultivators	Agricultural labourers	Other workers	Total
(1)	(2)	(3)	(4)	(5)	(6)	(7)	(8)
1951	361.1	1.25	298.6	69.9	27.3	42.8	140.0
			(82.7)	(49.9)	(19.5)	(30.6)	(100.0)
1961	439.2	1.96	360.3	99.6	31.5	57.6	188.7
			(82.0)	(52.8)	(16.7)	(30.5)	(100.0)
1971	548.2	2.20	439.0	78.2	47.5	54.7	180.4
			(80.1)	(43.4)	(26.3)	(30.3)	(100.0)
1981*	683.3	2.22	523.9	92.5	55.5	96.6‡	244.6
			(76.7)	(37.8)	(22.7)	(39.5)	(100.0)
1991†	846.3	2.14	628.7	110.7	74.6	128.8‡	314.1
			(74.3)	(35.2)	(23.8)	(41.0)	(100.0)
2001(P)	1027.0	1.93					

* Total and rural population of India in columns 2 and 4 includes population of Assam worked out by interpolation as 1981 Census could not be held in Assam due to disturbed conditions. The data on workers in columns 5-8 exclude Assam.

† Total and rural population of India in columns 2 and 4 includes the projected population of J & K as 1991 Census could not be conducted in J & K due to disturbed conditions. The data on workers in columns 5 –8 exclude J & K.

‡ Includes marginal workers.

Note: Figures in parentheses represent percentage of the total.

SOURCE: Registrar General of India, New Delhi.

according to the National Commission on Rural Labour (1991), during 1987-88, out of a total of 108.4 million rural households, 43 million households belonged to rural labour households and among them, agricultural labour households were of the order of 33.3 million. In relative terms, rural labour households accounted for 39.7 per cent of total labour households and agricultural labour households were of the order of 30.7 per cent. This implies that agricultural labour households constituted about 77 per cent of all rural labour households in 1987-88.

Characteristics of Demand and Supply

Demand Due to the seasonal nature of agricultural operations, the demand for agriculture labour is very uneven. There is peak demand during sowing and harvesting seasons. Demand is also high during

Table 13.2 Classification of Workers According to 1991 Census

(Thousands)

Sl. No.	State/UTs	Agricultural workers			Other workers	Total main workers	Marginal workers	Total workers
		As cultivators	As agricultural labours	Total				
(1)	(2)	(3)	(4)	(5)	(6)	(7)	(8)	(9)
1.	Andhra Pradesh	7891	11625	19516	8929	28445	1518	29963
2.	Arunachal Pradesh	236	20	256	135	391	9	400
3.	Assam	3559	845	4404	2588	6992	1097	8089
4.	Bihar	11165	9513	20678	4941	25619	2158	27777
5.	Goa	57	35	92	292	384	29	413
6.	Gujarat	4704	3231	7935	6161	14096	2525	16621
7.	Haryana	1830	897	2727	1992	4719	385	5104
8.	Himachal Pradesh	1125	59	1184	595	1779	435	2214
9.	Jammu & Kashmir	-	-	-	-	-	-	-
10.	Karnataka	5916	5000	10916	6376	17292	1595	18887
11.	Kerala	1016	2120	3136	5165	8301	845	9146
12.	Madhya Pradesh	12904	5863	18767	6168	24935	3406	28341
13.	Maharashtra	10172	8313	18485	12521	31006	2904	33910
14.	Manipur	437	47	464	224	708	67	775
15.	Meghalaya	396	90	486	230	716	42	758
16.	Mizoram	178	10	188	102	290	47	337
17.	Nagaland	372	7	379	132	511	5	516
18.	Orissa	4598	2977	7575	2803	10376	1505	11883
19.	Punjab	1917	1453	3370	2728	6098	164	6262
20.	Rajasthan	8181	1392	9573	4342	13915	3189	17104
21.	Sikkim	95	13	108	56	164	4	168
22.	Tamil Nadu	5664	7896	13560	9239	22799	1395	24194
23.	Tripura	306	188	494	308	802	56	858
24.	Uttar Pradesh	22031	7833	29864	11497	41361	3439	44800
25.	West Bengal	5845	5055	10900	9681	20581	1334	21915
UNION TERRITORIES								
1.	Andaman & Nicobar Island	15	5	20	71	91	8	99
2.	Chandigarh	2	2	4	220	224	1	225
3.	Dadra & Nagar Haveli	36	6	42	19	61	13	74
4.	Daman & Diu	3	1	4	28	32	6	38
5.	Delhi	33	25	58	2910	2968	12	2980
6.	Lakshadweep	-	-	-	12	12	1	13
7.	Pondicherry	18	77	95	167	262	5	267
ALL INDIA *		110702	74598	185300	100632	285932	28199	314131

* Exclude Jammu & Kashmir

SOURCE: Indian Agriculture in Brief, Directorate of Economics & Statistics, Ministry of Agriculture, Government of India, New Delhi.

Table 13.3 Characteristics of Agricultural Labour Households, 1964-65

Zone/State	Percentage of agricultural labour households to rural households	Percentage of agricultural labour households without land	Size of agricultural labour households				Wage-earners in agricultural labour households				Work participation rate in agricultural labour households (per cent)		Percentage of women labourers among agricultural labourers
			M	W	Ch.	Total	M	W	Ch.	Total	M	W	
Central Zone	15.9	49.2	1.25	13.8	18.0	4.4	11.9	0.70	0.12	2.01	88	51	34.5
Uttar Pradesh	13.9	46.1	1.45	1.39	1.81	4.6	1.23	0.55	0.12	1.90	85	40	28.5
Madhya Pradesh	20.3	53.1	1.28	1.29	1.62	4.2	1.14	0.92	0.15	2.21	89	71	41.7
Eastern Zone	23.9	45.0	1.33	1.41	1.96	4.7	1.17	0.51	0.07	1.75	88	36	28.0
Bihar	28.0	37.5	1.47	1.32	1.97	4.8	1.14	0.64	0.06	1.84	86	43	34.9
West Bengal	25.4	58.1	1.42	1.36	2.07	4.8	1.26	0.25	0.05	1.56	89	18	14.2
Orissa	24.7	45.3	1.33	1.35	1.74	4.4	1.17	0.50	0.10	1.77	88	37	27.2
Assam	4.9	43.2	1.49	1.20	1.83	4.5	1.25	0.44	0.03	1.72	84	37	25.2
Southern Zone	29.4	60.9	1.30	1.36	1.62	4.3	1.11	0.93	0.15	2.19	85	68	42.7
Andhra Pradesh	31.4	65.4	1.23	1.26	1.57	4.1	1.11	0.98	0.21	2.30	90	78	42.3
Tamil Nadu	28.0	68.5	1.25	1.33	1.43	4.0	1.05	0.94	0.11	2.10	84	71	45.0
Kerala	28.2	29.8	1.62	1.72	2.20	5.5	1.23	0.82	0.03	2.08	76	48	37.7
Western Zone	26.2	68.3	1.39	1.36	1.87	4.6	1.15	0.97	0.16	2.28	83	71	43.1
Gujarat	16.7	74.6	1.50	1.38	2.06	4.9	1.26	0.97	0.07	2.30	84	71	41.8
Maharashtra	31.0	68.4	1.39	1.40	1.81	4.6	1.16	1.00	0.18	2.34	83	71	43.5
Mysore	27.2	64.8	1.29	1.35	1.87	4.5	1.09	0.94	0.18	2.21	85	70	43.1
Northern Zone	8.5	75.1	1.56	1.39	2.05	5.0	1.29	0.43	0.12	1.84	83	31	22.2
Rajasthan	5.5	51.0	1.36	1.26	1.54	4.2	1.16	0.71	0.15	2.02	85	56	34.7
Punjab	14.3	87.7	1.68	1.48	2.34	5.5	1.37	0.29	0.11	1.77	82	20	14.9
All India	21.8	56.1	1.35	1.38	1.80	4.5	1.16	0.76	0.12	2.04	86	55	36.9

transplanting and weeding operations. Women are more suitable for certain jobs. Operations such as ploughing, levelling, digging trenches, lifting water from wells are done by men. The duration of employment in a year in different regions is unequal. It varies from 5 to 7 months in dry areas and 9 to 10 months in irrigated areas.

The demand for hired labour in the agricultural sector is limited due to the fact that the bulk of labour supply comes from the family of the farmer himself. Even if there is need for hired labour, small farmers mostly try to do without it, since they cannot afford to pay wages.

Supply The supply of labour is unevenly distributed over the country. The areas with high density of population have generally the agricultural labourers in excess. In some regions with low density of population, the labour supply is either just enough or shortages are left during parts of the year. There is a high percentage of female and child labour. Wages for this category are lower than those for men. Naturally they get some preference in employment in specific operations.

The period of complete inactivity in each agricultural region varies with the nature and variety of crops and cropping intensity. Broadly speaking, Indian cultivators are unoccupied anywhere from four to six months in a year excepting in places where they have taken to the cultivation to wet crops or where the area is double cropped. The cultivators' womenfolk are unoccupied for even longer part of the year.

GROWTH OF AGRICULTURAL LABOUR

Some of the important factors responsible for the growth of agricultural labour population during the last 100 years or so may be summarized as (1) disintegration of village communities of the pre-nineteenth century India; (2) change on the basis of landholding in the village communities; (3) decline of domestic industries; (4) land settlement under British rule; (5) disintegration of the peasantry; and (6) increase in rural population and pressure on land.

As per the second Agricultural Labour Enquiry report published in 1960, agricultural labour families constituted nearly 25 per cent of all rural families. The Report also stated that more than 85 percent of the rural workers were casual serving any farmer who was willing to engage them and only 15 per cent of agricultural labourers were attached to specific landlords. An analysis of 1991 census data focuses that agricultural labourers were 74.6 million (Table 13.2). As a percentage of total workers (main plus marginal) which were 314.1 million, agricultural labourers constituted 23.7 per cent of the total rural labour force. This implies that marginal farmers have been swelling the ranks of landless labourers. On account of the increasing economic compulsions in terms of past debts, they have been forced to sell their lands. This supports the popularly held view that the benefits of millions of rupees invested in irrigation, tube-wells, fertilizers or roads have gone to the big farmers. It also implies that cooperatives and rural banks have also helped the rich farmers. In fact, the problems of agricultural labourers arise not so much from the specific weaknesses and deficiencies of this class as from the basic maladjustment in the total economy due to lack of fast growth, along with appropriate structural and technological changes.

An important finding of the National Commission on Rural Labour (NCRL) was that whereas during 1977-78, the average days worked by men and women of agricultural labour households in agricultural wage employment were 230 and 184 respectively, in 1983 (4th Rural Labour Enquiry) there were 159 and 136 days. This decline in the employment days did produce an adverse effect on the earnings and indebtedness of the agricultural households.

It has also been found that the proportion of wage labour to total work force increased at the All-India level from 34.1% in 1972-73 to 41.4% in 1987-88. During the same period, the proportion of casual wage labour to total wage labour increased from 64.8% in 1972-73 to 75.8% in 1987-88. Explaining the growing trend towards casualization of agricultural labour, NCRL states unequivocally: "The technological change in agriculture, marginalization of small farmers, eviction of tenants, destruction of traditional cottage industries, inflation etc., are some of the important factors that are operating differently in different regions of India leading to the swelling of the number of agricultural labourers".

As regards regional distribution, the increase of agricultural labourers has not been evenly spread throughout the country. The problem of landless labourers is more acute in the former Bombay, Madras, and Central Provinces, which happen to be ryotwari regions. In most of these cases the proportion of agricultural labourers to working population is more than half. Similar is the case of Hyderabad and Mysore, though the proportion is somewhat less. The second region in importance comprises Bihar, Orissa, Bengal and Assam, i.e., the zamindari areas. In this region, the proportion of agricultural labourers to the total working population was between one-fifth and one-third in 1931. In UP and Punjab, i.e. Mahalwari tracts, the proportion was the smallest, i.e., less than one-fifth in 1931. Due to the exclusion of Sind, the position in the case of Bombay has undergone a change, but in other states the position remains more or less the same even after almost seven decades.

The correlation between the regions demarcated on the basis of the proportion of agricultural labourers and the form of land systems is so striking that it can hardly be dismissed as purely incidental. The number of agricultural labourers in ryotwari regions is greater because it was easier for the moneylenders to usurp the lands of the cultivators and force them to become agricultural labourers. This was more difficult in the joint village systems. On the other hand, the difference between zamindari and the joint village region, with regard to the proportion of agricultural labourers to the agricultural population, is accounted for by the fact that in the former areas British administration started earlier than in the latter ones. Thus, the village communities in the zamindari region disintegrated much earlier which led to the emergence of a larger number of agricultural labourers.

State Policy Towards Agricultural Labour

Till recently state did not pay much attention to agricultural labour. The Royal Commission on Agriculture suggested that the problem of agricultural labour was simply one of pressure of population on land, and the solution lay in relieving this pressure. The Congress Agrarian Reforms Committee observed: "To leave out the problem of agricultural labour in any scheme of agrarian reforms, as has been done so far, is to leave unattended a weeping wound in the agrarian system of the country". After independence, this class has been engaging the attention of the government.

One of the directive principles of the Constitution lays down that the state shall endeavour to secure, by suitable legislation or economic organization or in any other way, to all workers, agricultural, industrial or otherwise, work, a living wage, and conditions of work ensuring a decent standard of life and full enjoyment of social and cultural opportunities. The constitution has also declared the practice of serfdom an offence. It has abolished agrarian slavery including forced labour by law.

Land reform legislation on a comprehensive scale has been undertaken by different state governments to abolish intermediaries. These reforms have resulted in the improvement of the status of tenants who are not so distinctly different from agricultural labour. Besides these, tenancy laws have been passed in most of the states. Tenants' interests are sought to be protected by giving them occupancy rights, fair rent, security of tenure, etc. Under the UP Zamindari Abolition Act, the land on which the labourers' houses exist, now belongs to the labourers and the landlord cannot evict them from it. Formerly, the house belonged to the zamindar and the labourer depended always on the mercy of the landlord even for shelter. Under the moneylending and debt regulation acts, the agricultural labourer also enjoys protection as the farmer.

Forced labour in agriculture has been interwoven in the complex pattern of land tenure and tenancy system of India. Even though the abolition of intermediary tenures, merger of former princely states, and comprehensive tenancy reform led to the elimination of forced labour to a considerable extent, it still exists, as revealed by the first and the second agricultural labour enquiries in some form or the other, particularly under strong feudal influence. After independence, there has been such political awakening in the countryside that there are hardly any serfs in the sense described above. A loan is no doubt an occasion for entering into a contract for work as agricultural labourer but it would be wrong to say that such a labourer is a serf.

Despite taking various measure to alleviate the condition of agricultural labourers resorting to planned developments the National Commission on Agriculture (1976) observed that "neither general economic development nor agricultural development nor even agrarian reform measures has led to any improvement in the level of living of the bulk of agricultural labourers as the recent estimates of proportion of population below the poverty line show. The structural measure to realign the production relations within agriculture in favour of agricultural labourers and other weaker sections and legislative support to their wages have little to show by way of concrete results. Even the spectacular upsurge in agricultural production in the region of "green revolution" does not appear to have resulted in a uniform and substantial improvement in wages"[1]

Minimum Wage Fixation in Agriculture

The concept of Minimum Wages was first evolved by ILO in 1928 with reference to remuneration of workers in those industries where the level of wages was substantially low and the labour was vulnerable to exploitation, being not well organized and having less effective bargaining power. The need for a legislation for fixation of minimum wages in India received boost after World War-II when a draft bill was considered by the Indian Labour Conference in 1945.

On the recommendation of the 8th Standing Labour Committee, the Minimum Wages Bill was introduced in the Central Legislative assembly on 11-4-1946 to provide for fixation of minimum wages in certain employments. The Minimum Wages Bill was passed by the Indian Dominion Legislature and came into force on 15th March, 1948. Under the Act both State and Central Governments are "Appropriate Governments' for fixation/revision of minimum rates of wages for employments covered by the Schedule to the Act.

Thus, in India, Minimum Wages Act was passed in 1948 and pressure was brought upon the Government to extend the Act to cover agricultural labourer also. During the first five year plan attempts were made to ensure a minimum standard of living to agricultural labourer by fixing minimum wages under the Minimum Wages Act. However, there are still some states which have not brought large sections of agricultural labour within the ambit of the Act. Though some progress has been achieved in this respect, the implementation of the Act has brought to light some limitations. Merely prescribing a flat rate of

[1] National Commission on Agriculture, 1976-Abridged Report, p. 705.

agricultural labour is impracticable and ineffective. Agricultural conditions differ from region to region within a state, a level of minimum wage suitable for one region may be entirely inapplicable in another. The mere task of determining the required minima is thus immense.

Further, in a number of cases the minimum wages were fixed at an initially low level decades ago and have been revised only infrequently since then. This, and not effective enforcement, explains the prevalence of relatively higher level of prevailing wages in some states compared to minimum wages. As of now there is no uniform and comprehensive wage policy for all sectors of the economy in India. While wages in the organized sector are determined through negotiations and settlements between employer and employees, in the unorganised (e.g. agricultural labour) where labour is vulnerable to exploitation due to illiteracy, absence of knowledge of the existence of legislation, scattered nature of agricultural farms, casual nature of employment, and absence of bargaining power, wage rates are fixed/revised both by the central and state governments in the scheduled employment falling under their respective jurisdictions. The minimum wage rates fixed for different categories of workers under agriculture as fixed by the Central Government are shown in Table 13.4.

The rate of wages once fixed are revised at an interval not exceeding five years. The minimum wages were last revised in 1994 under Central sphere and preliminary notifications to this effect for further revision have already been issued. The range of wages for the unskilled workers as fixed/revised by various State Governments are at Table 13.5.

In practice the actual wages paid vary from district to district within a state and even from one village to another within a district. The wages are paid both category-wise, such as, field labour, other agricultural labour, skilled labour, herdsman, etc. and operation-wise, namely, ploughing, sowing, weeding, harvesting, etc. The prevailing daily rates, both category-wise and operation wise at the selected villages of the selected districts in a few states are shown in Appendices 13.1.

Real Wages for Unskilled Agricultural Labour

Despite marginal declines for the years 1994-95 and 1998-99, the all India average real wages for the unskilled agricultural workers have risen continuously and at an average rate of about 3 per cent per annum during the 8 year span of 1992-2000. However, as shown in Table 13.6 there are wide fluctuations among the various states over the years. These data are consistent with the reduction in poverty that has been noticed in the 1990s.

Social Security to Agricultural Workers

Though various social security laws have been centrally enacted, an inter-state consensus on preparing a legislative initiative for welfare

Table 13.4 Minimum Rates of Wages and Special Allowances Revised as on 1-10-2000

(Rs. per day/per worker)

Agriculture Category of worker	Area "A"			Area "B"			Area "C"		
	Basic wage	Revised Spl. allowance	Total wage	Basic wage	Revised spl. allowance	Total wage	Basic wage	Revised spl. allowance	Total wage
1	2	3	4	5	6	7	8	9	10
Unskilled	75.00	15.19	90.19	69.00	13.74	82.74	67.00	13.74	30.74
Semiskilled/Unskilled	83.00	16.64	99.64	77.00	15.19	92.19	70.00	14.47	84.47
Supervisory skilled/ Clerical	91.00	18.08	109.08	83.00	16.64	99.64	76.00	15.19	91.91
Highly Skilled	101.00	20.25	121.25	93.00	18.81	111.81	83.00	16.64	99.64

Note : Area A includes : Metropolitan Cities & Ahmedabad, Lucknow, Nagpur and Kanpur and Greater Bombay,
Area B Includes: 54 cities mainly with a population of 1 lakh
Area C Includes: All other areas
SOURCE: Wage Cell, Ministry of Labour
Author's SOURCE: Annual Report, 2000-2001, Ministry of Labour, Government of India.

Table 13.5 State-wise Details of Minimum Wages

Sl. No.	Centre/States/UTs.	No. of scheduled employments	Range of minimum wages per day (Rs.)	
			Minimum	Maximum
(1)	(2)	(3)	(4)	(5)
1.	Central Sphere	44	80.74	90.19
2.	Andhra Pradesh	61	27.00	63.19
3.	Arunachal Pradesh	25	35.60	37.60
4.	Assam	64	32.80	50.70
5.	Bihar	74	49.19	61.59
6.	Goa	18	21.00	125.00
7.	Gujarat	53	34.00	92.40
8.	Haryana	50	70.30	74.30
9.	Himachal Pradesh	24	26.00	51.00
10.	Jammu & Kashmir	18	30.00	-
11.	Karnataka	64	26.00	74.03
12.	Kerala	36	30.00	164.77
13.	Madhya Pradesh	36	50.46	56.46
14.	Maharashtra	65	42.46	108.65
15.	Manipur	5	44.65	55.00
16.	Meghalaya	24	50.00	-
17.	Mizoram	3	70.00	-
18.	Nagaland	36	40.00	-
19.	Orissa	83	42.50	-
20.	Punjab	60	69.25	151.32
21.	Rajasthan	38	47.05	60.00
22.	Sikkim (Minimum Wages Act, 1948 has not yet been extended and enforced)			
23.	Tamil Nadu	60	35.00	115.80
24.	Tripura	11	20.63	45.00
25.	Uttar Pradesh	62	42.02	70.62
26.	West Bengal	45	48.21	87.28
27.	Andaman & Nicobar Islands	5	50.00	86.76
28.	Chandigarh	44	81.65	-
29.	Dadra & Nagar Haveli	43	60.00	71.00
30.	Daman & Diu	71	50.00	60.00
31.	Delhi	29	93.00	-
32.	Lakshadweep	9	46.80	-
33.	Pondichery	4	19.25	65.00

SOURCE: Ministry of Labour, Annual Report 2000-2001.

Minimum Wages

Minimum wages help bolster low-paid workers and ensure that fair wages are paid. A statutory minimum wage refers to a legislated or national collectively agreed wage levels below which employers are not permitted to pay their employees: such minima now exist in 21 OECD countries. The ratio of the adult statutory minimum wage to median earnings of all full-time employees provides a measure of the relative importance of minimum wages in each country and of the extent to which it helps to prop up the wages of low paid workers.

Adult minimum wages appear to be highest in France and Australia, and lowest in Korea and Mexico (Chart II). It is generally found that the incidence of minium wage work tends to be highest among youth, women and part-time workers, and among those employed in relating, hotels and restaurants, and in smaller firms.

Negative employment effects are most likely to occur when minium wages are set at a relatively high level compared to average earnings, especially for low-wage workers such as youth and unskilled workers. Countries have sought to mitigate these possible 'disemployment' effects in a number of ways.

For example, minimum wages have been allowed to fall relative to average wages (for total labour costs) over time in many countries. In several instances, these trends have been accompanied by offering mechanisms to help shore up incomes of low-wage workers. The U.S. for example has introduced and expanded tax credits for low-paid workers while Belgium, France and the Netherlands have sought to lower the overall labour costs of hiring low-wage workers by cutting employer social security contributions rather than by lowering minimum wages in absolute or relative terms (Chart I).

Chart II

Ratio of adult minimum wages to median full-time earnings, mid-2000

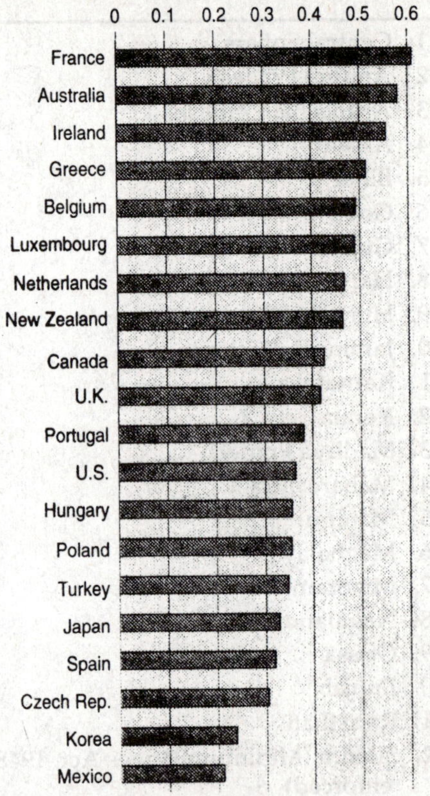

Chart I

Trends in the ratio of adult minimum wages to median full-time earnings, 1975-2000

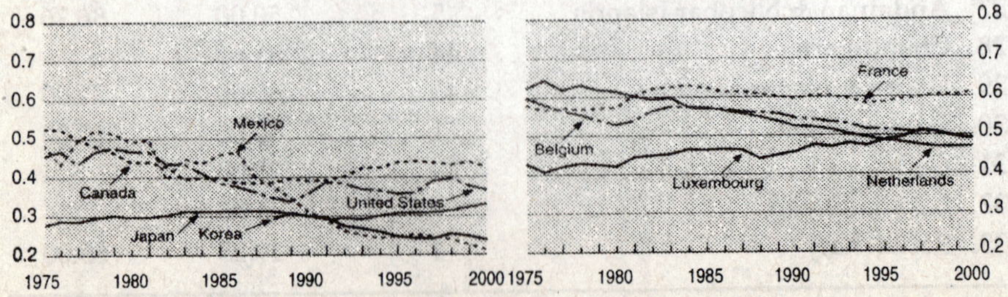

Table 13.6 Annual Percentage Change in Real Wages for Unskilled Agricultural Labour for Selected States

State	Percentage change for agricultural year (July to June) over previous year						
	1993-94	1994-95	1995-96	1996-97	1997-98(P)	1998-99(P)	1999-2000(P)
Andhra Pradesh	(+) 8.60	(+) 2.71	(-) 1.73	(+) 1.51	(+) 4.33	(-) 3.46	(+) 4.13
Assam	(-) 6.58	(-) 1.67	(+) 2.68	(+) 1.52	(+) 0.77	(+) 1.18	(-) 1.02
Bihar	(+) 5.98	(+) 1.69	(-) 2.30	(+) 15.15	(+) 4.70	(-) 5.70	(-) 3.26
Gujarat	(+) 2.86	(+) 1.27	(+) 2.92	(+) 5.08	(+) 14.43	(+) 7.37	(+) 10.14
Karnataka	(+) 41.31	(-) 15.60	(-) 8.61	(+) 21.39	(+) 17.05	(-) 2.83	(+) 8.42
Kerala	(-) 2.84	(+) 5.24	(+) 13.20	(+) 14.54	(+) 15.67	(+) 4.90	(-) 14.53
Madhya Pradesh	(-) 3.53	(+) 4.93	(+) 1.24	(+) 1.31	(+) 0.83	(+) 0.79	(+) 3.74
Maharashtra	(+) 25.58	(-) 0.68	(-) 7.89	(+) 8.31	(+) 8.78	(-) 5.41	(-) 10.84
Orissa	(-) 0.14	(-) 3.52	(+) 0.55	(-) 0.41	(+) 2.39	(+) 0.61	(-) 0.23
Punjab	(+) 1.51	(-) 1.17	(-) 6.50	(-) 0.42	(+) 0.56	(-) 2.92	(-) 0.74
Rajasthan	(-) 7.66	(+) 1.05	(+) 10.33	(+) 17.81	(+) 5.12	(-) 16.26	(+) 16.83
Tamil Nadu	(+) 11.60	(+) 1.03	(+) 3.63	(+) 7.90	(+) 13.39	(+) 2.63	(+) 16.84
Uttar Pradesh	(-) 6.77	(-) 2.31	(+) 14.78	(-) 6.39	(+) 17.36	(+) 0.38	(-) 5.61
West Bengal	(-) 6.50	(-) 5.29	(-) 0.28	(+) 11.15	(+) 3.02	(-) 3.14	(+) 0.65
All India.	(+) 5.61	(-) 0.39	(+) 0.72	(+) 6.37	(+) 7.17	(-) 1.56	(+) 1.15

(P) : Provisional

Notes: (i) Data on state average wage rates for unskilled agricultural labour in current prices are taken from the Ministry of Agriculture. The same have been converted into real wages by deflating with the State level Consumer Price Index Numbers for Agricultural Labourers (CPIAL) with 1960-61 as base. CPIAL has been sourced from Labour Bureau (Shimla). Having estimated real wages for agricultural year percentage change over previous year has been worked out.

(ii) New series of CPIAL with base 1986-87 – 100 were released w.e.f. November 1995. To maintain continuity of old series of CPIAL, the new series have been converted by using the linking factor of each state and then, the average for each state has been worked out on the basis of converted series.

(iii) The real wages for unskilled agricultural labour for each state have been weighted by total agricultural labourers of the state for working out all India average. The weighted average real wages for all India are based on 14 states as reported above. Having estimated weighted average real wages for all India, percentage change over previous year has been worked out.

SOURCE: Ministry of Agriculture and Labour.

Author's SOURCE: Economic Survey 2000-2001, Government of India.

of agricultural workers has so far not been possible. The states those are destination of migrant agricultural workers see the problem in a different perspective from others who originate the migrants. If agricultural workers remain outside any institutional mechanism of social security, then nearly two-third of the work force is denied the services that are available to other categories of workers.

Rural Workers Welfare Board

The Rural Workers Welfare Board carried out various welfare activities for agricultural labourers through 45 welfare centres in the country. Central Government provides 100 per cent grant-in-aid to this Board.

Seasonal Migrants Labour

About 1 per cent of India's population stay outside their place of residence—whether village or town, for 60 days or more in a year—in search of employment opportunities or for employment. On a base of around one billion people, this is no small figure: around 10 million Indians are what we could term as seasonal migrants. And out of them, as high as 78 per cent are from rural areas. Seasonal migration is probably not given its due by policy-makers, and the latest National Sample Survey figures on the number of these migrants only reiterate why they deserve a closer look.

An interesting evolution in seasonal migration that has occurred is the movement of migrants in gangs or groups. A revealing study on the nature of seasonal migration in West Bengal (EPW), December 2001) describes the nature of such migration over the years by migrants employed to transplant and harvest rice in central southern West Bengal. The number of these migrants have not only increased (estimated around five lakh in this region alone) but, contrary to popular conception, adult migrants take along their children in all seasons, no matter the hardships. Most migrants tend to be in the scheduled social groups: micro evidence to the macro data provided by the NSS shows that the percentage of seasonal migrants belonging to scheduled tribes, castes and other backward classes accounted for 70 per cent of them.

The study also shows that the functioning of labour markets for such seasonal gangs of migrants takes on its own peculiar character and has led to the evolution of certain self-regulating institutions. The Krishak Sabha, a leftist organisation of smallholder, cultivators and wage workers is one such, which has ensured a reduction of work hours per day for local labourers, in the male-female wage differential, and an increase in the cash component of the wage rate so that real wages are maintained. Migrants are also assured of an earning not less than that received by the local labourers per day.

Interestingly, the fact that this Sabha consists of landowners also, has ensured that employer's interests are simultaneously met—by relieving labour shortages in season and by providing them a higher bargaining power with local labourers to comply with work, using the threat of replacing them with migrants. Finally, the Sabha also appeases the local labourers by assuring them the migrants will be allowed to work only in the peak season.

The most significant development in seasonal migration is the movement in groups, which has important implications. The most striking of them is the presence of bargaining strength with employers, especially in the absence of collusion among employers. For instance, certain field observations in Maharashtra reveal that migrant workers are paid around 30 per cent more than local labour, mainly on account higher skills possessed by these workers. In the West Bengal region studied, there were no middlemen who fixed wages for the migrants—the group typically had a leader who did the negotiations. The main implication of an increasing group movement is the empowerment of immigrants, mostly belonging to scheduled classes, as it establishes strong identities.

Rehabilitation of Bonded Labour

Even after five decades of planned development, millions of landless labourers are still being treated as bonded contract labour. Bonded labour has existed in India for centuries. It is a peculiar phenomenon of our agricultural economy. The system grew out of extreme poverty and helplessness of scheduled castes, tribal and semi-tribal communities, who have always depended on wage-income which too they received during the peak agricultural season. When they needed foodgrains during the lean agricultural season or when they needed money for occasions like marriage or festival or for medical treatment, they had to borrow, but they had no security to offer, either in the form of land, or Jewellery, or any other property except their own labour. Accordingly, they `pledged' themselves. The money lenders and the high caste landlords took advantage of their helpless conditions and ignorance, and entered into repressive contracts. The wages were so low and rate of interest so high – often 25 to 50 per cent that the total loan got accumulated with the passage of time. In fact, the total burden of the loan became so huge that it could not be repaid even with the labour of many generations of the debtor's family.

In order to abolish the system of bonded labour and to rehabilitate them, Bonded Labour System (Abolition) Act was passed in 1976. Under this Act, the responsibility for identification, release and rehabilitation of bonded labour rests with the state governments. In 1978, Ministry of Labour formulated a Centrally Sponsored Plan Scheme (CSS) for rehabilitation of bonded labourers. In fact, the CSS supplements the State Governments efforts. Central and State Governments equally share the expenditure on this on 50:50 basis.

Under the scheme a bonded labour on release is paid immediately Rs. 1,000.00 as subsistence allowance and he/she is rehabilitated as per situation with a rehabilitation package of Rs. 10,000.00. Considering the demands by the state governments, the scheme has now been modified by raising the rehabilitation package to Rs. 20,000.00 per bonded labour released. State-wise distribution of bonded labour released and rehabilitated is given in Appendix 13.3. From the inception of the scheme in 1978-79 till March, 2000 nearly 2.8 lakh bonded labourers were identified and released. Out of that nearly 2.5 lakh labourers were rehabilitated. Thus, there were around 30,000 such released and not rehabilitated bonded labour which was causing a concern. Ministry of labour however, is addressing this problem through the implementing agency, the State Administration.

Poverty Alleviation Programme

As bulk of the agricultural labourer family are living below the poverty line, they are also the target group for most of the poverty alleviation programmes implemented by the State Governments. The programmes are (i) Swarnajayanti Gram Swarogar Yojana, (ii) Employment Assurance Scheme, (iii) Jawahar Gram Samridhi Yojana, (iv) Desert Development programme, (v) Wasteland Development Programmes etc. These programmes have been discussed in Chapter 21 entitled Rural Development and Panchayati Raj.

Land Reform

Landlessness is the root cause of economic hardship of the agricultural labourers. Land Reforms have however been on the National Agenda of Rural Reconstruction since independence. The major objectives of Land Reforms have been the reordering of agrarian relations in order to achieve an egalitarian social structure, elimination of exploitation in land relations, realizing the age-old goal of land to the tiller, enlarging the land base of the rural poor, increasing agricultural productivity and infusing an element of equality in local institution. Since the First Plan period, the Land Reform Division of the Ministry of Rural Development, Government of India has been playing a crucial role of evolving a National concensus at various fora for initiating effective land reforms.

Distribution of ceiling surplus land is one such measures to provide land to the landless labourers. Since inception till September, 2000, the total quantum of land declared surplus in the entire country is 73.49 lakh acres, out of which about 64.84 lakh acres have been taken possession and 52.99 lakh acres have been distributed to 55.10 lakh beneficiaries, of whom, 36 per cent belong to scheduled castes and 15 per cent, scheduled tribes.

Distribution of Governments' wasteland has been one of the key strategies of land reforms; it has been the accepted policy that wasteland at the disposal of the government should be distributed amongst eligible poor. So far, an area of 147.47 lakh acres of Government wasteland has been distributed amongst the landless rural poor.

Conferment of Ownership Rights to Tenants

Legislative provisions have been made in many states for conferment of ownership rights on tenants or allowing cultivating tenants to acquire ownership rights on payment of compensation. Some of the states have acquired ownership of land from land owners and transferred it to tenants. Till date 124.22 lakh tenants have got their rights protected over an area of 156.30 lakh acres.

Thus, despite taking various measures to alleviate the condition of the agricultural workers in the country, the problem has still remained gigantic. Siphoning of surplus agricultural labourers to other occupation by adopting a holistic all round rural development programme and limiting the family size through family welfare measures are also needed to improve the economic condition of the poorest of the poor in our society.

Unemployment

The unemployment problem in India is alarmingly pervasive in all sectors of the economy at, all levels of skills, and in all regions—and all the more elusive today, compared to what it was some 50 years ago, though we have an ever increasing stake in it and the research workers as well as policy makers have been devoting more and more resources to find a way out of it. Basically we appear to have engulfed ourselves in a plethora of institutional barriers and problems, and are unable to break the shell and seek rational solutions.

To an extent, even the academician engaged in research gets entangled in the web of tradition and looks for an already well-defined aspect of the problem rather than face the practical reality of the total problem at hand. For instance, a disproportionately large amount of effort is spent on defining the concept of unemployment. See Planning Commission (1970), Visaria (1972)[2] and Raj Krishna[3] (1973) for instance. True, there are a large number of persons "employed" in agriculture and services who do not have any work for almost six months, and there are "workers" who do not earn enough to pull them across the bare minimum of any poverty lines we may care to consider. It is, therefore, not altogether irrelevant to refer to the Time criterion and Income criterion of unemployment. But measurement of unemployment is not the ultimate purpose of analysis and the marginal social return from investments in such an endeavour cannot be commensurate with the costs involved. The problem is colossal whatever be the definition of unemployment.

---

[2] P. Visaria, A Survey of Research on Employment in India, 1972.

[3] Raj Krishna, Unemployment in India, Indian Journal of Agricultural Economics, 1973.

Trends in Unemployment

Trends in unemployment are affected by the changes in economic activity and factors influencing labour demand, specific labour market characteristics, demographic factors affecting labour supply, and social programme design. The unemployment rate in the OECD area in the Nineties was oscillating in the 5-10 percentage band before setting at 6.5 per cent in 1999 (Chart I). But there are variations among the constituents. Unemployment in the U.S. has fallen to historically low levels, to less than 5 per cent. In the EU, the jobless rate has been declining since 1994 though above the 1990 level. But in Japan, it has slightly risen since 1992.

Among individual countries, Spain had the highest unemployment rate of 15.9 per cent in 1999. The unemployment rate in France, Finland, Greece, Italy and Poland was around 10-11 per cent (Chart II)..

Generally, female unemployment trends are similar to overall unemployment trends, though at a much higher level in some countries. On an average, the gender gap in unemployment rates is less than one percentage point across the OECD, but averages nearly 3 per centage points across the EU.

Unemployment rates vary considerably across age groups and with worker characteristics such as skill levels. Disability and early retirement programmes have been used by workers in some countries (the Netherlands, Poland, Sweden and the U.K.) to withdraw from the labour market thereby shifting the unemployed to outside the labour force. Recently, social programme design in OECD countries is more focussed on increasing labour market participation of (older) workers and making work pay.

Chart I **Jobless Rate**

(As a percentage of labour force, 1999)

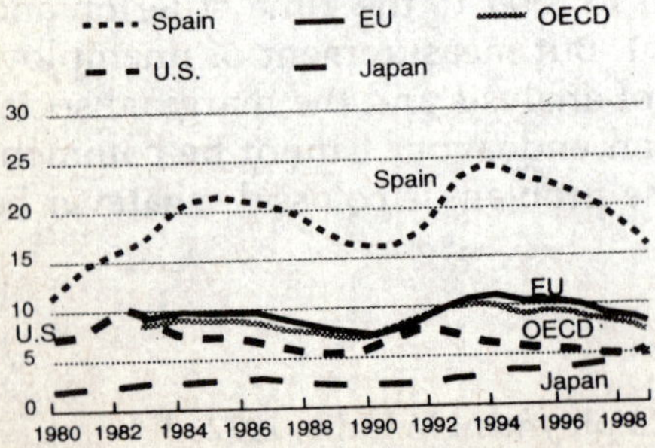

Chart II **Jobless Rate**

(As a percentage of the labour force, 1999)

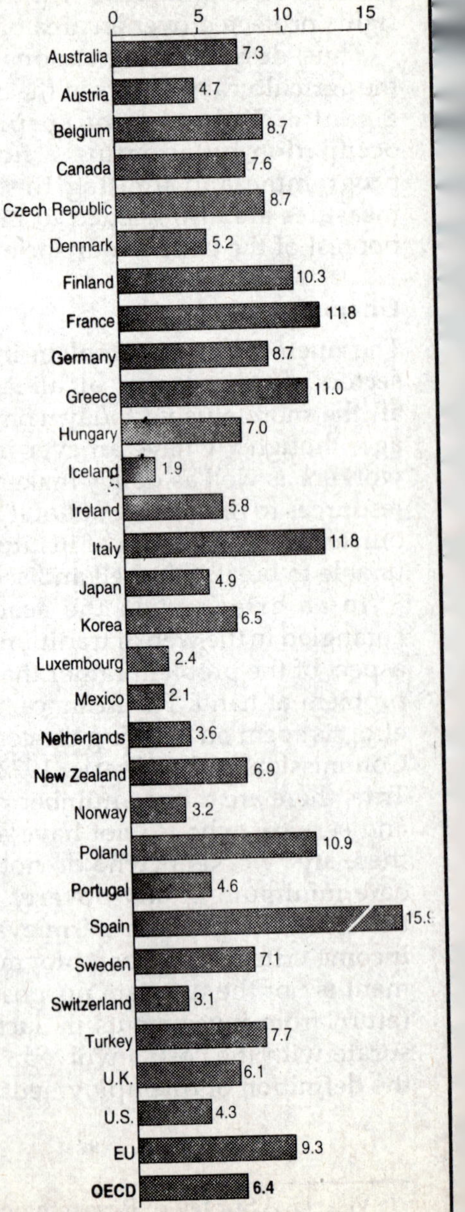

Appendix 13.1

Daily Agricultural Wages in Some States—Category-Wise

(In rupees)

State/ district	Village	Month and year	Normal daily working hrs	Field labour			Other agricultural			Herdsman			Skilled labour		
				Man	Woman	Child	Man	Woman	Child	Man	Woman	Child	Cobbler	Blacksmith	Carpenter
Andhra Pradesh															
Krishna	Ghantasala	Mar 2000	8	—	—	—	—	—	—	70.00	30.00	30.00	50.00	60.00	60.00
Guntur	Tadikonda	Mar 2000	8	50.00	40.00	35.00	75.00	65.00	60.00	50.00	40.00	35.00	75.00	75.00	75.00
Ranga-Reddy	Arutla	Mar 2000	8	40.00	25.00	18.00	40.00	30.00	20.00	40.00	30.00	20.00	40.00	50.00	60.00
Maharashtra															
Nagpur	Narkhed	Mar 2000	8	60.00	40.00	20.00	50.00	30.00	20.00	—	—	—	60.00	60.00	70.00

Appendix 13.2

Daily Agricultural Wages in Some States— Operation Wise

(In rupees)

State/District	Village	Month and year	Type of labour	Normal daily working hrs.	Plough-hing	Sowing	Weed-ing	Harve-sting	Other agricu-ltural labour	Herds-man	Skilled Labour Cob-bler	Black smith	Car-penter
Bihar													
Muzaffarpur	Narsingpur	Dec. 99	M	8	40.00	50.00	40.00	—	40.00	—	52.00	52.00	—
			W	8	—	—	—	—	—	—	—	—	—
Ranchi	Gaitalsood	Oct. 99	M	8	30.00	30.00	—	—	—	10.00	40.00	40.00	—
			W	8	—	30.00	—	—	—	10.00	—	—	—
Gujarat													
Panch-Mahal	Dohad												
		Dec. 99	M	8	40.00	40.00	40.00	—	—	—	75.00	75.00	60.00
Kaira	Petlad		W	8	—	40.00	40.00	—	—	—	—	—	—
		Dec. 99	M	8	—	35.00	—	—	35.00	—	80.00	80.00	60.00
			W	8	—	35.00	—	—	35.00	—	—	—	—
Haryana													
Panipat	Uggarkheri	Mar. 2000	M	8	100.00	100.00	80.00	—	80.00	—	—	—	—
			W	8	—	—	60.00	—	—	—	—	—	—

Appendix 13.2 *(Contd)*

Kerala													
Kozhikode	Koduvally	Dec. 99	M	4-8	135.00	140.00	—	140.00	140.00	—	170.00	—	—
			W	8	—	—	95.00	95.00	95.00	—	—	—	—
Palghat	Elapully	Dec. 99	M	4-8	80.00	80.00	—	—	80.00	—	125.00	—	—
			W	8	—	—	40.00	—	45.00	—	—	—	—
Madhya Pradesh													
	Sangakherak	Mar. 2000	M	8	85.00	—	—	—	40.00	35.00	100.00		
Hoshangabad	alan											100.00	60.00
			W	8	—	—	—	—	35.00	—	—	—	—
			C	8	—	—	—	—	—	35.00	—	—	—
Sarguja	Basdei	Mar. 2000	M	8	—	—	—	—	—	—	80.00	75.00	—
Satna	Kotar	Mar. 2000	W	8	—	—	—	—	—	—	—	—	—
			C	8	—	—	—	—	—	38.00	—	—	—
Syhopurkala	Bijapur	Mar. 2000	M	8	50.00	—	—	—	—	—	—	—	—
Orissa													
Bhadrak	Chandbali	Mar. 2000	M	8	50.00	—	50.00	50.00	—	50.00	100.00	—	—
			W	8	40.00	—	40.00	45.00	—	45.00	—	—	—
			C	8	—	—	—	45.00	—	45.00	—	—	—
Ganjam	Aska	Mar. 2000	M	8	40.00	40.00	40.00	40.00	50.00	40.00	80.00	65.00	60.00
			W	8	—	—	30.00	30.00	—	30.00	—	—	—
			C	8	—	—	25.00	25.00	—	25.00	—	—	—
Punjab													
Ludhiana	Pakhowal	June-99	M	8	—	—	—	—	80.00	—	165.00	165.00	—
Rajasthan													
Hanumangarh	Dulmana	Feb. 2000	M	8	65.00	65.00	65.00	—	—	—	140.00	—	—
		Mar. 2000	W	8	—	—	65.00	—	—	—	—	—	—
			C	8	65.00	65.00	—	65.00	—	—	140.00	—	—

Appendix 13.2 (Contd.)

Daily Agricultural Wages in Some States—Operation Wise

(In rupees)

State/District	Village	Month and year	Type of labour	Normal daily working hrs.	Ploughing	Sowing	Weeding	Harvesting	Other agricultural labour	Herdsman	Skilled Labour		
											Cobbler	Black smith	Carpenter
Tamil Nadu													
Tirunclveli	Malayan-kulam	June-99	M	5-7	—	—	—	—	—	—	75.00	60.00	50.00
			W	7	—	—	25.00	—	—	—	—	—	—
Thanjavur	Pulvanathan	June-99	M	5-7	—	—	—	—	—	—	100.00	100.00	—
			W	7	—	—	25.00	—	—	—	—	—	—
Tripura													
Govt. Agril. Farm	Lembuchera	July 99	M	8	50.00	50.00	50.00	50.00	50.00	—	—	—	—
			W	8	—	50.00	50.00	50.00	—	—	—	—	—
Uttar Pradesh													
Meerut	Ganespur	Feb. 2000	M	8	—	—	—	60.00	60.00	—	—	—	—

M-Man, W-Woman C-Child

SOURCE: Agricultural Situation in India, June 2000, Directorate of Economics & Statistics, Ministry of Agriculture, Government of India.

Appendix 13.3

Bonded Labourers Identified and Rehabilitated up to 31.3.2000 Since Inception of the Scheme in 1978-79

Name of States	*Number of bonded labour*		*Central assistance provided (Rs. in lakhs)*
	Identified and released	*Rehabilitated*	
Andhra Pradesh	36,289	29,552	680.10
Bihar	13,092	12,368	314.48
Karnatka	62,727	55,231	1383.14
Madhya Pradesh	12,822	11,897	146.35
Orissa	49,971	46,843	898.13
Rajasthan	7,478	6,297	69.02
Tamil Nadu	63,894	58,073	911.93
Maharashtra	1,384	1,300	8.25
Uttar Pradesh	27,797	27,797	533.22
Kerala	823	710	15.56
Haryana	544	21	0.42
Gujarat	64	64	1.01
Himachal Pradesh	3,526	1,416	70.84
Total	2,80,411	2,51,569	5032.45

SOURCE: Mid Term Appraisal of the 9th Five year Plan, Planning Commission, Government of India.

CHAPTER 14

Agricultural Research

HISTORICAL BACKDROP

Till about the end of the 19th century, technical change in agriculture was localized and farmer-driven. Growing population pressure and resulting intensification led to selection of better varieties and species of plants and animals, improved cultivation practices, reduction of losses in fields and stores, and development of simple but efficient soil and water management practices. Trade, invasions, and travel added exotic and higher yielding plants of amazing variety for various niches. Such informal processes sustained Indian agriculture for a very long time. Abundance of land and relatively low population growth facilitated this. The balance gradually broke down and massive famines started inflicting heavy toll. Towards the end of the 19th century, a view emerged that providing irrigation on a large scale, improvement in agriculture, and controlling losses due to pests and disease were basic to the solution of this problem.

Several unsuccessful attempts to introduce western farming techniques to improve Indian agriculture over a long period led the Government of India to the realisation that only the scientific study of the conditions of farming and experiments in agricultural practices in the Indian context would lead to any real improvement. Dr. Voelcker, an agricultural scientist who was invited to India in 1889 to advise on the steps to be taken to improve agriculture, stressed the need for research and this was later emphasised by the Famine Commission of 1910 and the Irrigation Commission of 1903. Subsequently, funds were provided for the development of agricultural research and education in the provinces and a separate Department of Agriculture was constituted in most of the provinces. Agricultural colleges were also founded in Pune, Kanpur, Nagpur, Lyallpur, Coimbatore and Shibpur (Howrah). Till the turn of the last century, however, the provincial departments of agriculture were small and were engaged largely in the collection of statistics of the area and production of crops and were least concerned with research.

The close of the nineteenth century witnessed a revolution in agriculture in the western world. The inventions of inorganic fertilisers by Liebig in 1861, study of agricultural chemistry and its scientific application to cropping pattern, application of guano, bone-meal and phosphates, improved breeding of livestock, etc., can be cited as a few examples. The beginning of the twentieth century marked a further awakening about technical improvements in agriculture in the West. With the munificence of Mr. Henry Phipps-an American-and a generous donation of thirty thousand pounds by him in 1903, agricultural research began on a more regular basis with the setting up of the Imperial (now Indian) Agricultural Research Institute at Pusa (Bihar) in 1905 (PUSA was named after him as Phipps from USA, P-USA). The Institute was transferred to New Delhi in 1936.

There was not much progress after this for some time. Even after the constitutional changes of 1919, under which agriculture was placed under the direct control of the Provincial Governments, the position did not take any positive turn and the stalemate continued until the famous Report of the Royal Commission on Agriculture, 1928, highlighted the backwardness of Indian agriculture and recommended the setting up of the Central Council of Agricultural Research with the following aims and objects:

1. To undertake aid, promote and coordinate agricultural and animal husbandry research and education.
2. To act as a clearing house of information not only in regard to research but also to agricultural and veterinary matters generally.
3. To establish and maintain a research and reference library in pursuance of the objects of the Council with reading and writing rooms and to furnish the same with books, reviews, magazines, newspapers and other publications.
4. To do all other things which the Council may consider necessary, incidental or conducive to the attainment of its objectives.

The two earliest institutions, Indian Veterinary Research Institute (IVRI) and Indian Agricultural Research Institute (IARI), were created with highly relevant mandates for Indian farmers; the former to address the problem of cattle plague and the latter to seek improvements in productivity of major crops. Research portfolios of these institutions, as revealed by the early documents, point unambiguously in these directions. The efforts in agriculture were based on Voelcker's prescription of bridging the gap between better performing and poorer regions through selection and adaptation of varieties and practices from the former to the latter; and using scientific advances in genetics, soil fertility, engineering, etc. Increased food production through scientific evaluation of indigenous practices and exploitation of new scientific principals was the goal. The beginnings of agricultural research in India were thus clearly focused on the peasantry because of the indigenous roots.

Pretty soon, however, commercial and trading interest of the colonial powers crept in. The Central Cotton Committee was created in 1921 to increase production of cotton – a major interest of British industry. It sponsored research and development in concerned provinces through respective departments of agriculture and their experimental farms.

On the recommendations of Royal Commission on Agriculture (1928), ICAR, the Imperial (now Indian) Council of Agricultural Research came into being in 1929 as a statutory body by an Act of the Central Legislature. Though agriculture was a state responsibility, the new Council under- took nationwide coordination of work carried by the Central Institutes and State Research Centres. Some research programmes were supported through Agriculture Produce Cess Fund. Further, duties like those of functioning as a link between agricultural institutions in India and those in foreign countries and education as well as development work were brought within the scope of the activities of the Council. It was by now grown into a premier organization which guides, finances, and coordinates research problems connected with agriculture and animal husbandry in the widest sense of the term.

The organizational functioning of the Council was arranged in such a manner that the research and technical side was being handled by technical experts and the administrative side by the Secretariat staff, the latter being part and parcel of the Central Ministry of Food and Agriculture. This separation of administrative and scientific duties was intended to help the technical persons to devote their undivided attention to scientific pursuits.

Central Research Institute

In the later years a number of Central Research Institutes were set up in various parts of the country to deal with different aspects of the problem to fulfil the dream of Lord Curzon.

Commodity Committees

Research work and coordination of the same with regard to particular crops are dealt with by the Central Commodity Committees which are semi-autonomous bodies and are generally located near the main production areas of the crop concerned. The commodity committees have, in most cases, also the Central Research Stations financed by them and working under their control. The Indian Central Cotton Committee was the first commodity committee and was established in 1921 (Table 14.1).

These Committees supported research either through their own Research Centres or by funding projects operated by the State Governments. The Government of India had also established under their direct control, a number of Research Institutes. Since the ICAR

Table 14.1 Commodity Committees in India

Name of the Committee	Location	Year of Starting
1. Indian Central Cotton Committee	Bombay (Maharastra)	1921
2. Indian Lac Cess Committee	Ranchi (Bihar)	1931
3. Indian Central Jute Committee	Calcutta (West Bengal)	1936
4. Indian Central Sugarcane Committee	New Delhi (Delhi)	1941
5. Indian Central Tobacco Committee	Madras (Tamil Nadu)	1945
6. Indian Central Coconut Committee	Ernakulam (Kerala)	1945
7. Indian Central Oilseeds Committee	Hyderabad (Andhra Pradesh)	1947
8. Indian Central Arecanut Committee	Kozhikode (Kerala)	1949

had limited control over the conduct of agricultural research in the country, the research efforts were fragmented, isolated, often duplicated and distributed in several functionary systems and Ministries.

In order to avoid a lack of coordination between the work of various commodities, a Board of Research and Extension has been constituted under the ICAR. All the Directors of Research Institutes and Secretaries of these commodity committees are represented in the Board. These committees have since been dissolved and are converted into Directorates.

As research on crops included in the commodity committees was looked after by them, ICAR paid special attention to problems of food crops like wheat, rice, barley, pulses, millets, maize, tuber crops, grasses and fodder crops, species, horticulture and other matters common to various commodities and such as control of plant diseases and pests, manurial trials, improved implements and dry farming in the field of agriculture, and investigation and control of animal diseases, animal nutrition, animal breeding and dairying in the field of animal husbandry.

ORGANIZATIONAL SET UP OF AGRICULTURAL RESEARCH IN INDIA

National Agricultural Research System (NARS)

The National Agricultural Research System (NARS), as it has evolved, has been developed over years of experience and experimentation and has undergone some major changes in concept, organization and activities. Since independence, it has made rapid strides, both in concept and implementation, towards becoming an effective system. It has withstood remarkably the test of time by remaining sensitive to the changing needs and challenges. Through the continuous development of newer technologies, and also adoption of exotic technologies, the present system is helping the nation to optimize the inputs and exploit the genetic and other resource potential.

In the present research system, the Indian Council of Agricultural Research (ICAR) at the national level aids, promotes and coordinates research and education activities in the country. It also undertakes research through its own institutions mainly on problems of national importance. The research and education responsibilities at the state level rest with the agricultural universities. In addition to these two main streams of research, some general universities and other agencies like scientific organizations related to agriculture, government departments, voluntary organizations, private institutions etc. participate in the nation's research efforts.

International cooperation has played a significant role in developing and strengthening the national agricultural research system in the country. Many developed countries, reputed institutions like Rockefeller and Ford Foundations, several international agencies of the United Nations and the International Agricultural Research Centres under the Consultative Group on International Agricultural Research (CGIAR) system have contributed extensively to India's efforts to develop its agricultural research infrastructure.

Strong working relationships and complementarity in research effort among the components of the national system have been built in order to optimize resources and make the system more effective. The ICAR as the coordinating agency has established close working relationships with agricultural universities and other agencies involved directly or indirectly in agricultural research through formal arrangements or informal exchanges. The details of the NARS are given in the Table 14.2.

ICAR System

As mentioned earlier, based on the recommendations of the Royal Commission on Agriculture in 1928, the Imperial (now Indian) Council of Agricultural Research (ICAR) was established in 1929 as a scientific society to promote, guide, and coordinate Agricultural Research and Education in the country. The Council was entrusted with the administration of funds to supplement research and education in its own Institutes and SAUs in the States. In the present research system, the Indian Council of Agricultural Research (ICAR) at the national level mainly aids, promotes and coordinates research and education activities in the country. It also undertakes research through its Institutions mainly on problems of national importance. The research and education responsibilities at the State level rest with the Agricultural Universities. In addition to these two main streams of

Table 14.2 National Agricultural Research system

	Crop Science	Horticulture	Animal Science	Fisheries	Soil, Agronomy & Agroforestry	Agril Engineering	Agril Education
National Institute	1		2	1			
Central Research Institute	8	8	6	5	8	5	1
National Bureau	1		1	1	1		
National Research Centre	7	10	7	1	3		
Project Directorate	5	1	2		2		
All India Coordinated Project	26	17	17		15	10	

General : 1. Indian Agricultural Statistical Research Institute
2. National Centre of Agricultural Economics and Policy Research
3. 29 State Agriculture Universities (SAUs)

SOURCE: ICAR and DARE Report, 1998-99, pp. 8
(Organisational set up of Agricultural Research System in India is shown in Figure-1 in Appendix 1).

research, some General Universities and other agencies like scientific organizations related to agriculture, Government departments, voluntary organizations, private institutions, etc. participate in the nation's research efforts.

The Council was reorganized from time-to-time to ensure efficient utilization of resources, better coordination of research, and integration of different scientific disciplines. The reorganization in 1965 was an important landmark. The Government of India entrusted to the ICAR Society the responsibility of managing Central Institutes engaged in agriculture, animal husbandry and fisheries research. Consequently, all the central Research Institutes under the Ministry of Food and Agriculture as well as those with the Commodity Committees were merged with the ICAR so that problems of agricultural research could be viewed in their totality. The Commodity Committees were abolished and the rules and bye-laws of the ICAR were revised to make it functionally more effective, technically competent and autonomous. They were renamed as Directorates. The Council was provided with a Director General as the Chief Executive at the top, and it remained attached to the Department of Agriculture in the Union Government. In the next step of reorganization or research in the country, the research farms in state control were transferred to SAUs of the respective states. With this, the SAUs and the ICAR became the two leading partners for Agricultural Research and Education in the country.

In 1973, the ICAR was reorganized for the second time so as to confer greater autonomy and flexibility in operation and management. The Department of Agricultural Research and Education (DARE) was constituted with the Director General of ICAR as its Secretary in the Ministry of Agriculture to provide the ICAR with the needed linkages to deal directly with States, Central Government and foreign agencies. Following this, the ICAR was given the concurrent responsibility to promote agricultural research and education in the country.

The composition of the ICAR was modified to make it a more businesslike body with the Minister of Agriculture as its President. The Governing Body was also restructured with the Director General as its Chairman. The management of its Research Institutes was streamlined by establishing Management Committees for administering them and to broad-base the decision making process. The personnel policies of the ICAR underwent a major change leading to the creation of a new All India Service called Agricultural Research Service in 1975. Consequently, a new Agricultural Scientists Recruitment Board (ASRB) with an eminent scientist as a whole time Chairman was established to recruit scientists to various positions in the ICAR. Recently, a high level committee has been appointed to review the present working of the ICAR for further improvement. As an autonomous national apex body, the mandate of the ICAR is as follows:

The Mandate of the Indian Council of Agricultural Research

(i) To plan, undertake, aid, promote and coordinate education, research and its application in agriculture, agroforestry, animal husbandry, fisheries, home science and allied sciences.

(ii) To act as a clearing house of research and general information relating to agriculture, animal husbandry, home science and allied sciences and fisheries through its publications and information system, and instituting and promoting transfer of technology programmes.

(iii) To provide, undertake and promote consultancy services in the field of education, research, training and dissemination of information in agriculture, agroforestry, animal husbandry, fisheries, home science and allied sciences.

(iv) To look into the problems relating to broader areas of rural development concerning agriculture, including post-harvest technology by developing cooperative programmes with other organizations such as the Indian Council of Social Science Research, Council of Scientific and Industrial Research, Bhabha Atomic Research Centre and the universities.

(v) To do other things considered necessary to attain the objectives of the Society.

Presently there are 42 Central Institutes, 4 National Institutes, 4 National Bureaux, 10 Project Directories, and 26 National Research Centres and 84 All India Coordinated Research Projects (AICRP) and many other National Research Projects under the control of ICAR. A synoptic view on them is as follows.

National Academy for Agricultural Research Management (NAARM) The NAARM established in 1976 as one of the National Institutes, provides management training to the agricultural scientists and research administrators of the ICAR as well as of the agricultural universities.

National Institutes The 4 other National Institutes – Indian Agricultural Research Institute (IARI), Indian Veterinary Research Institute (IVRI), National Dairy Research Institute (NDRI) and Central Institute for Fisheries Education (CIFE) have responsibilities for both research and postgraduate education in agriculture, animal husbandry and fishery. The IARI, IVRI, CIFE and NDRI have "Deemed University" status and offer their own degrees in various disciplines.

National Bureaux on Resource Conservation In order to collect, conserve and initiate such measures which lead to long term productivity of basic agricultural resources such as plants, animals, fishes and soils, the ICAR has established four National Bureaux, one in each of these areas.

Central Institutes In addition to these, the ICAR directly administers 42 central institutes for various disciplines. Each institute has a specific responsibility for research either on single or multiple crops/commodities or disciplines. Most of the institutes have substations in different parts of the country mainly to provide testing facilities under different agro-ecological situations and to conduct research on some of the regional problems wherever the local research infrastructure is inadequate. The institutes are organized into well defined divisions on the basis of disciplines.

National Research Centres Apart from the existing research infrastructure of research institutes, the ICAR has established single campus national research centres. The basic philosophy of these centres revolves around the need for concentrated attention with a mission approach by a team of scientists from different disciplines working under a senior leader on selected topics which have direct or indirect relevance to resolve national problems in particular crop or commodity or species. Unlike the institutes, these centres have neither the divisional set up nor regional stations. The National Research Centre for Groundnut was the first to be set up by the ICAR and there are now 26 such centres in the country.

All India Coordinated Research Projects A distinct landmark in the growth of agricultural research in India is the introduction of All India Coordinated Research Projects by the ICAR. These projects provide an opportunity for the scientists working in different institutions on similar problems to come together, discuss and exchange ideas, information and materials for mutual benefit. These are developed as multidisciplinary and problem-oriented projects with main emphasis on multi-locational testing of improved technologies developed by the ICAR institutes and agricultural universities under different agro-climatic regions in the country. The ICAR has initiated many such coordinated research projects and established a number of coordinating centres at its own institutes, agricultural and general universities. These projects constitute an effective national grid of coordinated experiments by integrating different disciplines and different research institutions in the country.

National Agricultural Research Project The agricultural universities which have a state-wide mandate for education, research and extension education did not have a strong base for agricultural research at the regional level. Most of the funds provided by the state governments and the ICAR was mainly utilized for developing the university main campus thereby neglecting the regional research needs. To rectify this, the ICAR, with World Bank assistance, had launched in 1979 a research scheme known as National Agricultural Research Project (NARP) mainly to strengthen the research capability of the agricultural universities to conduct location-specific, need based and production oriented research on the basis of identified agro-climatic zones.

Under the project, the country has been divided into 126 agro-climatic zones with 120 zones in 18 states and six zones in North Eastern region. Later on three more zones for Andaman & Nicobar Islands and two zones for Pondicherry were delineated. The project included the establishment or strengthening in each zone, a major regional station with a multidisciplinary team of scientists. Adequate infrastructure and physical facilities were provided in these stations so that they can function as well equipped and well manned units to tackle need-based and location-specific problems relating to a large number of crops and commodities of that region.

National Agricultural Technology Project (NATP) NATP sponsored by the World Bank (total funding of $238 million) was launched in November 1998 to address specific system constraints, weakness and gaps in research and extension. The NATP has made major strides towards full implementation of diverse activities of the project planned under 3 major components: Agro-ecosystem research; Innovations in Technology Dissemination and Organization & Management System.

Ad-hoc Research Schemes The ICAR is also continuing with its earlier practice of supporting ad-hoc research schemes from its Agricultural Produce Cess fund. It is sponsoring a large number of short-term, result-oriented ad-hoc schemes which aim at filling up critical gaps in the scientific field and in resolving problems limiting production in different disciplines of agriculture, animal husbandry and fisheries.

Krishi Vigyan Kendras In order to meet the mandate of application of science and technology, the ICAR has established Krishi Vigyan Kendras (KVK). The main functions of the KVKs are to (i) provide vocational training, (ii) carry out on-farm testing/research, (iii) organize front-line demonstrations and (iv) impart training of in-service extension personnel. Presently there are 261 KVKs which are fully functional. There are also 8 Trainers' Training Centres to provide scientific back up support to KVK staff. KVKs already organized 10696 Farmers' Training Courses, 1224 training programmes for in-service candidates and 2,076 vocational courses for rural youths.

Centres of Excellence Since 1971, the ICAR with UNDP support has established advanced centres for postgraduate agricultural education and research in selected subject matter areas. So far 28 such centres have been established and 17 of them are located in ICAR institutes. By and large, these centres have developed into Centres of Excellence. In view of the success experienced with these programmes, the international organizations involved decided to provide assistance for the establishment of eleven advanced centres which became operational from the beginning of 1987. One such advanced centre on agricultural education and research management is now operating at the National Academy of Agricultural Research Management.

Special Schemes The ICAR has launched a special programme known as `The Professor of Eminence and National Research Fellows

Scheme' mainly to identify individuals of outstanding merit who could provide leadership in the development of schools of thought in specific areas by undertaking fundamental research.

ICAR also provides Junior and Senior Research Fellowship for M.Sc. (Ag.) and Ph.D. students, selected through National level entrance test to encourage them in higher research.

International Collaboration The strength of the agricultural research system and the notable achievement in agricultural production, especially food production, have raised India's image considerably in the international scene. The international cooperation is now shifting towards sharing experiences and expertise not only with developing countries but even with technologically advanced countries in the world. The reciprocity and mutuality of interests are the essence of such cooperation which has played a significant role in developing and strengthening the research system in India.

The continuous multilateral cooperative programmes with the UNDP, UNESCO, SAARC, CGIAR, FAO, CABI helped the exchange of information on both research and education and exchange of experts and ideas.

At present there are more than 120 projects in operation with off shore collaborations; majority of them are with the USA, UK, Canada, Australia, Netherlands and many other countries.

Research Planning, Monitoring and Evaluation

At the national level, the ICAR is responsible for agricultural research planning. The research schemes received from the central institute, agricultural universities and private institutions are first technically examined by the concerned subject matter division in the ICAR headquarters and put up for consideration before the scientific panels. After the schemes are examined for financial implication by the Standing Finance Committee, they are finally placed before the Governing Body which approves them. In the ICAR, system, once the broad research programmes are decided by the ICAR, the responsibility of formulation of individual research projects are left to the institutes. Every year, scientists working in the institutes submit research projects with all details which are discussed by the divisional research councils in big institutes followed by the staff research council (SRC) for evaluation and approval.

The key to the success of the agricultural research efforts of the ICAR system has been the inbuilt mechanism of research monitoring and evaluation. At the institute level, these functions are carried out by the divisional and institute SRCs, and through a comprehensive review by specially constituted external quinquennial review teams (QRTs) once in five years. Different research schemes of the ICAR are monitored by the subject matter divisions in the headquarters and the overall implementation of the plan scheme through plan implementation and monitoring unit.

Personnel Policies of ICAR: Keeping in view its technical requirements, the ICAR has restructured its personnel policies which are designed to promote specialization and technical excellence of its scientific personnel. An all India service, known as Agricultural Research Service, was constituted in 1975 in order to bring about better focus and uniformity in its personnel management and for career advancement of its scientific manpower (Table 14.3).

Table 14.3 Scientific Manpower Position in the ICAR System

Sl. No.	*Class of post*	*Total posts sanctioned*	*Total employees in position*
1.	Experimental scientists	82	98
2.	Scientists	3969	3084
3.	Senior scientists	2097	1245
4.	Principal scientists	701	527
5.	RMP scientists	116	100
	Total	6965	5054

SOURCE: DARE and ICAR Annual Report 1999-2000. pp. 210

State Agriculture Universities System

In pursuance of the recommendations of the University Education Commission under the chairmanship of Dr. Radhakrishnan and other expert committees and teams (Joint Indo-American Teams, 1955 and 1959), the first agricultural university, patterned on the Land Grant System of Agricultural Universities in the U.S.A., was established at Pantnagar (Uttar Pradesh) in 1960. At present there are 28 SAUs and 1 Central Agricultural University, imparting agricultural research and education throughout the country. ICAR performs the role of SAUs same as the UGC performs to the General University. A typical SAU operates on the concept of integration of teaching, research, and extension function within a large number of specialized disciplines and departments.

Agricultural Research in SAUs

With the implementation of the National Agricultural Research Projects (NARP) from 1979 onwards, the research capability of each university has been strengthened not only at the main campus, but also expanded through a network of regional research stations, substations and centres to carry out relevant adaptive research and to provide facilities for communicating relevant information and arrange training meetings and test demonstrations.

The research system of an agricultural university operates in a manner so as to encourage projects to be formulated to solve current and emerging farm problems and test investigative findings through a systematic replicative process on experimental farms, laboratories and farmer's field. A research advisory committee is a statutory body within the university organization and is composed of Deans of constituent colleges, Director of Research, Director of Extension Education, Directors of departments of agriculture and animal husbandry and representatives of farmers with Vice-Chancellor as the chairman. The main function of this committee is to review from time to time the overall status of research activities of the university and determine their priorities and future direction.

Research projects are first examined in project review committee at the college level with respect to their objectives, research design, organizational and financial requirements and any interdisciplinary linkages which need to be established with the project. The projects are of two kinds—(a) those which relate to problems encountered within the state, and (b) those which encompass problems requiring an all-India coordinated effort. These projects are operated under the overall technical coordination and financial support of the Indian Council of Agricultural Research (ICAR).

A research evaluation committee provides the much needed in-house review mechanism within the agricultural universities to examine the findings and data support emerging from various research projects. Research findings are accepted as recommendations to be made to farmers only if sufficient data support is already available both from the experimental farms and farmers' field trials. A tentative package of recommendations to be made to farmers in every crop seasons as emerges from the proceedings of this committee.

Research—Extension Linkage

Current structure envisage permeation of the output of Research efforts from 'Top-to-Bottom'. Extension of Research is carried on with the help of Krishi Vigyan Kendras (KVKs) and Institute Village Linkage Programme (IVLP)—the principle route of course is the State Agriculture Departments's Extension machinery using by now well recognized Training and Visit (T&V) [Tour and Vanish for some] programme. All the sheen has gone away. What is largely left is an incoherent and in more than one way inadequate structure. There may be another way of looking at it. In matters of Transfer of Technology, we should consider consolidating and integrating many agencies operating in the area of Research Extension.

If Farm Plan approach is adopted, then the Extension Machinery, while drawing up farm plans for a group of villages or a region may end up with the problems, which become Research Issues at the local level—moving upwards till it reaches the National level thus determining the Agenda for Research Issues at local, regional, State, zonal and National level. These will call for restructuring the extension set up as well as the way we think. The latter shall involve bottom-to-top approach or adopting micro level building up to macro approach rather than the other way round.

There may also be a need to evaluate such effort using an independent agency to get a feedback from users. It could be an eye opener as well as a true test of efficacy of our extension effort.

There would be convergence in future of the extension system—whosoever carries out the Research—shall also undertake to take the results to the users—farmers in this case. What could happen is the State Agriculture University as an important player of total Research regime takes on the extension work totally. The two way communication highway between farmers and Researchers shall be a far more effective instrument and should do well without an uninterested (except his job) intermediary of the State's Agriculture Department. He is no stake holder in any sense of the term.

Importance of the use of Information Technology (TT) in extension need not be over emphasized. Use of electronic/print media, computers, toll-free-tele-sourcing from an Information Centre to give answers to the farmers' problems could endear the Researcher to the farmer as the Doctor does in respect of an ailing patient.

A beginning could be made by Mappii.g the Productivity levels of a given area based on given indicators. An analysis of the Indicator-led-Mapping is to quickly coming to know the area of concern, helping the programme Manager or Administrator to address that issue to help improve the productivity. Indicator led Mapping also help the Policy makers taking appropriate steps to remedy the situation. A continuous effort in this regard also helps maintain surveillance of the productivity levels.

In future, on account of several factors, basically exigencies, we envision three stage Research effort:

(i) Agri-Research and transfer centres in each district—single line.
(ii) Research effort at Research or Zonal level (zones being determined by agriconsiderations).
(iii) Coordinated All India projects.

Outcome of the Research effort of the latter two passed on the first for use and validation in the field.

A quick SWOT (strengths, weakness, opportunities and threats) analysis indicate that the potential for increasing productivity levels exist in the states/regions of Eastern UP, MP, Orissa, Bihar, North-Eastern States, Rajasthan, and some parts of West Bengal, Andhra Pradesh and Tamil Nadu. The lower productivity levels are clearly marked by related indicators of lower investments, lower farm credit, lower fertilizer consumption, lower availability of farm power and lower seed replacement and easily offers themselves as candidates for attention and growth. These are our opportunities.

Their strengths are fertile soils, good rainfall, very good irrigation potential both in respect of surface and ground water, handy farmers, and weakness is poor research-farmer extension linkage, resource poverty, lack of enterprise and investment in view of risks and poor marketing infrastructure for the marketable surpluses in the states like Bihar, Orissa and North Eastern States. Opportunity exists to address and remove the weaknesses, otherwise threat of abject poverty, squalor, malnutrition, illiteracy, etc., shall continue to loom large. For greater appreciation, micro level studies need to be carried out to specifically chalk out a plan of action for each region/sub-region. The farmer will never fail us-for us it is philosophy, for him it is life and death issue.

Agricultural Research by Governments and Other Agencies

Agricultural research is also being conducted under the Department of Agriculture of the Ministry of Agriculture, Government of India, at some centres other than its Central Research Institutes. Soil conservation research, for instance, is conducted under the soil conservation board of the Ministry. There are also certain other organizations specific problems like the Central Arid Research Institute at Jodhpur (Rajasthan) to undertake problems connected with desert and dry areas.

Each State Department of Agriculture conducts research on important crops grown in the state and also deals with the other problems of farming, in the field of agronomy, soil sciences, plant breeding, plant diseases, pests, fruit crops, etc. For important crops they have one or more experimental stations in the regions important for the crop. Usually for each subject there is a subject matter specialist at the state level but in the case of important crops there is more than one specialist in many states.

Research in agriculture or allied sciences is also receiving some attention in certain universities and laboratories or agencies endowed by private benefaction. Examples of these types are the Indian Institute of Science, Bangalore, and the Anand Agriculture Institute (Mumbai). Again tea, coffee, rubber and silk boards are functioning under the Ministry of Commerce although the problems tackled by them pertain mainly to agriculture.

Similarly, the Council of Scientific and Industrial Research (CSIR) is looking after certain research centres like the Central Food Technological Research Institute (CFTRI) at Mysore and the National Botanical Garden, Lucknow. The Atomic Energy Commission, through its Biological Wings, conducts research on irradiation and induction of mutants and related fundamental genetics research.

RESEARCH WORK AND ITS ACHIEVEMENT DURING POST-INDEPENDENCE PERIOD IN DIFFERENT AGRICULTURAL SECTOR

The decades immediately after Independence can be viewed as a watershed in the evolution and strengthening of a system of agricultural research in India. It was during this period that a number of commissions, committees, study teams were established which reviewed the prevailing agricultural situation in India. Some of the salient achievements of ICAR in this respect are;

- More than 180,000 germplasm accession of agri-horticulture and their wild relatives preserved in National Gene Bank.
- 2300 HYV/Hybrids of field crops developed.
- 460 HYV/Hybrids of Horticultural and Plantation crops developed.
- Region specific IPM modules developed.
- Adequate breeder seed production of clonal variants in rapeseed and mustard.
- Development high yielding crossbred cows, buffaloes, sheep and poultry breeds and used superovulation techniques for quick production of calves from superior bovine female using biotechnology.
- Soil maps of the country, States and agro-eco-regions developed.
- IPNS (Integrated Plant Nutrient System) and bio-facilities developed and popularized.
- Zero energy cooling chamber for on-farm cooling developed.
- Post harvest technology developed for minimizing wastes and byproducts.
- Utilization and value addition in crops, animals and fisheries.
- A large number of farm tools and implements developed for various field operations.
- Transfer of technology through Krishi Vigyan Kendras (KVKs) and Institute Village Linkage Programme (IVLP).
- Organization of computer based agricultural research information system.
- Developed VISION 2020 document for all the Institutes, SAUs and ICAR.
- Introduction of Organization and Management (O&M) reforms for better work culture.

Crop Sciences

The "Grow More Food Campaign" of the early forties was started with a high expectation but it did not pay off. But the Government of India and the ICAR did prove that right mix of policy and research helped in boosting foodgrains production in India. The introduction of improved dwarf varieties namely Mexican wheat and application of science and technologies in Indian agriculture brought about `Green Revolution' in late Sixties.

During the last three decades, the major objective of agricultural research and development was to achieve self-sufficiency in food. During the eighties, the goal was not only to further improve productivity and stabilize and diversify production, but also to generate rural employment and enhance consumption by increasing the purchasing power of the people. Development of high yield-cum-high stability production system, ensuring maximum utilization of available resources of soil, water and sunlight were the sheet-anchor of the agricultural policy. Land use planning, watershed management and farming system orientation to R &D efforts to maximize returns and minimize risks were some of the approaches for efficient utilization of resources. The emphasis also was given on sustainability in agriculture.

Special attention was paid to strengthen research in oilseeds and pulses to improve their production potential and to develop location-specific technology so as to help increase production of these crops. Maximization of biomass production, partitioning it along economically remunerative pathways, recycling of organic wastes and efficient transformation of all forms of cultural energy (i.e. all forms of energy introduced by man) into food energy were some of the complementary objectives. Emphasis was also laid on strengthening research on vegetables and horticultural crops.

Research in energy management in agriculture was considered as a new area to receive concerted attention. Efforts to harvest as much solar energy as possible through ago-physical devices and biological systems was intensified. Input utilization efficiency formed an important component of energy management system. This included water-use efficiency, fertilizer-use efficiency, etc. Efforts were directed towards harnessing organic and biological resources of nitrogen and developing technologies for recycling of phosphorous, a non-renewable resource. Integrated Pest Management (IPM) was another direction of pest research to reduce both cost and hazards of chemicalization of our agriculture. Studies on dynamics of labour availability and costs were undertaken to determine the desirability, extent and kind of mechanization of agriculture. Identification of constraints responsible for the gap between the potential and actual farm yields and causes of slow technology diffusion in some areas has been continuing as the prime concern. This would require more basic biological, agro-physical and socioeconomic research.

At present all major and minor cereals are a staple diet of a sizeable population, which is perpetually on the rise. In general there has been a marked increase in production of each one of them because of the development and wide adoption of genetically improved varieties and management technologies. However, except in Maize and to some extent in Bajra, the improvement in productivity in respect of other coarse cereals has not been very satisfactory.

Horticulture Sciences

Research on most Horticultural crops is not more than two decades old but India has achieved a significant position both in production and quality.

During 1996-97 India produced 46.97 million tones of fruits and 80.80 million tones of vegetables. In the year 1998-99 the country stood first in the production of total fruits, mango, banana, onion, cashew and in coconut production and stands second in total vegetable production after China.

Fisheries Science

Fishery research has given high priority to develop relevant technology for production, processing and marketing of both inland and marine fisheries. In the year 1998 India ranked seventh in the World and first among the Commonwealth countries in fish production. India is the second largest fish producer from inland sources after China.

Animal Science

Sustainable animal husbandry over the years has been a part of man-animal-plant-soil relationship where the animal has been an important integrating link sustaining animal and agriculture. Our agricultural operations have been traditionally much dependent on animal draught power.

Animal production has also always received special attention in dry and hilly areas. Silvi-pastoral system and agro-forestry programmes have been given attention since they were identified as a source of feed and fodder for livestock. Incentive prices are being ensured by developing marketing and trade on producer-oriented lines. Special programmes have been initiated to give export-orientation to agricultural production after meeting full home requirements. Table 14.4 indicates the growth of production of various agricultural and animal products in the country since 1951.

FINANCIAL SUPPORT TO AGRICULTURAL RESEARCH

Developing country like India always lacks resources to invest in research and development activities. They end up with underinvesting in these activities. In India, even though allocation for science and technology has increased in successive five year plans, the percentage allocation to ICAR, which is the largest individual sector, has actually fallen, sharpest during the seventh plan period which would be evident from Table 14.5.

Table 14.4 Trend of Production in Different Agricultural and Animal Husbandry Products

Year	Population (millions)	Foodgrains (mt)	Oilseeds (mt)	Milk (mt)	Egg (Billion nos.)	Fish (000' tones)	Potato (mt)	Onion (mt)	Sugar-cane (mt)	Cotton (million bales, each 170 kg
1951	363.2	50.82	5.16	—	—	752	1.66	—	57.05	3.04
1961	442.4	82.02	6.98	—	—	1160	2.72	—	110.0	5.60
1971	551.3	108.42	9.63	—	—	1756	4.81	—	126.37	4.76
1981	688.5	129.59	9.37	31.6	10.60	2444	9.67	2.50	154.25	7.01
1991	851.7	176.39	18.61	53.9	21.10	3836	15.21	3.23	241.05	9.84
1995	822.0	191.50	21.34	63.8	25.98	4789	17.40	4.04	275.54	11.89
1998-99	970.9*	203.61	24.75	74.7	30.1	5262	23.61	5.33	288.72	12.29
1999-2000(e)	986.0	208.87	20.87	78.1	31.5	5656	25.00	4.90	299.23	9.39

SOURCE: Economic Survey, 1998-99, Government of India
* estimated Population , e : estimated

Table 14.5 Allocations for Science and Technology in the Five Year Plans
(million rupees)

Plan	*Plan outlay S & T*	*ICAR*	*Percentage Share of total*
Fifth Plan	6930	1536	21.2
Sixth Plan	20160	3400	16.9
Seventh Plan	50870	4250	8.4
Eighth Plan	90420	13000	14.4
Ninth Plan	149735	N.A.	N.A.

N.A Not Available.
SOURCE: Various Plan documents and Policy Paper No. 3 prepared by National Centre for Agricultural Economics and Policy Research.

Out of the total plan budget of ICAR, about 60 per cent is spent on state agricultural universities (SAUs), either as direct assistance or through the research and extension schemes, including the National Agricultural Research Project. The extent of state support to the SAUs varies very widely. In some of the SAUs which receive substantial assistance from the state, the extent of ICAR assistance constitutes about 16 per cent of their total budget, while in some others this is as high as 53 per cent. The average is about 22 per cent. But a substantial growth in allocation of funding for Agricultural Research had been observed during the period of 4th and 8th plan. Growth in funding varies from one sectoral research to another according to the current need and priorities. Table 14.6 provides activity—wise break up of ICAR allocations on different research activities. Details about statewise growth rates and intensity of Govt. investment in research and education is given in Table 14.6A.

RESEARCH PRIORITIES AND NEW THRUST

During the last three decades, the major objective of agricultural research and development was to achieve self-sufficiency in foodgrains. During the eighties, the goal was not only to further improve productivity and stabilize and diversify production, but also to generate rural employment and enhance consumption by increasing the purchasing power of the people. Development of high yield-cum-high stability production system, ensuring maximum utilization of available resources of soil, water and sunlight were the sheet-anchor of the agricultural policy. Land use planning, watershed management and farming system orientation to R & D efforts to maximize returns and minimize risks were some of the approaches for efficient utilization of resources. The emphasis also was given on sustainability in agriculture.

Table 14.6 Activity-wise Breakup of ICAR Plan Allocations

(Rupees crore)

Plan	Research Crops	Horti-culture	Animal Science	Fisheries	Other Research	Total
IVth Plan (1969-74)	20.0 (21.9)	7.4 (8.1)	15.2 (16.6)	3.4 (3.8)	11.9 (13.0)	57.9 (63.4)
Vth Plan (1974-78)	31.9 (20.8)	9.3 (6.1)	25.9 (16.9)	8.1 (5.3)	17.9 (11.7)	93.2 (60.7)
VIth Plan (1980-85)	69.8 (20.5)	22.2 (6.5)	35.6 (10.5)	17.8 (5.2)	104.2 (30.6)	249.7 (73.4)
VIIth Plan (1985-90)	90.4 (21.3)	23.7 (5.6)	44.6 (10.5)	18.8 (4.4)	139.6 (32.9)	317.2 (74.6)
VIIIth Plan (1992-97)	322.8 (24.8)	100.0 (7.7)	140.0 (10.8)	65.0 (5.0)	323.3 (24.9)	951.2 (73.2)
IX Plan 1997-2000	525	213	275	125	460	1598
Per cent growth between IV and VIII Plans (at 1970-71 prices)	181	136	61	233	373	186

Note: Figures in parenthesis indicate the percentage break-up in each case
SOURCE: Research Priorities in Indian Agriculture; NCAP, New Delhi.

Special attention was paid to strengthen research in oilseeds and pulses to improve their production potential and to develop location-specific technology so as to help increase production of these crops. Maximisation of biomass production, partitioning it along economically remunerative pathways, recycling of organic wastes and efficient transformation of all forms of cultural energy (i.e. all forms of energy introduced by man) into food energy were some of the complementary objectives.

Starting from the base, the population of India by 2025 as projected by UNFPA is 1330 million and a cross section analysis by this author indicates the foodgrain demand will be 275 million tonnes by that time. This would mean the need of an annual additional production of say 3 million tonnes, which is to be achieved through increased productivity. Keeping this in view, emphasis of the present research is on bio-diversity, genetic engineering as well as improvement in the quality of the produce. Research on DNA fingerprinting is promising for restoration of indigenous germplasm.

The quality improvement researches are also thrusted on different commercial and export potential crops like jute development of high yielding varieties and improvement of retting of jute have received a special attention of research.

Table 14.6A ***State-wise Growth Rates and Intensity Ratios of Government Investment in Research and Education***

(Rupees in million)

Year	Growth rate (5) of real investment			Investment as % of AgGDP		Investment (Rs)/ha (at 1981/82 prices)		Investment (Rs)/ha (at current prices)		Investment/ scientist (000 Rs at current prices (1992-94)
	1960s	1970s	1980s	1980-82	1992-94	1980-82	1992-94	1980-82	1992-94	
Andhra Pradesh	– 0.09	12.18	7.48	0.17	0.26	5.40	12.90	5.32	32.23	357
Assam	7.49	– 0.09	6.25	0.30	0.41	11.19	20.88	11.12	51.81	291
Bihar	1.37	12.30	6.26	0.14	0.16	4.60	9.94	4.50	24.93	222
Gujarat	12.33	– 0.01	7.17	0.21	0.38	5.94	13.34	5.84	33.41	355
Haryana	—	31.25	4.69	0.30	0.31	11/52	17.91	11.31	44.86	227
Himachal Pradesh	—	– 0.12	9.39	0.67	1.23	21.59	51.88	21.21	130.16	225
Jammu and Kashmir	18.34	– 0.12	6.85	†	†	12.87	69.93	12.64	68.70	152
Karnataka	– 0.15	13.75	7.79	0.20	0.29	4.99	10.88	4.90	27.34	240
Kerala	2.06	21.12	7.42	0.33	0.49	18.10	42.94	17.77	107.50	488
Madhya Pradesh	– 0.08	– 0.08	13.32	0.07	0.14	1.08	3.36	1.06	8.35	145
Maharashtra	16.62	– 0.01	5.65	0.42	0.46	9.27	16.16	9.11	40.57	453
Orisa	– 0.05	7.19	7.01	0.11	0.21	2.40	4.67	2.36	11.64	196
Punjab	– 0.01	4.70	7.16	0.26	0.30	10.62	20.57	10.42	51.66	262
Rajasthan	– 0.02	4.46	9.32	0.13	0.21	1.92	4.45	1.90	11.16	241
Tamil Nadu	1.37	3.68	12.28	0.23	0.42	7.67	24.57	7.56	61.62	329
Uttar Pradesh	12.19	– 0.11	4.88	0.14	0.16	4.78	7.42	4.68	18.73	316
West Bengal	5.58	13.52	2.35	†	†	8.31	9.68	8.19	24.53	545
All India (Centre + State)	6.52	9.51	6.29	0.39	0.49	10.65	20.65	10.49	51.85	432

† Consistent AgGDP data were not available.

Note: Except growth rates, data are three-year averages.

SOURCE: B.K. Tamani, Agriculture in the 21st century, ICAR, 2001.

Though the oilseeds production has increased to a great extent, the ICAR has taken up a few micro-mission programme to achieve self sufficiency in edible oils. Researches are going on to improve the quality of oilseeds up to Double zero (containing low erucic acid) or the Canola type (containing low glucosinolate) and developing the Downy Mildew resistant varieties of sunflower. Emphasis is also laid on strengthening research on vegetables and horticultural crops, breeding of fishes and animals, improvement in production of milk and milk products etc. In the sector of Animal Sciences India has achieved a significant pace in the world not only in production but also in improvement of breeds, feeds and nutrition and disease eradication, curing and control.

Parallel to the research in these sectors, research on unconventional and under utilized crops like Amarantha species *Vigna umbellata, Vicia faba* which have a high nutritive value and other crops like *Fagopyrum* species which have a high medicinal value is going on with high priority. Fast expanding focus on research is also pointed to high demanding (both in home and abroad) crop like mushroom. Research on quality improvement of button mushroom and oyster mushroom has now been taken up with high priority throughout the country. Apart from this, floriculture has also received a high attention for the huge demand of flowers in the international market. Though the infrastructural facility of flower export is below par, a very high scope rests in this sector. With the globalization in agriculture and various provisions of the World Trade Organizations (WTO), exports of agricultural products from India have been facing tough competition from other agricultural exporting countries both in respect of quality and quantity. There is therefore a need for more emphasis on high quality research and technology in agriculture in order to face global competition. Main emphasis is now going on in the area of technology dissemination directly to the farmers field. Several projects including NATP are in operation for this particular purpose to foster the linkages between researchers and farmers.

Rice Wheat Consortium

For overseeing activities in the Indian subcontinent, the Rice wheat Consortium was established in 1994 as an eco-regional initiative of CGIAR and convened by CIMMYT. It is an alliance of scientific and technical experts from the national agricultural research systems of Bangladesh, India, Nepal and Pakistan. Its objectives are to improve the skills of NARS scientists, imparting a systems perspective in the research efforts and above all to address the issue of sustainability or rice-wheat cropping systems.

There is no hindrance to using and adapting RCTs like zero-tillage, surface seeding and bed planting to different crops. While, using them with rice is established worldwide, experimentation with wheat, soyabean and maize are on. These technologies are economical, environment friendly and allow more judicious use of natural resources. They are neither new nor something we have invented. What is new is adapting it to irrigated land areas of southeast Asia for rice-wheat cropping systems.

Some specific benefits of zero-tillage include water savings by 25 per cent in wheat crop, which can go up to 50 per cent in rice. A concern in India is that farmers resort to burning crop residue after the mechanical harvest of rice, leading to heavy carbon dioxide emission. Estimates state that 2 million hectares of zero-tilled land i.e., non-residue burning, can save up to 17 million tonnes of carbon dioxide emission. Also zero-till saves precious time between rice harvest and wheat sowing enabling wheat establishment in time. Timely sowing of wheat also increases yield. Hence, sustainability of crop yields with less farm inputs leading to improved profitability is the prime factor encouraging in average farmer to experiment with these techniques.

Rice feeds about half of the world's population, and 90 per cent of the total annual harvest comes from Asia. Not all research into new crop varieties involves genetic engineering, but the IRRI is helping with work on genetically-modified Vitamin A enriched rice, or "Golden Rice." This rice was developed by German scientists by implanting two genes from daffodil and one from a bacterium into a japonica rice variety called T309. This is a genetically—modified rice aimed at combating Vitamin A deficiency, responsible for half a million cases of irreversible blindness and up to a million deaths a year among the world's poorest people. The variety, rich in iron and zinc and known as IR 68144, was developed by cross breeding two varieties. We are not only developing higher yielding rice but also developing super value rice. The Institute estimates that about one third of the world's population suffers from anaemia, which impairs immunity and reduces physical and mental capacity.

Oilseeds

The most crucial issue before Indian agriculture today is that of oilseeds where despite the Technology Mission, the production having touched nearly 27 million tonnes in 1993-94, is hovering around 20-22 million tonnes. During the oil year 2000-01, oil imports touched an all time high of 5.0 million tonnes from just one million tonnes in 1994-95. During the course of past 50 years the country has moved from being an exporter of vegetable oils to the world's largest importer.

Indian oilseeds sector, the fourth largest in the world after USA. China and Brazil, accounting for an annual turnover of over Rs 60,000 crore, is at the cross roads. The Ninth Five Year Plan target of 30 million tonnes of oilseeds production is highly unlikely to be achieved with domestic production of around 20 to 22 million tonnes. India with 26 million hectares of area under oilseeds cultivation, today accounts for nearly 7 per cent of the world production of oilseeds, and 5.6 per cent oilmeal, 4.2 per cent of world oilmeal export, 5.7 per cent of world oil production, 10.6 per cent of the world edible oil consumption and as high as 15.6 per cent of world import of oils. With a steady growth of population and per capita income, Indian per capita consumption of edible oils has been growing steadily. Oilseeds output and in turn vegetable oil production has, however failed to keep pace with it necessitating increasing dependence on imports.

The world vegetable oil scenario is dominated by the shortfall in the production of sunflowerseed, the greater use of rapeseed oil in the production of bio-diesel in Europe, the higher production of palm oil during 2001 by Malaysia and Indonesia, the production of coconut and palm kernel oil at a high level during 2001 as a result of a prolonged spell of excellent rainfall, bumper soyabean crops in USA as well as in Brazil and Argentina and China's entry into the World Trade Organisation.

The edible oil policy is being run by five separate ministries each of whom does not know what the other is doing." Suggestions for the betterment of oilseeds and oils economy are to free up the development, propagation, and sale of seeds, continue to increase MSP for oilseeds at a rate greater than inflation and also greater than the rate of increase for cereals, take the bold step of scrapping archaic land ceiling laws, and the government must stop tinkering with edible oil policy on a weekly basis.

All these can at best be considered as stop gap arrangements. Let us accept that the so called 'yellow revolution' has withered away. This is a new challenge to agriculture research in India. With due consideration to the constraints suffered by the oilseeds, a concerted and high priority research effort is to be mounted to improve productivity per hect.

Hybrids and high yielding, disease and drought resistant varieties should be continuously evolved, and use of sulphur rich chemicals must be intensified. Since we are able to import edible oils easily, it is difficult to visualise the problems that this country would face when internationally oil prices touch $599 or more per tonne and the Indian production continues at the current level. The present value of import of Rs. 12,000 crore would not only double, but would go high with higher imports.

Genetically Modified Crops

Five years after the first commercialized crop—when the Flavr Savr tomato was engineered with the flick of a gene to keep longer-genetically modified organisms (GMOs) have won acceptance from many farmers and endorsement by most scientists. Doubts are being raised about the future of GMO crops. The question asked is whether we get beyond the initial wave of products like Bt (pest resistant) cotton or corn. Consumers in Europe and parts of Asia angered by what they see as products being foisted upon them without their consent, remain unconvinced. They have pushed for more testing, regulation, labelling and segregating or total bans.

In the corporate sector even Monsanto, the company most loathed by biotech opponents, has now acknowledged a public relation disaster and pledged to turn over a new leaf. There's a significant risk that the industry could still lose the credibility battle. We are at the same point with GMO crops that we were with pesticides 50 years ago. They were going to solve all the farmers' problems and pests were going to be a thing of the past.

The European Union which froze the approval of new GMOs three years ago, has tried to placate critics by proposing rules to label foods in which they make up more than one per cent. The United States says this is impractical and critics say it is too lenient. Brazil, on the verge of approving GMO soyabeans, has delayed again, Japan and south Korea's "zero tolerance" for StarLink corn—a genetically-modified grain which promoted widespread food recalls in the US because of fears of allergic reactions in some people has reduced sales of US corn to those top buyers in the past year. In the food industry, the consumer is king. So the vocal protests from consumer groups have prompted costly food recalls and a tangle of trade and intellectual property disputes.

Despite the storm, GMO use has not actually stalled. In 2001, plantings of GMO corn in the US accounted for 24 per cent of all corn acreage against 25 per cent a year earlier GMO soyabean acreage rose to 63 per cent from 54 per cent and GMO cotton acreage rose to 64 per cent from 61 per cent. Bt Cotton is commercially grown in countries as far flung as China, Mexico, South Africa and Argentina over a spread of over 2 million hectares. An Indian variety of the product—developed by the seed company Mahyco, in which Mosanto has a minority stake is undergoing large-scale field trials and is pending approval for commercialization. The need to adopt a tough and uncompromising line against the planting of illicit GM cotton in Gujarat stems not so much from the ecological risk it poses but the imperative of signalling that illegal genetic manipulation simply will not be tolerated. The International Service for the Acquisition of Agri-Biotech Applications (ISAAA) estimates that GMO plantings globally in 2001 would reach 50 million hectares up 10 per cent from the previous year.

Despite the ongoing debate about GMO crops, particularly in countries of the European Union, millions of large and small farmers in both industrial and developing countries continue to increase their plantings of GMO crops. The reason for the success of HMOs is economic. GMO soyabean growers in the U.S. claim savings of $5 to $20 per acre (0.447 hectares) from reduced fuel and herbicide costs. U.S. cotton growers report better yields and lower pesticide use from Bt cotton, which contains an insect-resistant soil bacterium.

Such lessons are not lost on the developing world. It is now widely recognized that we are at a post Green Revolution standstill and that yield ceilings of the main food crops have already been reached in conventional breeding programmes. We must look to genetic engineering to help to move beyond these plateaux. GMO research is advanced on canola, sweetcorn, raspberries, citrus and other crops that have an impact on rich consumers. But analysts say opportunities abound for researchers to score a victory by concentrating on the problems of developing countries. Some work is being done, with notable advances in GMO plants that have thrived in salty or low-nutrient soils.

But many high-impact solutions, such as controlling the striga weed that cuts corn yields by half in southern Africa, still await GMOs. The biotech industry made a mistake in trying to market itself as fighting world hunger and then not delivering. Monsanto, the holder of patents for GMO corn, soyabeans and cotton, has backed up its pledge to use its expertise for the hungry in the developing world after critics demonised it as the greedy, mad scientist of the new millennium. As the GMO standard bearer, Mosanto in August 2000 released its rice genome research to the public domain as a sign of its new open stance, swallowing significant expenses.

It has also pledged to drop the development of a "terminator" gene that aimed to block plants from producing next-generation seed that farmers could use without a fee. Mosanto is now working on producing "golden" rice in Asia and special mustard seed in India, both modified to include Vitamin A; virus resistant potatoes in Mexico and Kenya; virus resistant papaya in Hawaili and southeast Asia. The companies are struggling like mad- to solve a developing country food problem and are stuck in a 7 to 10-year development cycle. And none of the countries want to make a major blunder.

The other key to acceptance of GMOs lies with the consumer. GMO technology in modern medicines is rarely questioned by the consumer, where benefits are clear. Food is another matter. GMOs have so far been sold mainly as a benefit for farming or food processing, which urban consumers care little about. They emphasise the need for crops and new foods that clearly do benefit consumers. That is exactly what is targeted by the "second generation" of GMO crops now on the drawing board, with work on everything from cancer cures to snacks that reduce cholesterol levels. How about an oil with an omega 3-fatty acid, so that if you don not like fish you can still get an omega-3 fatty acid. Soyabean oil with the composition of olive oil? There are dozens of things being worked on tomatoes, potatoes, squash, coffee beans. Clearly, many are agronomic traits, because that is what is needed in the developing world. But others are clearly what consumers will want to buy.

At a larger level, it is time that India adopted a clear and unambiguous attitude with respect to the biotechnology sector—particularly in agriculture. Today, biotech crops are grown in 15 countries over a spread of over 50 million hect, a 30-fold increase since 1966. This is the highest adoption rate for any new technology by agriculture industry standards. Many other countries are poised to join this list and take the acreage much further. The potential of biotechnology to contribute to food security and the alleviation of hunger, as even the UNDP recently acknowledged, is something that can no longer be ignored. Over the next few years, decisions with respect to other GM crops will have to be taken—a transgenic variety of mustard is expected to come up for approval next year. While other countries have adopted relatively clear-cut and unambiguous attitudes towards bio-agriculture—either for or against—India continues to appear confused and uncertain about how to exploit this technology.

Bio/gene Technology

Biotechnology was defined as "any technique that uses living organism (or part of organism) to make or modify products, to improve plants and animals, or to develop microorganism for a special use." Later on in the year 1991, the US government redefined Biotechnology as "the industrial use of rDNA (recombinant DNA), cell fusion and novel bio processing techniques." The European Federation of Biotechnology has described it as "the integration of natural resources and engineering in order to achieve the application of microorganisms as well as parts there of and molecular analogues for products and services." Indeed it is a combination to the application of various principles of biology, chemistry, physics, mathematics, IT/computer science and engineering. We may, therefore, define Biotechnology as the interdisciplinary science using latest techniques for applying the same to organism or part thereof to identify, design and produce substances or to modify organism for specific use/application.

Application of Bio-Technology is the 'in' thing be it soil health measures or Plant Protection Measures. Currently the whole range of possibilities have not been exploited nor all the crops are covered. One of the principal requirement of future relates to sustainability which itself is related to reducing the use of chemicals be it in fertilizers or pesticides/insecticides/weedicides. Greater emphasis and attention shall have to be laid in application of biotechnology in agriculture. Genetic engineering offers limitless opportunities in increasing agricultural production. The famous debate and 'row' over genetically modified foods in USA versus. Europe really need not stymie our efforts but act only as a caution to limit our acts within a reasonable limit against what has been given to us by Mother Nature. Is it not surprising when it comes to application of gene technology in medicines and related areas—no noises are made except in cloning a human being—but loud noises are made on use of the technology in agriculture.

A breakthrough using the genetic route to get seed strains requiring less of fertilizer or water or pest resistant varieties can be a boon for many countries in Asia, Africa and South America. Thrust of research should be higher productivity with sustainability keeping within limits of environmental protection. If these limits are maintained then technology led breakthroughs, which will cover the gaps for the farmers, especially the poor, should be welcome anywhere—anytime and it is towards this that research effort should be directed. It would be of interest to learn that one-third of the global food production potential is lost due to pest infestation and other damages. Crop losses in India range from 10 to 30 per cent depending on the crop, region and severity of pest infestation. In monetary terms, the loss is estimated at more than Rs. 50,000 crore, and if half of this loss was reduced, a substantial quantity of food can be made available for human consumption.

India is fast emerging as an exporting country in the field of agriculture. Commodities with excessive pesticide residues are not accepted by most importing countries and act as a non-tariff barrier. This has caused considerable loss to the country and the grower and exporter. It is, therefore, of utmost concern that pesticide residues are kept below the prescribed MRL values both for domestic and export market. There is an urgent need to ban the use of pesticides which are toxic and whose residues persist for long duration in food commodities and environment. Any technology which reduces the ill effected pesticides would be welcome.

Power of genetic modification to do immense good to agriculture and food security is unlimited. It is now clear that the 21st century may witness changes in temperature precipitation, sea level and ultraviolet radiation, as a result of global warming. This led us to initiate an anticipatory research programme to breed salt tolerant varieties of mustard, and rice in coastal areas, in order to be prepared for sea water intrusion into farmland as a result of a rise in sea level. The donor of salt tolerance was a mangrove species. Transferring genes for tolerance to salinity from mangrove tree species to rice, mustard or tobacco is an impossible task without recourse to recombinant DNA experiments. Thus, the immense benefits that can accrue from genomics and molecular breeding are clear. What are the principal concerns?

Besides bio-safety concerns, the following three issues: *First*, India is a land of small farm holdings. There is concern that expansion of proprietary science and shrinking of "public good" research supported from public funds may lead to a situation where the technologies of the future remain in the hands of a few transnational corporations. Only resource-rich farmers may have access to them, thereby enlarging the genetic divide.

Second, the monopolistic control over crop varieties could lead to a situation where large areas are covered by very few genetic strains or hybrids. What will happen to the livelihoods of farm men and women operating small holdings with institutional credit and with no crop insurance cover, if GM cotton, maize, soybean, rice, potato or other crops are affected by serious diseases as a result of the breakdown of resistance? Hence, GM crops should be cultivated only with appropriate disease containment agronomy.

A *third* issue relates to the potential impact of GM foods on biodiversity. This aspect has two dimensions—one dealing with the replacement of numerous local cultivars with one or two GM strains, thereby leading to genetic erosion, and the other relating to equity in benefit sharing between biotechnologists and the primary conservers of genetic resources and the holders of traditional knowledge. At present, the primary conservers remain poor, while those who use their knowledge (for example, the medicinal properties of plants) and material become rich. This has resulted in accusations of bio-piracy. It is time that genetic engineers promote genuine bio-partnerships with the holders of indigenous knowledge and conservers of genetic variability, based on principles of ethics and equity in benefit sharing.

Unless research and development efforts on GM foods are based on principles of bio-ethics, bio-safety, bio-diversity conservation and bio-partnerships, there will be serious public concern about the ultimate nutritional, social, ecological and economic consequences of replacing numerous local varieties with a few GMOs. Also, under conditions where the market is the dominant factor in determining research priorities, "orphans will remain orphans" in terms of investment of research funds, unless the public sector steps in.

We should not throw the baby with the bath water. Genetic engineering is only a too for bringing about novel genetic combinations. Molecular genetics is the pathway to precision breeding. We should not condone unauthorised releases of GMOs, as in Gujarat. What is important is to put in place an objective and speedy risk-benefit analysis mechanism which inspires public trust. For this purpose, the government of India should set up without further delay a multi-stakeholder National Commission on Genetic Modification for Food and Health Security. Recent events with Bt Cotton in Gujarat underline the urgency of such a multi-stakeholder body which functions in a transparent and professionally credible manner.

This is much more important in the case of cotton where the livelihood of about 60 million people engaged in various vocations relating to farming, trade and textile industry are involved. India with an area of around 8.3 million hectares produces only 2.7 million tonnes of cotton, while China (its major competitor in the world) produces 50 per cent more cotton (4.2 million tonnes) in less than half the area of (4.1 million hectares). Thus, China has surpassed USA in productivity, which produce 3.9 million tonnes on nearly 5.8 million hectares. Besides low yields Indian cotton suffers from higher cost of production. Farmers have suffered heavy losses because of pest attacks and unfavourable weather. We have failed to tackle the menace of ball worms, despite coordinated research in pest management. We must meet the twin challenges—to improve quality and lower production cost by the use of technology. Bt. Cotton provides the answer.

A number of smaller players like Shantha Biotech, Bharat Biotech, Mahyco and Proagro have already entered the field of basic research. A list of the players in the field in given in Table 14.7.

Table 14.7 Indian Biotech Companies

Company	*Products developmen/uses of prod.*
Agri-tech:	
MAHYCO	Transgenic crops, plant bio-tech,
ITC Agrotech	Seeds
Monsanto chemicals	Herbicides, for food and crop protection
NOVARTIS	Herbicides, fungicides and agro-chemicals
AVENTIS Crop Sc.	Herbicides, fungicides and agro-chemicals
EXEL Industries	Bio-fertiliser (from waste) and agro-chemicals
Pro-Agro seeds	Hybrid seeds (rape and vegetable)
Spic	Hybrid seeds, transgenic crops.
Pioneer overseas	Seeds, transgenic plant products
DOW Agro Sciences	Agro-chemicals
Biajam Biosciences	Biotech agriculture
Classic biotech	Hightech agriculture
GVK Bio-Science	Bio-informatics
Trindus Biotech	Bio-informatics
DCM Sriram consolidated	(DSCL) cotton, sunflower, corn, bajra and jowar hybrids.

SOURCE: This is just an indicative list, compiled from different periodicals and news reports. (PNB) Monthly Review, September 2001.

Future Prospects

Present patent policies prevent international investments in R & D, however, it is expected that after 2005 expenditure in R & D will increase substantially. In USA 95% of the research is from universities and institutions. In India the research is at a low ebb, as there are missing links between industry and academy. There were 80 regulatory approvals for biotech products in the last five years against 40 in the last 13 years. The pace will accelerate as research increases. Marketing approvals of the biotech products are also to increase further with more than 350 products in clinical development. Biotech companies raised a record $40 billion worldwide in 2000. In the next five years, a rash of new drugs and therapies is expected as genomics and proteomics advance.

Government of India has also taken steps and the department of biotechnology, under the ministry of science is very actively involved. They are considering the UP Government's proposal of making Lucknow a biotech city and setting up biotechnology park at either Lucknow or Greater Nodia. UP with its abundant raw materials, manpower and prestigious R & D institutions has opened new avenues of opportunities. Punjab Government is promoting a project for" Green house cultivation of Vegetables" as a joint venture between Punjab Government, Centre's department of Science & Technology and a private promoter.

Companies strong in product-based R & D will have a distinct advantage. Among them are the companies that have access to their foreign parent's product. Companies that are working on biotech research include Monsanto Chemicals, Novartis and Aventis Crop Science. These companies are producing products for crop protection. There are a number of Indian start-ups, some with foreign collaboration, taking aim at the new kind of biotech-infotech convergence. Avestha Gengraine Technologies having Dutch connections (in short known as Avesthagen) is a biotech start-up trying to produce drought—and pest resistant rice. Avesthagen sourced experts from the bioinformatics faculty of Madurai Kamraj University.

A number of new projects are located and are likely to be located at Chennai, Hyderabad and Bangalore. As per media reports at least 50 entrepreneurs have displayed serious intent for biotech ventures since October 2000. Chennai and Bangalore are also witnessing similar rush. There will be a rush of contracting, subcontracting, collaboration, cooperation opportunities for the Indian biotech, IT, bioinformatics companies that choose to seek them. This scenario offers numerous opportunities to bankers/investors for financing and investment.

R & D Funds for Modified Crops

Noted agricultural research scientist LT Evans of Australia said (Nov. 2001) that while the next agricultural revolution depended on genetically modified seeds to increase agricultural output to feed the growing population in the world, developed countries and the World Bank are allowing lesser funds for research and development in agriculture. He said that in the more developed countries, the private sector has provided the substantial finance needed to develop GM crop varieties. In developing countries the funding of agricultural research and development has fallen sharply following serious cuts in foreign aid for R & D down by 57 per cent in the eight years between 1988 and 1996. Even World Bank funding for rural development fell by 47 per cent between 1986 and 1998. Agriculture according to him has had to compete with other issues such as maintenance of biodiversity, the amelioration of global warming, the promotion of sustainability, non-farm rural development etc. for foreign aid.

While the US has been opting for genetically modified (G.M) seeds with 54 per cent of the soyabean crop, 33 per cent of the maize crop and 72 per cent of the cotton crop grown from GM seeds, the European Union has since 1998 blocked the registration of any GM crops. He said that China has had lesser concern for over biosafety while countries like India, Brazil and Kenya have been depending on biosafety rules to delay the use of GM crops. China has modified 141 crops genetically, approved 45 for field trials and released 31 for commercial cultivation—compared to Indian development of only 16 GM plants, approvals of 10 for field trials and no commercial releases! Farmers here too appreciate the potential and importance of biotechnology. They no longer feel like waiting, as is evident in Gujarat and other states in the Bt cotton case.

FOCUS ON PRIVATE AGRICULTURAL RESEARCH

Paucity of public resources for investment and low efficiency of publicly managed systems have focused attention on fostering greater role for the private sector. In agricultural research too, which has been in public domain since the very beginning, a serious debate has started on the potential role for private sector. In developed countries, the U.S. for example, the private sector accounts for over 50 per cent of the total agricultural research expenditures.

Today, private entities are paying for and conducting a larger share of research, while many governments are scaling back the growth in or reducing their spending on agricultural R&D. Globally, the private sector spent an estimated $11.5 billion (1993 prices) on agricultural R&D in 1995, about one-third of the $33 billion public-private total. An overwhelming majority (94 per cent) of this private research is conducted in developed countries, where the private sector accounts for just over half the total agricultural research. In poor countries, private firms do less than 6 per cent of the agricultural R&D. Most herbicides, insecticides, and veterinary medicines have been developed by the private sector (though they drew on discoveries made by public research), and the private sector has developed many food storage, transport, and processing technologies. Changes in the world economy and in agriculture and science are having important implications for the funding, organization, and management of R&D. In many countries the emergence of modern biotechnology and a strengthening of intellectual property rights are giving rise to profound changes in both public and private agricultural R&D. Only a small part (12 percent) of private research concerns farm-level technologies for improving crop and livestock production. Much research relates to technologies embodied in purchased inputs as well as post-farm food processing and product development. Specialization has become the name of the game: in one country, firms may emphasize post-harvest research; in another, pesticides and herbicides. Research results tend to be rapidly transferred around the world.

In this changing research environment, a number of important policy questions must be addressed. How should resources for agricultural research be distributed among local, national and international research? How much agricultural research should be publicly funded? What role should multinational firms play? How should scarce research finds be distributed among sectors such as agriculture, forestry, fisheries, and livestock? Should a large part of agricultural research be directed toward environmental issues such as climate change, loss of biodiversity, and water pollution? Should research concentrate on short-term or long-term results? On improving the environment or increasing yields?

Private investment in any activity is determined by appropriateness, that is, the ability of the entrepreneur to capture the benefits arising from such investments, and the expected magnitude of these benefits. Many products of agricultural research, however, have the attributes of "public" goods, that is, benefits cannot be apportioned. Its use by one beneficiary does not reduce its availability to another. Crop management or new farming system information, generated from research, for example, are universally available to all potential users free of cost. These have social benefits, but no firm can capture any part of this. In this sense there is market failure. So, private sector will not invest in such research and there is no substitute for public intervention. Generally, however, there is some opportunity for appropriation of benefits and, therefore, some scope for private research.

Many developing countries (including India) had closed economies characterized by severe price, marketing and exchange rate distortions. When such economies are liberalized, there is a sudden spurt in appropriateness. Private sector can reap substantial profits with low-cost (largely adaptive) research even in areas where private research would not normally be undertaken. Growth in Chilean fruit industry and exports is a classic example of this phenomenon. Similar opportunities may exist in some exportable commodities in India also. However, such research is contingent upon existence of very high profits and cannot normally be sustained over time.

There is no single criterion to define the boundary between domains of public and private sector research. Opportunities for private sector research vary according to areas of research, type of technologies, farming systems, nature of commodity, etc. The above rationale and international experience (particularly from developed countries) help in identifying areas of research where private sector has some intrinsic advantage.

The view that privatization will enable reduction in public expenditures on research assumes that the two are substitutes. They are not, and the case for public research remains strong. The two are complementary and understanding the comparative advantage of each helps in avoiding duplication. This division of labour would enable the public sector to move away from some areas and use the resources so freed to focus more on basic research, frontier technologies, sustainability research, and so on.

Private sector research is nascent in India. Appropriate conditions must be created before a vibrant private system emerges. First, the process of liberalization of the economy, including reforms in the trade and exchange rate regimes, must continue apace. Access to world market creates strong compulsions for domestic R & D on the one hand, and international technology transfer on the other. Second, massive investment in basic (roads, markets, power, etc.) as well as modern (communication, information, specialized transport, cargo, and shipping etc.) infrastructure is crucial for efficient production and trade. These raise incentives for greater commercialization and improve returns to private R & D. Third, efficient patenting, registration, copyright and licensing laws are essential. These improve appropriateness by making imitation difficult. Fourth, direct incentives need to be provided to private relief, duty concessions on import of scientific equipment and supplies for research purposes.

Private sector research, moreover, is primarily concerned with technologies 'embedded' in seeds, chemical equipment and other inputs which they produce and other inputs which they produce and sell. Nowhere have they shown much interest in investing in research for better techniques of soil and water management, rainfed agriculture, cropping systems, environmental impact and long-term sustainability. Given that the performance of new varieties, and therefore their sales prospects, depend crucially on improvements in these spheres, private sector should be interested in them. But techniques in these areas are not marketable products; moreover the effective application of these techniques involves complex problems of adapting institutions and creating new institutions for managing common pool resources. These are beyond the spheres, and interests, of agri business corporations. Because of these considerations, research and action in these areas of necessity must be the responsibility of the public sector. And they must be seen as complementary to breeding better varieties.

Mehrauli-based food processing company Sterling Farms Research and Services Private Limited has come up with a unique item-soil substitute, which derives from coconut husk and pit. According to the chairman of this company, this product is being introduced in India for the first time. However, a similar product has been used in Sri Lanka since years. Outlining the features inherent to this product he further reveals this eco-friendly soil substitute, Neopeat, is four times lighter, more water-resistant than original soil and a bad conductor of heat.

Another special feature of this soil is that it is free from nematodes, worms, weed seeds, salmonella, *E. coli* and pathogenic fungi normally associated with soil. No chemicals are added to it as it lasts for about five to seven years. It is highly suitable for greenhouse farming, commercial plantation, flower beds, potted plants, horticultural crops, golf courses, landscaping, roof gardening and for nursery polybags.

He informs that this soil is available in various packs (bales). A 4.5-kg bale can produce about 80 kg of soil after adding 20 litres of water to it. The price of this pack is Rs. 125. Keeping in view the deficiency of good soil in metro cities, it is a good substitute for this. He says at Sri Wardhan Nursery in Maharashtra about 25,000 plants are growing on this soil. A golf course turf has also been developed from this in that area. Dabur is also using this soil and developing medicinal plants in Nepal. The company is also exporting this product to some countries like the Netherlands and the UK. The company's present turnover is Rs. 10 crore.

Poultry in the Private Sector

Prior to sixties, practically all the poultry services in the country were provided by the public sector, primarily through the Animal Husbandry departments of various state governments. Other than production (which was also in the nature of backyard poultry), private sector had practically no hand in research, breeding and disease control. There were hardly any feed-manufacturing units, or even testing laboratories in the country. It was only during the sixties that commercial poultry started in India and the credit for producing the first commercial egg goes to Rani Shaver Poultry Breeding Farms (P) Ltd., a Delhi-based private farm.

Today 16 pureline projects are being operated by 12 companies in private sector (Table 14.8). Subsequent to the recent liberalization, the grandparent broiler stocks have been imported by the breeding companies, viz. Eagle Agro-Farms, Pune, and Nasik Research Farms. The India Poultry Farms, Bangalore and Agritech Hatcheries, Ahmednagar are also in the process of importing grandparent stocks.

The Babcock BV 300, of Venkateshwara Hatcheries Groups is a highly pedigreed bird which lays up to 300 eggs. It commands almost 75% of the egg market. And it has made India the fifth largest producer of eggs in the world. Indian poultry has come of age today. Chicken and eggs meet international standards. High-quality feed is the order of the day. The smallest farmer has access to state-of the-art farming techniques at the Institute of Poultry Management of India, the only one of its kind in Asia. Reputed scientists discover remedies for poultry diseases at Poultry Diagnostic and Research Centres-practically all in the private sector.

Due to recent liberalization policies, pureline units in India are going to face a challenge from the imported grandparent stocks. The success or failure of each will depend upon the comparative performance, under the Indian agro-climatic conditions. In addition to progress of the poultry breeding industry, there are encouraging developments with regard to vaccine production. Vaccines produced by the private manufacturers are excellent in quality. Some of the big companies make use of Specific Pathogen-Free (SPF) eggs. One company is even maintaining a SPF chicken flock and is a supplier of SPF eggs. The pharmaceutical needs are also met by the Indian manufactures.

Table 14.8 Private Pureline Breeding Farms

Breeding farms	Brand	Name
M/s Kegg Farms Gurgaon (1970-71)	Keystone Kegbro	Layer Broiler
M/s Poona Pearls Poultry Breeding Farms and Hatcheries, Pune (1972-73)	Sonali Samrat	Layer Broiler
M/s Venco Research and Breeding Farms Ltd. (1981-82)	Vencob	Broiler
M/s Venkateshwara Research and Breeding Farms (1981-82)	BV 300	Layer
M/s Kasila Farms, Hyderabad	Hubchick	Broiler
M/s Basik Breeders Pvt. Ltd., Hyderabad (1987)	Starcross Starbro	Layer Broiler
M/s Tarakeshwari Hatcheries Pvt. Ltd., Delhi	Anak	Broiler
M/s Krishna Poultry Breeding Farms, Nasik	H and N	Layer
M/s Bovns Poultry Breeders, Hyderabad	Bovans	Layer
M/s Dekalb-Deejay Hatcheries, Bangalore	Dekalb	Layer
M/s Ross-Deejay Hatcheries, Bangalore	Ross	Broiler
M/s Select Breeders	Lohman	Layer

RESEARCH PRIORITIES

Though productivity has increased manifold, there exists still a wide gap between the productivity and actual potential in many areas. Nearly one-sixth of the land area has serious limitations like erosion, aridity, acidity, salinity and alkalinity which limit agricultural production. Focus of research should be on evolving strategies towards ecologically less endowed areas where the present level of productivity of crops is still low even though cultivated area under different crops is still large as rainfed areas.

The reasons for low productivity like low inputs, low quality of seeds, low level of seeds, low level of mechanization, inefficient plant protection measures, huge post-harvest losses etc. must be overcome.

By evolving better post-harvest technologies and processing the food items, post-harvest losses can be reduced. FCI godowns are overflowing with grains stored improperly, lying in open, exposed to sun and rain.

Due to piling up of grains, farmers should be made aware about diversification and going beyond crop raising i.e. horticulture, floriculture, sericulture, fisheries, genetic engineering, plastic culture, agribusiness, etc. The role of agriculture in the process of development has changed in the present system which has been affected by globalisation and liberalisation.

People are shifting from subsistence foods to basic food as their income is increasing. Due to vast diversity in the country's agro-climatic conditions, a variety of products can be produced. There is need to identify and exploit the areas of the domestic and international markets, plastic culture should be promoted so that farmers can turn towards earning more profits through commercial production for off season products.

The country's annual oilseeds output has remained virtually stagnant in the past decade despite several government initiatives. India produced 18.21 million tonnes of oilseeds in 2000-01 compared with 18.61 million a decade ago. Roughly 10 tonnes of oilseeds are needed to get three tonnes of oils. Yields have been stuck at around 850 kg per hectare through the past decade, well below the world average of about 1,500 kg. India's dependence on imported vegetable oils has risen to about 40 per cent from just three per cent in 1992-93.

Efforts should be made not only to maximise production but also to do it in a sustainable manner by searching innovative ways for reducing the use of chemicals through integrated pest management, integrated nutrients management, integrated crop-livestock management, use of biomass residues and renewable energy sources. On-farm biological production and recycling of inputs should be expanded, thus lowering off-farm, mineral fertilizers and other chemicals. Intensive cultivation of land without conservation of soil fertility and soil structure will lead ultimately to the springing up of deserts.

Research is also needed for improving irrigation water management, finding more economic ways of preventing deterioration of the existing water resources, development of simple, efficient and economical waste water treatment methods, waterlogging, conservation of rainwater, etc.

Biotechnology can contribute to more sustainable use of resources by gradually raising crops yields and reducing land requirements, thereby lowering the pressure or chemical inputs per unit of production.

The key link between the producer and the consumer is marketing. But in India inefficient transportation and marketing system results in the falling of cash prices and high wastage of farm produce. High losses can be attributed to poor transport facilities such as low quality and rough surface roads, exposure to high temperature, etc. An efficient marketing system decreases the number of intermediaries, minimizes the cost of marketing, increases the share of producer, reduces the effects of seasonal gluts and geographical differences and helps to handle the farm surpluses efficiently. There is then the need to provide for better transportation facilities like refrigeration vans, good quality roads and other infrastructure for storing, dry ports for airlifting perishable items for export and simplify the export procedures.

Concluding Remarks

Public sector research organisations in India—mostly ICAR and agricultural universities—now account for the bulk of the research spending on agriculture. The creation of this network has been one of the significant achievements of the last 50 years and it has contributed significantly to increasing output. However, one cannot claim that the performance of the public research system has been satisfactory.

Several weaknesses of the present system have attracted attention. For example, the uneven progress of varietal improvement across crops and regions; the rather anaemic results of research on techniques of soil and water conservation for rainfed land and control and application of water on irrigated lands; the neglect of crop systems research; and not-so-impressive results of local adaptive research. Many organisational weaknesses have also been noted: inadequacy of collaborative multidisciplinary research; weak interaction between researchers extension workers and farmers; excessive centralisation of planning and monitoring; and the lack of accountability for performance. Organisational issues have tended to dominate the reports of the two major reviews of the research system. There has been no substantive, independent professional assessment of the scientific quality of research, and even less of its impact in terms of expanding the limits of achievable yield, increasing efficiency of use of key inputs, and farmers' reactions to the varieties and techniques (in terms of knowledge, acceptance, adoption and productivity impact).

It is therefore not enough to assert the importance of public sector research in terms of financial allocations. Serious attention should be given to improving its performance and making it more accountable to the farming community. Its efficacy in developing better, more economical techniques for managing soil and water is critical for the effective exploitation of potentials made possible by plant breeding. Recognising this complementarity, ICAR now seems to be stressing ways of ensuring fruitful collaboration with, and participation of, the private sector in its research. But it is important to guard against the business interests of corporations determining the research agenda and priorities of the public research systems. Fruitful collaboration/interaction will call for credible public regulatory authorities to safeguard the requirements of bio-safety; screening of varieties and their performance before release; and addressing and resolving many issues concerning the principles governing the relation between public and private sector in funding and sharing the results of research.

Appendix 14.1

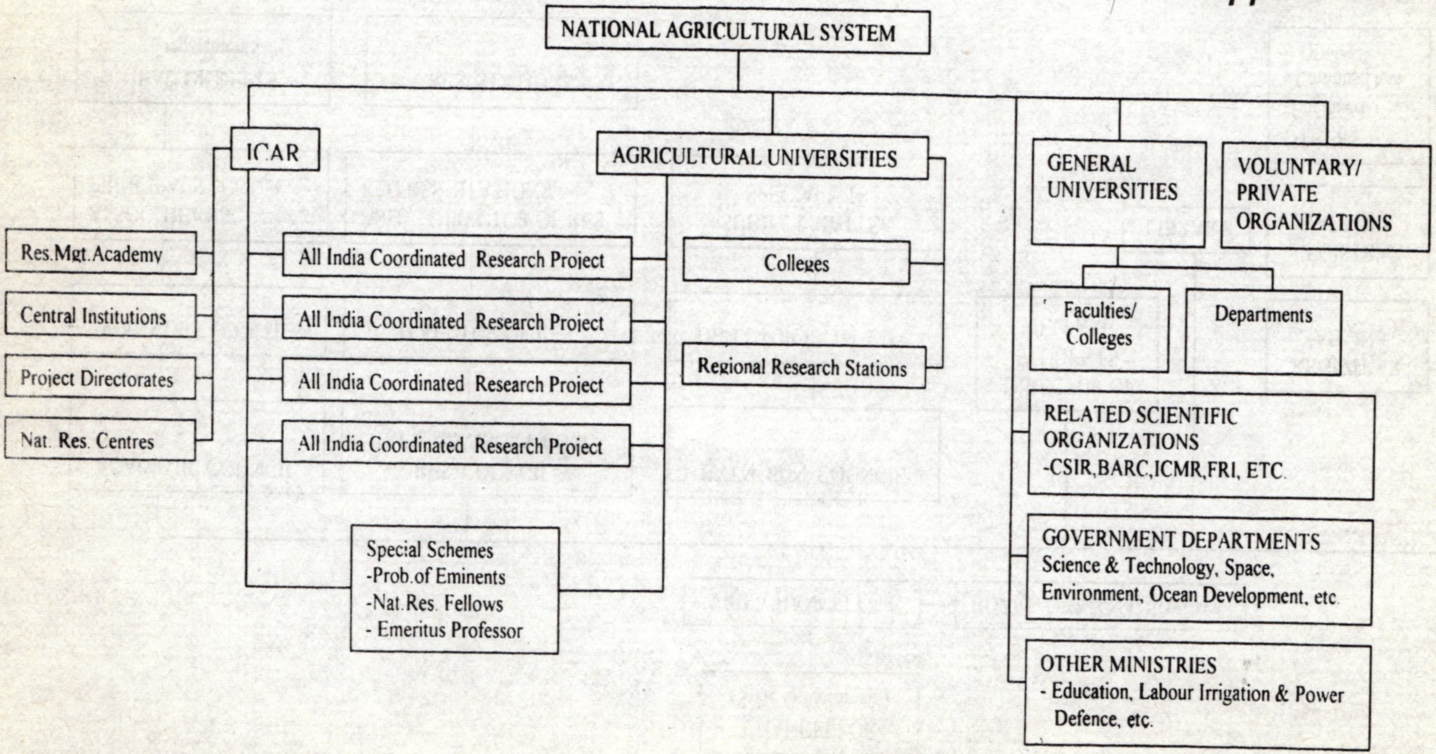

Agricultural research system in India

Appendix 14.2

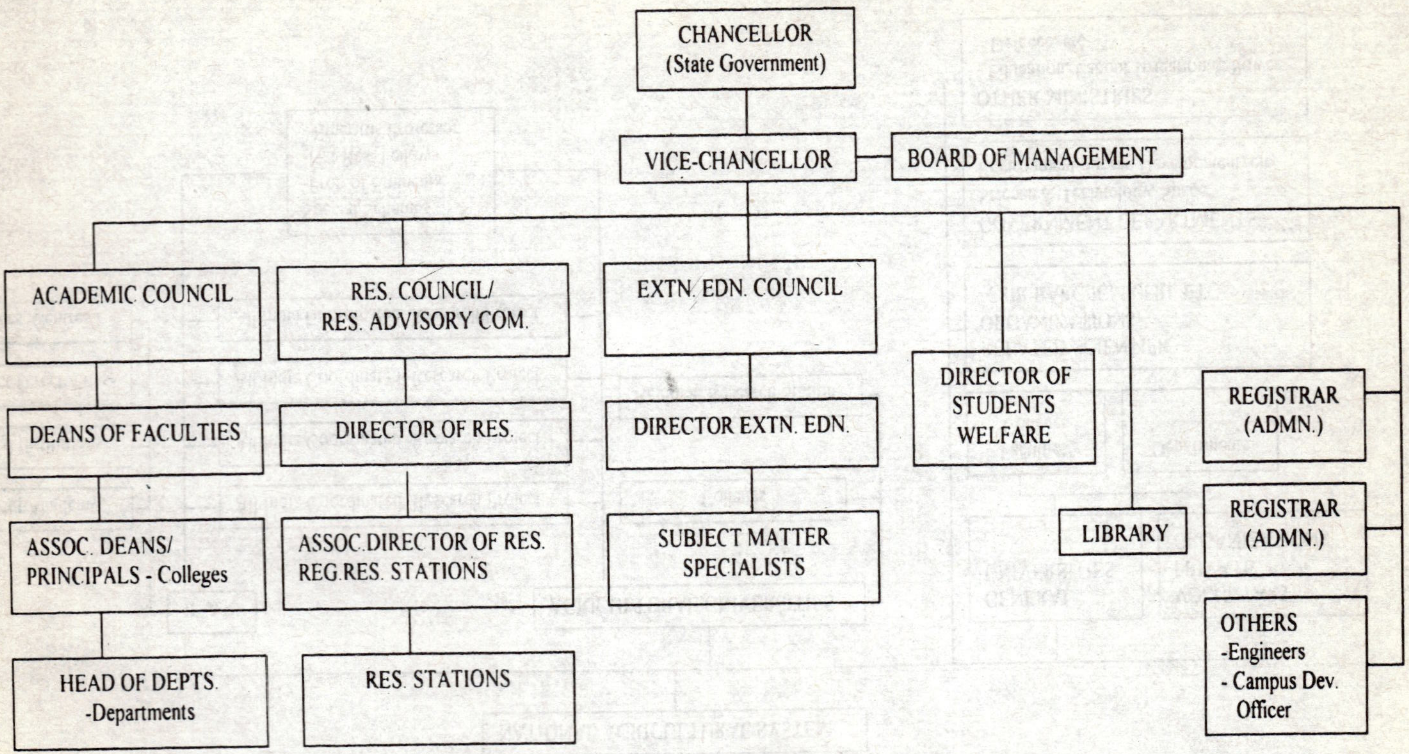

Organisational Structure of the State Agricultural Universities in India

Appendix 14.3

National Research Centres and Project Directorates

1. National Research Centre for Agroforestry
IGFRI Campus Pahuj Dam.
Gwalior-Jhansi Road
Jhansi (Uttar Pradesh) 284 003
E-mail: nrca@x400nicgw.nic.in
2. National Research Centre for Arid Horticulture
C-35, Sadulganj, Bikaner
(Rajasthan) 334 003
E-mail: nrch@x400nicgw.nic.in
3. National Research Centre for Banana
No. 4, Ramalingam Nagar,
Veluyur Road
Tiruchirapalli (Tamil Nadu) 639 103
E-mail:nrcbanana@x400nicgw.nic.in
4. National Research Centre for Cashew
Kamminje, Puttur
(Karnataka) 574 202
E-mail: nrccashew@x400nicgw.nic.in
5. National Research Centre for Citrus
Seminary Hills, Nagpur
(Maharashtra) 440 006
E-mail: nrccitrus@x400nicgw.nic.in
6. National Research Centre for Grapes
PB No. 3, Manjri Farm Post
Pune (Maharashtra) 412 307
E-mail: nrcgrapes@x400nicgw.nic.in
7. National Research Centre for Groundnut
Ivanagar Road, Timbawadi
PB 5, Junagadh (Gujarat) 362 001
E-mail: nrcg@x400nicgw.nic.in
8. National Research Centre for Integrated Pest Management
Lal Bahadur Shastri Centre for Biotechnology
IARI, Hillside Road, Pusa,
New Delhi 110 012
E-mail: nicipm@x400nicgw.nic.in
9. National Research Centre for Medicinal and Aromatic Plants
Boriavi Seed FArm, Boriavi,
Anand (Gujarat) 387 310
E-mail: nrcnap@x400nicgw.nic.in
10. National Centre for Mushroom Research and Training
Chambaghat, Solan
(Himachal Pradesh) 173 213
E-mail: nrcmrt@x400nicgw.nic.in
11. National Research Centre for Oilpalm
Ashok Nagar, Eluru
(Andhra Pradesh) 534 002
E-mail: nrcoilpalm@x400nicgw.nic.in
12. National Research Centre for Onion and Garlic
Rajguru Nagar,
Maharashtra 410 505
E-mail: nrconion@x400nicgw.nic.in
13. National Research Centre for Orchids
C/o Jt Director, ICAR Complex for NEH Region Regional Station,
Tadong, Gangtok (Sikkim(737 102)
E-mail: nrcorchids@x400nicgw.nic.in
14. National Research Centre on Plant Biotechnology
Indian Agricultural Research Institute,
New Delhi 110 012
E-mail: rps@x400nicgw.nic.in
15. National Research Centre for Rapeseed and Mustard
P B 41, Bharatpur
(Rajasthan) 321 001
E-mail: nrcseed@x400nicgw.nic.in
16. National Research Centre for Sorghum
Rajendranagar, Hyderabad
(Andhra Pradesh) 500 030
E-mail: nrcsorghum@x400nicgw.nic.in
17. National Research Centre on Soybean
Bhawerkua Farm, Khandwa Road
Indore (Madhya Pradesh) 452 001
E-mail: nrcsoya@x400nicgw.nic.in
18. National Research Centre for Water Technology
Eastern Region, Chandrasekharpur
Bhubaneshwar (Orissa) 751 016
E-mail: wtcer@x400nicgw.nic.in

19. National Research Centre for Weed Science
215, Ravindra Nagar,
C/o Department of Agronomy
JNKVV, Jabalpur
(Madhya Pradesh) 482 004
E-mail: nrcweed@x400nicgw.nic.in

Animal Sciences and Fisheries

20. High Security Animal Disease Laboratory
101, Kalpana Nagar, Bhopal
(Madhya Pradesh) 462 021
21. National Research Centre on Camel
Jobner PB 07, Bikaner
(Rajasthan) 334 001
E-mail: nrccamel@x400nicgw.nic.in
22. National Research Centre for Coldwater Fisheries
Sharv Cottage, Thandi Sarak
Nainital (Uttar Pradesh) 263 136
23. National Research Centre for Equines
Sirsa Road, Hisar (Haryana) 125 001
E-mail: nrcequines@x400nicgw.nic.in
24. National Research Centre on Meat and Meat Products
Rejendranagar, Hyderabad
(Andhra Pradesh) 500 030
E-mail: nrcmeat@x400nicgw.nic.in
25. National Research Centre on Mithun
ICAR Research Complex
Jharnapani, Distt Kohima
(Nagaland) 797 106
E-mail: nrcmithun@x400nicgw.nic.in
26. National Research Centre on Yak
West Kemeng, Dirang
(Arunachal Pradesh) 797 106
E-mail: nrcyak@x400nicgw.nic.in

General

27. National Centre for Agricultural Economics and Policy Research, IASRI Campus,
New Delhi 110 012
E-mail: ncap@x400nicgw.nic.in
28. National Research Centre for Women in Agriculture
93, Dharam Vihar, PO Khandagiri
Bhubaneshwar (Orissa) 751 001

PROJECT DIRECTORATES

Agricultural Sciences

1. Directorate of Cropping Systems Research
Modipuram, Meerut
(Uttar Pradesh) 250 110
E-mail: pdesr@x400nicgw.nic.in
2. Directorate of Oilseeds Research
Hyderabad
(Andhra Pradesh) 500 030
E-mail: pdoilseed@x400nicgw.nic.in
3. Directorate of Rice Research
Hyderabad
(Andhra Pradesh) 500 030
E-mail: pdrice@x400nicgw.nic.in
4. Project Directorate of Wheat Research
P.B. 158, Kunjpura Road, Karnal
(Haryana) 132 001
E-mail: dowr@x400nicgw.nic.in
5. Project Directorate of Biological Control
Bellary Road, P.B. 2491,
HA Farm Post,
Bangalore (Karnataka) 560 024
6. Project Directorate on Maize
Cummings Laboratory
Indian Agricultural Research Institute, New Delhi 110 012
7. Project Directorate on Soybean Processing and Utilization
CIAE Complex, T.T. Nagar,
Bhopal 462 018
8. Directorate of Water Management Research
WALMI Complex,
Phulwari Sharif PO
Patna (Bihar) 801 505
E-mail: pdwn@x400nicgw.nic.in

Animal Sciences

9. Project Directorate on Cattle
Ph-7, Pallavpuram, Phase II,
Modipuram, Meerut
(Uttar Pradesh) 250 110
E-mail: pdcattle@x400nicgw.nic.in
10. Project Directorate on Poultry
Agricultural University Campus
Hyderabad
(Andhra Pradesh) 500 030
E-mail: pdpoultry@x400nicgw.nic.in

Appendix 14.4

State Agriculture Universities

1. Andhra Pradesh Agricultural University (APAU)
   Hyderabad, AP – 500 030
   Telex: 0425-6936 APAU IN
   Phone: 040-245035
   Fax: 040-245031
2. Assam Agricultural University (AAU)
   Jorhat (Assam) 785 013
   Telex: 0287-206 AAU IN
   Phone: 0376-21100
   Fax: 0376-320919
3. Birsa Agricultural University (BAU)
   Ranchi (Bihar) 834 006.
   Phone: 0651-455510
4. Rajendhra Agricultural University (RAU)
   Pusa, Samastipur,
   Bihar 848 125
   Phone: 06274-226
   Fax: 0612-225364
5. Ch. Charan Singh Haryana Agricultural University (CCSHAU)
   Hissar , Haryana – 125 004
   Telex: 0345-216 HAU IN
   Phone: 01662-72640
   Fax: 01662-73552
6. Gujarat Agricultural University (GAU)
   Dantiwada , Gujarat-385 506.
   Phone : 027413-7171
7. Jawaharlal Nehru Krishi Vishwa Vidhayalaya (JNKVV)
   Jabalpur ,
   Madhya Pradesh 492 004.
   Telex: 0765-313 JKV IN
   Phone: 0761-343606
   Fax: 0761-343382
8. Indira Gandhi Krishi Vishwa Vidhyalaya (IGKVV)
   Raipur,
   Madhya Pradesh- 492 012.
   Telex: 775-7332 IGKV IN
   Phone: 0771-425219/425308
   Fax: 0771-424532
9. Kerala Agricultural University (KAU)
   Thrissur (Kerala) 680 654.
   Telex: 0887-268 KAU IN
   Phone: 0487-370034
   Fax: 0487-370019
   E-mail: HYPERLINK mailtokauhqr @en.nic.in kauhqr@en.nic.in
10. Konkan Krishi Vishwa Vidhalaya (KKVV)
    Dapoli, (Maharashtra) 415 712.
    Telex: 0190-3209 KKV IN
    Phone: 02358-82064
    Fax: 02358-82074

OTHERS

1. Punjab Agricultural University (PAU)
   Ludhiana, Punjab 141 004.
   Telex: 0386-473 COAE IN
   Phone: 0161-401794
   Fax: 0161-400945
2. Rajasthan Agricultural University (RAU)
   Bikaner, Rajasthan 334 001
   Telex: 0350-5205 RKVB IN
   Phone: (0151) 523977/523476
   Fax: 91-0151-522092
3. Tamil Nadu Agricultural University (TNAU)
   Coimbatore , Tamil Nadu – 641 003.
   Telex: 08558-360 TNAU IN
   Phone: 0422-431222
   Fax: 0422-431672
   E-mail: HYPERLINK mailto:S=TNAU%S=TNAU%GVC %OUI=A2530%VSNB@ MCIMAIL.COM S=TNAU%S= TNAU%G=VC%OUI=A2530% VSNB@MCIMAIL.COM
4. Tamil Nadu Veterinary and Animal Science University (TNV & ASU)
   Madras, Tamil Nadu 600 007
   Telex: 041-5049 MVC IN
   Phone: 044-581506/584954
   Fax: 044-560114/581886
5. Himachal Pradesh Krishi Vishwa Vidhalaya (HPKVV)
   Palampur,
   Himachal Pradesh – 176 062
   Phone: 01894-30521
   Fax: 01894-30511
6. Dr. Yashwant Singh Parmar University of Horticulture and Forestry (YSPUH & F),
   Solan,
   Himachal Pradesh- 173 230
   Telex: 01702-62363/2343
   Phone: 01792-852363/2359
   Fax: 01072-6-2242

7. University of Agricultural Sciences (UAS)
   Bangalore (Karnataka)-560 065.
   Telex: 0845-8393 UASK IN
   Phone: 080-3332442/3330153
   Fax: 080-3330277
8. University of Agricultural Sciences (UAS), Dharwad,
   Karnataka 580 005.
   Telex: 0865-244 AGCD IN
   Phone: 0836-347783
   Fax: 091-836-348-349
9. Mahatma Phule Krishi Vidhyapeeth (MPKV)
   Ahmednagar,
   Maharashtra 413 722
   Phone: 2046-43208/43302
10. Marathwada Agriculture Univerity (MAU)
    Parbhani, Maharashtra- 431 402
11. Dr. Panjabrao Deshmukh Krishi Vidhyapeeth (PKV)
    Akola, Maharashtra – 444 104
    Telex: 0725-215 PKV IN
    Phone: 0724-58219/58200-21 PBX
    Fax: 0724-58219
12. Orissa University of Agriculture and Technology (OUA & T)
    Bhubaneswar (Orissa) 751 003
    Telex: 0675-6446 OUAT IN
    Phone: 0674-402677
    Fax: 0674-407780
13. Chandhra Shekhar Azad University of Agriculture and Technology (CSAUA & T)
    Kanpur, Uttar Pradesh 208 002.
    Phone: 0512-294557
    Fax: 0512-210408
14. Bidhan Chandra Vishwa Vidhyalaya (BCKVV)
    Mohanpur, West Bengal - 741 252.
    Phone: 03473(O)/33275 (R)
    Fax: 03473-829772
15. Sher-e-Kashmir University of Agriculture and Technology (SKUA & T)
    Srinagar
    Jammu & Kashmir – 180 004
    Phone: 0191-30450/530450
    (O, Jammu)
    (471445 R, Srinagar)
16. Central Agricultural University
    Iroisemba, Imphal
    (Manipur) - 795 001.
    Phone: 0385-310636 (O)
    /31070 (R)
    Fax: 0385-310636
17. West Bengal University of Animal & Fishery Sciences
    68, Kshudirm Bose Sarani
    Belgachia
    Calcutta 700 037
    Phone: 033-5565021
18. National Centre of Agricultural Economics and Policy Research (NCAP)
    IASRI Campus, Library Avenue,
    New Delhi- 110 012.
    Phone: 011-5743036
19. National Academy of Agricultural Research Management (NAARM),
    Rajendhranagar, Hyderabad
    Andhra Pradesh 500 030
    Telex: 0425-6651 STAG IN
    Phone: 040-425070
    Fax: 040245912
    E-mail: HYPERLINK mailto:naarm @x400.nicgw.nic.in
    naarm@x400.nicgw.nic.in
20. West Bengal University of Animal & Fishery Sciences
    68, Kshudiram Bose Sarani
    Belgachia, Calcutta 700 037
    Phone: 033-5565021
21. Govind Ballabh Pant University of Agriculture and Technology (GBPUA & T)
    Pantnagar, Uttar Pradesh 263 145
    Telex: 0576-216 PANT IN
    Phone: 05946-33333/33500
    Fax: 05946-33473/33608
22. Narendra Dev University of Agriculture and Technology (NDUA & T)
    Farizabad, Uttar Pradesh-224 001.
    Phone: 0527-814862
    Fax: 0527-814947

Appendix 14.5

NATIONAL AGRICULTURAL TECHNOLOGY PROJECT

The National Agricultural Technology Project (NATP) is considered as a driving force for the growth of agricultural system with equity and social justice. The Project was jointly implemented by the ICAR and the Department of Agriculture and Cooperations. The progress made in three major components (Research, Innovation in Technology Dissemination and Organization and Management System in ICAR) of NATP is given here.

RESEARCH

The NATP funds are being utilized to complement existing resources and augment productivity in the National Agricultural Research System (NARS). This is being achieved by enhancing the availability of funds for research and upgrading of facilities and scientific skills.

The research programme under NATP is being executed under four different modes. viz. Production System Research (PSR), Cross-cutting Research in Mission Mode (MM), Strategic Research in a Team of Excellence Mode (ToE), and Competitive Grant Programme (CGP).

PRODUCTION SYSTEM RESEARCH

Rainfed Agro-Ecosystem Research

In all, 98 subprojects approved in 14 Scientific Advisory Panel (SAP) meetings were endorsed by Project Management Committee (PMC) at a total budget outlay of about Rs 1,000 million. In addition, some more subprojects in specified priority areas are in the pipeline for consideration and it is expected that PSR programme will eventually have about 110 subprojects, with an estimated budget outlay of Rs. 1,050 million.

The network developed for 98 projects covers 25 universities, 6 co-ordinated projects and 31 research institutes along with two traditional universities as partners. Other organizations involved include: State Ministries of Agriculture, Grain Storage and Research Institute, National Remote Sensing Agency, NGOs, Tata Energy Research Institute and Farm Science Centres (KVKs). The research work in all the subprojects is progressing well.

Irrigated Agro-Ecosystem Research

Three production systems, viz. rice-wheat, cotton-based and sugarcane-based, were identified for research support under irrigated agro-ecosystem.

Rice-wheat Production System It is the leading cropping system in 120 districts of the country, covering nearly 11 million ha area. Total

35 subprojects under PSR with a budget outlay of Rs 443-89 million were approved. It considered 20 subprojects directly related to rice-wheat production and 15 related to applied aspects such as horticulture, post-harvest processing, dairying and fisheries.

A number of biotic, abiotic and socio-economic production constraints that limit the sustainable growth of rice-wheat cropping system were identified and prioritized in terms of their impact on yield loss.

Of late, Total Factor Productivity (TFP) of important crops in Indo-gangetic region is showing disturbing trends. Data required for estimation of TFP index were collected for Haryana. West Bengal and Uttar Pradesh. And data collection for Punjab and Bihar is in progress.

Zero-tillage technology showed as advantage in raising wheat productivity and reducing cost of production and weed density. The bed planting system in whaat indicated better plant height, darker green foliage and lesser weed population than conventional method of sowing.

An international workshop for developing an action programme for farm-level impact in rice-wheat system was held during 25-27 September 2000. The recommendations and the work plan developed in this workshop provide guidelines for execution of research activities in this production system.

Cotton-wheat-based Production System Keeping in view to increase the productivity of cotton as well as wheat under cotton-wheat production system, nine subprojects with a budget outlay of Rs. 86.80 million were approved.

Of the large number of cotton varieties and hybrids screened against leaf-curl disease and whitefly under natural conditions, 165 lines were found free from and 19 varieties resistant to leaf-curl disease and 59 lines were totally free from and 10 varieties were tolerant to whitefly. Four genotypes showed resistance to leaf curl as well as tolerance to whitefly.

Azotobacter strains HT 57, E 12 and AC 18 were found useful in wheat in cotton-wheat-based production system.

Sugarcane-based Production System The principal factors for low production of sugarcane at farmers' fields are varied edaphic and climatic conditions, diversified cropping systems, planting season and input use. Hence seven research subprojects with a budget outlay of Rs. 85.12 million were approved.

The preliminary study indicated that sugarcane-based intercropping system involving Sesbania for green manure and cowpea for green pod appeared promising in controlling weeds in spring-planted sugarcane. An intercropped dual-purpose cowpea also showed scope of mid-season income generation.

A slit type-furrow opener was developed to open the furrows economically and eficiently in well-prepared field for sugarcane planting.

An information on availability of by-products available from sugarcane farms/industry and locally available feeds and fodders was generated through surveys. An average cane yield ranged from 88 to 120 tonnes/ha in Andhra Pradesh. Uttar Pradesh, Tamil Nadu and Maharashtra. The extract levels for baggase, molasses and pressmud from the cane were 33-43, 3-8 and 3-7% respectively. The yield of sugarcane top ranged from 15 to 20% of the whole cane.

Coastal Agro-Ecosystem Research

Under this agro-ecosystem, out of 74 subprojects received, 25 PSR subprojects were approved by SAP and PMC. These included 10 subprojects in horticulture and plantation crops, 6 each in field crops and fishery sciences and 2 in animal sciences. In addition, 1 subproject on Conservation of Eastern Ghats has also been approved. The subprojects are operating mainly in West Bengal, Orissa, Andhra Pradesh, Tamil Nadu, Kerala, Karnataka, Maharashtra and Gujarat. Some salient features of the progress are:

- Techniques for using pheromone traps to trap red palm weevil and rhinceros beetle are being standardized. These two pests have become very serious in Goa and Andaman and Nicobar Islands. Other than rhinoceros beetle, eriophyid mite is also becoming important. Release of baculovirus through infested beetles has shown promise in IPM strategy for rhinoceros beetle.
- Root samples of basal stem of rot-affected palm were collected and the pathogen was isolated and multiplied for further studies. Attempts are being made for genomic amplification of the pathogen.
- A technique for extraction of DNA from coconut palm tissues has been standardized for management of coconut root (wilt) disease.
- A benchmark survey at different locations in the coastal regions has been completed and locations for experimentation have been finalized for the development of integrated nutrient management and agronomic practices for rice-based cropping systems in the salt-affected coastal soils.
- A study was taken up to characterize Eastern Ghats into different zones and to suggest strengthening of the area-based research activities covering different zones of Eastern Ghats for natural resource management. On the basis of this report, a subproject on 'Improving the productivity of agri-horti in Eastern ghats Eco System' has been proposed with an outlay of Rs. 17.0 million.
- Arrangements for civil works for piggery and procurement of Yorkshire piglets have been completed. Local piggeries are also being studied for their cultural methods.
- Preliminary survey of duck farms in Kerala and Tamil Nadu is carried out. Traditional farming methods, feed habits and disease

occurring on these were identified. Local ducks are also being studied for their tolerance to the disease. Arrangements for culturing of ducks for experimentation have been completed.

- In tissue-culture programme, at Tuticorin Research Centre, CMFRI, pearl oysters mantle tissue was obtained wherein good proliferation of cell, formation of reticulate network and filling of interspace with organized matrix have taken place—an initial successful step towards the formation of pearl sac. Cell-division was prolific in the *in-vitro* culture. The excess cells were further preserved for studying revival, cell viability and total cells released. Experiments on comparison of mantle cells *in-vitro* and *in-vivo* cultures were conducted. Mantle cell was identified in both the cases and the presence of fibroblast cells was noticed under *in-vitro* culture.
- Lobster-holding facilities were selected for disease monitoring and evaluation of feeds. Methodologies for analysis of proximity composition (protein, fat, moisture, ash and minerals) of fish feed ingredient and prepared feed are being standardized.

Arid Agro-ecosystem

Fourteen research subprojects under agri-horti-pastoral production system and 11 under livestock and fish production system besides 2 subprojects of Technology Assessment and Refinement have been approved by SAP and endorsed by OMC. Two research subprojects under agri-horti-pastoral system were shifted to Mission Mode and one subproject on genetic identification of disease resistance in animals under livestock and fish production system was dropped, being a long-term study that could not be completed in the stipulated period of NATP. All the projects are showing good progresss.

Hill and Mountain Agro-ecosystem

As a prelude to the renewed research efforts under the NATP, problems and prospects of natural resource management in Indian Himalayas were analysed, research and development endeavours made in the past reviewed and vital statistics of Hill and Mountain ecosystem compiled and printed to set a baseline for monitoring and evaluation of the projects in future. This information was compiled according to prevalent major livelihood production system. The researchable issues for sustainable natural resource management to augment agricultural productivity in this ecosystem were identified and prioritized.

The research programme is being implemented as an integrated inter-disciplinary, inter-institutional and farming systems mode encompassing critical areas, such as resource inventory and documentation, watershed hydrology, land-use planning, crop production (maize, rice, wheat and vegetables), horiticulture (apple and nut fruits), livestock (pig, poultry, migratory buffaloes, goats and sheep), fishery and other small production systems of mushroom, rabbitry and bee keeping.

A total of 13 subprojects at a total cost of Rs. 133.7 million have been sanctioned. The research work is making satisfactory progress.

Technology Assessment and Refinement through Institution-Village Linkage Programme

The activities of 44 project centres are being carried out in 151 villages, covering 36.914 farmers with 1.428 technological interventions for Technology Assessment and Refinement. The main production system covered under irrigated agro-ecosystem includes rice-wheat, dairy, rice-cotton, rice-wheat-sugarcane, rice-wheat-dairy-fish based and rice-vegetable based system covering relevant thematic areas including IPM, NRM, IPNM, PHT and WM. In Rainfed agri-ecosystem, rice-based, nutrient cereal-based, oilseed-based, and rice-arable farming-livestock production system have been covered with a focus on NRM, IPM and IPNM thematic areas. The Agri-horti-livestock based coastal farming system was the major production system under Coastal agro-ecosystem, whereas Agri-horti-silvi-pastoral based production system was the major area under Arid and Hill Mountains Agro-ecosystem with a major focus on NRM, WM, IPM and IPNM.

TEAMS OF EXCELLENCE

In the main document of the NATP, 37 subprojects were identified under the Teams of Excellence (ToE) Mode. However, 26 projects were finally approved for implementation.

Out of 26 ToEs. 8 are exclusively for HRD activities. The total budget allocated under ToEs is Rs. 332.496 million. The activities under these projects are in full swing.

MISSION MODE PROGRAMMES

Crop Sciences

- The progress under Hybrid Crops includes (a) identification and release of male sterility-based hybrids (AAH 1 and PKVHy 5) in cotton for cultivation, (b) release of pearl millet hybrids (Pusa 605, Pusa 415, RHB 909 and HHB 94), (c) generation and evaluation of about 550 new hybrids of sunflower at different project centres. (d) initiation of development of early- and medium-duration hybrid resistance to wilt complex, i.e. Fusarium, Macrophomina root rot and nematodes, in castor, (e) initiation of work on Indian mustard at Ludhiana, Hissar and Bharatpur and on yellow sarson at Faizabad, (f) performance of GT 288 A, a CMS-based hybrid in pigeonpea, across different locations (100% male sterility).

- Design and synthesis of cry IF and cry 1 Ia5, genetic transformation of Indian genotype of cotton (LRK 516) and regeneration of pigeonpea *in-vitro* are significant achievements in Bt-transgenic project.
- Protease inhibitor proteins from indigenous legumes and amylase inhibitor from millets were isolated. Work on purification of these proteins is in progress.
- Phytochemicals from neem-seed kernels, Pongamia glabra and Madhuka indica were purified and evaluated for their insect-control properties.
- Under Plant biodiversity project, (a) undertaken more than 230 explorations, (b) collected more than 15,000 accessions, (c) received more than 11,000 accessions by the National Gene Bank for medium-term storage, (d) developed three softwares, (e) published nine documents, (f) prepared 10 guidelines, (g) 3 checklists prepared, (h) nine training schedules for grassroot-level workers prepared, (i) characterization of all newly collected material is in progress.
- Under Household food and nutritional security (a) life-support crop species for different regions identified, seed production work initiated, front-line demonstrations for improved production technologies arranged; (b) production and productivity of horticultural crops enhanced, quality seed and planting material supplied, location-specific technologies initiated through on-farm trials and front-line demonstrations; (c) work initiated to improve productivity of pig, poultry and sheep in tribal tracks; (d) programme to enhance freshwater fish production implemented. Ponds selected and stocked with fingerlings procured from the state fisheries department; (e) an information on food habit and other post-harvest practices adopted in tribal community of Madhya Pradesh collected and documented; (f) to understand the food security of the selected areas, required information is being collected at three levels, viz. district, village and household, on socio-economic conditions, infrastructure, resource-use pattern, agricultural productions, employment etc.

Horticulture

- Protocols for purification of citrus ringspot, citrus mosaic and potato virus Y standardized, polyclonal antibodies prepared and evaluated in ELISA and ISEM system. Viroids in citrus and potato diagnosed by R-PAGE technique.
- Significant progress made in development of hybrids in vegetable crops: (a) a large number of varieties and breeding lines of tomato screened against leaf curl virus, early blight, fusarium wilt and rot-knot nematodes etc. Crosses are also being attempted utilizing H 24 (PDVR) as one of the resistant parents:

(b) brinjal germplasm evaluated against phomopsis blight and root-knot nematode. Male-sterile (MS) lines developed for economic hybrid seed production; (c) genetic and cytoplasmic male-sterile lines of chilli from within India and foreign research institutions introduced. Genotypes screened under natural infection against anthracnose and Fusarium oxysporum; (d) available population of onion screened to identify natural male-sterile lines.

Animal Sciences

- Methods to assess microbial and antimicrobial titre, hormonal and pesticide residues, adulterants in food from livestock and poultry were standardized.
- Work on genetic characterization of endangered livestock and poultry breeds was carried out using microsatellite primers. The somatic cell isolation and primary culture methodology were standardized using samples from local slaughter houses.
- 'F' gene-based Polymerase chain reaction (PCR) was standardized.

Fisheries

- Under fish biodiversity project, survey on germplasm carried out in Western Ghats streams covering five river basins. Data and samples collected on riparian type, aquatic community and aquatic habitat parameters. For North-East India (Brahmputra and its adjoining tributaries), samples for DNA studies collected for several fish species. Work initiated on DNA sequence mation, DNA extraction and preservation.
- Under popularization of fish products, studies initiated on feasibility of using see-through retortable pouches for packing fish curry. Standardization of ready-to-serve freshwater fish (Rohu) in curry in retortable pouches being done. Physical properties of indigenous retort pouches studied.

Agricultural Engineering

- Whiteness and brightness of jute fibre improved. Effect of non-woven structure on composite development studied. A few experiments carried out with coir and jute as reinforcing material with synthetic resins.
- Under the project on 'Prototype Manufacturing of Agricultural Implements', the work to achieve the physical target, i.e. batch production (centre-wise) of prototypes initiated. Physical target (production of prototypes) for each centres fixed for the first year of the project.

- Experiments conducted on mechanized transplanting of rice and mechanization of direct dry-seeded rice and sprouted seeded rice. Observations on soil, crop and machine parameters are being taken. Work on introduction of self-propelled rice transplanter and manual transplanter as alternatre to hand transplanter to the farmers and field trials in progress.

Natural Resource Management

- Under 'Watershed Technology Project' (a) identification, selection and mapping of the watershed done; (b) collection of data pertaining to climate, topography, vegetation (land use), existing management practices and socio-economic conditions in progress; (c) survey of watershed for its characteristics in progress. (d) soil sample for physio-chemical analysis in progress; (e) Participatory rural appraisal (PRA) in Almas Waterhed (Dehra Dun) completed.
- Limited spectral signatures of the soil collected from the field and also measured in the laboratory using available coarse resolution spectro-radiometer. Spectral reflectance measurement of 34 samples in laboratory and 40) *in-situ* done. Correlation of special reflectance with soil properties also attempted with limited data.

Agricultural Extension

- Action initiated to notify for voluntary disclosure on indigenous knowledge.

Competitive Grant Programme (CGP)

Approximately Rs. 540 million for 5 years would be channelled through CGP.

The institutions interested in availing the CGP facility were invited to submit research proposals from any of the prioritized research area.

In the first round, Project Implementation Unit (PIU) received 1,495 researcg proposals under CGP in response to its first advertisement. A total of 79 projects were approved by Research Project Committee (RPC).

INNOVATIONS IN TECHNOLOGY DISSEMINATION (ITD)

This has two components, one being implemented by the Department of Agriculture and Cooperation. This report concerns only the activities under the ICAR component, which includes the following.

AGRICULTURAL TECHNOLOGY INFORMATION CENTRE (ATIC)

There are 40 Agricultural Technology Information Centres, which are being implemented by 25 State Agricultural Universities and selected

15 ICAR Research Institutes. All the centres have been sanctioned at a total budget of Rs. 171.95 million for a period of five years.

All the 40 centres have constituted Site Management Committee, consisting of Vice-Chancellor, SAU/Director, ICAR Institute and other senior officers of the University/Institute to guide direct the activities of the centre. Each centre is being managed by an ATIC manager, appointed by the Vice-Chancellor, SAU/Director, ICAR Institute, for day-to-day implementation of the activities. Besides, all the centres have already taken initiatives for completion of the formalities of floating national bidding for the construction of the building, other infrastructure and purchase of equipment. Many centres have started functioning to provide services for the benefit of the farmers.

Remandating Selected Zonal Agricultural Research Stations to Take up Functions of KVK

A total of 20 Zonal Research Stations of Phase I were remandated to take up the additional functions of KVK in February 1999. These centres became active and started taking action for the purchase of equipment and preparation of Action Plan for organizing training programmes, on-farm trials and front-line demonstrations. A launching workshop is being organized for orientation of the scientists working in all the 53 Zonal Agricultural Research Stations which will also include the centres of Phase II that have remandated to take up the additional functions of KVK during the current year.

Organization and Management Systems

Institutionalization of Research Priority Setting, Monitoring and Evaluation (PME) and Networking of Social Sciences

One of the objectives of the NATP is to initiate organization and management reforms to improve efficiency of the NARS. This project is one of the activities under reform process.

The National Centre for Agricultural Economics and Policy Research (NCAP), Indian Agricultural Statistics Research Institute (IASRI) and National Academy of Agricultural Research and Management (NAARM) are collaborating for this project with overall co-ordination by the NCAP.

NCAP Although the project was formally launched on 17 August 2000 in a workshop, a good deal of work has been done in the NCAP's component of macro-level priority setting, impact assessment and networking of social scientists.

National-level Priority-setting Exercise Preliminary results of cluster analysis of land-use data and congruence approach are now available.

Prioritization of Production Constraints A study was undertaken to identify and prioritize production constraints for the production system research. The study covered the Rainfed agro-ecosystem; rainfed rice, cotton, soybean, groundnut and sorghum-based production systems and the Irrigated agro-ecosytem: rice-wheat production system.

IASRI The IASRI has initiated the entrusted responsibility of monitoring and concurrent evaluation under PME component of NATP.

NAARM A number of programmes were initiated for implementation at the NAARM. These include the following:

(i) Institutionalization of research priority setting, monitoring and evaluation and networking of social scientists.
(ii) Human resource development (HRD) for agricultural research and education management.

Organization and Management Reforms

The progress made in different activities under the O&M Reforms component of NATP at ICAR Headquarters is:

Training, study tours and workshop: The comprehensive Training Plan was finalized and approved. A number of training programmes were held including international programmes. The training programmes on Hindi Word Processing. Procurement of Goods and Services for World Bank Loan for NATP, Globalization and Development, Management Development Programme on Computer in Accountancy, Attitudinal Transformation for Better Management, Enhancing Management Effectiveness for ICAR Officers and Finance and Accounts were held at the Electronics Trade and Technology Development Corporation Ltd. National Institute of Financial Management, National Institute of Advanced Studies, Institute of Applied Manpower Research, Management and Development Institute, Administrative Staff College of India and IMA International.

A post-training feedback form was prepared and circulated to all the participants of every training programme to obtain their valuable views which are being used to further improve the future plans for all categories and levels of staff.

Organization of Meeting and Workshop

In a workshop on ICAR-Private Sector Interface, five sectoral groups in the animal sciences, fisheries, crop science, horticulture and agricultural engineering developed an action with their Private Sector Partners.

In the first-ever annual interactive meet of the senior administrative and finance officer together with the brainstorming session, a feedback form was developed and circulated among the 80 participants. An overwhelming response was received, and the same is being analysed for organizing such interfaces in the future.

CHAPTER 15

Agricultural Education and Extension

DEVELOPMENT OF AGRICULTURAL EDUCATION DURING PRE-INDEPENDENCE PERIOD

Agricultural Sciences

Acute scarcity in food resulting serious famines in different provinces in India during second half of nineteenth century were the first to bring the focus on Agriculture for research & education. To mitigate this severe famine problem different Famine Commissions were formed. The Famine Commission, 1880, was the first to draw the attention of the Government to the need for agricultural schools for starting agricultural education. But no action was taken until 1890, when Dr. Voelcker's (Dr. Voelcker, an agricultural scientist, was invited to India in the year 1889, to advise on the steps to be taken regarding the improvements of Indian Agriculture) proposals with regard to agricultural education were examined by the representatives of the provincial Governments. The decisions taken by the provincial Governments were that:

(1) Agricultural degrees, diplomas, or certificates should be placed upon the same footing as corresponding science degrees, etc., in qualifying for admission to Government appointments and more particularly those connected with land-revenue administration.

(2) There should not be more than four institutions giving a high class diploma, viz., at Madras, Calcutta, Bombay, and some place in the North-Western Provinces, and that these should be utilised by other provinces.

(3) The diploma should eventually be compulsory in the case of certain appointments, e.g., agricultural teachers in training schools, assistance to the Director of Agriculture etc.

(4) Practical instruction of candidates for certain subordinate appointments at a school, or an experimental farm, should be further considered.
(5) A special school course leading up to the agricultural diploma, degree, or certificate, would be required.
(6) The practice of allowing school teachers, either before or after appointment, to pass through a course for a few months on a Government farm was one which would deserve consideration.

Consequently Government of India Resolution on Education Policy (1904) laid down a new policy regarding agricultural education at the collegiate level. There were only five institutions in British India which were imparting agricultural education, 219 students on roll in agricultural branches of the colleges of Pune and Shibpur (Bengal), the college of Agriculture at Saidapet (Madras) and the Agricultural Schools at Nagpur, and Kanpur. The agricultural branch of the Pune and Shibpur colleges was opened in the year 1879 and in the year 1899 respectively. It was only at Pune where the course extended over three years and L.Ag degree of Bombay University were awarded. The agricultural schools at Kanpur and Nagpur offered three types of courses, viz. (a) for training revenue subordinates, (b) for teachers and (c) for land holders.

The Resolution in reviewing the agricultural education facilities observed: "While the necessity for developing agricultural education is being recognised, India does not possess any institution capable of imparting a complete agricultural education. The existing schools and colleges have not wholly succeeded either in theory or in practice. They have neither produced scientific experts, nor succeeded in attracting members of the landholding classes to qualify themselves as practical agriculturists." It was suggested to:

(1) Create a central institute for training experts capable of studying the problems of Indian agriculture and of applying principles of Western science to bring about an improvement in the methods usually employed by Indian agriculturists;
(2) Create an agricultural college in each important province. It was further pointed out in the Resolution that research would ordinarily be more active and better sustained if it was associated with lecturing, which would check any tendency to the investigations of problems unlikely to lead to practical results; and
(3) Remove the defects of the agricultural college i.e. their failure in producing scientific experts and in attracting members of the landholding classes.

The Central Research Institute at Pusa (in Bihar) was created and named as Agricultural Research Institute (ARI) started its work in 1905. Then it was renamed as Imperial Agricultural Research Institute (IARI), which was transferred to Delhi in 1936 after the earthquake of 1934 in

Bihar. It was renamed as Indian Agricultural Research Institute after Independence. Organised instructions in agriculture in India thus began as early as the beginning of this century when five agricultural colleges were established during 1907 offering diploma courses. The first Agriculture College at Poona had, however, been opened in 1903. These institutions were later upgraded to degree level. The earliest postgraduate courses were organised towards the early twenties and it was only in 1930, when postgraduate colleges and institutes secured recognition for imparting training at M.Sc. and Ph.D levels in agriculture.

Veterinary Sciences

Organised training of veterinary personnel in India may be said to have started with the establishment of an Army Veterinary School at Pune in 1862, thus taking a lead over Agriculture Education. The first civil veterinary school was established at Babugarh (Uttar Pradesh) in 1877. The training imparted in these two schools was, however, of a low standard, more or less comparable to the present day courses for stockmen and compounders. Imperial Bacteriological Laboratory was set up at Pune and transferred to Mukteswar in 1893 and named as Indian Veterinary Research Institute (IVRI) in 1947.

The first Veterinary College to be set up in India was the Punjab Veterinary College, Lahore (now in Pakistan), in 1882. By 1903, four institutions were functioning, the three new colleges were at Bombay (1886), Belgacchia near Calcutta (1893) and Madras functioned as research institutes which over the years developed certain educational functions and continued to offer specialised postgraduate courses in veterinary sciences leading to awards of diplomas or certificates.

DEVELOPMENT OF AGRICULTURAL EDUCATION DURING POST-INDEPENDENCE PERIOD

The decade immediately after independence can be viewed as a watershed in the evolution and strengthening of a system of agricultural education and research in India. It was during this period that a number of committees, commissions, and study teams were formed which reviewed the existing agricultural situation in the country and the structure and form of the extension education.

When India attained independence in 1947, there were only 17 agricultural institutions offering degrees in Agriculture. Although higher agricultural education was costly and the resources available were rather limited, a large number of new agricultural colleges sprang up during post independence decade under the pressure of regional interests and in response to accelerated demand for agricultural graduates during this planning period. The number of agricultural colleges went up by about three times and that of veterinary colleges almost doubled. A number of affiliated private colleges sprang up without much planning and preparation. However, many of those colleges did not have adequate farm, laboratory, library, and technical manpower.

Most of the colleges referred to above were primarily concerned with the training of agricultural graduates. The State Departments of Agriculture and Community Development executed the programmes of research and extension respectively. The relationship between agricultural colleges and research departments, therefore, was not close enough to ensure maximum transfer of information in practice. The production technology developed at these educational institutions did not keep pace with the fast changing requirements of our agriculture. As a result of this it became hard to convince the State Governments for higher investments in agricultural education, and therefore, it remained deplorably low and virtually stagnant. Moreover this expansion took place along traditional pattern. It was not oriented to meet the needs of economic progress and change that was overtaking the country. It was soon realised that both the system of education as well as the setup of the institutions in the field of agriculture and animal sciences needed to be reorganised, if it was to serve as effective vehicle of agricultural progress and development.

Reorganisation of Agricultural Education and Development of Agricultural Universities

The need to bring about a rapid increase in food production in the years immediately following Independence necessitated re-examination of the existing system of agricultural education. It was soon realised that the goals of increased production could be achieved only through application of science and technology to agriculture and that trained personnel was vital for developing science-based agriculture. Accordingly, Government of India appointed in 1948-49 the University Education Commission headed by Dr. S. Radhakrishnan, our former President, which examined the entire pattern of higher education in India and made recommendations for improving it.

The recommendations for agricultural education were as under:

(1) Training of farmer's sons who will go back to their farms and work on them more efficiently.

(2) Training of persons for carrying the results of modern agricultural research to the peasant through extension work and demonstration.

(3) Training of persons for carrying on the work of research, developmental and fundamental, relating to problems of agriculture and animal husbandry.

The Commission recommended that the institutions that would take care of these three objectives would be (1) basic and post-basic schools, (2) farm institutes situated on model farms and associated with residential high schools, (3) rural universities for higher education, respectively. Acting on these recommendations different committees and teams were appointed for improving the facilities for agricultural education and research in India.

The Indo-American Team appointed by the Government of India in this regard suggested in 1955 that the Indian Council of Agricultural Education should play an increasingly important role in the development of higher education in agriculture, veterinary science and other related fields, both at the undergraduate and postgraduate levels. Having regard to the recommendations of the Team, the Government of India in consultation with the Indian Council of Agricultural Research, decided to make certain modifications in the constitution of the Council. The revised functions of the Council as announced on 8th January, 1957 were as follows:

(a) The Council will be purely an advisory body.
(b) It will coordinate agricultural education (including education in Animal Husbandry and Dairying) programmes so that a uniform standard of agricultural education may be achieved throughout the country.
(c) It will concern itself with only the broad principle of agricultural education and will advise State Governments on such problems as may be referred to it.
(d) It may prepare model syllabi for adoption in the various teaching institutions concerning agriculture, Animal husbandry and Dairying.

Second Indo-American Team on Agricultural Research and Education

As a result of the project for assistance to agricultural research, education and extension under the Technical Cooperation Programme between the Government of India and the Government of United States of America, a Joint Team consisting of five representatives of the Indian Government and three American specialists of Agricultural Research and Education was selected to make a comparative study of agricultural educational institutions. It reviewed the existing system of agricultural education and made certain recommendations. Some of these, which are of far-reaching importance are:

(1) The Team recognised the importance of the recommendation of the University Education Commission that the system of University examinations required rethinking and reorientation. Much study for agriculturally related higher education should be undertaken by the Indian Council of Agricultural Research, and suitable recommendations developed.
(2) The Team endorsed the view of the University Education Commission that a determination of a student's final standing

should be based not only upon the final examination but likewise upon the quality and character of his work in the college.

(3) In teaching institutions greatest care should be taken to ensure that the syllabus did not tend to become static, but kept pace with the advance of science and the progress of pertinent research.

(4) The Team believed that India had facilities and staff that were under-utilised in service to agricultural research and postgraduate education and recommended that the facilities of the Central Agricultural Institutes as well as those administered by agencies other than the Ministry of Food and Agriculture should be carefully considered by the Indian Council of Agricultural Research and cooriented in overall schemes for postgraduate instruction.

(5) The Team endorsed the recommendation of the University Education Commission that a Rural University would include "a ring of small resident, undergraduate colleges with specialised and University facilities in the centre."

The Team took the view that rural institutions were a half way house between the rural universities recommended by the University Education Commission and the Manjri type of vocational agricultural schools. The Team was of the opinion that each state should have a university and each district a Manjri type school.

The question of agricultural education was again examined by the Committee on Rural Education which submitted its report in 1958. They reviewed the position of all the four types of existing institutions, i.e., rural institutes, manjri type, basic agricultural schools and janata colleges. This Committee did not favour the view to combine agricultural schools and Extension Training Centres. It thus recommended that the establishment and continuance of agricultural schools should not be based on the number of gramsevaks required. The Committee was in favour of integration of the agricultural course in multipurpose Higher Secondary Schools and the Agricultural Schools. Janata Colleges, according to the Committee, had failed to fulfil their avowed purpose of providing mass adult education.

In pursuance of the recommendations of these commissions the first agricultural university was established in Pantnagar (UP) in 1960, patterned on Land Grant system of agricultural universities of USA. During that time P.G. School at IARI attained Deemed University status in 1958 and also marked the modernization of higher agricultural education in India.

Agricultural Universities Committee

With a view to providing a model legal base to Agricultural Universities, Government of India appointed an Agricultural Universities Committee in 1960. The report of the Committee submitted in 1962, provided the guidelines for developing the Model Act by the ICAR. This Model Act given out in 1966 provides in sufficient details, the legal framework for the development of an Agricultural University in India.

INSTITUTIONAL STRUCTURE OF AGRICULTURAL EDUCATION IN INDIA

Ralph W. Cummings Committee recommended the integration of teaching, research and extension in the State Agricultural Universities (SAU). This resulted in setting up of six agricultural universities during the Third Five Year Plan (1960-65). Subsequently, the Kothari Commission on Education in 1966 recommended the establishment of at least one Agricultural University in each state. Following this, the concept of SAU was fully developed and it grew rapidly with establishment of seven Universities during 1968-71, and another seven during 1972-78. At present there are 29 Agricultural Universities including one Central Agricultural University in North-Eastern region with headquarters at Imphal. The growth of SAUs/DUs/CAU from time to time is demonstrated in Fig. 15.1.

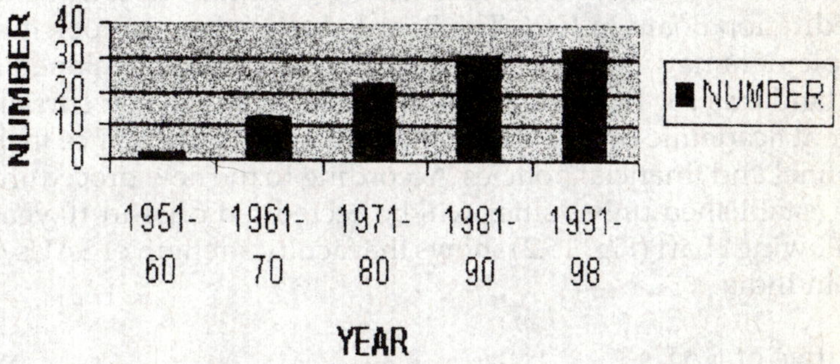

Fig. 15.1: Growth of SAUs, DUs and CAU

The general policy of having at least one SAU in each state has yet not been fully met. The States of Maharashtra and Uttar Pradesh, however, have set up 4 and 3 Universities respectively; Bihar, Karnataka, Madhya Pradesh have 2 SAUs in each state; West Bengal and Tamil Nadu also have 2 Universities each and one University for Veterinary and Dairy Sciences to meet the specific needs of different regions. Rest of the major states have at least one SAU except states like Goa, Sikkim and the states in North-Eastern region. The North-Eastern region possesses one central agriculture university.

The Indian Council of Agricultural Research (ICAR) is the apex organization for sponsoring, coordinating and promoting research, education and extension education in agriculture and allied fields in the country. In fact, in the field of agricultural education, ICAR performs a role similar to that of the University Grants Commission. Under the Council there are 46 Central Institutes, four National

Bureaux, 30 National Research Centres, 9 Project Directorates and 84 All-India Coordinated Research/Improvement Projects (AICRPs). The Council Assists 28 State Agricultural Universities (SAUs) and 1 Central Agricultural University and other leading institutions involved in agricultural education and research. During the Eighth Plan an amount of Rs. 750 million was provided for assistance to the SAUs to strengthen the infrastructural facilities.

Apart from the SAUs and the newly established Central Agricultural University, the four national institutes viz. (i) Indian Agricultural Research Institute (IARI), (ii) Indian Veterinary Research Institute (IVRI) (iii) National Dairy Research Institute (NDRI) and (iv) Central Institute of Fisheries Education offer postgraduate education in agriculture, veterinary & animal husbandry, dairy and fisheries. All these institutes have deemed university status and offer their own degrees in various disciplines. However there are 3 central universities each with a separate agricultural faculty viz. Aligarh Muslim University, Visva-Bharati, Benaras Hindu University confer degree up to PhD level in Agriculture.

For improvement and assurance of quality education in agriculture and allied sciences, ICAR under the new initiatives established the Accreditation Board in 1996. The Board, during the year took initiative to implement new process of accreditation and also developed norms and standards for higher agricultural education, coarse curricula for different academic programmes and university governance including personnel and financial policies. According to the new procedure, each of the established universities will be accredited once in 10 years.

Following chart (Fig. 15.2) shows the faculty strength of SAUs/DUs/CAU in India

Activities of SAUs

A typical Agricultural University operates on the concept of integration of teaching, research and extension functions within a large number

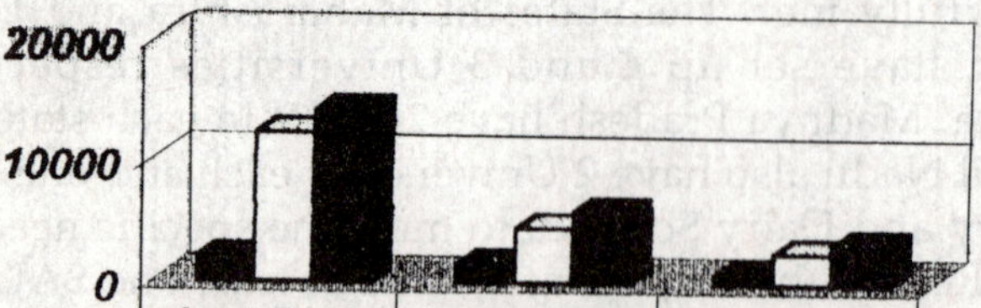

	Asst.Prof.	Assoc.Prof.	Professor
■ VACANT	1877	1413	685
□ FILLED	12217	4448	2456
■ TOTAL	14094	5861	3120

Fig. 15.2: Faculty strength and SAUs, DUS, and CAU in 1995-1996.

of specialized disciplines and departments. These are organizationally structured into five constituent colleges of Agriculture, Veterinary Science, Basic Science and Humanities, Agricultural Engineering and Home Science and the Directorate of Research and Extension Education. The research system at an Agricultural University operates in such a manner that it encourages projects to be formulated to solve current and emerging farm problems and test investigative findings through a systematic replicative process on experimental farms, laboratories and farmer's field.

The reform in agricultural education introduced in agricultural universities, besides improving in quality, has brought down to a large extent the wastage in higher education in agriculture. This not only saves costs but provides training opportunities for more students. These institutions today are serving as fountainheads of new knowledge earned through purposeful, problem-solving research and have become main centres of dissemination of useful knowledge to the farming community. Some of the best training for farmers is offered by the agricultural universities. A large number of functional specialists who have confidence born out of personal experience in successfully applying scientific knowledge to the solution of practical problems as well as those who have the competence to earn new knowledge that helps to enrich educational programmes are coming out of our agricultural universities.

With the good working conditions and incentives that they offer both to the faculty and the students, agricultural universities provide opportunities for productive and prestigious work, and foster unprecedented team spirit and healthy change in the outlook of all the teachers, the researchers, the farmers and the administration. They are winning the confidence of both the farmers and the Governments. They have already assumed leadership in sciences, education and extension in a number of cases and are producing future leaders for Indian agriculture. Their direct contribution to programmes like pedigree and production, fertiliser-use and National Crop Demonstration is highly impressive. Above all, they are aware that there is no substitute for quality, and competence and for this they are striving ceaselessly. In this connection the inter-institutional collaboration needs special mention.

Extension education activities of the agricultural universities are planned according to the zonal requirements and implemented by various transfer-of-technology projects. The activities are mainly divided into 3 categories, viz. (i) farm advisory services, (ii) farm training and (iii) farm information and communication. Besides implementing the ICAR's transfer of technology projects, the agricultural universities organise demonstrations, training programmes, farmers' fairs, national agricultural extension project, refresher courses, field-days, group discussions and campaigns and participate in many mass-media programmes including radio talks, TV programmes and publications of relevant technologies in regional languages.

Presently the project named as NATP (National Agricultural Technology Project, a project of Rs. 1000 crores, funded by the World Bank) is being implemented by ICAR and Department of Agriculture and Cooperation, which emphasizes on technology dissemination and improving the linkages between Research Extension and Client group.

Extension Education

As for as extension education, training and communication of information responsibilities are concerned, each university has established a Directorate of Extension Education with three functional units, such as, a communication centre, a farm advisory service comprising a team of extension subject matter specialists at district/regional/state levels and an extension training unit in addition to the academic department of extension education. Main activities of the Directorate of Extension Education at a University include:

(i) Organisation of farmers field days and farmers fairs on the university campus and regional research stations.
(ii) Offering diagnostic and other advisory service to farmers on demand.
(iii) Participation in training meetings at the state and district levels.
(iv) Arranging whole village demonstrations.
(v) Conducting adaptive research trials, crop outlook surveys and other field investigations.
(vi) Taking part in talks and discussions arranged by the state network of radio and television stations.
(vii) Publishing agriculture related magazines and bulletins.
(viii) Arranging in-service refresher courses for extension personnel and farmers on and off the campus.
(ix) Carrying out lab to land, operational research, national demonstration plots and such other extension projects sponsored by the ICAR.

Agricultural extension work responsibilities vest with the state departments of agriculture, horticulture, animal husbandry etc. They provide staff, resources and other facilities for planning and implementing extension programmes at various area levels such as the village or cluster of villages, a development block, subdivision, district, region and the state.

Revamping Extension Education

Four departments of the Haryana Government, i.e. Department of Agriculture, Command Area Development Authority, Department of Animal Husbandry and Rural Development, and Chaudhary Charan

Singh Haryana Agricultural University (CCSHAU), Hissar, have introduced and imbibed the concept of social marketing. This action was as a result of quick follow-up on the two-day workshop on "Revamping of Extension Education — Scope of Social Marketing Approach", which laid stress on conducting baseline survey effectively and pointed out that the ideas of the people, especially the target group, should be given greatest weightage and each project should be given a proper name and a logo as these would help in making them popular and enhance their acceptability.

The Directorate of Extension had already established a Social Marketing Cell at the campus. The varsity plans to depute a social marketing expert at each Krishi Vigyan Kendra besides publishing a resource book on social marketing. The Directorate of Extension Education also proposes to train in-service staff in the areas of agriculture, animal husbandry, social welfare and other developmental departments by making budgetary allocations from the next financial year. In its 10th Five Year Plan, the university submitted a proposal to start postgraduate diploma in social marketing at its Department of Home Science Extension. The Departments of Extension Education, Home Science Extension and Veterinary and Animal Husbandry Extension are revising the curriculum to include topics on social marketing.

Four technologies have been identified for Social Marketing. These include wheat sowing in zero tillage, furrow irrigated raised bed planting of wheat, laser assisted precision land levelling and leaf colour chart for use of fertiliser. Nilokheri and Nissing blocks had been identified as experimental blocks whereas those of Indri and Gharaunda were the control blocks. The leaders of the community like sarpanches, panchayat members, progressive farmers and educated young farmers would be responsible for the success of the campaign besides opinion makers like scientists and extension workers. In case of progressive and big farmers, the methods of communication could be scientists or extension workers, radio and television, vernacular media and pamphlets. Similarly, in case of small and marginal farmers, demonstration and field visits could be arranged besides seeking the assistance of service providers, radio, bhajan mandlis of Public Relations Department and progressive farmers. The message conveyed to the target farmers through folk songs sung by bhajan mandlis of Public Relations Department were very effective.

A campaign for Reclamation of Waterlogged Areas through Bio-Drainage, was necessary as out of 19 districts of the State, saline ground water was found in 12 districts and of these water table had been rising in Rohtak, Jind, Hissar, Bhiwani, Jhajjar, Fatehabad and Sirsa. As for, animal husbandry, there had been a tremendous increase in livestock and four fold increase in production of milk since the creation of Haryana in 1966, but no effective vaccine for foot and mouth diseases had been evolved. A survey conducted by the Department had revealed the need for cold chain up to the farmer and wholehearted approach for the implementation of various projects. Also, there had neither been any involvement of women farmers nor any linkage with other agencies like local bodies, panchayats, farmer cooperatives and Block Development and Panchayat Officers.

Affiliated Colleges of Agriculture and Veterinary Sciences

Although agricultural universities have been established in the states, about one-third of the agriculture and veterinary colleges still remain outside this orbit and are affiliated to traditional universities. They account for about 40 per cent of the total output of agricultural graduates. The ICAR, therefore, continues to give assistance for the development of such of these colleges which have the necessary potential for development. As in the case of agricultural universities, assistance was formerly given as per the UGC pattern. According to the revised pattern of assistance recently adopted by the ICAR, affiliated colleges will also receive assistance on 100 per cent basis on 11 selected items of development with an overall ceiling for the Plan period as well as for each item. With a view to bringing about uniformity, introduction of the three-year degree course (as well as four year degree course in some colleges) after 12 years of schooling has received special attention in the case of states' universities where it had not been adopted so far. It is intended to extend, through ICAR assistance, the concept of integration of teaching, research and extension to these colleges also. At present there are 48 colleges which are imparting agricultural education under general universities. Moreover, national institutes like IIT-Kharagpur also provide higher education in agriculture.

Agricultural Education at the School Level

At the school level in the existing system of education, agriculture forms part of the curriculum of studies in most general schools. It is one of the crafts studied in basic schools. It is an optional subject of study for matriculation in ordinary high schools and is one of the systems in four hundred out of the two thousand and odd multipurpose high schools in the country. Agriculture is taught as a vocation in a variety of special schools such as agricultural schools, Manjiri Schools or Rural Institutes and Gram Sevak Training Centres which have been established since 1952 with the implementation of Community Development Programme. Agricultural education up to the technician certificate or diploma level is imparted in the former institutions while the Gram Sevak Training Centres offer a two year integrated course for village level workers in agriculture and extension. The large number of schools and the variety of educational programmes have not assured the country a standard of agricultural education at the primary and secondary levels adequate to meet the needs of development. A reform of the school system of education is necessary along the lines indicated by the Education Commission, 1964-66, on the role of agriculture in general education.

The Commission recommended that in India some orientation in agriculture should form part of the general education at the school stage and at the university as well as at the teacher's training courses. In its view the period at school should be utilized to impart a sound general education with particular emphasis on mathematics and science to serve as a preparation for coping with the rapid scientific and technological changes that may be anticipated in Indian agriculture in the near future. The Education Commission further recommended the establishment of specialized institutions which would provide vocational education in agriculture at the post-matriculation level. These institutions, to be called Agricultural Polytechnics, would be responsible for training the nonprofessional specialists required as farm-mechanics, farm managers, craftsmen and technicians in agro-industries, assistants in agricultural credit and insurance organisations. The Commission suggested that the courses at these polytechnics should be practical in nature including a significant element of experience. They should be terminal in character and lead to specific and immediate employment. The training of village level workers is carried out in Gram Sevak Training Centres spread throughout the country. To increase the technical competence of the present village level worker following steps may be considered as very useful:

(i) Encouraging village level workers, who are eligible for admission to agricultural colleges, to study for their degrees.
(ii) Instituting an advanced Diploma Course of a year in agriculture for old village level workers and upgrading all the Gram Sevak Training Centres.
(iii) Increasing the number of refresher training programmes at all the centres so that all village level workers are able to attend them.

With a view to imparting practical and skill-oriented training to farmers' sons, village unemployed youths, school dropouts, etc., Krishi Vigyan Kendras (Farm Science Centres) have been established by ICAR in different parts of the country. One such centre started functioning in Pondicherry in March 1974. Six specialized Trainer's Training Centres were established during the Fifth Plan period in addition to the National Staff College.

DEVELOPMENT AND PRESENT SCENARIO OF OTHER SUBJECTS IN AGRICULTURAL EDUCATION

Dairy Education

The establishment of Imperial Institute of Animal Husbandry and Dairying in 1925 at Bangalore (later known as the Indian Dairy

Research Institute) was the first landmark in the history of Dairy Education in India. The first course in dairy farming was started in 1924. Later the Indian Dairy Diploma (IDD) course of two years' duration was started. In 1945, the Associateship course was initiated. The Institute has also been admitting honorary research workers who could earn M.Sc. and Ph.D. degrees of affiliated Indian universities. In 1955, the headquarters of the Indian Dairy Research Institute was shifted in Karnal in Punjab (now Haryana) and renamed as National Dairy Research Institute (NDRI). The Dairy Science College was organized as part of NDRI in 1957. The degree course in dairying was first introduced in that year itself under the auspices of the Punjab University. Now this has attained Deemed University status. This was a four year degree course. This course was later divided into two branches, viz., B.Sc. (Dairy Husbandry) and B.Sc. (Dairy Technology) in 1961. This was also the year for starting M.Sc. Dairy course. From the same year the IDD training was bifurcated into Indian Dairy Diploma (Dairy Husbandry and Dairy Technology). The education and research functions of the eight divisions of this Institute are fully integrated although the institute has a separate Division of Dairy Education and Training largely with coordinating functions. During the Fourth Plan period dairy education at NDRI was further strengthened adding three more divisions, viz., (i) Dairy Cattle Nutrition and Physiology, (ii) Dairy Cattle Genetics and Breeding, and (iii) Nutrition and Dietetics. The Institute continues to remain the strongest single centre of education and has provided most of the trained manpower available in this field in the country.

The Dairy Science College at Anand, started in the year 1961-62, is the only other Dairy Science College in the country. The college prepares students for IDD course and B.Sc. (Dairy Science) degree of the Ballabh Vidyapeeth, Anand. At present IDD course is offered at five centres including NDRI and Anand. Apart from these colleges D.Tech. and B.D.Sc and PG courses in Dairy science are offered in many of the SAUs in India.

Fisheries Education

Until the fifties, fisheries departments required graduates in zoology or biology. Some of them organised in-service training courses and also started polytechnics to award diploma courses in fishery technology and navigation. The Central Government also started the Inland Fisheries Training Course at Barrackpore and Marine Fisheries Training Courses at Mandapam in Tamil Nadu. By and large these ad hoc arrangements proved to be unsuccessful and had to be wound up. It was only in 1958 that the Government of India decided to take steps to organise fisheries education on a more permanent basis. The Central Institute of Fisheries Education at Bombay was set up in 1961 and the Central Institute of Fisheries Operatives, at Cochin in 1963. In the same year a postgraduate diploma course in Fish Processing and Technology was started at Mangalore by the Government of Mysore with Japanese collaboration. Some of the universities have since introduced Fish and Fisheries as a special subject in the M.Sc. course. Others have started fullfledged M.Sc. courses in Marine Biology and Oceanography. In 1969 the Calicut University started a B.Tech. Fisheries course and in the same year the University of Agricultural Sciences has started a fullfledged Fisheries College at Mangalore.

The Central Institute of Inland and Marine Fisheries training referred to above offers a number of Diploma and Certificate courses of duration varying from 6 to 15 months. Short courses of about one month duration in Fish and Technology are offered by the Central Food and Technological Research Institute, Mysore, as well as under the Indo-Norwegian Project. Though numerous number of Fisheries institutes have began Fishery study but there is no doubt that fisheries education needs to be strengthened considerably to meet the increasing demands for trained manpower in this field.

Agricultural Engineering Education

The Allahabad Agricultural Institute of the University of Allahabad was the first institution in India to offer the courses leading to the Bachelor's degree in Agricultural Engineering in 1942. The Indian Institute of Technology, Kharagpur, started a similar degree programme in 1952. Six more constituent colleges of agricultural universities—U.P. Agricultural University (Pantnagar), University of Udaipur (Udaipur, 1964), Punjab Agricultural University (Ludhiana, 1965), OUA & T (Bhubaneswar, 1966), JNKVV(Jabalpur,1967) and MPKV (Pune, 1969) also started an agricultural engineering college each. First central institute was set up in Bhopal, MP in 1976 (Central Institute of Agricultural Engineering). Presently, there are 21 agricultural universities and engineering colleges offering courses in agriculture engineering. Of these, 14 offer Masters and 5 Ph.D degrees. The country has capacity to train 800 graduates, 250 postgraduates and 75 Ph.D in agricultural engineering.

Home Science Education

Home Science education is not new and a large number of traditional universities have been offering education in Home Science for quite some time. However, in response to the need for orientation of Home Science education towards agriculture, three of the Agricultural Universities have organised constituent Home Science colleges after 1965 like Andhra Pradesh Agricultural University. Atleast five more agricultural universities have developed plans to start Home Science colleges in the near future. These colleges are organised around four main disciplines-Food and Nutrition, Child Care and Development,

Home Management and Clothing and Textiles. One of the main hurdles coming in the way of the development and growth of Home Science education for farm women is the paucity of trained personnel.

DIVERSIFICATION AND SPECIALISATION IN HIGHER AGRICULTURAL EDUCATION

With the advancement of science and technology and the need for greater degree of specialisation to tackle the new and complex problems that are coming up in the field of agriculture, there has been considerable diversification and specialisation in higher agricultural education in India. The subject of Agronomy which was organised only in late forties, as a distinct subject of Agriculture, has since developed into further fields of specialisation such as Crop Husbandry, Soil & Water Conservation, Weed Science. Another main discipline in Agricultural Science is Soil Science which further offers specialization in Physics, Soil Chemistry, Agril. Chemicals and Environment Sciences in different Agricultural Universities and Institutes. Likewise, the subject of Agricultural Botany has since grown into distinct fields like Genetics, Plant Breeding, Plant Physiology, Seed Technology and Biotechnology. Horticulture has developed further into Pomology, Olericulture, Floriculture and Fruit Preservation.

Apart from this, Social Science subjects like Agril. Economics and Agril. Extension and Plant Protection and subjects like Plant Pathology and Entomology are also the field of specialization in Agricultural education. A number of new subjects like Genetic Engineering, Food Technology, Human Nutrition, Business Management, Agricultural Credit and Nematology have come up in recent years. In the field of Veterinary and Animal Husbandry, new subjects like Poultry Science, Public Health, Animal Products Technology and Biochemistry have been added. With a view to reducing India's dependence on foreign training, the programme for the establishment of "Centres of Excellence" in selected but specialised areas has been taken up lately. Thus there has been considerable spurt in the diversification and specialisation of agricultural education in recent years. At present there are 11 subjects and 55 disciplines for specialization at the UG and PG level in agricultural education. Intake capacity of SAUs/DUs/CAU is given in Fig. 15.3.

Training for Farmers and Extension Workers

Training is an important and integral pat of extension. To provide training in Extension Management, Agricultural Technology and Extension Methodology, training institutions like National Institute for Management of Agricultural Extension (MANAGE), Advanced Centre of Training and Extension Education Institute have been established. Regular training courses are organized in these institutes,

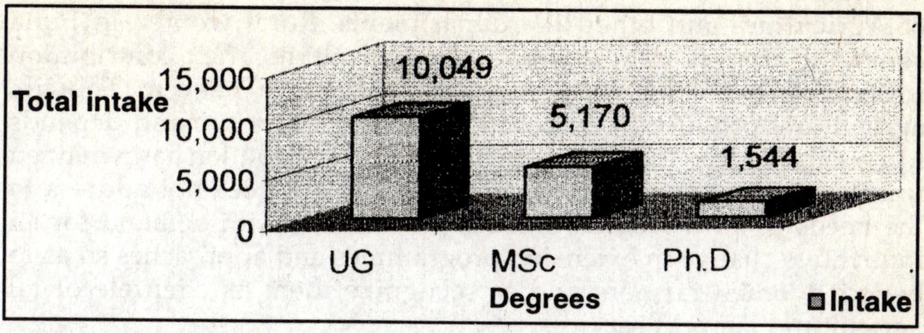

Fig. 15.3: Intake capacity of different degree courses in SAUs, DUs and CAU in 1995-96.

as well as in other research institutions for various level of extension personnel.

National Institute of Agricultural Extension Management (MANAGE)

The National Institute of Agricultural Extension Management (MANAGE) was established at Hyderabad to cater to the training needs of senior level extension managers on regional basis to provide training in communication technology and extension methodology to middle level extension functionaries working under States/UTs. Up to January, 2001, MANAGE organized 130 training programmes on management development under its banner, sponsored international consultancy cum training and western learning.

Centres of Excellence for Training (CETs)

Fifteen Centres of Excellence for Training (CETs) have been established to upgrade the competence of the subject Matter Specialists (SMSs) at Selected State Agricultural Universities, ICAR/ Central Institutes covering the subject matter areas of Rice, Sorghum, Plant Protection, Dryland Agriculture, Water Technology, Plantation Crops, Temperate Horticulture, Soyabean, Oilseeds, Kharif and Rabi Pulses. Another one centre of Excellence for training in vegetable production technology at Indian Institute of Vegetable Research, Varanasi, Uttar Pradesh is being shortly established.

Extension Education Institutes (EEIs)

To cater to the training needs of middle level extension functionaries in the areas of extension and communication, four Extension Education Institutes have been assigned the task of training at the regional level in the country. Ministry of Agriculture, Government of India has been making continuous efforts for creating professionally trained and competent cadre of extension personnel working in state Department of Agriculture and other like departments. Rural women in India constitute an important workforce in Agriculture. Their contribution in Agriculture is roughly estimated to be around 50 per cent. Though, agricultural production is basically a family enterprise and depends to a great extent on the farm women yet their contribution has remained unrecognized. As the present extension system does not address to the needs of farm women, there is a substitute with demand for an innovative change in extension programmes and approaches so as to benefit women farmers and to recognize them as clientele of all agricultural support services.

To bridge this gap and to provide training and extension support to farm women special sub projects with external assistance have been taken in six states of the country. Also, a Central Sector Scheme of Women in Agriculture is being implemented in one district each of 15 states of the country during ninth five year plan. Efforts to bring women farmers into the process of technology transfer have also been made through Farmers Training Centres (FTCs), Krishi Vigyan Kendras (KVKs); special sub projects and NationalAgricultural Extension Project.

With a view to imparting practical and skill-oriented training to farmers, women, unemployed village youth, school dropouts, etc. Krishi Vigyan Kendras (Farm Science Centres) have been established by ICAR in different parts of the country. Presently total 261 Numbers of KVKs are functioning throughout the country (1998-99). There are also eight Trainers' Training Centres to provide scientific backup support to KVK staff, Each year 2500-3000 farmers, farm women, rural youth and school dropouts are trained at every KVK in different courses. The courses are broadly categorized in crop production, horticulture, animal sciences, plant protection, home sciences and others which include agriculture extension, agricultural engineering, fodder production, soil sciences etc.

ICAR and Coordination of Agricultural Education

ICAR was established in the year 1929 in pursuance of the recommendation of the Royal Commission on Agriculture (1926). The main functions of the ICAR, inter alia, are to coordinate, aid and promote agricultural research and education and to serve as a clearing house of information relating to these functions. Although the statutory authority for coordination, accreditation, etc., of higher education rests with the University Grants Commission (UGC) in practice the coordinating functions in the field of technical, medical and agricultural education have been entrusted to the Central Ministry concerned. Accordingly, ICAR under the aegis of the Ministry of Agriculture, performs for all practical purposes, the same role in relation to agricultural education as the UGC does in the case of Basic Sciences and Humanities. The Council is responsible for coordination and promotion of higher agricultural education in the country. It provides incentives and leadership for the development of new and need-based agricultural education programmes, introduction of educational reforms, and institutionalisation of educational innovations. One of the important functions of the Council is to achieve uniformity of standards of agricultural education between institutions. The ultimate goal is to provide well trained manpower needed to give a sound, scientific and technological base to India's agriculture with a view to accelerating agricultural development and social transformation. The main emphasis in the programme of agricultural education is, therefore, on achieving 'excellence' and 'relevance'. For this, the Council gives assistance to agricultural universities and colleges for their development programmes, such as construction of the laboratories, hostels and purchase of books and equipment. It also provides technical guidance in the development of curricular materials, revision of syllabi and production of books. Organisation of Summer Institutes and in-service training programmes, award of scholarship and fellowships to the students, organisation of workshops, seminars and symposia and development of inter-institutional training programmes also fall under the purview of the activities of the Council. Provision of foreign training of faculty members and acquiring the services of foreign experts are some of its other important activities.

As mentioned earlier, the early post-Independence era witnessed rapid growth of higher education in agriculture and it became necessary for the Indian Council of Agricultural Research, in its capacity as national coordinating agency for agricultural education, to play an increasingly important role in the maintenance and improvement of standards of agricultural education. Accordingly, the Indian Council of Agricultural Research set up under its aegis, the Indian Council of Agricultural Education in the year 1951. The main functions of ICAE were: (a) to coordinate agricultural education programmes (including education in animal husbandry and dairying) so that uniform standards might be achieved throughout the country, (b) to prepare modern syllabi for adoption by various colleges, and (c) to advise the State Governments on problems of agricultural education and develop a consensus with regard to reforms that need to be introduced in agricultural education. The first meeting of the ICAE held at Hyderabad set up a Standing Committee with Dr. B.P. Pal as Chairman to ensure the follow up action and continuity of work between the Council meetings. Later, as per recommendations of the first Joint Indo-American Team, the composition and functions of the ICAE were further modified in the year 1957. *Inter alia* a whole-time Chief of Agricultural Education to serve as an ex-officio Secretary to the ICAE was appointed. A quarterly journal of the ICAE was also published from 1958 to 1964. With the reorganisation of ICAR in 1966, in pursuance of the recommendations of the Agricultural Research

Review Team (1963) and the formation of the Division of Agricultural Education in the ICAR, the ICAE has been replaced by the Standing Committee on Agricultural Education. This Standing Committee is assisted by the two Scientific Panels on Agricultural Education and Animal Sciences Education. According to the recommendations of the Education Commission (1964-66) it is envisaged that the ICAR will eventually have within it a body on the pattern of the UGC to advise on the development of Agricultural Education.

Financial Support for Agricultural Education

Until the later part of the Third Plan, Agricultural Education received little financial assistance from either the UGC or the Ministry of Agriculture. It was only towards the mid-sixties that a definite provision was made for giving financial assistance to agricultural universities and colleges on an ad hoc basis. After the reorganisation of ICAR and the establishment of Agricultural Education Division in the year 1966, concerted efforts have been made to develop agricultural education systematically and for this purpose financial assistance has been provided in a planned manner.

The funds advanced to the ICAR from the budget for agriculture and allied sectors have been 3.9% in the 4th Plan, 3.2% in 5th Plan, 6% in 6th Plan, 4% in 7th Plan and 5.8% in 8th Plan. The funds given were Rs. 914, 1536, 3400, 4250 and 13,000 million from 4th to 8th Plan respectively. Among the Rs. 13,000 million fund received by ICAR, Rs. 1554 million was spent on education which is 12% of ICAR spending.

Current levels of finance for Agricultural Research and Education have reached approximately 0.49% of Agricultural GDP. Although in the financial year 1993-94, around Rs. 526 crores were spent on SAUs but ICAR's contribution to Agricultural education at the SAUs was halved between the sixth and eighth plan. (All data are on 1970-71 prices).

In the year 1997-98 total GDP at factor cost of agriculture is Rs. 3595860 million (25.5% of total GDP) at current prices among which only Rs. 5745.2 million is allocated for agricultural research and education (0.2% of the total GDP of agriculture). ICAR allocation of funds in different sectors during 8th plan is furnished in Fig. 15.4.

Policy in the Plans

In the field of agricultural education, stress during the Plans has been on training farm graduates who can return to a career in farming. Krishi Vigyan Kendras have been developed to spread the latest technical skills to farmers and fishermen through the process of learning by doing. In addition to formal and non-formal education through Agricultural Universities and Krishi Vigyan Kendras, training programmes for developing cadres of self-employed soil-health care, plant-health care and animal-health care workers are also arranged.

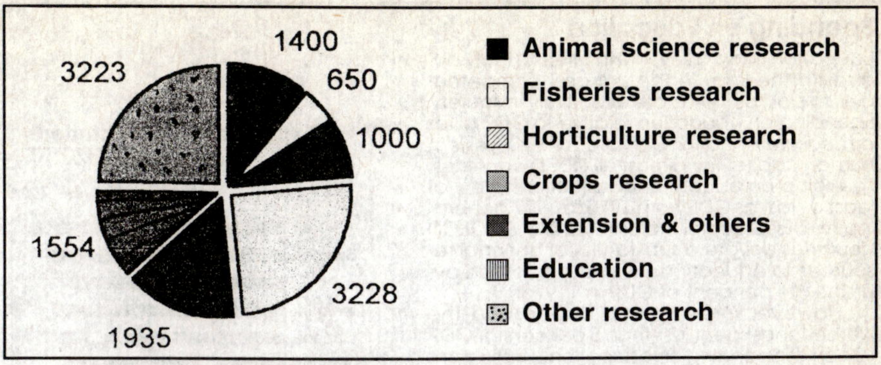

Fig. 15.4: ICAR allocation funds in different sector (Rs. in million).

The major training strategy in such programmes is to combine certain universal principles of soil health, animal and plant health, etc., with the unique practical problems faced by the farmers in the particular village where the trainee comes from. Extension Education programme is strengthened by enlarging the National Demonstrations Programme so as to include both systems and factor demonstrations. Mixed farming, freshwater aquaculture and mariculture demonstrations are the new feature of the programme.

International collaboration in research will be strengthened in an appropriate manner within the context of technological self-reliance. Technical cooperation among developing countries in agricultural research is being fostered. Linkages between research and development agencies will be strengthened through appropriate institutional devices. Manpower training programme is being accorded the highest priority. Wherever training facilities are not available, steps are taken to set up appropriate institutions. Research and training on specific problems of the northeastern Himalayan region, other hill and tribal areas will receive special attention.

A Glimpse on Present Educational Improvement Policy of ICAR

ICAR had taken different steps to improve and modernize Agricultural Education in India as well as to develop the human resources since its inception. Recently ICAR has taken several steps to improve the standard and infrastructural facilities to maintain the quality of agricultural personnel with the international level. The main steps already taken are as follows :

Norms and Standards for Improving Education

- Uniform academic regulations, examination and evaluation system in all SAUs adopted. Grading made uniform on 10 point scale GPA.

Spending on Education

Education plays a key role in offering individuals with the knowledge skill and competencies to participate more effectively in society. Spending on education relative to GDP gives a measure of how much a country invests in human capital. For almost all OECD countries, spending on educational institutions grew at least as fast as GDP from 1970 to 1977 according to OECD Social Indicators 2000. All OECD countries devote a substantial of national resources to educational institutions, on an average 6.1 per cent of GDP in 1997.

However, Greece, Italy, Japan and the Netherlands spent less than 5 per cent of GDP (Chart II). Spending on educational institutions is largely publicly financed and on an average amounts to 14 per cent of total government spending across the OECD. The proportion of education spending in all public spending has been growing everywhere except in Finland, Japan and Italy.

Levels of education spending differ across countries. These depend on the population of children, the number of years of compulsory education, class sizes, and differences in spending levels per student across different levels of education. Indeed, countries have adopted different policies regarding the distribution of resources among students at different education levels, though in all countries expenditure per student rise sharply with the level of education.

On an average, OECD countries spend $769 per student at the primary level, $5507 at the secondary level, and $10893 at the tertiary level of education. These averages mask considerable differences in expenditure per student across OECD countries. In 1997, spending per primary school student varied from $935 in Mexico to $6596 in Denmark, while per student at tertiary level spending varied from less than $3000 in Turkey to more than $17000 in the U.S. (Chart I). Obviously, overall spending will rise faster with growing number of university students than when a similar increase in primary school children occurs.

Chart II **Expenditure on Institutions**

(Per cent of GDP, 1997)

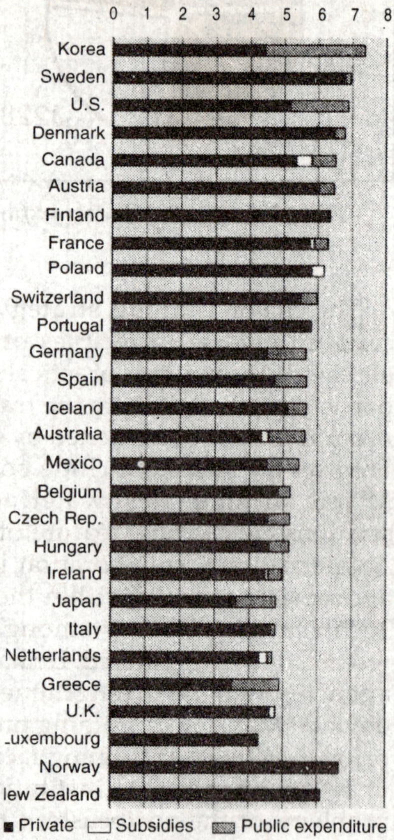

Chart I **Expenditure Per Student ($ PPPs) 1997**

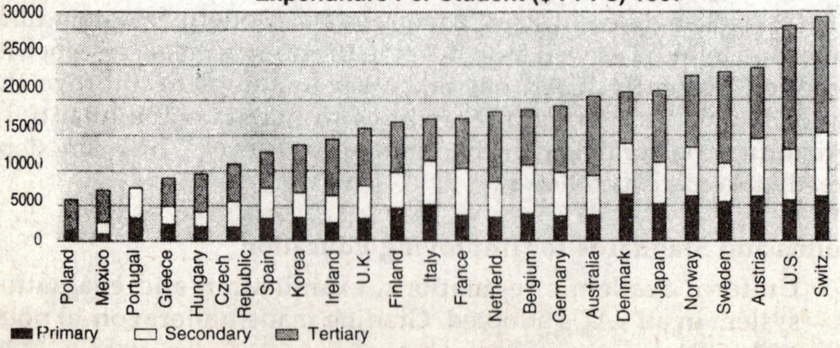

- The course contents and curriculum of UG programme revised and updated for adoption by SAUs from current academic session for agriculture, agricultural engineering, dairy technology, home science, horticulture, fisheries and forestry.
- Rural Agricultural work Experience (RAWE) for agriculture, Internship in Veterinary and Animal Sciences and In-plant Training programme for agricultural engineering and dairy technology made compulsory for 6 months for all UG students with stipend in all branches of agricultural and allied sciences for skill development.
- New Courses, viz. Computer Application, Bio-statistics, Biodiversity, Biotechnology, Principles of Ecology, Agri-Business Management, Marketing, and Environmental Sciences, incorporated in all degree programmes.
- Duration of Home Science degree programme enhanced to four from existing three years.

Capacity Building for Human Resources Development

- Modernization of students laboratory with latest equipment and classrooms through renovation and audiovisual aids.
- Library strengthening by providing international journals, computers, CD-ROM and interconnectivity.
- Establishment of students' computer laboratory at college level.
- Support provided for 'student' study and educational tours.
- Development of health centre and gymnasium for students.

Reduction of Inbreeding

- Arrangement of All India Competitive Examination each year to fill 15% of the seats in UG level and 25% of the seats in PG programme in all SAUs.
- Not more than 2 degrees from same institute is mandatory for getting SRF award.
- Appointment of Assistant Professor level in all SAUs only for NET qualifier.

Agricultural Administration and Extension

To promote the channelization of technology from laboratory to farmers land it is obviously necessary to have a strong administration with a planned set up. Agricultural administration has not been given the attention that was, in the past, given to revenue or police administration with the result that policy goals have not been supported with an implementation machinery capable of translating these goals into specific administrative practices and equipped with inbuilt devices to detect and correct shortcomings. Administrative skill is considered an important input in agricultural development, and it is the absence of this input rather than paucity of physical and intellectual resources that has acted as a constraint on faster growth. A strong administrative structure would be necessary to support the various programmes of agricultural growth. An effective transfer of known knowledge to the field would be essential for improving the productivity of the different farming systems in the country. This require the transformation of the administrative and extension machinery into a strong technical organisation so that the available knowledge does not remain unutilised and is pressed into service.

Reorganisation and rationalisation of agricultural administrative and extension setup initiated in some states during the Fifth Plan, has been progressively extended to cover the entire country, keeping the inter-regional diversity in view. Seventy to eighty per cent of all VLWs in the states would require to be placed directly under the State Agriculture Departments. Keeping in view the emphasis on an integrated and mixed farming approach, woven around the economy of the farm family, it is essential that the VLWs attend to the various farm production activities including crop production, animal husbandry, farm forestry and fisheries all the year round. The agricultural VLWs and other field level functionaries under various agricultural programmes would be integrated into a single organisation covering agriculture and allied activities. The VLW coverage of farming families will be rationalised so as to intensify extension efforts in areas having large agricultural development potential and under intensive agricultural programmes. The field-level extension functionaries would be supported by competent teams of specialists in agronomy, plant protection, farm management and other areas as per local requirements, State Seed/Demonstration Farms will be strengthened to carry out extensive adaptive trials of research findings of universities on an agro-climatic basis.

Educational and technical competence of the extension functionaries would need to be substantially improved through intensive pre-service and in-service refresher/specialised training courses and educational facilities taking into consideration the multidisciplinary role of the functionaries in the field of rural development. In order to meet the increasing needs of training of field level extension personnel and other functionaries, the Gram Sevak/Sevika Training Centres are proposed to be revitalised and suitably strengthened. The Agricultural Universities be involved to provide guidance in formulation of training programmes and also for providing training to the trainees. The Farmers' Training Centre will be established in areas not hitherto covered and where special programmes of rural development are taken up. The training of farm women and young farmers with emphasis on the development of skills in agricultural pursuits will also be taken up more vigorously. Besides, to enable technical officers to discharge their responsibilities efficiently as administrators of agricultural development programmes, it is necessary to provide suitable arrangements for their training in agricultural extension and management at an All India Institute of Agricultural Administration and Management, as recommended by the National Commission on Agriculture.

Keeping rapid technology transfer and improvement of linkages between researchers and farmers in mind, strengthening the organizational set up for management of extension is urgently needed. The Training & Visit system (popularly known as T & V system) of extension widely adopted in India was conceived over twenty years ago, at a time when the penetration of mass media, outside the areas with good communications, was minimal. But the recent growth in the availability of Radio, Television and Video in most of the villages - offer opportunities for new approaches in agricultural education.

Indian Farmers Fertiliser Cooperative Ltd (IFFCO) is forming a consortium with Indian Space Research Organisation (ISRO), Indian Council of Agriculture Research (ICAR), Indira Gandhi National Open University (IGNOU) and ministry of non conventional energy to invest Rs. 500 crore in an IT related agriculture company called Iffco-Agro Tech. The objective of this company would be to bring a wealth of data on crop yields, weather forecast, expected crop prices and satellite images of crop growth at the doorstep of farmers. The agro-tech company would provide online information to farmers on agricultural products, commodities, prices and weather conditions in their native language. The idea is to empower the farmers who are the backbone of the country with knowledge and information which can be easily accessed.

The administrative setup will have to be substantially strengthened at the state headquarters as well as divisional (if any), district and sub-divisional (in larger districts) levels with responsibilities increasingly assigned to senior technical personnel. Authority, responsibility and project planning and monitoring would be decentralised as much as possible. Linkages with village and block level panchayats and voluntary organisations would be strengthened. The Agricultural administration may be placed under the Zila Parishads in those districts where they are doing good work and have shown keen interest in agricultural development. The reorganised extension setup is to direct its special attention to the improvement of the economic conditions of the weaker sections of the rural community such as small and marginal farmers, agricultural labourers, rural women/ unemployed youth, tribal and hill farmers. Selective use of various communication media for effective extension would have to be ensured with special accent on inter-personnel communication methods. Consequently NGOs may have to work as the extension institute providing the farmers training and education as well as demonstration programme.

Interdepartmental coordination and linkages between extension, research and input agencies and farmers' and panchayat organisations will have to be ensured at appropriate levels. For this purpose, co-ordination committees should be set up at block and district levels to ensure adequate coordination amongst official and non-official agencies and autonomous bodies connected with agriculture and rural development.

Revitalizing Agricultural Research and Technology Dissemination

New agricultural technologies are increasingly complex, knowledge-intensive, and location-specific. They require a more decentralized research and extension system and more information and skills for successful adoption than did Green Revolution varieties and fertilizers. Extension and research that is driven by information from the bottom up could help farmers cope with the complexity of the new technologies. Private sector could also help revitalize agricultural research, though with some risks. Government is making it easier for the private sector to appropriate and use research results. And biotechnology innovations are likely to increase private-sector involvement in agricultural research. But the public sector will continue to play an important role in agricultural research because corporations may not want to invest in technologies that governments consider important for equity and poverty alleviation. Moreover, the private sector has generally shown little interest in increasing the yield of key commodities such as wheat or rice varieties adapted to Asian agroclimatic zones, and it has made virtually no investments in tropical crops, fruits and vegetables.

CHAPTER 16

Agricultural Prices and Price Policy

EVOLUTION OF POLICY

Agricultural price policy is basically aimed at intervention in agricultural produce markets with a view to influencing the level of and fluctuations in prices, and price spread from the farm gate to the retail level. As the price policy is required to reconcile the objectives of growth and equity, it has always occupied an important place in economic and political debates. This is because the perceived conflicting objectives need to be assigned weights which are often determined subjectively. The agricultural price policy and its instruments have been debated continuously and have remained under constant review. The primary role of price policy, till the end of the seventies, had been to subserve the national objective of making food available to consumers at reasonable prices. While until the mid-sixties, the instruments of price policy were mainly comprised of regulating the activities of private trade, imports and the distribution of cereals at below market prices, after the mid-sixties, when new seed-fertilizer technology became available, the price policy was assigned a positive role for augmenting the availability of food by increasing domestic production.

It is generally recognized that the post-Independence period growth in India owes much to a conscious and proactive policy of government for promoting agricultural development. Massive public investments in canal systems and rural electrification have resulted in a near trebling of irrigated area in the past five decades. The widespread nationwide network of specialized research stations under the ICAR and the agricultural universities, working with and through the national extension service, have contributed significantly to raising productivity by developing and diffusing better varieties and practices. Expansion and improvement of transport network, especially rural roads, has made it easier and cheaper for farmers to access inputs and market their produce. The state has actively encouraged the development of rural credit institutions. The supply of credit through cooperatives and nationalized banks has increased phenomenally and the costs of borrowing reduced.

In July, 2000 the Government of India came out with a National Agricultural Policy. It is a long-term policy for the next two decades. Its aims are to achieve a growth rate in excess of 4 per cent per annum in the agricultural sector; growth that is based on efficient use of resources and conservation of the soil, water and bio-diversity; growth with equity, i.e. growth which is widespread across regions and farmers; growth that is demand driven and caters to domestic markets and maximizes benefits from exports of agricultural products in the face of the challenges arising from economic liberalization and globalizations; and growth that is sustainable technologically, environmentally and economically.

Long before the formulation of a comprehensive National Agricultural Policy, it was conceived that three of the basic foundations needed for building a sound agricultural economy were production technology package, efficient delivery services and remunerative and stable market prices regimes. The market place in agriculture sector can indeed inflict undeserved losses on the farmer, even when he has applied modern technology and produced efficiently to meet the requirements of the economy. Therefore, a realistic price policy is essential in order to provide an assurance to the farmer of getting a remunerative price for his produce. However, it was also considered that too much reliance should not be placed on prices as a principal mechanism for augmenting production in a situation where there were overall shortages. Since such a policy added to price rise without yielding higher production, the increases in output and farmer's income would have to be brought about mainly through technological improvements and availability of crucial inputs rather than by manipulation of prices. At the same time, for encouraging investment in agriculture and for adoption of modern technology the assurance to the farmer would be essential. Hence, formulation of a policy of offering minimum support prices for the principal crops was of paramount importance. It may be reiterated that minimum price support policy was postulated as only one of the instruments for promoting agricultural growth, the main instruments being technological and institutional changes.

The inadequacy of marketing facilities in the countryside resulted in wide fluctuations in agricultural prices in the past. The biological character of agricultural production and its dependence upon weather conditions lead to variations in the volume of agricultural output from year to year. It has been observed that due to inadequacy of marketing facilities, in years of increased agricultural output, prices tend to fall sharply sometimes to such low levels that they act as disincentive to increase agricultural production, In subsequent years the farmer is tempted to slacken production efforts or to divert his land to other crops. Agricultural Price Policy aims at reducing the unduly large fluctuations in the prices of agricultural products, and the risk of loss to the producer would be minimised even in the event of an exceedingly good harvest.

The policy of fixing minimum guaranteed support prices can go a long way in creating a favourable climate for inducing the farmer to augment his investment in agriculture and to adopt improved technology. At the minimum support prices, Government undertakes to purchase all quantities offered to it so that the prices of agricultural produces do not fall below a specified level. The minimum support prices policy becomes essential in two ways; firstly it acts as a psychological incentive to the cultivator that his efforts in increasing production will not go in vain, and the level at which minimum prices are fixed also plays an important part in encouraging the farmer to undertake investment in improved technology. To reiterate, the main objective of price policy for agricultural produce are aimed at ensuring remunerative price to the growers for their produce with a view to encouraging higher investment and production and to safeguard the interests of the consumers by making available supplies at reasonable prices. The price policy seeks to evolve a balanced and integrated price structure in the perspective of the overall needs of the economy.

The National Commission on Agriculture (NCA), 1976 expressed that the agricultural price policy should keep in view its impact on the general price situation and on the economy as a whole. It should be in consonance with the country's overall economic policy and facilitate growth with stability. The major aim of agricultural price policy should be to correct distortions which are, in general, socially or economically harmful and which emerged from time to time because of the imperfections of the market mechanism. Being parts of the same policy, the interests of the producers should be safeguarded through price support operations when there was a sharp fall in prices, and the interests of the consumers, particularly the vulnerable sections of the population, should be protected through procurement and distribution of a part of the marketable surplus at below the market price when there was a sharp rise in prices of basic necessities such as cereals. The NCA's observation for a sound price policy could be justified both from the welfare angle i.e., for protecting the interests of the vulnerable sections of the community and also from the narrow economic stand-point, i.e., of keeping the impact of the supply –demand imbalance of prices within a reasonable limits.

Thus, the main objective of the Price Policy for agricultural commodities is to ensure remunerative prices to the growers for their produce, to encourage them to adopt improved inputs, and technology for higher levels of production for augmenting incomes and investment. The policy also safeguards the interests of consumers by making supplies available at reasonable prices. The thrust of the policy is to develop a balanced and integrated structure of agricultural economy to meet the overall needs of the economy as a whole with due regard to the interest of the producers as well as consumers. Towards this end, the government announces each season minimum support-prices (MSP) for major agricultural commodities and organises price support operations through public and cooperative agencies such as Food Corporation of India, Jute Corporation of India, Cotton Corporation of India, National Agricultural Cooperative Marketing Federation (NAFED), etc. The Government also stabilises the prices through Market Intervention Scheme (MIS).

AUTHORITY FOR RECOMMENDING MSP

The Government of India appointed the Foodgrains Prices Committee in 1964 under the chairmanship of Mr L.K. Jha, to advise on the determination of producers' prices for foodgrains on an all-India basis, the reasonable margins for the wholesalers and retailers, and the consumer prices for the 1964-65 crops. The Government also asked the Committee to suggest suitable terms of reference for an agency which would provide such advice on a continuing basis.

After a study of the trends in wholesale prices in the post-harvest periods, the Jha Committee recommended minimum support prices which were substantially higher than the averages of the post-harvest prices actually realized by the farmers in the immediate past. For instance, while he average wholesale prices of coarse paddy during the three post-harvest seasons, 1961-62 to 1963-64, ranged in different States between Rs. 28.56 and Rs. 38.36 per quintal, the minimum prices suggested by the Committee ranged between Rs.33.50 and Rs. 39.00 per quintal. In addition to the producers' prices, certain maximum wholesale and retail prices were also suggested by the Jha Committee for paddy and rice for the 1964-65 season. These were enforced after appropriate revision in the light of the views of the State Governments. In view, however, of the difficulty in enforcing the price ceilings, the maximum prices were subsequently withdrawn by most of the States.

The Jha Committee also suggested setting up of an Agricultural Prices Commission to advise, on a continuing basis, on price policy for the agricultural crops, with a view to evolving a balanced and an integrated price structure and resolving the claims of competing crops on limited resources in the perspective of the overall needs of the economy. The Agricultural Prices Commission was established early in 1965 to advise the Government on the price policy of agricultural commodities with due regard to the interest of the producer and the consumer. While recommending the price policy and the relative price structure, the Commission is required to keep in view:

(a) The need to provide incentive to the producer for adopting improved technology and for maximizing production;
  (i) The need to ensure rational utilisation of land and other production resources;
  (ii) The likely effect of the price policy on the rest of the economy, particularly on the cost of living, level of wages, industrial cost structure, etc.

(b) The need to ensure utilization of land and other production resources;

(c) The likely effect of the price policy on the rest of the economy, particularly on the cost of living, level of wages, industrial cost structure, etc.

CRITERIA FOR FIXATION OF MSP

In determining the level of minimum support prices, a number of factors have to be taken into consideration. These include prices of agricultural produce in the open market, returns from competing crops and also trends in the expenses of cultivation. In fact, the minimum support price should be fair to the farmer, and should cover his cost of production and allow him a reasonable margin of profit. Price fixation is to take into account the variations in the prices of inputs, and the output prices should not generally be out of alignment for long along with the package of input prices. The overall relationship between input and output prices within agriculture and the terms of trade between agriculture and other sectors of the economy should be such as to stimulate growth.

Increase in input prices would influence the capacity of the farmer to undertake technological changes in agriculture. Thus, the prices of important inputs such as fertilisers, pesticides and improved seeds would play an important role in encouraging the farmers to step up their utilisation. Inadequacy of supplies of inputs especially of fertilisers and pesticides, as well as improper coordination in the matter of supplies would hamper improvements in agriculture to a great extent. Price policy could, to that extent, play a secondary role if the other factors of cultivation are inadequate. Together with the inadequacy of input, there is also the problem of increased costs of input. A sharp rise in input prices may result in a corresponding increase in costs of cultivation leading in turn to the vicious circle of price increases of agricultural products, industrial goods, wages and agricultural inputs. It would be necessary to keep a close watch on the cost of inputs needed for increased production.

At present, there exists a practice of state-advised cane prices besides all-India statutory minimum price (SMP) announced by the centre every year. To ensure consistent rise in sugar output in the country it is important that the gap between the statutory minimum price and statutory advisory price of states is reduced. This is why the CAPC has been asked to bring about requisite changes in cane price for each zone. The union government has the idea to reform sugarcane pricing to make it uniform at least zone-wise instead of state-wise as at present. It may be mentioned that it is a long-standing demand of the indigenous sugar industry to make uniform cane pricing at least zone-wise.

It is also principally decided that the cane price may be fixed separately for different zones but within a zone all mills should be required to pay the same cane price which is to be based on the price realisations of the mills. This will ensure an uniform cane payoff by the mills located in a particular zone. Accordingly, instead of linking SMP to recovery percentage, SMP could be fixed on average sucrose content of cane and premium allowed on varieties with higher sucrose levels, it is felt.

Several instruments and complementary policies are used to achieve the objectives of agricultural price policy. Some of the important instruments currently in vogue include: the assurance of minimum support prices for certain commodities, selective market intervention for some other commodities; purchases of some commodities by public or cooperative agencies at market prices during the peak arrival period; open market sales by public agencies at fixed prices; buffer stocking of rice and wheat; procurement levy on rice mills and sugar factories and the distribution of subsidised foodgrains and sugar in limited quantities under the public distribution system.

The policy framework was modified in 1980 when the balance between the demand and supply of foodgrains was in sight (Ministry of Agriculture, 1980). The emphasis of the policy, as reflected in the revised terms of reference of APC, which was later renamed as Commission for Agricultural Costs and Prices (CACP), shifted from maximising production to developing production pattern consistent with the overall needs of the economy. It was based on the premise that the basic foundations needed for building a sound agricultural economy are a productive technology package, efficient delivery service along with remunerative and stable market prices for produce.

Further, the Commission was also asked to monitor the movements in the terms of trade for the agricultural sector, which reflected the emerging concern for the fair sharing of the gains arising from the application of technology and the public investment between farmers and consumers. The policy was reviewed in 1986 when a long-term perspective for the agricultural price policy was presented to the Parliament. It was emphasized that the policy should seek to build into the system the major factors, which, in the long run, influence the prices of agricultural commodities making the farm sector more vibrant, productive and cost effective. The policy was again subjected to rigorous review after the programme of economic reforms was launched in 1991 and India became a signatory to the new world trade arrangement, which, for the first time, included agriculture.

At the beginning only 19 commodities were identified for making price recommendations. They were paddy, jowar, bajra, maize, ragi, barley, gram, arhar, moong, urad, sugarcane, cotton tobacco, groundnut; sunflower, soyabean, rapeseed and mustard. The number has now been increased to 24 to include toria, sesamum, nigerseed and copra, etc. which cover altogether 82 percent of total cropped area and 75 percent of crop value. Other commodities like onion, potato, ginger, chillies, black pepper, castor seed and some fruits are included under the Market Intervention Scheme (MIS). This is much more flexible in terms of the period of support operations, coverage of area and the level of support prices. Support under MIS is provided at a mutually agreed price by the Centre and State Governments in the specified area during the predefined period. Losses, if any, are shared equally by the Centre and State Governments.

Since its inception, the Commission has been in constant examination of the trends in prices, production, etc., of the various agricultural commodities and has submitted to the Government a number of reports on price policy for the major crops. The Commission generally recommends the minimum support prices which are in the nature of an insurance against an excessive fall in prices in the wake of an increase in the output of agricultural commodities and also, in respect of foodgrains, the procurement prices at which the Government should procure the grains, keeping in mind the trends of market prices, the size of the crop and the need for public distribution. With a view to making price policy more effective, the Commission has also been making recommendations on related matters, such as agencies for procurement, storage and movement of the procured grains and development of facilities for quality assessment and orderly marketing of the agricultural produce. The actual policy announcements are made by the Government of India in the light of the recommendations of the Commission and after consulting the State Governments.

While making their recommendations, CACP not only looks into a comprehensive overview of the entire structure of the economy of a particular commodity, but a host of other factors like:

- Cost of production, changes in input prices, input-output parity, inter crop price parity, demand and supply scenario, effects on general price level and on cost of living, terms of trade and international market price situation.
- Cost of production covers not only paid-out costs, but also imputed value of owned assets including land and family labour for which the farmers do not incur expenses.
- Even though agriculture pricing policy was conceived during the Green Revolution era, the approach put-paid during the green and later yellow (oilseed) revolution eras. Green Revolution came

on the shoulders of high cost input intensive cultivation regime, adoption and spread of which would not have been possible in the absence of buyers. Hence, the need for thrust on three fronts i.e., popularisation of high cost and highly productive technology, development of markets to handle the marketable surpluses generated in many states and to ensure remunerative price for the produce. Any break in the chain would not only have set back the pace of progress but also rocked the very foundation of self-sufficiency on agricultural front and food security. The result of this integrated approach is for any one to see—bringing the foodgrain production of less then 90 million tonnes to around 200 million tonnes over a period of nearly thirty years—a record to be proud of by any standards.

For farmers, production means source of income, for the scientist, it means technology and for the state, it means ushering in an era of self-sufficiency and food security. But it is the 'psyche' of the farmer, which transforms the efforts and desires of the latter two into reality and he has one incentive—what he gets for the produce in the market. While overall growth is one part of perception, other equally important element is the perception of what commodity and at which scale we wish the farmer to produce. All other things are at par and in a free country, no coercive measure is possible. It is only through the 'price' mechanism, announced in advance of sowing, that state is able to project the anticipated production scenario for the ensuing year.

MACHINERY FOR IMPLEMENTATION OF MSP

Alongwith the announcement of agricultural prices, a public sector infrastructure, capable of launching when needed, an effective market intervention, is also necessary to translate the government's policy into meaningful price support for the farmers.

In order to achieve the above goals, organizations like Food Corporation of India, Jute Corporation of India and Cotton Corporation of India were created in 1960's itself. In the case of oilseeds and pulses, the government decided in 1985 to entrust the National Agricultural Cooperative Marketing Federation (NAFED) with the responsibility of price support. At present , the Government of India announces for each season minimum support prices for 24 agricultural commodities covering all important cereals as well as pulses, oilseeds cotton, jute, sugarcane and tobacco. The MSPs of major agricultural commodities fixed over the last five years are given in Table 16.1. A note giving details of Food, Cotton and Jute Corporations is given in Appendix A.

Announcement of Support Prices before Sowing

Another important aspect of the effectiveness of price support policy is the time of the announcement of minimum support prices. The policy can influence the decisions of farmers to allocate area and other resources to alternative crops only if the prices are announced well before the sowing season. We have looked at the dates of announcement of the minimum support prices for various crops during the last eight years (Table 16.2). In the case of rabi crops, the support prices were announced before or during sowing in 75 per cent of time period examined. However, for kharif crops, only in 38 per cent of time period examined, were the support prices announced before the sowing season.

BENEFITS TO THE FARMERS

The MSPs are perceived by the farmers as a guaranteed price from the Government. These help the producers to pursue his efforts with the assurance that the price of his produce would not be allowed to fall below the level fixed by the Government. The MSPs are fixed at the incentive level, so as to induce the farmer to make capital investments for the improvement of his farms and for expanding the use of inputs to step up production and thereby his net income. The price policy followed by the government has paid rich dividends. The average annual production of foodgrains has gone up from a level of 87.8 million tonnes during the triennium ending 1968-69 to 200.41 million tonnes during the triennium ending 1999-2000. The rising production alongwith higher productivity has resulted in enhancing the net income of the farmers. The National Agricultural Policy (July 2000) has also, inter-alia, mentioned that the Central Government will continue to discharge the responsibility to ensure remunerative prices for agricultural produce through the system of minimum support price.

It may be mentioned that though initially the MSPs were fixed at a lower level than the procurement prices, upward revision of the MSPs almost every year has brought them at par with the procurement prices and MSP has become the synonym for procurement price. It was conceived that since public distribution of essential commodities would be a permanent or a semipermanent feature of economic management in the country in the context of possible shortage and commitment to provide foodgrains at a cheaper rate to the vulnerable section of the population, procurement prices of cereals should be below the prevailing market prices in order to subserve the needs of the public distribution system. Since the issue prices have to be related to the purchasing capacity of consumers with low income, the minimum support prices/ procurement prices should not be much above the issue prices minus the cost of distribution plus, at least a small element of subsidy.

PITFALLS OF MSPs

Though the fixation of MSPs and elaborate arrangements for procurement of foodgrains and other commercial crops have helped,

Table 16.1 Minimum Support Prices (According to Crop Year)

(Rs per quintal)

S.	Commodity	Variety	1992-93	1993-94	1994-95	1995-96	1996-97	1997-98	1998-99	1999-2000	2000-01	Increase in latest Price over previous year: Absolute	Increase in latest Price over previous year: percentage
1.	Paddy	Common	270	310	340	360	380	415	440	490	510	20	4.1
		Fine	280	330	360	375	395						
		Superfine	290	350	380	395	415						
		Grade 'A'						445‡	470	520	540	20	3.8
2.	Coarse cereals (Jowar, bajra & ragi)		240	260	280	300	310	360	390	415	445	30	7.2
3.	Maize		245	265	290	310	320	360	390	415	445	30	7.2
4.	Wheat		330†	350	360	380	475*	510**	550	580		30	5.5
5.	Barley		260	275	285	295	305	350	385	430		45	11.7
6.	Gram		600	640	670	700	740	815	895	1015		120	13.4
7.	Arhar		640	700	760	800	840	900	960	1105	1200	95	8.6
8.	Moong		640	700	760	800	840	900	960	1105	1200	95	8.6
9.	Urad		640	700	760	800	840	900	960	1105	1200	95	8.6
10.	Sugarcane @		31.00	34.50	39.10	42.50	45.90	48.45	52.70	56.10	59.50	3.40	6.1

Table 16.1 Minimum Support Prices (According to Crop Year) (Contd.)

11.	Cotton	F-414/H777	800	900	1000	1150	1180	1330	1440 ++	1575 ++	1625 ++	50	3.2
		H-4	950	1050	1200	1350	1380	1530	1650	1775	1825	50	2.8
12.	Groundnut-in-shell		750	800	860	900	920	980	1040	1155	1200	65	5.6
13.	Jute		400	450	470	490	510	570	650	750	785	35	4.7
14.	Rapesed/mustard		760	810	830	860	890	940	1000	1100		100	10.0
15.	Sunflower seed		800	850	900	950	960	1000	1060	1155	1170	15	1.3
16.	Soyabean	Black	475	525	570	600	620	670	705	755	775	20	2.6
		Yellow	525	580	650	680	700	750	795	845	865	20	2.4
17.	Safflower		720	760	780	800	830	910	990	1100		110	11.1
18.	Toria		725	780	800	825	855	905	965	1065		100	10.4
19.	Tobacco (VFC)	Black soil (F2 Grade)	16.00	18.00	18.50	19.00	19.00	20.50	22.50	25.00	26.00	1.00	4.0
	(Rs. per kg.)	Light soil (L2 Grade)	17.50	20.00	21.00	21.50	22.00	23.50	25.50	27.00	28.00	1.00	3.1
20.	Copra	Milling	N.A.	2150	2350	2500	2500	2700	2900	3100	3250	150	4.8
	(Calender year)	ball	N.A.	2350	2575	2725	2725	2925	3125	3325	3500	175	5.3
21.	Sesamum					850	870	950	1060	1205	1300	95	7.9
22.	Nigerseed					720	720	800	850	915	1025	110	12.0

† Including a central bonus of Rs 25.00 per quintal. NA-Not announced

‡ Classified into two categories for the MSP purposes instead of existing three varieties from kharif season of 1997-98.

* Including a central bonus of Rs. 60.00 per quintal payable upto 30th June, 1997.

** Including a central bonus of Rs. 55.00 per quintal payable from 01.04.98 to 30.06.98.

++ For J-34 variety also.

@ Statutory minimum price linked to a basic recovery of 8.5% with proportionate premium for every 0.1% increase in recovery above that level.

SOURCE: Annual report 2000-2001, Department of Agriculture and Cooperation, Ministry of Agriculture, Government of India.

Table 16.2 Dates of Announcement of Minimum Support Prices

Year	Rabi crops*		Kharif crops**	
	DOS	DA	DOS	DA
1990-91	09-08-90	06-11-90	15-05-90	June 90
1991-92	25-09-91	17-03-92	15-03-91	04-08-91
1992-93	24-07-92	25-08-92	30-04-92	31-08-92
1993-94	29-07-93	07-10-93	19-03-93	22-07-93
1994-95	22-07-94	11-11-94	31-03-94	09-06-94
1995-96	28-07-95	01-02-96	31-03-95	04-08-95
1996-97	11-07-96	18-10-96	11-04-96	02-08-96
1997-98	31-07-97	17-11-98	27-03-97	30-06-97

D.O.S = Date of submission of recommendations by CACP
D.A. = Date of announcement of prices by the government
* Rabi Crops include wheat, barley, gram, mustard and safflower seed
** Kharif crops include paddy, jowar, bajra, ragi, maize, groundnut in shell, soyabean black, soyabean yellow, sunflower seed, arhar, urad, moong and cotton

SOURCE: Reports of CACP, Ministry of Agriculture, Govt. of India, New Delhi

inter-alia, in achieving quantum jump in production of various crops over the years, many distortion in the food and agricultural economy have lately surfaced. Between 1990-91 and 1999-2000, the MSPs for wheat, rice, cotton, coarse cereals, pulses and groundnut have increased by 158, 139, 137, 131,130 and 99 per cent respectively. According to the report of the CACP for crops sown during the 2000-01 season, the gross returns obtainable with respective MSPs at the national average yields for wheat, paddy, cotton, jowar, tur and groundnut correspondingly increased by 200,164, 143,145, 119 and 127 per cent. In terms of actual market prices, the real price of wheat and rice were around 25 per cent higher than the 1990-91 levels. This compares to a mere 8 percent increase in the real price of all agricultural commodities and a significant decline in that of oilseeds. This brought to an important fallout of the lopsided pricing policy of the government with respect to agricultural commodities.

A comparison of agricultural performance in the 1990s versus the 1980s shows that there was decelerating trend in yield of almost every crop in the 1990s. However, there was a trend towards greater diversification of agriculture during 90's decade. But a comparison of the first and second half of the 1990s reveals that there was only a fall in yields, this was accompanied by deceleration of the growth of area under non-foodgrains in the second half. The growth rate in the yield of foodgrains declined from 2.25 per cent between 1990-91 and 1995-96 to 1.79 per cent between 1995-96 and 1998-99, while that of area under foodgrains increased from (–) 0.78 per cent to 0.47 per cent in this period. On the contrary, the growth in index of area under non-foodgrains decelerated to 1.55 per cent in the second half from 2.02 per cent in the first half of the 1990s. This phenomenon leads to a conclusion that the so-called "Price incentives" through higher MSPs for wheat and rice have not led to any significant increase in yields; still worse, it is causing a serious imbalance in inter-crop parities. Another very important implication of the existing policy of fixation of MSP is in the area of environmental degradation. The states that hugely benefit from such price incentives in the case of rice are Punjab and Haryana, where a number of studies have pointed out that cultivation of rice should, in fact, be discouraged in view of the precarious agronomic and groundwater situation.

The entire edifice of public Distribution system depended on the premise that the public would receive foodgrains at prices that were substantially lower than the free market price, that periodical scarcity of short crop year would push up market prices and PDS would then be a source of cheaper foodgrains. But the present situation is quite different. There is no shortfall in supplies as domestic production has reached a level which is much more than what the market or PDS can absorb. Moreover, market prices are lower than the price at which foodgrains are sold under PDS to the consumers above poverty level (APL). Therefore, on the one hand Government is faced with the problem of carrying large surplus stocks, on the other hand, the offtake of foodgrains, particularly of wheat under PDS has been low in recent years on account of narrowing differential between the PDS and open market prices. The substantial annual increase in MSP unrelated to cost of production has led to serious misalignment between MSP, the consequent cost of FCI and the PDS issue prices. The rise in stocks with FCI has resulted a rise in storage costs as also loss due to deterioration in quality and, therefore a rise in the food subsidy bill of the Government. There is, therefore, a need to rationalize the present policy on fixing MSP/ procurement prices.

TERMS OF TRADE

Terms of Trade, for our purpose, could be defined to mean 'the ratio of indices of prices received and paid by the agriculture sector'.

Farmer's decision to produce is not governed by the price he receives for the produce but also the price he has to pay for goods and services purchased by him both for use in farm and for self-consumption—as the relationship or shift in relationship has a direct bearing on his life style.

Agriculture sector not only sells host of products/commodities/ services but also buys from other sectors. He sells his produce and purchases inputs and material for consumption like clothing, etc. It is also a well recognized fact that prices are determined by demand and supply scenario and the change in price of a commodity depends on the relative share of the commodity in the total sales or purchases made by the farm sector.

Relief lies in increasing agricultural productivity. Investments made by the state in the key areas of infrastructure like irrigation and rural roads, adoption of modern technologies, use of modern inputs, all help in increasing productivity. A point made in this regard is that when the State invests a substantial sum for which there is no direct returns, hence, the fruits of higher productivity need to be shared between the producer and consumer. There is a lot of merit in this argument.

Since agriculture still remains a gamble on monsoon, and 65% of the area is rainfed, hence, subject to vagaries of nature, terms of trade cannot be seen on a year to year basis. A medium term perspective in this regard shall be in order. It is important that price policy do take into consideration movement of prices of not only what the farmers sale but also what they purchase. Any dis-equilibrium over time can only help bring distortions. Terms of Trade were not favouring the agriculture sector based on 1970-71 prices (Table 16.3) but based on 1980-81 prices, terms of trade were found to be working in favour of agriculture sector (Table 16.4).

It needs to be appreciated that it cannot be the sole aim of the state to have a one-sided view, i.e., of taking care of the producer. What is true of agriculture is true of other sectors also. We may not all be producers, but consumers, as we are—the latter outnumber the former and yet, the development imperatives demand that producer is given his due not always necessarily at the cost of the consumer. CACP while making recommendation of MSPs takes all these into consideration.

It is in the country's and economy's interest that the terms of trade are continued to be maintained in some sort of equilibrium or at par by increasing the productivity, by modernising agriculture in the infrastructure sector.

The benefits of all this needs to be shared between the producer and the consumer for a harmonious and equitable economic growth.

It is undoubtedly clear that the price policy has played a pivotal role in helping adopt modern technology, maintained progress in satisfactory production of all commodities and helped maintain generally favourable terms of trade. At the same time they need an updated inputs to strengthen their database as well as diversify into making specific recommendations for export-oriented products/ commodities.

They must continue to do the excellent work started over thirty years ago.

CONCLUSION

The existing policy which is centred around procurement by official agencies at continuously rising minimum support prices, did have its use in the past. Indeed, it provided the ideal support to the spread of

Table 16.3 Index of Terms of Trade Between Agricultural, and Non-Agricultural Sectors

Year	Final consumption	Intermediate consumption	All commodities	Final consumption	Intermediate consumption	Capital formation	All commodities	Terms of trade
1981-82	216.6	235.4	224.2	249.1	296.4	392.5	270.5	82.9
1982-83	230.8	246.7	237.2	254.5	308.2	429.1	279.9	84.7
1983-84	253.0	273.2	261.1	278.4	325.6	454.2	302.6	86.3
1984-85	265.3	293.9	276.8	298.1	328.8	503.2	321.8	86.0
1985-86	282.4	271.5	278.0	313.2	343.3	524.5	337.4	82.4
1986-87	299.8	320.2	308.0	337.3	368.6	542.5	361.2	85.3
1987-88	328.7	377.0	348.2	382.7	387.6	574.8	400.5	86.9
1988-89	364.3	363.6	364.0	402.5	390.5	652.2	422.2	86.2
1989-90	384.3	407.2	393.5	440.2	401.4	692.5	455.1	86.5
1990-91	423.3	500.3	454.3	490.9	449.0	741.5	505.1	90.0
1991-92	502.8	567.3	528.8	549.9	524.4	834.7	570.1	92.7
1992-93	536.4	544.3	539.6	593.9	606.4	899.3	623.0	86.6
1994-95	641.7	721.2	673.7	693.9	759.5	1021.8	734.9	91.7
1995-96 (P)	683.7	775.2	720.6	762.5	791.0	1103.4	797.8	90.3
1996-97 (P)	747.7	732.8	741.7	793.2	839.3	1164.0	834.4	88.9
1997-98 (P)	806.9	739.5	779.7	828.7	926.9	1216.1	881.0	88.5

(P) Provisional

SOURCE: As compiled by CACP;

Table 16.4 Index of Terms of Trade Between Agricultural and Non-Agricultural Sectors

Year	Index of prices paid for			Combined index of prices paid	Index of prices received	Index of terms of trade
	Final consumption	Intermediate consumption	Capital formation			
1981-82	54.4	88.5	56.9	61.87	54.9	58.7
1982-83	58.8	91.1	62.6	65.92	60.3	91.4
1983-84	64.2	91.0	67.4	70.12	64.2	91.6
1984-85	66.6	92.3	72.5	72.45	68.0	93.9
1985-86	69.5	94.3	76.4	75.16	70.4	93.6
1986-87	74.8	98.7	78.8	80.14	76.7	95.6
1987-88	84.6	102.3	82.5	88.31	86.0	97.4
1988-89	90.4	96.9	90.9	91.79	90.3	98.3
1989-90	97.6	99.2	100.6	98.08	97.5	99.3
1990-91	112.1	104.0	108.5	110.13	112.3	101.9
1991-92	124.9	109.4	127.2	123.84	130.8	105.6
1992-93	131.5	139.5	137.5	133.51	138.4	103.7
1993-94	143.9	152.9	147.3	146.03	151.4	103.6
1994-95	159.0	166.1	158.4	160.51	171.1	106.6
1995-96	173.7	174.2	176.1	173.9	182.9	105.2
1996-97	181.6	185.6	183.1	182.5	187.7	102.8
1997-98	189.7	205.0	191.3	193.1	197.4	102.2

SOURCE: Directorate of Economics and Statistics, Ministry of Agriculture, Government of India.

the green revolution technology. Continuously rising procurement prices, and hence, continuously rising floor prices in the open market, guaranteed the farmers a remunerative price. The sustained growth in returns over a period of time improved the ability of the farmers to invest in the new technology. The higher output that resulted, most often meant that the farmers had to sell a substantial amount to the procuring agencies. The situation has become more critical when MSP actually became procurement price in 1991-92. As a consequence, the procuring agencies are saddled with large surplus food stock and government's subsidy burden has increased to a level when it has become fiscally unsustainable. If the surplus situation persists because of higher MSP and inability of the domestic market to adjust to each years's change in MSP, apart from India becoming internationally uncompetitive, there is a need to reformulate the price policy framework to make it more relevant in terms of the present domestic and global market realities.

Annexure 16.1

FOOD CORPORATION OF INDIA

The Food Corporation of India which was established in January, 1965 to undertake purchase, storage, movement, transport, distribution and sale of foodgrains has been gradually extending its scope of operations. It has set up a number of regional and district offices. Besides setting up modern rice mills and mechanical paddy dryers, the Corporation has been responsible for the supply of imported wheat to the roller flour mills and for the distribution of wheat products in various States. It played a major role for the first time in the procurement operations of wheat in Punjab and Haryana when production in these two States touched an all-time record.

The organisation of the Corporation was strengthened during 1969 with the transfer to it of a major part of the Food Department. With the completion and the transfer of the executive functions of the Department, the Food Corporation of India has become the sole agency of the Central Government for State trading in foodgrains. It serves the nation in the vital areas of food procurement, storage and distribution, protecting the interest of both the farmers and the consumers. The Corporation handles about fifty million tonnes of commodities like foodgrains, sugar and fertilizers. Besides the purchase of foodgrains, FCI also handles imported non-potassic fertilisers and levy sugar.

Food stocks are maintained by the Central Government to (i) meet the prescribed Minimum Buffer Stock norms for food security, (ii) for monthly releases of foodgrains for supply through the PDS, and (iii) for market intervention to augment supply so as to help moderate the open market prices. However, the FCI is now saddled with a large volume of stocks (nearly 46 million tonnes foodgrains on 1.1, 2001), much above stipulated buffer stock norms of 16.80 million tonnes due to higher procurement and poor offtake.

The Corporation has 25 modern rice mills in various States. Its solvent extraction plant at Samabanarkoil (Tamil Nadu) manufactures edible and industrial grade oil from rice bran. A dal mill has also been set up at Lucknow to meet the requirements of the Army Purchase Organisation.

JUTE CORPORATION OF INDIA (JCI)

In order to assure the jute grower a remunerative and fair price for his produce and thereby sustain his interest in jute growing, the Government has adopted a price support policy. Under this policy, minimum support prices are fixed in consultation with the CACP for delivery at Calcutta as well as for upcountry markets. Grade and variety differentials are also laid down to determine prices with reference to the standard, viz., bottom grade of Assam variety of white jute. Even before the CACP was set up, such an arrangement existed. It has thus been accepted that the primary requirement for attaining maximum production of fibre is the assurance of a fair price to the cultivator.

While dealing with the price support policy and the minimum support price for the 1968-69 season, the Agricultural Prices Commission recommended inter-alia that the Government might consider the advisability of charging some agencies with the standing responsibility for price support operations in raw jute and making it obligatory for such agencies to buy whatever quantities were offered for sale at the support prices at specified assembling points. Such a centralised purchase was necessary to ensure that market prices did not sag below the support price at any time. It was in this context that Government decided that a Jute Corporation should be set up for conducting price support as well as buffer stock operations which would impart stability to prices and contribute to the growth of jute production in the country.

The function of the Jute Corporation which came into existence on April 2, 1971 broadly are:

(i) To conduct commercial operations in a judicious manner;
(ii) To procure and maintain a buffer stock of fibre (including imported fibre, if necessary);
(iii) To import fibre, as and when necessary to supplement indigenous availability;
(iv) To export fibre (to the extent authorised by Government);
(v) To process and export jute goods.
(vi) To undertake export promotion measures for jute goods.

The Jute Corporation of India Ltd. is the only official agency of the government of India in implementing its policy of providing minimum support price to the jute growers and to serve as a stabilising agency in the raw jute sector. However, in years when prices of raw jute had ruled above the minimum support level the JCI had also undertaken commercial operation. It has completed 30 years of service to the jute growers in April, 2001.

Infrastructure

Currently JCI is operating through 171 purchase centres situated in 7 jute growing States, namely, West Bengal, Assam, Meghalaya, Bihar, Orissa, Andhra Pradesh and Tripura. In order to increase its market coverage, JCI has approached to the Apex Cooperative Societies of the jute growing States to participate in the MSP operation in raw jute/mesta through their centres. In response to this, 40 cooperative centres in West Bengal and 5 cooperative centres in Bihar are acting as agents of JCI in procuring raw jute under MSP operation. Apart from this, attempts were made to utilize the village level service societies to procure raw jute directly from the growers and to deliver the same to the nearest JCI/Cooperative centres. By this arrangement 5 village level service societies are procuring raw jute in Assam.

The Range of Services Provided by the JCI is as under

(i) MSP operation for the benefit of marginal jute farmers and commercial operation at prices above support level depending on the raw jute market situation.

(ii) Stabilising raw jute prices through sale of stocks procured at minimum support prices or higher in a phased manner to ensure that inventory level is kept at the minimum without adversely affecting the raw jute price situation. The JCI has also created a buffer stock from time to time in years of surplus.

(iii) Pioneering the establishment of BIS standard for raw jute grading. Due to strict quality control, jute purchased and packed by the corporation fetches a premium in the raw jute market.

(iv) Export and import of raw jute depending on domestic availability and international prices.

(v) Acting as Inspection Agency of the Government prior to export of raw jute as and when called for.

(vi) Providing services in the field of market research and acting as a decision support system in the field of agricultural marketing.

Government of India also entrusted JCI to function as a nodal agency for implementation of two projects—(1) for construction of 14 cost effective community retting tanks (5 in Assam, 5 in A.P. and 4 in Bihar) on 50-50 cost sharing basis between the Government of India and the respective State Governments. On completion of this project community retting tanks would be used by the local jute growers for jute retting, fishery and other household work. (2) A project on further development of a manual/power driven ribboner machine for extraction of fibre from green jute multiple jute plants. The machine was put to trial recently. NIRJAFT is working for further development of this machine.

COTTON CORPORATION OF INDIA

Cotton is one of the major crops cultivated in India. It accounts for about 81 per cent of the total fibre consumption in the spinning mills and 66 per cent of the total fibre consumption in the textile sector. In its report on the cotton price policy for the 1969-70 season, the Agricultural Prices Commission recommended, inter alia, setting up of an agency in the public sector for the purchase, sale and equitable distribution of domestic cotton and also to serve as a vehicle for the canalisation of import of cotton. The Government appreciated the recommendation of the Commission but, since the cotton season was then about to commence, it was decided to make every effort to evolve a new framework ready for introduction in the cotton season 1970-71.

The CCI was set up in 1970. It came into existence with the objective of acting as the canalising agency for import of cotton and undertaking purchase of raw cotton for giving necessary price support to enterprising cultivators growing new varieties of cotton developed as substitute for imported Long and Extra Long Staple Cotton and also for procuring raw cotton for textile mills both in public and private sector. Over the years, its operations have undergone significant changes in keeping with the development which have taken place in the Indian Cotton Economy during the past two decades. Subsequently, the CCI's role was expanded to carry out commercial operations for meeting the cotton requirements of institutional buyers and to fulfill the export quota allotted to it by the Government.

The Sales turnover of the Corporation was around Rs. 807 crore during the year 2000-2001 as compared to Rs. 546 crore in the year 1999-2000. The net profit after tax was Rs. 1.75 crore in the year 1999-2000 as against Rs. 12.91 crore in the previous year.

The CCI's sales of cotton to the quality conscious mills in the private sector (particularly the 100%) EOUs marginally declined from 72.2% during 1998-99 to 68.9% during the year 1999-2000. The sales to NTC mills registered a nominal increase from 13.6% to 15.04% during the year 1999-2000.

The CCI intensified its developmental activities during 2000-01 while continuing the existing activities and taking up new ones during the year. These were basically aimed at increasing production, productivity of cotton and also for improvement in the processing of cotton.

The developmental activities involved Village Adoption Programme for dissemination of technology to the farmers to increase the yield per hectare, production and distribution of genetically pure certified seeds, distribution of pesticides to cotton growers, production of genetically improved parental lines of DCH-32 variety, funding Research Projects for genetic improvement of parental lines of DCH-32 Hybrid cotton in Karnataka, crop surveillance Research Projects on naturally coloured cotton, promotion of medium staple cotton, bringing new areas under cotton, etc. For the various developmental activities listed above, the Corporation spent an amount of Rs. 1.34 crore during the year 1999-2000.

The CCI also implemented an Action Plan to modernize the Ginning and Pressing Factories with a view to ensuring contamination free processing of cotton for improvement in quality and also for ensuring that processing of cotton conforms of BIS norms. The CCI continued with this incentive scheme during 1999-2000 and incentive amounting to Rs. 29.98 lakh were given to Ginning and Pressing Factories in different States.

CHAPTER 17

Food Policy

THE INDIAN SCENARIO

Food and drinking water constitute the most basic need of a human being. Yet these needs are not met today all over the world. At the beginning of the first millennium, the Roman philosopher Seneca said "a hungry person listens neither to religion not reason, nor is bent by prayers", thereby stressing that where hunger rules, peace cannot prevail. In spite of this understanding, hunger and malnutrition were widely prevalent in the first millennium.

The situation continued in the second millennium although sometimes lack of food had an unexpected welcome outcome. One of the wars in Europe (1778-79) was termed Kartoffel Kreig, since the fighting ended when the Prussian and Austrian armies had consumed all the available potatoes in Bohemia. Towards the end of the second millennium, technological developments helped to improve food production substantially (popularly referred to as the Green Revolution), making it possible to raise the rate of food production above the population growth rate in most parts of the world. This helped to keep at bay the fears expressed by Thomas Malthus in 1798 concerning a potential mismatch between human numbers and the capacity to produce food. However, widespread poverty-induced protein-energy malnutrition (PEM) continued to persist. Mahatma Gandhi said in 1946, "to those who are hungry, God is bread".

The third millennium began with paradox of the coexistence of surplus grain and extensive endemic hunger, particularly in South Asia. Emerging technologies—in the areas of precision farming, ecotechnology, information, space and biotechnology and crop-livestock-fish integrated production systems—hold promise to foster an evergreen revolution in farming, rooted in the principles of ecology, economics, gender and social equity, energy conservation and employment generation. Hence, given appropriate blends of technologies, services and public policies, the physical availability of food can be ensured. The challenge lies in providing economic access to food through jobs or sustainable livelihood opportunities.

In India procurement, rationing and price control, which are the three pillars of food policy, have a long history. During the second world war alarming increase in the prices of foodgrains and also the cost of living caused a serious concern to the British Government. The position was aggravated following banning the movement of foodgrains by the principal governments and large –scale hoarding. The price control conferences which were being held at regular intervals recognized the vital importance of linking control over prices with control over distribution. Rationing was, therefore, introduced in 1942 firstly to meet the demands of essential services and non-producers of foodgrains and secondly to check inflationary prices. The first Foodgrains Policy Committee, 1943 recommended the formation of a Basic Plan to assess the food requirements of provinces and the surplus to meet the rationing requirement though the task of procurement was not very easy following their reluctance to abide by the provision of the Basic. The Government of India also could not do anything to ameliorate the situation as it was handicapped constitutionally in dealing with self governing provinces and states.

Partition of the country worsened the food situation further, population under rationing rose from 1.6 millions in 1943 to 148.7 millions in March 1947. After Independence, population under statutory rationing went up by about 1.3 millions. Though there was an overall decrease in the rationed population because of a fall in the non-statutory area, the Government's commitments were enhanced following an increase in the area under statutory rationing, as an assured supply of foodgrains was required to be issued to every ration card holder in such areas. The second Foodgrains Policy Committee 1947 recommended embarking a policy of partial decontrol. As a result, the population under rationing came down substantially. The immediate result of decontrol was however disastrous on prices of foodgrains which shot up markedly and the national government therefore re-imposed control in September, 1948. The obligations to meet the requirement of foodgrains supply to ration shops compelled the government to import. The situation was so grave that the country was considered far from self sufficient with the consequence that none thought of reducing food imports. However, in 1952 late shri Rafi Ahmed Kidwai took charge of food Ministry. He, after assessing the situation expressed the view that there was, in fact no shortage of foodgrains in the country and if at all there was any problem, it was one of purchasing power. Once this was realized, the next step, relaxation of controls, was but a simple process.

Early in 1954, food prices started falling below the economic levels, with the result that the Government had to announce a policy of price support for cereals and floor prices were fixed. The decontrol policy reached its climax in July, 1954 when all controls on rice were removed. However, in 1957-58, the production of foodgrains was 6 million tonnes less than in the previous year and in 1959-60 again, foodgrains was about 4 million tonnes less than in the previous year. These shortfalls and fluctuations in foodgrains production reached adversely on the price level as a whole. The level of foodgrains prices at the end of the second plan could not however be considered too high, but it was recognized that there were large fluctuations in the prices in course of the second plan period. The relative stability of foodgrains prices latterly was achieved by the large imports under P.L. 480.

FOOD POLICY—ITS OBJECTIVES

Thus, it was conceived that while food policy mainly confines to distribution, the agricultural policy pertains to production. Since both production and distribution are closely connected , a discussion on one of the aspects will overlap the other. The Foodgrains Policy Committee (1966) postulated three objectives of the food policy: to achieve self-reliance in production, to ensure equitable distribution, and to bring about price stability in the context of both production and distribution. The Committee went on to suggest that the latter two objectives could be achieved by planned management of supplies involving such measures as procurement, control of interstate movement of foodgrains, a system of public distribution and the building up of buffer stocks. Some of the measures recommended, and indeed actually in operation, such as control of interstate movement of foodgrains, were related to a situation of grave shortage coupled with the necessity of maximum procurement. If the situation changes, so must the strategy. Obviously management of food supplies has to be so formulated as to meet different situations, whether of deficits or of surplus. It must have a certain amount of flexibility. It must, at the same time, fit into the broad framework of economic policy. The main objectives of food policy may, therefore, be restated as:

(i) To ensure that consumer prices are stabilized and, in particular, that the interests of the low-income consumers are safeguarded;

(ii) To ensure that the producers get reasonable prices and continue to have adequate incentives for increasing production; and

(iii) To build up an adequate buffer stock of foodgrains with a view to ensuring both the objectives mentioned above by selling from the buffer stock to meet shortages and high prices, or buying to check prices falling below the remunerative level.

The Government has set before itself the goals of equitable distribution and stable prices to guide its food policy. These goals are unexceptionable, but the difficulties arise when they are spelled out in detail and are made to guide the actual policy decisions. The goal of equitable distribution has a relevance for the distribution over space, viz., interstate availability of the food grains has to be made more or less equal. It has also a relevance for intersectional distribution among various groups of population, especially for providing adequate foodgrains at reasonable prices to the poorer sections of the population. For fulfilling these goals monopoly of public agencies in the interstate trade on the one hand and a system of subsidized and regulated distribution of foodgrains by public agencies through fair price shops on the other are considered inevitable. The goal of stable prices has an obvious importance in an inflation-prone economy, especially when food prices exert a heavy weight on the wholesale price structure. Unchecked rise in the foodgrain prices will severely affect the development expenditure via a rise in wages and salaries. It will particularly hit hard the vulnerable sections of rural and urban population who are even as it is, at the margin of subsistence. The unchecked rise in foodgrain prices will also encourage speculative hoarding and other antisocial tendencies. Further, once the state takes over the responsibility of providing adequate foodgrains for the underprivileged sections, it will have to procure foodgrains, which it can seldom do at unrestrained market prices. Foodgrains for this section will have to be procured at a reasonable price if the public exchequer is not to be unduly strained. At the same time foodgrain prices cannot devoid of an incentive element for producers, or else the foodgrains production will suffer. A balance has to be struck in view of these conflicting claims.

Food Policy in Operation

Various instruments of policy have been devised with the objective of fulfilling these two basic goals of food policy. The important among these are: Procurement under the minimum support price operations and also through the statutory levy imposed by some state government on the millers and traders.

Procurement

Foodgrains are procured at the Minimum Support Prices (MSP) fixed by the government every year well before sowing seasons. The MSP for Common and Grade `A' paddy has been fixed at Rs. 510/- and 540/- per quintal respectively for the year 2000-2001 kharif marketing season (October – September). The comparative MSP of wheat and paddy from 1995-96 to 200-001 (marketing seasons) is shown below in Table 17.1.

There is however no levy on basmati rice, wheat, coarse grains and pulses. Government undertakes to purchase all wheat and paddy of prescribed specifications offered for sale by the farmers, thereby ensuring them a stable market for their produce. Non-basmati rice is procured for the Central Pool under statutory levy system imposed by the State Governments in exercise of powers conferred on them under the Essential Commodities Act, 1955. The Levy percentage prevailing various States/UTs pertaining to the Kharif Marketing

Table 17.1 Minimum Support Prices for Wheat and Paddy from 1995-96 to 2000-2001 (marketing seasons)

(Rs. per quintal)

Year	Wheat	Paddy		
		Common	Fine	Superfine*
1995-96	360	360	375	395
1996-97	380	380	395	415
			Grade `A'	
1997-98	475	415	445	
1998-99	510	440	470	
1999-2000	550	490	520	
2000-2001	580	510	540	

* Paddy was categorised into two varieties only in Common and Grade A from 1997-98 marketing year.

Season 2000-2001 is given in Table 17.2. The procurement of rice for the Central Pool (including paddy in terms of rice) since 1995-96 is shown in Table 17.3.

Procurement of Wheat

The State-wise procurement of wheat and the share of different States during the last 5 years is given in Table 17.4.

From 1985-86 marketing season, NAFED under the Ministry of Agriculture, was the nodal agency for procurement of coarse grains. In the kharif marketing season 1989-90, the FCI was entrusted with the task of conducting price support operation of coarse cereals in Punjab, Haryana and Uttar Pradesh., while the NAFED continued its procurement operation in other states. From 1990-91 Rabi marketing season, FCI has been made responsible for the procurement of Rabi and Kharif coarse grains for the whole country. Since the production of coarse grains are spread over a large number of markets, FCI makes arrangements with state agencies so that their widespread infrastructure is made use of in providing price support to the coarse grain producing farmers. All legitimate costs incurred by the state agencies are reimbursed by the FCI. As open market price of coarse grains generally rules much higher than minimum support price, not much of coarse grains is procured by the public agencies.

However, the Minimum Support Price of coarse grains, viz., jowar bajra, ragi and maize was fixed at Rs. 445/- per quintal, and for barley at Rs. 430/- per quintal for 2000-2001 Kharif/Rabi Marketing season, as against the procurement price of Rs. 415 per quintal for jowar, bajra, ragi and maize, and Rs. 385/- per quintal for barley in 1999-2000

Table 17.2 System of Procurement of Rice During 2000-2001 Kharif Marketing Season

Sl. No.	Name of the State/UT	Category	Quantum of Levy
1.	Andhra Pradesh	Millers/Dealers	50%
2.	Assam	Millers/Dealers	50%
3.	Bihar	Millers/Dealers	40% or 2500 qtls. Compound levy on millers. 25% or 500 qtls. Compound levy on wholesalers. (same % is applicable on paddy also)
4.	Gujarat	Millers	†
5.	Haryana	Millers/Dealers	75% @
6.	Karnataka	Millers/Dealers	33 1/3 %
7.	Madhya Pradesh	Millers/Dealers	50%
8.	Maharashtra	Millers	†
9.	Orissa	Millers/Dealers	75%
10.	Punjab	Millers/Dealers	75%
11.	Rajasthan	Millers/Dealers	25%
12.	Tamil Nadu	Millers/Dealers	50% (Exported on paddy)
13.	Uttar Pradesh	Millers/Dealers	60% (Western U.P.)
14.	West Bengal	Millers/Dealers	40% (Some Distts. In East U.P) ‡
15.	Chandigarh	Millers	50%
16.	Delhi	Millers/Dealers	†
17.	Pondicherry	Millers/Dealers	10% (20% Transport levy on Paddy/rice)

† Govts. of Delhi, Gujarat & Maharashtra have been granted levy exemption for the current kharif marketing season (KMS).

‡ These States have been given concurrence to grant levy exemption on non-basmati rice meant for export outside the States.

* Govt. of Punjab has been allowed to grant levy exemption at any time during the 2000-01 KMS.

Table 17.3 Procurement of Price (Central pool) (Marketing Season: October-September)

(In lakh tonnes)

Year	Procurement
1995-96	99.50
1996-97	122.22
1997-98	143.32
1998-99	117.89
1999-2000	172.74
2000-2001 (As on 20.2.2001)	153.33

Table 17.4 Procurement of Wheat for Central Pool—Marketing Season (April-March)

(In lakh tonnes)

State	1996-97	1997-98	1998-99	1999-2000	2000-2001
Haryana	20.22	22.90	31.58	38.70	44.98
Madhya Pradesh	0.04	1.07	5.31	5.42	3.50
Punjab	56.41	59.61	61.46	78.31	94.24
Rajasthan	2.29	3.20	6.67	6.37	5.38
Uttar Pradesh	2.61	6.18	21.41	12.61	15.45
Others	0.00	0.02	0.10	0.02	0.00
All India	81.57	92.98	126.53	141.43	163.55

Kharif/Rabi Marketing Season. During the Kharif/Rabi Marketing Season (2000-2001), 3.3 lakh tonnes of coarse grains were procured upto 20.02.2001.

Food Management

Procurement of rice is going ahead merrily, at the enhanced rate of Rs 530 and Rs 570 per quintal for coarse and fine varieties respectively. Since offtake from government stocks has been pathetic for some time and procurement is a function of political pressure on the central government rather than of buffer stocking requirements, at least 20 million tonnes of rice will be added to the Centre's stocks before the end of the current (2000-01) fiscal. In addition to artificially jacked up MSP, quality norms are also not strictly observed under political pressure. This additional procurement has to be financed. The cost of additional storage alone would be Rs 4,600 crore. Procurement, transportation and subsidy to the consumer would further jack up the Food Corporation of India's expenditure, Food credit, which has already swelled by over Rs 10,000 crore this year (2000-01), can easily go up by as much in the second half of the year.

Bank credit for procurement, stocking and distribution of foodgrains is provided to the Food Corporation of India (FCI) and state government agencies by a group of banks led by the State Bank of India (SBI). This consortium arrangement is regulated by the Reserve Bank of India (RBI). On October 19, 2001, food credit stood at Rs 50,280 crore as against Rs 33,845 crore a year ago-an abnormal increase of 48 per cent. This is likely to increase to a level for Rs 64500 crores by July 2002. Food credit carries a 11.65 per cent rate of interest. For all practical purposes, it is risk free, 'single entry' line of credit. This, for the commercial banks, is the goose which is currently laying golden eggs.

Foodgrains Management has unquestionably led to monstrous absurdities in recent years. Food procurement at minimum support prices, has reached mountainous scales, making a mockery of buffer stock norms intended to ensure food security for the vulnerable sections. Currently the stocks with the Centre are estimated at 65 million tonnes while the official reckoning of maximum storage capacity of reasonable quality is less than 30 million tonnes. In the absence of prudent and firm policy correction, the stocks could exceed 75 million tonnes by February 2002. At the current rate of lifting, it will take nearly seven years to remove the stock. By then six years of procurement would have added to the storage problem. This is a gigantic dilemma and the Centre has no clue to overcome this. It laid much emphasis on Prof Gopal Naik report and wanted to introduce an income insured scheme (IIS). But this was shot down by a high-level committee headed by Prof Abhijit Sen. A basic problem of agriculture is the absence of reliable marketing mechanism. A number of studies have shown that the grower receives a fraction of what the consumer pays. The cumbersome structure of middlemen eats away a big part. Before asking the farmers to shift to pulses and oilseeds, the Govt. must restore their confidence in the government's capacity to ensure a remunerative price and timely procurement.

The Union Food Minister, Mr. Shanta Kumar, addressing editors on the social sector broached a new policy framework gradually to unwind an increasingly unviable policy of centralised procurement of foodgrains in an obviously altered context of food surpluses or, at any rate, of widening mismatches between procurement and offtake from the Public Distribution System. The contradictions in the inherited policy matrix are well-known. Food subsidies which are supposed to benefit the poor mainly nourish the byzantine public sector Food Corporation of India in its vastly overextended procurement, storage and logistics operations. The concept of the MSP, originally intended to protect farmers against the contingency of farm price crashes, has largely helped the well-to-do among the farmers in Punjab, Haryana and Andhra Pradesh, sell wheat and rice without effort and not to look upon value-added crop diversification as a national opportunity. Above everything else, centralised procurement anchored in a politically-manoeuvrable MSP system, has distorted the constitutionally-designed sharing of functions between the Union and the States under which agriculture and food belong to the domain of the states.

As part of the agriculture sector initiatives, the government is also looking at introducing a policy of competitive procurement of foodgrains. This, however, would involve ending monopoly purchases by government agencies and hiring of private agencies for food procurement. It was suggested at the Cabinet Committee CCER meeting that the Food Corporation godowns with staff may be transferred to the States.

Fate of the farmer may, however, by summarised by saying that agriculture in North India is in a deep crisis. The only solution is total restructuring under tightly controlled conditions. Everyone knows the litany of woes. Punjab and Haryana grow too much wheat and rice. The government pays too much for the cereals of doubtful quality. The FCI is inefficient and burdens the Centre with huge losses. The open market prices are lower than the FCI grains offered on a no-profit, no-loss basis. Poor people do not have the purchasing power to draw these grains and escape hunger. The result? FCI godowns are bulging with wheat and rice in various stages of rotting and bank interest on loans is mounting. The wheat and paddy growers are angry, the consumer is angry. The kisan knows that the old arrangement of higher MSP to encourage higher production is dead and he has to prepare himself for a new regime. He is aware that there is no market for the cereals and there is no regulated market for pulses, oilseed and vegetables. He is painfully aware of what happened to potato growers this year (2000-01) in the Daoba region. What all this means can be compressed into four formations. One, the Punjab and Haryana farmer should shift from the paddy-wheat cycle and insert pulses or oilseed. His annual income will come down but the loss is bearable as the alternate is to suffer humiliation at the hands of petty FCI officials. The regional agricultural universities and government departments should stand by the kisan in this transition to a new world. Individual enterprises by the kisan has failed miserably as is evident in potato growing and grape farming. Farm experts should draw up a road map of the transition; otherwise the whole project will collapse. Finally, the governments at the Centre and the states should help in developing a dynamic market for non-cereal products. The crippling weakness of Indian agriculture is the underdevelopment of markets for vegetables, horticulture and floriculture products. If a kisan is sure that his labour will not go unrewarded, he is willing to take risks and help the country's policies to success.

Restrictions on the Movement of Foodgrains

The Essential Commodities Act, (1955) provides for control of production, supply and distribution of certain commodities identified as essential commodities under the Act to protect the interest of consumers. Several states have issued a large number of control orders under the existing legislation inhibiting free movement of certain food and agricultural produce. Since March 26,1993, the central Government has adopted the policy of treating the entire country as a single food zone for free movement of foodgrains and has directed all the States/UTs to remove all statutory restrictions which impede Inter-State and intra-State movement of foodgrains. Till recently, all States/UTs, except Andhra Pradesh, Jammu & Kashmir, West Bengal and Tamil Nadu, had no such restrictions. On the basis of consistent persuasion, the government of Andhra Pradesh have also removed the restrictions with effect from, July 27, 2000. The remaining three States want to keep the movement restrictions on account of local conditions.

The Minister of Consumer Affairs, Food & Public Distribution wrote a letter in November, 2000 to the Chief Ministers of all the state Governments to remove the existing restrictions, if any, on trade and industry dealing with wheat and wheat products, as free movement would help farmers in getting better remunerative prices for their produce. A similar letter was also sent to the Chief Ministers of all the States on 30.1.2001 to remove all restrictions on trade in rice. In the light of present ground situation, all restrictions on foodgrains regarding inter-State movement, stocking, exports and institutional credit and trade financing should be renounced. Free trade will help make-up the difference between production and consumption needs, reduce supply variability, increase efficiency in resource-use and permit production in regions more suited to it.

Public Distribution System

Procured foodgrains are distributed through the Public Distribution System (PDS). The PDS, which operates through a wide network of fair price shops (FPS), aims at making foodgrains, available at reasonable prices to the PDS consumers, most of whom belong to vulnerable sections of the society. Today, the Indian Public Distribution System, is the largest distribution network of its type in the world. The system is designed to help both the producers and consumers of foodgrains by linking procurement at support prices and ensuring their distribution alongwith other essential commodities at almost uniform and affordable prices throughout the country. PDS therefore continues to be the major instrument of government's economic policy for protecting purchasing power of the poor and for ensuring food security in the country. Truly speaking, it has assumed importance as one of the Government's most significant anti poverty programmes.

Targeted Public Distribution System (TPDS)

Despite its wide coverage, the PDS had been widely criticized for its failure to serve population below the poverty line, its urban bias, negligible coverage in the States with the highest concentration of the rural poor and lack of transparent and accountable arrangements for delivery. Realising this lacuna, the government streamlined the PDS by issuing special cards to families Below Poverty Line (BPL) and selling foodgrains to them at specially subsidized prices, with effect from June, 1997. In fact, under TPDS distribution of foodgrains operates under two tier system of delivery to households Below Poverty Line (BPL) and Above Poverty Line (APL), with BPL families receiving foodgrains at heavily subsidised prices. Under the Targeted Public Distribution System (TPDS), the States formulate and make foolproof arrangements for identification of the poor, and delivery foodgrains to Fair Price Shops (FPS) for its distribution in a transparent and accountable manner at the FPS level. The scheme is in operation in all states/UTs except Delhi and Lakshadweep.

The scheme, when introduced, was intended to benefit about 6 crore poor families for whom a quantity of about 72 lakh tonnes of foodgrains was earmarked annually. The identification of poor under the scheme is done by the States as per State-wise poverty estimates of the Planning Commission based on the methodology of the Expert Group on Estimation of Proportion and Number of Poor" chaired by Prof. Lakdawaia. The allocation of foodgrains to the States/UTs is made on the basis of average consumption in the past, i.e. average annual offtake of foodgrains under PDS during the past ten years. The quantum of foodgrains in excess of the requirement of BPL families @ 10 kg per family per month was provided to the States as transitory allocation for which a quantum of 103 lakh tonnes of foodgrains was earmarked annually. Keeping in view the consensus on increasing the allocation of foodgrains to BPL families and to better targetise food subsidy, the Government of India has increased the allocation to BPL families from 10 kg. to 20 kg. per family per month at 50% of Economic Cost and allocation to APL at Economic Cost with effect from 1.4.2000. The allocation for APL has been retained at the same level as at the time of introduction of TPDS.

The allocation of foodgrains for BPL families at the rate 20 kg. per family per month is being made from December, 2000 on the basis of population projection of the Registrar General, as on 1.3.2000 instead of the previous base of projected population of 1995 earmarked for poor families. The end retail price is fixed by the States/UTs after taking into account margins for wholesalers/retailers, transportation charges, levies, local taxes, etc., Under TPDS, the States are required to issue foodgrains at a margin of not more than 50 paise per kg. over and above the Central Issue Price (CIP) for BPL families. For APL families the States can fix the margin keeping in view the actual expenses incurred.

Thus, the implementation of the PDS and TPDS is the joint responsibility of the central and state governments and UTAdministration. While the responsibility of the central government is to procure, store and transport the PDS items up to the central godowns, the responsibility for actual distribution to consumers and administration of the PDS is that of the state governments and UT Administrations. They lift these commodities from the central godowns/mills and distribute them to the consumers through a network of fair price shops.

Problem of Targeting Poor Under TPDS

Various studies undertaken on the functioning of TPDS highlight that the performance of the new scheme has not been satisfactory so far. Although the ration quota has been increased to the poor (the BPL population), they are unable to make full use of this quota due to their limited purchasing power. The large difference between open market and TPDS price provided a great incentive for the diversion of grain to the black market. The selection of beneficiaries in many states is not transparent and the basis for selection is too complicated for the local officials to administer. The delivery system was usually weak in most of the states even before the introduction of TPDS and not much could be expected in terms of increasing the benefits to the poor.

It has been observed that one of the major problems with targeting the scheme specifically to the poor is the high cost involved in the correct identification of the poor. Narrow targeting at the level of the individual households, for example, requires very detailed data for all households and complex and expensive means testing in order to identify the eligible households. The effectiveness of such mechanism depends on the magnitude of two possible errors, the errors of exclusion and inclusion . The exclusion error indicates the extent to which poor are excluded from the list of beneficiaries and the inclusion error the extent to which non-poor are included in the list. Direct targeting of poor through means testing, involves high administrative cost due to the need for repeated periodic identification. The costs are further augmented due to widespread leakage to non-poor households by misrepresentation of information. Further, since a substantial part of poverty is transient in nature, targeting based on current consumption status (as it is done by the National Sampling Survey Organisation) is likely to have a lower impact on chromic poverty as compared to the case of uniform distribution of subsidies to the poor and the non-poor.

Suggestion for Improvement

In order to improve targeting, alternative indirect identification mechanisms can be used, which are based on the observed correlation between different socioeconomic characteristics of the population and their poverty status. Such characteristics may include the household's housing condition, access to electricity, irrigation facilities, drinking water, use of cooking fuel etc.

Geographical targeting that uses the place of residence as the main criterion for eligibility can provide an effective way of reaching the poor when there are substantial disparities in living conditions across geographical areas. Targeting selected regions with a high concentration of poverty can be an effective mechanism for transferring a greater share of benefits to the poor while keeping the total number of beneficiaries unchanged. Further, targeting smaller administrative areas, such as villages identifying regions with greater concentrations of the poor increases. This would help in increasing the coverage of the poor while reducing that of the non-poor.

Finally, in regions with greater concentration of poverty the high cost of identification and administration of TPDS can be avoided since the leakage of benefits to the non-poor will be small for these regions. Universal provision of subsidies to these regions is thus likely to be cost effective. For the remaining regions suitable self-targeting mechanisms can be used. For example, for the least poor group of regions, PDS could supply only coarse cereals so that there is self-selection of the poor. Or, the supply of foodgrains could be linked to employment generation programmes, which also have the self-selection property. In addition to this, other targeting criteria can be used such as landlessness, widowhood, old age, etc. Geographic targeting would also ensure supply of grains in remote and inaccessible rural hilly and tribal areas where markets are underdeveloped or even nonexistent.

Revamped Public Distribution System (RPDS)

The scheme was launched in January 1992 to improve the reach of the PDS to the consumers living in the areas of relatively economic disadvantage showed remarkable progress. Additional allocation of foodgrains and their distribution at reduced prices, creation/expansion of storage facilities, opening adequate number of Fair Price Shops including mobile shops, doorstep delivery, etc. were the core elements of RPDS. The two centrally sponsored schemes, viz, Purchase of mobile/trucks and construction of godowns were under implementation in all the identified RPDS areas. Following the introduction of TPDS in 1997 the scope of these schemes has been extended throughout the country with effect from 1998-99.

The network of fair price shops has been expanding over the years. As per the latest available reports there are nearly 4.63 lakh fair price shops in the country. Mention may be made that increased emphasis has been laid in the last few years on improving the reach of the PDS to remote, far-flung and inaccessible areas.

Antyodaya Anna Yojana

A National Sample Survey exercise points towards the fact that about 5% of the total population in the country sleeps without two square meals a day. This section of the population can be called as "hungry":. In order to make the Targeted Public Distribution System (TPDS) more focused and targeted towards this category of population, the Prime Minister has launched the "Antyodaya Anna Yojana" on the 25th December 2000.

The Antyodaya Scheme contemplates identification of one crore poorest families out of a total of 6.52 crore BPL families covered under TPDS and provide them with an additional quantity of 5 kgs foodgrains per family per month over their normal monthly entitlements of 20 kgs of foodgrains per family per month. In addition, these identified poorest families will be provided foodgrains at rates below the rates charged for the BPL families viz., Rs. 2/- per kg. for wheat and Rs. 3/- per kg. for rice against the Central Issue Price of Rs. 4.15 per kg. for wheat and Rs. 5.65 per kg., for rice for the BPL families (ex-FCI godowns).

Citizen's Charter

The Citizens' Charter, issued in November 1997 for adoption by the State Governments, is an important milestone in the ongoing efforts of the government to provide services under the PDS in a more transparent and caring manner. This Charter is intended to be a model for the State Governments. It contains, inter alia, basic information of interest to the consumers and a model procedure and time schedule for the services. The Charter contains essential information, viz., entitlement of BPL families, fair average quality of foodgrains, information regarding FPS, procedure of issue of ration cards, inspection and checking, right to information, vigilance and public participation.

Buffer Stocking Policy

Food stocks are maintained by the Central Governmental to (i) meet the prescribed minimum buffer stock norms for food security, (ii) for monthly releases of foodgrains for supply through the PDS/welfare schemes, (iii) to meet emergent situations arising out of unexpected crop failure, natural disasters, etc., and (iv) for market intervention to augment supply so as to help moderate the open market prices. One of the problems faced by the FCI during past few years is that it is saddled with large volume of stocks, particularly of wheat, much above the stipulated buffer stock norms. This is largely due to considerably higher procurement because of attractive Minimum Support Prices (MSP) fixed by Government. Offtake under PDS has also come down due to open market availability. The Government has fixed minimum requirement of stock for the Ninth Five year Plan (1997-2002) as under:

(In Million Tonnes)

	January	*April*	*July*	*October*
Wheat	8.4	4.0	14.3	11.6
Rice	8.4	11.8	10.0	6.5
Total	16.8	15.8	24.3	18.1

How Relevant is PDS?

Public distribution had its origin in the scarcity regime of pre-Independence period when the then government was forced to introduce rationing after the Bengal famine. During this period, not only was every urban resident entitled to buy from ration shops, but he was forced to do so as free market sales were not permitted. During the

'60s, this was also the mechanism of selling the foodgrains received as aid by the government. Since the cost of getting the grain was negligible, the subsidy given to urban consumers did not burden the government's budget. On the contrary, since the food aid was virtually free, even at the highly subsidised ration prices, the government generated surplus from it, which came handy in financing development expenditure.

The NSSO's 42nd round household survey data throw much light on the coverage of cereals distribution through the PDS. The data show that:

(i) In the northern big states Punjab, Haryana, UP, Bihar, Orissa and MP, more than 90 per cent of the population do not purchase any cereals from the PDS. Except for urban Delhi and Jammu & Kashmir, the PDS is almost irrelevant as far as cereals are concerned.

(ii) Distribution of cereals through PDS is not particularly targeted to the poor. In fact, in almost all states, persons belonging to the bottom 70 per cent of the population get more or less the same amount.

(iii) Barring Andhra Pradesh and Kerala, the levels of implicit subsidy are very low except for a small fraction of the households in a few more states.

(iv) The cost-effectiveness of reaching the poorest 20 per cent of the households through PDS cereals is very small. For every rupee spent less than 22 paise reaches the poor in all states excepting in Goa. Daman and Diu where it is around 28 paise. Thus, PDS support is provided to the poor at a very high cost.

(v) There is some indirect evidence to suggest that the free market price is not lower where the PDS exists. In fact, Dantwala (1967) had suggested that the free market price would be lower in the absence of PDS.

Our past experience with the PDS/RPDS shows that other than being a populist programme, even theoretically speaking. PDS has no relation with poverty alleviation. In its present form, it is likely to prove counterproductive and can be considered as a poverty perpetuation programme.

We must be clear that poverty and hunger are not synonyms. The solution to hunger would therefore, lie first in identifying the real hungry and undertake micro level development studies of the area, which will put more income in the hands of the people by cost-effective technologies in agriculture and introducing intermediate technology in the non-farm rural sector. This must be accompanied by the development of an efficient infrastructure and appropriate health delivery system. It may not be out of place to mention that despite all the rhetoric about progress made. India is not really a healthy nation. Its health status is worse than those of Ghana, Vietnam, the Philippines or Mexico.

Micro level development plans should be prepared for the identified pockets and these should then be translated into action programmes. All the identified hungry in that area should be provided employment in these programmes and given adequate wages (part in cash and part in foodgrains) to enable them to have a reasonable standard of living over and above their basic needs of food, most of the activity being in the nature of food for work programme. Since the programme will be restricted to only 51.1 million its budgetary implications will be manageable. It could actually be met from the existing IRDP funds for the area. Since the development will be for the whole area—say a block, it will be a time bound programme with a clear visibility. A programme of this nature should be completed in a period of about two years by which time the sub-region would have already created self-sustainable activities of its own. It should be possible to cover the whole lot of these 10 million hungry (poorest of the poor) families in one plan period. This is how PDS can be merged with IRDP. In its present form, as an independent programme, it is really not effective, rather, irrelevant.

Food Subsidies

Another important component of food policy is food subsidies. Sale and purchase being the two sides of the same transaction, 'what the farmer receives the consumer has to pay, unless there is a benevolent 'middleman' who is all the time prepared to lose. Government had created such a middleman way back in 1965 and named it the Food Corporation of India (FCI).

The FCI buys from the farmer and sells to the fair price shops for distribution to the consumer. The costs incurred by the FCI in procuring, paying state taxes, transporting, handling and storing of foodgrains constitute FCI's acquisition cost which in 2000-001 accounted for 84 per cent of the economic cost of wheat. The balance 16 per cent of cost was distribution cost. The two together i.e., the acquisition cost and distribution cost constitute the economic cost. The economic cost, FCI's average sales realization and consumer subsidy on wheat and rice since 1991-92 are shown in Table 17.5.

In recent years, annual increase in Minimum Support Prices (MSP) have been substantial and at times much above the inflation rate. Higher procurement prices invariably cause FCI to procure more than what is required for food security, leading to much higher commitments for Government subsidy, while lower volumes stocked by trade means higher market price during lean season. In addition, the carrying cost of buffer stocks (comprising freight, storage, interest charges etc.) also included as part of food subsidy add further to the subsidy burden.

The gap between the economic cost incurred by the FCI towards procurement storage, distribution and wastage of foodgrains and its average realization based on the issue prices under PDS is filled by

Table 17.5 Economic Cost and Consumer Subsidy

(Rs/Quintal)

Fiscal year	*Economic cost*		*FCI's /Average sales realisation*			*Consumer subsidy*	
	Wheat	*Rice*	*Wheat*	*Rice*		*Wheat*	*Rice*
1991-92	390.79	497.04	251.68	365.58		139.11	131.46
1992-93	504.10	585.27	279.36	442.40		224.74	142.87
1993-94	532.03	665.10	355.88	500.42		176.15	164.68
1994-95	551.17	694.71	407.89	600.75		143.28	93.96
1995-96	583.95	762.82	411.94	613.34		172.01	149.48
1996-97	640.16	847.69	433.20	610.57		206.96	237.12
1997-98 BPL	786.35	939.33	250.00	450.00		536.35	589.33
APL			450.00	673.68		336.35	265.65
1998-99 BPL	797.16	1026.67	249.57	401.81		547.59	624.86
APL			449.57	751.81		347.59	274.86
1999-2000 (RE)							
BPL			261.29	366.77		563.45	728.26
APL	824.74	1095.03	693.29	921.77		131.45	173.26
APL (NE)			824.74	716.77		—	378.26
2000-01 (BE)	830.00	1130.00	415.00	565.00	BPL*	450.00	590.00
					BPL**	415.00	565.00

* upto 24.7. 2000

** w.e.f. 25.7.2000

SOURCE: Economic Survey 2000-2001, Government of India.

the Central Government through the consumer subsidy. The consumer subsidy together with the buffer carrying cost constitute the food subsidy. The subsidy on foodgrains incurred by the Central Government since 1991-92 is given in Table 11.1.

Where does the Government itself get the money to subsidise the FCI? From taxation, of course. To buy food at lower prices, the consumer has to pay higher taxes. Probably, the only consolation is that those who pay the bulk of taxes are not necessarily those who consume the bulk of grain sold through the fair price shops.

So, to pay a higher price to the farmer and charge a lower price to the consumer, Government needs huge amount of money. There are limits to how much Government can tax only to subsidize food. The money is required for several other uses, like irrigation and power, steel and coal, etc., which are even more important. The food subsidy is a mere consumption expenditure, a device to redistribute income in society. It does not at all add to the cake that is to be shared. On the contrary, money spent by Government on irrigation, power, industry, etc., creates assets and simultaneously jobs. If for instance, the Rs. 7,800 crore, which are spent on subsidy to keep food prices down, were to be invested in industry, the number of jobs, that would have been generated each year would have exceeded 1 million.

Hence, in order to reduce the economic cost and thus the subsidy burden, efforts are required to be made to reduce the costs incurred by FCI through more efficient management in handling losses, transportation costs, storage and also maintenance of quality stock. This may be an arduous task if FCI is forced to procure stocks below the prescribed standard quality under political pressure. The price of subsidy is no doubt heavy. Obviously therefore, the issue price of foodgrains must rise relatively more than the procurement prices so that the subsidy is generally reduced and ultimately eliminated. Lastly, but not the least, inadequate purchasing power among the poor leads to low overall demand for foodgrains. So long as the incomes of the poor fail to grow adequately the need for food subsidy remains and improving the efficiency of the system and reducing the incentives for corruption is the only way to reduce food subsidy bill.

Availability of Foodgrains

Keeping in view the food policy adopted so far in the country it would be prudent to consider what has been the per capita availability of foodgrains over the years. India's population has been growing very fast. In fact, between 1951 and 2001, India's population has almost trebled with an average exponential growth rate of almost 2 per cent. During this period though the compound growth rate in cereal production has been quite satisfactory being at the rate of 2.86 per cent per annum, growth rate in pulses was disappointing being only 0.55 per cent. A noticeable feature in the growth rates of cereal as well as pulses production were that during the pre-green revolution period i.e. 1949-50 to 1964-65, these were higher (being 3.21 and 1.41 respectively) than those of the post green revolution period i.e. 1967-68 to 2000-2001 when the growth rates were 2.79 and 0.85 respectively. The higher growth rates in pre-green revolution period were attributed mainly to additional area under foodgrains and better management practices. However, during the period from 1960 to 1967 production of foodgrains remained almost stagnant. In fact, due to severe drought, production markedly declined in 1965-66 and 1966-67.

Thus, the per capita availability of foodgrains and other essential items depended on the rate of population growth, annual production and net import of the commodities. Table 17.6 shows year-wise net availability and average daily per caput availability of cereals and pulses. It may be seen that daily per caput availability of cereals and pulses and the foodgrains as a whole was 334.2 gm, 60.7 gm and 394.9 gm respectively in 1951. In 1965, the availability increased to 418.6 gm, 61.6 gm and 480.2 gm respectively. In 1966 and 1967 due to sharp decline in production following unprecedented drought, per caput

Table 17.6 Net availability of Cereals and Pulses

Year	Population (million)	Cereals				Pulses	Per Caput Net Availability per day (in gm)		
		Net production	Net imports	Change in government	Net availability**	Net availability	Cereals	Pulses	Total
		(million tonnes)							
1	2	3	4	5	6	7	8	9	10
1951	363.2	40.1	4.1	(+)0.6	44.3	8.0	334.2	60.7	394.9
1961	442.4	60.89	3.49	(-)0.17	64.55	11.14	399.7	69.0	468.7
1962	452.2	61.85	3.64	(-)0.36	65.85	10.24	399.0	62.0	461.0
1963	462.0	60.19	4.55	(-)0.02	64.76	10.08	384.0	59.8	443.6
1964	472.1	61.79	6.26	(-)1.24	69.29	8.81	401.0	51.0	452.0
1965	482.5	67.33	7.45	(+)1.06	73.72	10.85	418.6	61.6	480.2
1966	493.2	54.60	10.34	(+)0.14	64.80	8.68	360.0	48.2	408.2
1967	504.2	57.65	8.66	(-)0.26	66.57	7.30	361.7	39.7	401.4
1968	515.4	72.58	5.69	(+)2.04	76.23	10.57	401.1	56.0	460.1
1969	527.0	73.14	3.85	(+)0.46	76.53	9.06	397.9	47.3	445.2
1970	538.9	76.83	3.58	(+)1.12	79.29	10.20	403.1	51.9	455.0
1971	551.3	84.53	2.03	(+)2.57	83.99	10.32	417.6	51.2	468.8
1972	563.8	82.32	(-)0.49	(-)4.69	86.52	9.70	419.1	47.0	466.1
1973	576.7	76.23	3.59	(-)0.31	80.13	8.66	380.8	41.1	421.9
1974	589.8	82.82	5.16	(-)0.40	88.38	8.76	410.7	40.5	451.2
1975	603.2	78.59	7.54	(+)5.56	80.56	8.76	366.1	39.7	405.8
1976	619.9	94.50	6.91	(+)10.74	90.67	11.42	401.6	50.6	452.2

Table 17.6 Net availability of Cereals and Pulses (Contd.)

Year	Population (million)	Cereals				Pulses	Per Caput Net Availability per day (in gm)		
		Net production	Net imports	Change in government	Net availability**	Net availability	Cereals	Pulses	Total
		(million tonnes)							
1	2	3	4	5	6	7	8	9	10
1977	630.8	87.33	0.47	(-)1.63	89.43	9.96	388.5	43.3	431.8
1978	645.0	100.13	(-)0.84	(-)0.25	99.53	10.69	423.0	45.2	468.2
1979	659.4	104.75	(-)0.98	(-)0.36	103.41	10.79	429.6	44.9	474.5
1980	674.1	88.49	(-)0.48	(-)5.78	93.78	7.63	380.0	30.9	410.9
1981	688.5	104.1	0.5	(-)10.2	104.8	9.4	417.3	37.5	454.8
1982	703.8	106.6	1.6	(+)1.3	108.8	10.1	415.6	39.2	454.8
1983	718.9	103.0	4.1	(+)2.7	104.4	10.4	397.8	39.5	437.3
1984	734.5	122.0	2.4	(+)7.1	117.4	11.3	437.8	41.9	479.7
1985	750.4	116.9	(-)0.3	(+)2.7	113.9	10.5	415.6	38.4	454.0
1986	766.5	119.9	(-)0.1	(-)1.6	121.5	12.3	434.2	43.9	478.1
1987	782.7	115.2	(-)0.4	(-)9.5	124.4	10.4	435.4	36.4	471.8
1988	799.2	113.2	2.3	(-)4.6	120.1	10.7	411.8	36.7	448.5
1989	815.8	136.6	0.8	(+)2.6	134.7	12.5	452.6	41.9	494.5
1990	832.6	138.4	neg.	(+)8.2	132.3	12.5	435.3	41.1	476.4
1991	851.7	141.9	(-)0.6	(-)4.4	145.7	12.9	468.5	41.6	510.1
1992	867.8	136.8	(-)0.7	(-)1.6	137.6	10.9	434.5	34.3	468.8
1993	883.9	145.8	2.6	(+)10.3	138.1	11.7	427.9	34.2	464.1

Table 17.6 ***Net availability of Cereals and Pulses*** *(Contd.)*

1	2	3	4	5	6	7	8	9	10
1994	899.9	149.6	0.5	(+)7.5	142.6	12.2	434.0	35.2	471.2
1995	922.0	155.3	(-)3.0	(-)1.7	154.0	12.7	457.5	37.8	496.3
1996	939.5	147.1	(-)3.6	(-)8.5	152.1	11.3	443.6	32.6	476.2
1997	655.2	162.0	(-)0.6	(-)1.8	163.2	13.0	468.2	37.3	505.5
1998	970.9	156.9	(-)2.8	(+)6.1	147.9	11.7	417.3	33.1	450.4
1999(P)	986.6	164.7	(-)1.5	(+)7.0	156.2	13.2	433.7	36.7	470.4
2000(P)	1002.1	168.7	(-)1.0	(+)8.7	159.1	11.4	434.8	31.2	466.0

(P) Provisional. Neg. Negligible

Notes:

1. Midyear Population figures from 1971 to 1980 are based on projections made by the office of the Registrar General of India: Estimates for 1981 onwards are provisional and are worked out by taking 1991 Census provisional population figures.
2. Production figures relate to agricultural year July-June : 1951 figures correspond to the production of 1950 -51 and so on for subsequent years.
3. Net production has been taken 87.5% of the gross production, 12.5% being provided for seeds, feed requirements and waste.
4. Figures in respect of change in stocks with traders and producers are not known. The estimates of net availability above should not, therefore, be taken to be strictly equivalent to consumption.
5. Net imports from 1981 to 1994 are only on Government account and from 1995 onwards the net Imports are total Imports and Exports of the Country.

SOURCE:- Directorate of Economics & Statistics, Department of Agriculture & Cooperation.

availability of foodgrains recorded a precipitous fall at 408.2 gm and 401.4 gm respectively. Thereafter, however, due to increase in production of cereal crops, per capita availability hovered between 400 gm and 468 gm in case of cereals and 460 gm and 505 gm in case of total foodgrains till 1977 though there were years of abrupt decline in the availability following poor harvest of food crops. In recent years 1998 to 2000) per capita availability of foodgrains again declined due to near stagnant foodgrains production.

A steady decline in the availability of pulses over the years is a cause of concern since it is not only the major item of daily consumption of the of the by and large vegetarian population of the country, it is also considered as the poor men's protein. In the fifties, the daily availability of pulses improved from 61 gm in 1951 to 75 gm in 1959. But thereafter the availability recorded a steady decline with occasional marginal size following imports. Presently (2000 AD) the per caput availability of pulses is a meagre 31 gm. Indeed, the green revolution in foodgrains has totally by passed pulses crop, and unless there is improvement in yield rate through technological innovations, per caput availability may further decline.

In this context it may be stated that the mounting buffer stocks of foodgrains (nearly 62 million tonnes in August 2001) may appear at the outset to be incompatible with a declining per capita availability of foodgrains. These stocks are more a reflection on the purchasing power of consumers than the adequacy of food stuffs from a nutritional point of view. Given the widespread poverty, unemployment and the resultant skewed distribution of income and consumption, the majority of the population is not in a position to satisfy their biological demand for food in its entirety. Should purchasing power improve, we might find that the present surpluses are rendered notional. Thus, this depression in effective demand has led to both stockpiling of foodgrains as well as relative price stability.

Further impetus to agricultural growth can come from two major factors. The first is an increased availability of irrigation. Possibilities of major irrigation projects transforming large areas are extremely limited, with the exception of the Narmada and the Rajasthan canal projects. Ground water exploitation is both costly and energy-intensive. The second major factor is a technological breakthrough with or without the availability of water. We have been particularly hoping for an improvement in rainfed agriculture, but the laboratory results are yet to percolate to individual farmers. Farm operations in large tracts of the country are still a gamble on the monsoon.

It would thus appear that a complacency on the food front is not warranted. Although Indian agriculture may not undergo violent fluctuations on account of climatic factors as it did in the past, any talk of the future Indian agricultural problem being one of managing the plenty is perhaps premature.

Food Security

According to definition emerging out of World Food Summit 'Food Security exists when all people, at all times, have physical, social and economic access to sufficient, safe and nutritious food which meets their dietary needs and food preferences for an active and healthy life. Household food security is the application of this concept to the family level with individuals within households as the focus of concern.' As can be seen, Food Security has been made very broad based to include the question of access in all its forms, and is meant to encompass nutrition security as well. Another important ingredient of food policy in the Indian context has, however, concentrated on a rather narrow definition of making available foodgrains or rather cereals to the vulnerable sections of the society at subsidized prices. The primary instrument of this programme is the Public Distribution System (PDS), which had its origin in the scarcity regime of pre-independence period when the Government was forced to introduce rationing after the Bengal Famine. For many years India had been suffering from shortages off foodgrains, and the only solution to keep prices within reach of particularly the urban low-income group was to build up public sector stocks by procurement and imports in case of shortfalls to meet PDS commitments.

Today, we have surplus foodgrains. Our food godowns are overflowing. We do not have sufficient storage capacity to keep the surplus. Public sector stocks are estimated at over 62 million tonnes. At the same time National Sample Survey Organization (NSSO) data show that per caput consumption of cereals has steadily declined and now stabilized around 11 kg/caput/month in urban areas and 14 kg in rural areas. The number of those getting two square meals throughout the

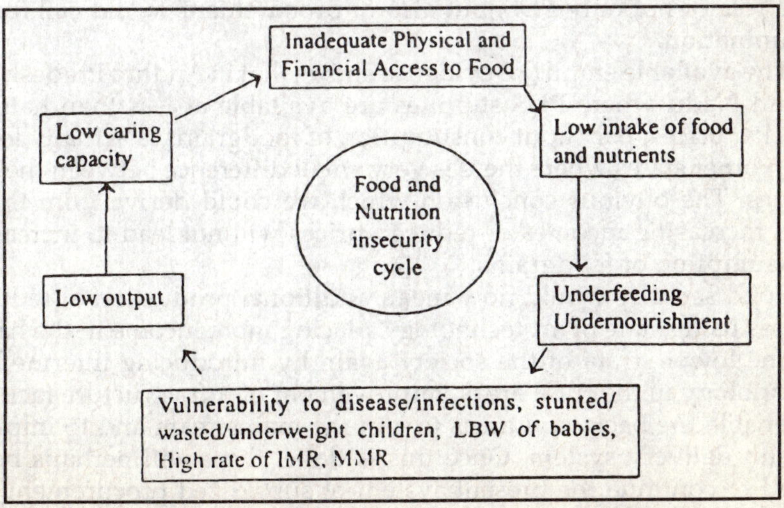

SOURCE: B.K. Taimni, Food Security in 21st Century, 2001.

year increased from 81.1% in 1983-84 to 92.3% in 1992 for rural India with corresponding numbers of 93.2 and 97.3%, respectively for urban areas (Table 19.4). Food consumption basket of an average Indian has diversified to include higher levels of fruits, vegetables, milk, meat, egg, oils, sugar, etc.

Food security, therefore, will have to be redefined and new solutions found to tackle the issue. Let us first have a critical look at PDS. Political parties of different hues are vying with each other to reduce issue prices and increase the scope of PDS under what is called the revamped PDS, a targetted PDS (TPDS) without a proper diagnosis of the problem. We must first of all understand why offtake of foodgrains has today come down to around 40% of the allocation. It is not due to either the inability of the poorer classes to purchase or price difference between PDS and open market being negligible, because even under the rural development programmes, where issue prices are much lower than PDS, the story is the same. The real problem with the PDS however, is:

1. Quality of PDS supplies is rather poor, price being comparatively higher for comparable varieties.
2. PDS supplies are not regular.
3. A daily wage-earner cannot afford to buy his full quota for a month or a fortnight at one go.

If NSSO data are to be believed, and we have no reason to disbelieve it, the consumer even in the lower income group is neither prepared to take any junk, nor waste his time to pay frequent visits to the ration/ fair price shops. He is possibly prepared to pay the price for the quality he is wanting to have. PDS in its present form has not only failed to serve its purpose, but has outlived its utility and become redundant. We have to look for solutions other than the PDS to have a tab on prices. The role of not only PDS, but also of procurement would call for re-examination.

The available empirical evidence shows that in Andhra Pradesh and Tamil Nadu where PDS supplies are available at less than half the market prices, per caput consumption of foodgrains is actually lower than other states where there is very small difference between the two prices. The obvious conclusion which we could derive from this is that increasing incomes or reduced prices will not lead to increasing consumption of foodgrains.

Food security would now mean additional production at reduced prices using state of art technology, placing more income in the hands of the lower strata of the society again by introducing intermediate technology in the rural areas, improvement of infrastructure facilities to enable the backward areas to join the mainstream and to improve health delivery system. Once this is done, there will perhaps be no need to continue the present system of subsidized procurement and distribution. The system being suggested is self sustaining and in tune with the new economic policy.

Grain Banks

The FCI can be gradually dismantled and procurement decentralised through the creation of foodgrain banks in each block/village of the district, from which people may get subsidised foodgrains against food coupons. The food coupons can be numbered serially to avoid frauds. The grain storage facilities can be created within two years under the existing rural development schemes and the initial lot of grains can come from the existing FCI stocks. If culturally acceptable, the possibility of relatively cheap coarse grains, like bajra and ragi and nutritional grains like millets and pulses meeting the nutritional needs of the people can also be explored. This will not only enlarge the food basket but also prevent such locally adapted grains from becoming extinct. The community can be authorised to manage the food banks. This decentralised management will improve the delivery of entitlements, reduce handling and transport costs and eliminate corruption, thereby bringing down the issue price substantially. To enforce efficiency in grain banks operation, people can also be given an option to obtain foodgrains against food coupons from the open market, if the rates in the grain banks are higher, quality is poor or services are deficient. A fund can be set up to reimburse the food retailers for the presented coupons. This competition will lead to constant improvement and lower prices. It must also be mandatory to maintain a small buffer stock at the State level, to deal with exigencies.

The scheme will have to be backed by local communities and one will also have to ensure that it helps in restoring livelihood of the people. The Govt. plans to allocate initially one million tonnes of foodgrains and Rs. 60 crore to meet the transport cost. The community grain banks should not be conceived as an emergency operation, but are to be structured in a manner that they become the hub of a sustainable and replicable community nutrition and ecological security system.

Such banks can perform multiple functions depending upon local needs and opportunities. In the area of health, the control of tuberculosis and leprosy can be speeded up if foodgrains can be given to those whose economic circumstances do not permit taking drugs regularly over many months. The Tuberculosis Research Centre at Chennai is initiating an imaginative programme in collaboration with the U.N. World Food Programme, for using foodgrains to encourage the regular intake of the needed drugs. Similarly, in the area of education, economic and social conditions prevent many children, belonging to the category of child labour, as well as adolescent girls, from continuing their school education. By introducing carefully-designed food for education programmes, substantial progress can be made in reducing the prevalence of such school push-outs.

Another area of nutrition security which can be strengthened through community grain banks is the introduction of a whole lifecycle approach to overcoming malnutrition during various stages in one's life, ranging from pregnant mothers and infants to old and infirm persons. This will help bring down speedily the incidence of low birth weight children and infant and maternal mortality rates. This will call for steps which can foster the integrated implementation of numerous ongoing nutrition intervention programmes.

Strengthening ecological security will be another lasting benefit from the use of grain for the conservation and enhancement of natural resources. The new tribal area grain bank programme would be structured in such a manner that foodgrains are used to establish field level gene banks to conserve local agro-biodiversity, seed banks and water banks. Community grain banks can then promote concurrent progress in achieving desirable goals in conservation, education and nutrition. The storage bins can be designed according to local climatic conditions and separate bins can be fabricated locally for different grains. The Save Grain programme of the Government of India can be used for training and capacity building in storage methods. The Rural Godown Scheme can be integrated with community grain banks.

Grain banks already exist in different parts of the country, set up and operated by both Government and non-governmental agencies. The Madhya Pradesh Government has institutionalised the grain bank (called Anna Kosh) programme. The Government of Rajasthan is planning to integrate the community grain bank initiative with the ongoing Gandhi Gram Yojana, which has several social and ecological objectives including local level water security. The available experience stresses the need for community control and involvement to ensure sustainability and replicability. Otherwise, the grain banks will vanish when Government support ends.

Community grain banks should become central to community-managed nutrition and ecological security programmes. Only then will transaction costs become affordable and the programme replicable. These banks provide opportunities for achieving convergence and synergy among the numerous yojanas initiated in recent years, including Annapoorna and Antyodaya Anna Yojana. The time is opportune for unifying all of them under the supervision of gram sabhas into a community nutrition security system based on a whole lifecycle approach.

In continuation of the present policy to use the surplus grain stocks in a manner that lasting benefits accrue to the people and to the nation, or wood. This will help restore the degraded mangrove ecosystems, control sea erosion and revitalise the habitats of migratory birds, in addition to promoting sustainable capture and culture fisheries. Similarly, a separate allocation of 2 million tonnes of foodgrains for the eco-restoration of hydrologic and biodiversity "hot spots" in the Himalayas (including the Northeast), and Western and Eastern Ghats regions will confer several invaluable long term and downstream benefits. Cherrapunji in Meghalaya, which has a very high annual rainfall, will then no longer remain "thirsty" during summer months. Thanks to the impressive grain stocks, we have for the first time in the history of Independent India an opportunity to leapfrog in achieving freedom from poverty-induced hunger, illiteracy and ill-health.

Cost-Effective Technologies

Our unit cost of production of various agricultural commodities at the farmer's level is increasing. This results in substantial increases in the procurement prices by the Government, which in turn results in higher issue prices, and still higher open market prices. The net result is that both the farmer as well as the consumer are unhappy. Our future agricultural policy has to be cost-effective and aiming at reducing unit cost of production so that a healthy situation is created in the Indian Economy.

Even a cursory analysis of cost of production data indicates that there does exist a considerable scope for reducing the cost of production. For example, in Andhra Pradesh, during 1983-84, the cost of production of paddy on 15% of holding having least cost, averaged at Rs. 1,060-1,480/tonne whereas for the entire sample, it averaged at Rs. 1,410-1,530/tonne. This difference in the cost of production was on account of difference in the pattern and level of use of inputs and the agronomical practices followed. It is indicative of the potential which exists for reducing the unit cost of production. The situation may not be much different in case of other crops in other areas. Such studies should be undertaken which should come up with specific recommendations.

New Zealand Method of Wheat Growing

Dr. Chowdhary, a native of Pakistan and agriculture expert in New Zeland invented "zero till drill" machine for the cultivation of wheat. Under the scheme, as soon as the fields are cleared of paddy, the land will be tilled with this machine and paddy straw in the fields utilized as manure to strengthen the soil and make it more productive. Expenses on cultivation of wheat in this case go down because it saves time and water for preparing the fields. Diesel and water expenses also go down. Use of insecticides is comparatively lesser and the Gulli Danda problems will also diminish by 30 per cent. Paddy straw which otherwise is set on fire and thus polluting the atmosphere is avoided.

The experiment has been a success in Haryana where 2000 acres of land was tilled with this machine during 1996 which has gone up to 1.2 lakh acres during the current (2001) year against 20,000 acres last year. The experiment has yielded dividends and farmers of Punjab in Patiala and Sangrur districts have 70 such machines. Punjab Agriculture University has also invented ship drill machine on the pattern of the "zero till drill" machine. But it costs Rs. 40,000 approximately. The machine is useful for farmers with large landholdings. It carries a subsidy of 50 per cent.

UP Maize

In what is being termed as a major development for increasing coarse grain production, India has established a world record of 80 quintal per hectare in yield of maize in kharif season. Demonstrations in selected areas of Lucknow, Barabanki andAligarh in Uttar Pradesh by technology mission on oilseeds, pulses and maize (TMOPM) resulted in yield of maize spiralling to 80 quintals per hectare against a national average of 18 quintals. Just by proper use of inputs in an optimal combination, ensuring sowing of seeds at a critical time, planing hybrid seeds and giving technical advice, there has been a record increase in yield.

What has astonished even American scientists is that the 80 quintal per hectare yield was achieved for kharif maize and that too without any major technological changes. This was because 30 per cent increase in yield is possible with the same inputs provided the cultivation procedures are fine tuned. Over 1,000 acres in the three districts of UP had been made to grow maize under the mission's supervision and close monitoring. Five different varieties of double cross hybrids had been employed in various plots of these districts to achieve maximum possible yield. Close monitoring ensured that sowing of seeds was done 20 days before the expected rains which was one of the reasons for the quantum increase in yields.

The extension machinery in the country may even not be aware of these issues. The question of their advising the farmer as to how efficiency of input use could be raised so as to reduce the unit cost of production, does not arise. Even otherwise we have not yet been able to realize more than 35% of the potential of known technology. According to an IARI study when full potential of known technology is used it should help reduce the costs. Excessive use of pesticides, fertilizers and water by the farmers, being unaware of actual requirement of crop, not only increases unit cost of production, but also leads to soil degradation and depletion of underground water resources.

An experiment on group farming tried during rabi 1990 season in a small village Peraikonam in Kerala produced a record 6,250 kg of rice/ha. It increased productivity by an average of 20-25% and also lowered the cost of production by Rs. 1,000/ha. Use of right seed and right method of cultivation were the key to success. There exists a large scope for more efficient input use. Report of the Commission for Agricultural Costs and Prices on Price Policy for kharif crops for the year 1985-86 highlighted that it is possible to obtain much larger incremental levels of output within the framework of available technology through a more efficient use of inputs.

Technology is available in the country by which we can increase the yield by 10-12 quintals/ha without any additional investment. Bidirectional sowing of wheat in Punjab can give an increase of 5 quintals/ha. Timely sowing can increase the yield to the extent of 3.75

quintals/ha every week over the late sown. An additional 2-3 quintals of raya crop per hectare can be taken by sowing 9th row alternatively in wheat. Similarly application of one-fourth of required dose of nitrogen at first irrigation before the preparatory tillage has given more than 3% increase in wheat yield. Various other methods also exist by which yield in other crops can be increased without additional investment. If Indian agriculture becomes a professional avocation, it would also strive to optimize gains from technological developments and promote production patterns where the country has comparative advantage. Such a move should help increase the export of farm commodities, traditional as well as non-traditional, both of primary produce and the value-added processed products.

Intermediate Technology

Harmonious development of the Indian economy is hindered by the existence of a technological duality in the economic structure. This duality is reflected in the coexistence of both aeroplanes and rickshaws, handploughs and tractors and the service of traditional vaidyas and modern doctors. In these circumstances, our concept of appropriate technology, comes into conflict with the techno-economic policies followed hitherto which accept the above technological duality. Therefore, R&D institutions are encouraged to direct their resources towards raising productivity of employees rather than increasing the efficiency of capital. Such income disparities are the inevitable outcome of the policies that have been followed so far. If this trend is to be reversed, the concepts and significance attached to savings and labour productivity may have to undergo changes and the entire economy should be viewed as a single entity.

What is then required under the present situation is to improve the efficiency of both labour and capital by the use of appropriate technology. With the help of improved technology, we have to improve the productivity as well as quality of the product of rural artisan. The main attraction to the village industries is their capacity to contribute value addition when the raw materials are processed in the villages besides providing employment to the rural people. This not only keeps the idle hands busy in the rural areas, but also give the rural people capacity to purchase their daily requirements. This also brings in social change and arrests concentration of money power in very few hands. Such intervention may take 4-5 years after which the individuals will not depend on any type of subsidized supplies. They will generate sufficient income to make the system self-sustaining.

Infrastructure

Development of infrastructural activities is the basic requirement for the development of any region. In the absence of any efficient communication system, surpluses of the region cannot move out and necessary inputs cannot move in at competitive prices. All the efforts leading to additional production will be of no use if technological changes are not accompanied by infrastructural development.

Sound Health

Democratic developments in the world have not eradicated but may actually have reinforced poverty. As per report of World Health Organization (WHO), poverty is by far the most important underlying cause of death and disease. The report notes that the much anticipated peace dividend that was to follow democracy in many countries has failed to materialize. Poverty on the other hand, has increased.

The report further says that more than a fifth of the population in the world lives in extreme poverty and almost a third of the world's children are undernourished and half of the global population lacks regular access to the most essential drugs. Poverty is the main reason why babies are not vaccinated, why clean water and sanitation are not provided, why curative drugs and treatment are not available and why thousands of mothers die at childbirth.

The WHO report summarizes the Indian ground situation more vividly. Poverty today is not of people starving for cereals or of absolute unemployment. There is, however, rampant malnourishment and underemployment with low levels of income. The dual objective of providing education and health facilities can be achieved by giving midday meals to school children and subsidized food to the Anganwadi beneficiaries and all the pregnant ladies in selected backward areas. In the first exercise, the scheme should be made applicable to those blocks where, (i) irrigation facilities are less than 10% of the cultivated area and average rainfall is less than 70 cm, (ii) electricity is not available and infrastructural development is nil, (iii) illiteracy among the females is high and (iv) birth and death rates are high.

Some other indicators can also be worked out. The idea here is that targeting should be on area basis rather than the individuals. Health and poverty are highly correlated. Poverty alleviation programmes will, therefore, have to stress on a sound health delivery system. It would perhaps be a sound policy to involve the corporate sector in such developmental activities by handing over the charges of a block each to them.

Therefore, keeping in view the NSSO data indicating that majority of the people in India are not only having two square meals a day but are also having full-time employment, and in view of the ever increasing public sector stocks of foodgrains, the concept of food security and its basic components of procurement and PDS needs complete re-examination. Despite the production and availability of sufficient quantities of foodgrains, there are wide income disparities.

Agriculture which supports nearly 70% of the population shares less than 30% of the Gross Domestic Product (GDP) and there is a further skewed distribution within the sector. Agricultural technology must be cost effective, and enable the farmer to stand on his own in the competitive market. Simultaneously additional incomes have to be placed in the hands of the ruralite, in particular, again by improving technology and rural arts and crafts. This must be accompanied by immediate infrastructural development activities and identifying areas at the block level using various visible and identifiable indicators. High priority should be attached to improve health delivery system particularly in rural areas.

A programme of this nature cannot show results overnight. A regime of subsidies has perpetuated poverty and the present procurement system and PDS have created centres of corruption. They must all be done away with. An open economy based on competitive efficiency must be allowed to flourish. Let the farmers diversify according to market signals and the inefficient ones come up by adopting the available technologies. This is the most opportune time to implement a programme of this nature, when the country has more than sufficient stocks to play the game. Let the Food Corporation of India (FCI) operate within a given band of prices to watch the interest of the producers on the principle of minimum support prices and that of the consumers according to their purchasing power capacity.

Economic Security

In the context of the prevailing situation when over 62 million tonnes of foodgrains are lying in public sector storage, food security really means economic security. About 74% of the population live in rural areas who could broadly be classified into three categories namely the farming class, people engaged in service sector and landless agriculture class. Economic security of all these three classes closely associated with what happens in agriculture sector. We have also seen that a large number of submarginal farmers could really fall into landless agriculture class de facto. They are completely unorganized enjoying at the most an indifferent health and nutrition status, literacy levels and access to basic amenities. It is also true that in a market economy, things can be subsidized but there is nothing like 'free-lunch'. Security, thus, has to be purchased which means they must get gainful avocations to pay for various facilities starting with food, health, drinking water, etc.

Hardly any opportunity exists for shift to non-agriculture sector vis-a-vis employment and the scenario on the horizon does not offer any bright future in this regard. We also know that the rate of population growth in rural areas, for socioeconomic reasons, is higher than their urban counterparts. All this centres on one aspect and that is, they have to find their fortune and salvation in the agriculture sector.

Currently there are two major opportunities for employment in rural sector—one in the agriculture sector and the other under the poverty alleviation programmes.

In this scenario, there is all the more reason for the system to go in for a massive irrigation programme, helping the cropping intensity, thus, offering employment opportunities to the people in rural areas almost around the year. It is possible to achieve higher levels of agriculture production/growth, touching almost all the areas, leaving only a smaller section of the population untouched by its effects. Agriculture in this country is not to be seen as supplier of food vegetable, fruits, milk, meat and fish to the urban population and also servicing the agro based industries, but be seen as a sector where largest section of the nation resides and contributes to the Economic might and Food Security of the Nation. They are human beings—not so articulate and vociferous as some of the other in urban areas and their friends in organized sector. This sector normally gets attention before elections—promising, normally, wrong things we quote from Prof. Galbraith who said, "over the years, I have found virtue—at election times, in the views of (politicians), —of some exceptional illiteracy, economically speaking."[1]

It is this exceptional illiteracy—'economically speaking', which, perhaps, explains the current status of largest number of people engaged and dependent on this sector. Modern age is recognized by a common factor, the power of protection—in fact improve upon—of the income levels in the organized sector, who determine for themselves as to what their income levels should be. It suits all the politicians, the babus, organized unions in public and private sector, thus ensuring their economic security. But for the phenomenally large number of people dependant on (agriculture—directly and indirectly) and that too as individual units (not organized)—this manifestation of free market economy (the power to protect their income levels) has stayed as an infirmity.

Obverse side of the coin is to make agriculture a profitable enterprise for all and not only for certain states or certain areas/pockets by providing them a package of incentives including subsidized inputs and transfer of technology and the reverse side is to create wherewithal for around the year avocation for almost 50% of the rural population who are landless agriculture labourers. Irrigation holds the key, which, accompanied by increasing cropping intensity, addresses the question of giving them long-term employment opportunities in toto. It is their economic security. It is their life as citizens of the country to live a decent life—eat two square meals a day, give their children education and have shelter. Instead of making them dependent on cheap facilities,

[1] We have discussed Chapter 18 the need to diversify agriculture and also rural economy.

it will be appropriate if they are made to earn, to meet their basic needs, which not only will give a fillip to the economy but also bring a self-respect in this class so that they can say, they have not lived on charity but earned whatever they have.

Forward Market in Foodgrains

When the government decides prices there are bound to be distortions; and, when those prices are critical, the distortions give rise to grave problems. That is exactly what has happened to the prices of foodgrains. The regulation of foodgrains prices was motivated by the need to guarantee a minimum price to the farmers, create a buffer stock for distribution of grain through the public distribution system (PDS) and thus ensure a stable price for the consumer.

Over the years, in spite of the increase in production, farmers have been able to get away with bloated prices and Food Corporation of India (FCI), as result, forced to carry excessive stocks. The price to the consumer has not kept pace with the cost and the government consequently has been burdened with excessive subsidy. In the current year (2001-2002), it is conservatively budgeted at Rs. 13,675 crores but will be undoubtedly surpassed by a wide margin.

Prices should cover cost. That is what the Agricultural Prices Commission was expected to do and would have faithfully recommended. But that was not to be the last word. The final prices have been decided by the central government under political pressure from the producer states. In spite of the good crop and large buffer stock of foodgrains, prices have risen far more than prices in the rest of the economy, except fuel.

Prices of food articles, in the last years, rose 78 per cent; prices of industrial goods only 44 per cent. The terms of trade between agriculture and industry moved against the latter. About 25 per cent more industrial goods exchanged for the same amount of food articles. Even in respect of foodgrains the prices of which are controlled by the government, the rise in prices was 31 per cent more than those of industrial goods.

This had two serious consequences. First, it meant that food articles, in spite of having the first claim on the expenditure of the people, went beyond the reach of a large section of consumers. This is precisely why Food Corporation of India accumulated nearly 70 million tonnes of stock when quite a few people, with low incomes, were forced to miss their meals. Had the excess 30 million tonnes stock with FCI come to the market instead, foodgrains prices would have been down to a more reasonable level and prevented the starvation deaths that occurred.

Second, the relatively higher increase in the prices of food articles transferred purchasing power from urban consumers to rural producers. On an average, about 40 per cent of the income in urban areas is spent on food articles. With the rise in their prices by 34 per cent more than those of industrial goods the share of income available to be spent on manufactured articles would have, to that extent, shrunk.

Of course, this transfer of purchasing power would not have been totally lost to industry. For, a part of that money in the hands of the farmers, will have been spent on industrial goods. The difference is that in the urban sector 60 per cent of the total expenditure is on industrial goods; in the rural sector it is only 40 per cent. So, industry would have missed nearly 20 per cent of the demand that would have been generated from the additional money that went into the pockets of the farmers with surplus grain to sell. That would have been responsible for the slowdown the industry has been experiencing for quite some time. The increase in prices of foodgrains was not justified either on the basis of the cost of production or the terms of trade between industry and agriculture. For instance, against the 75 per cent increase in foodgrain prices, prices of fertilisers and pesticides, the important inputs for agriculture, increased by only 57 per cent, of tractors 54 per cent and of agricultural implements 19 per cent.

Obviously it is not the cost but the political pressure that has led to the excessive rise in foodgrains prices and inflated the subsidy that the government has to shell out. Prices of foodgrains have to be completely exposed to the market while assuring the farmer a price for his product without loading Food Corporation of India with involuntary stocks and consequently the government with excessive subsidies.

All this will be possible with the introduction of forward market for foodgrains. That market will decide the price which is fair and which is known in advance to help the farmer plan is crop. Improved communication systems through the use of information technology may help them get a better deal for their produce. Crop insurance schemes can be promoted with government meeting a major part of the insurance premium to protect the farmers against patural calamities. FCI will hold the minimum necessary stock to meet eventualities and to distribute grain through the public distribution system to below-poverty-line consumers. That will minimise the food subsidy as well.

There is a need to shift from the existing expensive, inefficient and corruption ridden institutional arrangements to those that will ensure cheap delivery of requisite quality grains in a transparent manner and are self-targeting. Futures market and free trade: The present system marked by input subsidies and high MSP should be phased out. To avoid wide fluctuations in prices and prevent distress selling by small farmers, futures market can be encouraged.

CHAPTER 18

Hunger, Poverty and Malnutrition

Poverty, hunger and malnutrition are not really synonymous. Each one of them has different meaning even within the same environment. Poverty, for example, is a relative term. There are poor in every society. An advanced country like the United States has around 11% poor. Hunger can theoretically be described as a situation where the individual concerned does not have sufficient purchasing power to meet his or her requirement of energy for normal activity even from the cheapest sources available. Here again income criteria alone will not suffice. While every hungry person would be 'poor', the reverse may not be so. A person may be depriving himself and his family of his basic need, but wasting a major part of his income on drinking or some other wasteful or non-healthy activities. Similarly malnutrition is significantly influenced by attitudes and habits. In fact, malnourishment is more pronounced among the well off societies.

In the light of this, for purposes of our present discussion, we will forget for a moment income or even the calory criteria-both of them being misleading. A person can be considered as hungry who is not having at least two meals a day and his normal activity of life suffers as a result thereof. If the cheapest source of energy in a region is, say coarse cereals or some root crop, and the individual being not addicted to some vices, allocates his resources judiciously so as to provide the minimum energy requirements for himself and his family, we will not consider him hungry. It would mean under this definition that the mere fact of the availability of such commodities in sufficient quantities is not enough. All the people should have easy access to it and every rational consumer should have sufficient purchasing power to secure these commodities to satisfy his/her minimum requirement.

FOOD PRODUCTION

If so, we will leave out cases like those of Bengal Famine or a family which has a completely irrational approach to his way of life. Looking at the availability aspect at the international level, world population has today increased to over 6.0 billion from 2.5 billion fifty years ago in 1950. As against this, food production has expanded from an average level of 707 million tonnes during the quadrennium 1948-49 to 1952-53 to over 2000 million tonnes today. The comparatively higher increase of 183 % in food production as against 140% increase in population is a really welcome sign, disproving Malthus and other pessimists of their creed. The net result is that per capita availability of foodgrains is more than what it was 40 years back. Accordingly an average person in the world today can be assumed to be better fed and clothed.

It is further interesting in this context to note that the total area under foodgrains during the period increased only by 25 per cent. Most of the gains in the production of foodgrains have been achieved through the continued upswing in productivity. The secret behind this success lies in the story of Green Revolution - new seeds, more fertilisers and better water usage technology.

As for India, forgetting the period before 1969-70, we find that production of foodgrains has increased from 99.5 million tonnes during that year to around 209 million tonnes during 1999-2000. The production of fruits, vegetables, milk, eggs, meat, fish vegetable oils and sugar has also shown increases more than the population growth (Table 18.1) At the same time stocks of foodgrains have crossed the minimum stock level requirement by more than 100% and crossed 60 million tonnes in November 2001. By the end of the year, they may be over 75 million tonnes. This would mean that the criteria of availability is more than fulfilled at the country level not only for foodgrains, but also for other protective foods.

HUNGER IN INDIA

Despite this happy situation, we often come across statements like 300 or odd million starving people in the country, not only from politicians, who can be excused, but also from serious students of economics. Let us examine this issue in some details. The only source of information which can throw some light on the consumption pattern of people in the country is the national sample survey data. A study for the period 1970-71 to 1999-2000 (*see* Tables 18.8 and 18.9) shows that per capita consumption of cereals has shown a declining trend in all the states without exception. NNMB data shows that with increasing incomes consumption of cereals declined while consumption of other protective foods increased (Table 18.2). This also goes well with Engel's law which says the same. The case of Kerala is peculiar where tapioca is being substituted by foodgrains. It would then mean that but for Orissa and West Bengal, the remaining part of the country has by and large started substituting foodgrains by other protective foods. One interesting feature of a study of the data is that per capita consumption of foodgrains has started declining even in these three states from 1989-90 onward.

Table 18.1 Per Caput Availability of Food Items

Item	1970-71		1994-95		1997-98	
	Total availability	Per caput (kg/year)	Total availability	Per caput (kg/year)	Total availability	Per caput (kg/year)
Total Population (million)		548.2	-	910.7		955.2
Production of milk (million tonnes)	20.1	36	65.8	72.0	70.8	74.1
Fruits (million tonnes)	12.0	21.89	33.0	36.24	43.3	45.3
Vegetables (million tonnes)	27.3	50	71.0	77.96	72.7	76.1
Eggs Number (million tonnes)	6282	11.4	24753	27.18	28567	29.9
Meat (million tonnes)	0.8	1.39	4.2	4.61	4.2	4.4
Fish (million tonnes)	1.8	3.2	4.8	5.27	5.4	5.6
Vegetable Oils (million tonnes)	1.6	3.0	6.83	7.5	7.2	7.5
Sugar (million tonnes)	3.7	6.75	14.6	16.03	13.85	14.5

Table 18.2 Average Consumption of Foodstuffs (g/cu/day) According to Per Caput Income (PCI) During 1988-90

PCI (Rs./ month	*N*	*Cereals*	*Pulses*	*GLV*	*Other vege- tables*	*Roots and tubes*	*Nuts oil- seeds*	*Condiments spices*	*Fruits*	*Fish*	*Other flesh foods*	*Milk, milk products*	*Fats and oils*	*Sugar and jaggery*	*Protein (g)*	*Energy (kcal)*
< 30	143	475	25	10	34	36	7	14	16	6	3	42	9	16	53.3	2026
30-45	372	509	33	9	34	27	6	18	23	5	2	45	7	20	56.5	2172
45-60	550	490	29	9	44	31	8	17	23	6	1	51	8	0	55.8	2131
60-90	1137	478	29	9	40	37	10	16	28	9	3	62	9	23	55.6	2130
90-150	1424	479	29	9	48	41	14	16	26	14	4	86	11	17	59.4	2213
150-300	1056	452	33	14	54	44	20	15	28	14	6	121	14	33	60.8	2254
>300	499	454	43	14	67	56	29	19	43	20	12	230	25	39	70.3	2595

SOURCE: NNMB Repeat Survey, 1991, NNMB, National Institute of Nutrition, ICMR; Bansil P.C, Agricultural Statistical Compendium, vol. 1 and Supplement, 1996.

Again, we have additional information from NSSO when they asked the question from the sample households, are you having two square meals a day". We observe (Tables 18.3 and 18.4) that while in Orissa. West Bengal and Bihar, during 1983 around 40 per cent of the people in rural areas and 7-16% in urban areas were not having two square meals throughout the year, their number was drastically reduced during 1991 to less than 10% in Bihar and 16 and 21 per cent in West Bengal and Orissa respectively in rural areas. The corresponding figures for urban areas for these 3 states were 4.8, 11.3 and 4 per cent respectively. At the all India level number of those having two square meals throughout the year increased from 81.46 to 94.5 per cent during 1983-98 for rural and the corresponding figure for urban India was 93.25 to 98.1 per cent. This would mean that those who were really hungry during 1998 constituted hardly less than 2 per cent of the population in Urban and 5.5 per cent in Rural India. By now this number would have certainly been reduced further. At the state level; the problem states are Orissa, West Bengal and Bihar where 15.4, 11.4 and 6.6 per cent of rural and 1.7, 2.0 and 2.0 per cent urban respectively were suffering from partial or extreme hunger.

In fact, these 3 States put together constituted nearly 50 percent of the total hungry people in the country. The most critical section which falls under our definition of 'hungry' or 'starvation' is 0.9% (5.2 million) in rural India and 0.2% (0.45 million) in urban India who were not having two square meals even in some months of the year- majority of them are in these very 3 states. Total population suffering from hunger-partial and extreme-during 1998 works out to 4.6% of the total population of 40.4 million during 1998 as against 26 percent below the poverty line during 1999-2000. With the developments during the last 2-3 years, there is every reason to believe that there must be a further decline in the number of those suffering from hunger. This could possibly be in the range of 30.0 million or so, say, around 3 per cent of the total population (Tables 18.5 and 18.6).

POVERTY DEFINED

There is no dispute that to be poor is to be unable to manage the basic elements of human subsistence. No per capita income figures, no indices of calorie consumption can capture the wretchedness that is the lot of the poor, whether destitute amidst the dust of rural India or begging on the side-walks of its teeming cities. To be poor is to be born of a malnourished mother in conditions where ones survival is uncertain; to survive with inadequate food, clothing and shelter, without the stimulation of learning or play; to grow unequipped intellectually or physically to be a productive member of a striving society.

We all know that man does not live by bread alone. Of course we must end poverty, and give men and women enough bread to live on. But music, dance, art and the telling of stories are indispensable to

Table 18.3 Proportion of Hunger (Rural) 1983, 1991 to 1994 and 1998 Percentage Distribution of Households by the Type of Response to the Question-whether all Members of the Household GOT Square Meals a Day

(Percent)

State/Union Territory	Throughout the year				Only some months of the year				Not even in some months of the year				Not Reported
	1983	1991	1993	1998	1983	1991	1993	1998	1983	1991	1993	1998	1993
Andhra Pradesh	84.32	97.0	96.2	96.6	14.69	4.0	3.6	1.7	0.82	0.3	0.2	1.2	.5
Assam	83.87	84.5	90.4	90.1	12.49	10.9	9.0	6.1	3.58	4.6	0.6	0.3	.8
Bihar	62.51	90.8	91.0	92.8	31.81	8.1	8.2	5.1	5.42	0.5	0.8	1.5	.6
Gujarat	96.92	98.4	99.2	97.6	2.78	1.6	0.8	0.9	0.07		0	0.4	1.1
Haryana	98.61	98.7	99.2	99.2	0.73	0.9	0	0.8	0.12	0.4	0.8	0.0	0
Karnataka	80.91	89.9	93.8	96.0	17.81	9.6	5.9	2.7	0.93	0.5	0.3	0.8	.4
Kerala	80.80	85.7	91.2	91.0	15.29	10.7	8.2	7.4	3.68	3.4	0.6	0.4	1.2
Madhya Pradesh	84.34	93.5	96.2	97.0	13.35	5.3	3.5	2.5	1.72	1.2	0.3	0.3	.1
Maharashtra	85.80	96.7	97.4	95.4	13.42	2.8	2.4	4.1	0.68	0.5	0.2	0.4	.1
Orissa	62.79	78.7	83.5	84.4	31.80	18.9	15.7	14.9	5.02	2.4	0.8	0.5	.2
Punjab	98.26	99.7	100.0	99.9	1.35	0.3	0	0.1	0.24		0	0.0	0
Rajasthan	95.95	98.7	99.6	98.5	3.11	1.3	0.4	0.6	0.69		0	0.0	.8
Tamil Nadu	82.10	92.7	94.9	96.9	16.06	7.0	5.1	1.5	1.36		0	0.9	.7
Uttar Pradesh	88.24	96.3	98.6	96.3	10.39	3.3	1.2	2.9	0.62	0.3	0.2	0.5	.3
West Bengal	60.31	84.0	81.4	85.6	31.10	14.8	17.4	11.1	8.60	1.2	1.2	0.3	.4
All India	81.46	92.8	93.8	94.5	16.19	6.4	5.4	4.2	2.35	0.7	0.8	0.9	.4

SOURCE : NSSO and Bansil P.C, Agricultural Statistical Compendium, vol 1 and Supplement, 1997.

Table 18.4 ***Proportion of Hunger (Urban) 1983, 1991 to 1994 and 1998. Percentage Distribution of Households by the Type of Response to the Question—whether Members of the Household GOT square meals a day.***

(Percent)

State/Union Territory	Response type												
	Throughout the year				Only some months of the year				Not even in some months of the year				Not Reported
	1983	1991	1993	1998	1983	1991	1993	1998	1983	1991	1993	1998	1993
Andhra Pradesh	92.94	96.4	99.0	98.3	6.93	2.7	1.0	0.9	0.04	0.9	0	0.7	.1
Assam	90.77	93.8	98.0	98.1	7.23	1.3	2.0	1.2	1.79	4.9	0	0.6	.1
Bihar	87.60	94.4	96.8	97.0	9.14	5.0	2.7	1.1	2.89	0.6	0.5	0.9	.9
Gujarat	98.18	98.5	98.3	98.4	1.05	1.5	1.5	0.8	0.09	--	0.2	0.7	0
Haryana	99.47	98.1	100.0	99.4	0.53	1.9	0	0.6	0.00	--	0	0.0	0
Karnataka	88.65	96.4	97.4	98.6	10.37	2.8	2.6	0.1	0.58	0.8	0	0.3	.1
Kerala	86.05	95.2	92.5	93.9	11.67	4.8	5.5	4.8	1.85	--	2.0	1.1	.2
Madhya Pradesh	94.21	97.7	98.8	98.8	4.86	1.8	1.2	0.9	0.37	0.5	0	0.3	0
Maharashtra	94.50	98.7	98.6	98.5	5.00	1.1	1.1	1.1	0.42	0.2	0.3	0.4	0
Orissa	87.41	88.7	93.2	95.8	11.33	11.3	6.6	1.3	5.00	--	0.2	0.7	.2
Punjab	96.80	99.8	99.5	99.8	1.80		0.5	0.1	0.84	--	0	0.1	.1
Rajasthan	96.98	98.0	99.4	99.2	1.18	2.0	0.4	0.2	0.82	--	0.2	0.0	.7
Tamil Nadu	91.28	96.6	95.8	97.7	7.15	2.8	4.0	0.1	0.27	0.2	0.2	0.6	.7
Uttar Pradesh	95.17	97.6	99.1	98.5	3.86	.2	0.9	0.8	1.05	2.2	0	0.2	.5
West Bengal	91.88	95.9	94.0	96.0	6.14	3.3	5.4	0.2	0.71	0.7	0.6	1.5	.5
All India	93.25	96.9	97.7	98.1	5.56	2.1	2.1	1.1	0.77	0.9	0.2	0.5	.3

SOURCE: NSSO and Bansil P.C, Agricultural Statistical Compendium, vol 1 and supplement.1997.

Table 18.5 Hunger and Poverty in Rural India

State	Population (Million)				Extreme hunger(%)				Number for extreme hunger (Million)				Partial hunger (%)				Number for Partial hunger (Million)				Total hunger (%)				Below poverty line (%)
	1983	'91	'93	'98	'83	'91	'93	'98	'83	'91	'93	'98	'83	'91	'93	'98	'83	'91	'93	'98	'83	'91	'93	'98	'87-88
Andhra Pradesh	44.02	48.6	50.1	54.2	0.82	0.3	0.2	1.2	0.36	0.15	0.10	0.65	14.69	4.0	3.6	1.7	6.47	1.94	1.80	0.92	15.51	4.3	3.8	2.9	33.8
Assam	18.55	19.9	20.8	22.8	3.54	4.6	0.6	0.3	0.66	0.92	0.12	0.07	12.49	10.9	9.0	6.1	3.32	2.17	1.87	1.39	16.03	15.5	9.6	6.4	24.5
Bihar	63.60	75.0	78.3	24.3	5.42	0.5	0.8	1.5	3.45	0.38	0.63	1.26	31.81	8.1	8.2	5.1	20.23	6.08	6.42	4.30	37.23	8.6	9.0	6.6	42.7
Gujarat	24.41	27.1	27.8	30.9	0.07		0	0.4	0.02		0	0.12	2.78	1.6	0.8	0.9	0.68	0.43	0.22	0.28	2.85	1.6	0.8	1.3	21.2
Haryana	10.48	12.4	12.8	14.6	0.12	0.4	0.8	0.0	0.01	0.05	0.10	0.00	0.73	0.9	0	0.8	0.08	0.11	0	0.12	0.85	1.3	0.8	0.8	11.7
Karnataka	27.44	31.1	32.1	35.2	0.93	0.5	0.3	0.8	0.26	0.16	0.10	0.28	17.81	9.6	5.9	2.7	4.89	2.99	1.89	0.95	18.74	10.1	6.2	3.5	35.9
Kerala	21.49	21.4	22.0	23.4	3.68	3.4	0.6	0.4	0.79	0.73	0.13	0.09	15.29	10.7	8.2	7.4	3.29	2.29	1.80	1.73	18.97	14.1	8.8	7.8	16.4
Madhya Pradesh	43.22	50.8	52.8	59.4	1.72	1.2	0.3	0.3	0.74	0.61	0.16	0.18	13.85	5.3	3.5	2.5	5.77	2.69	1.85	1.48	15.07	6.5	3.8	2.8	41.5
Maharashtra	42.39	48.4	49.8	54.8	0.68	0.5	0.2	0.4	0.29	0.24	0.10	0.22	13.42	2.8	2.4	4.1	5.69	1.36	1.20	2.25	14.1	3.3	2.6	4.5	36.7
Orissa	24.17	27.4	28.3	30.6	5.02	2.4	0.8	0.5	1.21	0.66	0.23	0.15	31.80	18.9	15.7	14.9	7.69	5.18	4.44	4.56	36.82	21.3	16.5	15.4	48.3
Punjab	12.61	14.3	14.6	16.3	0.24		0	0.0	0.03		0	0	1.35	0.3	0	0.1	0.17	0.04	0	0.02	1.59	0.3	0	0.1	7.2
Rajasthan	28.11	33.9	35.7	40.1	0.69		0	0.0	0.19		0	0	3.11	1.3	0.4	0.6	0.87	0.44	0.14	0.24	3.8	1.3	0.4	0.6	26.0
Tamil Nadu	33.73	36.8	37.7	40.1	1.36		0	0.9	0.46		0	0.36	16.06	7.0	5.1	1.5	5.42	2.58	1.92	0.60	17.42	7.0	5.1	2.4	39.5
Uttar Prades	94.52	111.5	116.2	131.5	0.62	0.3	0.2	0.5	0.59	0.33	0.23	0.66	10.39	3.3	1.2	2.9	9.82	3.68	1.39	3.81	11.01	3.6	1.4	3.4	37.2
West Bengal	41.70	49.4	51.0	56.0	8.60	1.2	1.2	0.3	3.59	0.59	0.61	0.17	31.01	14.8	17.4	11.1	12.93	7.31	8.87	6.22	39.61	16.0	18.6	11.4	30.3
All India	546.06	628.7	651.6	721.4	2.35	0.7	0.8	0.9	12.83	4.40	5.21	6.49	16.19	6.4	5.4	4.2	88.41	40.24	35.19	30.30	18.54	7.1	6.2	5.1	33.4

SOURCE: NSSO and Bansil P.C. Agricultural Statistical Compendium Vol 1 and Supplement. Last Column from Planning Commission.

Table 18.6 Hunger and Poverty in Urban India

State	Population (million)				Extreme hunger(%)				Number for extreme hunger (million)				Partial hunger (%)				Number for Partial hunger (million)				Total hunger (%)				Below poverty line (%)
	1983	'91	'93	'98	'83	'91	'93	'98	'83	'91	'93	'98	'83	'91	'93	'98	'83	'91	'93	'98	'83	'91	'93	'98	'87-88
Andhra Pradesh	13.39	17.9	18.5	20.0	0.04	0.9	0	0.7	0.005	0.161	0	0.140	6.93	2.7	1.0	0.9	0.928	0.483	0.185	0.180	6.97	3.6	1.0	1.6	26.10
Assam	2.20	2.5	2.6	2.8	1.79	4.9	0	0.6	0.039	0.123	0	0.017	7.23	1.3	2.0	1.2	0.159	0.033	0.052	0.034	9.02	6.2	2.0	1.8	9.40
Bihar	9.35	11.4	11.8	12.7	2.89	0.4	0.5	0.9	0.270	0.046	0.059	0.114	9.14	5.0	2.7	1.1	0.855	1.042	0.319	0.140	12.03	5.4	3.2	2.0	30.00
Gujarat	11.36	14.2	14.7	16.2	0.09		0.2	0.7	0.010	0.000	0.029	0.113	1.05	1.5	1.5	0.8	0.119	0.213	0.221	0.130	1.14	1.5	1.7	1.5	12.90
Haryana	3.03	4.0	4.2	4.7	0.00		0	0.0	0.000	0.000	0		0.53	1.9	0	0.6	0.016	0.076	0	0.028	0.53	1.9	0	0.6	11.70
Karnataka	11.50	13.9	14.4	15.8	0.58	0.8	0	0.3	0.067	0.111	0	0.047	10.37	2.8	2.6	0.1	1.193	0.389	0.374	0.016	10.95	3.6	2.6	0.4	24.20
Kerala	5.11	7.7	7.9	8.4	1.85		0.2	1.1	0.095	0.000	0.016	0.092	11.67	4.8	5.5	4.8	0.596	0.370	0.434	0.403	13.52	4.8	7.5	5.9	19.30
Madhya Pradesh	11.35	15.3	15.9	18.0	0.37	0.5	0	0.3	0.042	0.077	0	0.054	4.86	1.8	1.2	0.9	0.552	0.275	0.191	0.162	5.23	2.3	1.2	1.2	21.30
Maharashtra	23.57	30.5	31.4	34.6	0.42	0.2	0.3	0.4	0.099	0.061	0.094	0.138	5.00	1.1	1.1	1.1	1.179	0.336	0.345	0.381	5.42	1.3	1.5	1.4	17.00
Orissa	3.33	4.2	4.4	4.7	5.00		0.2	0.7	0.167	0.000	0.001	0.033	11.33	11.3	6.6	1.3	0.377	0.475	0.290	0.061	16.33	11.3	6.62	2.0	24.10
Punjab	4.98	6.0	6.1	6.8	0.84		0	0.1	0.042	0.000	0	0.007	1.80		0.5	0.1	0.090	0.000	0.030	0.007	2.64	0.0	0.5	0.2	7.20
Rajasthan	7.73	10.1	10.6	11.9	0.82		0.2	0.0	0.063	0.000	0.021		1.18	2.0	0.4	0.2	0.091	0.202	0.042	0.024	2.00	2.0	0.6	0.2	19.40
Tamil Nadu	17.10	19.1	19.6	20.8	0.27	0.2	0.2	0.6	0.046	0.038	0.039	0.125	7.15	2.8	4.0	0.1	1.223	0.535	0.784	0.021	7.42	3.0	4.2	0.7	20.50
Uttar Prades	21.33	27.6	28.7	32.5	1.05	2.2	0	0.2	0.224	0.607	0		3.86	0.2	0.9	0.8	0.823	0.055	0.258	0.260	4.91	2.4	0.9	1.0	27.20
West Bengal	15.49	18.7	19.3	21.2	0.71	0.7	0.6	1.5	0.110	0.131	0.116	0.318	6.14	3.3	5.4	0.2	0.951	0.617	1.042	0.042	6.85	4.0	6.0	1.7	20.70
All India	171.22	217.6	225.4	249.5	0.77	0.9	0.2	0.5	1.318	1.958	0.451	1.248	5.56	2.1	2.1	1.1	9.520	4.570	4.733	2.744	5.33	3.0	2.3	1.6	20.10

SOURCE: NSSO and Bansil P.C: Agricultural Statistical Compendium, Vol 1 and Supplement

humanity's ability to cope with the human condition. After all, why does man need bread? To survive. But why survive, if it is only to eat more bread. To live is more than just to sustain life-it is to find meaning in life. And the poorest men and women in the developing world feel the throb of culture on their pulse, for they tell stories to their children as their fires are lit at dusk and the shadows fall—stories of their land and its heroes, stories of the earth and its mysteries, stories that have gone into making them what they are.

It is necessary, too, to tackle poverty on a broad front. After all, what is the use of providing a farmer with high yielding varieties if his crop cannot fetch a fair price? What is the point of providing development aid when poor countries lose more to trade barriers and declining commodity prices? What could be more cruel than immunizing a child only to see it die of starvation? What is the use of education if unemployment is the only reward awaiting the educated. Indeed, there are broader questions too, that one would tend to ask whenever poverty is discussed—questions of sustainable development and of good governance, what is the merit of economic growth if it benefits only the rich? Who can sustain creative energy under conditions of instability or corrupt institutions.

For whom, after all, is development? It is not an abstract endeavour of states, a set of figures on GNP tales. Development is about people—human beings with needs and rights. Without culture, development becomes mere materialism, a subject for economists and planners rather than a matter of people. And if people are to develop, it is unthinkable that they would develop without culture, without song, and in turn, without expressing their views on their present lot and their future hopes. Development implies dynamism, requires freedom—the freedom to create.

Let us not forget that there exist, around us, many societies whose richness lies in their soul and not in their soil, whose past may offer more wealth than their present, whose culture is more valuable than their technology. We must strive to eradicate poverty, but we must also ensure that poverty of the spirit that ultimately is as harmful to humanity as lack of food or medicine. Let us work for a world in which we can fill both stomachs and souls at the same time.

It must be appreciated that poverty is no longer inevitable. For the first time, long—cherished hopes of eradicating poverty seem attainable, because the world has the material, natural and technological resources to do so within a generation—provided that concerted political will and sufficient resources are brought to the task. This is not just rhetoric: over the last three decades, more than 20 industrial states, and more encouraging, more than a dozen developing countries, have eliminated absolute poverty. Others can do it too.

The wealth of nations has increased seven-fold since 1945. The astonishing proliferation of billionaires is not the only indication of that. Overall, the proportion of people living in poverty has declined; yet thanks to population increases, the number of poor has risen considerably. Almost one-quarter of the world's population still lives in poverty. Income disparities between the richest 20 per cent and the poorest 20 per cent of the world's population have doubled since 1960 from 30:1 to 61:1. The statistics point to the increasing number of people (1.5 billion today) with incomes of less than $1 a day; about three billion people, half the world's population, live on less than $2 a day.

There are 750 million people unemployed and another 750 million underemployed. Some 160 million children are moderately or severely malnourished. About 110 million do not attend school. Another 1.5 billion are without clean drinking water, 800 million have no health services whatsoever, 35 million people suffer from HIV/AIDS. And poverty in old age remains the most common human experience around the world.

HUNGER AND POVERTY

Number of the persons below the poverty line as calculated by the Planning Commission is based on the value attached to an average consumer basket at average unit prices, providing specified number of calories for rural and urban population. It would be appreciated that there is some sort of arbitrariness in this calculation at every stage. A study by Subramanian and Deaton (Table 18.7) , shows that on an average rural Maharashtra households in 1983 spent Rs. 1.14/1000 calories, with the poorest decile paying just Rs. 0.88 and top one Rs. 1.5. If so, the calory criteria and the values attached to determine the number of those below the specified level as of those below the poverty line would not appear to be correct. The same NSSO source gives information about the hungry in India, as discussed here already. We have concluded that there would hardly be 3 per cent of the population who are hungry as against 26 per cent below poverty line.

It would then seem that if poverty line is intended to define those suffering from hunger, there is something wrong somewhere down the line. Our calculations are from the same source as an answer to a direct question and Planning Commission calculations represent a derived number from the same source with a number of assumptions. Certainly, we should depend more on a direct answer. Therefore, there is an urgent need to look into the issue immediately when the Tenth Plan is being formulated. It will have a number of implications for the new policy framework. Latest data from the 55th Round should be analysed immediately at the sub regional level.

The first step for a solution of the problem would be to locate the areas where a majority of these hungry people are concentrated in Assam, Bihar, Kerala, M.P., Orissa and West Bengal. Employment generating programmes and infrastructural development in the selected

Table 18.7 ***Expenditure Patterns, Calorie Consumption, and Prices Per Calorie, Rural Maharashtra, 1983***

	Expenditure share (%)			*calorie share (%)*			*Price/calorie (Rs/1 000 calories)*		
	Mean	*Bottom 10%*	*Top 10%*	*Mean*	*Bottom 10%*	*Top 10%*	*Mean*	*Bottom 10%*	*Top 10%*
Food groups									
Cereals	40.7	46.0	31.0	70.8	77.3	57.3	0.64	0.51	0.79
Pulses	8.9	10.2	7.8	6.6	6.2	7.2	1.51	1.44	1.60
Dairy	8.1	4.9	11.8	2.8	1.3	4.9	3.69	3.59	3.92
Oils and fats	9.0	9.2	9.2	5.9	4.8	7.6	1.74	1.67	1.81
Meat	5.1	3.4	6.4	0.7	0.4	1.0	11.7	11.0	12.2
Fruit & vegetables	10.5	8.5	12.0	3.5	2.3	5.4	3.90	3.83	3.85
Sugar	6.5	7.4	5.9	7.2	7.0	8.0	1.01	0.94	1.09
Other food	11.3	10.4	16.1	2.5	0.8	8.6	17.4	16.8	15.9
Cereals									
Rice	11.6	9.0	10.9	15.2	10.1	16.5	0.95	0.89	1.02
Wheat	5.6	3.8	7.9	8.5	4.7	14.4	0.79	0.73	0.82
Sorghum	18.2	27.4	9.3	37.8	52.9	21.6	0.50	0.43	0.55
Pearl millet	3.0	2.7	1.3	6.6	4.9	3.2	0.48	0.48	0.50
Other coarse cereal	1.2	2.8	0.3	2.2	4.5	0.6	0.66	0.58	0.99
Cereal substitutes	1.1	0.5	1.3	0.6	0.2	0.8	2.23	2.22	2.22
Total food (or total	67.4	73.4	54.1	2.120	1.385	3.382			
calories)				2.098	1.429	3.167			

Mean refers to mean over the whole sample, bottom 10% to mean over households in the bottom decile of per caput household expenditure, top 10% to mean over households in the top decile of per caput household expenditure. The figures in the last row of the middle panel are unadjusted and adjusted total calories respectively, where the adjustment corrects for meals given to others or not received from others. Shares of calories and of expenditures are calculated on an individual household and are averaged over all appropriate households. Calorie prices are averages over consuming households.

pockets should then be mounted. Most of the activity can be in the nature of 'Food for Work' programme, part of the wages being paid should be in the shape of 'food coupons' which the target population can cash from a designated shop in the area. The whole question of TPDS etc. will perhaps have no meaning. The issue is restricted to only these 30 million or odd persons who are concentrated in certain pockets of these few states. It is heartening to note that these very so called backward states are coming up fast in agriculture, the backbone of the economy. Farmers in the most fertile part of the country, the green belt, which stretches over UP, Bihar, Orissa and West Bangal were slow in adopting the high yielding technology. In the seventies, however, the green revolution first spread to western UP and then to the eastern part. In the eighties, West Bengal experienced impressive gains in agricultural production. Now it appears that agricultural growth is picking up in other eastern states, the most backyard part of the country, as well.

MALNUTRITION

The problem of malnutrition and the solutions are quite different from those of hunger. We will restrict ourselves here to only those who cannot afford to purchase sufficient quantities of necessary protective foods and vitamins etc. or are living under unhygienic conditions, exposing themselves to nutritional and other diseases. We may define malnutrition as a pathological state resulting from a relative or absolute deficiency of one or more essential nutrients, proteins, minerals, vitamins and energy. It results from interaction of several factors-ignorance, illiteracy, and poverty which lead to inadequate feeding. The traditional beliefs, taboos, food fads, customs and infection are the other major contributing factors in malnutrition. There are an estimated 60 million malnourished children in India, of whom nearly one lakh are dying every month.

It can be due to specific vitamin/mineral deficiencies. The deficiency of vitamin A, for example, leads to grave complications, like blindness and an estimated 2.5 million children are threatened in this respect. Of these, 12000 may loose their sight by 2002 year end. Protein Energy Malnutrition (PEM) comprises of a variety of very closely interrelated syndromes like, Kwashiorkor which is probably the result of consumption of low protein diet providing just enough energy to satisfy the needs of the child and is usually in children aged 1-4 years. Again marasmus is a clinical form of protein malnutrition primarily due to gross deprivation of calorie, usually occurring in the age group 6 months to 5 years. Similarly vitamins B, C, D, and iron as well as Iodine deficiencies lead to various other body problems.

---

* List of various nutritional programme is at Appendix A 18 1.

Nutrition—Relevant Actions

The Government of India has taken up a major programme called the Integrated Child Development Services Scheme (ICDS). ICDS was initiated in India in 1975, and has thus been operational for over 25 years).* It happens to be the largest single programme in the area of child development anywhere in the world. It includes service not only to children, but also to pregnant and lactating women. ICDS delivers a package of services comprising of supplementary nutrition, immunization, health checkups referral services, and health and nutrition education to children under 6 years of age, pregnant and nursing women, and preschool education to children between 3 and 6 years of age. Thus, it adopts a holistic approach to improve child development by reduced incidence of mortality, morbidity, malnutrition and school dropouts. The integrated package of services offered under the ICDS addresses all three issues of concern i.e. care factors (through the education/information component), health and to a lesser extent, household food security (through supplementary feeding).

The GOI rightly followed gradual ICDS expansion policy, based on two kinds of targeting: first to the most disadvantaged areas and second, within them to vulnerable preschool children and pregnant and nursing women. The initial geographic focus was on tribal, drought-prone areas and blocks with a significant proportion of scheduled caste population. The programme is also targeted towards malnourished children, but in practice most beneficiaries of supplementary feeding are not selected through nutritional screening. Selection criteria generally depend upon a combination of individual worker's perceptions of which are the poorest households and overall quotas which the central and individual state governments set for supplementation. Similarly the Tamil Nadu Integrated Nutrition Project (TINP), a World Bank/IDA assisted health and nutrition intervention offers a package of health and nutrition services to young children and pregnant and lactating women in rural Tamil Nadu. The first TINP project has been followed up with a second generation TINP-II.

TINP-I was targeted at 6-36 month old children, and lactating women. Project activities were started in October 1980 in one Pilot block, and extended gradually to cover 177 out of a total of 385 rural blocks in the state, by 1989/90. Of these, 31 rural blocks have been subsequently converted to ICDS, so that a total of 146 blocks are covered by TINP-I. Area-targeting was attempted inasmuch as the poorest districts not covered by ICDS were selected for preferential coverage under TINP-I. Universal growth monitoring and promotion, well-targeted selective short-term supplementary feeding complemented with a strong information-education-communication component, are among the critical/unique design features of this programme.

The Project had four major components: nutrition services, health services, communications, and monitoring and evaluation. The main project strategies were to provide nutrition education and primary health care to pregnant and lactating women and children of 6-36 months; to monitor the growth of children in this age group through monthly weighing and growth charting; and to provide supplementary feeding and health checks to children with faltering growth, as well as intensive counselling to their mothers. To provide these services, nutrition centres staffed by part-time women community nutrition workers were set up in about 9000 villages. These were to be assisted by local women's groups created under the project and strengthened health outreach and referral services. As a result of these interventions and other activities, there is some improvement in the nutritional standard. The NNMB has been conducting some surveys in this direction. Their results for 8 states present a comparative picture of nutritional status during the period 1975-79 and 1988-90 and 1996.

Growth Status of Pre-school Children

Weight for age status (Gomez classification): Young children (1-5 years) were classified into different nutritional grades based on their weight for age. Normals (90% and above), mild (75-89%), moderate (60-74%) and severe (below 60%). The percentage of normal children increased from 5.9 in 1975 to 8.9 in 1996, although it shows a little decline from 9.9% in 1988. The prevalence of severe malnutrition has declined from 15 to 6.2% during the period. In all the states the proportions of normal and mildly malnourished children increased while those of 'moderately' and severely malnourished decreased (except in Orissa where moderately malnourished showed an increase). The decline of severe grades was highest in Maharashtra, whereas Gujarat is the only state where percentage of severely malnourished children has not only increased substantially, but is the highest in the country.

The second National Family Health Survey of India (1998-99) report reveals that in Punjab a state higher on per capita income levels 80, per cent of the children in the age bracket 6-35 months are anaemic and even 41 per cent women suffer from some degree of anaemia. Despite claims of the best health facilities, the nutritional status of children is low. At least 29 per cent of them, under three years, are underweight. An equal percentage are stunted. The high rate of vaccination notwithstanding, 13 per cent of the girls compared to only 5 per cent of the boys did not receive the required vaccination.

When it came to the prescribed health indicators, it was seen that on the weight-for-height index 17 per cent of the some were undernourished. Though Punjab has generally a healthy population, the survey revealed certain morbidity patterns—1 per cent each suffered from asthma, malaria and jaundice, 0.5 per cent from tuberculosis and 28 per cent of the women suffered from one or the other reproductive health problem, including abnormal vaginal discharge, urinary tract infection and pain or bleeding associated with intercourse. Surprisingly, 41 per cent of such women did not seek any medical advice or treatment. This practice was more pronounced in poor or middle class households. Nearly 28 per cent of the men above 15 years consumed liquor. Punjab and Goa are the highest drinkers of alcohol. Smoking is also widely prevalent.

It is interesting to observe that high income states have higher number of malnourished children. Malnutrition is also not related to calory intake. Tamil Nadu and Kerala which are lower on the calory scale have the least number of undernourished. The only possible explanation could be better health delivery system and higher per child public expenditure in these states (Tables 18.8 and 18.9).

Stunting, Wasting and Undernourished Profile

Standard deviation classification is given in Table 18.10 for different types of malnutrition stunting (height for age), wasting (weight-for-

Table 18.8 Distribution (%) of 1-5 Year Children (Boys and Girls) by Nutritional Status* (Weight for Age)-Gomez Classification

State	*Period*	*N*	*Nutritional Grades*			
			Normal	*Mild*	*Moderate*	*Severe*
Kerala	1975 +	737	7.5	35.7	46.5	10.3
	1988 +	882	17.7	47.4	32.9	2.0
	1996 +	886	22.2	50.7	25.1	2.0
Tamil Nadu	1975 +	1183	6.2	34.2	47.0	12.6
	1988 +	3337	8.0	42.0	45.8	4.2
	1996 +	819	14.4	49.2	35.5	2.9
Karnataka	1975 +	1065	4.6	31.1	50.0	14.3
	1988 +	2035	4.8	38.1	48.8	8.3
	1996 +	1684	9.4	39.0	45.4	6.2
Andhra Pradesh	1975 +	809	6.1	32.4	46.1	15.4
	1988 +	2838	8.7	39.5	44.3	7.5
	1996 +	1962	7.2	38.1	47.6	7.1
Maharashtra	1975 +	760	3.2	25.4	49.5	21.9
	1988 +	1666	6.7	38.0	47.5	7.8
	1996 +	1015	7.4	35.5	49.5	7.7
Gujarat	1975 +	718	3.8	28.1	54.3	13.8
	1988 +	1262	7.3	33.9	45.8	13.0
	1966 +	647	4.5	31.8	47.0	16.7
Orissa	1975 +	371	7.5	35.9	41.7	14.9
	1988 +	1175	8.1	34.6	46.6	10.7
	1996 +	1651	3.3	42.2	50.4	4.1
Pooled	1975 +	6248	5.9	31.6	47.5	15.0
	1988 +	13432	9.9	37.6	43.8	8.7
	1996 +	8664	8.9	40.6	44.3	6.2

* National Centre for Health Statistics (NCHS) Standards used

SOURCE: Report of Second Report Survey, National Nutrition Monitoring Bureau, Institute of Nutrition, Hyderabad, 1999.

Table 18.9 Inter-state Variations in the Incidence of Malnutrition and its Correlations

State	Percentage of moderately or severely malnourished				Per consumer unit calorie intake (k Cal/day)			Infant morality rate/ 1000 live births			
	1975-79	1988-90	1990-91*	1996	1976-79	1986-90	1990-91*	1977-79	1987-89	1992	1996
States with high per caput SDP											
Maharashtra	71.4	55.3	71.9	57.2	2300	2211	1929	92	64	59	48
Gujarat	68.1	58.8	60.8	63.7	2162	2375	2002	128	91	67	61
States with medium per caput SDP											
Tamil Nadu	59.6	50.0	52.4	36.4	2275	1871	1950	103	73	58	53
Karnataka	64.3	57.1	62.8	51.6	2932	2431	2293	83	76	73	53
Kerala	56.8	34.9	35.6	27.1	1978	2140	2055	44	25	15	14
Andhra Pradesh	61.5	51.8	50.8	54.7	2447	2340	2247	116	81	71	65
States with low per caput SDP											
Madhya Pradesh	61.3	54.9	50.7		2283	2614	2397	145	119	104	97
Orissa	56.6	57.3	57.7	54.5	—	—	—	143	123	115	96

(a) 1991-92 for Maharashtra, Gujarat, Orissa, West Bengal and Uttar Pradesh

Source: NNMB : Report of Repeat Surveys (1988-90), NIN, Hyderabad, 1991

NNMB : Annual Survey Report (1990-92), NIN, Hyderabad, 1993

*List of various nutritional programmes is at Appendix A 18.1.

Table 18.10 Distribution (%) of Pre-school Children According to Standard Deviation (SD) Classification

SD classification according to	Period	N	< – 3 SD	– 3 SD to – 2 SD	– 2 SD to – 1 SD	– 1 SD Median	> Median
Weight/age	1975-79	6.428	38.0	39.5	18.3	3.3	0.9
(under weight)	1988-90	13.432	26.6	42.0	24.2	6.0	1.2
Height/age	1975-90	6.428	53.3	25.3	14.6	4.8	2.0
(stunting)	1988-90	13.432	36.8	28.3	21.0	9.9	4.0
Weight/height	1975-79	6.422	2.9	15.2	44.3	29.0	8.6
(wasting)	1988-90	13.422	2.4	17.5	44.0	27.6	8.5

height) and undernourished (weight-for-age). Children falling between median - 2 SD and median - 3 SD are considered as moderately malnourished while those below the median -3 SD are classified as severely malnourished. The NCHS values are used as reference for this purpose. This clearly shows that there has been 'substantial' reduction in the percentage of children suffering from severe forms of 'underweight' 'stunting' as well as 'wasting with corresponding increases in the milder forms over the period-a trend similar to that of Gomez classification.

CONCLUSION

Our discussion in the preceding pages shows that we have to guard against the confusion of treating poverty, hunger and malnutrition as the same. They are clearly three different identities-the symptoms and remedies for each are clearly defined. Poverty being a relative term, we have neither defined it, nor attempted to make any calculation. In fact, any society can put a break at any point according to its socio economic milieu and the solutions would lie in overall economic development with emphasis on those who constitute the lower income groups. The position of those who are hungry or malnourished is different. They must get high priority and any egalitarian society cannot afford to neglect the claims of this highly vulnerable section.

The number of hungry in the country during 1993 was just 40 million, which during the last 8 years must have declined further. The number of malnourished children and women has also come down. Their location and problems are different than those who are hungry. We understand that the Ministry of Health has concluded a country-wide nutritional survey. This provides information about the present state of affairs. Since the information collected and analysed is districtwise, it is of much more relevant for further policy programmes.

The real solution to hunger and malnutrition lies in putting more incomes in the hands of the people by cost effective technologies in agriculture and introducing intermediate technology in the non-farm rural sector. This has to be accompanied by the development of an efficient infrastructure and appropriate health delivery system. With regard to health delivery system it may not be out of place to mention that despite all the rhetoric about progress made, India is not really a healthy nation. Its health statistics are worse than those of Ghana, Vietnam, the Philippines or Mexico. The cumulative impact of little planning and a feckless leadership is an inefficient delivery system. It is more comfortable controlling disasters than developing a preventive health mechanism. Since our individual targeting approach has not succeeded to bring the desired results, we strongly feel that area approach will be the correct answer to tackle the immediate problem before us.

Appendix 18.1

Important current government (including collateral programme) for addressing nutrition problems

Integrated Child Development Services (ICDS)	Provides a package of services including supplementary nutrition to control nutritional and health problems; implemented by Ministry of Human Resource Development, Department of Women and Child Development.
Administration of Vitamin A	To address blindness among children due to Vitamin A deficiency; a concentrated dose of Vitamin A is given orally every six months through peripheral health workers; implemented by Ministry of Health and Family Welfare.
Distribution of Iron and Folic Acid Tablets	To prevent nutritional anaemia amongst women and children; distribution is done through health centres; implemented by Ministry of Health and Family Welfare.
Pilot Programme against Micro Nutrient Malnutrition	To improve micro-nutrients status among school children, adolescent boys and girls, women of reproductive age and elderly population; implemented in five districts in the

	States of Assam, Bihar, Orissa, Tripura and West Bengal; implemented by Ministry of Health and Family Welfare.
National Iodine Deficiency Disorders Control Programme (NIDDCP)	To focus on provision of iodized salt consumption; most States have banned use of salt other than iodized salt for edible purpose; over 600 private manufactures have been licensed by the Salt Commissioner to produce iodized salt; more than 500 of them have also commenced production; about four million tonnes of iodized salt is now being produced; implemented by Ministry of Health and Family Welfare.
National Programme of Nutritional Support in Primary Education	This is a nationwide programme started in 1995 as a measure of contributing to universalisation of primary education and of simultaneously improving the nutrition of children in primary classes. Foodgrains (Wheat/Rice) @ 3 kgs per student per month is distributed based on linkage to attendance to children in primary classes. The stipulation is that the children should put in a minimum attendance of 80%. Previous month's attendance is taken into consideration. All children in the primary classes of all Government, Government aided and local body schools are covered. Foodgrains are given free of cost to implementing agencies. Cost of transport of foodgrains is also reimbursed; implemented by Ministry of Human Resource Development, Department of Education.
National-Social Assistance Programme (NSAP)	The NSAP was launched on 15th August 1995 as a centrally sponsored programme with 100% central funding to States and UTs. It has, inter alia, a maternity related component namely, National Maternity Benefit Scheme (NMBS). The objective is to give financial assistance to pregnant women of households living below the poverty line; implemented by Ministry of Rural Development.
Annapoorna Scheme	The scheme aims at providing food security at 10 kgs foodgrains per month to all those who,

	though eligible for old age pensions, remaining uncovered under the National Old Age Pension Scheme; implemented by Ministry of Rural Development.
Accelerated Rural Water Supply Programme	The programme is meant for assisting State Governments in provision of drinking water to all rural habitations in the country; implemented by the Ministry of Rural Development, Department of Drinking Water Supply.
Rural Sanitation	The scheme is for supplementing the efforts of State Governments in providing sanitation facilities to the rural masses. The scheme envisages achievements of at least 35% coverage of rural population by the end of the Ninth Five Year Plan. The scheme has also been restructured so as to be community led and people centred. Rural school sanitation is also a major component, the objective being facilitation, at the entry point, of wider acceptance of sanitation among rural masses; implemented by Ministry of Rural Development, Department of Drinking Water Supply.
Urban Water Supply and Sewerage	The scheme, provides assistance and technical guidance to States and Union Territories for formation of water supply and sanitation programmes through Central Public Health and Environmental Engineering Organisation; implemented by Ministry of Urban Development.
Support to Water Supply Scheme of Major Cities Facing Acute Water Shortage	Scheme is self-explanatory; implemented by Ministry of Urban Development.
Special Scheme for Solid Waste Management and Sanitation	Scheme is self-explanatory; implemented by Ministry of Urban Development.

CHAPTER 19

Demand for Foodgrains by 2020 AD

Starting from Malthus, the question of feeding the ever growing population has been engaging the attention of politicians and academicians alike. At the international level, the history of global carrying capacity estimates goes a century back. Nobody could make reliable global appraisals until there was at least basic information regarding the extent of cultivated and potentially cultivable area, typical yields of dominant cereal crops, and their likely future increase. As with so many other developments, the time for projecting the total population that the planet could support came during the last decades of the nineteenth century. Ravenstein (1891)[1] perhaps the first researcher to investigate the limit, came up with a maximum total of just under 6 billion people. Shortly afterwards, Pfaundler (1902)[2] assuming no extension of the then existing 2,174 million hectares (Mha) of cropland and good grazing land, average density of 5 people per hectare supported by traditional farming methods, and recycling of organic matter-ended up with a minimum of 11 billion people. Numerous other estimates followed, and those vary from 10 to 40 billion people[3]. Such is the diversity of these estimates. The position is more or less the same in India. Demand projections for foodgrains vary widely (179 to 241 million tonnes) even for the year 2000 AD (Table 19.1).

The position is all the more complicated for the year 2020. Although there is no dearth of 'doomsday' crystal gazers in India, the position in the country today is that stocks of foodgrains are overflowing and the issue is one of its disposal. It is, therefore, necessary to examine the issues involved in the estimation of future requirements of foodgrains and come up with somewhat realistic estimates for 2020. Demand projections for foodgrains have two broad components—Human consumption and feed, seed and wastages, etc. While sufficiently reliable data are available on long term series regarding human consumption, the other segment—feed, seed and wastages, etc. is a completely unexplored area.

Table 19.1 Comparison of Studies for Demand Projections for Foodgrains in 2000 A.D.

(Million tonnes)

Studies	*Human demand*	*Domestic demand*
1. National Commission on Agriculture, 1976		205-225
2. Working Group (Requirement)	Foodgrains	179
Demand at Physiological Level	Foodgrains	219
3. World Bank, 1981		191-205
4. IFPRI study (for Asian Development Bank), 1984		210
5. Planning Commission, 1985		240
6. Radhakrishna & Ravi, 1990, Centre for Economic and Social Studies, Hyderabad	205[b]	234[e]
7. G.S. Bhalla	Foodgrains	263
8. Radhakrishna & Ravi (1994)	Foodgrains	230.22
Cereals	217.94	
Rice	106.37	
Wheat	83.99	
Coarse Cereals	27.58	
Pulses	12.28	
Foodgrains		238.52 - Expenditure growth
Cereals		Rate 5% 224.54
Foodgrains		237.02-30% Reduction in Giri Rate
9. Sarma and Gandhi	176[a]	220[c]
10. IFPRI,1990	183[b]	227[c]
11. P.C. Bansil, 1996		198[d]
12. Praduman Kumar, 1996	182[b]	209[e]
13. IARI-IFPRI study		205[c]

[a] Without change in income distribution

[b] With change in income distribution.

[c] Projected the requirements for seed, feed, industrial use and wastage. Feed demand is computed using the feeding ratio (that is, the quantity of feed required to produce one unit of livestock products).

[d] Using incremental demand model by providing additional requirement for household and non-household over the base year demand

[e] Using a grossing factor of 1.143 to account for non-household demand.

Bansil, P.C. (1996): 'India's Demand for Foodgrains in 2000AD—Simple Incremental Demand Model'. Indian Farming, February, 1997.

Bhalla, G.S. (Ed.) Economic liberalization and Indian agriculture. Institute for Studies in Industrial Development, New Delhi, 1994.

Government of India (1976): Report of the National Commission on Agriculture part III: Demand and Supply, Ministry of Agriculture and Irrigation, New Delhi.

J.M. (1994): Food Exports and Food Requirement, Economic and Political Weekly, Vol. XXIX, No. 35, pp.2261.

IFPRI (1984), Assessment of Food Demand-Supply Prospects and Related Strategies for Developing Member Countries of the Asian Development Bank. International Food Policy Research Institute, Washington. D.C., mimeo.

Kumar, Praduman, Mark W. Rosegrant and Howarth, E. Bouis (1996), Demand for Foodgrains and Other Food in India, Indian Agricultural Research Institute, New Delhi and International Food Policy Research Institute, Washington. D.C., mimeo.

Radhakrishna, R & Ravi, C. (1990): Food Demand Projections for India, Centre for Economic and Social Studies, Hyderabad.

Radhakrishna, R & Ravi, C. (1991): Food demand projections for India, Centre for Economic and Social Studies, Hyderabad.

Radhakrishna, R. & Ravi, C. (1992): Effects of Growth, Relative Price and Preferences on Food and Nutrition, Indian Economic Review, Vol. XXVII, pp. 303.

Radhakrishna, R & Ravi, C. (1994): Food demand in India: emergence trends and perspectives, Paper presented at the International Conference on Economic Liberalisation in South Asia, Australia South Regional Centre, Australia National University, 30 November-2 December, 1994.

Radhakrishna, R & Murty, K.N. (1995): Econometrics of complete demand systems with illustration for India, Centre for Economic and Social Studies, Hyderabad.

Sarma, J.S. and Vasant P. Gandhi (1990): Production and Consumption of Foodgrains in India: Implications of Accelerated Economic Growth and Poverty Alleviation. International Food Policy Research Institute, D.C.: Research Report No. 81.

World Bank (1991): Country economic memorandum, Vol. II.

World Bank (1992): Market outlook for major primary commodities, Report No. 814/92.

HUMAN CONSUMPTION

As regards the demand for human beings, one of the constraints relates to human behaviour which changes not only from place to place, but also from time to time. Any change in income or living conditions reflects itself profoundly in food habits. In other words, food consumption levels are closely connected with the standard of living and the environment. Urban people with higher income, for example, consume less cereals than people in the villages. The change is not only in quantity but also in the quality of the grain consumed. Rice and wheat which account for more than 80 per cent of foodgrains constitute the staple of majority of the people in India. Next come coarse grains and then there is a small section of the people in certain parts of Kerala whose chief subsistence is still on root crops like tapioca and sweet potato, commonly known as subsidiary foods. This is not in any way peculiar to India. In China, the consumption level of wheat determines the social status of a family[4].

Every increase in income thus has a two-way effect on food. First of all fine grains are substituted for the coarse ones as well as tubers and then the cereals are themselves replaced to a smaller or greater extent by protective foods like milk, fruits and vegetables depending on the income, customs, habits and taste of the people. We will examine the future food consumption levels with due consideration to the changing economic scenario likely to take place in the country.

Engel's Law

This is just in keeping with the Engel's law of consumption which, as stated by Carl Clark Zimmerman[5],

(a) "the poorer a family, the greater is the proportion of the total outgo which must be used for food; and

(b) the proportion of the outgo used for food, other things being equal, is the best measure of the material standard of living of a population."

Engel's Law as further elucidated by Zimmerman has three phases appropriate to different ranges of income[6]:

(i) "Once the starvation level is passed, additional increments of income are associated, for a period at least, with increase of the proportion expended for food. This occurs when the food expense is so low that the population feels underfed and intensely desires more appetising food."

(ii) "Additional increases in income are associated with an increasing amount spent for food, but at a rate which gives a decreasing proportion of the total income. These relations occur among populations securing food sufficient for existence and comfort".

(iii) "Finally, as income increases further, there is sufficient evidence that the amount spent for food may actually decrease. The upper sedentary and rich classes are in this category."

It would be clear that Engel's law is nothing but the general economic law of substitution. Every individual tries to distribute his income in such a way as to derive maximum utility from the total money at his command. With every increase or decrease in income he substitutes one thing for the other so that there is no diminution in the total utility.

Schultz and others of his school of thought did place India in the first phase[7] (out of the three referred to above) and thus arrived at a conclusion which is not consistent with present reality. Even if their findings were partially true in the early fifties, the changes during the past 5 decades would call for a re-examination, particularly in the context of the real ground situation as it exists today.

Available Data Source

For purposes of this study we are making use of two sets of data. Availability based on Balance Sheet, being calculated by the Directorate of E & S, Ministry of Agriculture, and Private Final Consumption Series of CSO—both having been derived from production sources. The NSSO (National Sample Survey Organization) and NNMB (National Nutrition Monitoring Board), however, conduct regular field surveys—the former throughout the country on an annual basis and the latter in selected States.

In the case of NSSO, annual data series are primarily in terms of expenditure, but for selected years quantitative information is also available. A careful study of the CSO, Directorate of E & S, NSSO and NNMB data leads us to the conclusion that there is hardly any possibility of an increase in the per capita consumption of foodgrains:

1. National Accounts (CSO) data shows that the share of private final consumption expenditure at constant prices declined by 10.5 per cent for food and 23.6 per cent for cereals between 1980-81 and 1994-95.[8]
2. Similar result is available from NSSO data where we find that the average monthly per capita expenditure on cereals as a percentage of total MPCE, declined from 40.6% (1972-73) to 24.2% (1993-94) for rural areas and from 23.3% to 14% for urban areas during the same period. Although there is a decline in the share of total expenditure on food, there is a corresponding increase in expenditure on non-cereals as well as non-food items.
3. Distribution of household consumption expenditure for population group below the poverty line came down from 80.25% in 1977-78 to 75.77% (Rural) and 75.19% to 73.68% (urban) during the same period.[8A] Lipton (1983) takes 20% as being the irreducible proportion of income spent by the poorest in a wide range of countries on non-food essentials[9]. Given the tendency of food requirement figures to overestimate real food needs, especially in relation to people living in warm climates, Lipton suggests that it might be more realistic to work with 80% of the (FAO/WHO 1973) weight-adjusted dietary energy requirements. This leads to a double 80 rule, according to which people are judged to be ultra poor if 80% of their income is insufficient to purchase 80% of these FAO/WHO energy requirements[9].
4. Per capita availability of foodgrains remained around 470 grams per day since 1961 by which time comparable data series for food production stabilised.[10] It did cross this number in a few years, a part of which could be explained by changes in private stocks for which no information is available. As against this, per capita availability of milk, eggs, fish, fruits, vegetables, sugar, oils, tea and coffee has increased many fold. Availability of potato increased by about 12 times, milk 7 times and meat nearly 10

times against a population increase of two and a half times (Tables 19.2 and 19.3; Fig. 19.1).

5. A study of the net availability of various food items at physiological level[11] for the TE ending 1993 shows that an average Indian has a total availability of 964.6 gm of all food items providing 2400 calories and 64.9 gm of proteins.
6. Comprehensive NSSO data series are available up to the year 1999-2000. A study conducted by the Techno Economic Research Institute for US AID[12] converted value data into quantities and found that even in the case of lowest 3 deciles, per capita cereal consumption both in the urban and rural areas declined in all the states during 1961-62 to 1983. The pattern was the same in the poorest states as well.

6a. According to CSO data, expenditure on food actually declined by 1.4 per cent in '00-01 in nominal terms and by 2.7 per cent in inflation-adjusted terms. Since these figures refer to total consumption, this would mean that Indians are on an average, or on a per capita basis, are less in 2000-01 since population increased during that year. It has been known for some time now that the consumption basket of the average Indian has changed in recent years in favour of healthcare, transport and communication services at the cost of the basic necessities of food and clothing. But the recent CSO data show that this pattern has accelerated significantly during '00-'01). Except for fruits and Vegetables—where expenditure rose 5 per cent (real terms)—all other major food categories have seen the expenditure falling. Moreover, the private final consumption expenditure (PFCE) on food products has actually declined during the year. This is the first time since '76-'77 that the expenditure on food has actually fallen in nominal terms.

Table 19.1A Composition of PFCE (%)

	'93-94	'99-00	'00-01
Food, Beverages and Tobacco	54.8	51.5	48.1
Of which, food	50.6	46.0	42.8
Clothing and Fotwear	11.9	10.1	11.3
Furniture and appliances	3.1	2.8	3.0
Healthcare	3.4	6.6	7.3
Transport and Communication	11.3	12.8	13.3
Recreation and education	3.1	3.6	3.7

7. A FAO sponsored study by the Indian Association for the Advancement of Science on Food and Nutrition Status observes that "The poverty indication gives large population as threatened by malnutrition or undernutrition, but ground reality is different. Most of poor consume many local products which are not reflected in their income or even various consumer surveys. Their traditional knowledge also helps them to eat locally available foods and minor forest products, not recorded otherwise. There are, however, better off households whose average dietary intake is low."

Table 19.2 Meat Production—All India

('000 tonnes)

Year	Population million	Beef & veal	Buffalo & lamb	Mutton meat	Goat meat	Pig meat	Poultry	Total (kg)	Per capita
1971	551.3	179	—	371	—	52	36	588	1.28
1976	617.2	70	116	117	273	60	103	789	1.20
1981	668.5	78	127	125	277	75	130	802	1.20
1982	703.8	80	130	132	298	30	130	850	1.21
1983	718.9	80	132	134	302	30	137	865	1.20
1984	734.5	149	148	135	346	82	150	1010	1.38
1985	750.4	150	152	141	358	85	161	1047	1.40
1996	766.5	160	163	147	370	86	180	1106	1.44
1987	782.7	239	207	162	380	80	193	1261	1.61
1988	799.2	232	290	148	378	357	225	1630	2.04
1989	815.8	845	936	160	385	359	289	2974	3.55
1990	832.6	852	952	162	410	360	334	3070	3.69
1991	851.7	857	978	166	361	420	368	3150	3.70
1993	833.9	860	1010	170	425	361	400	3226	1.65
1995	916.0		1085	182	481		710	3680	4.02
2000	1000.0	2000		700		400	900	4050	4.05

SOURCE: Report of the Technical Committee of Direction for Improvement of Animal Husbandry and Dairying Statistics, Ministry of Agriculture, 1993.

Table 19.3 Production and Per Capita Availability (PCA) of Fruits and Vegetables, Milk and Eggs in India

Year	Population (million)	Fruits '000 tonnes	PCA (kg)	Vegetables '000 tones	PCA (kg)	Milk '000 tonnes	PCA (kg)	Eggs (billion)	PCA (No.)
1950-51*	361.1	12000	33.2	1000	27.7	17000	47.1	1.832	5
1983	718.9	22176	30.8	45971	63.9	38800	54.0	12.792	18
1990	832.6	28540	34.3	56577	68.0	53900	64.7	21.101	25
1991	851.7	29359	34.5	57761	67.8	55700	65.4	21.983	26
1992	861.7	30903	35.9	58962	68.4	58000	67.3	22.929	17
1993	883.9	31850	36.0	60010	67.9	60600	68.6	24.167	27
1995-96	922.0	41507	45.0	71594	77.6		71.8		29
1996-97	939.5	40458	43.1	75074	79.9	69100	73.5	27.496	29
1997-98	955.2	43263	45.3	72683	76.1	70800	74.1	28.567	30
1998-99	970.9	44042	45.4	87536	90.2	74700	76.9	30.150	31

SOURCE: 1. Selected indicators of food and agriculture development in Asia (RAPA), food and agriculture organisation of the United Nations, Bangkok, 1994.
2. Annual reports, deptt. of animal husbandry and darying, Ministry of Agriculture, Government of India.

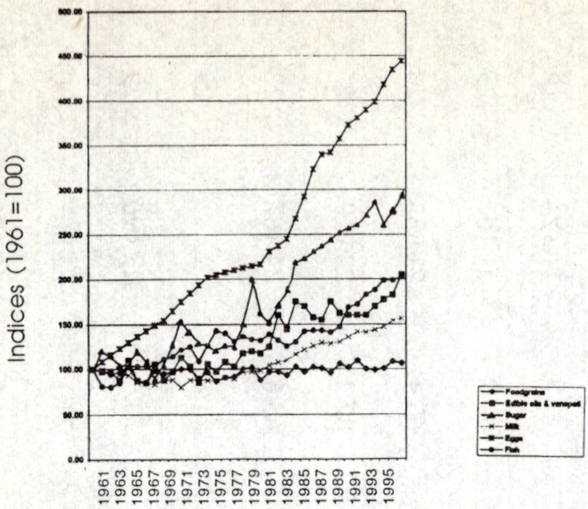

Fig. 19.1 Per capita availability of various food items

8. While per capita income at constant (1980-81) prices has more than doubled during 1951-2000, a time series data of cereal consumption under NSSO is quite revealing. Over a period of 38 years 1961-62 to 1999-2000, there is a steady decline in the per capita consumption of cereals at the all India level. At the same time there is a shift in the pattern as between the different grains both in the rural and urban areas. Share of rice having remained more or less constant, wheat has substituted coarse grains to a large extent (Table 19.4 and Fig. 19.2).
9. This decline in cereal consumption is over all the deciles during 1987-88 to 1999-00. This being much sharper (Tables 19.5 and 19.6) in the top deciles and marginal in the lower ones. This is accompanied by a corresponding increase in non-foodgrains. While a plateau has been reached at below 11 kg of cereals for urban areas, the decline for cereals is sharpest for top deciles in rural India.

9a. According to Economic Survey 2001-02 the National Sample Surveys show that the proportion of household expenditure on items other than food has been increasing. Conversely, household expenditure on food has fallen as a proportion of their total expenditure from 60 per cent in 1977-78 to 48.1 per cent in 1999-2000 in urban areas, and from 64.3 per cent to 59.4 per cent in rural areas. With rising incomes, peoples' diets are becoming more diversified. The share of cereals in their diet has been falling, being substituted by other foods. Expenditure on cereals in total household food expenditure has fallen from 40.8 per cent in 1977-78 to 31.8 per cent in 1999-2000 in urban areas, and from 50 per cent to 44.1 per cent in rural areas. Correspondingly, substantial increases have taken place in the proportion of food expenditure on other foods such as fruits, vegetables, meat, eggs, fish and milk. Hence, although it is essential to ensure food security through adequate production

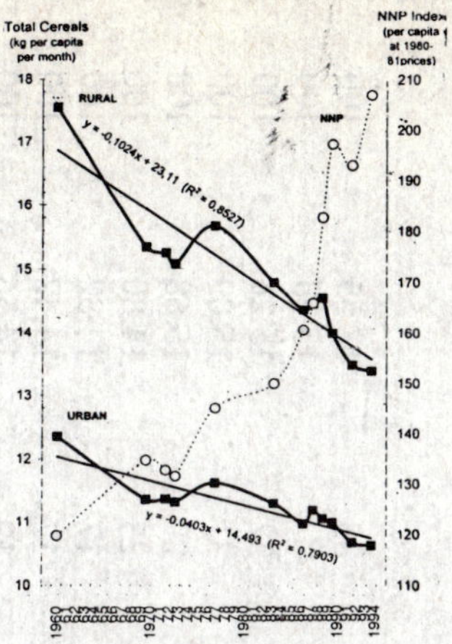

Fig. 19.2 Consumption pattern of cereals

SOURCE: NSSO Survey of Consumer Expenditure various rounds

of foodgrains in the country, the thrust of agricultural policy now must shift to accelerating the growth of non-cereal food products. The growth experienced in the production and consumption of milk, poultry, fish and meat suggests that there is great potential for further growth in these products. Increasing incomes and urbanisation are also providing the demand stimulus for greater production and consumption of fruits and vegetables. As urbanisation proceeds, there will be an accelerating need for basic processed foods as well.

9b. Really speaking, average daily calorie intake went up from 1,981 kcal in the period 1961-63 to 2,090 in 1979-81 and further to 2,235 kcal in 1988-90. There is no evidence that consumption inequality has increased in India. In fact, if at all it is the other way round - the nutrition level has improved and hunger situation has eased.[13]

10. Even the State level study for the period shows that during the period 1970-71 to 1991-92, both in the rural and urban areas, but for a few states- Kerala, Orissa and West Bengal, there is clear decline in the per capita consumption of cereals. If we take into consideration the latest 55th Round data, even Orissa shows a decline. A study of the consumption patterns of Kerala and Andhra, both of which are much below the all India per capita income, but have the best P.D.S. would be of interest. If consumption of cereals is stabilising little above 13 kg (Andhra) and 10 kg (Kerala) in the rural areas and 11 kg (Andhra) and 9.5 kg (Kerala) in the urban areas, at highly subsidised prices, the argument that consumption levels will go up with increasing incomes, will not hold good (Tables 19.7 and 19.8).

11. Recent evidence[14,15,16] thus shows that trends in cereal consumption appear not to be in line with income growth. Such counter-intuitive findings are also not explained by food

Table 19.4 **Consumption Pattern of Cereals by Period in Rural and Urban India (Monthly Per Capita in kg)**

NSS round	Year	Rice	(%)	Wheat	(%)	Coarse cereals	(%)	Total cereals	(%)
(1)	(2)	(3)	(4)	(5)	(6)	(7)	(8)	(9)	(10)
		Rural							
17	1961-62	8.77	50	2.63	15	6.15	35	17.55	100
	1970-71							15.35	100
27	1972-73	8.56	56	3.83	25	4.84	32	15.26	100
28	1973-74	6.90	46	3.52	23	4.67	31	15.09	100
32	1977-78	7.12	45	4.05	26	4.51	29	15.68	100
38	1983	6.63	45	4.46	30	3.71	25	14.80	100
42	1986-87	7.11	49	4.77	33	2.49	17	14.37	100
43	1987-88	7.04	49	4.94	34	2.49	17	14.47	100
44	1988-89	7.07	49	4.73	32	2.76	19	14.56	100
47	1991	7.10	49	4.60	32	1.70	12	13.8	100
48	1992	7.20	49	4.50	31	1.70	12	13.8	100
49	1993	7.20	49	4.50	31	1.60	11	13.6	100
50	1993-94	7.00	52.2	4.40	32.8	2.00	15	13.4	100
51	1994-95	7.10	49	4.30	30	1.40	10	13.2	100
52	1995-96	7.00	48	4.20	29	1.50	10	12.9	100
53	1997	6.70	46	4.50	31	1.40	10	12.8	100
54	1998	6.80	47	4.30	30	1.20	8	12.5	100
55	99-2000	6.78	53.3	4.55	35.8	1.39	10.9	12.72	100

(1)	(2)	(3)	(4)	(5)	(6)	(7)	(8)	(9)	(10)
		Urban							
17	1961-62	6.16	50	4.10	33	2.09	17	12.35	100
	1970-71							11.36	100
27	1972-73	4.94	43	4.82	42	1.61	14	11.37	100
28	1973-74	5.38	48	4.32	38	1.62	14	11.32	100
32	1977-78	5.48	47	4.87	42	1.27	11	11.62	100
38	1983	5.32	47	4.82	43	1.16	10	11.30	100
42	1986-87	5.33	49	4.82	44	0.83	8	10.98	100
43	1987-88	5.35	48	4.98	45	0.86	8	11.19	100
44	1988-89	5.35	48	4.81	43	0.90	8	11.06	100
47	1991	5.20	47	4.90	44	0.40	4	10.70	100
48	1992	5.20	47	4.90	44	0.40	4	10.70	100
49	1993	5.30	48	4.50	41	0.60	5	10.50	100
50	1993-94	5.28	49.7	4.72	44.4	0.63	5.9	10.63	100
51	1994-95	5.10	46	4.90	44	0.60	5	10.70	100
52	1995-96	5.30	48	4.70	42	0.40	4	10.60	100
53	1997	5.20	47	4.60	42	0.40	4	10.30	100
54	1998	5.30	48	4.70	42	0.40	4	10.40	100
55	1999-2000	5.22	50.0	4.77	45.8	0.43	4.13	10.42	

43rd Round : July 1987–June 1988
47th Round : July 1991–December 1991
48th Round : January 1992–December 1992
52th Round : July 1995–June 1996
53rd Round : January 1997–December 1997
49th Round : January 1993–June 1993
50th Round : July 1993–June 1994
51st Round : July 1994–June 1995
54th Round : January–June 1998
55th Round : July 1999–June 2000

Note: Percentage of total cereal consumption.
SOURCE: NSSO, Survey on consumer expenditure, various rounds.

Table 19.5 Quantity (kg) of Consumption of Cereals, Pulses and other Items Per Person for 30 Days Each Monthly Per Capita Expenditure Class

All India Rural *(In kilograms)*

Items	Monthly per capita expenditure for different detail class (Rs.)													
1987-88	*Less than 65*	*65-80*	*80-95*	*95-110*	*125-140*	*125-140*	*140-160*	*160-180*	*180-215*	*215-280*	*280-385*	*More than 385*	*All classes*	*C.V. across Expenditure Class*
1	2	3	4	5	6	7	8	9	10	11	12	13	14	15
1993-94 1999-2000	*Less than 120*	*120—140*	*140—165*	*165—190*	*190—210*	*210—235*	*235—265*	*265—300*	*300—355*	*355—455*	*455—560*	*560 & Above*	"	"
Total Cereals														
1987-88	9.84	11.86	12.90	13.67	14.27	14.75	15.21	15.54	16.04	16.45	17.10	20.58	14.57	17.61
1993-94	9.7	11.3	12.0	12.7	13.2	13.4	13.8	14.1	14.5	14.7	15.1	16.0	13.5	12.50
1998-99	9.78	11.15	11.64	12.27	12.56	12.89	13.03	13.36	13.45	13.67	13.73	14.19	12.72	
Total Pulses														
1987-88	0.38	0.52	0.63	0.69	0.77	0.82	0.88	0.94	1.07	1.20	1.37	2.01	0.87	44.61
1993-94	0.42	0.50	0.84	0.67	0.68	0.74	0.79	0.83	0.94	1.01	1.17	1.48	0.79	32.93
1999-00	0.38	0.51	0.59	0.63	0.70	0.73	0.81	0.84	0.96	1.15	1.13	1.30	0.81	
Total Other Food Items														
1987-88	1.92	2.84	3.72	4.47	5.52	6.54	7.51	6.92	10.71	13.20	16.63	25.09	7.68	73.59
1993-94	3.03	4.22	5.17	6.37	7.39	8.60	10.03	11.60	13.64	17.09	20.93	27.71	10.81	62.78
Total Food														
1987-88	12.14	15.22	17.25	18.83	20.56	22.11	23.60	23.40	27.82	30.85	35.10	47.68	23.12	38.07
1993-94	13.15	16.04	18.05	19.70	21.29	22.72	24.59	26.57	29.08	32.84	37.21	45.14	25.05	34.81

1	2	3	4	5	6	7	8	9	10	11	12	13	14	15
Rice as % to Cereals														
1987-88	37.8	46.2	47.4	50.3	51.6	50.0	50.6	49.5	47.0	46.6	46.7	43.9	48.3	7.58
1993-94	41.8	48.4	53.0	55.1	56.8	55.6	54.8	54.2	52.4	47.4	48.1	45.8	52.2	8.79
1999-00	60.1	58.2	57.0	57.0	56.8	56.0	53.0	51.1	51.2	48.2	47.1	45.1	53.3	
Wheat as % to Cereals														
1987-88	28.7	29.2	30.7	30.8	31.2	32.3	32.3	35.6	36.7	39.1	40.9	44.5	33.9	14.04
1993-94	27.4	30.3	29.2	28.0	28.1	30.2	31.1	32.1	34.3	39.2	39.9	43.6	32.7	15.58
1999-00	24.9	28.8	30.7	32.2	32.6	33.3	35.0	37.3	38.1	42.1	44.1	47.5	35.8	
Rice+Wheat % to Cereals														
1987-88	66.5	75.4	78.1	81.1	82.8	82.3	82.9	85.1	83.7	85.7	87.6	88.4	82.2	7.07
1993-94	69.2	78.7	82.1	83.2	84.9	85.8	85.8	86.4	86.8	86.6	88.0	89.4	84.9	6.20
1999-00	85.0	87.0	87.7	89.2	89.4	89.3	88.0	88.4	89.3	90.3	91.2	92.6	89.1	
Cereals to All Food														
1987-88	81.0	77.9	74.8	72.6	69.4	66.7	64.5	66.4	57.7	53.3	48.7	43.2	63.0	17.48
1993-94	73.8	70.6	66.7	64.3	62.1	58.9	56.0	53.2	49.9	44.9	40.6	35.3	53.7	20.41
Pulses to All Food														
1987-88	3.1	3.4	3.7	3.7	3.7	3.7	3.7	4.0	3.8	3.9	3.9	4.2	3.8	7.13
1993-94	3.2	3.1	4.7	3.4	3.2	3.3	3.2	3.1	3.2	3.1	3.1	3.3	3.2	12.31
Other Food Item to - All Food %														
1987-88	15.8	18.7	21.6	23.8	26.8	29.6	31.8	29.6	38.5	42.8	47.4	52.6	33.2	35.10
1993-94	23.0	26.3	28.7	32.3	34.7	37.8	40.8	43.7	46.9	52.0	56.2	61.4	43.2	28.83

SOURCE: Computed based on tables Government of India, Department of Statistics, level and pattern of consumer expenditure, 5th quinquennial survey 1987-88 and 1993-94.

Note: While the actual quantity of consumption for cereals and pulses was available from the original source, the quantity for sepecific (Group of) items in the category of other food items has been estimated by the authors.

Table 19.6 Quantity (kg) of Consumption of Cereals, Pulses and other Items Per Person for 30 Days Each Monthly Per Capita Expenditure Class

All India Urban

(In kilograms)

Items		Monthly per capita expenditure class (Rs.)													
	1987-88	Less than 90	90-110	110-135	135-160	160-185	185-215	215-255	255-310	310-385	385-520	520-700 700	More t han 700	All classes	C.V. across Expenditure Class
1		2	3	4	5	6	7	8	9	10	11	12	13	14	15
	1993-94	Less than 160	160—190	190—230	230—265	265—310	310—355	355—410	410—490	490—605	605—825	825—1055	1055 & Above	"	"
Total Cereals															
1987-88		9.17	10.65	10.98	11.20	11.50	11.24	12.25	11.69	11.62	11.36	11.19	12.32	11.21	6.93
1993-94		8.92	10.11	10.61	10.75	10.88	10.99	10.92	10.95	10.74	10.66	10.18	10.28	10.64	5.30
1999-00		8.99	10.15	10.25	10.75	10.61	10.80	10.69	10.66	10.50	10.52	9.94	9.72	10.42	
Total Pulses															
1987-88		0.46	0.58	0.66	0.77	0.85	0.92	1.07	1.15	1.25	1.32	1.57	1.74	0.94	36.82
1993-94		0.43	0.58	0.64	0.71	0.78	0.87	0.93	1.00	1.08	1.20	1.28	1.45	0.92	31.96
1999-00		0.49	9.50	0.65	0.80	9.86	0.92	1.07	1.03	1.08	1.27	1.28	1.38	0.96	
Total Other Food Items															
1987-88		2.71	3.91	4.99	6.22	7.43	9.03	10.77	12.87	14.78	17.62	22.55	31.13	10.06	67.30
1993-94		3.44	4.74	6.01	7.34	8.72	10.45	12.03	13.89	16.29	20.25	25.16	31.69	12.78	62.22
Total Food															
1987-88		12.34	15.14	16.63	18.20	19.78	21.19	24.09	25.71	27.65	30.30	35.31	45.19	22.21	36.82
1993-94		12.79	15.45	17.29	18.83	20.41	22.35	23.92	25.89	28.15	32.15	36.67	43.47	24.38	35.05

1	2	3	4	5	6	7	8	9	10	11	12	13	14	15
Rice as % to Cereals														
1987-88	45.47	45.16	48.82	48.74	48.52	49.56	45.06	46.45	47.76	48.86	44.86	46.35	47.73	3.53
1993-94	41.37	48.37	51.84	52.56	51.93	50.14	50.46	50.50	48.88	47.84	46.86	46.11	49.62	6.13
1999-00	49.38	48.86	51.41	52.65	50.80	49.54	50.80	49.15	50.76	50.19	47.98	45.88	40.09	
Wheat as % to Cereals														
1987-88	36.97	40.28	41.44	43.11	42.17	43.33	43.18	48.25	47.42	47.54	52.64	51.46	44.42	9.97
1993-94	40.47	39.96	39.68	40.37	42.10	44.04	44.23	45.11	47.21	49.16	50.29	52.43	44.36	9.36
1999-00	43.38	46.60	43.61	42.32	44.49	45.27	45.28	47.47	46.38	46.96	50.00	52.26	45.78	
Rice + Wheat % to Cereals														
1987-88	82.4	85.4	90.3	91.9	90.7	92.9	88.2	94.7	95.2	96.2	97.5	97.8	92.1	4.99
1993-94	81.84	88.33	91.52	92.93	94.03	94.18	94.69	95.62	96.09	97.00	97.15	98.54	93.98	4.70
1999-00	92.76	95.46	95.02	94.97	95.29	94.82	96.08	96.62	97.14	97.15	97.98	98.14	95.87	
Cereals to All Food														
1987-88	74.3	70.4	66.0	61.6	58.1	53.0	50.9	45.5	42.0	37.5	31.7	27.3	50.5	28.23
1993-94	69.7	65.4	61.4	57.1	53.3	49.2	45.7	42.3	38.2	33.2	27.8	23.6	43.7	30.05
Pulses to All Food														
1987-88	3.7	3.8	4.0	4.2	4.3	4.3	4.4	4.5	4.5	4.4	4.4	3.9	4.2	6.45
1993-94	3.4	3.8	3.7	3.8	3.8	3.9	3.9	3.9	3.8	3.7	3.5	3.3	3.8	5.13
Other Food Item to All Food %														
1987-88	22.0	25.8	30.0	34.2	37.6	42.6	44.7	50.1	53.5	58.2	63.9	68.9	45.3	32.55
1993-94	26.9	30.7	34.8	39.0	42.7	46.8	50.3	53.67	57.9	63.0	68.6	72.9	52.4	29.04

SOURCE: Computed based on tables Government of India, Department of Statistics, level and pattern of consumer expenditure, 5th quinquennial survey 1987-88 and 1993-94.

Note: While the actual quantity of consumption for cereals and pulses was available from the original source, the quantity for sepecific (Group of) items in the category of other food items has been estimated by the authors.

Table 19.7 ***Per Caput Consumption of Cereals (Urban) from 1970-71 to 1991-92, 1997-98 and 1999-2000***

(kg/month)

State	1970-71	1972-73	1973-74	1977-78	1983-84	1986-87	1987-88	1989-90	1990-91	1991-92	1997-98	1999-2000
Andhra Pradesh	13.31	12.68	13.07	12.83	11.95	11.37	11.70	11.74	11.70	11.57	11.30	10.94
Assam	11.91	12.55	12.31	13.44	12.78	11.89	12.39	12.34	12.08	11.53	11.00	12.26
Bihar	13.68	13.49	13.22	14.06	13.44	12.90	13.37	13.50	12.85	13.66	13.28	12.70
Gujarat	10.35	10.77	10.71	10.17	9.61	8.81	9.44	9.48	9.55	8.88	9.06	8.49
Haryana	11.90	11.86	12.23	12.24	11.59	10.61	10.98	10.24	10.11	9.90	11.14	9.36
Himachal Pradesh	11.30	11.97	12.57	11.62	11.79	11.44	13.28	N.A	N.A	N.A	N.A.	10.33
Jammu & Kashmir	14.62	14.16	14.31	13.16	13.80	14.62	14.09	N.A	N.A	N.A	N.A.	12.84
Karnataka	11.91	11.32	11.24	12.68	11.69	10.37	11.06	10.71	10.40	10.44	10.38	10.21
Kerala	7.55	8.17	7.93	8.91	10.12	9.55	9.60	9.88	9.60	9.73	9.68	9.25
Madhya Pradesh	12.88	12.88	12.53	12.61	12.32	11.70	11.89	11.63	11.54	11.46	10.72	11.09
Maharashtra	9.75	8.95	9.24	9.92	9.90	9.23	10.18	10.18	9.74	9.42	8.86	9.35
Orissa	13.22	13.77	13.42	13.96	14.19	13.98	13.74	14.39	13.94	13.36	13.35	14.51
Punjab	11.25	10.71	11.03	10.80	9.94	10.25	9.74	9.40	9.06	8.85	9.67	9.21
Rajasthan	13.03	13.21	12.97	12.55	12.95	13.32	12.73	11.76	12.03	11.62	10.35	11.56
Tamil Nadu	10.63	11.12	11.39	11.05	10.39	9.93	10.14	10.26	10.14	9.98	9.48	9.65
Uttar Pradesh	11.79	12.24	12.48	12.27	11.66	11.77	11.63	11.33	11.14	11.42	11.34	10.79
West Bengal	10.88	10.53	10.92	11.92	11.80	12.75	11.71	12.12	11.78	11.30	10.95	11.17
All- India	11.36	11.24	11.32	11.62	11.30	10.94	11.19	11.04	10.87	10.68	10.42	10.42

* Statistically significant at 5% level

SOURCE: Radhakrishna R, Indian Journal of Agricultural Economics (January- June 1996); Bansil P.C, Agricultural Statistical Compendium, Vol. 1 and Supplement, NSS 55th round, level and pattern of consumer expenditure in India, 1999-2000.

Table 17.8 ***Per Capita Consumption of Cereals (Rural) During 1970-71 to 1991-92, 1997-98 and 1999-2000***

(kg/month)

State	*1970-71*	*1972-73*	*1973-74*	*1977-78*	*1983-84*	*1986-87*	*1987-88*	*1989-90*	*1990-91*	*1991-92*	*1997-98*	*1999-2000*
Andhra Pradesh	16.05	15.25	15.80	15.85	15.37	13.99	14.35	14.31	13.62	13.60	13.02	12.65
Assam	15.70	14.81	15.33	14.38	14.23	13.24	14.23	13.93	13.63	13.20	12.56	12.63
Bihar	16.39	15.58	14.99	16.16	15.77	15.25	15.39	15.14	16.45	15.00	14.08	13.75
Gujarat	15.00	13.32	13.87	13.44	12.56	11.05	12.00	12.22	11.75	11.10	9.27	10.19
Haryana	18.13	17.57	16.56	15.22	14.54	14.84	15.02	13.74	14.55	10.20	11.48	11.37
Himachal Pradesh	17.64	18.06	16.30	15.47	16.06	14.32	16.06	N.A	N.A	N.A	N.A	12.86
Jammu & Kashmir	20.14	18.72	19.09	17.99	17.59	17.82	17.26	N.A	N.A	N.A	N.A	14.68
Karnataka	15.71	15.63	15.61	15.01	15.03	13.16	13.75	12.11	11.62	12.30	11.21	11.53
Kerala	7.99	7.97	7.69	9.18	10.01	10.28	10.36	9.75	10.73	10.00	9.90	9.89
Madhya Pradesh	16.51	17.28	17.12	16.08	15.83	15.14	15.39	16.60	15.22	14.30	12.51	12.94
Maharashtra	12.83	12.60	13.45	13.52	13.79	11.84	13.03	11.89	11.48	11.70	10.45	11.32
Orissa	16.12	15.22	15.88	15.97	15.61	16.02	15.72	16.52	15.98	17.10	15.87	15.09
Punjab	15.46	15.38	14.89	14.35	13.52	11.86	12.41	12.29	11.69	12.00	9.77	10.58
Rajasthan	17.91	18.17	18.76	18.18	17.19	16.69	16.62	15.54	15.75	14.90	12.72	14.19
Tamil Nadu	13.95	14.53	14.72	13.85	13.05	12.27	12.24	12.43	12.20	11.60	11.28	10.66
Uttar Pradesh	16.32	16.83	16.24	16.57	15.17	15.48	15.32	14.77	14.79	13.70	12.83	13.62
West Bengal	13.35	13.64	12.97	14.74	14.28	15.41	15.12	15.44	15.06	14.20	13.74	13.59
All- India	15.35	15.26	15.09	15.25	14.80	14.28	14.47	14.00	14.06	13.5	12.47	12.72

Note: Statistically significant at 5 percent level.

SOURCE: R. Radhakrishnan. Indian Journal of Agricultural Economics January-June 1996 and Bansil P.C. Agricultural Statistical Compendium. Vol. 1 and Supplement, NSS 55th round, level and pattern of consumer expenditure in India, 1999-2000.

expenditure elasticities, which are supposed to be generally high. Rather, a part of the explanation lies not only in changes in taste and preferences but also development of rural infrastructure and mechanisation which again would reflect that during the late eighties the country was already in the 2nd stage of Engel's law. A trend analysis suggests a distinct shift in consumption patterns away from cereals since the mid-1970s uniformly across all expenditure groups, including the poorest (Tables 19.9A and 19.9).

12. NNMB latest available Report for 1988-90 says that the average calorie consumption of rural households during sixties was around 2070 kcal/CU/day at aggregate level. The figures reported by NNMB for the seventies was 2350 kcal. This increase of 280 kcal/CU/day is quite substantial. However, there was no further change during the subsequent period. While the earlier surveys of NNMB showed an increase of 110 kcal between 1975 and 1980, the repeat surveys in 1988-90 showed a decrease of 57 kcal. These changes, however, are marginal and statistically not significant as the standard deviation for the difference of means was 175 kcal after correcting for family size.[16] In other words, it can be concluded that at the aggregate level, there has been little change in the average calorie intake of rural households during the last 15 years.
13. NSSO data (Tables 19.10 to 19.11) further show that the share of persons having two square meals a day has increased from 93.05% in 1985 to 99.7% in 1993 (urban) and from 81.46% to 93.8% (rural) during the same period. Recently the Institute conducted a survey for the FAO on Food Security. More than 98 per cent of the respondents reported having two square meals, but aspired for better health facilities, skill upgradation and improved infrastructure. Their perception of `two square meals', however, was limited to the desired/required quantities of cereals.[17]
14. NNMB data for 1988-90 shows that a person with per capita per month income of less than Rs. 30/- or less than Rs. 2000/- per annum per family, was consuming 500 grams of foodgrains per cu. per day. Since the nineties have witnessed a faster growth in the availability of non-cereal foodstuff, there is very little possibility of their increasing the consumption of foodgrains further.
15. Repeat surveys of NNMB further show that an average person in the surveyed areas was having invariably more than the RDA in terms of energy, proteins, iron etc. severe deficiency was with regard to Thiamine only.
16. A study by the NCAER[18] shows that during 1992-93, the lowest income group people (household having income below Rs. 11000/- at 1987-88 prices) purchased 1.85 million transistor

Table 19.9A Per Capita Calorie Intake by Bottom Groups from Cereals only and from all Food Groups

State	Calorie intake from cereals (kcal/caput/day)				State average % of calorie inake from cereals out of all food groups				Total calorie intake calculated using state average % of calorie intake from cereals out of all food group (kcal/caput/day)			
	Rural		Urban		Rural		Urban		Rural		Urban	
	1983 (1)	1993/94 (2)	1983 (3)	1993/94 (4)	1983 (5)	1993/94 (6)	1983 (7)	1993/94 (8)	1983 (9) = (1)/(5)	1993/94 (10) = (2)/(6)	1983 (11) = (3)/(7)	1993/94 (12) = (4)/(8)
Andhra Pradesh	1221	1304	1210	1187	89	74	68	65	1526	1752	1779	1818
Assam	1361	1309	1586	1344	80	76	72	66	1701	1713	2203	2052
Bihar	1586	1344	1356	1359	76	78	72	67	2087	1734	1883	2025
Gujarat	1219	1094	998	980	65	60	54	49	1875	1836	1848	2004
Haryana	1392	1243	1189	1160	64	59	58	56	2175	2107	2050	2086
Karnataka	1304	1259	1144	1148	76	72	63	61	1715	1739	1815	1870
Madhya Pradesh	1509	1385	1200	1253	77	75	66	62	1959	1845	1818	2008
Maharashtra	1412	1160	1133	1105	73	67	56	54	1934	1737	2024	2060
Punjab	1672	1106	913	953	58	51	54	50	2883	2183	1690	1904
Rajasthan	1716	1508	1352	1273	73	67	64	60	2351	2247	2113	2131
Tamil Nadu	1146	1137	1006	1017	76	71	55	60	1508	1594	1828	1690
Uttar Pradesh	1436	1423	1218	1239	73	69	65	59	1967	2073	1874	2087
West Bengal	1150	1473	1194	1311	81	78	66	62	1420	1899	1809	2101
All India	1391	1363	1185	1202	75	71	61	59	1855	1919	1942	2054

Food Groups: I cereals, potato, sugar, jaggery and cereal substitutes; II Pulses and nuts; III Milk and milk products, meat, egg and fish; IV Edible oil, oil seeds; V Fruits, vegetables, spices and prepared foods

SOURCE: Calculated according to Joshi 1998, various tables. Our source: Nutritional products and role of Pos, Zhang-Yue Zhou *et al.*, Indian Agriculture Policy, S.S. Acharya and D.P. Chaudhri.

Table 19.9 Percentage Distribution of MPCE over Broad Groups of Items for Different NSS Rounds in Rural and Urban Areas—All India

Item group	Average monthly per capita consumption as percentage of total MPCE																	
	Rural									Urban								
	43rd round	47th round	48th round	49th round	50th round	51st round	52nd round	53rd round	55th round	43rd round	47th round	48th round	49th round	50th round	51st round	52nd round	53rd round	55th round
(1)	(2)	(3)	(4)	(5)	(6)	(7)	(8)	(9)	(10)	(11)	(12)	(13)	(14)	(15)	(16)	(17)	(18)	(19)
Cereals	26.3	24.0	26.4	25.9	24.2	24.3	23.3	21.9	22.2	15.0	13.9	14.9	15.2	14.0	14.4	13.1	13.3	12.4
Gram	0.2	0.2	0.2	0.2	0.2	0.2	0.2	0.2	0.1	0.2	0.2	0.2	0.2	0.2	0.2	0.1	0.2	0.1
Cereal subst	0.1	0.1	0.1	0.1	0.1	0.1	0.1	0.1	0.1	0.1	0.1	0.1	0.1	0.1	0.1	0.1	0.1	0.1
Pulse & Prod.	4.0	4.2	3.9	4.0	3.8	3.7	3.7	3.8	3.8	3.4	3.4	3.2	3.1	3.0	3.0	3.1	2.8	2.8
Milk & Prod.	8.6	9.0	9.4	9.4	9.5	8.9	9.4	10.0	8.8	9.5	10.0	10.4	10.7	9.8	9.7	9.4	9.7	8.7
Edible oil	5.0	5.5	5.0	4.7	4.4	4.6	4.6	4.1	3.7	5.3	5.8	5.1	4.6	4.4	4.5	4.1	3.7	3.2
Meat, egg, fish	3.3	3.4	3.4	3.6	3.3	3.2	3.2	3.0	3.3	3.6	3.6	3.6	3.7	3.4	3.4	3.2	3.0	3.1
Vegetables	5.2	6.0	5.4	5.7	6.0	5.6	5.7	5.3	6.2	5.3	5.5	5.1	5.2	5.5	4.9	5.0	4.7	5.1
Fruits & nuts	1.6	1.6	1.7	1.7	1.7	1.4	1.5	1.7	1.7	2.5	2.3	2.5	2.8	2.7	2.5	2.2	2.2	2.4
Sugar	2.9	2.6	2.6	3.1	3.1	2.9	2.6	2.7	2.4	2.4	2.1	2.1	2.5	2.4	2.2	2.0	1.9	1.6
Salt	0.2	0.2	0.2	0.2	0.2	0.2	0.2	0.2	0.2	0.1	0.1	0.1	0.1	0.1	0.1	0.2	0.2	0.2

(1)	(2)	(3)	(4)	(5)	(6)	(7)	(8)	(9)	(10)	(11)	(12)	(13)	(14)	(15)	(16)	(17)	(18)	(19)
Spices	2.7	2.7	2.8	2.7	2.5	2.4	2.3	2.2	2.7	2.2	2.0	2.2	2.1	1.9	1.9	1.6	1.6	2.1
Beverages etc.	3.9	3.8	3.8	3.9	4.2	3.8	3.7	3.7	4.2	6.8	7.0	6.6	7.3	7.2	6.6	6.1	6.3	6.3
Food total	64.0	63.1	65.0	65.2	63.2	61.0	60.3	58.7	59.4	56.4	56.0	56.0	57.6	54.7	53.4	50.1	49.6	48.1
Pan, tobacco & intox.	3.2	4.5	3.3	3.3	3.2	3.0	2.7	3.0	2.9	2.6	2.6	2.3	2.5	2.3	2.1	1.9	1.9	1.9
Fuel & light	7.5	7.0	7.0	7.6	7.4	7.0	7.1	7.2	7.5	6.8	6.4	6.3	7.0	6.6	6.7	6.4	7.1	7.7
Clothing	6.7	5.0	5.6	5.2	5.4	7.0	7.7	7.0	6.8	5.9	5.7	5.4	4.9	4.7	5.5	7.1	5.8	6.0
Footwear	1.0	0.7	0.8	0.8	0.9	1.0	1.1	1.2	1.1	1.1	0.9	0.9	0.9	0.9	1.0	1.2	1.0	1.2
Misc. goods & services	14.5	13.0	14.1	14.2	17.3	15.4	16.1	18.2	19.1	23.2	19.8	20.9	19.6	27.5	21.9	22.5	24.6	26.3
Rent	*	0.3	0.3	0.3	*	0.2	0.3	0.3	0.4	$	3.7	3.5	4.2	*	4.3	3.8	4.4	4.5
Taxes & cesses	*	0	0.0	0.1	*	0.1	0.1	0.1	0.2	*	0.3	0.3	0.3	*	0.6	0.6	0.6	0.7
Durable goods	3.1	6.3	3.8	3.3	2.7	5.2	4.5	4.4	2.6	4.1	4.6	4.3	3.0	3.3	4.5	6.5	5.0	3.6
Non-food total	36.0	36.9	35.0	34.8	36.8	39.0	39.7	41.3	40.6	43.6	44.0	44.0	42.4	45.3	46.6	49.9	50.4	51.9
Tot.con.exp.	100.0	100.0	100.0	100.0	100.0	100.0	100.0	100.0	100.0	100.0	100.0	100.0	100.0	100.0	100.0	100.0	100.0	100.0

* Clubbed with miscellaneous goods and services.

43rd Round : July 1987–June 1988
47th Round : July 1991–December 1991
48th Round : January 1992–December 1992
49th Round : January 1993–June 1993
50th Round : July 1993–July 1994
51st Round : July 1994-June 1995
52nd Round : July 1995–June 1996
53rd Round : January 1997–December 1997
55th Round : July 1999–June 2000

Table 19.10 Proportion of Household Getting Two Square Meals a Day—Urban Hunger

(Percent)

State/ Union Territory	Response type: Throughout the year				Only some months of the year				Not even in some months of the year				Not reported
	1983	1991	1993	1998	1983	1991	1993	1998	1983	1991	1993	1998	1993
Andhra Pradesh	92.94	96.4	99.0	98.3	6.93	2.7	1.0	0.9	0.04	0.9	0	0.7	.1
Assam	90.77	93.8	98.0	98.1	7.23	1.3	2.0	0.2	1.79	4.9	0	0.6	.1
Bihar	87.60	94.4	96.8	97.0	9.14	5.0	2.7	0.1	2.89	0.6	0.5	0.9	.9
Gujarat	98.18	98.5	98.3	98.4	1.05	1.5	1.5	0.8	0.09	--	0.2	0.7	0
Haryana	99.47	98.1	100.0	99.4	0.53	1.9	0	0.6	0.00	--	0	0.0	0
Karnataka	88.65	96.4	97.4	98.6	10.37	2.8	2.6	0.1	0.58	0.8	0	0.3	.1
Kerala	86.05	95.2	92.5	93.9	11.67	4.8	5.5	4.8	1.85	--	2.0	0.1	.2
Madhya Pradesh	94.21	97.7	98.8	98.8	4.86	1.8	1.2	0.9	0.37	0.5	0	0.3	0
Maharashtra	94.50	98.7	98.6	98.5	5.00	1.1	1.1	0.1	0.42	0.2	0.3	0.4	0
Orissa	87.41	88.7	93.2	95.8	11.33	11.3	6.6	1.3	5.00	--	0.2	0.7	.2
Punjab	96.80	99.8	99.5	99.8	1.80		0.5	0.1	0.84	--	0	0.1	.1
Rajasthan	96.98	98.0	99.4	99.2	1.18	2.0	0.4	0.2	0.82	--	0.2	0.0	.7
Tamil Nadu	91.28	96.6	95.8	97.7	7.15	2.8	4.0	0.1	0.27	0.2	0.2	0.6	.7
Uttar Pradesh	95.17	97.6	99.1	98.5	3.86	.2	0.9	0.8	1.05	2.2	0	0.2	.5
West Bengal	91.88	95.9	94.0	96.0	6.14	3.3	5.4	0.2	0.71	0.7	0.6	1.5	.5
All India	93.25	96.9	97.7	98.1	5.56	2.1	2.1	1.1	0.77	0.9	0.2	0.5	.3

SOURCE: NSSO and Bansil P.C, Agricultural Statistical Compendium, vol 1 and supplement.

Table 19.11 ***Proportion of Household Getting Two Square Meals in Day—Rural Hunger***

(Percent)

State /Union Territory	*Throughout the year*				*Only some months of the year*				*Not even in some months of the year*				*Not reported*
	1983	*1991*	*1993*	*1998*	*1983*	*1991*	*1993*	*1998*	*1983*	*1991*	*1993*	*1998*	*1993*
Andhra Pradesh	84.32	97.0	96.2	96.6	14.69	4.0	3.6	0.7	0.82	0.3	0.2	1.2	.5
Assam	83.87	84.5	90.4	90.1	12.49	10.9	9.0	6.1	3.58	4.6	0.6	0.3	.8
Bihar	62.51	90.8	91.0	92.8	31.81	8.1	8.2	5.1	5.42	0.5	0.8	1.5	.6
Gujarat	96.92	98.4	99.2	97.6	2.78	1.6	0.8	0.9	0.07		0	0.4	1.1
Haryana	98.61	98.7	99.2	99.2	0.73	0.9	0	0.8	0.12	0.4	0.8	0.0	0
Karnataka	80.91	89.9	93.8	96.0	17.81	9.6	5.9	2.7	0.93	0.5	0.3	0.8	.4
Kerala	80.80	85.7	91.2	91.0	15.29	10.7	8.2	7.4	3.68	3.4	0.6	0.4	1.2
Madhya Pradesh	84.34	93.5	96.2	97.0	13.35	5.3	3.5	2.5	1.72	1.2	0.3	0.3	.1
Maharashtra	85.80	96.7	97.4	95.4	13.42	2.8	2.4	4.1	0.68	0.5	0.2	0.4	.1
Orissa	62.79	78.7	83.5	84.4	31.80	18.9	15.7	14.9	5.02	2.4	0.8	0.5	.2
Punjab	98.26	99.7	100.0	99.9	1.35	0.3	0	0.1	0.24	—	0	0.0	0
Rajasthan	95.95	98.7	99.6	98.5	3.11	1.3	0.4	0.6	0.69	—	0	0.0	.8
Tamil Nadu	82.10	92.7	94.9	96.9	16.06	7.0	5.1	1.5	1.36	—	0	0.9	.7
Uttar Pradesh	88.24	96.3	98.6	96.3	10.39	3.3	1.2	2.9	0.62	0.3	0.2	0.5	.3
West Bengal	60.31	84.0	81.4	85.6	31.10	14.8	17.4	11.1	8.60	1.2	1.2	0.3	.4
All India	81.46	92.8	93.8	94.5	16.19	6.4	5.4	4.2	2.35	0.7	0.8	0.9	.4

SOURCE: NSSO and Bansil P.C, Agricultural Statistical Compendium, vol 1 and Supplement.

radios, 0.68 million black and white TV sets, 0.67 million pressure cookers, 4.12 million torches, 2.46 million bicycles, over 5 million wrist watches and 1.8 million electric fans. Thus even among those in the lowest level of income, there are a sufficient number of those who aspire and are able to purchase products which offer convenience and comfort. Low income households, owned 37 per cent of group I durable goods, (costing less than Rs. 1000) 24 per cent of group II goods, (costing Rs. 1000 to Rs. 6000) and 10.5 per cent of group III goods (value Rs 6000/- and above). This shows that durable goods are owned at all income levels in significant numbers. Even at the lowest income levels, on the basis of national average and a proportionate allocation to each income class, the data show that about 18 of the durable goods are actually owned by the poor. This would show that those in the lowest group also, having satisfied their minimal food requirements, are venturing to spend on white goods.

DEMAND ELASTICITIES

Demand projections for various food items for human consumption are often based on demand elasticities and available data on income and expenditure structure. NSSO being the only source of such data series, researchers have been calculating such demand elasticities since the First Plan. These elasticities are supposed to be nothing more than an illustration of Engel's Law of Consumption as discussed earlier. Some of the functions used for calculating these elasticities have been based on log inverse, log log inverse, semi log and logarithmic, etc.

In so far as cereal consumption is concerned, all such calculations made so far have shown that:

1. Urban elasticities are always lower than rural.
2. Elasticity at different points of time beginning with the First Plan has regularly come down for cereals. This was 1.0 in the fifties, 0.65 in the seventies and sharp decline to 0.3 in the eighties.

With this premise before us, one thing is clear that any long term projections based on this 'scientific tool' are bound to go wrong. If the National Commission on Agriculture (1976) projected the demand for foodgrains for 2000 at 240 million tonnes according to the calculated elasticity of 0.65, it must not be considered valid even by 1987-88 when the elasticity had already come down to 0.3. Similarly all long term projections based on such elasticities will not be valid 20 years hence.

Normally one should assume that when it is only the N.S.S.O. data as the source for calculating expenditure elasticities, the results should be the same. This is not, however, so. Variation in the elasticities calculated by different authors is from -0.037 to 0.18 for urban and—007 to 0.29 for rural (Table 19.12). It is then left to the judgement of any individual to take which one out of them suits him/her. If so, all these numbers lose their sanctity as a scientific tool.[18B]

Table 19.12 Expenditure and OWN Price Elasticities Based on FCDS by Rural, and Urban Population, India

	Expenditure elasticity		*Own price elasticity*	
	Rural	*Urban*	*Rural*	*Urban*
Rice	0.064	0.016	– 0.282	– 0.288
Wheat	– 0.056	– 0.080	– 0.242	– 0.217
C.cer.	– 0.151	– 0.165	– 0.268	– 0.309
Pulses	0.309	0.214	– 0.524	– 0.516
Milk	0.458	0.372	– 0.636	– 0.667
Oil	0.389	0.234	– 0.567	– 0.522
Veg.	0.385	0.253	– 0.601	– 0.567
Fruits	0.442	0.360	– 0.641	– 0.683
Meat	0.848	0.633	– 0.879	– 0.885
Sugar	0.133	0.057	– 0.405	– 0.394
Others	0.945	0.695	– 0.967	– 0.967
Non-Food	2.251	1.874	– 1.241	– 1.235

SOURCE: Praduman Kumar *et al*, Demand for Foodgrains and other Food, Sept. 1994.

As for the future, all the researchers were using the calculated elasticities for 1987-88/1993-94 as applicable even 20-25 years hence. In some cases elasticities for 2020 have now been reduced arbitrarily saying that they are the "best guesses".[18C] Murty using different elasticities under different methods gives demand projections for cereals for 2020 which vary from 188.7 to 354.0 million tonnes.[18D] All such calculations will then lose the label of so called scientific approach.

There are three more theoretical problems with these elasticities. Firstly, while the elasticities are calculated from expenditure, for projecting the demand, income is being used as a proxy for expenditure. This is not in keeping with the facts. Figure 19.3 shows that total expenditure moves within the narrow band of Rs. 3000 to Rs. 6000/- per capita per annum, irrespective of income. The gap between income and expenditure goes on widening once income crosses the Rs. 7500 mark at 1993-94 prices. As seen earlier, expenditure on cereals starts declining even earlier. Secondly while elasticities have been calculated at some constant prices, all income projections are at current prices of the target year.

Thirdly there is a limit to the total calories which an average human being can consume under given climatic conditions. There is no built in formula in the elasticities referred to above where elasticity coefficient becomes zero and takes negative value once the satiation point is reached. As an answer to this problem, some demand studies centred around complete demand system taking into account mutual interdependence of a large number of commodities in the budget

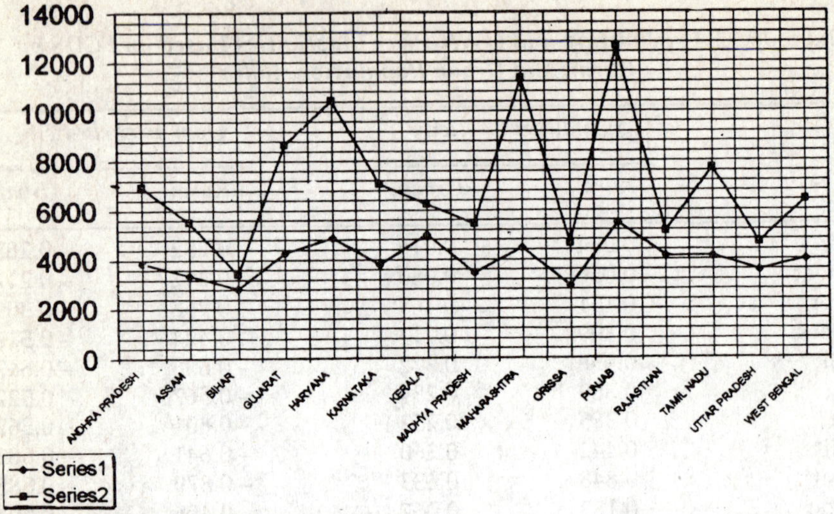

Fig. 19.3 Per capita income expenditure relationship

decisions of the consumer were undertaken by some experts. The important models which received considerable attention are the linear expenditure system (Stone, 1954) and 'almost ideal demand system (AIDS)' (Deaton and Muellbaur, 1980). These models were generally used for estimating demand equation for a group of commodities and not for commodities at a disaggregate level. But they also do not allow increasing or decreasing income elasticities.

The 'Normalized Quadratic Demand System (NQDS)', 'Generalised Leontief Demand System (GLDS)' and 'Transcendental Logarithmic Demand System (TLDS)' suggested by Swamy and Binswanger (1983) are the models which satisfy all general restrictions of demand theory and also allow for estimation of cross-price elasticities within a group of close substitutes or complements, and do not assume additivity. These models also include linear and squared income terms which allow more flexibility in the response of consumer items to changes in income. In addition to econometrics models, Bouis (1991) suggested a non-econometric model based on demand characteristics known as 'Food Characteristic Demand System (FCDS)'. This model requires far less data than the usual econometric approaches and so may be implemented relatively quickly and cost-effectively. Several studies in literature have shown that demand elasticities can vary widely across income groups and by regions as production environments and tastes change. FCDS can be used easily for these subset of consumers.

Under the FCDS system, three characteristics- energy, variety, and tastes of individual food-are assumed to be additive in the utility function. Energy and variety enter the utility function in such a way that utility from consumption of one food depends on the level of consumption of all other foods. By specifying an explicit functional form for these characteristics in the utility function, it turns out that the entire matrix of price and income elasticities can be derived for a system of `n' food and one non-food from prior knowledge of just $K + 4$ elasticities in the $(n + 1)$ by $(n + 2)$ matrix of price and income elasticities, where 'K' is the number of broad non-staple food groups. Staple foods such as rice, wheat, coarse grains which are consumed primarily for their calorie content are treated in a unique way in the FCDS[18E].

This conforms to Engel's Law of consumption, that is, although the food basket of an average person undergoes changes with changes in income, once the consumption of cereals is stabilized, income calories elasticity becomes zero. This situation has not only been reached at the all-India level, but is also confirmed in so far as hunger and poverty are concerned.

When ground situation both at the All India level and State level shows that there is a steady decline in the per capita consumption of cereals over the last 38 years and it has reached a level of saturation, any model which goes against this ground situation has to be rejected.

The calculated elasticities on the basis of the FCDS system discussed above for 1987-88 (Table 19.12) show that both for wheat and coarse grains they were negative and marginally positive for rice. Since the share of rice was 36% and that of wheat and coarse cereals 38% in the total calories in rural areas and more or less similar pattern in urban India, the overall elasticity coefficient for cereals for India as a whole would be negative. This would mean that every real increase in per capita income will result in a decline in the per capita consumption of cereals. A comparison of the 50th and 55th Rounds NSSO data (1993-94 and 1999-2000) shows the same trend.

Our discussion in the preceding pages shows that in keeping with the Engel's Law, the behaviour of food consumption in India has dramatically changed over the last 25 years. The consumer food basket of an average Indian has not only replaced coarse cereals by fine grains to a large extent, but has also reduced the quantity of foodgrains consumed. At the same time, the share of total expenditure on food has also decreased with a corresponding increase on non-food. This has happened in response to increasing per capita income, urbanisation, changes in food habits and tastes, etc. with per capita income having nearly doubled at constant prices there is a declining trend in cereal consumption. During this period the share of people below the poverty line has come down from above 50 percent to around 19 percent according to old methodology of the Planning Commission and 39 per cent as per Expert Group estimates. We will therefore, be justified to assume that the most optimistic assumption would be that the future consumption level of cereals will remain more or less stable at the 1993-94 level or say 14 kg per capita per month for rural India and 11 kg per capita per month for urban areas.

CALORIE CONSUMPTION

The other most important consideration in the consumer behaviour is the limit beyond which total calories consumed by an average person will not increase. A study of the 50th Round NSSO data shows that per capita/day consumption of calories (2418) rural in the most prosperous state (Punjab) is lower than J&K (2507), Haryana (2491) and Rajasthan (2470).As for Urban areas, Punjab (2089) is lower than 11 other States including Bihar (2188) and Orissa (2261). Even with regard to intake of proteins, Punjab is way behind some other states both in rural and urban areas, although the intake of fats (59.8 gm/day) is the highest in rural Punjab. This only shows that the intake of total calories or for that matter other constituents of the food basket is also not related to income only. Punjab (both rural and Urban) has, for example lowest share of calories from cereals but highest from milk in the country. Similarly with regard to meat, fish and egg, it is Kerala which comes to the top followed by Assam and West Bengal both in rural and urban areas (Fig. 19.4).

This discussion would help to reach the conclusion that (i) though there is a limit beyond which intake of total calories will not go, neither the number nor its composition is a function of income alone. So, many other considerations-climate, food habits/tastes, nature of activities and easy availability of various consumption items in rural areas, price relationship between foodgrains, non-foodgrains and non-food items, changes in energy requirement due to relief in heavy manual labour and climatic variations, changes in the wage payment systems, improvements in health status and resulting efficiency in conversion of food into energy play their own role.

Despite lower income levels, Himachal Pradesh and Jammu & Kashmir consume higher calories both in Rural and Urban India, primarily because of colder climate. At the same time, per capita intake of both proteins and fats is also one of the highest in these two states. Another interesting feature of the inter state consumption pattern is that while the total calory consumption is within a band of 1922 to 2416 (urban) and 1939 to 2507 (rural), per capita incomes vary between Rs. 1042 (Bihar) to 4053 (Punjab).

This is further confirmed at the international level, where availability of total calories in each country is more than required. Although per capita income of Papua New Guinea is more than double that of China, the availability of calories in the former is 30% less than China. The highest level of calories available is in Malaysia (2790) followed by China (2709) although per capita income of China is six and a half times less than that of Malaysia. Same applies to the composition of the total consumer basket among different countries (Fig. 19.5).

This understate comparison within India and international comparison among the countries in the Asian Region is more than sufficient to prove that irrespective of the income of a family, there is a

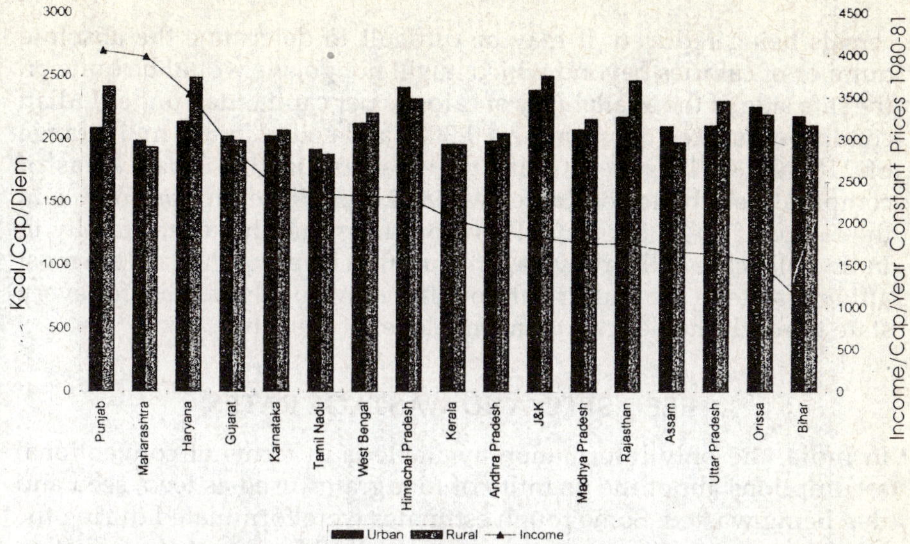

Fig. 19.4 Per capita income and calory intake 1993-94

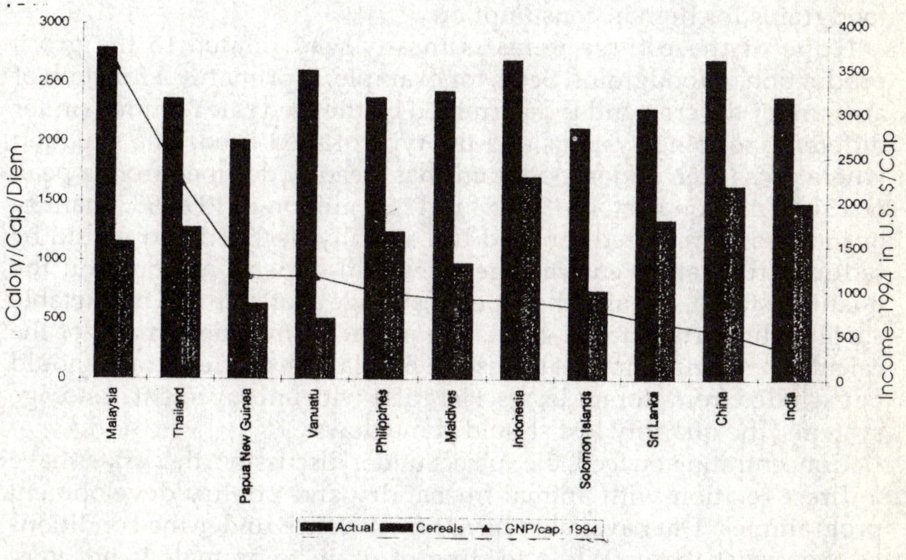

Fig. 19.5 Per capita income and calory consumption relationship in selected countries 1993-95

limit beyond which calorie consumption will not go. If at all, there is an inverse relation between income and calories consumed. But there is again a limit at which it will tend to stabilise. There is, however, sufficient evidence available to prove that composition of the food basket does undergo changes with increasing incomes-the share of cereals being reduced. It may be difficult to determine the absolute number of calories beyond which it will not go, we would be quite on the safe side, if the availability of calories per capita/day under Indian conditions is fixed at around 2900-3000 and actual intake in the range of 2100-2400. This is actually the position in the urban areas of comparatively better off States where expenditure on non-food is in the range of 40-45 per cent. This would assume that every family in India will achieve the present consumption levels of Punjab- the most affluent state in the country although it may not be possible for every state to reach the per capita income level of Punjab.

FEED SEED AND WASTAGE RATES

In India, the only information available is in terms of conventional assumptions about the quantity of foodgrains used as feed, seed and that being wasted. Some rough estimates were formulated during the late fifties aggregating to a broad average of 12.5 per cent of production as accounting for feed, seed and wastages. For all official calculations, this is the netting factor being adopted to calculate the availability of foodgrains for human consumption.

None of these three items is in any way related to the gross production of foodgrains. Seed, for example, is primarily a function of area under the crop and is determined by the seed rate required under different cropping systems and the type of seed used. In a situation where gross area under foodgrains has steadily declined from a peak of 131.16 million hect. in 1983-84 to 124.1 million in 1997-98, quantity of foodgrains required for seed has actually declined and would be reduced further. Even wastage rates will depend not only on the quantity stored, but also the types of storage available and marketable surplus. Imported stored grains are not at all included in any of the calculations being made at present. Similarly exported grain should be excluded from storage losses. Here also with improvement in storage systems, the quantity lost should come down.

Concentrating on feed, the subject under discussion, these rates have a direct relation with animal husbandry and poultry development programmes. Data available have no relevance under the conditions as they exist today. While feeding of gram to animals is not very common these days, the consumption of maize has gone up appreciably because of poultry development.

At the international level, according to FAO estimates, as much as 39 per cent of cereals were used as feed during 1984-85 for the whole world. This according to them came down to 34.6 percent during 1995-96. It looks interesting because even the physical quantity of foodgrains is less by 2.0 million tonnes. Estimated consumption of wheat, coarse grains and rice for feed during 1994-95 was 647.0 million tonnes as estimated by the FAO when the world production of meat, milk and eggs was less than that of 1995-96. The Story is a bit different according to USDA sources.

Data from the two sources do not tally which is possible because the methodology in each case may be different. But what is important in the two sources is that while according to FAO the total quantity of coarse grains, wheat and rice fed to animals came down from 622 to 620 million tonnes during the 11 years period, the corresponding figures for USDA are 608.7 and 641.9 million tonnes. A long time data series of USDA shows that the consumption of wheat for feed increased from 60.6 to 97.2 million tonnes (62.3%) and coarse cereals from 336.4 to 568.4 million tonnes (59.2%) during 1968-69 to 1995-96. There is a steady increase up to 1987-88 when estimated feed (wheat and coarse grain) peaked at 661.5 million tonnes. Eight years later (1995-96), the estimate is only 641.9 million tonnes-nearly 20 million tonnes less than the base 1987-88.

According to USDA rice is not being fed to animals anywhere in the world, but FAO shows that this has increased from 7.0 to 9.0 million tonnes during the same period. Our studies in Punjab, Haryana and Uttar Pradesh show that small quantities of rice are being consumed by livestock in India. But most interesting case is that of China where during 1993 as much as 20.0 million tonnes of rice was consumed by the animals. Again a study by IFPRI shows that the estimated consumption of paddy for feed uses was 32.0 million tonnes representing 8.0 per cent of production during 1980. Total consumption of cereals according to the IFPRI study during that year as feed was 681.0 million tonnes. This included 17% by-products of cereals, giving net cereal consumption of 565.6 million tonnes. The IFPRI study does not make it clear whether the original figure of 681.4 million tonnes includes by-products of this very grain or is additional from outside. Normally, in India, for example, grain is fed to livestock as whole and additional by-products like bran/choker etc. are also fed. For purposes of comparison, it is assumed that whole grain equivalent of consumption during 1980 was 681.4 million tonnes including by-products according to IFPRI, representing 40.5 per cent of total production.

A comparison of these three sources of data FAO, USDA and IFPRI depicts a rather confusing picture. IFPRI does not give any annual data series. But for 1980 its estimate is 681.4 million tonnes as against 559.6 million tonnes by USDA. Again for 1984 FAO estimate is 622 million tonnes against USDA 582.2 million tonnes. Besides these varied estimates, one striking feature is that while cereal feed consumption according to FAO and USDA has come down during the last 10-11 years, world production of eggs, meat and milk increased many fold during the same period. IFRPI appreciates that the use of cereals for livestock feed is growing rapidly in developing countries and is reaching significant proportions and that this fact has profound implications for food security of low-income people, employment, and the size of markets available to exporters of cereals and did undertake a few studies, but no one has tried to go to the field to find the real ground situation which has its own peculiarities.

INDIAN SCENE

Most of the researchers engaged in projecting the demand for foodgrains for India, base their calculations on the experience abroad and come up with conclusions which have no relevance to the ground situation. China is perhaps the only country in the Asian Region where the quantity of foodgrains fed to livestock is rather high. But without understanding the implications of Chinese data, our researchers also project much high requirements for India on this account. The fact is that even there, leaving aside projections, current consumption estimates vary widely between different sources.[20A]

In India, there is only one study which was conducted by Techno-Economic Research Institute, New Delhi, under the sponsorship of the Planning Commission to address itself to this specific question. The study was based on an interview of 1800 farmers spread over 15 districts in Punjab, Haryana and Western Uttar Pradesh during 1986-87. The results throw an interesting sidelight. Against a total of 5 per cent of food grains for feed under the conventional estimates, the survey results show only 3.24 per cent and a total of 9.78 per cent for feed, seed and wastages as against 12.5% normally assumed.[21]

Peculiar Indian Conditions

Let us examine the problem involved in estimating the demand for feed. Normally the farmer either buys the concentrate from the market or prepares it himself according to his own experience and circumstances. Such decisions certainly have inter- and intra-regional/ country variations. Theoretically animal nutritionists have laid down recommended composition of concentrates containing specified quantities of digested crude proteins, total digestible nutrients, etc. They are grouped into some sort of maintenance for mature animals, growing calves, milk production etc. Now these are available from oilcakes, foodgrains, fish meal, pulses, root crops like cassava and various agricultural wastes. Composition among various commodities will depend upon easy availability of a particular item, traditional feeds and systems, inter-commodity price differential, economics of feeding livestock, changes in the production pattern of livestock products.

It is true that we cannot produce milk or meat just on air and water. But it is also true that various factors referred to above play a very significant role. If China produces 150 million tonnes of sweet potato and potato, no wonder if half of this is fed to animals. In India if the prices of foodgrains go up, it is uneconomical for the farmer to give concentrates to animals which give say 1-2 kg of milk. Instead, he may keep them on grazing, dry fodder, some green fodder, if available, plus by- products of foodgrains, kitchen or other agricultural wastes etc. This type of flexibility is much more easier with regard to dairy animals and piggery, but in the case of poultry -layers (particularly the organised sector) and broilers, research so far available shows that a certain percentage of maize is quite essential. This would then mean that there is nothing like a fixed relationship between the various constituents of the concentrate at a given time. This will vary from time to time, depending on the specific factors mentioned earlier. The problem is further complicated in the case of India where we have our own peculiarities as:

1. Major part of the milk in India is produced by the animals which yield less than 2-2.5 kg/day. It is neither economical nor practical to give them any concentrates.
2. There is double counting in so far as wastage and livestock feeding is concerned. Major part of the so-called wasted grain is fed to livestock.
3. Out of a total of around 3.5 million tonnes of meat, major part of the 3.1 million (other than chicken) is a by-product of the livestock industry. We do not have separate beef or pig fattening programmes. Major part of the sheep or goat are also not stall fed. Even with regard to chicken meat, not more than half is broilers which have to be fed to get good results. The remaining half is from the culled layers which again is a by-product.
4. With regard to egg production, at least 12% are coming from *desi* birds, where the productivity is only 40 eggs/annum/bird compared with around 240 eggs of the organized sector. Desi birds just scavange around and live on kitchen waste if at all. No additional concentrates are given.
5. Obviously, all studies which convert livestock products into meat livestock units and calculate feed requirements on theoretical norms are bound to go wrong.
6. In India, draught animal power (DAP) of bullocks (72 million) and buffaloes (8 million) as well as equines (1 million of horses and donkeys) and camels (1 million), make available 50,000 million units of energy per year, worth Rs. 100,000 million. Draught animals plough 100 million ha. of farm land, forming 60% of the area cultivated. Draught animal power saves 6 million tonnes of petroleum per year, worth Rs. 40,000 million in foreign exchange. Draught animal power is an appropriate technology, inevitable for 60 million small farms and for small-scale transportation. Asset value of draught animal power is Rs. 200,000 million, and replacement by mechanised system would need Rs. 1,000,000 million. The Institute of Economic Growth made a study and found that to replace our draught animals, we would

require about 20 million tractors and the petroleum products worth $20 billion. Another study by Dr Jugner Lansh, who stayed in Indian villages for 3 months found that if the cattle were to be eliminated, 100-200 million of people would migrate to cities. With more of tractorization, the importance of draught animal power will, however, be decreasing in the future.

Research in the Pipeline

While projecting the demand for feedgrains for livestock feeding in the developing world, one has also to take into consideration the likely impact of research activity which aims at providing the required DCP/TDN from sources other than foodgrains like:

1. Debate is going on today that a large proportion of cereals can be saved in poultry feeding by increasing the caloric density of the diet. To replace cereals for poultry feeding, other alternative sources include fats and oils, preferably the nonconventional ones like mahua/mustard oil, which are very rich source of energy in poultry rations. Since vegetable oils are mostly used for human consumption, the importance of rendered animal fats may be a better proposition. Despite social constraints for the use of rendered animal fats, the organised feed industry can make use of this product which is being practically wasted today. Failing this, import of mutton tallow holds a promise for maintaining poultry production at the desired levels.[21A]
2. Present research efforts have to be intensified to sustain animal production on crop residues and industrial by-products. The present research on animal nutrition and physiology promoting traditional feeding system will no longer deliver high productivity levels as the basic raw materials have a low digestibility (2-3%). However, a major reserve of energy is found in the untapped plant cell wall in terms of ligno-cellulose complex and, if tapped, will yield enough energy to feed all the 400 million livestock. But this will require large investments in research on feed biotechnology, manipulating and constructing microbes which can digest the lignin ring. Current nutrition research has to focus on this area to generate and release carbohydrates from plant cell wall. A method has to be found to remove various chemical moieties like tannin and other antigrowth factors from cakes and meals so that the abundant protein in the meal is made available to livestock.[21B]
3. New technologies are being developed to improve the utilization of crop residues. Fodder production and cut-and-carry systems offer an alternative to communal grazing. The quality of crop residue (i.e straw) can be improved by urea treatment to improve its nutritive value. Agricultural waste can be successfully

converted into useful animal feed by the use of selective microbes. With new developments in molecular biochemistry throwing up exciting possibilities of breaking down lignocellulose—the most important compound generated in agricultural waste—it is indeed challenging times for biochemists. A highly successful and acceptable urea-molasses-mineral block-lick has been developed for improved utilisation of straws by growing animals. The supplement can be used during natural calamities to save the animal. Compact straw blocks supplemented with urea, mineral mixture, and molasses, cakes, bran and green fodder have been developed to act as a complete feed for different categories of dairy animals. Similar low cost feed & fodder are to be developed. Increased milk yields of 20 percent as a result of using urea-molasses blocks have been reported.

The application of bypass protein technology in combination with straw has been found to quadruple the efficiency of supply of amino-acids from feed to milk production. Bypass protein technology, which refers to the use of special protein sources (e.g. brewer's grain, corn gluten meal, cotton seed cake, soybean meal) and processes (e.g. heating) to reduce the digestive losses in the rumen and improve the efficiency of protein utilization, under experimental conditions, has reportedly allowed the reduction of concentrate requirement by 40 per cent, the increase in the conversion of protein in dry matter by over 30 per cent, and the reduction of dry matter requirement by 24 percent.[21C] Important constraints to the utilization and dissemination of these technologies however, still remain. These include the applicability of these technologies to high yielding crossbred cows only, their commercial production and utilization potential, and weaknesses in the existing technology transfer system which could introduce such technologies to farmers.

4. Extensive research and feeding trials have been conducted on many agro-industrial by-products and non conventional feeds to use these as protein and energy supplements, such as apple pomace, groundnut hulls, mesta cake, mahua cake, neem cake salseed meal, leaucena leaf meal, soya pulp, rice bran, brewery waste, etc. The compounded feed industry has been greatly benefited by these findings. Appropriate technologies have been developed for detoxifying toxins in certain agro-industrial feeds like mahua cake, neem cake and sal seed meals for providing cheep alternative feed to growing calves. The development of cheap good quality feed is going to be a great challenge for the scientists in the coming years.*

---

* Shiv Kumar Gupta - Dairy in Next Millennium- The Challenges, Yojana, Vol. 43, No. 11, November 1999.

5. In Cuba, farmers add pumpkin (squash gourds) to the birds feed. They chop and dry pumpkins and feed them to laying hens with good results. Pumpkins have as much or more protein and fat as maize and cassava flours which are used to feed chicken. Taro is another plant which is used to feed poultry. Taro (*Colocasia esculenta*) is a tuber also known as dasheen or coco yam. The taro is ground into flour. Add 15% of this flour to the diet of chicks between the age of one day and four weeks. Chickens must eat well from an early age. Chickens gain weight quickly-they can gain 10 times their weight in the first four weeks of life. Similarly an alternative feed for pigs is using local plants as feed substitutes. One of the plants is `cassava' (*Manihot esculenta*). It can be used to replace maize or other grains. The farmers gather cassava tubers, leaves and the juicy parts of the stem. They boil them together in water. They add a little salt and a little amount of fish meal. The fish meal provides protein which is an essential part of the pigs' diet.[21D]

   It is hoped that over a span of more than two decades, the dissemination of results of researching under way would reduce substantially the use of cereals in animal food, leading to the utilization of alternative sources of energy and protein.

Some Problems

Besides this, there is the problem of some of our experts[20A] using certain coefficients for converting milk, meat and egg, etc. into foodgrains which have neither any scientific basis behind them, nor take into consideration peculiar Indian conditions. The net result is that the projected demand figures present some sort of imaginary number, giving completely wrong signals to the policy makers.

It is unfortunate that over the last 5 decades, no serious effort has been made in India or for that matter in other developing countries to establish any empirical basis in this respect. Firstly, it is wrong to lump up feed with seed and wastages for the reasons given in the opening paras of this paper. They are not grouped together anywhere else. Secondly, all those engaged in the projections studies, go about the business by pure guess work-raising the magical figure of 12.5 percent (which itself has no basis) to anything like 15 percent for say the year 2000 and more for subsequent periods. Fallacy of such an exercise is obvious. During the last 50 years milk production has increased by 4 times, egg by over 15 times, chicken from 0 to 0.4 million tonnes, (of course with about 4 times increase in food production), the conventional adjustment factor of 12.5 percent has been assumed to remain constant. One would then wonder why this should be assumed to go up to 15 or 20% in the coming few years, particularly when foodgrains production is also assumed to grow more or less at the prevailing rates or even a bit higher.

THE MODEL

There is no empirical study available which can give any idea about the consumption levels of foodgrains by the livestock.[22] To overcome this problem, a Simple Incremental Demand Model has been developed to project the demand for foodgrains by 2020 AD. The year 1993 is taken as the base. The production of foodgrains during the year was 179.5 Mt., milk 58 Mt., eggs 23 billion (1.15 Mt.) and meat 3.5 Mt. To meet the human as well as livestock requirements at the then existing pattern of consumption, existing levels of prices and poverty (whatever its dimension and definition) the system could not absorb the available quantity. As much as 9.6 million tonnes were added to public sector stocks. With imports of 2.4 million tonnes, total quantity of foodgrains available in the system was 172.28 million tonnes (Table 19.13).

Starting from this base, the population of India by 2020 as projected by UNFPA will be 1280.4 million, which will be equally distributed

Table 19.13 Consumption Pattern of Foodgrains During 1993-94

Million tonnes

Human Consumption (million tonnes)	
Rural (675 @ 168 kg./annum.)	113.40
Urban (225 @ 132 " " ")	29.70
Total (900 @ 159 " " ")	143.10
Pulses (total production)	13.30
Poultry (million tonnes)	
(1.54@ 1.2 tonnes/tonne)	1.85
Seed	5.00
Wastage (@ 1.5% for total production + net imports (181.9 million tonnes)	2.73
Total	165.98
Total availability 179.48-9.6 (public sector stocks) 169.88 + 2.4 imports	172.28
Balance for milk and other meat and workforce	6.30
Work force	2.0
Breeding bullocks	0.8
Other meat	1.0
Total	3.8
Balance for milk	2.50
Total production (million tonnes) of milk during 1993-94	= 60.6
Milk produced/kg. foodgrains consumed.	24.24 (kg)

between rural and urban. Human cereal consumption levels both for rural and urban India will not remain constant at the 1993-94 levels of 13.4 kg per capita per month (rural) and 10.63 kg per capita per month (urban) since past experience is a clear indicator of further decline. Well fed states like Punjab (10.78 kg Rural and 9.01 kg Urban), Haryana (11.92 kg Rural and 10.46 kg Urban) or Gujarat (10.66 kg Rural and 8.96 kg Urban), Maharashtra (11.39 kg Rural and 9.37 kg Urban) have registered a steep decline in their consumption pattern of cereals. We will then be within reasonable limits to assume that per capita per month consumption of cereals for the country as a whole will not be more than 12 kg (rural) and 10 kg (urban)—somewhat above the present consumption levels of these states. This may actually be reduced further.

Recent studies throw an interesting sidelight by establishing an inverse relation between consumption of cereals and availability of labour saving devices like increase in the horse power tractors and pumpsets. Same is the position with regard to increase in road length in rural areas (Table 19.14 and 19.15). After discussing other indicators like higher nutritional efficiency, etc. Prof. Hanumantha Rao concludes that it is thus interesting, though it may appear paradoxical that, upto a point, a reduction in the intake of foodgrains on certain counts should in fact be associated with improvement in human welfare. For our future projections, rural and urban consumption levels are assumed to be 12 kg (rural) and 10 kg (urban) respectively as mentioned above. This would mean a reduction of only 5% for urban and 10% for rural areas over the 1993-94 consumption levels of cereals over a period of 27 years. This may actually stabilise at lower rates.

Based on the assumptions as below, production targets for various livestock products are determined. Although major part of additional production of livestock products is likely to be continuously produced under the existing systems, it is assumed that the total additional production will be under the improved system.

1. Availability of milk hovered around 40 kg per capita per annum upto 1977-78, when it started moving up steadily. It rose from 44 kg to 65.6 kg during 1992-93 an annual compound growth rate of 2.8 percent in response to a per capita income growth rate of 2 percent. Production of milk during this 15 year period increased at an annual compound rate of 4.9 percent. There has, however, been a deceleration in the growth pattern during the nineties when production increased at the rate of around 3 percent per annum. There is an all round increase in milk prices and synthetic milk is being produced in large quantities, particularly in North India, the milk bowl of the country. Special efforts will have to be made to remove constraints in production due to breeding, feeding, management and disease control problems. With due consideration to the demand, targeted growth rate has to be at least 3 per cent. This is an important issue for consideration by the

Table 19.14 ***Correction Ratio Between Rural Cereal Consumption and Related Variables***

1992-93	*Rural per capita cereal consumption 1993-94*							
	Bottom % 30	*Middle % 40*	*Top % 30*	*All*	*Bottom % 30*	*Middle % 40*	*Top % 30*	*All*
Total Expenditure	0.4647 (1.8922)	0.2601 (0.9712)	0.1521 (0.5549)	0.2688 (1.0062)	– 0.4492 (– 1.8128)	– 0.6417 (– 3.0167)	– 0.6114 (– 2.7858)	– 0.6301 (– 2.9257)
Price	– 0.8792 (– 6.6533)	– 0.8382 (– 5.5416)	– 0.7420 (– 3.9906)	– 0.8531 (– 5.8954)	0.0032 (0.0115)	0.0179 (0.0645)	– 0.0939 (– 0.3401)	– 0.0244 (– 0.088)
Road Length	– 0.5901 (– 2.6354)	– 0.7983 (– 4.7792)	– 0.7420 (– 3.9906)	– 0.7449 (– 4.0756)	– 0.6545 (– 3.1212)	– 0.5918 (– 2.6471)	– 0.5930 (– 2.6553)	– 0.6142 (– 2.8062)
Tractor and pumpsets	0.1368 (0.4979)	0.0475 (0.1715)	– 0.0385 (– 0.1389	0.0481 (0.1736)	– 0.3091 (– 1.1719)	– 0.3709 (– 1.44)	– 0.3684 (– 1.4788)	– 0.3592 (1.3877)

Figures in the parenthesis are t-ratios.

SOURCE: C.H. Hanumantha Rao, Presidential address delivered at the 13th National Conference on Agricultural Marketing, held at N.I.R.D., Hyderabad, on 12 October, 1999.

Table 19.15 Road Length ad Horse Power from Tractors and Pumpsets

State	Road length (km/000 SQ km)		HP from tractors and pumpsets	
	1975-76*	1991-92*	1972*	1987**
Andhra Pradesh	379.0	556.0	133.4	551.4
Assam	689.0	878.0	9.5	18.4
Bihar	536.0	504.0	83.5	313.5
Gujarat	248.0	472.0	258.9	530.7
Haryana	583.0	673.0	343.1	1572.2
Karnataka	525.0	711.0	121.8	354.2
Kerala	2248.0	3534.0	87.5	519.5
Madhya Pradesh	211.0	309.0	40.0	248.8
Maharashtra	368.0	799.0	116.3	204.7
Orissa	310.0	428.0	17.0	43.1
Punjab	797.0	1116.0	763.5	1666.2
Rajasthan	164.0	358.0	51.6	400.3
Tamil Nadu	847.0	1434.0	731.0	1143.3
Uttar Pradesh	653.0	756.0	146.2	960.3
West Bengal	610.0	665.0	10.4	723.4
All India	380.0	628.0	153.7	761.8

Note: 1. Pump sets including both electric and diesel pumpsets
2. *Data used for '72-73. ** Data used for '93-'94.
3. In case of Orissa, the total road length in 1991-92 is arrived at by assuming the growth rate of road length.

Source: 1. For Cols. 1 and 2: Centre for monitoring Indian economy (1996), Infrastructure in India, CMIE, November, 1996.
2. For Cols., 3 and 4: C.S.O., Ministry of Planning and Programme Implementation, G.O.I., Statistical Abstract of India, 1997, Vol. I.

TRRI SOURCE: C.H. Hanumantha Rao, Presidential address delivered at the 13th National Conference on agricultural marketing, held at N.I.R.D., Hyderabad, on 12 October, 1999.

policy makers. If so, milk production target for 2020 will be 163 million tonnes. Although the organised sector today contributes hardly 10-15 percent of total milk output, to produce the whole of additional (163 – 58) = 105 million tonnes, in the organised sector, the recommended norm of 14.45 kg of milk for 1 kg of foodgrains will apply[21C]. Hence, additional requirement will be 7.27 million tonnes of foodgrains.

It would be of interest to learn that the compound animal feed industry in India has been growing at an average rate of 10-12 per cent annually. In order to feed the growing population with nutrition, diet with adequate calories and protein, it was necessary to bring about a revolution in agricultural production, animal husbandry and aquaculture. The compound animal feed industry has utilized the nutritional qualities of various conventional and non-conventional raw materials and scientifically compounded them to prepare animal feed according to the nutritional requirements of the animals. It has thus contributed in achieving the main objective directly by increasing yield and production of animal protein and indirectly by sparing and thus augmenting food grains and edible oil bearing material useful for human consumption by reducing their use in feeding animals. Thus, from less than about 50,000 tonnes of production per annum in the early sixties, the compound animal feed industry in India has grown to produce about 8m tonnes of compound feed annually. The Indian compound animal feed industry has also been improving the quality of compound food. Efficiency of animal feed is always expressed in terms of feed conversion ratio, i.e. output (animal production) in relation to input (feed) per unit.

To produce a balanced feed for animal, poultry or aqua the main oilmeals used are soybean meal, groundnut meal, sunflowerseed meal, rice bran extraction, rapeseed meal, cottonseed meal. India produces 32m tonnes of oilseeds and oil bearing material which gives about 20/22 tonnes of oilcake/meal. The current production of oilmeal is about 10 m tonnes out of which about 3 m tonnes is exported. Exploiting the full potential of oilmeals will go a long way to save foodgrains and improve animal nutrition.

2. In 1993, annual per capita availability of eggs was 28. With the growth rate of 5-6 percent in production during the past few years, and increasing incomes supported by the educational campaigns by the National Egg Coordination Committee (NECC) and improved infrastructural facilities for rural poultry development, demand is projected to go up by over 3 times to say 90 eggs per capita per annum. This would mean a production target of 119.7 or say 120 billion (6.0 million tonnes) eggs. It may be noted that the present annual per capita consumption in rural India is only 10 eggs and in urban area 80 eggs. Demand for foodgrains at 1.2 kg of foodgrains for 1 kg (20) eggs for additional 92 billion eggs will calculate to 5.5 million tonnes[23]. This is when the total production of eggs will be in the organised sector. The present free range system at the village level which provides about 12% of total eggs will be completely eliminated.

3. Per capita availability of poultry meat during 1993 was 517 grams per annum. Demand for poultry meat is increasing fast at around 12-14 percent. Assuming an annual growth of around 9 percent, for the whole period, total availability of poultry meat is projected at 6.5 million tonnes. This will provide 5.0 kg per capita or nearly 10 times the consumption levels of 1993. Of the total poultry meat of 454 thousand tonnes available during 1993, only 254 thousand tonnes was from broilers and the remaining 200 thousand tonnes from culled layers after 18 months of their productive life. Assuming that all the additional egg production of 92 billion will come from pedigree hens given over

240 eggs each, the total number of hens will work out to around 400 million. At 2 kg per bird, they will give 800 thousand tonnes of chicken meat. Additional chicken meat which will be produced by broilers will calculate to 6500 – (454+ 800) = 5246 thousand tonnes. To produce this quantity of broiler meat, foodgrains requirement at 1.2 kg foodgrains for 1.0 kg meat, will work out to 6.3 million tonnes.

4. There is a debate going on today that a large proportion of cereals can be saved in poultry feeding by increasing the caloric density of the diet. Since the availability of cereals for poultry feeding would continue to be a problem, the other alternative source is to use fats and oils, may be the nonconventional ones like mahua oil, mustard oil, etc., which are a rich source of energy in poultry rations. But vegetable oils are mostly used for human consumption. The importance of rendered animal fats may then be a better proposition. Although social constraints exist for the use of rendered animal fats, there should be no problem for the organised feed industry to make use of this product which is being practically wasted today. Failing this, import of mutton tallow holds a promise for maintaining poultry production at the desired levels.[24]

5. Meat from culled birds and other animals like buffalo etc. is a by-product of the livestock industry. Concentrates are also not being given to sheep, goat and piggery. Of the total meat production of about 3.5 million tonnes during 1993, the share of goat, sheep and pig was about a million tonnes. There are no well-focussed programmes to increase the production of these categories of meat. The most optimistic assumption can be to add another 1 million tonnes of meat from these sources. While sheep and goat will continue to be raised as before, piggery can be assumed to be taken by the organised sector to some extent. This would possibly need a total of around 2 million tonnes of additional foodgrains.

6. India has a special place for draught animals and breeding stock with increasing mechanisation of agriculture, the demand for draught power should possibly be decreasing, but a provision of 2.0 million tonnes as calculated by us (Table 19.13) for 1993-94 has already been made. Similarly with increasing application of artificial insemination , the number of breeding bulls might also decrease and allocations already made for 1993-94 should be sufficient to meet the requirement of food on this account.

7. Since a major part of the so called wastage in foodgrains is used to feed livestock, and there is a strong possibility of new technology being introduced both in the public and private, storage losses on this account will be the minimal. Even then, it would be better to allow for wastages on the additional production of 69.0 million tonnes.Aprovision for additional 1.5 million tonnes on this account has been made.

8. Seed requirements are related to the area under cultivation. Total area under foodgrains peaked at 131.16 million hect. during 1983-84

and steadily came down to 124.1 million hect. in 1997-98. There being hardly any possibility of any increase in the area under foodgrains, no allowance is being made for additional seed requirements.

9. Another area - industrial uses - is likely to become very important in the times to come. Industrial uses of foodgrains can be divided into two categories - indirect human consumption like biscuits, bread etc. and non-human consumption like starch and malt. The demand for starch has to go up primarily with the development of textile and paper industries, although small quantities are also used for glucose, cosmetics and pharmaceuticals. Estimated production of starch for the year 2000 is around 637 thousand tonnes[24A]. With an annual increase of about 40 thousand tonnes projected production by 2020 may then be placed at about 1.5 million tonnes. The source for the production of starch today is tapioca and maize. Although human consumption of tapioca in Kerala is decreasing, more or less same is the position regarding production. There are, however, other states like Tamil Nadu where the production of tapioca is increasing. Additional starch requirement will be (1.5 – 0.637) 0.863 million tonnes. Part of it being supplied by tapioca, maize required for the purpose will work out to say 1.0 million tonnes.

Industrial units manufacturing beer, nutritious food products, pharmaceutical items and even cattle feed also use malt in different proportions. Total demand for malt today is 2.5 lakh tonnes for which the source is primarily barley. Since the demand for these products using malt has a very high growth rate-over 10 per cent – malt requirements are likely to go up to around 2.5 million tonnes. Total production of malt in the country is hardly 1.7 lakh tonnes and the rest is being imported. If the total demand of 2.5 million tonnes of malt is to be produced in India with barley as the base, it will be an impossible task to produce the required quantities of 3.5 million tonnes of barley for the purpose. The present production of barley in India is around 1.6 million tonnes which has come down from over 3.0 million tonnes 50 years back. Since it is basically rain fed crop, it is replaced by wheat or even mustard to some extent once irrigation facilities are available. The possibilities of increasing the production of quality barley to meet the total demand for malt are remote. As imported barley is superior to the one produced in India for the purpose of making malt and costs less than the material available at home, the imported barley-based units can also earn considerable quantum of foreign exchange, particularly when the Union and State governments have delicensed the manufacture of beer.

In the light of all this, there will be only two options left for the malt manufacturing companies. Either to import barley from outside or shift to other bases like molasses and beat root etc. at least for non beer uses. A provision for a total 4.5 million tonnes of foodgrains (3.5 for malt and 1.5 for starch) is being made. All other industrial uses like biscuits etc. are included in the calculations for human consumption of cereals.

10. Requirements for human consumption do not include pulses. Demand for this commodity has been assumed to go up by around 50% per capita. Efforts will have to be made to find alternative sources like soya cake, etc. as a substitute for pulses for any additional demand because of production constraints. Against the availability of 12.8 million tonnes, in 1998 and the highest ever production of 14.26 million tonnes, we have provided for 20.0 million tonnes under the model.

Summarising the position (Table 19.16), gross requirement of foodgrains will not exceed 241 million tonnes. This would mean an additional production of 40 million tonnes during the coming 20 years from today or say 2 million tonnes annually. Having already achieved

Table 19.16 Demand for Foodgrains by 2020 AD

Item	*Population (million)*		
	Urban	*Rural*	*Total*
1993	221	663	884
2020	640	640	1280
1993-2020*	419	– 23	446
Additional Foodgrains Requirement (million tonnes)			
Human Consumption			
Cereals	48.6	– 14.3	34.3
Pulses	20-12.8		7.2**
Milk (additional 105 million tonnes)			7.27
Eggs (additional 92 Billion eggs)			5.5
Chicken (additional 4.4 million tonnes)			5.3
Other meat			2.0
Draught and other animals			.5
Wastage			2.5
Industrial uses			1.5
Total Quantity available in the system during 1993			69.07
179.48-9.6 (Public sector stock) =169.88 + 2.4 (Imports) =			172.28
Grand Total			241.35

* Additional population during period

** Present per capita consumption of pulses is 10.3 kg/annum for urban and 9.1 kg/annum for rural areas. Calculated at this rate, total demand for pulses works out to 13.0 million tonnes. Our estimated demand at 20.0 million tonnes gives an increase of over 50%.

a production of nearly 209 million tonnes during 1999-2000, this should be within reasonable limits of achievement. Each of the assumption made above with regard to demand errs, if at all, on the higher side. This is because, total additional production of livestock products is assumed to be produced under the modern organised sector. This has resulted in an allocation of over 32% of the additional production of foodgrains for livestock feeding. This is not likely to happen and new researches in the pipeline aiming at substituting foodgrains for livestock feeding have not been taken into account. These projections would, therefore, be the optimistic ones. The reconstituted food basket for 2020 (Table 19.17) gives a total per capita availability of 2849 calories. Total availability of protein is 89.4 gm and the share of calories from animal sources is 14.4% as against 7.8% during 1993 Fig. 19.6.

Table 19.17 Available Consumer Basket - 2020

Item	*Total Production (million tonnes)*		*Per Capita Availability*			
			Annual	*Daily*		
	TE-ending 1993	*2020*	*Kg*	*Gms*	*Calories*	*Proteins Gms*
Cereals*	123.30	169.00	132.03	361.7	1266.0	31.2
Pulses	13.0	20.0	15.62	42.8	150.9	9.0
Milk	53.90	163.2	127.50	349.3	366.5	12.7
Oils	6.2	14.96	11.69	32.0	288.0	--
Egg	1.1	5.98	4.67	12.8	23.1	17.8
Meat	3.08	12.24	9.56	26.2	29.5	5.4
Fish	3.09	10.88	8.50	23.3	23.4	4.1
Fruits	24.12	62.56	48.88	133.9	100.2	1.4
Vegetables	43.02	140.08	109.144	299.8	185.0	7.8
Sugar**	20.36	40.8	31.88	87.3	346.2	--
Total				1369.1	2778.8	89.4
Miscellaneous not already covered					70.0	
Grand Total					2848.8	

SOURCE: * This is the actual consumption level for humans.
** Includes jaggery
a. Per capital consumption of milk in Delhi during 1996-97 was only 282 gms.

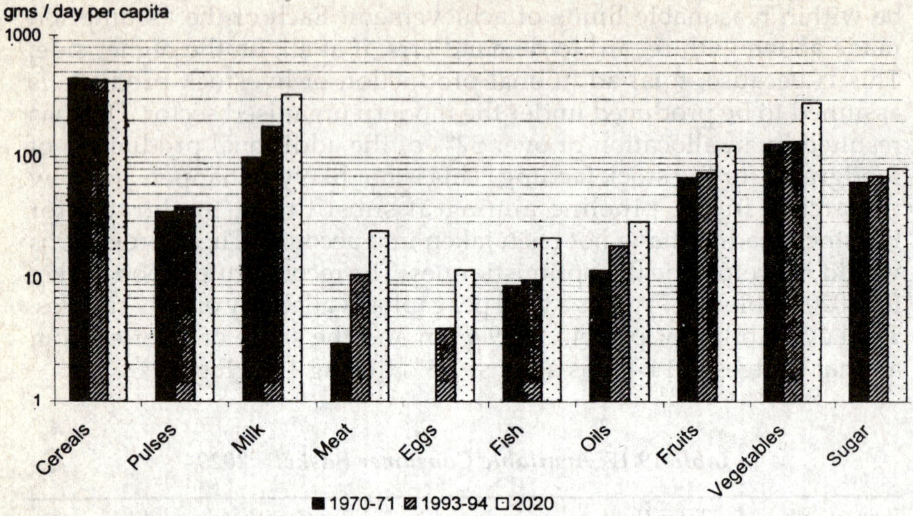

Fig. 19.6 Consumption (cereals)/availability (others of various food items

It must be highlighted that the northern region which has so far contributed more than 50 percent in the average incremental production of foodgrains during 1962-65 to 1990-93 (Table 19.18) will not be able to maintain its performance. Western, Southern and Central Regions also do not give much hope. We will have to depend for a major contribution, on the Eastern region only. During the 27 years (1962-66 to 1990-93), when the previous 7 years happened to have good monsoons in a row, additional foodgrain production totalled, 91.7 million tonnes, with the full benefit of the green revolution. We will now have to add another 41 million tonnes during the next 20 years (2000-2020), the period under discussion. No complacency will, therefore, be called for on the food front. While Krishi Bhavan need not loose its sleep, it certainly cannot afford to sleep over the matter.

CONCLUSIONS

An effort has been made to prepare optimistic demand projections both for human consumption and other uses. An allocation of 23.6 million tonnes of foodgrains for feed alone, from the additional production of 69 million tonnes (over 32.0 percent) would certainly be the highest. Most of the other estimates of total demand for foodgrains being thrown out by the national and international agencies being much higher, this exercise raises important policy issues. A target of say 241.0 million tonnes of foodgrains, for 2020 AD although within achievable limits, will need special efforts. Actual requirements will certainly be much less because of the assumptions (giving higher

Table 19.18 Average and Incremental Production of Foodgrains Regionwise 1962-65 to 2001.

(Million tonnes)

Year	North-Western Region	Eastern Region	Central-Wes-tern Region	Southern Region	All-India
		Average production			
1. 1962-65	20.9	19.7	23.5	18.7	82.8
2. 1970-73	32.5	23.0	26.0	21.1	102.6
3. 1980-83	47.0	23.4	34.4	24.5	129.3
4. 1990-93	67.8	33.8	43.0	28.5	173.1
5. 1994-97	74.8	38.0	47.8	29.4	190.0
		Incremental average production			
2 Over 1	11.6 (58.6)	3.3 (16.7)	2.5 (12.6)	2.4 (12.1)	19.8 (100)
3 over 2	14.5 (54.3)	0.4 (1.5)	8.4 (31.5)	3.4 (12.7)	26.7 (100)
4 over 3	20.8 (47.5)	10.4 (23.7)	8.6 (19.6)	4.0 (9.1)	43.8 (100)
4 over 1	46.9 (51.9)	14.1 (15.6)	19.5 (21.6)	9.8 (10.9)	90.3 (100)
5 over 4	7.0 (41.4)	4.2 (24.9)	4.8 (28.4)	0.9 (5.3)	16.9 (100)
5 over 1	53.9 (50.3)	18.3 (17.1)	24.3 (22.7)	10.7 (9.10)	107.2 (100)

Note: North Western — U.P., Punjab, Hayana, Himachal Pradesh and J & K
Central Western — M.P., Maharashtra, Gujarat and Rajasthan
Southern — A.P., Karnataka, Kerala and Tamil Nadu.
Eastern — Arunachal Pradesh, Assam, Manipur, Meghalaya, Mizoram, Nagaland, Tripura West Bengal, Orissa and Bihar.

estimates) made under the model. We will then be playing safe. But if the target is fixed much higher, as proposed by many others,[20A] there is an obvious danger of giving wrong signals to the development strategy which might lead to distortions and ill advised wasted efforts.

The purpose of this paper which is of an indicative nature is to serve as an input in this major controversial issue of national importance. The country would be interested in having realistic estimates. There is an urgent need to undertake comprehensive studies on livestock feeding, the only major grey area in the country. The ground situation in India is very much different as mentioned in the introductory section. At the same time, a micro level study about the problems, constraints and potentials of production of foodgrains at the regional and subregional levels is another area where research is called for. Really speaking, time has come when we must get out of the orthodoxy of regional self-sufficiency and come up with an optimal cropping pattern with due consideration to optimising production potential in the country.

In the end, it may be stated that there is today a need to mount special studies to have a much more detailed information about the existing food basket of people in the various strata of the society. The available information is not sufficient to provide an answer to this most important issue. There are a number of scattered micro level studies available[25] which are quite revealing. Both human beings and livestock are consuming a large number of locally available material which does not figure any where in our production estimates. Even the NSSO methodology as it exists today cannot provide any answer to these intricate issues. The things as they stand, models imported from outside and developed by various interests, will continue to keep the controversy alive so as to confuse the issue. There is otherwise no reason that some responsible quarters should have projected the foodgrains demand for 2000 at something like 240 million tonnes as the minimum, only a few years back. They have already been proved wrong today. Their projections for the future will then be equally wrong.

REFERENCES

1. Ravenstein, E.G. 1891. "Lands of the globe still available for European settlement," Proceedings of the Royal Geographic Society 13: 27-35,64.
2. Pfaundler, L. 1902. "Die Weltwirtschaft im Lichte der Physik," Deutsche Revue 22, no. 2:29-38, 171-182.
3. Brown, H. 1954. The Challenge of Man's Existence.
4. Cf., Martin C. Yang, A Chinese Village, p. 34.
5. Ernest Engel's "Law of Expenditure For Food" Q.J.E. No. XLVII, November 1932, pp.78-101. Quoted by E.M. Ojala, Agriculture and Economic Progress, p. 87.
6. Bansil, P.C., India's Food Resources and Population, 1958,
7. Theodore W. Schultz, The Economic Organisation of Agriculture, p.245,237 goes so far as to place the income elasticity for home grown food, in India, at as high a figure as 1.0 (Income elasticity means the relation between a certain ratio of change in income and the ratio of the resultant change in expenditure on any item. This relation is unity when any change in income results in a proportionate change in the expenditure for the item). Also cf., Demand for Food in the Second Five Year Plan, Agricultural Situation in India, October 1956.
8. Various issues of National Accounts, C.S.O.

8A. Report of the Expert Group on Estimation of the proportion and Number of Poor, Planning Commission, 1993.

9. FAO/WHO (1973) Energy and Protein Requirements, Report of a Joint FAO/WHO Ad Hoc Expert Committee, March 22-April 2,1971, FAO

Nutrition Meetings Report Series No.522, Rome, Italy; Geneva, Switzerland.

10. Bansil, P.C., Food Statistics, Sankhya, December 1956.
11. Report of the Working Group on Foodgrains Requirements by the year 2000 A.D., Ministry of Agriculture, April 1994.
12. Bansil,P.C., Agricultural Statistical Compendium, 1990.
13. Dr. Y.K. Alagh, Export Peripheral to Farm Growth, Economic Times, 31/10/1994. Alagh, Y.K. (1985).`Institution for Price Policy and Supply Management of Food in India.' Paper presented at the Seminar on the Role of Foodgrain Agencies in Food Security in Asia and the Pacific sponsored by FAO, AFMA and FCI. 23-25 April, New Delhi.
14. Radhakrishna,R. (1992) Trends in nutrition: Emerging challenges; and Nutrition: Need for effective intervention, The Economic Times, New Delhi, February 10 and 11 1992.
15. Radhakrishna, R. and C. Ravi, 1992. Effects of Growth, Relative Price and Prefereances on Food and Nutrition. Hyderabad: Centre for Economic and Social Studies and 25 years of National Monitoring Bureau, 1997.
16. Vinodini Reddy, Nutrition in India, National Institute of Nutrition, Hyderabad, India, December 1992.
17. Bansil P.C., Food Security - Perceptions and Aspirations of villagers, Techno Economic Research Institute, 1997 (Memeo)
18. S.L. Rao, Consumer Goods Market, Economic Times, Sep. 30, 1994.

18A. Praduman Kumar, Demand for Foodgrains and other Food in India, 1997, E.P.W.

18B. Bansil P.C., Demand for Foodgrains by 2020, E.P.W., March 7, 1998.

18C. Prospects for India's Cereal Supply and Demand to 2020, International Food Policy Research Institute.

18D. Foodgrains Demand in India to 2020, Economic and Political Weekly, November 14,1998.

18E. Praduman Kumar, Demand for Foodgrains, 1994.

19. Ceng Guoquian, Market Prospects for Upland Crops in China, Working Paper 24, The CGPRT Centre, 1997.
20. Memed Gurgaon, Market prospects for Upland crops in Indonesia, Working Paper 25, the CGPRT Centre, January 1997.

20A. Bhalla G.S., Demand for Foodgrains to 2020 (E.P.W) Dec. 1997 and Rejoinder P.C. Bansil (E.P.W. March 7,1998).

21A. World Bank, India Livestock Sector Review, 1996.

21B. J.S. Sarma and V.P. Gandhi, IFPRI Research Report No. 81.

21C. Bansil's P.C, Feed, Seed and Wastage Rates-A Regional Study, 1985, Techno Economic Research Institute and Bansil P.C., Inter Country Comparisons in Feed Production and Consumption, 1998, Memeo.

21D. Honey Bee, April-June 1999—Developing Countries Farm Radio News work, Canada.

22. Bansil, P.C. -Agricultural Planning for 700 millions in India, 1971, Bansil P.C., Future Feed Seed and Wastage Rates, Indian Journal of Agricultural Economics, July-September, 1959 and Bansil P.C., Inter Country Comparisons in Feed Production and Consumption, Sponsored by the ICSSR, 1998, Memeo.

22A. C.H. Hanumantha Rao, Presidential address delivered at the 13th National Conference on Agricultural Marketing, held at N.I.R.D., Hyderabad, on 12 October, 1999, Declining per capita Demand for Foodgrains in India: Why and What Does This Imply.

23. Bansil P.C. and Bhat P.N., Problems and Prospects of poultry Industry in India, Indian Journal of Animal Production, Dec. 1996.

23A. Bansil P.C., Feeding for Livestock, Indian Farming, October 1997.

24. Richard Arnold, and Dr. S.P. Netke, Big Leap in Poultry Industry, National Livestock Feed Symposium, Rendering Association, June, 1991.

25. Bansil, P.C., Food Resources of India and Population, 1958 Wisner Charlotte Viall, Foods of a Hindu Village of North India, Bulletin No. 2, (Bureau of Statistics and Economic Research U.P.) Allahabad, 1936.

CHAPTER 20

Indian Farmer in the New Millennium

Rural prosperity in the Indian context goes with bumper agriculture. This is because over 70 per cent of the rural workforce draws its livelihood from this sector. But how far agriculture can go to bring rural prosperity and overall improvement in the quality of life of a farmer is an issue which needs further probing. It is one of the laws of economic development that as an economy grows, there will be a shift in the workforce from agriculture to industry (or from the agriculture sector to the manufacturing sector) and to the services sector. Increase in the productivity of the workforce in the non-services sector is responsible for such shifts as demonstrated by the historical experience of the advanced Western economies where the share of workforce in agriculture declined from 65 per cent in the 19th century to about 20 per cent in the mid-20th century and even further down subsequently very sharply in some instances. This is true for even some of the countries like Korea and Malaysia (Table 20.1).

INDIAN SCENE

It is interesting to note that while the share of agricultural workforce in India has remained more or less constant at around 70 percent over the decades since independence (Tables 20.2 and 20.2A) its contribution to gross GDP has slid by more than half from 56 (1950-51) to 28.7 per cent by 1990-91 and 24.2 percent now. Future projections show that this will further go down to, may be 12-15 per cent in the coming decade (Table 20.3).

Production and Value addition

There was no acceleration in the growth of agriculture despite the fact that the share of value of modern inputs (fertilisers, pesticides, electricity and diesel oil) at constant 80-81 prices to the value of gross

Table 20.1 Comparative Study of Agricultural GDP and Labour Force

Country	Share of Agriculture in GDP %			Agricultural Labour Force in Total %	
	1965	1991	1994	1965	1994
1. Bangladesh	55	35	30	84	65
2. China	39	27	19	81	72
3. India	47	32	30	73	64
4. Indonesia	56	19	17	--	55
5. Japan	9	3	2	24	7
6. Malaysia	28	22	14	50	27
7. Nepal	65	59	43	94	94
8. New Zealand		9	7		10
9. Pakistan	40	26	25	60	52
10. Philippines	26	21	22	58	46
11. Rep. of Korea	38	10	7	55	18
12. Sri Lanka	28	27	24	56	48
13. Thailand	32	12	10	75	64

SOURCE: Selected Indicators of Food and Agriculture Development in Asia-Pacific Region, FAO, Various Issues

Table 20.2 Occupational Distribution of Working Population 1901-1961

(Per cent)

Sector/Industrial categories	1901	1911	1921	1931	1951	1961
Agriculture sector	71.7	74.9	76.0	74.8	72.1	71.8
Cultivators	50.6	49.8	54.4	45.1	50.0	52.8
Agricultural labourers	16.9	21.6	17.4	24.8	19.7	16.7
Livestock, forestry & others	4.2	4.5	4.2	4.9	2.4	2.3
Industrial sector	12.6	11.1	10.5	10.2	10.7	12.2
Mining & quarrying	0.1	0.2	0.3	0.3	0.6	0.5
Large & small industries	11.7	9.9	9.3	8.9	9.0	10.6
Construction	0.8	1.0	0.9	1.0	1.1	1.1
Services sector	15.7	14.0	13.5	15.0	17.2	16.0
Trade and commerce	6.1	5.5	5.7	5.6	5.2	4.0
Transport, storage and communication	1.1	1.1	0.9	1.0	1.5	1.6
Other services	8.5	7.4	6.9	8.4	10.5	10.4
Total	100.0	100.0	100.0	100.0	100.0	100.0

* Based on 5 percent sample data. Includes marginal workers also.

SOURCE: Registrar General, India.

Table 20.2A Sectoral Distribution of Workers

(Millions)

Year		Workers	Cultivators	Agricultural labour	Livestock, forestry, fishing, hunting, etc.	Total Agriculture	Mining & quarrying	Manufacturing, proessing & H.H. industry	Servicing, repair other than H.H. industry	Construction	Trade & commerce	Transport, storage & communication	Other services
(1)	(2)	(3)	(4)	(5)	(6)	(7)	(8)	(9)	(10)	(11)	(12)	(13)	(14)
1971	Total	180.4 (33.06)	78.2 (43.34)	47.5 (26.38)	4.3 (2.38)	130.0 (72.05)	0.9 (0.51)	6.3 (3.52)	12.5 (6.94)	2.2 (1.23)	8.2 (4.57)	4.4 (2.44)	15.8 (8.74)
1981	Main	222.5 (33.45)	92.5 (41.58)	55.5 (24.94)	5.0 (2.26)	153.0 (68.78)	1.2 (0.53)	7.7 (3.47)	17.4 (7.84)	3.7 (1.67)	14.1 (6.33)	6.1 (2.76)	19.1 (8.59)
	Marginal	(3.32)											
1991	Main	285.9 (34.18)	110.7 (38.72)	74.6 (26.09)	6.0 (2.11)	191.3 (66.92)	1.8 (0.61)	6.8 (2.38)	21.9 (7.65)	5.5 (1.94)	21.3 (7.45)	8.0 (2.80)	29.3 (10.25)
	Marginal	(3.32)											

N.B.: Figures in bracket percentages.
SOURCE: Registrar General, India.

Table 20.3 Relative Income of Agricultural workers (Including Both Cultivators and Labour)

	Share(%) of Agriculture in			*Ratio per worker income in agriculture to non-agriculture sector at*	
	SDP at 1980-81 Prices	*SDP at Current Prices*	*Work force*	*1980-81 Prices*	*Current Prices*
1960-61	45.9	43.0	69.5	0.37	0.33
1970-71	39.7	42.4	72.05	0.28	0.32
1980-81	34.7	34.7	68.78	0.27	0.27
1990-91	28.7	28.3	66.92	0.23	0.23

SOURCES: Calculated from National Accounts Statistics, CSO, and Population Census. Bansil P.C., Agricultural Statistical Compendium, Vol. I, Techno Economic Research Institue.

agricultural output marginally increased from an average 11 percent during 1985-91 to 13 per cent during 1991-96. More so, per hectare consumption of fertilisers rose perceptibly from 56.7 kg to 70.6 kg in the periods under comparison. In fact, the compound growth rate of foodgrains production dropped to 1.66 percent per annum during 1990-98 from the peak level of 3.54 per cent per annum during 1980-90 and the average growth rate of gross value of output of agriculture at 1980-81 prices in the reform period was lower at 3.1 per cent per annum than that during the earlier period at 4.3 per cent.

With sectoral distribution of workforce remaining more or less unchanged, per worker value added in agriculture which was 28 and 24 per cent of that in the secondary and tertiary sectors in 1987-88 declined to 27 and 22 percent respectively in 1993-94. The relative per worker value added in agriculture vis-a-vis the non-agricultural sectors became more adverse in 1998-99 with the former coming down to 23 and 18 per cent respectively of the secondary and tertiary sectors. Per worker (agriculture) value added was just about half the level for the economy as a whole. On the other hand, per worker production in secondary and tertiary sectors was more than three to four times as compared with the primary sector and this gap further widened during 1994-97 (Thamarajakshi). Since the organised industry is not employment intensive, the world is witnessing `jobless economic growth'. The average annual growth rate of per worker value added in agriculture during 1993-99 was less than that during 1987-94, whereas the corresponding growth rates in secondary and tertiary sectors in the recent period were higher than the respective rates in the earlier period. In both periods, the growth rate in the case of the agricultural worker was less than that of his counterparts in non-agricultural sector (Table 20.4).

Table 20.4 Per Worker Value Added (Rs. at Constant 1993-94 Prices)

	1987-88	*1993-94*	*1998-99*
Agriculture	8404	10435 (4.0)	12179 (3.3)
Secondary	29519	38684 (5.2)	53276 (7.5)
Tertiary	34719	46724 (5.8)	66074 (8.3)
All	17022	22160 (5.0)	29353 (6.5)

Notes: (i) Gross value added at 1993-94 prices derived for 1987-88 on comparable basis.
(ii) Workforce pertains to 15 + age groups.
(iii) Figures in brackets refer to average annual growth rates over the preceding period.

SOURCE: (i) CSO, Revised estimates of National Accounts at 1993-94 prices and earlier issues of National Accounts.

NSSO: (ii) Employment-unemployment Survey: 50th round (1993-94) and 53rd round (1997). Assumed 1997 WFPRs obtain for 1998-99.

This is notwithstanding the improvement in agriculture's (particularly foodgrains) barter terms of trade during the nineties. The improvement in foodgrains terms of trade along with the observed deterioration in relative per worker value added in agriculture certainly, had impact on the poorer sections of the agricultural population who are net purchasers of foodgrains.

Size of Holding

An obvious conclusion is that an average farming family is getting poorer and poorer as compared with the non-farmers. The biggest danger to the unity and stability of the country will then emerge as the rural and urban divide. That is not all. There is again a skewed distribution of this paltry kitty among the farmers. Marginal holdings (less than one hect.) constituting 59.0 per cent of the total, operated only on 14.9 per cent of the area, while the large (10 hect. and above) holdings constituting only 1.6 percent had control over as much as 17.4 per cent of the land (Table 20.5). This resulted in the average size of only 0.4 hect. for the marginal farmer against 17.33 hect. of the larger one. The trend in a prosperous State like Punjab is no better. Against 38.6 per cent farms below 2 hectares in 1981, the number has gone up to 44.7 per cent in 1990-91. On the other hand the percentage of medium and large farms have declined over this period. Out of 12 lakh operational holdings expected to be in 2000-2001, every year 8,982 farmers get added to which small farmers increase still faster while

Tables 20.5 Operational Holding (1960-61 to 1990-91)

A. Number of Holdings

Category of farmers	*Million Numbers*						*As % of total*				
	1960-61	*1970-71*	*1976-77*	*1980-81*	*1985-86*	*1990-91*	*1960-61*	*1970-71*	*1976-77*	*1980-81*	*1990-91*
Marginal	19.90	35.68	44.52	50.12	56.15	62.11	40.7	50.6	54.6	56.4	59.0
Small	10.88	13.43	14.73	16.07	17.92	19.97	22.3	19.1	18.0	18.1	19.0
Semi-medium	9.22	10.68	11.67	12.45	13.25	13.91	18.9	15.2	14.3	14.0	13.2
Medium	6.57	7.93	8.21	8.07	7.92	7.63	13.4	11.2	10.1	9.1	7.2
Large	2.31	2.77	2.44	2.17	1.92	1.67	4.7	3.9	3.0	2.4	1.6
All groups	48.88	70.49	81.57	88.88	97.16	105.29	100.0	100.0	100.0	100.0	100.0

B. Area Operated

Category of farmers	*Million hectares*						*As % of total*				
	1960-61	*1970-71*	*1976-77*	*1980-81*	*1985-86*	*1990-91*	*1960-61*	*1970-71*	*1976-77*	*1980-81*	*1990-91*
Marginal	8.78	14.55	17.51	19.73	22.04	24.62	6.7	9.0	10.7	12.0	14.9
Small	16.00	19.28	20.90	23.17	25.71	28.71	12.2	11.9	12.8	14.1	17.3

Semi-medium	26.23	30.00	32.43	34.65	36.67	38.35	20.0	18.5	19.9	21.2	23.2
Medium	40.07	48.23	49.63	48.54	47.14	45.05	30.4	29.7	30.4	29.1	27.2
Large	40.38	50.06	42.87	37.71	33.00	28.89	30.7	30.9	26.2	23.0	17.4
All groups	131.46	162.12	163.34	163.80	164.56	165.60	100.0	100.0	100.0	100.0	100.0

C. *Average Size of Holding*

Category of farmers	*Area per operating holding (hectares)*						*Percentage change*		
							1970-71 over	*1980-81 over*	*1990-91 over*
	1960-61	*1970-71*	*1976-77*	*1980-81*	*1985-86*	*1990-91*	*1960-61*	*1970-71*	*1960-61*
Marginal	0.44	0.41	0.39	0.39	0.39	0.40	-7.6	-3.5	-9.3
Small	1.47	1.44	1.42	1.44	1.43	1.44	-2.4	0.4	-2.1
Semi-medium	2.84	2.81	2.78	2.78	2.77	2.76	-1.3	-0.9	-3.0
Medium	6.10	6.08	6.05	6.01	5.96	5.90	-0.3	-1.1	-3.3
Large	17.48	18.07	17.57	17.38	17.21	17.33	3.4	-3.8	-0.9
All groups	2.69	2.30	2.00	1.84	1.69	1.57	-14.5	-19.9	-41.6

SOURCE: Bansil P.C., Agricultural Statistical Compendium, Techno Economic Research Institute.

the larger holdings are sharply declining year after year. The situation is still worse if the ownership distribution is also viewed on every operational holding, there being 1.37 owners who share the produce. Further, every farm has an average of 1.83 adult male members wholly dependent upon farming.

At the all India level, all this will calculate to an average farming family being poorer by 2.7 times as compared with non farming family and those large farmers among them getting more than 44 times. This is the position of those having at least some piece of land to sustain, the fate of nearly 24 percent of those who are agricultural labourers will, of course, be beyond description.

Real Wages of Agricultural Labourers and Poverty

There has also been an increase in the proportion of casual labour mainly at the cost of the self-employed; of the workforce, about 34 per cent of rural males and 46 per cent of rural females are casual workers. While this has been accompanied by a rise in real wage earnings, this is a continuation of the uptrend that started in the eighties, and the rise in the six-year period of 1987-94 was only 5.9 per cent. Besides, the absolute levels of rural wages in 1993-94 were lower than the minimum levels to assure a reasonable level of living, let alone a reasonable level of social security for the agricultural labourers. (Thamarajakshi and Ruddar Dutt). Further it may be that but for the improvement of foodgrains terms of trade in the nineties, real wage increase would have been higher. A slackening in the rate of annual growth of real wages from 4.8 per cent in the eighties to 2.4 per cent in the nineties so far has also been noticed (NCAER). Although there is an estimated fall in poverty ratios, the percentage decline in rural sector has been less at 4.6 per cent, compared to 15.2 per cent for urban sector in the recent period, 1987-94.

This is despite the disbursements in this period of a total sum of Rs. 14,000 crore (at 1981-82 prices) for rural poverty alleviation programmes. There is also a view that there is no strong evidence of a decline in the incidence of rural poverty since 1993-94.

EMERGING ISSUES

The discussion in the preceding pages would show that despite high rate of growth in agriculture over the decades, an average worker in the agriculture sector is much poorer as compared with his counterpart in the secondary and tertiary sectors. Firstly we may examine the employment potential, under the existing intensive cropping system. Even after some shifts in the occupational structure during the last two decades, agriculture still occupies a predominant place in the employment structure, employing about two-thirds of the total workers. It is agriculture which has shown the lowest and rapidly declining employment potential in the recent past. According to Eighth

Plan a major reason for this lies in the sharply declining employment potential in the regions with high output growth. Employment growth accompanying a one per cent growth of output was found to be as low as 0.00, 0.07 and 0.19 in Punjab, Haryana and Uttar Pradesh respectively. In these areas, the source of growth is now turning to be labour substituting.

Quite often a case is made that there are possibilities of raising the income of a small /marginal farmer by the introduction of a highly intensive cropping pattern. Appropriate changes in cropping patterns can lead to additional employment opportunities and incomes. Horticulture crops which occupy nearly six million acres of area in this category are often quoted as most important. Some of the enterprising farmers have achieved tremendous success. There is the example of a farmer in Nasik who produced 1 to 1.5 kilograms a piece of pomegranate. Similarly, there are vegetable cooperatives near Ranchi where small farmers are growing four to five crops of different vegetables simultaneously throughout the year on their tiny farms. There is quite a large number of similar examples of intensive and innovative agricultural production systems in the so-called backward state of Bihar alone and many other parts of the country. But if we want to apply the same pattern on a large scale, we are bound to face immense difficulties. Unless there is a guaranteed supply of water and an assured market, along with a fully trained manpower, a small farmer may end up in losses because of the very perishable nature of fruits and vegetables. These enterprises can then be given only to some of the selected families who have the necessary wherewithal and can fulfil other conditions.

Even otherwise, a highly intensive system of agricultural production is not able to sustain a small/marginal farmer. Rough calculations show that a farmer owning 2.5 hectares of irrigated land in Punjab after toiling hard under unhygienic conditions and subject to high degree of risks, gets about Rs. 5,000 per month which is almost equivalent to the monetary gains of a fresh appointed clerk (Joginder Singh).

Again various cost of cultivation studies give an estimate of mandays requirement in respect of different crops. Utilizing the results of such studies in U.P., one finds that requirement of human labour in one hectare of holding varies from 88 mandays in Jhansi district to 206 mandays in Muzaffarnagar district (Table 20.6).

Muzaffarnagar represents an agriculturally very developed area with a very high cropping intensity and cropping pattern which is highly tilted towards a cash crop like sugarcane. If sugarcane is counted as a kharif as well as rabi crop, cropping intensity becomes 210 per cent.

This shows that even a highly developed district like Muzaffarnagar cannot exclusively keep a family fully employed with one hectare of land where he has an additional animal providing work opportunities of 50 to 60 mandays. Both these activities would give an average farmer

Table 20.6 Expected Number of Mandays Required for the Present Cropping Pattern in Some Different Districts of U.P.

Sl. No.	Districts	Present Intensity of Cropping (%)	Mandays required per hectare of net cropped area
1.	Muzaffar Nagar	160	206
2.	Farukhabad	151	157
3.	Sultanpur	149	159
4.	Gorakhpur	147	166
5.	Jhansi	133	88
6.	Almora	167	174

gross income of not more than Rs. 5000/-, much below the poverty line. Marginal/Small farms under normal cropping systems even if irrigated would not be in a position to generate sufficient income to sustain the farm family. Some of the meticulous studies undertaken by Late Dr. Dharam Narain showed that more than half of the marginal and small farmers were net buyers of foodgrains.

Even a simple statewise correlation study between persons below the poverty line and share of marginal/small farms in the total number of operational holdings (Table 20.7) gives positive results indicating thereby that small/marginal holdings have a direct relation with poverty, or non-sustainability, in other word.

HARVESTING MICROORGANISM WEALTH

The general view now is that small-size agriculture can maximise per acre employment and output (income) if its microorganism wealth is harnessed. The challenges now facing Indian agriculture are daunting in that research and extension system as they are practised today are not percolated. Interaction with the domestic industry is still far short of what it could be. The annual industrial production based on the CSIR technology has gone up, of course, but modestly. Far too many domestic companies still prefer intellectual piracy and reverse engineering and so are not willing to either pay for technology and perhaps even absorb it.

Technology adoption and dissemination becomes the biggest problem of Indian agro-industries. For example, the technology developed by the Central Institute of Medicinal and Aromatic Plants for the cultivation of geranium has not reached the farmers. With this technology a farmer could earn about Rs. 1.40 lakh per acre but the farmers take it unbelievable as no industry ensures them for the purchase of their geranium crop for finished product (perfume oil). Consequently, India is forced to import geranium oil worth over Rs. 100 crore annually. Same is the case of the *guldaudi* crop which is in

Table 20.7 Rural Poverty and Marginal Holdings

Sl. No.	*Name of the State*	*Rural Poverty 1983*	*Bank*	*Marginal Holdings*	*Bank*	*D*	*D2*
1.	Andhra Pradesh	34.6	11	51.8	5	6	36
2.	Assam	48.8	7	59.4	4	3	9
3.	Bihar	70.1	1	76.0	1	0	0
4.	Gujarat	36.0	10	24.3	11	-1	1
5.	Haryana	23.8	12	32.2	9	3	9
6.	Karnataka	40.1	9	34.5	7	2	4
7.	Madhya Pradesh	59.9	5	32.8	8	-3	9
8.	Maharashtra	53.9	5	29.4	10	-5	25
9.	Orissa	64.8	3	46.8	3	-3	9
10.	Punjab	18.3	13	19.2	12	1	1
11.	Rajasthan	41.8	8	29.4	11	-2	4
12.	Tamil Nadu	56.8	4	69.7	3	1	1
13.	Uttar Pradesh	49.6	6	70.6	2	4	16
14.	West Bengal	65.4	2	69.7	3	1	1
						D2	125

$$\text{R. Correlation} = 1 \frac{6\text{ D2}}{\text{N3-N}} = 1 \frac{6(125)}{(14)3-(14)} = 1 \frac{750}{2744-14} = 1 \frac{750}{2730} = 1 - 0.27$$

$$= 0.73$$

heavy demand in the USA and European countries. It gives an insecticide which destroys mosquitoes, cockroaches, etc.

Technology may, therefore, change the life of farmers but the "lab-to field" programme has completely failed in India. Almost in every state an agro-industries corporation is functioning but none has come to the rescue of the hapless peasantry. Central Medicinal and Aromatic Plants Research Institute, Lucknow, has demonstrated the cultivation of mint at Jennabad village, 11 km from Lucknow. Thirty-year-old young farmer Ram Lakhan owns half an acre of land. His five- member family is leading a very happy life on this piece of land by cultivating mint. The comparative economics of mint farming is very interesting. One hectare of potato crop fetches Rs. 20,000 and the same amount is available from wheat or gram crop. But mint crop gives Rs. 40,000 per hectare.

The farmer can earn even more from mint if he installs an oil extracting plant at his farm. After extraction if he converts the oil into crystal form, his income will go up to four-five times. The future of small farmers thus lies in value addition of their crops. Sustainable agriculture in the 21st century will be based on appropriate use of biotechnology, information technology and ecotechnology. Practical achievement in bringing about the desired paradigm shift will, however, depend upon public policy support and political action.

Not perennial Green Revolution for food production but the gene revolution for biological sovereignty should be the aim of Indian agriculture for the 21st century. A new scientific discipline of genomics has arisen. This discipline will contribute to powerful new approaches that can be used in agriculture as well as medicine and will help to promote the biotechnology industry in India, but for this we have to prepare our small farmers which will be the central force to transform India into a strong economy in the next century. It is, however, essential to take following steps for optimising our microorganisms wealth:

- The farmers should be educated in this respect through a strong extension machinery.
- Training programmes should be organised for farmers to take up the processing of their raw produce with *swadeshi* technology.
- Credit and subsidy should be made available to farmers.
- An effective market promotion needs priority.

MIXED FARMING

The potential of this sector for income and employment generation can hardly be overemphasised. Based on some recent studies by the National Dairy Development Board (NDDB) and the earlier estimates by the National Commission on Agriculture, it is estimated that the animal husbandry sector, even with the existing stock, can generate employment in processing and marketing of milk and milk products. It is claimed by experts that a much higher growth than in the past can be attained in this sector, raising productivity and income levels of those engaged in it, as well as creating new employment opportunities.

Mixed farming is an age old practice in Indian agriculture. In areas where irrigation is available, dairying is a feasible proposition. There are a number of options, depending upon the availability of fodder for a small/marginal farmer. If only a part of the area is devoted to fodder, he can have a minimum of one animal unit providing an additional employment for 50 to 60 days. With additional area under fodder, there could be a possibility of rearing additional animals, thereby generating more employment potential and increased income.

Recent studies at the National Dairy Research Institute (NDRI), Karnal, have shown that while a buffalo or a crossbred cow is a viable unit, a jersey cow is not. Even if 50 per cent of the irrigated land holders (numbering over 33 million) is to be provided the dairying activity, there will be a need to have many additional crossbred animals or buffaloes . Second, to get optimum returns from these animals, they have to be fed properly. We must then have adequate supplies of green fodder to give them proper feed. Since it may not be possible to meet all these requirements adequately, we will also have to think of other alternatives in the mixed farming system. Introducing poultry, piggery and fisheries should prove to be quite handy. Here again, we will have to face economic, social and religious problems. Third, there will be the need for backward and forward linkages before any such programme can be thought of.

With only 28 per cent of small and marginal holdings as wholly irrigated and hardly another 21 per cent as partially irrigated, the problem in respect of this big section of the farming community is much more complicated. Despite all the improved techniques of dry farming in use now, there is not much scope to recommend a mixed farming system to provide additional employment and to generate additional income (Table 20.8).

Poultry farming needs to be placed on a new technological and commercial footing if it is to have any major impact on the income of the poor. The requirements include: (a) new, tested technology that uses improved poultry strains to raise yields of meat and eggs; (b) a system to deliver credit, feed supplies, and veterinary services; (c) a marketing and transport system to handle processing, cleaning, grading, and delivery of output; and (d) a cooperative organisation to make these services available to small producers. How far we are in a position to provide these conditions is debatable.

The investment costs of commercial poultry activities have hitherto been too high for the rural poor to afford. The economies of scale also seem significant. On the basis of a study in Jabalpur, Madhya Pradesh, in 1978-79, Karanjkar and Soni (1980) report that the optimum scale of business seems to be around 1,000 birds. To set up and operation of this size would require an investment of around Rs. 30,000 which is an unthinkable sum for most small farmers. Obviously, the rural poor can neither undertake such enterprises by themselves nor can they easily compete with those already in operation.

Fishery, it is maintained, can grow as fast as seven per cent per annum because about two-thirds of the existing marine and inland potential is unexploited. In fact, a high growth of value-added agro-business, including animal husbandry, fishery, horticulture and aquaculture, offers scope for employment expansion in the immediate future.

AGRICULTURE ALONE NOT THE ANSWER

This leads us to the obvious conclusion that whatever we might do to improve agriculture, (highly intensive with mixed farming) an average person engaged in agriculture, particularly the subsistence and marginal farmer will become poorer and poorer as compared with his better off counterpart even in the agriculture sector not to speak about the other sector. Not only that, with the increasing flux of population where agriculture continues to remain as the dumping ground for all the rejects in other sectors and shrinkage of available land as a result of urbanization and industrialisation, an average person in agriculture will become further poorer.

Table 20.8 Distribution of Number and Area of Operational Holdings by Irrigation Status for All Social Groups (1985-86)—All India

Number in thousand and Area in thousand hectares

Sl. No.	Size class (ha.)	Total holdings		Wholly irrigated holdings		Wholly unirrigated holdings		Partly irrigated holdings		Holdings receiving irrigation		
		Number	Area	Number	Area	Number	Area	Number	Total area	Irrigated area	Number	Net Irrigated Area
1.	0.02-0.5	35705 (37.6)	8857 (5.4)	11902 (47.1)	2873 (10.8)	18831 (36.7)	3567 (4.7)	4132 (24.9)	1013 (2.9)	524 (3.8)	16034 (38.3)	3397 (8.4)
2.	0.5-1.0	18194 (19.2)	13152 (8.0)	5442 (21.5)	3675 (13.8)	9453 (18.4)	5687 (7.5)	2972 (17.9)	2028 (5.7)	989 (7.1)	8413 (20.1)	4664 (11.5)
3.	1.0-2.0	17922 (18.9)	25708 (15.6)	4152 (16.4)	5475 (20.6)	9941 (19.4)	12162 (16.1)	3532 (21.3)	4708 (13.3)	2181 (15.7)	7684 (18.3)	7656 (18.9)
4.	2.0 - 3.0	9736 (10.3)	21123 (12.8)	1677 (6.6)	3749 (14.1)	4985 (9.7)	10183 (13.5)	1960 (11.8)	4351 (12.3)	1906 (13.7)	3636 (8.7)	5655 (14.0)
5.	3.0 - 4.0	4515 (4.8)	15543 (9.4)	803 (3.2)	2516 (9.5)	2519 (4.9)	7205 (9.6)	1154 (7.0)	3566 (10.1)	1512 (10.9)	1957 (4.7)	4028 (10.0)
6.	4.0 - 50	2914 (3.1)	12932 (7.9)	432 (1.7)	1948 (7.3)	1620 (3.2)	5963 (7.9)	787 (4.7)	3113 (8.8)	1272 (9.1)	1268 (3.0)	3220 (8.0)

Table 20.8 Distribution of Number and Area of Operational Holdings by Irrigation Status for All Social Groups (1985-86)—All India (Contd.)

7. 5.0 - 7.5	3454 (3.6)	20972 (12.7)	476 (1.9)	2575 (9.7)	1957 (3.8)	9820 (13.0)	992 (6.0)	5311 (15.0)	1991 (14.3)	1468 (3.5)	4566 (11.3)
8. 7.5 - 10.0	1549 (1.6)	13239 (8.0)	182 (0.7)	1372 (5.2)	880 (1.7)	6074 (8.1)	475 (2.9)	3526 (9.9)	1202 (8.6)	657 (1.6)	2574 (6.4)
9. 10.0 -20.0	1553 (1.6)	20585 (12.5)	148 (0.6)	1676 (6.3)	911 (1.8)	9322 (12.4)	482 (2.9)	5375 (15.2)	1652 (11.9)	631 (1.5)	3328 (8.2)
10. 20.0 -30.0	238 (0.3)	5612 (3.4)	19 (0.1)	367 (1.4)	145 (0.3)	2393 (3.2)	72 (0.4)	1350 (3.8)	379 (2.7)	91 (0.2)	747 (1.8)
11. 30.0 -40.0	67 (0.1)	2258 (1.4)	5 (0.0)	124 (0.5)	44 (0.1)	966 (1.3)	17 (0.1)	453 (1.3)	125 (0.9)	22 (0.1)	240 (0.6)
12. 40.0- 50.0	27 (0.0)	1182 (0.7)	2 (0.0)	61 (0.2)	18 (0.0)	487 (0.6)	7 (0.0)	213 (0.6)	59 (0.4)	8 (0.0)	120 (0.3)
13. 50.0 & above	34 (0.0)	3365 (2.0)	2 (0.0)	140 (0.5)	24 (0.0)	1604 (2.1)	7 (0.0)	436 (1.2)	116 (0.8)	9 (0.0)	256 (0.6)
All Sizes	94907 (100)	164529 (100)	25292 (100)	26552 (100)	51329 (100)	75434 (100)	16589 (100)	35442 (100)	13909 (100)	41880 (100)	40461 (100)

Note: Totals may not tally due to rounding off. Figures in paranthesis represent % share.
SOURCE: All India Report on Agricultural Census, 1985-86, Deptt. of Agriculture & Co.op.,

If so, we have to frame our policies so that the small and marginal land holders and landless labourers are encouraged to get into occupations other than agriculture in the rural area itself without moving to the cities. The steps taken in this direction in the past show more or less a complete failure of our rural development programmes where a multiple number of schemes quite often working at cross roads, are being implemented in rural India. Starting from the Community Development Programmes of early fifties, we have sunk under these programmes billions and billions of rupees without any visible impact on the rural economy or even in any pocket of the country. A Reserve Bank analysis shows that the share of households below the poverty line in rural India is highest among those engaged in agriculture (Table 20.9).

Available skills in rural areas are not capable to adopt modern technologies in any of the rural activity. We need to have a clear policy to introduce an integrated programme to cover:

1. Micro level assessment of human and natural resource base.
2. Provide appropriate training facilities so as to exploit the full potential of all the available resources and
3. Introduce appropriate technologies directed to generate off farm employment and additional income.

To comprehend the importance of Small Scale Industries (SSI) sector these facts may be considered. SSI units account for 95% of the

Table 20.9 Structure of Rural Poverty

Household (hh) type	*Percentage share in all rural hhs.*	*Incidence of poverty within each hh. type*	*Percentage share in a rural hhs. below poverty line*	*Percentage share of each hh. type in the total unemployed days*
1. Self-employed Agriculture (cultivators)	40.7	24.1	32.0	16.3
2. Self-employed in non-agricultural operations	11.7	16.9	10.3	8.5
3. Agriculture labour hhs.	30.7	45.5	45.6	59.5
4. Other labour hhs.	6.6	27.9	6.0	10.2
5. Other rural hhs.	10.3	18.3	6.1	5.4
6. All rural hhs.	100.0	30.6	100.0	100.0

SOURCE: Dev et al, 1991: Agricultural policy in India, Context, Issues and Instruments, H.V. Nadherni, Department of Economic Analysis and Policy, Reserve Bank of India, Bombay, February 10,1993.

industrial units in India, contribute to 40% of the output in the manufacturing sector and provide employment to over 18 million people. Most importantly, this sector accounts for 35% of India's exports. Indian banks are required, by law, to provide 40% of their net bank credit to the priority sector which includes agriculture, the SSI units, small businesses, services and other programmes for poverty alleviation. This is where the political catch comes. Though the intent was good, over a period of time, the SSI sector has become a politically sensitive issue. There was an advantage in keeping the sector small, almost forever. However, as competition intensified, anomalous policies in subsequent years harmed the sector. But now there are no subsidies and incentives to stay small and as the WTO (World Trade Organization) provisions have come into play, everything has changed. The world has become one market and there is no point in staying small. This does not mean that all small units should become big. They can be ancillaries to the large industries. Today, it is the age of contract manufacturing. For instance, the watch industry in Switzerland entirely depends on the small scale industry. As the WTO rules come into force, SSI units find it increasingly difficult to survive the way they are now. Change is essential. So SIDBI, as a financier, promoter and facilitator has its work cut out. While introducing off farm employment activities in the rural sector, one will have to take these factors into consideration.

Even smaller countries like Korea, Indonesia and Thailand have implemented such programmes with success. There is no reason that India will not succeed. The future, therefore, lies in an optimum blend of technologies, old and new which can lead to a new paradigm of rural development based on the principles of ecological sustainability, economic viability and social equity. The corporate sector can take a lead in such technology blending.

INTERNATIONAL EXPERIENCE

The problem of small marginal holders is not peculiar to India alone. The 170 million subsistent farmers, pastoralists, and landless groups, that represent about three-quarters of the agricultural households in developing countries, are expected to increase by 50 million to nearly 220 million by the end of this century. Without adequate opportunities to earn a living, these resource-poor households will be caught in a poverty trap that induces them to over-exploit existing resources just to survive. This is not to suggest that all resource-poor, small scale farmers and pastoralists degrade the environment. These rural households have often developed highly efficient agricultural and livelihood systems that make the most rational and conservative use of the scarce resources available to them. Traditional systems are often optimally adapted to the prevailing environmental conditions, even though they function under the constraints of marginal land, little capital, and virtually no modern inputs. But the sustainability of many resource-poor farming and pastoral systems can be easily undermined, aggravating the poverty of rural households and the degradation of the environment (World Bank).

South Korea

There are a number of countries in South-East Asia where the problem is acute but has been mitigated to a large extent. The experience of South Korea in this connection will serve as a good example. The small holder agriculture of South Korea has witnessed a rapid rate of both horizontal and vertical diversification. The share of agriculture in GDP declined from 38 percent in 1965 to 7 percent in 1994 and the proportion of agricultural labour force to total labour force declined from 55 per cent in 1965 to 18 per cent in 1994 Agro-industrial output is rising at the annual rate of about 13 per cent, while the annual growth rates of output of fruits, meat, milk and fish also provided phenomenal support to provide additional income to small holders (Haque).

It is a land of small holdings. But because of a sharp decline in the number of farm households and farm population on the one hand and a well-thought-out policy of rural industries fully integrated with farm economy on the other hand, there has been a steady increase in the size of the average holdings since 1970. The number of small farmers owning less than 0.5 hectare of land declined by 26.8 per cent during 1970 to 1981 and the trend has continued. This is despite the fact that the area under total farm land declined during this period because of sufficient parts of agricultural lands having been taken over by the non-agricultural sector, rural/urban households, industries and roads.

One noteworthy policy introduced in the area of rural development in South Korea was the implementation of `Saemaul Undoung' during the early 1970s. Today, this has taken firm roots in the rural areas and has become the base for stable growth of agricultural production by consolidating its foothold as an agrarian, cultural and spiritual movement. The Saemaul movement has brought about sweeping changes among the rural communities. The development of Saemaul factories has reduced the urban-rural income gap through increased non-farm income for farmers and increased employment by utilising idle rural work force. This development has discouraged the movement of the rural populace towards cities, increased financial revenues for provincial administration and created self-sustaining rural communities. The normal income per farm household increased by 14.4 times during 1970-1981, more than one-third of this being contributed by the non-farm sector (FAO).

This has brought about such a dramatic change that, while in the second half of the 1960s, average farm household's income was 60 per cent below that an urban worker, during the mid-1970s, it outpaced that of urban workers by over 10 to 15 per cent. In addition to the

Saemaul rural factories, the policy was also directed towards greater participation of farm women in the productive activity so much so that their share of farm labour increased from 32 per cent in 1970 to 42.6 per cent in 1980.

Network Alliance Scheme

It might be of interest to study another highly simplified concept `Network Alliance Scheme' (NAS) of the Japanese model. This is being adopted with some modification to suit the cultural and social environment in Thailand, Indonesia and even China. Thailand has implemented the scheme in a bold and imaginative way.

In Indonesia, the network system called `Bapak Angkat' (Father Unit) and `Anak Angkat' (Related Units) successfully and effectively covers large sections of industry and agriculture. As a matter of fact, Indonesia's most prestigious Presidential Awards recognise accomplishment in this manner of employment generation and value addition.

In addition to contractual networking, the Bapak Angkat provides technical and financial assistance, leases plant equipment and trains people. This eventually leads to higher employment and a lowering of the cost of production. Indonesia's experience so far shows that the output-network alliances achieve a cost advantage which can be as high as 30 per cent. This is, indeed, impressive when considered along with the fact that such networks generate three to fourfold increase in employment compared to fully integrated units.

The average farm size there is as low as 0.99 hectare and farm families possessing more than 2 hectares of land are very rare. The small farms in Java today earn as much as 70 per cent of family income from non-farm activities. During the Fifth Five Year Plan covering the period from 1989-94, there was renewed emphasis on diversification of the rural economy, involving activities ranging from introduction of new technologies into existing farming system to development of off-farm employment opportunities.

TAIWAN

That a strategy based on rural small scale industries can be made to work is evident not only from experience in the Indian Punjab but also from developments in several Southeast Asian economies, including China, the Republic of Korea, Malaysia and Taiwan.

Ho has shown that in Taiwan, non-farm sources of income increased from 25 per cent of total farm household income in 1962 to 43 per cent in 1975. Although total rural employment grew at a slower rate than urban employment, employment in many rural industries grew more rapidly (manufacturing employment in rural Taiwan grew at 7.2 per cent between 1956 and 1966) and led to a large shift towards non-agricultural rural jobs. In 1956, agriculture employed 73 per cent of the rural labour force. By 1966, this share had fallen to 54 per cent, with the rest employed in manufacturing, commerce and services. Further, industrialisation has not been accompanied by a concentration of non-agricultural employment in major metropolitan areas.

In rural areas, small scale units with low capital intensity predominate, establishments with fewer than 10 workers employed 41 per cent of the manufacturing workers in rural Taiwan. Fixed assets per person employed in rural areas were half of those in urban areas, the output capital ratios were higher in some industries, and the ratio of net value added to fixed assets did not differ much from those in urban Taiwan. These facts suggest that rural-based industries used capital as efficiently as, if not better than, urban-based industries.

The impact on rural employment was particularly significant. With the labour force growing by over 2.5 per cent and the size of holdings averaging about one hectare (Fei, Ranis and Kuo, 1979), increasing non-farm employment enabled farm households to combine farming with part-time or full-time employment (for some members of the household). This eased the pressure on land and on rural-urban migration. In 1960, 45 per cent of all farm households relied exclusively on farms, while 23 per cent earned more income from non-farm activities. By 1970, these ratios stood at 30 and 29 per cent, and contributed to the greater equality of total incomes in rural areas. Non-farm activities grew by 12 per cent a year between 1960 and 1970.

Rural Industry in China

Rural linkages and non-farm activities are strongly emphasised in China. Although non-crop agricultural activities have always been important (especially pig iron production) they have been accelerated and integrated since the 1970s at both the private and the communal level. Non-agricultural rural employment, for example, rose from about 15 per cent of the labour force in 1957 to over 24 per cent by 1975 (Bansil).

More than 100 million people worked in China's non-farm rural sector in 1975, reflecting a growth rate of over seven per cent a year between 1957 and 1975. The expansion was most marked in collective commune industries in rural areas. Trade, food processing, personal and financial services, health, education, transport, and communication-all showed above average rates of growth (Rawski, 1979). Social services-health, education, and population control-have been actively encouraged and have grown rapidly.

One unique feature of rural development in China has been the promotion of rural small-scale industries designed to meet local production (intermediate) and consumption (final) demand locally. A second unique feature has been the integration of these activities with agricultural seasons; in the slack period much of the labour force is employed in non-crop and non-agricultural rural activities. Communes and `brigades' run small scale enterprises organised on this basis. In the 1980s these were largely decollectivised through the use of the Personal Responsibility System (PRS). These enterprises almost doubled in number and in the value of their output between 1975 and 1978.

These activities were expected to contribute about half the total value of the communes' output by 1985 (Perkins and Yusuf, 1984).

The Chinese have also gone to unusual lengths to promote indigenous intermediate technologies in support of the official strategy. Locally developed methods, equipment and adaptive innovatives are encouraged (Riskin, 1978). As a direct consequence, in addition to the considerable intensification of agriculture, the vast rural economy not only absorbed nearly 100 million new entrants into the rural work force between 1957 and 1975, but also raised the average number of days of employment for the entire farm labour force of more than 300 million men and women (Rawski, 1979).

Between 1978 and 1987 the value of gross agricultural output grew at 6.8 per cent a year in real terms, the gross value of industrial output in rural areas grew at more than 23 per cent a year in real terms, while rural employment in industry, commerce, transport, and construction increased by 124 per cent. The growth of value added in industry during recent years is around 15 per cent. This tremendous growth of rural, industrial and other activities has been accompanied by a large increase in personal incomes and in the demand for rural housing and consumer goods. As a result, millions of new Township and Village Enterprises (TVEs) have emerged to meet this demand. Large increases in rural credit have been provided to the TVEs by the expanding banking system and internal accumulation of funds has been generated in part by concessional tax treatment. Rapid growth in income in the rest of the economy (at rates of more than 10 per cent a year) together with high investment demand (gross investment to GDP ratios in China in the 1980s exceeded 30 per cent a year) have helped support this expansion.

The growth in the TVE section has also brought about massive shifts in the rural labour force. In 1978, about 11 per cent of the total rural labour force of around 306 million was in non-farm activities. By 1986, this share had grown to about 20 per cent of a total rural labour force of 380 million.

Dabur Experiment in Nepal

For any agro business to be successful, a sound backward integration policy is a must, and that is what Dabur Nepal has charted out for itself. The company has not only created separate division for honey bee but has brought in a new technology for boosting honey production in the country. It has distributed thermocol box with plastic frames and queen bees among farmers. The entire kit costs Rs. 15,526. The farmers can earn it back from one crop. There is a honey buyback guarantee but the farmers are free to sell honey to anybody.

In Nepal there are three crops of honey from eucalyptus, tori (mustard) and leechi. From each crop, upto 50 kg of honey can be extracted. The queen bees are raised at the Dabur Apiculture Centre in the valley of river Naraina, which falls on the highway connecting Kathmandu to the famous Chitwan National Park. The centre is engaged in developing bee colonies and educating farmers in latest techniques of bee keeping, producing organic honey and other honey bee products.

The boxes are made at Dabur's Birganj unit. With a capacity of 1 lakh beehives a year, the unit plans to use the equipment to build over 5 lakh bee colonies over the next five years. The company is exporting mustard honey to Europe and Australia and queen bee to Poland. The bee project was started early in 2001 on a mustard plantation of 1.4 lakh hectare. Around 3.4 hives can be kept per hectare. The honey processing is done at the Birganj unit which has a capacity of 200 tonnes per month. For expansion of the project they have tied up with NGOs. Right from training farmers to transportation of hives and leasing of land is done by Dabur in association with the NGOs. Dabur's success has reaffirmed the fact that there is good scope for agro-based industries in rural areas.

CONCLUSION

The Ninth Plan does appreciate the crucial need for exploring the potential of non-farm sector for those engaged in agriculture. It says that since the inception of IRDP- till 1996-97, 50.99 million families have been covered under IRDP at an expenditure of Rs. 11434.27 crore. The total investment during this period has been Rs. 28047.65 crore which includes a subsidy component of Rs. 9669.97 crore and a credit disbursement of Rs. 18377.68 crore. Of the total families assisted under this programme 44.75 per cent were Scheduled Castes/Scheduled Tribes and 27.07 per cent women. Actual amount invested (sunk) by all the rural development Programmes really calculates to around Rs. 90,000 crores upto the end of 8th Plan. The ground situation does not, however, support any such physical achievement.

Based on the position as it exists today and international experience, one could come across any number of developmental models in the world which may or may not have a potential applicability under specific Indian conditions, but could possibly be applied with certain modifications. We will, however, have no hesitation to say that unless we succeed in providing additional employment to this huge chunk of underemployed marginal/small farmers, the prosperity of agriculture and hence rural India in the country will remain only a dream.

The Indian situation stands out as being somewhat unique and it is imperative for us to find solutions relevant and sustainable within our own agro-climatic and socioeconomic framework. What we are struggling to achieve will undoubtedly be recorded by historians as one of the greatest economic and social experiments-to achieve economic growth, fair income distribution and social upliftment, concomitantly with the highest traditions of democratic commitment in which the individual remains supreme. In other words, we have chosen the path which is time consuming and where risks are high but in the long run more rewarding.

If we mean business, it has to be realised by the policy makers that the problem is of such a nature which calls for immediate political and economic solutions. Indian agriculture has certainly gained strength, but if farming is to emerge as an honourable and respectable avocation, immediate attention is called for to improve the economic conditions of the farmer. Small and marginal farmers will not change their farming practices and current uses of the resource base unless they have the appropriate economic incentives to do so. Even if we want to recommend any change, it would be necessary to undertake a proper economic analysis of various policy options and their impact on marginal/small farmers. All this will require appropriate data, methodology and analytical tools for economic evaluation of the recommended package and its environmental impact at the micro level.

With due consideration to all these aspects, we will have to find solutions outside the agriculture sector which are completely indigenous and germane to our heritage. They will vary from region to region and even within the sub-regions according to various agro-climatic, socio-economic and cultural situations. A number of studies have possibly been already conducted all over the country looking into the problems of one or other aspect of this class of cultivators. It would perhaps be advisable to compile all this information at one place so as to derive some meaningful results for various policy options in each case. There would certainly remain many gaps to complete the story. There will then be a need to undertake specific studies which should cover:-

1. A critical study of the present farming practices including livestock as well as non-farm activities of marginal/small farmers.
2. An evaluation of the rationale for different practices being followed by these farmers in the same area under more or less similar conditions.
3. Resource base of the farmers in terms of human skills and aptitudes and that of the region in terms of the availability of raw materials etc., for processing.
4. An inventory of the schemes to be introduced which are technically and economically feasible and socially desirable as well as acceptable.

5. The possibility of such programme being integrated into the local economy as well as environment.

REFERENCES

1. Bansil P.C. Agricultural Statistical Compendium Volume I, Techno Economic Research Institute, 1992.
2. Bansil P.C. Rural Labour and Employment Opportunities paper in Challenges Facing Agriculture and Rural Development, T.K. Velayudham, 1994.
3. Bansil P.C. Sustainability and Viability of Small/Marginal Farms, Paper read at a NIRD Seminar.
4. C.S.O., National Accounts.
5. Dev. et.al:, 1991: Agricultural policy in India, Context, Issues and Instruments, H.V. Nadkani, Department of Economic Analysis and Policy, Reserve Bank of India, Bombay, February 10,1993.
6. Fei, John C.H. Gustav Ranis, and Shirley W.Y. Kuo, 1979, Growth with Equity: The Taiwan Case, New York: Oxford University Press.
7. FAO, Poverty Alleviation in Korea, 1984, Selected Indicators of Food and Agriculture, Various Issues.
8. Government of India, Agricultural Census, Livestock Census, Economic Survey Various issues. Annual Reports of Ministry of Rural Development, Agriculture in Brief.
9. T. Haque, Small Farm Diversification: Problems and Prospects, National Centre for Agricultural Economics an Policy Research.
10. Ho, Samuel P.S. 1979. Decentralised Industrialisation and Rural Development: Evidence from Taiwan, Economic Development and Cultural Change, 28(I) October.
11. Inderjit Singh, The Great Ascent, The Rural Poor in South Asia, World Bank, 1990.
12. Joginder Singh & Jasbinder Singh Kular, Policy Paper, PAU.
13. NCAER (National Council of Applied Economic Research). 1974, Credit Requirements for Agriculture, New Delhi.
14. NCAER, Towards Rural Development and poverty Reduction', paper presented at the NCAR-IEG- World Bank Conference on Reform in the Agricultural Sector for Growth: Efficiency. Equity and Sustainability, New Delhi, April 15-16.1999.
15. Perkins, Dwight H., and Shahid Yusuf. 1984. Rural Development in China, Baltimore, Md: John Hopkins University Press.
16. Planning Commission, Eighth Five Year Plan, Ninth Five Year Plan, 1999.
17. Planning Commission, Ninth Plan and Ruddar Dutt, `Labour and Employment in the Ninth Plan', paper presented at the National Seminar on Ninth-Five Year Plan. Challenges and Strategies', Indian Economic Association Trust for Research and Development, New Delhi, April 1999.
18. Rawski, Thomas, G. 1979. Economic Growth and Employment in China, New York, Oxford University Press.
19. Riskin, C. 1978, "Intermediate Technology in China's Rural Industries". World Development 6(11-12)
20. Thamarajakshi R, Growth Employment and Productivity, The Economic Times, February 20, 1999, Agriculture and Economic Reforms, EPW, August 14, 1999.

21. World Commission on Environment and Dev., Oxford, Oxford University Press, 1987, Our Common Future.
22. Pramila B, Problems and Prospects of Agri-business in Selected Developing Asia-Pacific Countries Proceedings of the APO Seminar held on August 4-14, 1992, Jakarta.
23. World Bank, World Development Report, 1999.

CHAPTER 21

Rural Development Programmes and Panchayati Raj

Economic planning may be stated as an action with a socioeconomic purpose. In other words, the object of planning is not simply to achieve economic progress but also balance such progress with social justice. Social justice presupposes that opportunities in a greater measure must be provided to the poor so that they may become increasingly better off. The underprivileged class must get opportunities to rise to higher strata. Provision of basic minimum to all in respect of life and living and facilities for promoting one's own values and inner worth are essential content of social justice. In India, the mainstream political movement was deeply influenced by the Gandhian approach which emphasised the need to uplift the social and economic status of the poorest of the poor, or `*antyodaya*'. Emphasis on an egalitarian social order was reflected in the policy documents which were produced by the Indian National Congress.

Economic Programme Committee appointed by the president of the congress party, immediately after independence, in November 1947 also reiterated the national objective of economic justice . While stating the aims and objective of the economic programme for independent India, the first recommendation of the Committee was: "A quick and progressive rise in the standard of living of the people should be the primary consideration governing all economic activities and relevant administrative measures of the Central and Provincial Governments. The achievement of a national minimum standard in respect of all the essentials of physical and social well being within a reasonable period must be pursued as the practical goal of all schemes for economic development". This was really the birth of what may be called as 'Rural Development' although some stray experiments like those of Gurgaon Experiment had been tried earlier.

Developing countries have realized that the process of rural development is complex and multidimensional with diverse socioeconomic and technological issues involved. The objective conditions, however, differ from one area to another. The specific goals to be achieved and strategies to be adopted vary from situation to situation depending on the circumstances. The complex and multidimensional process involving multilateral interactions on economic, political, social, technological and administrative decisions are often not properly visualized and perceived. However, rural development objectives can be sought in various ways once there is a firm commitment and people's participation. The critical elements in rural development, to be specific, are : (a) basic needs, (b) full employment, (c) local participation and (d) micro-level planning. In this chapter we will examine the various rural development programmes which have been formulated and implemented and the extent of local participation both in formulation and implementation of the programmes.

RURAL DEVELOPMENT PROGRAMMES

Community Development Programmes

During the fifties two great rural programs were sponsored by the Americans: community development (CD) and agricultural extension (AE). The former was newly fashioned by American sociologists, while the latter was an old product of the American land-grant colleges. Both CD and AE were generously supported and carefully supervised by American advisors. Rural Reconstruction Programmes of pre-Independence period had two approaches-British view of the philosophy of F.L. Brayne and nationalist view of M.K. Gandhi. Brayne wanted to uplift the villagers by sending an official guide-philosopher-friend. Gandhi wanted to do that by sending a constructive worker. Following the footsteps of Brayne and Gandhi, CD relied mainly on a government village-level worker (VLW) as the agent of change. Sending a missionary outsider was considered essential in every case. The VLW, like Brayne's guide, was advised to collaborate closely with the local gentry, the established or "natural" leaders. Evidently, the VLW came to help everybody, not by fighting for the weak against the strong, but by uniting all of them, weak and strong, into a fraternal community.

This was the most significant development programme initiated during the first five year plan to embody India's methods of approach to the problems of improving rural life under conditions of democratic planning. Community Development, in fact, was a concept, a movement and revolution. It had a crucial significance in our plans and from the point of view of both economic progress and social justice, its role was therefore of supreme importance.

Before initiating the first five year plan rural development programmes had been undertaken at many centres in the country by

Government and voluntary agencies. Although the models differed in content, they aimed at tackling the four major problems, the emergence of which was acknowledged by the British administrators. They were: the recurrence of famine, the inequity of land tenure, ever-increasing peasant indebtedness, and smouldering disaffection with the government. In the third and last phase the rural problems were magnified and the administrators encountered fundamental challenges—political, economic, and moral—to the ideology of the empire. Their efforts often on a small scale, had given indications of the approach and the methods most likely to succeed when development was taken up on a national scale. The lessons derived from these were summarised in the First Five Year Plan document on the following lines.

(1) When different departments of the Government approach the villager, each from the aspects of its own work, the effect on the villager is apt to be, confusing and no permanent impression is created. The peasant's life is not cut into segments in the way the Government's activities are apt to be, the approach to the villager has, therefore, to be a coordinated one and has to comprehend his whole life. Such an approach has to be made, not through a multiplicity of departmental officials, but through an agent common at least to the principal departments engaged in rural work.

(2) There has to be a dominant purpose round which the enthusiasm of the people can be aroused and sustained, a purpose which can draw forth from the people and those who assist them on behalf of the Government, the will to work as well as sense of urgency. The aim should be to create in the rural population a burning desire for a higher standard of living - a will to live better.

(3) Programmes which have been built on the basis of self help and cooperation of the people have greater chance of abiding success than those which are imposed on them from outside.

(4) While the official machinery has to guide and assist, the principal responsibility for improving their own conditions must rest with the people themselves. Unless they feel that a programme is theirs and are prepared to make sacrifices for carrying it out, no substantial results will be gained.

(5) The best results will be gained if programmes are pursued intensively, and every family has its own contributions to make through village organisations which they regard as their own.

(6) The approach to the villagers should be in terms of his/her own experience and problems, conceived on the pattern of simplicity, and avoiding elaborate techniques and equipment until he/she is ready for them.

The aim of the community projects and national extension service programme was to apply these principles progressively throughout the country. Community Development programme began in a modest way on October 2, 1952 when 55 areas comprising 27,388 villages and a population of 16.7 million were selected to rejuvenate economic and social life in the rural areas. The emphasis was on infrastructure building at the local level and investment in human resource development through the provision of education and health services.

In this context it may be pointed out that Community Development has to be distinguished from mere rural reconstruction or village development programme. Rural reconstruction has been in India since time immemorial. In earlier periods in history, kings and monarchs and philanthropists had undertaken many works of charity, and many had been noted for their extraordinary munificence. Even in British days, there was no dearth of rural reconstruction programmes and there was quite a remarkable progress in many directions during that period. Not that community development excluded those rural reconstruction programmes, it very much included them. But the distinction was that community development was something more than those programmes. Basically, Community Development was investment in man—an effort to build up a new man out of men and thereby create a new and better human potential. It thus aimed at creating a new sense of purpose, and that also by a process of full involvement and participation by the people.

The community development programme was the first organised attempt to lift the centuries old stagnant rural economy from the morass and inertia of the proverbial fatalist outlook and to the extent it generated some awakening and visible changes in the social and cultural mores, it was successful. But the major stumbling blocks in the programme were the weight of the colonial traditions of Government administration, and the lack of a sound technological base for improving productivity and incomes of the rural population. Further once the programme was expanded to cover the whole country, the weaknesses of the socioeconomic system, of the administrative structure geared to targetry, of the social structure dominated by caste hierarchies, of an economic system characterised by rent seeking tendencies-came to the surface. There was also lack of people's participation at the desired level in the programme. The Programme, therefore, failed to provide the impulse for sustained growth of all round rural scenario.

The programmes so well conceived just floundered under the weight of over administration. By 1960 CD was demoted and the American concept of Agricultural Extension became the senior partner. Careful analysts found that CD had four crucial imperfections:

(a) It promoted welfare activities more effectively than productive activities. Particularly, it seemed incapable of solving the national food crisis.

(b) CD did not succeed significantly in forming harmonious communities. It did not secure general participation. The poorer classes remained as they were, apathetic and skeptical.

(c) CD's reliance on its own agents and total collaboration with established leaders further confirmed the elitist and paternalist bias, a colonial heritage, and inhibited the growth of true local initiative.

(d) CD's role as a generalist captain and coordinator was not acceptable to the specialist departments. Agricultural experts especially complained about the inadequacy of a multipurpose VLW as their agent.

Recent experience clearly shows that for a project to be successful, it has to be based on the principle of local participation, control, and authority, and supported by an approach to project design that emphasises learning over blueprints. In short major part of the success of a project will depend on how far people influence or control the decisions that affect them. Once they have a greater stake in the outcome, they will work harder to ensure success.

Rural Development Programmes in Sixties

While the first phase of Rural Development during the fifties emphasised on redistribution of land to improve the plight of poor tenants, the second phase popularly known as Poverty Alleviation Programme (PAP), stressed on intensive agriculture as a strategy for the sixties since the country started facing acute food shortage. Truly speaking, rural development became agricultural development. The strategy was to concentrate the flow of resources in the already better endowed areas. Thanks to the discovery of high yielding varieties of wheat and its spectacular productivity improvement. It no doubt paid dividend, but widened the gap between better endowed and poorer areas. This type of regional imbalances led to serious political and economic ramifications. It was also causing concern that there was no sign of decline in rural poverty in the country. Thus, as a general strategy for poverty alleviation, an emphasis on more equitable distribution of ownership and access to land, reforms in the credit delivery system to enable the poor command over productive resources; and a public distribution system for foodgrains to contribute to improvement of nutritional standards of the poor by bringing down the real cost of foodgrains, have all played an important role in poverty alleviation in the country. However, their less than satisfactory impact demands a closer look at the efficacy of these programmes.

Rural Employment Programmes

The Second phase directed as it was to address exclusively the poor in rural areas, resulted in a target group approach to create new employment opportunities. It was identified that one of the main causes of rural poverty was the lack of purchasing power of the majority of the rural people in the absence of employment opportunities. Rural Manpower Employment Programme in 1960 was the first attempt on an all-India basis to create employment opportunities. In 1971-72, the Government of India launched the Crash Scheme for Rural Employment (CSRE). The Scheme envisaged execution of essentially labour intensive projects in all the districts of the country. As a part of this Scheme, Pilot Intensive Rural Employment projects were taken up during 1972-73 for a period of three years in 15 selected blocks. These had a limited object to collect necessary data providing full employment to everyone who was willing to work.

During seventies, a few state governments also launched rural employment programmes. In fact, Maharashtra was the first state to introduce at the state level an Employment Guarantee Scheme (EGS) in 1972. The EGS provides a guarantee of employment to all the adults above 18 years of age who are willing to do unskilled manual work on piece rate basis. The main objective of the EGS is to sustain household welfare in the short run (through provision of employment) and to contribute to the development of rural infrastructure. Mention may also be made about the Land Army Corporation of Karnataka (1974, revamped in 1983), State Rural Employment Programme in Tripura (1981-82), and Village Development Council of Nagaland (set up under the Village Area Council Act of 1978). These efforts finally culminated in the Integrated Rural Development Programme (IRDP) and National Rural Employment Programme (NREP). Unfortunately, experience of the past was that all these programmes were Government sponsored and there was precious little participation of the people in formulation or implementation of the schemes.

Food for Work Programme

The programme was started during 1977-78. The scheme was designed to offer gainful employment to the rural poor and improve their income level, through the development of infrastructure and durable community assets. In order to improve the nutritional standards of the rural poor, the scheme provided for payment of part of wages in kind by utilising surplus foodstocks available in the country. The programme, in the initial years did gain momentum and created substantial additional employment in the rural areas during lean periods besides making a favourable impact on stabilisation of wages in the rural areas. However, it also suffered from severe limitations in respect of planning and supervision of works. Further, the operation of this programme on year to year basis had resulted in uncertainty about its continuance for the full plan period. No serious attempt also appeared to have been made by the state governments to implement the programme at block level resulting in taking up works of low priority with dubious utility at several places. In fact, it was an official programme with complete absence of people's participation.

Anti Poverty Programmes

It was realised in the seventies itself that the economic development as such could not make much dent on the gargantuan problem of rural poverty. " Trickle down effect" was the basic aim of investment in agriculture, land development, terracing works, rural access roads, irrigation, soil and water conservation works, afforestation, etc. But all these created more inequalities in the rural areas and menacing rural poverty persisted unabatedly.

Removal of rural poverty through `direct attack' therefore, has become the key issue in the rural development programmes since the eighties onward. During the Sixth Plan, the Government adopted a two pronged strategy to deal with the problem of poverty. While laying emphasis on accelerated growth in agriculture with the expectation that it would have a long lasting beneficial effect on raising the standard of living of the lower strata of the rural society, it was also decided to fortify and expand the scope of target oriented poverty alleviation programmes in rural areas. Consistent with this approach, the Seventh Five Year Plan laid emphasis on accelerated agricultural growth, increased productivity of various agricultural commodities, developing potential of dry land agriculture, adoption of special measures to increase and expand irrigation facilities. It also included a number of anti-poverty and employment generation programmes especially designed to raise incomes and productivity of people below the poverty line.

During the Sixth Plan the National Rural Employment Programme (NREP) and the Rural Landless Employment Guarantee Programme (RLEGP) were implemented replacing the earlier Food for work programme. However, in the last year of the Seventh Five Year Plan, i.e.. from April 1989, these two programmes were merged into a single programme known as Jawahar Rozgar Yojana. Besides generating additional gainful employment for the unemployed and underemployed men and women in rural areas, the programme had also five other secondary objectives. These were: (i) creation of sustained employment by strengthening the rural economic infrastructure; (ii) creation of community and social assets; (iii) creation of assets in favour of the rural poor for their direct and continuing benefit; (iv) positive impact on wage levels; and (v) overall improvement in the quality of life in rural areas.

In 1993-94 the scheme was revised to be implemented in three streams. The first stream would consist of general work under the programme and the two sub-schemes, viz, the Indira Awaas Yojana (IAY) and the Million Wells Scheme (MWS). The second stream (also called Intensified Jawahar Rozgar Yojana) was implemented in 120 backward districts with additional allocation. The third stream of JRY consisted of special and innovative projects. From 1995-96 IAY and MWS were being implemented as separate schemes and no longer formed part of the JRY. Later on, the centrally sponsored Rural Housing scheme was also merged with the IAY.

The Employment Assurance Scheme (EAS) was also launched in 1993 to provide 100 days of assured employment to the rural poor in the lean agricultural season in selected blocks. Subsequently, the second stream of JRY was discontinued by merging the backward districts under EAS.

Self-Employment Programme

The Integrated Rural Development Programme (IRDP) was launched in all the blocks of the country on October 2, 1980, as a major credit linked self-employment programme for alleviation of poverty. Access to assets other than land could provide additional income to the poor. A very wide range of such assets can be listed. They may include livestock, raw material for arts and crafts for artisans, small implements or even a better means of transport (a bullock cart or bicycle). In some cases these assets may provide substantial income even to those households who primarily depend on land. The most important programme which is aimed at providing additional income to the poor by giving them productive assets of the type listed above is the IRDP. The objective of IRDP is to enable identified rural poor families to augment their income and cross the poverty line through acquisition of credit based productive assets which would provide self-employment on a sustained basis. Assistance in the form of subsidy by the Government and term credit are advanced by financial institutions (viz. commercial banks, cooperative and regional rural banks) for income generating activities in the primary, secondary and tertiary sectors of the rural economy.

There are also two subschemes under IRDP, namely (i) Development of Women and Children in Rural Areas (DWCRA) and (ii) Training of Rural youth for Self-Employment (TRYSEM). While the objective of the former is to provide income generating skills and activities to poor women in rural areas, thereby improving their social and economic status, the objective of the latter is to provide technical and entrepreneurial skills to rural youth from families below the poverty line. All these programmes have since been merged with Swarnajayanti Gram Swarozgar Yojana (SGSY).

Swarnjayanti Gram Swarozgar Yojana

A new self-employment programme namely Swarnjayanti Gram Swarozgar Yojna (SGSY) has been launched w.e.f. April 1,1999. As a result, the erstwhile programmes viz. Integrated Rural Development

Programme (IRDP), Development of Women and Children in Rural Areas (DWCRA), Training of Rural Youth for Self-Employment (TRYSEM), Supply of Improved Toolkits to Rural Artisans (SITRA), Ganga Kalyan Yojana (GKY) and Million Wells Scheme (MWS) ceased to be in operation. It may be pointed out that SGSY has been devised keeping in view the positive aspects and deficiencies of the earlier programmes. The earlier programmes were originally viewed as complementary to each other to achieve the larger goal of poverty alleviation. But over the years, each one of these started operating almost as a separate and independent programme. Obviously, the concern was more for achieving individual programme targets. The desired linkages among the programmes and the much needed focus on the substantive issue of sustainable income generation were missing. SGSY accordingly came into being after restructuring of all these programmes.

SGSY has a definite objective of improving the family income of the rural poor and, at the same time, providing for a flexibility of design at the grassroots level to suit the local needs and resources. The objective of the restructuring was to make the programme more effective in providing a sustainable income through micro-enterprise development, both land based and otherwise. In doing so, effective linkages have been established between various components such as capacity building of the poor, credit, technology, marketing and infrastructure.

Expansion of Employment Insurance Scheme (EAS)

During 1994-95, EAS was extended to 409 blocks under DPAP/DDP and Modified Area Development Approach (MADA) blocks having larger concentration of tribal population. In March, 1995 the scheme was further extended to 256 blocks (233 flood prone blocks in the States of Uttar Pradesh, Bihar and Assam, and 23 blocks of Jammu and Kashmir in view of the special conditions prevailing there). The Intensified Jawahar Rozgar Yojana (IJRY) was merged with EAS w.e.f. 1.1.1996. Consequently. 722 non-EAS blocks in 120 IJRY districts were also covered under EAS. On universlisation, the remaining blocks were covered under the scheme in two phases, i.e. 1123 blocks in 1996-97 and 1121 blocks in 1997-98. At present, the scheme is being implemented in all the 5448 rural blocks of the country.

Based on the experience of last five years of implementation of the programme, EAS has been restructured w.e.f. April 1,1999 to make it a single wage employment programme. While the basic parameters have been retained, the allocation to the States/Districts is more definitely applied. In keeping with the spirit of democratic decentralisation, the Zila Parishads have been designated as the "Implementing Authority" under the programme.

Million Wells Scheme

Million wells Scheme (MWS) was launched as a sub-scheme of National Rural Employment Guarantee Programme (RLEGP) during 1988-89. It continued as a sub-scheme of Jawahar Rozgar Yojana from April 1989 to 31-12-95. From 1-1-96, MWS was an independent scheme. The scheme has since been merged with Swarnjayanti Gram Swarozgar Yojana with effect from April 1,1999.

Objectives The objective of the scheme was to provide open irrigation wells free of cost to poor, small and marginal farmers who were below the poverty line and freed bonded labourers.

Performance under Million Wells Scheme From inception of the scheme in 1988-89 till 1998-99, a total of 12,63,090 wells were constructed under MWS with an expenditure of Rs. 4728.17 crores. The total number of beneficiaries was 12,63,090.

Drought Prone Area Programme (DPAP)

Drought Prone Area Programme is one of the area development programmes launched by the government in 1973-74 to tackle the special problems by those fragile areas which are constantly affected by severe drought conditions. These areas are characterized by large human and cattle populations which are continuously putting heavy pressure on the already fragile natural resource base for food, fodder and fuel. This continuous biotic pressure is leading to fast and continuous depletion of vegetative cover, less and less rainfall, increasing soil erosion and fast receding ground water levels due to continuous exploitation without any effort to recharge the underground acquifers.

Objectives The basic objective of the programme is to minimise the adverse effects of drought on production of crops and livestock and productivity of land, water and human resources, ultimately leading to the drought proofing of the affected areas. The programme also aims to promote overall economic development and improving the socioeconomic conditions of the resource poor and disadvantaged sections inhabiting the programme areas.

Strategy The common guidelines for Watershed Development provide for a uniform strategy in the implementation of all the area development programmes, viz. DPAP, DDP, IWDP and EAS. The main features of this strategy are:

- Area development programmes to be implemented on watershed basis.
- Programme activities to be confined to the identified watershed of about 500 hectares and are to be executed in a project basis spanning over a period of four years.
- Watershed project to cover a village as far as possible.
- Elaborate institutional mechanisms at various levels clearly defined for effective participation of the local people and the Panchayati Raj Institutions in all stages of project management.

- DRDA/zilla parishad is the nodal Government agency at the district level to act as a facilitator and provider of finances and technical assistance to the people's organisations executing the watershed projects.

Coverage At present, DPAP is in operation in 961 blocks of 180 districts in 16 states. The corresponding physical area for treatment under the programme works out to approximately 7.46 lakh square kilometres. The states where DPAP is under implementation along with number of districts and blocks may be seen in Table 21.1.

Table 21.1 State-wise Number of Districts and Area Under DPAP

Sl. No.	States	No. of Districts DPAP	No. of Blocks DPAP	Area in Sq. km. DPAP
1.	Andhra Pradesh	11	94	99218
2.	Bihar	6	30	9533
3.	Chhattisgarh	8	29	21801
4.	Gujarat	14	67	43938
5.	Himachal Pradesh	3	9	3319
6.	Jammu & Kashmir	2	22	14705
7.	Jharkhand	12	91	34843
8.	Karnataka	15	81	84332
9.	Madhya Pradesh	23	105	89101
10.	Maharashtra	25	148	194473
11.	Orissa	8	47	26178
12.	Rajasthan	11	32	31969
13.	Tamil Nadu	16	80	29416
14.	Uttar Pradesh	15	60	35698
15.	Uttaranchal	7	30	15796
16.	West Bengal	4	36	11594
TOTAL		180	961	7,45914

Desert Development Programme (DDP)

Over the years, the increase in human and livestock population in desert areas has placed the natural resources of the regions under great stress. The major problems are continuous depletion of vegetative cover, increase in soil erosion and fall in ground water table. All these factors account for diminishing productivity of land and loss of natural resources. The problems would have been worse but for the introduction of some specific highly focussed area development programmes in these areas. On the recommendations of the National Commission on Agriculture (1976), the Desert Development Programme (DDP) was started in the year 1977-78. The programme was started both in the hot desert areas of Rajasthan, Gujarat and

Haryana and the cold desert areas of Jammu & Kashmir and Himachal Pradesh.

Objectives In broad sense, the objectives of the programme are to promote the economic development of village community, restore ecological balance and improve the economic conditions of the resource poor and disadvantaged sections of society through creation, widening and equitable distribution of resources and increased employment opportunities. DDP has been envisaged as an essentially land based activity and conceived as a long-term measure for restoration of ecological balance by conserving, developing and harnessing land, water, livestock and human resources. Objectives of the programme have been recast as under:

- Combating drought and desertification.
- Encouraging restoration of ecological balance.
- Mitigating the adverse effects of drought and adverse edapho-climatic conditions on crops and livestock, and productivity of land, water and human resources.
- Promoting economic development of village community.
- Improving socioeconomic conditions of the resource poor and disadvantaged sections of village community viz. assetless and women.

Coverage Under DDP 227 block of 40 districts having an area of 457, 432 sq.km. in 7 states are covered. The states where DDP is under implementation are Andhra Pradesh, Gujarat, Haryana, Himachal Pradesh, Jammu & Kashmir, Karnataka and Rajasthan.

Poverty Status

Starting from the first poverty estimates of 1972-73 when 51.5 percent of the population was estimated below the poverty line), this came down to 35.97 per cent by 1993-94. According to the latest estimates (55th round), this number has been further reduced to 26.10 per cent on a 30 days recall method (Table 21.2) and 23.33 per cent on a 7 day recall method (Table 21.3). The Prime Minister now says, "Let us make rural prosperity the *mantra* of the decade. (Details of the programmes are given in Appendix 21.1).

VILLAGE PANCHAYATS

Before Independence, Mahatma Gandhi's programme of rural rejuvenation based on Panchayati Raj *nee* grassroot democracy of Gram Swaraj alone held the national ground as the ideal for a free India. For, the realities of the freedom struggle admitted no other alternatives. It was stressed in the First Five Year Plan that progress in rural development depended largely on the existence of an active organisation in the village which represented the community as a whole and could bring the people together in common programmes to be

Table 21.2 Number and Percentage of Population Below Poverty Line by States-1999-2000 (30-Day Recall Method)

No.	States/UTs	Rural		Urban		Combined	
		No. of persons (lakhs)	% of persons	No. of persons (lakhs)	% of persons	No. of persons (lakhs)	% of persons
1.	Andhra Pradesh	58.13	11.05	60.88	26.63	119.01	15.77
2.	Arunachal Pradesh	3.80	40.04	0.18	7.47	3.98	33.47
3.	Assam	92.17	40.04	2.38	7.47	94.55	36.09
4.	Bihar	376.51	44.30	49.13	32.91	425.64	42.60
5.	Goa	0.11	1.35	0.59	7.52	0.70	4.40
6.	Gujarat	39.80	13.17	28.09	15.59	67.89	14.07
7.	Haryana	11.94	8.27	5.39	9.99	17.34	8.74
8.	Himachal Pradesh	4.84	7.94	0.29	4.63	5.12	7.63
9.	Jammu & Kashmir	2.97	3.97	0.49	1.98	3.46	3.48
10.	Karnataka	59.91	17.38	44.49	25.25	104.40	20.04
11.	Kerala	20.97	9.38	20.07	20.27	41.04	12.72
12.	Madhya Pradesh	217.32	37.06	81.22	38.44	298.54	37.43
13.	Maharashtra	125.12	23.72	102.87	26.81	227.99	25.02
14.	Manipur	6.53	40.04	0.66	7.47	7.19	28.54
15.	Meghalaya	7.89	40.04	0.34	7.47	8.23	33.87
16.	Mizoram	1.40	40.04	0.45	7.47	1.85	19.47
17.	Nagaland	5.21	40.04	0.28	7.47	5.49	32.67
18.	Orissa	143.69	48.01	25.40	42.83	169.09	47.15
19.	Punjab	10.20	6.35	4.29	5.75	14.49	6.16
20.	Rajasthan	55.06	13.74	26.78	19.85	81.83	15.28
21.	Sikkim	2.00	40.04	0.04	7.47	2.05	36.55
22.	Tamil Nadu	80.51	20.55	49.97	22.11	130.48	21.12
23.	Tripura	12.53	40.04	0.49	7.47	13.02	34.44
24.	Uttar Pradesh	412.01	31.22	117.88	30.89	529.89	31.15
25.	West Bengal	180.11	31.85	33.38	14.86	213.49	27.02
26.	A & N Island	0.58	20.55	0.24	22.11	0.82	20.99
27.	Chandigarh	0.06	5.75	0.45	5.75	0.51	5.75
28.	Dadra & Nagar Hav	0.30	17.57	0.03	13.52	0.33	17.14
29.	Daman & Diu	0.01	1.35	0.05	7.52	0.06	4.44
30.	Delhi	0.07	0.40	11.42	9.42	11.49	8.23
31.	Lakshadweep	0.03	9.38	0.08	20.27	0.11	15.60
32.	Pondicherry	0.64	20.55	1.77	22.11	2.41	21.67
	All India	1932.43	27.09	670.07	23.62	2602.50	26.10

Table 21.3 Number and Percentage of Population Below Poverty Line by States-1999-2000 (17-Day Recall Method)

No.	States/UTs	Rural		Urban		Combined	
		No. of persons (lakhs)	*% of persons*	*No. of persons (lakhs)*	*% of persons*	*No. of persons (lakhs)*	*% of persons*
1.	Andhra Pradesh	48.14	9.15	55.96	24.48	104.10	13.79
2.	Arunachal Pradesh	3.23	34.00	0.15	6.29	3.38	28.41
3.	Assam	78.27	34.00	2.00	6.29	80.27	30.64
4.	Bihar	322.96	38.00	43.64	29.23	366.60	36.69
5.	Goa	0.23	2.80	0.40	5.03	0.62	3.90
6.	Gujarat	36.87	12.20	24.80	13.76	61.66	12.78
7.	Haryana	11.13	7.71	4.33	8.02	15.46	7.79
8.	Himachal Pradesh	4.63	7.61	0.24	3.95	4.88	7.27
9.	Jammu & Kashmir	3.10	4.14	0.42	1.70	3.52	3.53
10.	Karnataka	47.02	13.64	39.35	22.33	86.36	16.58
11.	Kerala	18.20	8.14	17.73	17.91	35.93	11.14
12.	Madhya Pradesh	202.78	34.58	74.93	35.46	277.70	34.81
13.	Maharashtra	109.25	20.71	96.81	25.23	206.05	22.61
14.	Manipur	5.54	34.00	0.56	6.29	6.10	24.21
15.	Meghalaya	6.70	34.00	0.29	6.29	6.99	28.75
16.	Mizoram	1.19	34.00	0.38	6.29	1.57	16.50
17.	Nagaland	4.42	34.00	0.24	6.29	4.66	27.73
18.	Orissa	131.63	43.98	23.92	40.33	155.55	43.38
19.	Punjab	8.53	5.31	4.03	5.40	12.56	5.34
20.	Rajasthan	48.97	12.22	25.36	18.80	74.33	13.88
21.	Sikkim	1.70	34.00	0.04	6.29	1.74	31.03
22.	Tamil Nadu	73.19	18.68	45.81	20.27	119.00	19.26
23.	Tripura	10.64	34.00	0.41	6.29	11.05	29.24
24.	Uttar Pradesh	379.41	28.75	110.82	29.04	490.23	28.82
25.	West Begal	154.04	27.24	31.06	13.83	185.10	23.43
26.	A & N Island	0.52	18.68	0.22	20.27	0.75	19.13
27.	Chandigarh	0.06	5.40	0.42	5.40	0.48	5.40
28.	Dadra & Nagar Hav	0.26	15.31	0.02	10.89	0.28	14.84
29.	Daman & Diu	0.02	2.80	0.04	5.03	0.05	3.92
30.	Delhi	0.12	0.63	6.52	5.38	6.64	4.75
31.	Lakshadweep	0.02	8.14	0.07	17.91	0.10	13.72
32.	Pondicherry	0.58	18.68	1.62	20.27	2.20	19.83
	All India	1713.35	24.02	612.57	21.59	2325.92	23.33

carried out with the assistance of the administration. In other words, the village panchayat was to be the foundation of the entire administrative structure for national development. In 1958 the evaluators of CD pointed out that the primary need of rural areas was institutional. Instead of building a lot of "brick and mortar" projects, as CD was doing, panchayats and cooperatives should be organized or strengthened. Disappointed with American-sponsored CD, the planners turned back to older traditions. The reasons for emphasizing local government appeared more urgent than before. It was essential that the rural people identify themselves with their government; otherwise there would be instability. The rural people must assume responsibility for planning and financing their own development; otherwise the central government could do very little. Self-reliant local institutions obviously were the best means for popular participation and general mobilization. If the reasons were the same as before, unfortunately the impediments also were the same. Colonial traditions of centralism, elitism, and paternalism still prevailed.

Experience in the initial years of development planning indicated that while a number of panchayats provided good leadership, invariably panchayats were handicapped on account of insufficient experience of development activities. The idea of the village panchayat being given the opportunity to share fully, along with the village cooperative, the responsibility for social and economic activities of the village community has not been achieved to any extent. No doubt, there are cases, though a few, where the village panchayats organised their members for contributing voluntary work for the building of roads, planting of trees and other works of interest to the community.

The Second Five Year Plan set out certain functions of village panchayats in relation to rural development which were as follow:

(1) framing programmes of production in the village;
(2) in association with cooperatives, framing budgets of requirements for supplies and finances for carrying out programmes;
(3) acting as a channel through which an increasing proportion of Government assistance reaches the villages;
(4) developing common land such as waste lands, forests, abadi sites, tanks, etc. including measures for soil conservation;
(5) construction, repair and maintenance of common village buildings, public wells, tanks, roads, etc.
(6) organization of mutual aid and joint efforts in all activities;
(7) promotion of cooperative societies;
(8) organising voluntary labour for community workers;
(9) promoting small savings; and
(10) improvement of livestock.

The Third Five Year Plan document actually felt satisfied when it said that "the people in the rural areas are now coming into their own.

Direct responsibility for the administration of their affair is being passed on to them as panchayati raj gets established in one state after another. The transformation now occurring at the base of the country side, and emerging from panchayati raj, is intended to facilitate the fuller play of the energy and initiative of the people in dealing with the tasks which lie close to them in the villages of the country. Conditions are being created for a fuller use of the manpower and other resources in order to secure more rapid development in every direction. This will also widen very much the opportunities of public cooperation".

Unfortunately, this remained as pious wishes as the panchayati raj institutions in most of the states were in doldrum. Even where there was semblance of the institution, there was no election for years together and remained under the grip of the rural politicians who had vested interests in them.

It may be reiterated that putting people first in development projects comes down to tailoring the design and implementation of projects to the needs and capabilities of people who are supposed to benefit from them. No longer should people be indentified as "target groups". Rather, if we must speak of them abstractly, we should consider them as "intended beneficiaries". They are to be benefited, rather than "impacted". In design and implementation we have only intentions, since our knowledge of how to improve the productivity and wellbeing of the poor majority is limited. We can and should be clear about whom we expect to benefit, and how, but we cannot be certain that our efforts will bear the desired fruits until the processes of economic and social change have been put in motion. Fortunately, some of the anticipated outcomes can be favourable. The probabilities of gaining momentum, rather than losing it, in the course of carrying out projects should be greater to the extent that the mode of design and implementation reflects a "learning process" approach. This enlists the participation of intended beneficiaries as much as feasible in all aspects of project operations.

Efforts have since been made to give more powers to the panchayat and streamline the system. The passage of the Constitution (73rd Amendment) Act, 1992 certainly marks a new era in the federal democratic set up of the country and to provide constitutional entities to the Panchayati Raj Institutions (PRIs). Consequent upon the enactment of the Act almost all the States/UTs (except Jharkhand, Arunachal Pradesh, Punjab and Pondicherry) have enacted their legislation and completed the elections in their respective States/UTs. As a result, about 2,27,698 Panchayats at village level, 5,906 Panchayats at intermediate level and 474 Panchayats at the district level have been constituted in the country. These Panchayats are being manned by about 34 lakh elected representatives of Panchayats at all levels, comprising, 31,98,554 persons at village level, 1,51,412 persons at the intermediate level and 15,935 persons at the district level. Thus, this is the broadest representative base which exists in any country of the world-developed or underdeveloped.

The EAS funds are, for example being distributed among different DRDAS/Zilla Parishads, Intermediate Panchayats/Village Panchayats in the district in the ratio of 20:15:65. The responsibility for implementation of EAS in respect of the district share of funds rests with DRDA/Zilla Parishad. The resources allocated to DRDA/Zilla Parishad, intermediate panchayat and gram panchayat are to be spent within the geographical boundaries of the unit and cannot be diverted under any circumstances except where two or more district/panchayats decide to pool the resources together to take up a work for common benefit of the concerned districts/panchayats. A recent study conducted by the ORG for District Meerut shows that even this experiment has not succeeded fully. Quality of work was poor primarily because community effort was missing. Thus, we find that though the village panchayats are responsible for implementation of the wage employment programmes at the grass root level, it is not very clear what is the say of the targeted people in taking up a particular project for implementation. As discussed under in PAPSL programme, we have to perhaps review and re-examine the very philosophy behind the innumerable rural development programmes and the existing Panchayati Raj. Failing which we will continue to waste our scarce resources for another fifty years.

Panchayati Raj as a Developmental Vehicle and Food Security

Having a close link with the rural fabric, Panchayats with their network are most suited to undertake responsibility not only in enhancing agricultural production, but also ensuring food security by streamlining the PDS—a most abused system as at present. The 11th schedule of the constitution has recommended vital areas of agricultural operation to be brought under the panchayats (1) Agriculture, including agricultural extension, (2) Land, improvement, implementation of land reforms, land consolidation and soil conservation, (3) Minor irrigation, water management and watershed development, (4) Animal husbandry, dairying and poultry, (5) Fisheries.

They are also entrusted with the responsibility of preparing plans for economic development and social justice in respect of these areas and are expected to act as the implementation agencies of schemes and plans related to the these areas. Such institutions can serve as an effective medium for bringing about technology transfers in the areas of agriculture. Being in close contact with ground realities they can ensure that inputs meet local requirements. Also they can provide valuable feedback for agricultural universities and research institutes to help develop technology and inputs suited to regional variations.

The importance of land reforms in ensuring higher production and thus contributing to food security cannot be overstated. Land reforms provide the rural poor (small and marginalised farmers) with greater income and consequently enhanced purchasing power. The state of West Bengal is the best example. The land reforms through the famous operation barga was successful because of "pressure from below", i.e., the Panchayati Raj institutions. PRI's in West Bengal were crucial in sustaining grass roots pressure in favour of the reforms during their first term (1978-1983). The extent of land reforms in West Bengal can be gauged from the fact that while Bengal has only 3.5% of the country's cultivable land, it contributed 20.77% of the total ceiling surplus land distributed in the country. The beneficial impact of land reforms on agriculture is evident from the significant improvement in agricultural production in the post 1983 period, when panchayati raj had established itself. If the growth of rice production in West Bengal in 1950-60 was 1.01 percent, it reached 6.41 in 1980-81.[1] A visit to West Bengal countryside is a refreshing experience where one can see the linkage between increased agricultural production, land utilisation and relatively self-content village population dependent on agriculture related activities and vibrant panchayati raj system. Functions performed by line departments are now brought under the gram panchayats and in close proximity with community problems, giving space for constructive activity.

Greater involvement of panchayati raj institutions with the PDS can again help in ensuring food reaching the needy and that is why the PDS has been explicitly included in the list provided in the 11th schedule. In order to actualise this provision there is a need for furthering experiments like that attempted in the Keonjhar district of Orissa. Under section 44(1)(x-3) of Orissa Gram Panchayat Act, 1965; PDS is an obligatory function of the gram panchayat. Under this provision it is the duty of the gram panchayat, within the limits of funds, to undertake control, administer and be responsible for the PDS in the village. Making use of this provision the gram panchayats in Keonjhar were entrusted with the retail of the goods through the PDS by replacing private retailers. Observers argue that this not only helped generate funds for the panchayats but also brought down corruption drastically by bringing in greater transparency and accountability.[2]

In the case of Rajasthan, the government has been utilising the gram sabha as a public forum for selecting people below poverty line (BPL) for the purposes of the Integrated Rural Development Programme (IRDP). Under the "Annapoorna" scheme gram panchayats are to identify, prepare and display a list of beneficiaries after wide publicity.

---

[1] Bandyopadhaya, D. (2000); Land Reforms In West Bengal, *Economic and Political Weekly*, May 27.

[2] Garg, Saurabh; "Gram Panchayats As Retailers of Public Distribution System Commodities" (2000-2001) *Compass*, Monsoon Issue.

It has been observed that the BPL identification process by the gram sabha has been generally fair and in conformity with the programmatic guidelines.

The recently published report of the Task Force on Devolution of Powers and Function upon Panchayati Raj Institutions has identified the various functions that can be performed by different tiers of PRIs.[3] The report sought to give concrete shape to activities to be performed by PRIs under the PDS. They are: (1) Availability and movement of essential commodities and demand assessment under the PDS programme; (2) Transport, storage and delivery system; (3) Vigilance and enforcement aspects; (4) Linking PDS with poverty alleviation programmes. Within these broad activity areas the report seeks to identify tasks that can be performed by each tier.* An analysis of these tasks reveals that District Panchayats have been generally deemed to be suitable for performing overall planning and assessment tasks. Thus, for instance, District Panchayat has been assigned the task of preparing a district map of PDS outlets and deciding the opening of new shops. Intermediate level panchayats can assist in the performance of these planning and assessment tasks by undertaking these activities in the areas under their jurisdiction and also providing a link between district panchayats and gram panchayats.

The task assigned to Gram Panchayats are more related to supervision and control of functioning of Fair Price Shops (FPS). Being closest to the people it is seen as crucial in identifying the beneficiaries as well as eliminating bogus ration cardholders. The Report of the Task Force contains no major surprises. As early as January, 2000 the Ministry for Consumer Affairs and Public Distribution had released a six-point action plan empowering the gram panchayats to supervise and regulate the working of Fair Price Shops. The Report of the Task Force is, however, a comprehensive attempt at giving shape to the activities of the PRIs while also delineating the various powers and sources of finance which need to be devolved with each activity. In that sense the latest report in some ways represents the collective wisdom gained by the fore mentioned initiatives and experiments as well as the critical role of the local self government institutions in this vital area.

Access to Food

Increased income generation amongst the rural poor is a sine qua non for ensuring food security. For it is only if the people have adequate

[3] *Report of the Task Force on Devolution of Powers and Function upon Panchayati Raj Institutions*, Government of India, Ministry of Rural Development, Department of Rural Development (Panchayati Raj Division) (2001), Krishi Bhavan, New-Delhi, August.

* Details given in Annexure A.

purchasing power can they have economic access to the food requirements. The recent starvation deaths in Kashipur, Orissa highlight the disastrous consequences of inadequate purchasing power amongst the rural poor. It also highlights the failure of welfare and development schemes initiated from above without giving power to the people through the panchayats. The PRIs can help break the nexus between the corrupt local officials and the rural elite by both empowering the weak and marginalised sections of society and bringing in greater accountability and transparency. As is well known PRIs provide an excellent opportunity for ensuring greater participation of the hitherto marginalised sections of society. Panchayati raj institutions can further ensure accountability of Fair Price Shops and the PDS system through effectively implementing the right to information and by conducting social audit.

The former finance minister, Mr P. Chidambaram, in fact argued in favour of replacing the PDS with "food-for-work" programmes run by panchayats.[4] These programmes are crucial for ensuring the food security of the rural poor who have neither work nor food. However, in order to ensure that these programmes are effectively implemented Mr. Chidambaram had called for a greater role for panchayats than that has been hitherto assigned to them. He argued that adequate quantity of wheat or paddy should be transported to the drought-affected areas and the stock should be entrusted to the panchayats. The panchayats should then decide what works they should take up and fix the wage for each unit of work in terms of wheat or rice. Thus, the goals of rural development and food security would be met simultaneously by the panchayats.

Decentralised Planning—Fortifying Food Security

The preceding discussion highlights the numerous ways in which PRIs can contribute to ensuring food security. These are however unlikely to materialise or lead to long term benefits if unaccompanied by a genuine empowerment of the people at the grass roots levels. It is impossible to imagine starvation deaths in a community where local bodies have the autonomy and the power to decide their development priorities, projects and their implementation and the entitlements of the poor. For no sensitive community today is likely to condemn its members to starvation. Empowerment of local communities through grass root democracy, decentralised planning is therefore the best guarantee of food security. The experience of Kerala in the last five years highlights the fact that if there is scientific, participatory planning from below, decentralisation is the best means of ensuring the development of the people including enhanced food production.

---

[4] Chidambaram, P., "Problem of Plenty" (2201), *India Today*, September 24.

In 1996 the LDF government in Kerala, for the first time in the country decided to earmark 35–40% of the outlay of the state's Ninth Five Year Plan for the local bodies. Moreover, in order to ensure maximum autonomy for local bodies it decided to provide 75% of the funds in the form of grant-in-aid as 'untied'. The only restriction was that the local bodies should spend at least 40% on productive sector (agriculture and allied activities, industries and self-employment, etc.). Through people's plan campaign a decentralised approach to planning was developed which highlighted the differences that existed between the people's perception of their needs and priorities and those perceived by a centralised bureaucracy. A comparative analysis of the decentralised plan prepared by the panchayats with that of the state that existed earlier, reveals the shift in priorities. Local bodies gave a much higher priority to agriculture than the state plan—19% of the local outlay compared to 10.5% in the state plan.[5]

Animal husbandry received a greater share (7.57%) which is significant considering that dairy farming in Kerala is not undertaken on a large scale commercial basis.[6] It was found that ideally it suited the raising of income of small and marginal farmers. Numerous case studies are indicative of how agricultural productivity can be boosted through the efforts of PRIs. For instance, the Kanjikuzhy Panchayat (Alappuzha, Kerala) has successfully revived the traditional vegetable cultivation. Technical input and guidance was provided by the Krishi Bhavan while the Panchayat provided the funds and mobilised the community through an awareness and mass contact programme. The programme was a resounding success. A drop in the local prices of vegetables to the extent of 20-30% was observed during the 3 month harvest period. Similarly minor irrigation projects and other infrastructural support for agriculture received greater attention. This illustrates the priority people place on food security. Thus given a chance they can to a large extent ensure food security for the local community provided the local government institutions are empowered to plan and execute projects required to meet their needs and priorities. At the implementation stage, in order to ensure accountability and transparency several measures were taken up resulting in less corruption and "leakages". Thus, decentralisation ensured that development programmes not only reflected people's priorities to a greater extent but also increased their efficacy. This is significant for, as shift in priorities discussed above indicated, food security is a priority area for the people, particularly the rural poor.

---

[5] Thomas Isaac, T.M. and Franke, Richard W.: *Local Democracy and Development-People's campaign for decentralized planning in Kerala* (2000), LeftWord Books, New-Delhi, pp. 205.

[6] *Ibid* p. 8, pp. 206.

PARTICIPATORY ASSESSMENT AND PLANNING FOR SUSTAINABLE LIVELIHOODS (PAPSL)

The concept of participatory development was introduced by Brazilian educator Paulo Freire in 1970. In his book, Pedagogy of the Oppressed, Freire describes what he calls "training for transformation," a methodology for teaching illiterate adults how to think critically about themselves and their circumstances. More recently, such ideas have been carried forward and expanded by Robert Chambers of the Institute for Development Studies at Sussex University, UK. Chambers is coauthor with Gordon Conway of a widely-read paper published in 1992, "Sustainable Rural Livelihoods: Practical Concepts for the 21st Century." He is best known for his more recent book, "Whose Reality Counts? Putting the First Last".

An assessment process jointly worked with the help of villagers to produce their action plans would be a fusion of three development methodologies: training for transformation, which seeks to "awaken" and "empower" the poor to take charge of their own development; participatory rural appraisal, a system of research and information gathering involving local people in a detailed study of their community and livelihood systems; and a planning methodology designed to produce strategies for action.

Integrated Rural Development - the so called panacea for rural poverty elimination-is inherently `top-down'. The approach is no doubt based on consultation but rarely participation. The new approach to development PAPSL goes a step further, when it takes its starting-point not poverty but the "wealth" of the poor: the knowledge, skills and adaptive strategies that have enabled the poor to survive over the years, often against terrible odds. Adaptive strategies-the changes and adjustments people make in their livelihood systems in order to cope under difficult circumstances-serve as the "entry-point" of the SL approach.

The sustainable livelihoods process trains its facilitators to help people look at themselves and the world in a new light. The planning process is designed to create self-awareness within communities. Once people realize that they can do things for themselves and create the necessary leadership and organizations for this, nothing stops them. They use every possible resource available. They change the world around them. The advantage that one sees in sustainable livelihoods is that it moves beyond the traditional sectoral or thematic approaches that development work has been locked into for so long. In organizations like ours, it becomes very difficult to realize the wholeness of a community's situation. We tend to separate everything into watertight compartments-gender, environment, income-generation, and so on. We have to, in short, stick to adaptive strategies and sustainable livelihood system. The people must feel that they are a part of the system, not `parcels' in the system-that is PAPSL.

A CRITIQUE

Apart from the expansion of the "nation building" departments (agriculture, education, health, etc.), four attempts have been made to reform the nature and approach to rural administration. The first attempt was made by the colonial Rural Reconstruction (RR) Movement, the second by CD, the third by the local government (LG) programmes and the fourth Integrated Rural Development Programme (IRDP). Colonial RR gave a new dimension to the district officer. Besides being a magistrate and collector, he was to become the father of development, the guide-philosopher-friend of the villagers. Obviously the RR reform was confined to attitudes. On the one hand, it did not in the least interfere with the paternalist framework. On the other hand, it brought idealistic reinforcement.

Thirty years later, CD pointed out the need for a new orientation for administrators. It criticized them for the "law and order" mentality. Development required much more than obedience and submission for the people. It required active participation. This point was further emphasized by the proponents of local government. They said that the rural people and their resources could be mobilized only through strong, self-managed, self-supporting local institutions. Government departments should be synthesized with and work through these institutions. CD and LG laid the foundation of a rural administrative infrastructure. But, after five decades of expansion and reform, rural administration still displays serious faults. IRDP (now SGSY) came in the Eighties. This has proved to be only integrated in name. At the field level, it continues to be a disintegrated approach as before.

All these efforts have generally failed to deliver services and supplies promptly and equitably. The failure is due partly in inadequate resources, partly to an elitist bias, and partly to lack of coordination. And rural administration generally fails to secure popular participation. Traditional attitudes have prevented any synthesis with local institutions or a real partnership with the people. The inhibiting influence of paternalistic centralization, which prevailed in the past, has not yet disappeared. Villages were economically depressed by the colonial connection and further degraded by urban domination. It is said that the rural people suffered from an exterior as well as an interior colonialism, and even when the former went away, the latter stayed on.

We have discussed in brief some of the important programmes implemented under the broad head-Rural Development, from time to time, and the genesis of Panchayati Raj . A complete list is, given at Table 21.4 for the benefit of the readers. One interesting feature of these 30 or odd programmes (the list being not complete any way) is that there have been so many changes/mergers/bifurcations etc. that there is a complete confusion at the village level. In addition to the Ministry of Rural Development, there are a number of other Ministries-Human

Table 21.4 Rural Development Programmes under the Ministry of Rural Development

		Year
1. National Extension and Community Development Programme.	CDP	Oct. 1952
2. Village Housing Scheme	VHS	1957
3. Rural Manpower Employment Programme	RMEP	1960
4. Drought Prone Area programme	DPAP	1970-71
5. Crash Scheme for Rural Employment	CSRE	1971-72
6. Rural Water Supply Programme	RWS	1972-73
7. Pilot Intensive Rural Employment Programme	PIREP	1972-73
8. Food for Work Programme	FWP	1977-78 Merged into NREP and RLEGP
9. Desert Development Programme	DDP	1977-78
10. Training for Rural Youth for Self-Employment.	TRYSEM	15th Aug.1979
11. Integrated Rural Development Programme	IRDP	1980 Merged with SGSY in April, 1999.
12. National Rural Employment Programme	NRDP	1980 Merged with JRY from April 1 989
13. Distribution of Surplus Land	DSL	1980
14. Rural Landless Employment Guarantee Programme	RLEGP	1983 Merged with JRY from April 1989.
15. Development of Woman and Child in Rural Area	DWCRA	1982-83 Merged with SGSY in April, 99
16. Council for Advancement of Rural Technology	CART	1983
17. People's Action for Development of India.	PADI	1983.
18. Rural Roads Programme	RRP	During 5th Plan
19. National Wastelands Development Board	NWDB	1985
20. Council for Advancement of Peoples Action for Rural Technology	CAPART	1986 By merging PADI & CART
21. Rural Sanitation Programme	RSP	1986
22. National Drinking Water Mission (Renamed in 1991 RGNDWM)	NDWM	1986
23. Jawahar Rozgar Yojana	JRY	April 1989 Merged with JGSY
24. Supply of Improved Tool kits to Rural Artisans.	SITRA	July 1992.Merged with SGSY In April 99

Table 21.4 Rural Development Programmes under the Ministry of Rural Development (Contd.)

		Year
25. Jai Parkash Rozegar Yojna	JPRY	March 2002
26. Employment Assurance Scheme	EAS	1993
27. Intensified JRY	IJRY	1993 Merged with EAS in 1996.
28. National Old Age Pension Scheme	NOAPS	15th Aug.1995
29. National Family Benefit Scheme	NFBS	15th Aug.1995
30. National Maternity Benefit Scheme	NMBS	15th Aug.1995
31. Indira Awas Yojana (Sub-Scheme of IRDP)	IAY	Jan.1996} Merged from
32. Million Wells Scheme	MWS	Jan.1996} JRY
33. Ganga Kalyan Yojana	GKY	1997
34. Swarnajayanti Gram Swarajgar Yojna	SGSY	April 1999
35. Jawahar Gram Samridhi Yojana	JGSY	April 1999

Resources and Ministry of Welfare, for example- and also individual State Governments which are running a number of their own programmes. Neither field worker nor the villager is clear about their content. Targets come from the top even if a particular scheme is not relevant to the area. It is strange that the valuable lessons drawn from the pre-independence programmes and highlighted in the First Plan document, were completely forgotten.

If so, the immediate question which any right thinking person will pose is - where do we stand today after 50 years of independence. The country (only Rural Dev. Miny) has invested a total sum of over Rs. 116 thousand crores (Table 21.5) on all these programmes. It would be a matter of interest that East Asia which started much behind us even in 1960, is now 27 times ahead in terms of its average per capita income. The per capita commercial energy consumption in India (not considered very important) increased from a lowly 111 kg of oil equivalent in 1971 to a mere 242 kg in 1993 whereas the corresponding values for China, Thailand and Malaysia have been from 278 to 628; 178 to 678 and 436 to 1,529 kg of oil equivalent. Fifty years back, India was considered as the leader in all respects in the Asian region. It is now ranked 139 out of a total of 174 countries in the Human Development Index and 128 under the Gender Related Development Index.

Today our female literacy (above + 15) is less than 34, with BIMARU States less than 20. Infant mortality for male (73) and Female (75) with States like Madhya Pradesh 106 and Orissa/Uttar Pradesh 100, is a blot on us. With as much as 53% of malnourished children in India, their proportion here is much higher than even the poorest countries of Sub-Saharan Africa. The incidence of maternal mortality rate ranges

Table 21.5 Expenditure on CD/Rural Development Programme

(Rs. crores)

	C. Development/ IRDP		*Land Reforms*		*Special Area Programme*		*Total*
	Outlays	*Actual*	*Outlays*	*Actual*	*Outlays*	*Actual*	
1951-56		116					116
1956-61		197					197
1961-66	288						288
1966-69	99						99
1969-74		115.2					115.2
1974-78		99.3		126.7			226.0
1978-79		40.8		47.0			87.8
1979-80	58.6		48.3				106.9
1980-81		887.8		44.6		206.4	1138.8
1981-82		919.9		52.9		258.5	1231.3
1982-83		1076.2		62.3		335.1	1473.6
1983-84		1263.6		66.6		356.9	1687.1
1984-85		1845.8		77.5		423.6	2346.9
1985-86	8510.30*	2151.20	395.80*	74.90	2803.59*	447.33	2673.43
1986-87		2586.80		80.80		627.60	3295.20
1987-88		3049.10		97.40		677.05	3823.55
1988-89		2875.01		107.33		926.51	3908.85
1989-90		3946.91		127.89		903.18	4977.98
1990-91	4149.44	4007.43	152.76	142.51	1037.26	986.33	5136.27
1991-92	4260.76	3984.91	181.53	156.68	1142.93	1067.28	5208.87
1992-93	4379.08	4830.58	157.12	179.39	1179.83	1153.91	6163.88
1993-94	5998.97	6860.74	188.65	172.62	1405.61	1363.59	8396.95
1994-95	8429.93	8506.31	197.42	210.79	1547.54	1428.24	10145.34
1995-96	9685.92	9741.89	236.83	225.27	1780.18	407.84	10375.00
1996-97	10756.67	9312.00	285.65	251.11	1824.66	449.12	10012.23
1997-98	11156.00	10074.00	200.58	264.09	780.85	874.00	11212.09
1998-99	12203.00	10985.00	340.45	340.45	1535.00	1184.00	12509.45
1999- 00 RE	7517.00	7517.00	N.A	N.A	1630	1630.00	9147.00

* Total plan outlay

between 400 and 800 per lakh live births, compared to less than four in the developed countries. Haemorrhage accounts for one in four deaths and anaemia for one in five. Other causes include toxaemia, illegal abortions, sepsis and rupture of the uterus. All these causes are avoidable. The number of people below the poverty line increased from 16 crore in 1951 to 23 crore in 1997 (30-day recall method) and the number of illiterates increased from about 23 crore in 1951 to 34 crore in 1991. The number of unemployed increased from 2.3 crore in 1992 to 5.8 crore in 1997, that is, during the eighth Plan in which employment generation was the thrust area. It is estimated that at this rate the unemployment figure will be over nine crore by the year 2002.

There are villages in Mewat Region of Haryana where additional funds of a few hundred crores have been sunk in the name of development, but literacy level is 8 percent for females. In these very villages, average family size is more than 7 and T.B. is rampant. It's not as if we have not made our own share of pledges. As early as 1944, the Post-War Plan of Education Development had recommended a speedy introduction of a system of universal, compulsory and free education of all boys and girls between ages six and 14. Six years later, the same vow surfaced as a Directive Principle. Article 45 of the Constitution which sets down that "the State shall endeavour to provide within a period of 10 years from the commencement of this Constitution, for free and compulsory education for all children until they completed the age of 14..." This promise has been repeated from time to time. The Prime Minister has again promised at the Red Fort to provide free education to girls upto college level. Let us see when it is realised. For so long as we do not educate our people, particularly women followed by their participation and stake in the development activity, we will continue to live in the land of dreams - Panchayats or no Panchayats.

There is a general feeling that all poverty alleviation programmes are ineffective and the beneficiaries are middlemen and very junior local officials. The fault can be traced to three sources. Most of the schemes are unfeasible, that means they cannot reach the poor and provide them help. Two, there is no administrative mechanism to deliver the benefit to the poor and, three, the states which are the implementing agencies have no funds either to build infrastructure or a delivery system. The result is alarming. The poor are getting poorer. And they are in very backward states like Orissa, Bihar, eastern UP and Rajasthan. Concentration of the economically deprived but culturally rich people in congested pockets spells risks of social unrest, if not combustion. Various Union Ministries spend about Rs. 35,000 crore on fighting poverty. If this amount is distributed directly to the 25 crore very poor, they can buy three kilos of foodgrains daily from the open market at Rs. 7.50 a kilo. If this is sustained over the 10th Five Year Plan, poverty level will come down by 10 percentage points—from the present 26 per cent (7-day recall method) to about 15 per cent. Increasing poverty in certain states in rural India cannot be fought with the present mindset. Economic growth at the national level is calculated by measuring industrial and service sectors performance. The poor in villages have no role to play in this growth and receive no benefit. The point is, involve them in economic growth and ensure that they gain from it. From the way industrialisation is going on, the rural poor have no chance of participating in it for years.

Not only pro-poor schemes do not succeed but they also create fresh problems. Take, for instance, the Integrated Rural Development

Programme (IRDP), under which banks distributed money to ruralites to supplement their income by buying cows and buffaloes or setting up small service centres. These ventures have collapsed for a variety of reasons and farmers are saddled with heavy debts. Instead of being of any help, the IRDP loan has added to the misery of the rural people. Some of the employment guarantee programmes have proved to be a perfect waste of money or a gift to the rural rich. For instance, in the mid-seventies the Planning Commission found the Maharashtra scheme helped rich landlords in the western part of the state to get irrigation to their fields, though the landless poor did not draw any benefit. In other states the so-called food-for-work programmes have ended up as thoroughly useless exercises or as enriching the contractors. Despite this, one may recommend the revival of the food-for-work programme in the name of the creating community assets. Sadly, there is no scope for this in the highly populated states in the Hindi heartland.

Panchayat Representatives View

Are the panchayats any different now that the passage of the 73rd Constitution Amendment is entering the tenth year? Have the last nine years lent certainty, continuity and strength to them? To discuss this issue about 1,500 elected panchayat representatives came together in New Delhi on December 22-23, 2001. Although, there were positive notes about some achievements since the early 1990s, the general mood of this assembly of the grassroots democracy representatives was one of despondency. They have no funds, they have no functions, they have no functionaries. The Constitution had given the panchayats the status of self-government institutions but they were nowhere near this ideal. Some States such as Kerala and Karnataka, which had earlier taken long strides towards decentralising the powers making the panchayats the third tier of governance, are now faltering. When in the Opposition our political leaders are extremely vocal about giving powers to the local bodies. The moment they grab power, they change colour. It is such lip service to panchayats that tends to undermine them.

Defying the constitutional provisions (in this context Part IX) has become routine with most States. The State Governments are required to constitute District Planning Committees (DPCs) under the Constitution to facilitate decentralised planning. Nine years have passed. Andhra Pradesh, Assam, Bihar, Goa and Gujarat are yet to constitute the DPCs. In many States, DPCs are being chaired by members of the State Government, although it is against the spirit of the 73rd Amendment. In Tamil Nadu operational orders for DPCs are yet to be issued. Another area of utter neglect is the States' Finance Commission reports for devolution of funds to the panchayats. They are not taken seriously at all by the State Governments. Yet another disturbing trend is the emergence of parallel bodies to delimit the powers of the panchayats. Both Central and State Governments are trying to outdo one another. The Janmabhoomi programme of Andhra Pradesh, the Gram Vikas Samitis of Haryana, the Joint Forest Management Committees of Gujarat, Rajasthan's Watershed programme, the Water User Groups and Site Implementation Committees of Uttar Pradesh and the District Governments in Madhya Pradesh are some cases in point. These are blatant attempts by the State Governments to strengthen the hands of Ministers, other powerful elements nominated to these parallel bodies and above all, the District Collectors. The politicians and the political parties (both at the Centre and in the States) obviously prefer the collector raj to panchayati raj.

The Central Government is not lagging far behind in strengthening parallel structures. For example, the Ministry of Rural Development is doing everything to fortify the District Rural Development Agencies handling thousands of crores of rupees meant for rural development bypassing the panchayats. Had the Central Government and the Ministry taken the 73rd Amendment seriously the DRDAs would have been rendered obsolete. Instead, the move is to maintain a distinctive identity for DRDAs from the panchayati raj institutions in the name of professionalising and strengthening the administration.

The most damaging measure taken by the Centre and Parliament to emasculate the panchayati raj institutions was to place at the disposal of Members of Parliament Rs. 1,580 crores a year for local areas development. Citizens are agitated over the fact that the MPLADS has not only compromised the moral authority of Parliament and the Centre to enforce the relevant provisions of the Constitution 73/74th Amendments by allowing MPs to undertake local development schemes outside the purview of the panchayats/municipalities, but also strengthened the hold of the bureaucratic machinery. "This is even more outrageous to the modesty of institutions of self-government which they themselves created under Article 243G," according to another document submitted to the Constitution Review Commission.[7]

CONCLUSION

We have observed that rural development programmes since Independence are being implemented in a haphazard and incoherent manner. In fact, till the third five year plan most of the rural development programmes were enshrined in the community development programme. Emphasis was also laid on land reforms in order to establish an egalitarian rural society which however still remained a far cry. It was assumed that the "trickle down" effect of the

[7] George Mathew, *The Hindu*, 2002.

various sectoral developmental programmes themselves would take care of all round rural development. However, as the condition of rural masses continued to remain alarming with persistent lack of essential rural infrastructure and avenues of employment, new ideas of rural development took birth in seventies in the shape of employment generation programmes, with emphasis on development of rural infrastructure; and later, removal of rural poverty became the 'mantra' of the planners and policy makers.

We find that the rural development programmes are now synonymous with anti-poverty programmes. The anti-poverty programmes are of two categories: self employment and wage employment, although some social security schemes like National Social Assistance Programme and special programmes like Member of Parliament's Local Area programme are also there. Although all these are basically employment oriented or security based, they are essentially ad-hoc and not well designed or planned with little or no involvement of the local people at the project formulation stage. Prof. Oommen states that "IRDP is a bureaucratic programme in which the innumerable steps involved, from identification of beneficiaries to marketing, one very demanding and indeed baffling. Subsidies have become the really rallying point where the views of various actors from officers to bankers, beneficiaries and local politicians coincide. Given the fact that except states like Kerala, most others have not constituted the District Planning Committee as per Article 243ZD, the question of reorienting the anti-poverty programmes in favour of local development planning following the 73rd and 74th constitutional Amendments seems to recede into the horizon."

With this scenario before us, it is time for retrospection and heart searching. Where have we gone wrong and where do we go from here. Nobody is clear today as to who and how many are poor. Every one of the organisations has different concepts, definitions and even the numbers. The basic lesson learnt long back-people's participation and prioritisation of the development activity according to the requirement of the poor - is missing till today. As discussed earlier what is more important is Participatory Assessment and Planning for Sustainable Livelihood (PAPSL)—a concept which takes as its starting point not poverty, but the wealth of poor-the knowledge, skills and adaptive strategies that have enabled the poor to survive over the years, often against terrible odds. Panchayats cannot thus be effective as they stand today and empowerment of women will remain a pipe dream with the present level of literacy.

Appendix 21.1

Current Rural Development Programmes

- *Sampoorna Grameen Rozgar Yojana*—outlay of Rs. 10,000 crore per annum—provides 100 crore mandays of employment with food security. 50% of funds earmarked direct to Panchayats.
- *Swarnjayanti Gram Swarozgar Yojana* providing sustainable income to rural poor through Self-Help Groups. 14 lakh Self—Help Groups, one in each Habitation, targeted by 2004.
- *Shelter for all by 2007*—Construction of 25 lakh houses per year in rural areas.
- *Pradhan Mantri Gram Sadak Yojana* providing an all weather road to all rural Habitations with a population of 500 by 2007. 21,000 projects already taken up.
- *Safe Drinking Water* by 2004 for all villages. 87.9% villages fully covered and 10.9% partially covered so far. Sector Reforms in 62 pilot districts with an outlay of Rs. 1800 crore under implementation.
- *Total Sanitation Campaign* launched in 200 districts, Project cost Rs. 1195 crores.
- *New Watershed Development Projects* taken up to develop 62 lakh hectares of wasteland/degraded lands.
- National *Old Age Pension Scheme* provides social security to 44 lakh destitute persons above 65 years. 10 kg free foodgrains per month to identified poor under *Annapurna Scheme*. Under *National Maternity Benefit Scheme* Rs. 500/- to women below poverty line during maternity. Assistance of Rs. 10,000/- to the family of deceased bread earner under *National Family Benefit Scheme*.
- Massive *Food for Work Programme* introduced in calamity affected States. 25.13 lakh tonnes of food grains valued at Rs. 2353 crores released.
- Nation wide programme to *computerize land records* for empowerment of farmers.
- A number of *insurance schemes* started for providing social security to weaker sections; *Bhagyashree Child Welfare Policy* for girl child, *Rajrajeshwari Mahila Kalyan Bima Yojana* for women, *Janashree Bima Yogjana* for Labour in Unorganised Sector, *Khetihar Mazdoor Bima Yojana* for agricultural labours and *Shiksha Sahyoa Yojana* for education allowance to poor children.
- Corpus of *Rural Infrastructure Development Fund (RIDF)* with NABARD for creating infrastructure in rural areas increased to Rs. 5000 crores.
- 1.94 crore farmers already covered under *Kisan Credit Card*. All eligible farmers to be covered in next three years. *Life Insurance Cover* to Kisan Credit Card holders.

- *Comprehensive Crop Insurance* to farmers against calamity and loss of crop.
- *Decentralisation* and *devolution* of powers, funds and functions to the *Panchayati Raj Institutions* being pursued vigorously with the States.

CHAPTER 22

Agricultural Marketing and Marketing Institutions

Agricultural production function is incomplete without proper marketing of the produce. It is not enough to produce a crop or animal product, it must be marketed as well. Production and marketing are two equally important wheels of the vehicle, on which agricultural development of the country is structured. Unless and until matching importance is given to the agricultural marketing policies and programmes, the production programmes are bound to suffer setbacks. An efficient marketing system can be an effective agent of change and an important means for raising the income levels of farmers and satisfaction level of consumers.

Agricultural marketing includes all aspects of market structure and systems, both institutional and functional, pre and post-harvest operations, assembling, grading, processing, storage, transport and distribution. Increased production resulting in greater percentage increase in marketable surplus, accompanied by the increase in demand from urban population, calls for a rapid improvement in the existing system.

The outlook of the farmer is now changing. He has realized the importance of adopting new techniques of production and is yearning for more income and higher standards of living. In consequence, the cropping pattern is no longer dictated by what he needs for his own personal consumption but what is responsive to the market in terms of prices received by him, yet he is not conversant with the complexities of the marketing system which is becoming more and more complicated. While the trade is very well organized, the farmers are not. There is, therefore, no wonder that many practices in vogue in the markets completely ignore the interests of the farmer. By dint of remunerative prices of farm produce, agriculture is today increasingly being looked upon as a commercial proposition. Marketing, in fact, is now being considered as an integral part of production process itself.

The movement of the produce from the field to the consumer in adequate quantities and of appropriate qualities at minimum incidental cost, and a reasonable margin of profit to the trader, presupposes the existence of an efficient marketing system. Thus, the final disposal of agricultural commodities produced involves the activities of real (primary) producer, small and big traders and finally consumers at different points of time and place. In between the points of origin to final distribution for consumption of such commodities there are several functionaries which help the producers by mobilizing the produce to the market place on the one hand, and making them available their consumption and production requirements on the other. To mention some of these market functionaries, they are commission agents or *arhatiyaṣ*, wholesale traders, *dalals* or brokers, processors, mill agents, weighmen, *palledars*, etc.

Since the produce is not immediately disposed of to the ultimate consumer, the problem of storage naturally comes in. Even the movement of such produce from the primary traders to the secondary traders or from the primary markets (hats) to the secondary markets (*arhat* or *gola*), involves a time lag, the cost of storage becomes a part of the price to be included at the point of sale. Sometimes some secondary markets do have, however, adequate storage facilities like pucca godowns and cold storages but most of the time in primary market centres miserably inadequate storage facilities become chiefly responsible for the rat nuisance or deterioration by rottening of the produce. Underdeveloped or undeveloped infrastructure of such markets is accountable for loss to the primary producer or primary trader, less price to the farmers and, what is more important, the wastage of foodgrains and other agricultural produces.

Disposal of the produce from producers to the distributors or consumers involves other important problems such as cleaning, processing, grading, and weighing. In the absence of an established and functioning regulated market all over the country middlemen in the form of distributive agencies take undue advantage of the ignorance of the farmers. Due to lack of effective market intelligence services, ignorant peasants are exploited in terms of low price for their produce. Different types of weighing is always a matter of dispute between the producer and the tradesman. From the point of view of distribution of agricultural inputs also, a developed market is an incentive to produce more. The extension and regulation of all agricultural markets is thus a necessary requirement of the optimum production process.

MARKETING ORGANISATIONS

Prior to 1928, agricultural marketing received little attention in India. However, in 1928, the Royal Commission on Agriculture in its report drew pointed attention to the serious disadvantages suffered under the unorganized marketing of agricultural products in the country and emphasized the need for evolving an efficient marketing system for agricultural products. The Commission recommended the appointment of marketing experts in the Agriculture Departments of all the major "provinces". Till that time there was no official agency directly concerned with agricultural marketing. The Central Banking Enquiry Committee, in 1931 while endorsing the recommendations of the Royal Commission, further recommended the setting up of a central agency for initiating and coordinating state activities relating to the development of agricultural marketing. As a result of these recommendations, the Government of India set up in 1935 a central organization known as the "Office of the Agricultural Marketing Advisor to the Government of India". The organization later expanded and was renamed as Directorate of Marketing and Inspection (DMI). It is presently under the Ministry of Agriculture.

THE DIRECTORATE OF MARKETING AND INSPECTION

The Directorate endeavours to bring about integrated development of agricultural marketing system in the country. It envisages safeguarding the interests of producer-sellers; as well as the consumers. It maintains a close liaison between the central and the state governments in the implementation of agricultural marketing policies in the country. The Directorate works under the Ministry of Agriculture, and is headed by the Agricultural Marketing Adviser.

The Directorate has its Head Office at Faridabad (Haryana) and Branch Head Office at Nagpur (Maharashtra). It has eleven Regional Offices and 37 sub-offices. A network of 22 Agmark laboratories operate under the CAL, Nagpur headed by the Director of Laboratories. The activities of the Directorate include: (i) Rendering advice on statutory regulation, development and management of agricultural produce markets to the States and Union Territories (ii) Promotion of grading and standardization of agricultural and allied products under the Agricultural Produce (Grading & Marking) Act, 1937 as amended in 1986; (iii) Market Research, Surveys and Planning; (iv) Training of Personnel in agricultural marketing; and (v) Administration of Meat Food Products Order, 1973.

Grading and Standardisation

The grade standards notified under Agricultural Produce (Grading and Marking) Act, 1937 as amended in 1986 are popularly known as Agmark Standards and such grade standards for 162 agricultural and allied commodities have been notified under the Act so far. The purity standards under the provisions of the Prevention of Food Adulteration (PFA) Act, 1954 and Bureau of Indian Standards (BIS) Act, 1986 are invariably taken into consideration while framing the grade standards. The important commodities graded under `Agmark' for internal consumption include cotton, vegetable oils, ghee, cream, butter, wheat, atta, suji, maida, besan, pulses, cotton, eggs, ground nut, spices and honey. For securing adequate return to farmers, 4181 grading units at production level were functioning by the end of March 1998. A special scheme for grading of seed cotton (kapas) at producer's level was in operation in 25 centres spread over several stages. Compulsory grading and pre-shipment inspection prior to exports was in force in respect of 40 commodities. During the year 2000-01 (upto September, 2000), commodities valued at Rs. 3500 thousand were graded for export.

The network of Regional Agmark Laboratories (RAL) under the Central Agmark Laboratory (CAL) which is the Apex Laboratory helps to check and ensure the purity and quality graded under Agmark. The CAL and the RALs at Mumbai, Delhi, Kolkata, and Chennai are also provided with veterinary biological control testing units. Besides the authorized packers, State Marketing Departments, etc. have also set up laboratories. Presently, 511 laboratories of the authorized packers, 46 commercial laboratories, 14 States Grading Laboratories and 12 Cooperative Laboratories (total 683) are engaged in testing of products and assigning the Agmark grader.

Regulation of Markets

The DMI, as central advisory organization, has been providing technical assistance and advice to the States in framing suitable market legislation. For this purpose, the DMI has framed a "Model Act" which provides guidelines for framing of legislation. Due to constant endeavour of DMI, all States and UTs except Manipur, Kerala, Andaman & Nicobar Islands, Lakshadweep and Dadra & Nagar Haveli have enacted legislation. The Jammu & Kashmir Assembly has passed the Bill on Market Regulation in the State. The DMI is pursuing with remaining States/UTs for enactment of necessary legislation.

Training of Personnel

Personnel from different states are provided training in various fields of agricultural marketing by the Directorate of Marketing and Inspection and the National Institute of Agricultural Marketing (NIAM). During the year 2000-01, NIAM planned to conduct 129 training programmes covering most of the states in the country. Of these 48 training programmes were conducted till November, 2000.

Market Extension

With the object of developing orderly marketing, extension work among the producers and consumers is carried out by the Directorate through various media like documentaries, cinema slides, exhibitions and printed literature. The DMI organized two `AGMARK' exhibitions during 1999-2000 and participated in the India International Trade Fair,

2000 and AHARA - 2000 at New Delhi. As part of its programme to create awareness about quality, the DMI conducted 788 programmes in different schools/colleges during 1999-2000. A quarterly Journal "Agricultural Marketing" is brought out by DMI for the benefit of farmers, traders and consumers.

Market Research and Survey

Four studies relating to the planning of wholesale markets for fruits and vegetables are at various stages of completion. Marketing Planning and Design Centre (MPDC) of DMI prepares State Master Plan for the development of Agricultural Produce Markets and imparts training to the personnel of State Governments/Marketing Boards for the preparation of State Master Plan. Draft of the Master Plan for Market Development in Mizoram State is almost complete.

The NIAM has also taken up long-term projects for the formulation of State Master Plans for the Development of Agricultural Produce Markets in the States of Madhya Pradesh and Tripura. Further, the Institute has taken up case studies on post-harvest management of various commodities and formulation of integrated action plan for promotion of handlooms and handicrafts in Varanasi (Uttar Pradesh) and Nadia (West Bengal) districts in collaboration with the Institute of Rural Management, Anand. Apart from this, NIAM has taken up Research Projects on the Action Plan for Horticulture Produce Marketing and an All India Research Study on Cost and spread of margins in vegetables. The NIAM has also taken up case studies on the following subjects:

- Study of Chilli production, procurement and marketing in Tonk District of Rajasthan.
- Problem areas in the development of spices in Rajasthan.
- Marketing practices and problems of fruits and vegetable growers in Jammu & Kashmir.
- Study of oilseed production of Rajasthan.
- Spatial distribution of markets in Southern Jaipur.
- Organizational and functional pattern of Chaksu market.

The Institute has also undertaken Online Market Information System for the States of Maharashtra and Uttar Pradesh. The project for the state of Maharashtra was hoisted in the month of May, 2000. Project for Uttar Pradesh is in progress. A scheme for estimation of marketable surplus and post-harvest losses in foodgrain was launched by the Ministry during the year 1995-96 in 100 selected districts of 25 States. An amount of Rs. 3.43 crores has been released to Designated State Agencies for conducting the field survey under the scheme. The Directorate has regularly been undertaking commodity marketing surveys and indepth studies of marketing system in respect of various agricultural commodities. More than 325 reports covering nearly 50 important commodities have been published so far.

Regulatory Measures

The government monitors market conduct through an imposition of several regulatory measures. The regulatory framework consists of two distinct sets of measures. The first set of measures is the development and regulation of wholesale markets, popularly called 'Regulated Markets' and the second is the regulation of market conduct through a series of legal instruments. The regulation of marketing practices in wholesale markets, in the form of Agricultural Produce Market Acts of various state governments, was adopted so as to create an orderly marketing system for farmers at the primary market level. As the programme was a development-cum-legal measure, it took considerable time to broaden its scope. The programme developed momentum after the mid-sixties and now, out of 7169 wholesale markets in the country, as many as 7001 are encompassed by the market regulation programme. During 1992-93, agricultural commodities worth Rs. 62000 crores were traded in these wholesale markets. This was around 58 per cent of the total value of marketable surplus of agricultural commodities.

The term 'regulated markets' in India results from a Royal Commission Report and refers to institutional arrangements. Regulated markets are in the nature of physical and institutional infrastructures and represent the first contact point for farmers to encash their market surpluses. The infrastructure created in these markets includes suction platforms, parking spaces, traders shops and farmers rest-houses. This apart, a management committee, with more than half the number of members from amongst farmers, prescribes the market fee and charges for various services. It also specifies procedures for the settlement of disputes among sellers and buyers. In return for these services, the regulated market committees charge a fee varying from 0.5 per cent to 2.0 per cent ad valorem from the buyer or seller of the produce in these markets. The type of infrastructure created in these markets depends on the expected scale of arrivals. Out of 7001 regulated markets, a higher-level infrastructure has been provided for in 2281, which are called 'market yards', whereas, a lower level of infrastructure exists in 4720 of these markets, which are known as 'sub-yards'. If may be mentioned here that apart from 7169 wholesale markets, there are around 27040 locations (haats, shaties or shandies) in rural areas where farmers and other rural people congregate periodically to sell their surpluses and purchase articles. Out of these, only about 15 per cent are reported to have been provided with the physical infrastructure needed so far. The periodic markets operate on specified weekdays and are located on barren land or along side village pathways.

Apart from the Agricultural Produce Market Acts of various states, the activities of market functionaries are regulated by several other legal instruments, which are also promulgated by the Centre and the State governments. These apart, various state governments also issue

Orders/Notifications under the Essential Commodities Act so as to regulate the conduct of market functionaries. These include the following:

Agriculture Produce (Grading and Marking) Act, 1937, 1986
Prevention of Food Adulteration (PFA) Act, 1954, 1964, 1976, 1986
Essential Commodities Act, 1955
Solvent Extracted Oil, Deoiled Meal and Edible Oil (control) Order, 1967
Meat Food Products Order, 1973
Standards of Weights and Measures Act, 1976
Pulses, Edible Oilseeds and Edible Oils (storage control) Order, 1977
Vegetable Oil Products (control) Order, 1977
Prevention of Black Marketing and Maintenance of Supply of Essential Commodities Act, 1980
The Cold Storage Order, 1964, 1980 (rescinded in 1997)
Consumer Protection Act, 1986
Bureau of Indian Standards Act, 1986
Milk and Milk Products Order, 1992
Fruit Products Order (FPO), 1955, 1997.

Cold Storage and Meat Products

The Cold Storage Order, 1980 which was uniformly applicable throughout the country except in the States of Haryana, Punjab, Uttar Pradesh and West Bengal. It was promulgated under Section 3 of Essential Commodities Act, 1955 to ensure hygienic and proper refrigeration conditions in the cold storages all over the country. This has been repealed with effect from 27th May, 1997 with a view to removing the controls laid down in the said Order in the areas of licensing, price control and requisitioning of cold storage space etc. and allow functioning of free market mechanism for demand based growth of cold storage industry in the country free from all kinds of administrative interference.

The objective of the Meat Food Products Order, 1973 is to ensure quality control and hygienic manufacturing conditions of meat food products for domestic consumption and the Order is applicable all over the country. A total of 173 licences have been issued to the manufacturers operating under the Order. Necessary amendments are being proposed to be made in the Order to streamline the implementation of the Order in a broad based manner, keeping in view the interests of the manufacturers and licence holders in the meat food products industry.

MARKETING COOPERATIVES

Generally speaking, prior to Independence, only a few sporadic efforts were made in the development of cooperative marketing. In 1945, the

Cooperative Planning Committee recommended that, within 10 years, 25 per cent of the total annual marketable surplus should be sold through cooperative organization, and, for this purpose, a marketing society should be organized at each of the 2,000 mandies in the country; it appeared that no planned efforts were made to implement this recommendation. Cooperative marketing did not make much headway until independence in 1947. In fact, at the time of independence, the annual value of all types of agricultural produce marketed by co-operatives in the country did not exceed even 7 per cent of the total market produce. In 1951, when the All India Rural Credit Survey was carried out, it was observed that out of 75 districts selected for the survey, there was no cooperative marketing in as many as 63 districts. Out of the remaining 12 districts, the share of cooperatives in the marketing of agricultural produce exceeded one per cent of the total sales to all agencies in only 5 districts.

The All-India Rural Credit Survey Report of 1951-52 recommended that for an effective solution of the marketing and credit problems of farmers, there should be proper integration of cooperative credit societies and cooperative marketing societies in the rural areas. The successive five year plans have also repeatedly stressed the need for development of cooperative agencies for handling marketable surpluses in agricultural crops. Before 1954, separate cooperative marketing societies were established as distinct from the cooperative credit societies. Since 1954, however, multipurpose societies have been started with the purpose of giving credit to the farmers and marketing their surplus produce.

The cooperative marketing society functions in the following manner. The members of the society agree to sell their surplus produce to the society. As soon as they supply the produce to the society, they get an advance to carry on with their agricultural operations. The society collects the produce of all the members as also of the nonmembers of the village who are willing to sell their produce, often processes the produce and then disposes it of in the mandi. It does away with many of the middlemen. If the current prices are not favourable and if it is anticipated that prices may rise in the future, the society may decide to stock the commodity. As soon as the produce is sold, the society pays the farmers the balance of the amount due to them. An important feature of the marketing society is that it is managed by paid staff. Usually a society covers a number of villages so that it may be effective and successful.

Advantage of Cooperative Marketing Societies

In some of the Western countries, cooperative marketing has been extremely successful. Denmark has been well-known throughout the world for cooperative marketing of dairy products. Many advantages are claimed for agricultural marketing on cooperative basis. They are:

(a) The marketing society substitutes collective bargaining in place of individual bargaining. The farmer by himself is weak but the marketing society is said to be strong.
(b) It advances loans to the farmers and enables them to wait for better prices. Besides, it lends to them for their other needs. Thus, cooperative marketing societies can link credit, farming, marketing and processing to the best advantage of the farmers.
(c) It can have its own storage and warehousing facilities, it can thus remove the damage to agricultural produce through rats, ants, dampness etc.
(d) It can arrange to have quick and cheap transport and sometimes it can even have its own transport.
(e) It can encourage the farmers to produce graded and standardized products and discourage them from adulterating their produce.
(f) It can control the flow of supplies and thus influence the prices.
(g) It can eliminate many of the middlemen and thus remove their large-profit margins.
(h) Apart from selling the produce of the farmers it can supply them such essential goods as seeds, fertilizers, implements, etc. Thus the cooperative marketing society is probably the best method to reorganize rural marketing and promote planned growth of our rural areas.

Development of Cooperative Marketing

There is great scope for the development of cooperative marketing societies. In the first place, there is the necessity to coordinate better farming, finance and marketing. At present efforts are being made to have one society which will perform all the three services for the farmers. Secondly, the marketing societies increasingly undertake processing of agricultural goods. Several agricultural goods can be more favourably marketed if they are processed before sale. Cotton can be ginned and pressed; oilseeds can be crushed and oil may be sold; jute can be processed and baled; and so on. Thirdly, the cooperative marketing societies can attempt to sell agricultural goods to consumers directly (wherever this is possible) and thus eliminate the middlemen and their commission.

Fourthly, the cooperative marketing societies should be made to grade their goods. The grading facilities may be made available to them by the Government through the Agricultural Marketing Department. Grading will not only help the societies to secure better prices for their produce but also induce them to bring pressure upon their members to improve the quality of their products through the use of improved seeds, etc. Fifthly, the cooperative marketing societies are going for their own storage and warehousing facilities in the rural areas and "mandis". This may be promoted through the provision of grants and subsidies by the Government or through cheap finance provided by the State Bank and the Reserve Bank of India. Sixth,, the area of operation of the cooperative marketing society should be expanded to cover many villages (if necessary, even a tehsil) so that it may render effective marketing service to the farmers. This will also enable it to engage qualified men to manage its affairs.

Seventh, there is very great scope for cooperative marketing societies to supply inputs to their members, such as fertilizers, certified quality seeds, agricultural machinery and implements, pesticides etc. Nearly 47 per cent of the total fertilizers distributed in the country are sold through cooperative marketing societies. Finally, the government should use the cooperative marketing societies whenever it is possible and necessary. The Food Corporation of India should buy foodgrains from the cooperative marketing societies and thus eliminate the usual channels of trade. This will encourage the formation of cooperative marketing societies.

Diversification of marketing is an important task which should be taken up by the cooperative. For this product identification is a must, i.e., where we can produce efficiently on the basis of comparative advantage. The product obtained in this way will have ample export potential—a need of the hour when the world is globalizing at a faster pace. The cooperative, therefore, would have to undertake a survey of total agricultural scenario to identify the possibility of export of agricultural commodity from one state to another and finally within the state: and also to other countries. The task is complex owing to vast range of agricultural produce grown in this country.

Progress in Cooperative Marketing

Over the last five decades, the cooperative marketing infrastructure has covered almost all the important wholesale assembling markets in the country and the cooperative marketing societies have also attained significant growth in their business. However, the progress of cooperative marketing has not been evenly spread throughout the country. The bulk of cooperative marketing is confined to only five states, namely, Maharashtra, Uttar Pradesh, Gujarat, Punjab and Karnataka. These five states account for nearly 80 per cent of the agricultural produce marketed by all the cooperatives in the country.

Further, the commodity spread of cooperative marketing is also still restricted mainly to foodgrains, sugarcane and cotton. Among these, cooperatives have gained importance in foodgrains mainly as state procurement agencies under the levy as well as price support scheme. The sugarcane supply societies have developed in the major sugarcane growing states of Uttar Pradesh, Bihar, Punjab and Haryana, largely in response to the restriction imposed on sugarcane growers to supply cane to the nearest sugar factories only. In cotton, the State Monopoly Procurement Scheme in Maharashtra, which enjoins all cotton growers to sell kapas only to the state government, has boosted the cooperative sales. Among other commodities, cooperatives have made hardly any progress, particularly, in oilseed, jute and even horticultural crops.

The network of cooperative marketing structure now comprises over 6,000 primary marketing societies, of which 3,500 are special commodity marketing societies, at the district level, there are 160 central marketing societies, covering nearly all the important mandis in the country; at the state level, there are 29 special purpose state level Cooperative Marketing Federations and 16 special Commodity Marketing Federations.

Role of NAFED

In 1958, an organization called National Agricultural Cooperative Marketing Federation Ltd. (NAFED) was established at the centre, to coordinate the activities of the State Marketing Federations and also to render advice and technical guidance to these societies. NAFED promotes cooperative marketing of agricultural produce for the benefit of farmers through its Headquarters at Delhi, four regional offices at Delhi, Mumbai, Kolkata and Chennai and 32 branches located in the state capitals and other important cities, five Agro Service Centres, four sales outlets of processed foods and five Industrial Units. This organization has also been undertaking export and interstate trade of agricultural commodities.

An organization called National Cooperative Development Corporation (NCDC) was set up in 1963, to finance and coordinate the activities of cooperative institutions. Its main functions are to plan and promote programmes for production, processing, marketing, storage and advance loans and/or grant subsidies for financing the cooperative institutions for development. This is an organization interposed between the states and central government in channelling finance and rendering technical guidance for development of marketing and processing cooperatives. While the functioning of the NCDC encompasses the activities of all types of cooperative institutions in their entity, the functioning of the NAFED limits itself to the agricultural marketing sphere (NCA, 1976).

It exports agricultural produce like onion, pulses, chillies, ginger, garlic, cardamom and potato etc. to many countries. It also undertakes movement of essential commodities from surplus areas to scarcity areas and helps in easing consumer supplies. NAFED is a central nodal agency for undertaking price support operation for pulses and oil seeds and market intervention operation for pulses, oil seeds and horticulture items like kinoo/malta, potato, black pepper, onion, grapes and red chillies etc. In general NAFED has played a useful role in establishing market prices of such commodities like onion and potatoes in principal producing areas through strategic market interventions. Under the guidance of NAFED, most of the state cooperative marketing federation have set up technical and promotional cells which offer the services of refrigeration, engineering oil and fruit processing export market specialist, cost accountant etc.

Cooperative Marketing of Agro-inputs

With the introduction of new agricultural technology need for intensive application of inputs such as fertilizer, seed etc. was felt. Moreover, need to bridge the gap between the fertilizer demand and supply was also realized. Thus the government of India in the year 1965, invited private as well as the cooperative to play their role in manufacture and distribution of fertilizers; and since 1975 its plants situated at Aonla and Phulpur (U.P.) Hazira, Kalol and Kandla (Gujarat) started functioning. Through these production units IFFCO contributes 22 per cent together of manufacture and distribution of different types of fertilizers. IFFCO is also carrying out farming as well as environment related work. Cooperative is also working in the field of distribution of improved seeds, but it has not been taken up seriously. Distribution of pesticides is limited to the states of Andhra Pradesh, Kerala, Madhya Pradesh, Punjab, Tamil Nadu and Uttar Pradesh.

Cooperatives Allowed to Become Companies

In August, 2001, the Cabinet cleared amendments to the Companies Act, 1956, that would allow major cooperatives such as Gujarat Cooperative Milk Marketing Federation, the makers of Amul dairy products, to convert themselves into companies and thus become eligible for institutional financing.

The registration as companies would also take these cooperative societies out of the purview of State Cooperatives Act and/or Multi-state Cooperatives Act as applicable and give them operational autonomy. This would imply Registrar of Cooperative Societies would not be able to interfere in the affairs of a cooperative company or a producer company, dissolve it or supersede it. Most importantly, these cooperative bodies would be freed from political interference.

As per the draft Bill to amend the Companies Act any cooperative which have objects/operations extending beyond boundaries of one state would be eligible for conversion even if all its members are drawn from a single state. The proposed amendment would largely benefit milk cooperatives, many of which have been lobbying for this option, as well as cooperatives of other agriculture produce such as sugarcane.

However, even as a cooperative society converts itself into a company, they would continue to retain certain characteristics of a cooperative. For instance, voting rights would be based on the principle of one vote per member, irrespective of their shareholding. Proxy voting would not be allowed. In a public or private company, voting rights are determined by the shareholding. Shareholding in a producer company would be restricted to the members.

A cooperative seeking to convert itself into a company would be required to adopt a resolution in favour of the transformation with at least two-thirds majority at a general body meeting. Reconversion of a producer company into cooperative would be difficult.

Under the proposed amendments, the producer company would be required to appoint full time professional as chief executive to direct the day-to-day management of the business, make arrangements for maintenance of proper books of accounts, preparation of annual accounts, audit of the annual accounts and discharge other duties, and exercise other powers as may be set out and delegated by the board.

TYPES OF MARKETS

Agricultural marketing is a process which starts with decision to produce a saleable farm commodity and involves all aspects of marketing structure or system, both functional and institutional, based on technical and economic considerations. In India, marketing channel starts traditionally either in the village or in the nearest `hat' or `shandi' where the goods are exchanged into cash. The system of marketing of farm produce that developed in this country during the last century or more was, by and large, dictated by the socioeconomic conditions that prevailed during that period. As a result of the changes in the pattern of agricultural production from the level of village self-sufficiency to that of export-oriented commercial farming, many market centres sprang up during the first half of the nineteenth century at convenient points where transport and communication facilities were available. Each market centre initiated and developed its own trade practices and code of business.

Markets for agricultural commodities can be broadly classified into three groups: (i) hats and shandies: (ii) wholesale markets or mandies; and (iii) retail markets. Hats and shandies are markets periodically held, the former usually once or twice a week and the latter either at longer intervals or on special occasions.

A High Power Committee on Agricultural Marketing was constituted in January, 1992 under the chairmanship of Mr Shankarlal Guru, former chairman of Council of State Agricultural Marketing Boards (COSAMB), New Delhi, to review the present State Market Acts and working of various agricultural marketing bodies and to recommend appropriate measures for streamlining and strengthening the set up for marketing of agricultural produce. The High Power Committee in their report has submitted 81 recommendations to the Government, out of which 58 recommendations have been accepted and 21 recommendations rejected. The accepted recommendations have been communicated to the State Governments/UT administrations for implementation. Further, the recommendations have been discussed in the first meeting of Ministers-in-charge of Agricultural Marketing of all States/UTs held on 30th January, 1997 at New Delhi.

The States/UTs have been directed to implement the recommendations of the High Power Committee as early as possible.

Most mandies, particularly those in the producing areas, function as both primary and secondary markets. Primary markets are those where the bulk of the produce is brought for sale by the producer himself. The primary markets serve as feeding centres for the secondary markets which are usually wholesale markets and serve as the second point of assembling, the first being the primary market. Terminal markets are those from where the produce is exported outside. Such markets could also be primary and secondary markets.

Bulk of marketed surplus of the farmers is usually sold in the village. The All-India Rural Credit Survey shows that about 65 per cent of the total sales of crops are effected in the village. There are many reasons for the bulk of the produce being sold by the farmer in the village. The farming units are small and many farmers do not possess any transport and road development is not quite adequate. Farmers are illiterate and the market information service is yet to have its ramifications in the villages. The system of agricultural credit is defective. The farmer has still to depend on the village merchant for loans and quite often the farmer gives an undertaking to the merchant that he will sell his produce to the latter.

In many areas keen competition among the buyers makes the village prices quite fair and attractive as compared with the prices in mandies. It is only in backward areas that the margin of difference between the village and market price is large and the prices offered to the former are unfavourable as compared with the prices in the mandi. The conditions of marketing in the mandies are not always attractive to the small producer. He gets less attention, there are a number of unauthorized deductions and he fails to understand the complicated sale system in the mandi. This happens mainly due to absence of regulated markets or non-functioning of the regulated markets.

Rural Market

There are nearly 5,65,000 villages in the country. Over 60 per cent of the villages have fewer than 500 people each, accounting for 20 per cent of the rural population. Nearly half the rural population lives in villages which have a population between 1,000 and 5,000 each and 4,000 of the bigger villages, with other 5,000 people each, account for less than 10 per cent of the country's population. Moreover, thousands of villages are well outside the reach of the railway, and roads are the only way of reaching them. The roads, being in poor shape, are unusable during the monsoon. The multitude of levies, permits, and licences constitute a major impediment in the free movement of goods from villages to the urban areas and from one state to another. Surely the advantages of developing a region outweigh the extra income accruing from such levies and tolls.

Road transport and the freer movement of goods play crucial role in hastening the pace of industrialization. On the road transport industry will fall a large share of the burden of opening up rural markets and its past record entitles it to encouragement. There is the difficult problem of ascertaining new ways of communicating with the villagers. There are, however, two hopeful factors. One, the younger generation are becoming educated and, two, in the well-to-do rural communities between 80 and 90 per cent of the villagers own radio sets. Radio coverage now caters to a population of 97.3 per cent spread over 90 per cent area of the country. Similarly Doordarshan covers 87 per cent of population and 70% area. However, despite All India Radio's rural programmes, the potential of the radio as a means of educating the rural masses has barely been tapped. It has been found that one of the best ways of communicating with the illiterate villager is through the medium of films carried by mobile vans. The government should adopt this method more widely for educating and informing the farmer. Television has also made very good inroads in the rural areas. This medium also may be fully utilized for making the producer-sellers more knowledgeable.

Socioeconomic surveys have revealed that there is a great deal of difference in the prosperity of different districts-not all rural areas are poor as is generally believed. There are variations in the incomes of farm families in different districts. Surveys have also revealed that the first priority on surplus income is food and the next priority is farm inputs-tube wells, pumping sets, implements, hybrid seeds, and grain storage. In other words, if our planners improve the infrastructure of development, such as roads, water, and power supply, the farmer himself will put 25 to 60 per cent of his surplus income into agriculture. This in turn will increase the demand for agricultural inputs and help to raise per capita income in the rural areas (Fig. 22.1).

Trends indicate that the rural markets are coming up in a big way and growing twice as fast as the urban, witnessing a rise in sales of hitherto typical urban kitchen gadgets such as refrigerators, mixer-grinders and pressure cookers. According to a National Council for Applied Economic Research, (NCAER) study, there are as many 'middle income and above' households in the rural areas as there are in the urban areas. There are almost twice as many 'lower middle income' households in rural areas as in the urban areas. At the highest income level there are 2.3 million urban households as against 1.6 million households in rural areas. Money available to spend on FMCG (Fast Moving Consumer Goods) products by urban India is Rs. 49,500 crores as against is Rs. 63,500 crores in rural India.

As per NCAER projections, the number of middle and high income households in rural India is expected to grow from 80 million to 111 million by 2007. In urban India, the same is expected to grow from 46 million to 59 million. Thus, the absolute size of rural India is expected

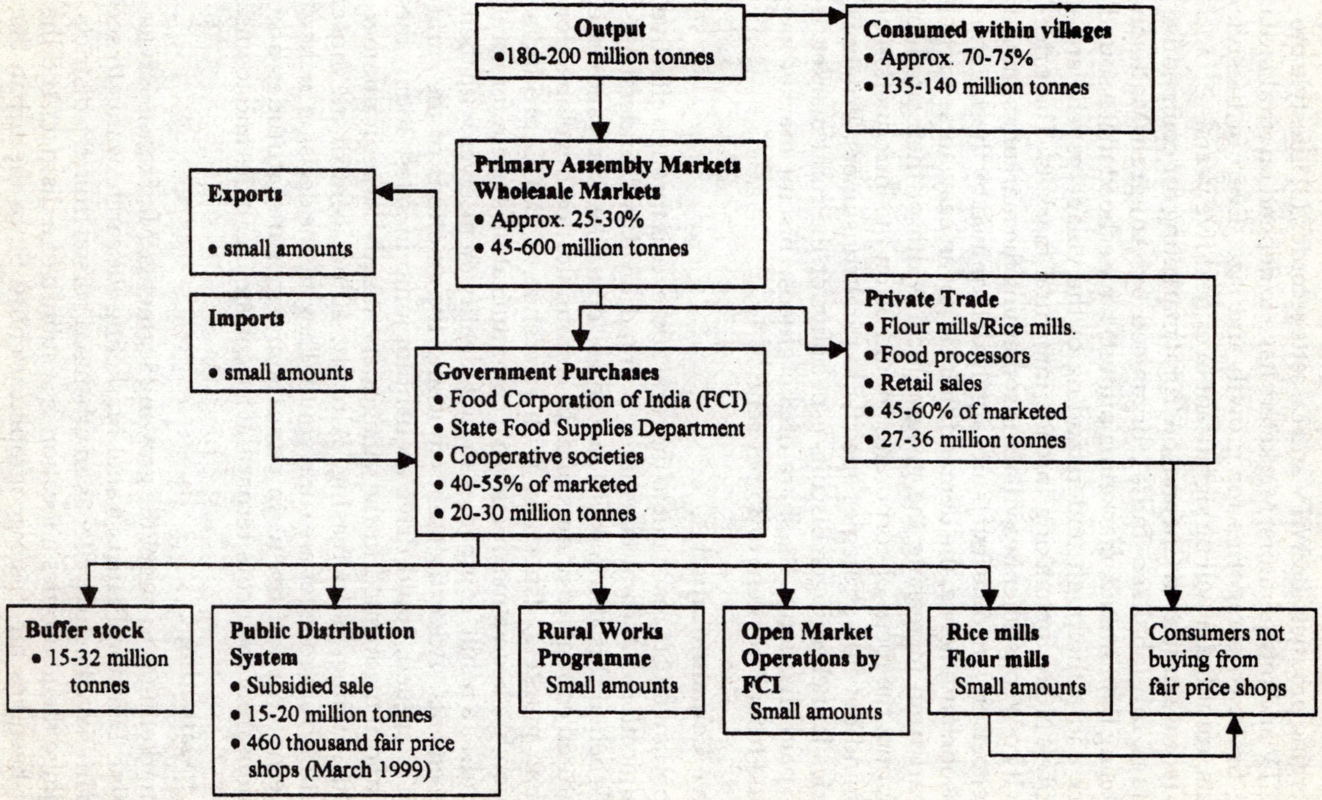

Fig. 22.1 An overview of grain marketing in India in the 1990s

SOURCES: 1. Chaudhri (1988), 'Food price policy in India and Indonesia', pp. 58-59; 3. GOIb, Bulletin on Food Statistics, various issues.

to be double that of urban India. The study on ownership of goods indicates the same trend. It segments durables under three groups: (1) necessary products-Transistors, wristwatch and bicycle, (2) Emerging products-B&W TV and cassette recorder, (3) Lifestyle products-CTV and refrigerators, Marketers have to depend on rural India for the first two categories for growth and size. Even in lifestyle products, rural India will be significant over next five years.

At a recent seminar in Chennai on 'rural marketing for competitive advantage in globalised India', organised by Anugrah Madison Advertising Pvt Limited, marketing pundits have echoed that a sound network and a thorough understanding of the village psyche are a SINE QUA NON for making inroads into rural markets. The price-sensitivity of a consumer in a village is something the marketers should be alive to. Rural income levels are largely determined by the vagaries of monsoon and, hence, the demand there is not an easy horse to ride on. Apart from increasing the geographical width of their product distribution, the focus of corporates should be on the introduction of brands and develop strategies specific to rural consumers. Britannia Industries launched Tiger Biscuits especially for the rural market. It clearly paid dividend. Its share of the glucose biscuit market has increased from 7 per cent to 15 per cent.

Effective Communication

An important tool to reach out to the rural audience is through effective communication. "A rural consumer is brand loyal and understands symbols better. This also makes it easy to sell look-alike. Rural audience has matured enough to understand the communication developed for the urban markets, especially with reference to FMCG products. Television has been a major effective communication system for rural mass and, as a result, companies should identify themselves with their advertisements. Advertisements touching the emotions of the rural folks, it is argued, could drive a quantum jump in sales. Today, the young and the educated in the villages are already large in number. And this number is increasing. Already, 40 per cent of all those graduating from colleges are rural youth. They are the decision makers and are not very different in education, exposure, attitudes and aspirations from their counterparts at least in smaller cities and towns.

District Marketing

Since marketing is to target the growing segments, Mr. Francis Xavier, Managing Director, Francis Kanol Marketing Research, wants to see the urban-like village dweller as an urbanised person from the districts. The village then becomes a location or a suburb of a district. And the district becomes the basic geographical entity. Since the urban-like populations in the villages are taken as a part of the district, they will represent the dominant part of the market in most of the districts. This will compel the kind of attention that it deserves. A districts perspective removes the complexities, heterogeneity, access and targetability that have hindered rural marketing initiatives. He feels that rural marketing requires every element of marketing including product, pricing, packaging, advertising, and media planning to have the rural customer as the target. And, this becomes possible when we have districts marketing as a separate entity.

Impact of Globalisation

The impact of globalisation will be felt in rural India as much as in urban. But it will be slow. It will have its impact on target groups like farmers, youth and women. Farmers, today 'keep in touch' with the latest information and maximise both ends. Animal feed producers no longer look at Andhra Pradesh or Karnataka. They keep their cell phones constantly connected to global markets. Surely, price movements and products' availability in the international market place seem to drive their local business strategies. On youth its impact is on knowledge and information and while on women it still depends on the socioeconomic aspect. The marketers who understand the rural consumer and fine tune their strategy are sure to reap benefits in the coming years. In fact, the leadership in any product or service is linked to leadership in the rural India except for few lifestyle-based products, which depend on urban India mainly.

Road-links and Transport

A market, particularly a rural one cannot be effective unless it is connected with a network of feeder roads with its hinterland. In agriculture, transportation is an indispensable input in the pre and post-harvest operations. Transportation bottlenecks adversely affect the production and marketability of goods and lead to heterogeneous market condition. Inadequate transport facilities are largely responsible for the slow rate of increase in marketing efficiency and for the continuance of subsistence farming in many areas. A well developed and efficient system of transport helps in expanding the size of market, reduces the transit time and economic cost of transportation. In fact, diffusion of agricultural innovation and the adoption of new agricultural practices is necessarily a function of good transportation. Overall growth of rural areas has been constrained by poor transportation services as people experience difficulties in procuring input materials and disposing of output, obstacles to penetration of new agricultural knowledge into villages, inability to implement improved margins due to high cost of production and lower output prices.

It may however he mentioned that since the beginning of the plan era efforts have been made to link all the villages, particularly those having a population of above 1500 with all weather roads. At the beginning of the eighth plan (1992-97), only about 10 per cent of the villages with a population of 1500 and above still remained unconnected, though in Bihar, Mizoram and West Bengal their proportion was 34, 42 and 40 per cent respectively. In the population category of 1000-1500 the target of covering 50 per cent of the villages had exceeded with the exception of Mizoram covering 44 per cent only (Government of India, 1992). Quoting from the study of Tata Consultancy Services Ltd., 1990, Sidhu (1990), however, states that present situation of linking the villages with all- weather roads is not at all satisfactory except in a few states like Punjab, Haryana and Kerala where almost all the villages have been connected with all-weather roads. On the other extreme are the states like Orissa, Rajasthan, Madhya Pradesh, where hardly 15, 21 and 23 per cent of the villages were connected by all-weather roads. He iterates that but for this, the market remains a dead weight particularly in the eastern region of the country where the directed price signals do not reach the farmers effectively to induce production through the adoption of new technology in agriculture.

Pradhan Mantri Gram Sadak Yojana

Keeping in view the fact that Rural Roads are vital to economic growth and to measures for poverty alleviation in the villages, Government's resolve to provide total Rural Connectivity was indicated in the Address of the Hon'ble president to the Joint Sitting of Parliament on 25th October, 1999, when a Programme of construction of all-weather roads in the rural areas was announced. The Rural Roads Programme as a component of the Pradhan Mantri Gramodaya Yojana (PMGY) was announced by the Finance Minister in his Budget Speech, 2000-2001. The Department of Rural Development had in January, 2000, set up a National Rural Roads Development Committee under the chairmanship of Mr Nitin Gadkari to assess the magnitude of the task, the volume of funds required and to suggest Implementation Strategies as also suitable Agencies for the same. The Committee submitted its Report in May, 2000. The gist of its recommendations are enclosed at Annexure 22.1.

In April, 2000, the Union Cabinet decided that 50% of the Diesel Cess would be set apart for Rural Roads and made available to the Ministry of Rural Development. In December, 2000, Parliament enacted legislation imposing Diesel Cess and earmarking 50% of the Cess to the Development of Rural Roads. In his Address to the Nation on 15th August, 2000, the Prime Minister stated: "For the first time since Independence, the Central Government has devised a well conceived and time-bound programme for rural roads. This hundred percent Centrally Sponsored Scheme, which is called the "Prime Minister's Rural Roads Scheme", aims to connect within the next three years, every village that has a population of more than one thousand, through good all-weather roads. By 2007, every village with a population more than five hundred will be similarly connected."

This Ministry of Rural Development, accordingly, drew up a Programme, the Pradhan Mantri Gram Sadak Yojana (PMGSY) which envisages an investment of about Rs. 60,000 crores to achieve the objectives outlined by the Prime Minister. The Pradhan Mantri Gram Sadak Yojana was launched by the Honb'le Prime Minister on 25th December 2000. Guidelines of the Programme have been issued to all the States/UTs. The primary focus of the programme is on construction of new roads. It is proposed to connect about 1 lakh villages in the next seven years. Besides, upgradation (to prescribed standards) about 5 lakh kilometres of existing roads will be taken up under the Programme, so as to achieve connectivity through a good All-weather roads. The key elements of the Pradhan Mantri Gram Sadak Yojana are as follows:

- Preparation of Master Plans- District Rural Roads Plans to be generated, based on Block-level Plans;
- Project Implementation Units to be formed to ensure professional and timely completion;
- Execution on a Project Mode;
- Ensuring Standard Specifications, including adequate cross-drainage works;
- Time-bound Execution- completion in 9-12 months; Penalty clauses for time overruns; No Escalation permitted;
- Strict Quality Control - independent Monitors to inspect works.

The Programme further envisages:

- Ready availability of Land for the Roads;
- Maintenance of the Roads by Panchayati Raj Institutions;
- Encouraging use of locally available materials for construction of roads;
- Planting of trees on either side of the roads.

Proposals worth about Rs. 658 crores had been approved by the end of January- 2001. It is assumed that the entire allocation of Rs. 2500 crores available for 2000-2001 had been released to the States.

MARKET FUNCTIONARIES

The human agency in the marketing process is an important consideration. The functionaries of the various marketing activities at market places adopt their own techniques of operation, procedure of business, and trading practices. Techniques of marketing and organization vary in accordance with the economic conditions, nature of the marketed product, the area and location of marketing, marketing agencies, and the rate of technical and commercial development.

There are several types of functionaries in the mandi such as arhatiyas or commission agents, dalals or commodity brokers, general agents, and agents for specific commodities and purposes.

Arhatiyas are of two kinds, namely kutcha and pucca. The kutcha one is primarily concerned with the assembling of the produce. He sometimes advances loans to the village merchants and traders on the condition that the produce purchased by them in the villages is sold in the mandi through him. Kutcha arhatiyas are more active in the vegetable and fruit markets. The pucca arhatiya acts on behalf of outstation buyers as well as on his own account. He makes advances to kutcha arhatiyas for purchases made on behalf of his clients. A dalal or broker is a person with no establishment of his own; his function is to bring together the sellers and the buyers. In addition to arhatiyas and brokers, as already mentioned, there are weighmen, sweepers, and labourers for stitching bags, loading and stocking of bags and bales.

The agencies in the chain of marketing from the producer to the manufacturer and the consumer depend upon the nature of the crop also. Paddy usually passes from the village merchant to the mill or to the wholesale dealer in the assembling market; and, from the mill, rice passes on to the wholesale dealer in the consuming market and then through one or more retailers to the consumer. Between the wholesaler or the miller on the producing end, and the wholesaler at the consuming end, a host of intermediaries exist and execute orders on the strength of samples.

In the case of groundnut, the route taken comprises the grower, the village merchant, the broker, the decorticating mill, the exporter's agents, and finally, the exporter. Similarly, in the marketing of tobacco, except in the case of cigarette tobacco which is bought by the manufacturers directly from the growers through depots established in the growing areas, many intermediaries exist between the producer and the assembling market. The existence of a long chain of intermediaries naturally reduces the share received by the actual cultivator out of the price paid by the ultimate consumer. In regulated markets there are paid marketing secretaries and other assisting staff.

Place and Time of Sale

Village sales account for a major part of the marketed agricultural produce. According to the Rural Credit Survey nearly 65 per cent of the total sales in 1951 were made in the village. This is, however, only an overall position. The marketing studies carried out by the Directorate of Marketing and Inspection, indicate considerable local variations in this respect. In Punjab, for instance, 35 per cent of paddy was estimated to have been brought to the assembling markets by cultivators as against only 3 per cent in some parts of Kerala. The direct sale by cultivators in the assembling markets depends on various factors. In some districts of Punjab with well-developed means of transport and communications, about four-fifths of the wheat crop is sold by the grower directly in the assembling markets. On the other hand, in other districts of the same state, lacking these facilities, the corresponding proportion is insignificant. A similar variation exists among districts in Uttar Pradesh. In the western Uttar Pradesh about one-third of the local surplus is estimated to be taken to the assembling markets by the growers. This proportion is very small in the eastern districts.

Marketing Charges

Since the bulk of the marketed produce comes to the assembling market for disposal, whether brought by cultivators themselves or by other agencies operating at the village level such as itinerant merchants, it is necessary to analyse the marketing charges for the assembling of produce. The main elements in these charges are arhat (commission), dalali (brokerage), karda (trade allowance), hamali (handling charges), tulai (weighing charges), and miscellaneous charges such as deduction for charities, market fees, fees levied by commission agents to cover the wages of his apprentices, payment to water-man, cook, sweeper, etc. Karda or trade allowance is a deduction in kind payable by the seller in order to compensate the buyer for loss in weight on account of impurities, driage, etc.

A noteworthy feature of these market charges is that they differ from market to market in magnitude and may be payable by the seller in some places and by the buyer in others. In Punjab, for instance, in some of the markets, commission charges are paid partly by the seller and partly by the buyer while in other markets it is paid solely by the former. Handling charges comprise of wages paid to labourers for unloading the cart, dressing the produce, and cleaning, etc. These charges are paid by sellers at some places and by buyers at other places. Deduction for charitable purposes forms a regular item in the list of customary marketing charges in almost all markets. The purposes for which this collection is made are numerous-social , educational and religious purposes being the most important.

In the post-assembling stage of marketing, marketing charges include expenses of transportation and handling from the point of delivery to the buyer's premises, the expenses of packing commission and brokerage, etc. As a general rule all these charges are paid in cash by the wholesaler or his agent. Although there are variations in these charges from market to market, these are not so pronounced as assembling costs. The reason for this is that the contracting parties in wholesale markets are more evenly matched than those in the assembling markets.

Defects in Marketing

However, there has been a change in the market structure since mid-sixties with the entry of various government agencies like Food

Corporation of India, Jute Corporation of India, Cotton Corporation of India, etc. and many of the intermediaries have been eliminated resulting in improvement of the producer's share in the consumer's rupee.

The defects in marketing of agricultural produce can be classified into two broad groups. The first group consists of various types of malpractices prevailing in the markets such as: (1) manipulation of weights and scales against the seller, (2) the practice of taking large quantities as sample, (3) arbitrary deductions from sale proceeds by the market functionaries under various pretexts, (4) sale under cover keeping the seller ignorant of price, and (5) discriminatory marketing charges. The extent of these malpractices varies from market to market and it is difficult to measure it with any precision. Some typical instances of these malpractices may be noted. The arhatiyas' commission is usually higher for small cultivators as compared to village merchants who, because of their large turnover, get better terms from the arhatiyas. This is also true of trade allowance or karad. Even in well-organized markets like Hapur and Ghaziabad, the cultivators ordinarily pay twice as much as the charges paid by village merchants.

The second group of defects in the marketing of agricultural produce arises out of inadequate facilities for transport and storage. This results in the simultaneous existence of pockets of scarcities and surpluses leading to wide inter-regional variations in prices. Another consequence flowing from preponderance of sale immediately after the harvest is wide inter-seasonal fluctuations in prices.

It has not been established that there is a direct relationship between the agricultural growth and availability of adequate marketing facility. This is quite evident from the fact that in the regions with high agricultural growth like northern, central and southern zones, the markets are much more developed than those of low growth region like eastern and northeastern regions. Even in the high growth regions, some of the available marketing facilities have become non-functional. For example, in Punjab, the markets which were established in the sixties and the seventies became outdated and too small to accommodate increased arrivals since eighties. In future, the markets need to be designed with a scope for expansion so that they are functional for at least four to five decades.

National Institute of Agricultural Marketing (NIAM)

The Institute started functioning at Jaipur (Rajasthan) with effect from 8th August 1988. It is managed by a Governing Body under the Chairmanship of Minister of Agriculture. All the executive and financial powers of the Institute are vested in the Executive Committee subject to the directions of the government of India and Governing Body. Director General is the Chief Executive of the Institute. The Main objectives of the Institute are as follows:

(i) To undertake a study of applied and operational research in problems of agricultural marketing.

(ii) To act as a national nodal point for coordination of various research studies and dissemination of technologies relevant to agricultural marketing in the country.

(iii) To undertake adaptive research aimed at vertical and horizontal integration of the marketing functions and functionaries so as to reduce the cost of marketing thereby ensuring a fair price to the growers and consumers.

(iv) To provide specialized training in agricultural marketing designed to develop leadership potential in the management of agricultural marketing enterprises and services.

(v) To undertake research in agricultural marketing for Government, Cooperatives and other institutions, both on public funding and by contract.

(vi) To offer other specialized marketing courses at various levels as may be necessary to supplement existing facilities.

(vii) To help State Governments and Urban/City authorities to formulate proposals for institutional funding from national and international agencies for their development projects relating to agricultural produce markets, on consultancy basis.

(viii) To study the internal market and distribution infrastructure for agricultural and allied products and suggest proposals for their improvement.

(ix) To offer technical services for the study, analysis and planning of physical distribution systems for agricultural produce on a State, Regional and National basis to State Governments, Public Sector Undertakings, Development Authorities and other State and Central agencies, both on public funding and by contract.

STORAGE

An important adjunct of efficient agricultural marketing is the adequate availability of scientific storage facility in the villages as well as in the market yards. Besides preventing losses, storage function performed with technical and economic efficiency, is expected to smoothen the availability of produce over different periods of the year and over several years, and also acts as cushion against intra-seasonal price fluctuations. The construction of large scientific storage started in the sixties, when public agencies took advantage of the huge marketable surpluses triggered by the adoption of new technologies, particularly in rice and wheat and entered the market in a big way for procurement of these commodities. The main agencies responsible for building storage capacity are Food Corporation of India (FCI), Central Warehousing Corporation (CWC) and State Warehousing Corporation (SWC). Besides, some state Marketing Federations, State Civil Supplies

Corporation and State Civil Supplies Departments have also built stores, though in a smaller scale.

To total storage capacity available with FCI as on 01-12-1999 was 24.5 million tonnes. Out of this, 10.0 million tonnes was hired from Warehousing Corporations, State Governments and Private Owners (Tables 22.1A and 22.1B). Notwithstanding the expansion in storage capacity over the years, there was a great strain following spectacular growth in foodgrains production with the wider diffusion of modern technology and the capacity continued to be insufficient. Hence, a sizeable portion (20.8 per cent) of foodgrains stock was kept stacked

Table 22.1A Storage/Warehousing Capacity with Public Agencies

(In lakh tonnes)

Agencies	*As on 31-03-1996*			*As on 31-03-1997*		
	Owned	Hired	Total	Owned	Hired	Total
FCI	124.14	82.52	206.66	124.23	50.53	194.76
CWC	51.30	18.45	69.75	51.93	19.26	71.19
SWCs	79.06	33.00	112.06	80.37	29.13	109.50
Agencies	*As on 31-03-1998*			*As on 31-03-1999*		
	Owned	Hired	Total	Owned	Hired	Total
FCI	124.34	67.26	191.60	125.03	66.53	191.56
CWC	52.29	19.99	72.28	53.65	19.83	73.48
SWCs	81.60	26.20	107.80	79.59	34.30	113.89
Agencies	*As on 01-12-1999*					
	Owned	Hired	Total			
FCI	125.69	68.63	194.32*			
CWC	53.80	20.06	73.86			
SWCs	84.66	35.31	119.97			

* The capacity of FCI includes 33.07 lakh MT capacity hired from the CWC and SWCs.

Table 22.1B Cap storage Capacity Owned

(In lakh tones)

Year	*Owned*	*Hired*	*Total*
1995-1996	16.02	41.42	57.44
1996-1997	14.94	14.72	31.66
1997-1998	15.53	16.56	32.09
1998-1999	16.30	25.55	41.85
1999-2000 (upto 01-12-1999)	20.01	31.08	51.09

under CAP (covered and plinth) and was exposed to rains, storms and bird damage. According to some estimates, out of the total storage losses, 92 per cent occurred to stock stacked under CAP, and only eight per cent in the godowns. The huge losses under CAP point to the necessity of building more scientific storage capacity.

REGULATED MARKETS

Most markets in India were unregulated till recently. Once the farmer goes with his produce to the market for any dispute arising between him and the middleman or the purchaser, he has to depend on the decision of his broker and arhatiya. The facilities for parking carts, drinking water, sanitation, etc., are not good. As mentioned earlier, there is considerable room for improvement in market places and sale procedure, system of payment of price, etc.

When the sales are not done by the open auction system, the farmer's interest is often lost sight of. Even in open auctions there may be a tacit understanding among the bidders not to bid high. For putting these malpractices to an end, marketing committees with strong representation of farmers' interests are necessary. A number of unfair practices like short weights, unwarranted deductions and higher rates of commission and other market charges prevalent in most of the mandis take away a substantial share of the price paid by the purchasers and place the farmers at a disadvantage vis-a-vis the more organized section of the trading class. The purpose of law and regulation is to improve competition, to strengthen bargaining power of the producer-seller and thus ensure a fair deal to the farmer. During the British regime, the regulated markets came into existence to help exports of industrial raw materials to England. But today the regulated markets have to play a positive role in the orderly development of marketing.

The anxiety of the British rulers to make available supplies of pure cotton to the textile mills at Manchester, originally motivated the desire for improving and regulating the marketing functionaries at the level of `Mandis'. Karenja was the first regulated market to be established in 1886 under the Hyderabad Residency's order. Subsequently, a special law known as "The Cotton & Grain Markets Law" was enacted in Berar, then known as "The Hyderabad assigned District" in 1897. The institution of regulated market thus came into existence. Having due regards to the socioeconomic conditions prevailing in they country, this type of reform at the primary level of marketing was first recognized for general adoption in the country by the central cotton committee, appointed by the government of India in 1918 and later it received wider recognition following the recommendation of the Royal Commission in Agriculture in 1928. Hyderabad was the first state in India to pass Agricultural produce Market Act in 1930. In that decade Madras, Central Provinces, Bombay, Mysore and Punjab enacted the necessary legislation.

The National Commission on Agriculture (1976) recommended that the facility of a regulated market should be available in general within a radius of 5 km or so. Though this target has remained still elusive, there has been phenomenal progress in the establishment of regulated markets since independence. Regulation of markets and market practices is now done under the Agricultural Produce Markets Act. The Directorate of Marketing and Inspection renders the necessary guidance and assistance to states in forming market legislation and its enforcement. Excepting the states of Mizoram and Jammu & Kashmir, all states have passed legislation for market regulation. Out of 7245 wholesale assembling markets in the country, the total number of regulated markets at the end of March 1994 was 6809, this increased to 7075 by March 1999.

The various state governments and union territories have enacted state Agricultural Produce Marketing Acts with the avowed object to provide for better regulation of sale and purchase of agricultural produce. There are 23 Agricultural Produce Market Acts in force in various States/UTs. The states of Jammu and Kashmir and Mizoram and the union territories of Andaman & Nicobar Islands, Dadra & Nagar Haveli and Lakshadweep have not passed the Act as yet. With a view to protecting the interests of the producer-sellers, the regulated markets aim at improving the efficiency of marketing at the assembling points which form the base of the marketing machinery. This is achieved by creating healthy competition. In fact, the establishment of well-organized markets is the first step for providing the much needed infrastructure. Its necessity has further enhanced with the spurt in production following technological breakthrough in a few crops (Table 22.2)

The legislation to regulate markets generally covers all the agricultural, horticultural, livestock and livestock products. The Act authorizes the state government to establish a market committee for every notified area consisting of representatives of cultivators, traders, local bodies, cooperative marketing societies, and the government. The principal aim of legislation is to ensure fair marketing conditions for cultivators through elimination of malpractices and unauthorized deductions. It stipulates the sale of produce through open auction in the presence of a representative of the market committee who notes down the particulars of buyers, quantity sold, price etc. It provides for licensing of market functionaries such as commission agents with provision for revocation of license if the market functionary is found to follow unfair practices. It also prescribes that no allowances other than those stipulated in the legislation shall be levied. In addition to the responsibility to ensure fair practices, the market committee is also entrusted with the function of hearing the disputes between buyers and sellers and giving decisions on them which would be binding on the parties.

Table 22.2 Number of Wholesale Assembling Markets and Regulated Market as on 31.2.1994.

Sl. No.	*State/U.T.*	*Whole Sale Markets*	*Regulated Markets*		
			Principal	*Sub-markets*	*Total*
1.	Andhra Pradesh	821	244	577a	821
2.	Arunachal Pradesh	--	--	--	--
3.	Assam *	172	15	19	34
4.	Bihar	443	122	706	828
5.	Goa	11	1	4	5
6.	Gujarat	377	155	222	377
7.	Haryana*	273	99	174	273
8.	Himachal Pradesh*	28	7	22	29
9.	Jammu & Kashmir	26	APMR ACT NOT YET PASSED		
10.	Karnataka	429	122	307	429
11.	Kerala	348	5	--	5(b)
12.	Madhya Pradesh*	633	290	293	583
13.	Maharashtra	833	256	566	822
14.	Manipur	20	--	--	--
15.	Meghalaya	111	--	--	--
16.	Mizoram	8	APMR ACT NOT YET PASSED		
17.	Nagaland	11	--	--	--
18.	Orissa	163	46	87	133
19.	Punjab*	667	143	524	667
20.	Rajasthan *	388	138	250	388
21.	Sikkim	10	--	--	--
22.	Tamil Nadu*	300	270	--	270
23.	Tripura	84	21	--	21
24.	Uttar Pradesh	645	262	383	645
25.	West Bengal*	214	41	415	456
26.	A & N Islands	--	APMR ACT NOT YET PASSED		
27.	Chandigarh*	3	1	2	3
28.	D & N Haveli	--	APMR ACT NOT YET PASSED		
29.	Daman & Diu	--	--	--	--
30.	Delhi	25	6	10	16
31.	Lakshadweep	--	APMR ACT NOT YET PASSED		
32.	Pondicherry	4	4	--	4
	TOTAL	7047	2248	4561	6809

* Figures are provisional;

(a) Represents additional markets at places other than headquarters of market committees.

(b) In Kerala markets are regulated under Commercial Crops Markets Act, 1933, in the Malabar Region of erstwhile Madras State.

Note: In some cases sub-yards include rural markets or cold stores and hence figures of total regulated markets and wholesale assembling markets are not comparable.

SOURCE: Directorate of Marketing & Inspection, Govt. of India.

The regulation of markets has been helpful in securing reduction in village sales, systematization of methods of sale and weighment, and reduction in market charges. Reduction in charges has varied from 33 to 66 per cent and unauthorized deductions have been completely eliminated. There has been a progressive increase in the produce brought to the regulated markets by the growers.

The National Commission on Agriculture (1976) recommended that the facility of a regulated market should be available in general; within a radius of 5 km or so. However, it was realizes that market regulation *ipso facto* does not provide a remedy to improve the sale and purchase operations in the market. The market should be able to provide adequate facilities, services and amenities to attract more and more market users. The Market Committees are not financially sound to take up development works to create the necessary infrastructure. During the seventies, the government of India launched a scheme of central assistance for the development of selected markets satisfying certain prescribed parameters. However, the amount granted was intended to serve as "margin money" for the Market Committees to enable them to approach the commercial banks for obtaining development loans. The main emphasis of the scheme has been on development of regulated periodic markets where predominantly small and marginal farmers bring their marketable surpluses for sale and, in turn, buy necessary articles and agricultural inputs.

A stage has come when these committees should play a more dominant part in improving the marketing structure than what they have been playing so far. They should serve as focal points for initiation and development of programmes not only in respect of marketing but also in terms of the overall development of agriculture in surrounding rural areas. In addition to providing the usual facilities and amenities, regulated markets should earmark sites for location of shops which may stock different agricultural inputs like improved seeds, fertilizers, pesticides, etc., needed by the farmers. The shops should also stock pumping sets and other small implements and machinery required by the farmers.

SOME STRUCTURAL CHARACTERISTICS OF AGRICULTURAL PRODUCE MARKETS

The conduct and performance of the market depends on the structure of the market, which varies from commodity to commodity. Several structural characteristics of the Indian agricultural produce market need to be noted. First, though Indian farmers do not sell the total output they produce, the size of the marketed surplus is quite large. According to one estimate, the value of farm products entering the marketing system during 1990-91 was Rs. 1067 billion which was around 64 per cent of the total value of agricultural output (Acharya,

1994).[1] Secondly, notwithstanding the direct intervention by the government, the markets for agricultural products in India have remained dominated by the private sector. According to one estimate, the quantity of agricultural produce handled by government agencies has been not more than 10 per cent of the total value of marketed surplus. Further, around 10 per cent of the marketed surplus was handled by the cooperatives (Acharya, 1994)[1]. Thus, private trade handles 80 per cent of the marketed surplus of agricultural products in India. Even in the case of cereals, the share of private trade is quite large and is on the increase. Of the estimated marketed surplus of cereals, the share of private trade, which was 72.5 per cent during Triennium Ending (TE) 1982-83 went upto 74.0 per cent during TE 1996-97. Out of the incremental output of 57.4 million tonnes between TE 1982-83 and TE 1996-97, the quantity handled by the public agencies was around 8 million tonnes. With larger quantities, which need to be handled by private trade, the size and structure of the open market, which was initially quite large, has considerably expanded further.

Third, for trade in foodgrains there are around two million wholesalers and five million retailers. Retailers include 4.10 lakh fair price shops operating under the PDS of which nearly three-fourths are in the private sector. On an average, there is one retail shop of foodgrains for a population of 200. Fourth, apart from wholesalers and retailers, processors enter the market as bulk buyers and sellers. In the case of paddy/rice, there are 91801 hullers, 4538 shellers, 8365 huller-cum-shellers and 34688 rice mills, which process the entire output of around 120 million tonnes of paddy. Nearly 30 per cent of paddy is milled by hullers and/or shellers which are less efficient than rice mills. It is estimated that around 4 million tonnes of rice is lost due to less efficient rice milling technologies. In the case of wheat, milling is done by 266000 chakkies and 812 roller flour mills. Chakkies operate on a very small scale. Roller flour mills buy, process and sell 10.5 million tonnes of wheat and wheat products. Out of the total output of pulses, nearly 75 per cent is processed in the organised as well as the unorganised sector. The number of organised pulse (dal) mills is now more than 10000.

Fifth, the Indian fruit and vegetable market is mainly a market for fresh products. Nearly 98 per cent of the fruits and vegetables produced in India are traded as fresh products. The commercial processing segment accounts for only two per cent of the total output. Though the processing capacity for fruits and vegetables has gone upto 19.1 lakh tonnes, due to the seasonality in production and lack of farmer-processor linkages, only half of the capacity is utilised at present.

---

[1] Acharya, S.S. Marketing Environment for Farm Products—Emerging Issues and Challenges, *Indian Journal of Marketing*, Vol. 8 No. 2, July–Sept. 1994.

Sixth, the market structure for meat includes 3600 slaughter houses, six modern abattoirs and 25 meat processing plants besides several poultry dressing units. There are 104 licensees functioning under the Meat Food Products Order, 1973. The structure of the processing capacity needs to be examined in relation to the total meat output in the country, which is estimated at 3.9 million tonnes. Seventh, apart from meat, the poultry sector is also emerging as one of the fastest growing sectors in India. The current production is 30 billion eggs and 350 million broiler and the sector is growing at a rate of 20 per cent per annum. The poultry network includes 600 hatcheries and 130 feed mills.[2]

Annexure 22.1

GIST OF RECOMMENDATIONS OF THE NATIONAL RURAL ROADS DEVELOPMENT COMMITTEE (MAY, 2000)

Mission

In order to free each and every village in the country from the handicaps and deprivation of lack of access and to provide all the facilities like health care, education, etc. To the entire rural population, the Government should take up on priority the task of providing good All-weather roads to each and every village in the country. A time bound programme should be drawn up for the task. Such roads should be very durable and should need no maintenance for several years after construction.

Phasing

Considering the huge magnitude of the task, the programme should be taken up in two phases. In Phase-I, all the villages with a population of 500 or more should be tackled. In Phase-II, the remaining villages may be taken up. During Phase-I, if any smaller villages are found to lie close to a road being constructed in that Phase, such smaller villages may also be tackled in Phase-I for ease of construction and economy. If it is found during detailed planning that any area or pocket with smaller villages is especially deprived, the culverts and small bridges on the proposed alignments for approach roads to such villages may be taken up in Phase-I. The work should be started by tackling about 40 to 50 districts at the outset, each State to have 7 districts with larger States getting an additional district.

---

[2] For more details refer to S.S. Acharya, *Indian Agricultural Policy at the Crossroads*, 2001, Rawat Publications, New Delhi.

Specifications

These roads should have a black top surface in view of the fast moving, pneumatic-tyred and heavy vehicles, which are plying even in rural areas today. The width of the carriage way should be 3.75 metres and the width of formation should be 7.5 metres. All the necessary cross drainage works and minor bridges should be constructed. The objective should be to ensure that in no case should the traffic be held up for more than 24 hours at a time and not more than six times a year even on the village roads. In some special cases, even major bridges may be constructed to ensure proper connectivity.

Authority

In order to ensure speedy and systematic execution of the programme, the Union Government should set up "National Rural Road Development Authority". Its Chairman should be of the status of a Cabinet Minister of the Union Cabinet, considering the onerous task entrusted to it.

Finances

The Authority should be authorized to raise finances for the programme by borrowing from suitable sources. The Union Government should guarantee the release of such loans. The Authority may also be given full freedom to tap any other sources of fund, which it may find suitable. The earmarked portion of special cess on petrol and diesel collected every year should be made available for this Scheme. The Rural Development Department should also make available to the Authority Rs. 2,500 crores each year from its outlays. This should be non-lapsable. The Central Government should also raise Rs. 5,000 crores by issuing tax-free bonds @ maximum 8% for the first 5 years. Interest on these bonds as well as guarantee for repayment should be given by the Central Government. However, principal repayment would be arranged by the Authority from its funds.

Execution

In order to ensure full accountability of the Authority to the lenders regarding the quality and proper standards of these works, the Authority should itself execute the programme with full cooperation from the State Government/Zilla Parishads. The Authority should not be only a machinery for reimbursement of expenditure on road works over which it has no control. Full cooperation of the State Government and the Zilla Parishads should be secured for the programme. Fixing the alignment of the road, should be done in consultation with Zilla Parishads and the State Government. The land acquisition will have to be done by the State Government. The State Government should also provide experienced personnel on deputation to the Authority whenever asked by it.

The Authority should carry out the works under this Programme in the districts where the local Zilla Parishads and the State Government permit the Authority to carry out these works. Where such permission is not forthcoming, the Authority should not carry out any work. For managing the actual construction of these roads in the districts, the corporation may set up its cells in each district. This cell should have bare minimum staff. For detailed field working, services of suitable qualified consultants may be used freely. In special difficult areas, the construction work could be entrusted to the BRO.

The Authority must carry out these works to a high standard of workmanship using modern machinery and latest methods. It should also strive to achieve all possible economy by using suitable technologies and materials. The Authority should have full freedom to decide the methodology of carrying out the survey and execution of the works. It should be made mandatory for the owner of the land required for these road works, to hand over the land without demur or protest. He should have no right to contest the need for alignment. He shall have full freedom to contest the amount of compensation. Project estimate shall provide for cost of acquiring land for the project. Environmental and forest clearances should be made automatic wherever they are required as per the law. Project Implementation Authority shall be bound to take the mitigation measures. Quarry permission as well as explosive permits and blasting permissions must be issued very expeditiously.

Online Management and Monitoring

The Authority should set up a computer based and internet based, detailed online management and monitoring system. The responsibility for coordinating the design, development and delivery of the entire Online Management and Monitoring System for the programme should be allocated to Centre for Development of Advanced Computing (C_DAC), Ministry of Information Technology, Government of India, in view of their general expertise and experience in handling Electronic Governance projects and more specifically, the project for Statewide Computerization of Public Works Department, Government of Maharashtra. Keeping in view the time-critical nature of the project, C-DAC may in turn involve their Authorized Training Centres across the country to provide support at the district locations through the availability of highly trained manpower.

Monitoring and Quality Audit

There should be a separate organization for quality audit and monitoring of the road works of this Authority in each district. This organization could draw experienced and retired persons from the Army and the BRO. In each District, an Advisory committee may be set up to review the progress once a month, occasionally visit the works, take not of the grievances of the local people and suggest suitable actions for redressal.

Maintenance

After completion of the works, the completed roads should be handed over to the State Governments/Zilla Parishads for further maintenance. It should be ensured that adequate provision is made for the maintenance.

Iron-Tyred Carts

The Government should encourage the development and use of pneumatic-tyred carts instead of the iron-tyred ones, presently in use by way of subsidies towards conversion and tax-exemption on tyres.

CHAPTER 23

Post-Harvest Management and Food Processing Industries

INTRODUCTION

Indian agriculture has progressed remarkably during the last few decades and there has been all-round growth in production, whether it is production of foodgrains, commercial crops, horticulture, livestock or fisheries. The country has achieved food self-sufficiency and has built up a large buffer stock of about 62 million tonnes of foodgrains. Per capita availability of foodgrains increased from about 400 gm per day in 1967/68 to about 500 gm in 2000-2001. However, at the same time the country has about 26 per cent of the population below the poverty line. In terms of absolute numbers, this means that almost 260 million persons are below the poverty line in the country. A large proportion of this population lives in rural areas. It is estimated that almost 193 million persons out of the 260 million persons below the poverty line live in rural India. Agriculture provides the source of livelihood to most of these persons.

Though there has been spectacular success in production front in respect of many of agricultural and horticultural products, post harvest management of these products has not made a commensurate progress. The post-harvest losses in the agriculture sector are still very high. Such losses for foodgrains, according to a World Bank Study, are estimated to be 7 to 10 per cent at the farm to market level and another 4 to 5 per cent at the market and distribution level. For the system as a whole, the losses equal to 12 to 16 million tonnes of grains- all grains – per year including 3-4 million tonnes of wheat and 5-7 million tonnes of rice.[1] With an average per capita consumption of about 15 kg of

[1] World Bank : India Foodgrains Marketing Policies: Reforming to Meet Food security Needs.

foodgrains a month, these losses are enough to feed about 70 to 100 million people, about one-third of India's poor, or the states of Bihar and Haryana together, for about one year.

In case of horticulture crops, it is estimated that the losses could be anywhere between 20-40 per cent. The financial implication of the post-harvest losses cannot be visualized through the percentage figures alone. Indeed, the post harvest losses are enormous and take away large amount of money from the pockets of the cultivators. For example, the value of production of cereals in the year 1999-2000 was approximately Rs 856 billion. The reduction in post harvest losses by 5 per cent would mean an additional income to farmers of approximately Rs. 43 billion. In case of pulses, the corresponding figures are Rs. 125 billion and Rs. 6 billion respectively. The value of total output of fruit and vegetables in the country is estimated to be approximately Rs. 560 billion. If the post-harvest losses in this sector are assumed to 20 per cent and if it is possible to cut these losses to 5 per cent, it would mean a generation of additional income to the horticulturists of about Rs. 84 billion. Evidently, the farming community of the country is losing a sizeable amount of money because of high post-harvest losses. In fact, it is not only a loss to the farming community but also a loss to the economy as a whole. In this background, post-harvest management assumes special significance.

Of the total Indian food market, the processed segment is only 10 per cent, the semi-processed is 15 per cent and the remaining 75 per cent constitutes fresh food. Food processing in India is presently dominated by the unorganised sector. The organised agro-food processing sector comprises of 261.79 units producing more than Rs. 9000 crore worth of processed foods. Owing to the increased urbanization and rise in income levels, the demand for processed foods is rising at a fast rate. The processing segment of the food market is projected to increase by 200 per cent by the year 2005 with a very high investment potential which is being placed at Rs. 140000 crores. The segment is attracting massive investment and since July 1991, several ventures in the private, joint and cooperative sectors, some with foreign collaboration and with 100 per cent export oriented units, have been approved, sanctioned or commissioned.

Oilseeds and vegetable oils constitute another important segment of the Indian agricultural market. The oilseed processing industry consists of mechanical crushing and solvent extraction units. The mechanical crushing units include 20000 expellers and 131600 cottage level crushers (ghanies). The number of solvent extraction units is 761. In addition, there are 130 oil refining and 145 hydrogenation units. However, the present capacity utilization of the industry is less than half. An important structural change observed in the last decade in the oilseed processing sector is that the share of cottage level units in the total volume of crushing is going down. The capacity utilization in cottage units is reported to be around 10 per cent, whereas it is 30 per cent for expellers, 34 per cent for solvent extraction units, 50 per cent for oil refining and 37 per cent for hydrogenation units.

India's agri-business contributes to roughly one fifth of the export earnings. The major products exported include cereals, tea, coffee, oil cake, fruit and vegetables, sugar and molasses, processed foods, fish products, poultry and dairy products and flowers. Out of the total exports of agro-allied products, the share of processed products however constitute only about 8 per cent. Though India's agro-food processing industry is estimated at Rs. 75,000 to Rs. 80,000 crores, quantitatively India processes only about 1% of its total agricultural production. Its share in world food processing industry is less than 1 per cent and value addition of food production is a mere 7 per cent compared to 23% in China, 45% in Philippines and 88 per cent in U.K. India is one of the biggest emerging markets with a population of over one billion with a strong middle class of over 350 million, food processing can add value and find good business opportunity. A massive thrust to food processing and other agro-based industries will add value to the product, thereby increasing the income of farmers, creating employment opportunities, diversifying the rural economy and fostering rural industrialization.

Some More Issues

Indian agriculture is at present riddled with several weaknesses like very low productivity for many agro-products, lack of pre and post-harvest management practices, lack of infrastructure and absence of awareness and knowledge about the requirements of global trade. In fact, following liberalization the Indian agricultural markets are being increasingly integrated with global market. Developing countries like Thailand, Chile, Mexico and Brazil could overcome the initial difficulties as we are experiencing now and boost their trade. India should follow the examples of these countries by better post-harvest management of her agricultural products. Indian agriculture is now at a critical juncture. The changing character of agriculture especially of the foodgrains sector for instance is creating new demands on the post-harvest management and marketing systems.

Despite government intervention in pricing and procurement of foodgrains, primarily wheat and paddy, India continues to suffer heavily on account of losses and wastages incurred during the post-harvest period. Attention to the concept of reduction of post-harvest loss of food as a significant means to increase availability was drawn by the World Food Conference held in Rome in 1974. The seventh session of the U.N. General Assembly in 1975 passed a resolution calling for a 50 percent reduction in post-harvest losses by 1985. In the FAO, food loss prevention became a priority area and an Action Programme became operational in early 1987. The Food Loss Prevention Programme of FAO earlier focused on the durable foodgrains, because of their prominence in our daily diet. However, in May 1980, an Expert Consultation on Food Loss Prevention in perishable crops mainly covering fruit and vegetables was held. It goes without saying that fruit and vegetables being highly perishable, call for instant post-harvest handling.

Obviously different agricultural produce require different post-harvest management practices to reduce losses. However, there may not be common prescription for all the crops, fruits, vegetables, spices, etc. But there are a few general issues which have relevance for most of the agricultural produce. Sometimes the linkages between production practices and post-harvest losses are ignored. Agriculture and horticultural produces in general, are like living organisms which breathe. The produce continue to have changes even after the harvest till these reach the consumer or the processor. Moisture plays an important role in determining the keeping quality of agricultural produce. Therefore the season of harvest becomes important. If harvesting is done during rains, the moisture content is high and the keeping quality deteriorates, increasing the post harvest losses. Use of balanced nutrient for producing the crops is another important factor which has bearing on the keeping quality. According to crop scientists, use of nitrogen higher than what is required and lower availability of potassium, calcium and zinc increase the post harvest losses. The incidence of pests and diseases leads to post-harvest losses in terms of quality and quantity. Then we have varieties in crops which give output which are less prone to post harvest losses. Thus, when we discuss the issue of post-harvest management with a view to reducing the post harvest losses, we should also take into account the pre-harvest factors which have a bearing on the post-harvest management in general and losses in particular.

The post-harvest technologies of agricultural produces, and more particularly, because of the perishable nature of horticultural produces, have to match with the production. It is a great challenge that always keeps the scientists, the technologists and the engineers attentive in looking for innovative methodologies and technologies towards making this happen with cost effectiveness built into it and at the same time value addition and the by-product utilization of these commodities. There is a challenge for quality parameters which the world is bench marking for a common harmonization protocols for the global market.

Presently there are a number of hi-tech agri-business projects, capital intensive but risky as well and have targeted the export market. In these projects sophisticated technology is used in production, processing and distribution. The hi-tech technologies in agriculture are to increase the efficiency of production, enhance quality and ensure uniformity of products and make the Indian products globally competitive. The hi-tech technologies that are now being applied in this area include ultra high-density farming, greenhouse floriculture, controlled environment livestock farming, genetic engineering, hybrid seed production technology, tissue culture, embryo transfer technology, micro propagation of bio-fertilizers and bio-pesticides, drip irrigation, and cultivation of mushrooms in climatically controlled conditions, etc. All these are concerned with increasing efficiency of production.

One aspect of utmost importance will be to ensure optimum return for the farmer for his produce. The post-WTO phase has witnessed liberalization of imports by the developing countries on the one hand, and increasing use of sanitary, phyto-sanitary and non-tarrif barriers by developed countries against exports by developing countries on the other. Market competitiveness has become a creed as never before. The Indian farmers particularly belonging to the small and marginal category seem to have been placed in an unenviably disadvantaged position when placed alongside the farmers with hi-tech commercial intensive agriculture.

Hi-tech post-harvest agricultural (including horticultural) products includes, inter alia, washing and waxing facilities, cold chains, controlled atmosphere storage, retortable and flexible packing, CA packaging and mechanized grading and handling which are concerned with improving the shelf life and preservation of products.

POST-HARVEST LOSSES

The problem of hunger and malnutrition has been hunting the human race since long. The pertinent and most controversial question that is posed to us today is : whether man could maintain a balance between food production and the sustained increase in demand for food, current estimates of the situation in the world indicate that over 500 million people do not consume enough calories per day and are considered undernourished, or are not able to consume the nutrients needed for an adequate diet and are therefore malnourished[2].

It has already been pointed out that over the last five decades since independence India has made a significant stride in agricultural sector. But, the existing post-harvest management system, structures and policies are unequal to new challenges. Despite playing an important role by the government in pricing and procurement of foodgrains, India continues to suffer heavily on account of losses and wastages incurred during post harvest period. We have already stated that the magnitude of losses is colossal. In case of foodgrains, what is contributing to continuing losses and wastages are to a large extent, government policies and their implementation, which even stunt growth and modernization of grain markets and processors. The changing character of agriculture especially of the foodgrains sector is creating new demands on the

[2] Report of Food and Agricultural Organization (1989).

post-harvest management and marketing systems. This calls for adjustment to foodgrains policies. Government of India interventions influence prices, volume, quality, storage, processing and distribution of wheat and rice. The public procurement, distribution, and buffer stocking programmes of the government stood in the way of growth and modernization of private foodgrains marketing undermining its potential contribution to long term food security.

FCI's procurement and distribution operations under the Public Distribution System (PDS) have created an extensive public marketing channel, leasing the private sector to function only in FCI's residual market. Illegitimate trade, which flourishes on leakages from government food programmes, however, undermines the effectiveness and raises the cost of the public programmes. The existing stunted private trade discourages much needed modernization. Market congestion, heavy handling and storage losses, high transport costs and low recovery rates in processing wheat and rice, all urgently call for improved post-harvest management technology and infrastructure.

Losses in Pulses

India has the distinction of being the world's largest producer of pulses. The role of pulses in providing the much needed protein to our population hardly needs to be emphasized. Although, the production of pulses has remained virtually static whereas the population, as mentioned earlier, has trebled since independence. The near stagnation in pulse output has adversely affected the nutrient content of available food. The per capita availability of pulses has declined from 60.7 gm/day in 1951 to less than 40 gm/day in 2000 as against the FAO/WHO recommendation of minimum requirement of 85 gm/per day per capita.

The National Commission on Agriculture (1976) projected that about 25 million tonnes of pulses would be required to meet the protein requirement of the country by the end of 2000 A.D. But as there has so far not been any perceptible breakthrough in the productivity of pulses, producing 25 million tonnes may remain a far cry. Under the circumstances the country cannot afford to incur large post-harvest losses which is presently estimated to be to the extent of 10 per cent of the production. The prevention of waste and loss of pulses at post-harvest could be best achieved in the process of threshing, winnowing, handling, transport and storage, etc. This will prevent huge pulse losses which is at least equal, if not more, our annual pulse imports. In fact, saving of even small proportion of the total pulse losses will have a significant impact on the overall pulses availability in the country and this will also save precious foreign exchange.

Losses in Fruit and Vegetables

India produces about 132 million tonnes of fruit and vegetables. Unfortunately, unlike other horticulturally rich countries, average Indians do not get the basic daily requirement of fruit and vegetables since a considerable amount is lost due to improper post-harvest operations. Due to the perishable nature of the fruit and vegetables, the post harvest losses of these commodities is four to five times higher than in foodgrains. According to a joint study conducted by the management consultancy firm, MC Kinsey & Co. and the Confederation of Indian Industry (CII), at least 50 per cent of the production of fruit and vegetables in the country is lost due to wastage and value destruction. The wastage cost is estimated to be Rs. 23,000 crore each year.

POST-HARVEST OPERATIONS

Post-harvest operations consist of threshing, winnowing, transport, storage, packaging, standardization and grading, etc. Of these, storage, standardization and grading, and transportation need special discussion as these are essential operations for avoidance of major losses and maintenance of quality of the produces.

Storage

The function of storage is that having the product available at the desired time. It is the function which matches the pattern of production to the pattern of consumption from the stand point of time. Storage over a period of several years is not a normal situation for agricultural commodities. Carryovers from one production season to another under freely operating market situation are usually only enough to assure continuity of processing and distributive operations. The public's idea of huge storage holdings of agricultural products has stemmed to some degree from the operation of the price support programmes of the government.

There are two general types of normal storage operations. One is that which equalized seasonal production to the pattern of demand. The other is storage at all times within trade channels which is necessary to keep the marketing system operating without interruption. Much of the output of agriculture is harvested during relatively short periods of the year. The foodgrains, jute, cotton, tobacco, fruits and vegetables are all highly seasonal in nature. Even the production of livestock, eggs and dairy products, though continuous throughout the year, has wide variations between the high and low periods of production. The demand for these products, however, is often quite constant throughout the year.

To the extent that products are not perishable, they can be placed in storage at harvest and then released slowly as the year progresses. In this way storage stocks tend to equalize the amounts available for consumption throughout the year. In the case of storable crops which are harvested during a very short period of the year, the entire production need be stored and released for consumption throughout the remainder.

Where Commodities are Stored

Because of great number of places where goods can be stored, an accurate inventory of storage capacity in the country for various agricultural commodities is almost impossible. The most important single storage facilities are for the on-farm storage of grains. This does not, however, include open-air storage. The use of open-air storage is often temporarily quite great especially during the harvest season. Commodities, of course, change hands and place of storage during the season. Grain may be retained in farm storage. It then may be moved to village haat and primary markets, then to secondary wholesale markets and finally to millers and processors.

India's Storage Problem

As the farm storage in India is generally unscientific, there is quite a substantial loss of agricultural commodities both in quantity and commodity. Storage loss due to thefts, damage and leakages is a matter of great concern. As mentioned earlier, although there are no detailed national statistics on private sector storage, most of it is known to be small scale, low-quality structures such as covered and plinth (CAP) storage or covered godowns. CAP storages involve seeking grain in bags in a pyramid shape. This is mainly in private sector paid by various government agencies. This type of storage itself results in estimated 20 per cent losses. Extensive use of covered and plinth (CAP) storage unnecessarily increases losses and enhances difficulties in implementing the first-in, first-out principle of inventory management. According to the official information half of the FCI stock is at least 2 years old; 30 per cent between 2 to 4 years old; and some grains as old as 16 years. The loss in value due to quality deterioration and aging in storage and weaknesses in inventory monitoring and control raise FCI's operating cost.

Cold Chain Concept

Now with branded food being sold on a large scale, an integrated viable cold chain concept has to be developed. With the development of technology there are presently better methods of preserving and storage of foods to make it available throughout the year. As the loss in perishables like fruit and vegetables is very large, there is an urgent need to adopt the concept of cold chain which includes pre-cooling, cold storages, refrigerated transport and air-conditioned outlets. The cold chain helps in keeping the quality of the produce over a long duration, making it available in off-season, helps in avoiding glut and distress sale and support processing industries by assured supply of raw materials. India has so far not developed a viable cold chain system. Cold storages were built largely to store potatoes, apples and oranges. But the concept of cold chain is almost nonexistent with a few exceptions, such as, the one set up by the Maharashtra Grape Growers Association. As a scientific post-harvest management practice, cold chain system needs to be urgently developed, particularly in perishable commodities.

Transportation

Products must be moved from where they are produced into the areas where they will be consumed. Transport is therefore important in agricultural produce marketing, not only as an integral link in the marketing chain, but also because of its strategic implication for cost. At every stage in the distributive sequence there is some dependence on transport. Adequate and efficient transportation is a cornerstone of our modern marketing system. The grower carries his produces from the field to the farm sheds and thence to the local buyer i.e. primary wholesalers, itinerant traders, etc. Large scale transportation is undertaken by local buyers, wholesalers, exporters and importers. When it is realized how many times the product has to be moved, not only the importance of appropriate packing is evident, but also the importance of suitable means of transport. Improper or careless handling of many agricultural produces, particularly, the horticultural produces during transportation can lead to damaged cargoes and extensive losses. The inadvertent destruction is often due to incorrect temperature and humidity setting during transport. It can also occur when products which ought to be stored separately are mistakenly put together.

Transport may be effected by hand, by pack animals, by horse or motor vehicle, country boat, railway. In each case, the primary requirement is that the product must stand up to the transport satisfactorily; secondly, that it can be moved as efficiently as possible. There is a wide range in transport efficiency in the country, a sign that there is much scope for improvement. A large number of villages in the country lack a reliable all weather connection with nearby markets and towns. Some areas like North-East and Jammu & Kashmir have remained physically and emotionally isolated because the transport system has not linked them with the rest of the country. In fact, had there been efficient and easy transport system in those areas, many of the agricultural and horticultural crops could be grown more extensively which would have acted as a catalytic agent for faster economic development of the areas.

Damage to the product, breakage of the containers, inefficient working methods, unnecessary movement, careless loading and unloading, and rough handling are all every day events and the causes of serious losses. The situation can often be improved by a few simple alterations which may reduce costs considerably. In India losses in transport add to the cost of products significantly. The movement of small lots over short distances and the transport of large units over long distances merit consideration separately.

Management of Small Lots

For short distances of transport, the main considerations are protection of the produce, more particularly fruit and vegetables, against mechanical damage and against exposure to contamination and to extremes of temperature. It is imperative that workers, while loading and unloading realize that the product is vulnerable and cannot stand rough handling. Transport should follow a preconceived plan. The precise destination for each consignment should be carefully specified, otherwise time and again further shifting will be necessary increasing the transport loss. The system should be such that the produce is moved in a consistent direction as much as possible and does not retrace its tracks.

Non-motorized transport modes, powered by human and animal energy like bicycles, rickshaws, carts, etc. could play a big role in the developing transport scenarios of the country. Animal carts are an essential part of the rural agricultural economy. But, unfortunately, the elitist approach has not focused on the development of these modes of transport as much as are the formal motorized modes, despite their manifold benefits like relatively lesser cost, simple technology, large employment potential, non-polluting operations, etc. The provision of simple technological inputs of improved designs, standardization of spare parts and ensuring safe and smooth movement could go a long way in improving the transport system from farm yard to primary markets and even from primary markets to nearby secondary markets.

Long Distance Transport

Trucks have made the greatest inroads in the transportation of products from primary markets to secondary and terminal markets. In the long-distance transport of agricultural produces by trucks, there may be losses due to poor packaging, pilferage, rain soaking, etc. In case of horticultural produces, deterioration can take place due to variety of causes, for instance; mold development in fruits, wilting in vegetables, excessive heating (due to respiration) in produce such as leafy vegetable and beans; softening and ripening of fruit at high temperatures. The successful transport of horticultural produce over long distances requires skill, experience, and special equipment. It is a subject which has commanded much scientific attention in many countries. However, to overcome the risks, several procedures are often adopted. Some of these are:

(i) Pre-cooling of some fruits before transportation
(ii) Ventilation of unrefrigerated transport vehicles
(iii) Cooling (often by ice) of road and rail vehicles, and

(iv) Automatic cooling and also heating of vehicles for the transport of bananas, since this fruit is easily damaged at temperatures below about 12°C and will tend to ripen at temperatures of 15-18°C;

We have already stated that transportation cost is one of the major items of the cost structure of agricultural produce. High perishability is one of the basic reasons for expensive transportation. But poor quality products are more perishable than top quality products. An expended programme of farm selling on grades might result in products being more closely graded before transportation. Only those products best able to stand up during movement may be sent to long distances. Those which might deteriorate more quickly would be sold in the nearby market.

Grading and Standardization

Standards are yardsticks of measurement. In agricultural marketing two types of standards are of major concern-the standards for weights and measures and those for quality. Grading refers to the sorting of products into the various categories (referred to as grades) which are established by the standards for quality. For example, standards have been established for the various qualities of grain. In grading grain, it is sorted into the various grades which have been set up.

In a complex marketing machinery, the possibilities of waste, confusion, and downright chicanery are great. Keeping such practices to a minimum is one of the purposes of an adequate and workable system of standards and grades. As one author phrased it, standardization furnishes the ethical basis for making a transaction. Without such a system, the rule "caveat emptor" ("let the buyer beware") must prevail along with all of its confusion and unfairness[3].

The principal objective of an ideal standard should be to aid the consumer in telling the producer what he considers desirable in a product for the particular use to be made of it. Ideal standards set up a chain of information between the consumer and the producer.

Grading of agricultural products is a method of differentiation of the products to meet the various desires of the consumers. We have learned that consumers are characterized by a large range of incomes and preferences. Some desire and can pay for the highest quality. Others must be satisfied with a somewhat lower quality at a lower price. A grading system attempts to differentiate the product in such a way that the various consumers are tapped for all that they will pay. Or from the consumers' point of view, a grading system attempts to aid the consumer in obtaining the particular product he desires. The best

[3] Edward A.Duddy and David A. Revzan, Marketing, An Institutional Approach (New York, McGraw-Hill, 1947), p. 59.

grading system will be such that it will move the greatest total amount into consumption and secure the greatest total price for that amount[4]. The purpose of grading is not to assure the marketing of only top quality products. Those who conceive a grading system as a vehicle for the elimination of lower quality products are ignoring the wide range of consumer preferences and uses which exist.

The major problem in developing grading standards then becomes one of determining differences in products which are economically significant and then developing methods for measuring these differences in the products. Only differences which users are willing to pay for are pertinent to the establishment of grades. Whims and desires not backed by the willingness to pay are not justifications for grade differentiation. Neither are the opinions of a few "experts" of what should be desired workable foundations for grades.

Criteria for Good Standards

The development of a system of perfect and ideal standards is highly improbable. Each agricultural product presents different problems. Realizing that it is very improbable that any standards will meet them all, the following may be used as criteria upon which to judge the adequacy of standards.[5]

1. Standards should be built on characteristics which the users consider important as indicated by their willingness to pay different prices, and these characteristics should be easily recognizable.
2. Standards should be built on those factors which can be accurately and uniformly measured and interpreted. If the major part of the standard consists of subjective measurements, uniform application by different graders or at different points will be very difficult.
3. Standards should use those factors and terminology which will make the grade meaningful to as many users of the product as possible. The ideal situation would be that in which the same grade terminology is used at all levels of the marketing channel from the consumer to the producer. This, of course, is complicated by the fact that many products have several different uses.
4. Standards should be such that each grade classification includes enough of the average production so as to be a meaningful category on the market. Though grading standards should be

[4] L.J. Norton, "Differentiation in Marketing Farm Products," Journal of Farm Economics, Part 1, August, 1939, pp. 587-594.

[5] Discussion of this area and many other articles pertinent to the subject of standards and grading can be found in the report of the 1951 Marketing Research Workshop, Market Demand and Product Quality, USDA, Agricultural Research Administration, processed.

consumer oriented, they cannot ignore the real facts of production. Consideration must be given to the quality of the product which is produced. It is of little purpose to have a standard for the top quality set up in such a fashion that very little of the actual production can meet the standards.

Probably the best practical test of the adequacy of standards is their acceptance and use by the various marketing agencies. If the grading standard is widely used, it is probable that the standards are fairly adequate and economically meaningful. However, if large segments of the trade do not use the standards, then it usually may be assumed that some of the criteria are not adequately met.

Farm Selling on a Graded Basis

Only if the farmer sells on the basis of grades, fullest benefits of the grading system as a method of consumer-producer communication will be realized. Yet it is true that a great many-perhaps a majority-of products are sold by farmers on an ungraded or partially graded basis. The wider the practice of selling on a graded basis the less is the possibility for fraud and deceit in the selling of goods by farmers. However, it is probably also true that not all farmers stand to gain from selling on a graded basis. The farmers which produce the higher quality products would gain at the expense of those producing the lower quality products.

Producing high quality products usually is not costless. Usually more careful, and often more expensive, handling is required. In some areas of agricultural production, the extra cost would probably outweigh the extra returns. In these situations, farm selling on a graded basis has little attraction. However, to the individual farmer such production may be a sideline enterprise which receives little attention. Generally, the larger specialized producers to whom the product is financially important are more receptive to the idea of graded selling. Also, usually those producers who are farthest from market are more interested in such a programme. In that way, the best can go forward and the poorer quality products be sold nearer home. This enhances the competitive position in the distant markets. It also reduces the relative transportation costs, since it generally costs the same amount to ship high quality, high-valued products as it does the lower quality, lower-valued products.

There is evidence that a programme of graded selling raises the quality of the goods sold. This usually comes about as the producer realizes the things which he can do which will produce a crop of higher quality. Many of these things represent only changes in present practices and not adoption of new or additional ones. For example, picking fruit and vegetables at the proper degree of ripeness may reduce spoilage. Such practices as these might become more widespread if what constituted higher quality and higher valued products were known.

Quality programmes should not be built on the premise that only the highest quality is desirable or marketable. As we have seen, there is a wide variety of consumers and users for each commodity. Many of these can pay only for something less than the best. The farmers' objective is to maximize incomes, not quality alone.

Standardization System

A number of organizations in our country are responsible for the formulation of grade standards and monitoring their quality. These can be basically classified into two: (1) Mandatory and (2) Voluntary.

Mandatory provisions are being implemented through a number of legislative measures. Some of these are mentioned below:

(a) Prevention of Food Adulteration Act 1954 and the rules framed thereunder:

(b) Essential Commodities Act 1955 and the various orders issued under it, like:

- (i) Fruit Products Order, 1955;
- (ii) Solvent Extracted Oils, Deoiled Meal and Edible Flour Control Order, 1967;
- (iii) Milk and Milk Product Order, 1992;
- (iv) Vegetable Products Control Order, 1975;
- (v) Meat Food Products Order, 1973;
- (vi) Sugar Control Order, 1966.

(c) Weights and Measures Act, 1977 and the rules framed thereunder;

(d) Infant Milk substitutes, Feeding bottles and infant foods (Regulations of Production, Supplies and Distribution) Act, 1992, and

(e) Export, Quality Control and Inspection Act, 1963.

Under the voluntary system there are two main organizations i.e. Directorate of Marketing & Inspection through APGM Act 1937 popularly known as "Agmark" and the other is Bureau of Indian Standards through BIS Act 1986 popularly known as "ISI". Apart from these two organizations under the present concept of self quality assurance certification system, a number of other agencies have been authorized to certify the quality of a product.

International standards are now being recognized as means to overcome technical barriers that result in difference of various grade standards being adopted by different countries. This has lead to most national standard bodies to align their grade standards with the international standards as well as promulgation of GATT standards code which recognizes international standards as suitable code standards for harmonizing among national rules and regulation. The GATT standard code has recognized International standard of the

International Organization of Standardization (ISO) and International Electro-Technical Commission (IEC), as suitable means of achieving necessary harmonization amongst National Standards and Technical Standards. The increased acceptability of international standards in the world market has prompted many countries to the GATT standard codes to participate effectively in International Standardization Process, so that potential obstacles in international trade could be eliminated.

The present day view is that National standards should be aligned with International standards for giving impetus to exports. Though the developing countries have become conscious of the economic growth yet they have to identify their products fully through international standards in the world market to gain economic advantage. It is, therefore, necessary to adopt International standards as a starting point without going into costly exercise for preparation of national standards in alignment with international standards for which they often lack the necessary infrastructural facilities.

Under the present quality concept system, it is not only necessary to standardize a product, but standardization of inspection techniques, test procedures, sampling technique, packaging material and other processes are necessary for successful marketing of a product up to the satisfaction of consumer acceptability. The process of standardization has in fact to start right from the production level up to the entire processing till the product is marketed and consumed.

The mechanism of grading and standardization is a continuous process and the same needs review and changes depending upon the technological changes and requirements. But it has been observed that such process through research and developmental activities has not been given much importance in our country and in most of the cases, standards are being adopted depending upon minimum requirements without a proper scientific study.

Major Issues

Post-harvest handling of the foodgrains is another area of concern. Huge amount is being spent by the procurement agencies on packing and transportation of foodgrains. A bag of foodgrain is loaded and unloaded many times before it reaches the final consumers. Cost of handling a bag of foodgrains is almost equal to the cost of foodgrains. Post-harvest management can be made efficient by mechanisation of operations by procurement agencies, development of economic transportation models and public and private investments in the storage infrastructure. Efficiency in this aspect will make the local agricultural products cost effective, thereby can go a long way in checking the threat of cheaper imported goods.

Presently all the farmers rush to the markets after harvest of the crop. This leads to excessive supply in the markets and exploitation of the farmers by middlemen. Even procurement agencies find it difficult to handle the produce, thereby leading to the huge losses in quantity and quality of foodgrains. This problem can be diluted by encouraging big farmers to develop storage facilities on the farm and sell the produce later when market prices are suitable. Even the higher MSP should be assured in later parts of the year after harvest of the crop.

Present crisis has once again pointed towards drying government investments in the agricultural infrastructure, and development. This trend needs to be reversed immediately, otherwise the agriculture sector will become highly vulnerable to the external forces. This crisis has raised many issues which needs to be addressed properly before it is too late.

FOOD PROCESSING INDUSTRIES

The agro and food processing industry in India is of utmost significance in terms of employment and income generation, poverty alleviation, export promotion and foreign exchange earnings. There is vast scope for improvement in value addition in agricultural products, creation of new employment especially in the small towns and rural areas, improvement in the nutritional status of rural women and the poor, and availability of cheaper and better products for the consumers. A well run food processing industry ensures that the producer gets remunerative prices for his product and the consumer buys less for higher and assured quality. In India, fruits and vegetables are generally marketed immediately after the harvest and hardly 2 per cent of the production is commercially processed, whereas more than 50 per cent of the produce is processed in developed countries. The unnecessary wastage of valuable commodities can be avoided if they are processed in value added products or adequately distributed in different parts of the country. There is a great scope of domestic and export trade by improving the post-harvest distribution and processing facilities of the highly perishable horticultural commodities. The country provides great opportunities for investment and growth in agro-processing sector. A massive thrust to food processing and other agro-based industries will add value to the product thereby increasing the income of farmers, create employment opportunities, diversify the rural economy and foster rural industrialization. India is one of the biggest emerging markets with a population of over one billion with a strong middle class of over 350 million, food processing can add value and find good business opportunity.

Status of Food Processing Industry

The Food processing industry which has taken off recently in India, has still a long way to go. The All India Food Preservers Association (AIFPA), which has members mainly from the fruits and vegetables industry, is striving to develop this particular sector. The present installed capacity of fruits and vegetables processing industry has increased from 9.0 lakh tonnes (1990-91) to 21.0 lakh tonnes (1999-2000). However this capacity is not being fully utilized. Actual utilization of this capacity is only about 45.0 per cent. Most of the units are in tiny or small sector accounting for nearly 90 per cent in number but have a cumulative output of 2.5 lakh tonnes representing 12 per cent of the total installed capacity.

Although the domestic food processing industry is growing at a rate of about 20%, it is stated to have run into some problems because of the introduction of central excise taxes at multiple points. The total taxes, including the ones charged on the packaging material and also on the declared minimum retail price (MRP), works out to about 30 per cent which is mainly passed on to the consumers making the processed foods unaffordable to the common man. For exports, the exporters can avail of duty drawback. But the process is time consuming. As the MRP keeps on changing every now and then, it results in a lot of paperwork affecting the operation of the trade and industry.

According to the Ministry of Food Processing Industries, the government has so far approved investment proposals of over Rs. 73,000 crore (Table 23.1) in the food processing sector. As many as 6,587 industrial entrepreneurs' memoranda involving an investment of Rs 53,869 crore with a potential to employ 11.7 lakh persons have also been filed with the Food Processing Department. The Ministry has already prepared a national food processing policy and processed food development act to create the environment for investment and sustained growth of the food processing industry.

The Government of India has also approved setting up of food processing projects to enable entrepreneurs to set up a cluster of food industries in selected areas and 20 such projects have so far been approved. During the four years of the Ninth Five Year Plan, a sum of Rs. 140 crore has already been provided as assistance for various projects.

The theme of the 21st India International Trade Fair which opened its doors to both business visitors and public during Nov. 2001 was 'Agro Product and Processed Food'. As the third largest food producer in the world, agricultural sector has particular significance for India and the fair is an opportunity for displaying technological updates and launching new products and services. The fair featured exhibits from over 6,500 Indian and foreign companies.

Food processing holds the key to prevent wastage of food items. Massive investments are called for to save food through processing. The present level of processing is limited to 2 per cent. If it is to be raised to 10 per cent in 10 years, this will need an investment of Rs 1.4 lakh crore. It seems that we are not prepared for the requisite investment to bring India at par with the developed countries in food processing industry.

Table 23.1 Investment in the Processed Food Sector (Since Liberalization in July, 1991)

(*Rs. in crores*)

S. No.	Sector	Industrial Entrepreneur Memoranda (till Dec. 2000)		Industrial Approval (100% Export Oriented Units/ Industrial Licence (till Nov. 2000)		Total		Foreign Investment out of total Investment
		No.	Invest.	No.	Invest.	No.	Invest.	
1.	Grain milling and grain based products	334	5800	98	988	432	6788	1118
2.	Fruits and vegetable products	1717	3314	413	5141	2130	8455	1066
3.	Meat and poultry products	77	383	58	1393	135	1776	209
4.	Fish processing and aquaculture	105	460	190	2171	295	2631	548
5.	Fermentation industry	820	7436	211	2073	1031	9509	4493
6.	Consumer industry including soft drinks/ waters/confectionery etc.	612	9266	78	5814	690	15080	2146
7.	Milk and milk products	1087	13744	25	961	1112	14705	914
8.	Other including food additives, flavours etc.	—	—	62	860	62	860	498
9.	Edible oil/oil seeds	1675	13416	—	—	1675	13416	—
	Total	6427	53819	1135	19401	7562	73220	10992

Since the peasants are basically the primary producers and do not have the wherewithal to process, the benefits of value added to the product only accrues to the manufactures. For example, the Indian farmer is forced for distress sale, now just throwing his wheat at any price between Rs 450 and Rs. 600 per quintal. But Britania Biscuits Factory is selling its biscuits at Rs 11,000 to Rs. 15,000 per quintal.

Opportunities for exporting fresh fruits and vegetables are quite high. With the new food for 'organices', the chances are still brighter. Namdhari Seeds, one of the largest producers and distributors of hybrid vegetable seeds in India has plans to aggressively market fresh high-end vegetables to Europe, the Middle-East and the US, as well as the domestic market this year, (2001). After its success in the seed market, the Rs. 50-crore company has diversified into production, distribution and export of fresh vegetables and fruits under the brand name Namdhari's Fresh. Capitalising on the availability of hi-tech infrastructure such as continuous cold chain facility right from production till it reaches the consumer, Namdhari's Fresh is planning to go global in a big way.

It was just a wish to do something different. There is good scope in Europe where most of the tropical vegetables come from South American or African nations. Now that they have the infrastructure in place in India to export fresh vegetables, they decided to foray into exports. The Namdhari range of vegetables includes baby corn, French beans, peas, zucchini and also tropical vegetables like brinjals and orka. The company now exports about two tonnes a week "but in a couple of years they plan to export at least 20 tonnes a week".

These products are available in big departmental stores such as Tesco. Sainsbury and Asda in UK. These stores are finicky about their brand image, so they send the products in two-kg packages to company's importers who in turn re-pack and brand them in smaller containers. For some markets, such as the middle-east,, they do the packing and branding in small containers and export directly. The European market being highly quality-conscious, the company lays special emphasis on quality specifications as specified by the EU regulations and also the British retail consortium. Every second or third shipment undergoes quality tests. So the company has to be very careful. Moreover, the market for organic vegetables is growing at a spanking pace of five to 10 per cent. To expand its high value products market in the West, the company believes it should achieve competitive pricing through increased volumes so that the air-freight costs come down.

These high-end vegetables are also available in leading domestic departmental stores. The company is also planning to give the same international quality vegetables to Indian consumers, such as 'topped and tailed' beans, seedless water melons, lettuce, asparagus, leek and broccoli. At present, these are available in departmental stores in

Bangalore and also sent to 5-star hotels in Mumbai. It plans to open its own retail shop in Bangalore in the next three months where vegetables of international standard will be sold and displayed. Namdhari Seeds commenced operations in 1985 with its contract seed production wherein MNCs gave the parents which were then developed in India because of the favourable climatic conditions and cheap manpower. This still constitutes 30 per cent of Namdhari's business.

Such success stories apart, price fluctuations in the international market also play quite an import role. Take the case of international seafood export business which has been on a tailspin since November 2000. Since September it has crashed like never before by 45 per cent. In September 2000, 16/20 headless Black Tiger was quoted at $17.40 per kg in November 2001 this had slumped at $9.50 per kg. Prices just before September 11 was pegged at around $11 per kg.

Shrimp farmers are now selling at almost below cost and the industry does not have deep pockets to sustain this recession. Many farmers will be forced to exit the business. The association is planning to urge the government to step in and increase DEPB (Duty Entitlement Pass Book) scheme rates from 4 per cent to 10 per cent on exports to provide marginal relief to all sections of the industry. Mr Ramalingam, President, Seafood Exporters Association of India, West-Bengal Region said. "MPEDA (Marine Products Export Development Authority) does encourage processing plants with capital subsidies but this time exporters feel they need revenue subsidies." This region is expected to lose about Rs. 100 crore in exports due to price revision in the coming months. About I lakh people from the rural and urban areas are involved in this segment.

The position is not very different for horticulture which lags on price disadvantage. The new WTO order has important implications for the country's horticulture sector, which has the potential to become a major source of export revenues. Processed exports since 1991 has increased significantly—from Rs 102.96 crore in 1990-91 to Rs. 829.86 crore in 2000-01, but this still falls far behind the potential—India being the largest producer of fruits and second-largest producer of vegetables in the world (Table 23.2). The horticultural sector includes the entire gamut of fruits, vegetables, mushrooms, flowers, plantation crops like cashews, spices, medicinal and aromatic plants, of which fresh fruits and vegetables constitute as high as about 90 per cent of the total production of this sector.

A study commissioned by the ministry of agriculture on the export potential of five significant commodities in the category—grapes, mango, apple, banana and onions—for the period 1980-96 shows that barring export of grapes to the Middle East, the liberalised regime has not really helped exports of these commodities. This has been attributed to India's disadvantage on the price front. In fact, in the case of mangoes

Table 23.2 Export of Processed Food Including Marine Products

(Rs. in crores)

	1993-94	1994-95	1995-96	1996-97	1997-98	1998-99	1999-2000	2000-01*
A. Processed Foods								
1. Processed fruits and vegetables	268	348	492	474	750	678	656	522
2. Animal products	374	448	683	804	926	859	879	950
3. Other processed foods	457	416	1172	1836	1140	1166	1695	
4. Rice								
(a) Basmati	1061	865	850	1247	1685	1866	1736	
(b) Non-Basmati	225	340	3717	1925	1685	4335	1369	
B. Marine products	2504	3576	3501	4121	4697	4627	5117	5875
Grand total	4889	5993	10415	10407	11183	13531	11452	

* Estimated

and onions, a non-tariff barriers index devised for the study shows that it has a negative effect on exports of these crops.

Fruits typically have long gestation periods in production and are characterised by yearly fluctuations in output. A mango cultivator, for instance, has to plan for a suitable mix of plants maturing at different points of time so that he has a reasonable return from the activity at all times. Further, a study of rates of return to important fruits and vegetables shows there are significant variations among stages: the internal rate of return (IRR) on grapes in Andhra Pradesh varies between 35 per cent and 6.2 per cent, while in Maharashtra, it varies between 24 per cent and 42 per cent.

If one included production and marketing, the IRR goes down further; in Himachal Pradesh, IRR to apple production is 21-32 per cent, whereas the IRR to production and marketing drops to 18-25 per cent, reflecting high marketing costs, especially in hilly regions. An important technological change that is yet to pick up in a big way that could improve IRRs is the use of water-saving devices like drip irrigation. The study reports that use of drip irrigation is water saving to the extent of 45 to 48 per cent and raises productivity by one-and-a-half times.

GROWTH OF FOOD PROCESSING INDUSTRIES

Grain Processing

Due to the efforts made by the Department from time to time, the number of modern/modernised rice mills has gone up from practically nil in 1970 to 35088 as on 01.01.2001. The Rice Milling Industry (Regulation) Act, 1958 has since been repealed. The information about the number of modern/modernised rice mills etc. are not forthcoming from State Governments/UTs. As a result of improved availability of bran from these modern and modernised mills, the processing of bran is estimated to be around 34 lakh tonnes.

Thirteen Regional Extension Service Centres have been set up in various states with Agricultural Universities/Research institutions for propagating the benefits of modernisation of rice milling industry and by-product utilisation through organising seminars, group discussions/setting up demonstration units and preparation of technical literature etc. Post Harvest Technology Centre at Indian Institute of Technology (IIT), Kharagpur offers training courses on long term duration leading to M.Tech., Ph.D and Post Doctoral Degree and also short term courses for managers/mill operators etc. At present 11 M.Tech., 11 Ph.D are undergoing courses at the centre. Besides teaching activities, the centre is also engaged in Research and Development work on the engineering aspects of the rice processing and byproduct utilisation etc. The centre also undertakes research and development projects as per need of the industry. During 1999-2000, the centre had also conducted two training programmes on "Home Scale Food Processing and Preservation techniques" and "Processing of minor Millet" and also organised seminars on "Oilseeds" and "Kodo puffing and popping".

No licence is required for manufacture of wheat products. There are no controls on price and distribution of wheat products. The mills have been given a free hand to obtain their requirements of wheat from any source, thereby avoiding their dependence on government for supply of raw materials. Nearly 10.5 million tonnes of wheat is converted into various wheat products by about 820 roller flour mills in the country every year against an installed capacity of 19.5 million tonnes.

Consumer Food Industries

The consumer food industry mainly consists of ready-to-eat or ready-to-cook products such as pasta products, cocoa based products, bakery products, biscuits, soft drinks, etc.

Bakery Bakery industry in India is probably the largest among the processed food industries, production of which has been increasing steadily in the country. The two major bakery industries, viz., bread and biscuit account for about 82% of the total bakery products. The annual production of bakery products which include bread, biscuits, pastries, cakes, buns, rusk, etc., most of which are in the unorganised sector, is estimated to be in excess of 30 lakh tonnes. 'The production of bread and biscuits in the country, both in the organised and unorganized sectors, is estimated to be around 15 lakh tonnes and 11 lakh tonnes respectively. Of the total production of bread and biscuits, about 35% is produced in the organised sector and the remaining is manufactured in the unorganised sector. Another wheat based product known by its generic name, pasta products, comprising of noodles, vermicelli, macaroni and spaghetti is gaining popularity.

Cocoa Products There are 20 units engaged in the manufacture of cocoa products like chocolates, drinking chocolates, cocoa butter, cocoa butter substitutes, cocoa based malted milk foods with a production of approximately 34 thousand tonnes.

Soft Drinks The estimated production of soft drinks have increased from 6230 million bottles in 1999-2000 to 6540 million bottles during the year 2000-2001.

Beer and Alcoholic Drinks At present, there are 36 units manufacturing beer under license from Govt. of India having an estimated output of 4.00 lakh KL per annum. On the other hand, the production of alcoholic drinks from non-molasses sources is very small in the country compared to the total production of alcoholic drinks. However, with various foreign companies producing non-molasses alcoholic drinks such drinks are gaining popularity in the domestic market.

Fruit and Vegetable Processing Industries

The estimated installed capacity of fruit and vegetable processing industries has increased from 21.00 lakh tonnes in 1999 to 21.10 lakh tonnes in 2000. The production of processed fruits and vegetables in the country has increased from 9.8 lakh tonnes in 1999 to 9.9 lakh tonnes in 2000. During the same period the number of licenses issued under Fruit Product Order (FPO), 1955 has increased to 5293 from 5198.

Milk and Milk Products

India's milk production is expected to touch 81 million tonnes during 2000-2001 from 78 million tonnes during 1999-2000.

There has been increase in the estimated production of milk powder including infant milk food from 2.25 lakh tonnes in the year 1999 to 2.30 lakh tones in the year 2000 and the estimated production of malted food product has increased from 66,000 tonnes in the year 1999 to 67,000 tonnes in the year 2000. The production of cheese in the organised sector in the year 2000 has been estimated as 7,500 tonnes. The estimated production of condensed milk has increased from 11,000 tonnes in the year 1999 to 11,500 tones in the year 2000.

Meat and Poultry Processing

The production of meat and meat products has shown steady increase from the year 1994 till the year 1998. The details of production of meat and meat products from 1994 to 1998 are given in Table 23.03.

Table 23.3

(In thousand tonnes)

	1994	1995	1996	1997	1998
1. Mutton and goat meat	637	647	669	670	675
2. Pork meat	366	420	420	420	420
3. Poultry meat	442	578	480	580	600
4. Cattle meat (beef)	1290	1292	1292	1292	1295
5. Buffalo meat	1200	1204	1204	1205	1210

The total meat production in the country is of the tune of 4.5 million tonnes per annum. This includes meat products also. The slaughtered rate in relation to the population of animals is about 6% in the case of cattle, 10% in the case of buffalo, 99% in case of pigs, 31% in case of sheep and 39% in case of goat. The production of value added meat and meat products is also steadily increasing.

Broiler and Egg Production With the growth of poultry in the country, there has been a sharp rise in the availability of egg and broilers. The production of eggs and broiler meat from 1989-90 onwards are given in Table 23.4.

Table 23.4

(In millions)

Year	*Egg production*	*Broiler production*
1989-90	20,204	190
1990-91	21,101	215
1991-92	21,983	210
1992-93	22,929	235
1993-94	24,202	275
1994-95	26,049	330
1995-96	27,275	350
1996-97	27,530	400
1997-98*	28,567	450
1998-99*	29,000	475
1999-2000*	30,000	500

With the increase in availability of eggs in the country and demand of egg products in Europe, Japan and other countries, six egg processing units were established in the year 1994 to 1996. These units have started export egg products like egg powder, albumin powder and frozen yolk. Though initially there was a boom in the export of egg products but in 1997, a sudden downfall occurred in the demand of egg products. The export has got a setback and only three units in the country are running with 20 to 25% capacity.

Fish Processing

55% of the production of fish in India is from marine sources. Production of fish from both marine and inland source has decreased from 5.39 million tonnes in 1997-98 to 5.26 million tonnes in 1998-99.

Processing of marine products into canned and frozen forms is carried out almost entirely for the export market. In all, there are 388 freezing units, 12 caning units, 156 ice-making units, 12 fish meal plants and also about 482 frozen storage units in this sector (up to September, 2000).

Exports Export of processed fruits and vegetables in 2000-2001 is estimated to be around Rs. 525 crores as against Rs. 656 crores in 1999-2000. Export of animal products is estimated to be around Rs. 950 crores in 2000-2001 as against Rs. 879 crores in the last year. Export of processed foods (including cereal based products) is estimated to be around Rs. 4895 crores in 2000-2001 as against Rs. 6335 crores in 1999-2000 and export of marine products is expected to increase from

Rs. 5117 crores to Rs. 5875 crores during the same period. Year-wise details of export of processed foods is shown at Table 23.2.

MINISTRY OF FOOD PROCESSING INDUSTRIES

The Ministry of Food Processing Industries was set up in July, 1988 to give an impetus to the development of food processing industries in the country. A strong and effective food processing sector plays a significant role in diversification and commercialization of agriculture, improves value addition of the agricultural produce, generates employment, enhances income of farmers and creates surplus for export of agro foods. The Ministry of Food Processing Industries is concerned with the formulation and implementation of the policies and plans for the food processing industries within the overall national priorities and objectives.

Goals and Objectives of the Ministry

The Ministry of Food Processing Industries is the nodal agency of the Government of India for processed foods and is responsible for developing a strong and vibrant food processing sector.

In the era of economic liberalization where the private, public and cooperative sectors are to play their respective role in development of food processing sector, Ministry acts as a catalyst for bringing in greater investment into this sector, guiding and helping the industry in a proper direction encouraging exports and creating a conducive environment for healthy growth of the food processing industry. Within this overall objective, the Ministry aims at:-

- Better utilization and value addition of agricultural/ horticultural produce for enhancement of income of farmers.
- Minimizing wastage at all stages in the food processing chain by the development of infrastructure for storage, transportation and processing of agro-food produce.
- Introduction of modern technology into the food processing industries from both domestic and external sources.
- Maximum utilization of agricultural residues and by-products of the primary agricultural produce as also of the processed food industry.
- To encourage R & D in food processing for product and process development and improved packaging.
- To provide policy support, promotional initiatives and physical facilities to promote value added exports.

Reasons' for Low Profile of Processing Industry

Most of the units with medium to high capacity which are export oriented, are either not doing very well or have gone sick. The major reasons for sickness of industry are:

1. Backward integration for timely availability of raw material is not properly planned. There is need for strong extension services to educate farmers.
2. Breach of marketing agreement with the collaborators leading to stocking of the finished products over longer period.
3. Inadequate funding backup for working capital. It takes a minimum of Rs. 20 lakh to start a small scale food processing unit. The money has to be raised from banks and financial institutions at the same rate at which it is lent to other sectors. No concessions are extended on account of the seasonal and cyclical peculiarities of the business.
4. Most Indian food processing companies are small and medium enterprises (SMEs) and, consequently, are midgets compared to the global biggies. None of the SME companies come anywhere near international levels in terms of either size or technology.
5. Lack of modern production and quality control technology.
6. Absence of facilities to process multiple fruits.

An analysis of tiny and small scale sector shows that the investment being low and the product range being wide it is possible for the small units to survive. Most of these units do not use any fixed assets worth mentioning and the owners and the family members are employed to process the raw material into finished products. Hence, the direct costs of such employment is never loaded on to cost of production. Most of the processed products are sold in local or nearby markets, still reducing the overheads and keeping the profit margins high.

Most of the smaller units are unable to bear the burden of heavy taxation. Rationalization of the central and state taxes will definitely help. Imposition of central excise at multiple points is one of the major problems faced by the industry. The incidence of taxes on packaged processed foods works out to about 30 per cent. This takes our products out of reach of the common man. According to a section of small-scale food processors, the laws and regulatory measures governing the food processing industry, framed in 1955, have remained mostly unchanged. Despite repeated representations from the industry for necessary amendments to take on the challenges thrown up by MNCs and foreign brands, no sincere attempt has been made by the Centre and the states so far to this effect. Incoherent policies, bureaucratic red tape, heavy taxation and official apathy have conspired to stagnate and, at times, even suffocate the country's nascent food processing industry. The situation has become all the more critical as India has become a party to the WTO agreement which allows automatic foreign equity participation to the extent of 51 per cent in the organized sector and a maximum of 24 per cent in the small scale segment.

A common complaint against the banking sector is that it has not tried to understand the special needs of the food processing sector. The industry has to carry a very large inventory as the processing season is very short (two to three months for any particular fruit). In the West, institutions like Rabobank (The Netherlands) cater to the special financial needs of the agricultural sector. The closest Indian equivalent of Rabobank is NABARD. It might be a good idea if Nabard uses its experience to develop special models to address the specific financial needs of the farm and food processing sectors. The entry of multinationals like Hindustan Lever, Nestle, Kelloggs, Coca-Cola, Pepsi and Cadbury and large Indian groups like Godrej and ITC - and the use of well known international brand names - has resulted in some improvement in the ground situation but problems remain.

Quality is the first and most basic of these. Most SMEs do not maintain good government practices (GMP) or good hygiene practices (GHP). The food testing labs are out of reach of these units and as a result, only about 25 per cent of the companies in the organised sector use these labs or implement GMP or GHP. A second major problem faced by small companies is the absence of a steady supply of fruits of consistent quality at reasonable prices. The managing director of a Delhi-based small scale unit complains: "We have to take whatever fruit we get. There's very little choice. Thus, we can't guarantee the quality of the finished product. Besides, prices fluctuate wildly between seasons, making cost planning hazardous".

Red tape and corruption, the old enemies of the Indian business class, are making their presence felt in this sector as well. According to Kolkata based promoter of Crusher Fruit Juice Company which produces sauces, pickles, mixed spices and squashes, small food processing units are not allowed to increase production in reaction to market trends. In a throwback to the Licence -Permit Raj, any production in excess of the permissible limit (in accordance with the regulatory measures framed in 1955) is deemed "illegal". Another major problem is the concentration of demand in urban pockets of the country.

Finally, there is very little R & D in this area. Consequently, Indian entrepreneurs have to perforce, remain dependent on products developed and popularised by MNCs. At the same time Indian fruit processors are rendered uncompetitive against their foreign rivals mainly because of the low yields of Indian fruits.

In the absence of these very basic backward linkages, it is not surprising to find the industry languishing. However, the first strands of silver are already visible through the dark clouds. The powers that be are beginning to realise the potential of the food processing sector and are looking to give it its due. Karnataka which contributes a sizeable chunk of India's fruit and vegetable crops has recently become the first state in the country to come out with a separate policy for the food processing sector, though it may take some time for the policy vision to translate into real achievements on the ground.

For starters, the Union as well as the state governments will do well to identify a few fruits and vegetables and concentrate on pushing them both in India and abroad. In recent times Indian industry has moved up the value chain and has started making products like frozen pulps and vegetable curries in pouches and canned mushroom and mushroom products. Despite the current less-than-healthy state of the Indian food processing industry, things are likely to get better in future. Changing attitudes and lifestyles not only among the urban elite but also down the social hierarchy can only lead to a higher demand for value added products. The low base also points towards this. The future can only get better*.

NATIONAL POLICY FOR FOOD PROCESSING—THE NEED AND STEPS TAKEN

Then Union Minister for Agriculture Mr Nitish Kumar while inaugurating a National Conference on "National Policy on Food Processing" said that the policy should create an impact at the grass root level to enable the producers of agricultural produce derive full advantage. Panchayat level institution's must be involved so that the development can have a uniform spread. Location specific system based technologies must be adopted to have a holistic approach. Government is prepared to have a proactive industry oriented approach to enable the industry to grow in a modern, scientific and well planned manner.

Challenges of WTO regime have to be taken as an opportunity rather than a challenge. With the opening of the global markets, we will be in a position to derive maximum advantage in case our food processing sector is appropriately developed with a network of laboratories and R& D institutions to achieve the highest standards of manufacturing practice and the final product. The deliberations of this Conference will enable the country to evolve an appropriate National Policy on Food Processing so as to create a win-win situation for all the players in the field, namely, farmers, processors, industries and the ultimate consumers.

The Department of Food Processing Industries has been operating a number of Plan Schemes to develop the infrastructure for processing and post harvest management. Number of research institutions were also assisted to enable processed food to be of a high and acceptable standard. A special programme was also launched to formulate effective strategies to eliminate micro-nutritional deficiency. Further, this sector is totally delicensed and deregulated to enable establishment of more and more such industries.

Value addition to the raw produce in the country is hardly 7 per cent. Small scale and unorganized sector accounts for more than 75 per cent of the food processing industry. Intermediaries deny our

* Economic Times, August 9, 1999.

farmers from getting remunerative prices. Another issue on which focused attention is required is regarding the multifarious laws and plethora of agencies administering them. There is an urgent need not only to harmonize these laws but to simplify them so as to make these laws easy for compliance. A single comprehensive legislation could be introduced to relieve the industry from the throes of multitudes of legislations.

Food Processing Industry has been identified as a thrust area for development as it involves many types of value addition to the agricultural and horticultural produce starting at post-harvest level. It is a matter of concern that only 2 per cent of fruits and vegetables in our country are processed. The wastage levels are as high as 30 to 40 per cent of production equivalent to the annual consumption in the United Kingdom or Australia. In Rupee term, this wastage works out of nearly Rs. 25,000 crores. Even if half of this is converted into value added commodities, it would add a high degree of impetus to the economic development of the country.

The processed food sector provides a high index of employment. For every thousand crores of rupees invested, this sector generates employment to 39,000 persons in comparison to 31,300 jobs in the textiles and 22,300 in the paper industry. Some of the specific steps taken during the past decade with regard to this sector are –except for alcoholic beverages, the rest of the sector has been delicensed and deregulated; Fruit Products Order have been simplified to facilitate quality production under hygienic environment ; 100 per cent foreign direct investment (FDI) has been allowed in the sector; facilitating environment for domestic and foreign investments is made; and Plan schemes and pattern of assistance has been geared up to give a boost to the sector.

The policy has attempted a bottom up matrix of development as against the top down system and has attempted to involve village level and Panchayati Raj institutions. Attention is focused now on location and product specific system based technologies so as to have a holistic approach in formulation of the policy to make it viable for this promising and growing industry.

Imperatives for Food Processing Industry are waste reduction, remunerative prices to farmers, price stability, employment potential and challenges of WTO. The suggestions received from the industry representatives are concept of cluster development, creating centres of excellence, harmonization of laws-single act, simplification of procedures, market intelligence, strong database, specialized packing development, focus on area specific fruit/vegetable, processing near farms, linkage between farmer and the processor, future trading, equalization and development funds, establishment of cold chains, new technologies, tax holiday for 5-10 years and standards-compulsory and in line with codex.

Opportunities in Food Processing

India is one of the world's largest food producers. With a food industry business estimated at US$ 72 billion (1), to which 26% of the nation's GDP and 61% of employment is linked, food is the most important aspects of the Indian economy. The study report (1996) of the Confederation of Indian Industries (CII) and consultant firm M.C Kinsey has thrown up many interesting facts on India's food industry, some of which are as follows:-

a. India is the most richly endowed agricultural nation in Asia-having 75% more available land than China and almost as much all of East and South East Asia put together. In contrast, India's output is 30% less than that of China. This offers immense opportunity, with very high scope for improvement in output.

b. The Indian food processing industry is on the brink of a revolution that will modernise the entire food chain. This will need lot of capital-human, technological and financial which will require at least US$ 40 billion in the next ten years.

c. India's output multiplier for food is the highest of any sector-at 2.4. So, for a US$ 29 million growth in food, the Indian economy grows by a US$ 69 million-making food a national priority. Of course, food habits are changing rapidly, with a clear leaning towards value added products.

Tables 23.5 and 23.6 depict the position of India in different food products as well as their projections.

Table 23.5 India's Share of World Production

Sl. No.	*Commodity*	*% Share*	*Rank in the World Production*
1.	Fruit & Vegetables	9	1
	a) Fruit	8	1
	b) Vegetable	12	2
2.	Rice	21	2
3.	Tea	28	1
4.	Milk	10	1
5.	Sugar	11	1

This shows that India is the world's largest producer of indispensable agricultural commodities like sugar, rice, milk, tea and fruit/ vegetable etc. According to the said Report the value added food sector in India will present dramatic growth possibilities, say three times more in 10 years (Table 23.6).

Table 23.6 Growth of Value Added Food Sector of India

Sl. No.	Year	Sector worth (US $)
1.	1995	22.86 billion
2.	2005	64.29 billion (Projected)

1. Draft Report on Integrated marketing Master Plan for Jammu & Kashmir, Vol. III; National Institute of Agricultural Marketing, Jaipur.
2. Ibid.

CONCLUSION

The growth of the food processing industry will bring immense benefits to the economy raising the agricultural yields, ushering new opportunities, creating employment and raising the standard of large number of people throughout the country especially in the rural areas. Economic liberalization and rising consumer prosperity is opening up new opportunities for diversification in food processing sector. Liberalization of world trade has opened up new vistas for growth. There is enormous potential in India to make profitable business in food processing. To enable appropriate environment for entrepreneurs to set up food processing industries, the Central Government and the state governments will have to work in a close interactive manner and evolve joint efforts to provide conducive atmosphere for the production of safe, hygienic, healthy and high quality, processed foods conforming to international standards at a competitive and economic costs. This will make available processed foods at a reasonable cost to the consumers as well as stimulate demands in the domestic and overseas markets. Extensive training should be provided to the farmers and cooperatives in the area of post harvest management of agro produce to encourage creation of preprocessing facilities near the farms which include provision for washing, fumigation, packaging etc. Efforts should be made to encourage setting up of agro processing facilities close to the area of production to avoid wastages and transportation of raw materials to far away places and to ensure increased value addition especially for horticultural produce. Application of bio-technology, remote sensing technologies, pre and post harvest technologies, energy saving technologies and technologies for environmental protection should be encouraged. This will reduce poverty by providing opportunity for gainful employment to the rural masses with income distribution among the poor class society. By adopting these measures, India will become stronger economically, socially and politically among the developing nations of the world as the safe, hygienic, healthy and nutritious food is essential for healthy survival of any nation and its citizens.

CHAPTER 24

Globalisation of Agriculture and World Trade Organization

Though the realization that a major change of the economy was essential had been gaining ground in policy making circles from mid eighties, the macroeconomic crisis of 1991 compelled the then government to take advantage of the changed outlook and initiate a wide-ranging reform programme with devastating speed. Liberalization, privatisation and globalisation are the three pillars on which the edifice of the economic reform policy has been erected since 1991. Of these three, globalisation has become the present day buzzword. The term globalisation means the integration of Indian economy with the world economy. It has been deemed as panacea for solving all problems because it presupposes promoting competition, efficiency, productivity, cost effectiveness, technological upgradation, modernization and growth. In fact, any country that wants to achieve economic development and modernise its productive processes has to globalise - not only in its outlook but also its economic policies. Various attempts have since been made to globalise the Indian economy through industry, trade, investment and other channels essentially aiming at integrating India with the rest of the world.

As in other sectors, it has been necessary to globalise in agriculture also, though agricultural reform is very complex, involving changes in other policies and cooperation of states. But it was assumed that there would be no long-run insuperable opposition, since the opening of trade would more than compensate most farmers for loss of subsidies if any, and the poor could be compensated in various ways for a rise in cereal prices. In fact, globalisation of markets leads to competition in farm production and the products marketed at a competitive price. In such a situation for agriculture, the best option, as has been envisaged, is to enhance net monetary returns per unit area, input and time. In the coming years agriculture will certainly face more challenging situations on the ecological, global, climatic, economic, social justice, energy, and employment fronts. This calls for realization of competitive quality of produce to ensure better returns on investment thereby securing improved living standards for those engaged in agriculture. This will no doubt need careful phasing and coordination of several ministries as well as states. There is however, no need of having an over-arching institution to steer the process of globalisation in agriculture.

AGRICULTURAL TRADE

A conventional version of the changes in agricultural trade pattern during the course of economic development will suggest that with the growth of an economy not only does the share of agriculture in GDP declines, so does the share of agricultural exports to the total merchandise exports. As the economy gets diversified, non-agricultural items and the processed agricultural products acquire greater importance in the product mix, and also in exports. One of the reasons for relative decline in agricultural commodities in a developing economy may be attributed to rising share of processed agricultural products. On the import side, with larger share of purchased inputs in the input base of agriculture, the quantum of imports of inputs such as fertilizers, pesticides, farm machinery, etc. rises. However, as the import intensity of agricultural production is low, earnings from exports outpace the outlay on imports. Most of the developing countries still maintain a favourable trade balance in agriculture in an environment of globalised economy.

However, India like several other large countries, is not an export-oriented economy. This is particularly true of agriculture. In recent years the ratio of agricultural exports to agriculture GDP has seldom exceeded 3 per cent. The Indian export basket has a composition that has virtually remained unchanged over the years with low-value added commodities predominating. Even when volumes are rising, unit realizations have been going down showing that our competitiveness is unduly dependent on low prices and not on other parameters like quality or technology. Quality standards of agricultural products are becoming an increasingly important factor in world trade. Indian exports of rice and other agricultural products, for example, have to meet quality standards in importing countries, particularly in the developed world. But relying on the quality certification mechanisms of the developed world to decide on the quality of Indian agricultural exports has at least two very serious shortcomings. First, if a consignment from one exporter does not meet the quality standards, there is typically a tendency to blacklist all Indian exports of the product. Second, quality standards developed in the importing country could be designed to protect that country's producers.

There cannot be two opinions that quality enforcement in agricultural exports is essential, but it should be transparent, efficient and quick. Perishables can perish if the inspection is not done properly. The unfair manner in which restrictions are imposed on Indian agricultural exports need to be recognized and commercial policy and economic and diplomatic policy initiatives taken. Globalisation, per se, may not help in inculcating dynamism in agricultural trade. The country needs to follow through the vicissitudes of the global economy. The accepted economic wisdom today is that there is no future for a country which does not integrate its economy with global economy and learn to face and survive competition on a global scale. In fact, globalisation is a part of a process of progressive integration of the world economy through falling barriers to trade and exchange and greater mobility of capital. In India, with its economy newly opened-up internally and externally, export competitiveness has been given a top priority in the economic agenda of the government. However, there is a need for commitment, clarity and systematic approach to various impediments for achieving global competitiveness. The economic environment for agricultural trade is changing in a remarkable way due to changes in the domestic policies as well as international trade arrangements and India should join countries pushing for aggressive liberalization of trade in agricultural commodities, particularly in the world market.

Since the philosophy behind trade liberalization is the maximisation of global welfare through efficiency gains, mapping out comparative advantages across countries for different commodities in a dynamic setting is necessary as a basis for meaningful negotiation in the WTO.

WORLD TRADE ORGANIZATION (WTO)

The Genesis

The principle of comparative advantage which is built on the basis of the inter-country differences in costs and returns between different commodities abstracting from taxes and subsidies influencing these costs and returns is the foundation of international trade. However, the principle of comparative advantage is denied a free play in two ways. Firstly, if some rich countries because of their ability to subsidize agriculture can sell their produce at artificially lower prices and thus undercut the market for the genuinely efficient or low cost producers, then the playing field is highly uneven and the principle of comparative advantage is not followed or is even thrown overboard. On the other hand, there are several countries which have only recently emerged from long period of colonial rule and they have to go a long way to achieve a level playing field vis-à-vis developed countries in regard to infrastructure, technology and skills. These countries need protection for some time in certain specified areas before they can harness their potential and attain the position to compete with the advanced countries as trading partners on an equal footing. It is therefore essential to make some institutional arrangement like WTO for ensuring level playing field so that considerations of comparative advantage can have a free and fair play.

A world body however, was created (in 1947) after the second world war, called General Agreement on Tariffs and Trade (GATT). The GATT was engaged in efforts at promoting multilateralism in world trade through reduction of tariff and non-tariff barriers to trade. It provided a forum for the countries to discuss and overcome their trade problems and negotiate to enlarge international trading opportunities. Domestic policies and matters outside of goods trade were regarded as beyond the orbit and competence of GATT. The first seven rounds of GATT, ending with the Tokyo Round in 1979, conformed to this traditional GATT paradigm and confined themselves to tariff cuts and reduction of non-tariff barriers with a view to liberalizing global trade in goods. In the eighth round in 1986 held at Puntadel-Este of Uruguay unexpectedly proposals were made in the form of Annexures. Annexe IA was on Trade-Related Investment Measures (TRIMs); 1B on Trade in Service (GATS) and on Trade Related Intellectual Property Rights (TRIPs), thus annexing all aspects of the economy which include patent, insurance, banking, agriculture, etc.

The proposals were opposed by the developing countries led by India and Brazil and no decision could be taken. Ultimately it was left to the chairman of GATT, Arthur Dunkel to prepare a draft for discussion. The developed countries, led by the U.S., Japan Canada and what later became the European Union, decided that GATT should expand its responsibilities. They were keen that GATT introduce global rules that would make it easier for all kinds of products and services to be sold in countries around the world. No longer was GATT's work to be only about customs duties on products like clothes, toys and electronic goods. It was also about the rules for allowing global banks to establish branches around the world, about how governments could provide patents on everything from seeds to medicines, about what prices governments could give farmers for their crops and more. It was also decided then that the era of special concessions to developing countries would end. The draft was completed in December 1991 and was accepted subduing all resistance. GATT was dissolved (January 1, 1995) giving birth to a new world body, World Trade Organisation (WTO) or new GATT with 143 countries including India and China with its headquarters at Geneva. This new body, unlike GATT, did not become a voluntary forum for persuasion but a legal entity empowered to prosecute and punish. However, India does not project the WTO as some sort of international court. She believes that the political and negotiating character of the WTO should not be subordinated to the dispute resolution role of this organization.

The significance of the Uruguay Round agreements concluded in Marrakesh in April, 1994, can be appreciated once it is recognized that for the first time agriculture is brought under the GATT discipline and there was an elaborate Agreement on Agriculture (AoA). Until the Uruguay Round of trade negotiations, the contracting parties to GATT had reconciled to a waiver on agricultural trade obtained by the United States of America (USA), which was also used by other countries. The situation has changed, ironically, at the instance of the USA which, in fact, pleaded for complete removal of all interventions in agriculture. The proposal to bring agriculture under GATT discipline evoked a responsive chord in several countries which were concerned with the rising burden of subsidies in their budgets. However, since agriculture is brought under the new rules of world trading system for the first time, as expected, there are a few problems in implementation of this AoA.

After lengthy and tortuous negotiations under the Uruguay Round, agreements were reached on several important areas. These include: (a) reduction in farm subsidies; (b) enhanced market access; (c) sparing use of sanitary and phytosanitary import barriers; and (d) introduction of intellectual property rights.

Reduction in Farm Subsidies

World trade in agriculture has been so far influenced by the several government interventions. Mostly these aim to protect the domestic producers by one or other kind of producer-subsidies. This support consisted of measures such as high support prices for farm produce and export subsidies which are now shifted to direct measures for income support under the so called Blue Box, such as deficiency payments in the US, and compensations to the farmers in the European Union via acreage and headage premiums which are exempt from reduction commitments. As it is well known, these subsidies cause a barrier to trade as the tariff and other quantitative restrictions do. Due to strong political opposition from the farmer lobbies most of the developed nations were reluctant to reduce the subsidies. In fact, a major issue of contention during the Uruguay Round negotiations was the high domestic support being provided to agriculture in the developed countries, especially the European Union in the west and Japan in the east.

Thus the main issue in the negotiation was the extent of reduction in the trade distorting subsidies. Not all subsidies are to be reduced. Briefly following types of support measures will be reduced, but not entirely eliminated. (i) Levies imposed on agricultural products, (ii) Marketing and transport subsidies (not applicable to developing economies), (iii) Subsidies to exports i.e. export sales at prices below the domestic prices and subsidies to inputs of the exportable, and (iv) Payments related to export achievements or performance.

It may be noted that the following types of supports and subsidies are not covered in the total measure of support, called Aggregate Measure of Support (AMS).

(a) General, environmental and other product specific research and development, (b) health safety standardisation extension and advisory services training, (c) infrastructural services (d) pest and disease control (e) marketing and promotion advisory services, (f) public stock holding for security purposes, (g) domestic food aid and public distribution for weaker sections, (h) income support not attached to production or price considerations, (i) Government supported income insurance schemes and income safety net programmes within the limits of 70% of net loss and only for losses exceeding 30% of the average gross income, and (j) payments under environmental and conservational programmes and regional assistance for such purposes.

AMS and Subsidies in Agriculture

As per WTO agreements, country whose product specific and non-product specific AMS does not exceed 10 per cent of the total value of agricultural product in the case of a developing country (5 per cent for developed countries), is not subject to any reduction commitments. If, on the other hand, the AMS exceeds the de-minimis level, the country is committed to reduce domestic support: by 13.3 per cent in case of a developing country over 10 years and 20 per cent in case of a developed country over six years. It may be noted that the obligation is on total AMS and within that there is flexibility to choose products covered and extent of support measure and quantity of products that benefit from them.

The withdrawal of the subsidies will enhance the potential scope for increased agricultural exports, provided a conscious attempt to seize the opportunity is undertaken. It should be noted that the recent agreement on phasing out of subsidies has three aspects. (i) phasing out will take place in stages and there are many who will strive to benefit at each level and stage. Hence it will intensify the competition; (ii) there will be attempts to create some technical barriers in spite of or rather within the agreed framework on phyto-sanitary provisions. It is, however clear that phasing out of subsidies will create sizable opportunity for increasing our agricultural exports; and (iii) as per the definition of the subsidy Indian agriculture has been receiving negative subsidy. Hence we have no immediate obligation to reduce any subsidy. On the contrary we can raise the same till its negative character vanishes plus the limit available in different phases.

Keeping the above in view, it may be pointed out that in India, non-product specific support amounts to 7.5 percent of the value of agricultural production, the aggregate measure of support (AMS) to Indian agriculture is still well below the deminimis of 10 per cent according to Uruguay Round stipulations. In its proposals on the negotiations on WTO Agreements on Agriculture, India has suggested that the AMS may be calculated as a sum of the product specific and non-product specific support. If the product –specific support is still negative in the case of India, then the aggregate measure of support would be below 7.5 per cent of the value of agricultural production. As it is, input subsidies to resource poor farmers which come under non-product specific support are exempt from reduction commitments under the WTO provisions. If India avails of this, the non-product specific support may come down to less than half of what is being shown today. In view of this, it may not be of India's interest to fight within the WTO for greater domestic support to agriculture. For its further growth, Indian agriculture is in need of substantial public investments in irrigation, power, roads, and agricultural research and extension, rather than subsidies on inputs. Indeed, there is a consensus now among planners and policy-makers that the declining investment in agriculture is basically attributable to the mounting subsidies on irrigation, power and fertilizers.

In the developed countries agriculture is highly input-intensive, and a large complex of agro-industries having backward linkage with agriculture as input suppliers constitute the highly organized and vocal sections of these farm lobbies. Moreover, these countries are in any case, incurring huge expenditures on social security for the unemployed in the rest of the economy. The difference is that in the case of the farm sector, these payments take the form of compensation for lower farm prices, thus providing incentive for committing resources beyond what would otherwise have been allocated if farm prices were allowed to be determined by the market forces.

However, it is expected that the situation will change in course of time following pressure from the members of the WTO. There is already a marked shift away from support prices and export subsidies, which are considered highly trade distorting, towards direct payments in the form of deficiency payments and compensations related to acreage and livestock numbers, which are considered `minimally trade distorting' and hence placed under `Blue' and `Green' boxes which are exempt from reduction commitments. This is because such payments, unless they are fully decoupled from the use of inputs, do influence the allocation of resources, in the sense that in the absence of such payments, fewer resources would be committed to agriculture, leading to lower output, higher prices and smaller export surpluses.

In this context , it may be highlighted that in EU countries, where the distortion in the allocation of resources are found to be highest, there is a significant scope for reducing unit cost through wider application of known technologies. There is also a large potential for reducing unit costs through vertical integration of agro-processing industry-the growth of which has been surprisingly slow with farming operations. The ongoing biotechnological revolution promises to work in the same direction. In such an event India must prepare itself for competing with low-cost farm products rather than expecting a significant rise in their prices through reform induced reduction in the surplus from the developed countries.

Market Access or Tariffication

At the beginning of the Uruguay round the border measures in support of the domestic producers were limited to unbound or bound tariffs for approximately two thirds of all agricultural tariff lines of the participating countries. In the rest of the one third tariff lines, border measures or interventions in the form of the non tariff barriers were operative. In these tariff lines, the present protective measures will now be converted into equivalent single new tariff which will roughly provide same degree of protection. Such tariff, can be either advalorem or specific duty. The new tariffs resulting from tariffication together with other tariffs are to be reduced by a simple average of 36 percent in six years in the case of the developed countries and 24 per cent in ten years in case of developing countries. In the case of least developed countries no reduction is required.

This tariffication package includes the MARKET ACCESS (both current and minimum market access) and the right to use the SPECIAL SAFEGUARD PROVISIONS. As per these provisions if the conditions relating to import acceleration or surges or decline in import prices are met, the countries are allowed to impose the additional duties to the bound rates. For products covered under the tariffication process, in all the cases where current market access is less than 5 percent of the domestic consumption it will be maintained. Similarly at reduced tariff rates minimum access tariff quotas will be established. Over the implementation period these minimum tariff quotas will be increased from 3 percent to 5 percent.

India has already negotiated tariff findings at the level of 100 per cent for raw commodities, 150 per cent for processed agro-commodities and 300 per cent for most edible oils. These are considered sufficient to protect the relevant commodities from the onslaught of cheaper imports sustained by high domestic support in the countries of their origin. In fact, major challenge to the viability of agriculture of most developing countries, including India, is posed by the high domestic support, export subsidies and denial of market access through various tariff and non-tariff barriers in the developed countries. India has been fighting in league with other developing countries in the WTO for the removal of such barriers. In the process of bargaining and in India's own interest, the rate of protection to its industry which used to be among the highest in the world has been brought down to less than half of its earlier level. Indian agriculture is a major beneficiary from this reduced protection to industry.

Sanitary and Phytosanitary Requirements and other Quality Restrictions

Exports of the fresh agricultural produce have to meet the phytosanitary standards. So far there existed no specific agreement that covered these phytosanitary measures. With the inclusion of agriculture in the scope of multilateral treaty some broad understanding regarding these standards is essential.

A number of imported agricultural products particularly plants, fresh fruits and vegetables, meat, meat products and other food products may be required to satisfy sanitary and phytosanitary regulations as well as product standards. In addition, many countries restrict the export of these products if they do not meet the quality requirements specified by regulations. The following paragraph illustrates how these regulations can affect international trade.

Knowledge of Health and Sanitary Regulations is important in planning for exports. This can be further explained with the case of fruits and vegetables. A number of major importers of fresh fruits and vegetables have strict regulations on plant protection. These countries require fresh commodities infected with specific pests, especially the fruit fly of the Tephridiate family, to be treated to prevent the establishment of the pests in their territories. In the past, ethylene dibromide (EDB) was widely used for the fumigation of such produce prior to importation. The prohibition of EDB by the United States, Japan, and other countries jeopardized trade in fresh fruit and vegetables originating from tropical and semitropical countries. Alternative treatments to EDB fumigation such as vapour and dry heat treatment, hot water dips, refrigeration at near zero degree centigrade for a specific duration, and treatment with other chemicals such as methyl bromide, phosphine and cyanide, are now used with varying degrees of success.

The Agreement on the Application of Sanitary and Phytosanitary Measures, which was negotiated in the Uruguay Round, specifies the principles and rules, which member countries must follow in regulating imported products. The Agreement define sanitary and phytosanitary measures as measures taken to protect human, animal or plant life or health,

- "From risks arising from the entry, establishment or spread of pests diseases, diseases carrying organisms or diseases causing organisms;
- From risks arising from additives, contaminants, toxins or disease causing organisms in food, beverages or foodstuffs;
- From diseases carried by animals, plants or products thereof".

India's agricultural and horticultural products often encounter strict sanitary and phytosanitary tests introduced by WTO. India's mango exports were getting blocked for not meeting WTO requirements on these aspects and it directed the country to improve its phyto-sanitary regime with the help of Food and Agricultural Organisation (FAO). Further, a new set of stringent norms by the European Union (EU) threatens to shut off exports of edible groundnut from India to that region. The legislations proposed by EU aims at lowering the aflatoxin (a carcinogenic agent) limits in edible nuts from 15 parts per billion (ppb) to 10 ppb measure. The EU has asked the Indian Government to introduce new standards and procedures for production, packaging and pre-shipment inspection for edible peanuts so as to conform to the EU specifications.

Trade Related Aspects of Intellectual Property Rights (TRIPS)

Most of the above agreements are found to be serious impediments for growth of international trade in Indian agriculture. The most serious of the agreements is TRIPS which was signed in 1995 at Marrakesh and as stated earlier, is an annexure to the Marrakesh agreement establishing the World Trade Organisation. As per this agreement India will be required to amend its PATENT ACT 1970 to provide for the product patent and extend the patent protection to the plants. However, the contracting parties will be required to provide for the sui generis system of protection of the newly developed varieties. Intellectual Property Rights were first raised as a multilateral trade issue in 1986 under the General Agreement on Tariffs and Trade (GATT) to crackdown on counterfeit goods. But with many developed countries interested in negotiations on trade liberalisation to tighten control over technology, this narrow focus was soon extended to include many other areas. Although each country implements the Intellectual Property Rights law at the national level, the TRIPS agreement imposes minimum standards on patents, copyright, trade marks and trade secrets. These standards are derived from the legislation of industrial companies, applying the form and level of protection of the industrial world to all WTO members.

This is far tighter than the existing legislations in most developing countries and often conflicts with their national interests and needs. Tightened property rights raise the price of technology transfer, blocking developing countries from the dynamic knowledge sectors. The TRIPS agreement enables multinationals to dominate the global market more easily. In fact, the two US firms patented India's age old agricultural products like `turmeric' and `basmati rice' in which the country has the geographical advantage. However, after a vehement protests and legal battles these patents have since been cancelled. Similarly though India is considered to be the largest source of neem, and has developed and used this plant since centuries for natural cure of a number of ailments, thus having the natural patent, is being pirated and patented by a US based company. Such `biocolonialism' in regard to gene patents is even being condemned by many developed countries and in fact, the European Council has extended its support to India for safeguarding her patent rights. Thus, it is observed that lucrative products belonging to developing countries are being acquired with impunity through the magical instrument of Intellectual Property Rights (IPRs).

India Mooted Changes in WTO Patenting Norms

At a review meeting of WTO TRIPS committee, prior to Seattle, India proposed changes to article 27.3 (b) of the TRIPS Agreement in connection with patenting of life forms, microorganisms, and plant varieties.

India proposed that the review could see whether and what form of exclusion from patentability should apply to plants and animals "per se"; as well as the effect of protection granted to macro-organisms and non-biological and microbiological processes (scope and definition of microorganism); and also whether and what form of protection of plant varieties through "sui generis" systems was an effective form of protection (effectiveness of plant variety protection).

India's paper to TRIPS stated that developing countries could not accept any further strengthening of the protection to life forms at present. In these countries, laws in this area are in the process of being developed and they need more time to acquire experience on the level of protection necessary and desirable as well as the exceptions and balances necessary for ethical, social and economic needs of their peoples. The paper called for re-examining the need to grant patents on life forms anywhere in the world. It advised that there be a standstill on giving patents until such systems were in place, and advisable to:

- exclude patents on all life forms,
- and if this is impossible, to exclude patents based on traditional/ indigenous knowledge and essentially derived products and processes from such knowledge.
- at least there should be an insistence on disclosure of the country of origin of the biological resource and associated knowledge, and obtention consent of the country providing the resource and knowledge, to ensure equitable sharing of benefits.

India considers that there could be two dimensions on the patenting of life forms - the ethical question of private ownership that could be extended to life forms and the use of intellectual property rights (IPRs) concept as understood by industrialized countries and its appropriateness in the face of the larger dimension of rights on knowledge, their ownership, use, transfer and dissemination. India proposed that TRIPS should have another look on the scope of patentability of microorganisms and non-biological and microbiological processes with many grey areas in defining the scope of patentable microorganisms and microbiological processes multilaterally.

India called for making a difference between discovery and invention, with only "invention" being allowed to be patented. India also questioned the patentibility of biological material such as cell lines, enzymes, plasmids, cosmids and genes, unless they fell in the category of microorganisms. A gene could not be patented except if it was also qualified as a microorganism that was patentable under the "natural law". India felt it should be left to the national policy to decide what were patentable macro-organisms. The same goes for plant varieties, which should be left to member countries to decide what system it would like to choose for providing protection of plant varieties in accordance with a country's own legal system and practice. India's paper leaves countries to develop their own models, which are effective "sui generis" systems under TRIPS.

Finally, perhaps few would underrate the key role that agriculture has played, first in the making and then in the functioning of the WTO. However, the tardy implementation of the more crucial provisions of the Agreement on Agriculture (AoA) now poses several challenges to this new world body. The AoA was concluded with the understanding that the market distortions plaguing the agricultural sector would progressively be removed through the adoption of two broad sets of policies. The first was to be in the form of reining in the subsidies, which were responsible for distortion of market prices. The second set of policies involved the adoption of relatively more open trading regime through the removal of all non-tariff barriers and replacing these by appropriate level of tariffs. On both fronts, however, the implementation by the developed countries has been far removed from what was anticipated during the negotiations on AoA.

In fact, there are now four sharp divergently opposed blocks among the members of the WTO. Apart from the views of the CAIRNS* Group and the United States as well as diametrically opposed views of the European Union (EU), Japan, Norway and Switzerland, two other blocks have come up: those of developing countries like India, whose large rural population depend on agriculture not only for rural employment but a way of life, and call for food security and necessity to develop agriculture, as well as another group-that of net food importing developing countries. The CAIRNS Group wants that provisions with regard to AoA to be detailed and specific on objectives (such as bringing into line with individual products), on the scope of issues to be included such as substantial reduction and immediate elimination of market subsidies, and special and differential treatment (including market access for developing countries as well as their own commitments), substantial reduction in support and protection for exports. The US also wants trade in biotechnology, including genetically modified products not to depend on consumer concerns but to be governed as a rational basis. The opposing view of the EU and supporters is that there should not be any further amendment to the provisions laid down in Article 20 of the AoA. Norway does not endorse the view that agriculture to be treated as industry.

Developing countries such as India, Egypt, Jamaica, Honduras and Pakistan call for greater flexibility in treatment, as the present system

* A group of 15 countries formed after a meeting in Cairns, Australia, in 1986 to push aggressively for liberalization of trade in agriculture. The members are Australia, Argentina, Brazil, Canada, Chile, Columbia, Fiji, Indonesia, Malaysia, New Zealand, Paraguay, The Philippines, South Africa, Thailand and Uruguay.

is biased against them for such lower limits on trade distorting subsidies for use in rural employment, poverty alleviation and increasing agricultural productivity permitted to them. India advocates that support given by food insecure countries for maintaining enhanced domestic production for domestic consumption should be entirely exempt from provisions of the Agreement on Agriculture. Developing countries with predominantly rural economies dependent on agriculture should be given greater flexibility so that they can address non-trade concerns such as food security and rural employment. This should not come under the AoA aggregate measure of support (AMS) requirements.

With the more dominant players in the global agricultural scenario intent upon keeping their market share in a manner that blatantly violates the AoA, the possibilities of additional market access for the developing countries that could take advantage of a genuine opening up of trade in this sector have remained a mirage. In fact, the problems faced by the developing countries, India- not excluding, arising from the implementation problems could be two-fold. One, they would not get the desirable share of the market because of the continuing policies of protectionism. And, two, their own markets may be targeted by the subsidized products from the developed countries.

Seattle Meeting and WTO Doldrum

The WTO ministerial meeting in seattle held on 30th November to 3rd December, 1999 failed to reach any agreement. The developing countries were, in fact, on the receiving end in Seattle as the US, along with the European Union, decided to bring on to the agenda three contentious issues. On top of this list was the issue of labour standards. The efforts of the US towards this end were helped by the protests made by the country's trade unions. The trade unions argued that the businesses took advantage of "sweat shops" which offered employment on low wages, thus depriving the work force in affluent countries of their jobs.

The second issue was the establishment of the working group on biotechnology, which was to oversee the trade in genetically modified food. This initiative of bringing the issue of bio-safety in the WTO, can be considered as a part of the familiar "forum shifting" agenda of the US. Bio-safety issues are currently at an advanced stage of negotiations under the UN sponsored Convention on Biological Diversity (CBD). The US has, however, not yet ratified the CBD since it views the CBD to be serving the interests of the developing countries.

The third issue that was raising its head, much to the discomfiture of the developing countries, was the linking of trade with environment. The European Union seemed quite keen to bring this agenda on to the WTO. The negotiators of the European Union opined that the protection of the environment was not possible without the use of trade sanctions, a position most developing countries rejected ever since trade and environment were considered by the WTO.

Beside the Agreement on Agriculture, India has also been arguing for a review of the Agreement on Trade Related Aspects of Intellectual Property Rights (TRIPs) to take into consideration several of its concerns. In the first place, the agreement on TRIPs needs to be amended to take on board the rights of the local communities in so far as they are the custodians of traditional knowledge systems. Secondly, the agreement was required to provide effective protection to geographical location of the produce. And, finally, the rapid move towards patenting of life forms, a process that was set in motion by the TRIPs Agreement by bringing in microorganism under the ambit of patenting, needed to be reviewed.

Doha WTO Meet

After the Seattle doldrums in 1999, the fourth ministerial conclave of the 143 member countries of WTO was held in November, 2001 at Doha in Qatar to discuss on major trade issues. The Doha agenda calls for negotiations in four areas: trade liberalization, trade and environment, WTO rules in certain areas and the Dispute Settlement Understanding (DSU). The mandate on trade and environment and WTO rules is truly narrow and DSO negotiations are part of the Uruguay Round built-in agenda. This leaves trade liberalization as the main negotiating item on the agenda. There were continuing negotiations on WTO Agreement on Agriculture also. Since India is concerned with regard to implementation of the provisions on textiles, clothing, agriculture, subsidies, countervailing measures and dumping, the Doha meet gave the country a real opportunity to redress some of the wrongs of the Uruguay Round. The real gains in the agreement is expected to come from TRIPS where the TRIPS council would examine contentious issues such as the compatibility with the convention on bio-diversity and traditional knowledge. The ministerial decided that around 40 implementation and other issues would be considered by the relevant WTO bodies. These bodies would report to the Trade Negotiating Committee by the end of 2002 for appropriate action.

The most contentious issue is that of antidumping. The United States feels that developing countries that apply their laws do not have the same transparency, information standards, standards of analysis and methods of review. Thus, there is a need to discipline their application of antidumping, which can only be done through negotiations. However, the US also feels that sufficient safeguards on the necessity of anti-dumping measures has been introduced in the ministerial declaration on the preservation of the principles and objectives of these instruments.

In fact, the draft declaration for Doha specifically addresses the issue of the misuse of the antidumping device by many countries. The developed countries, therefore, have a far greater responsibility in outlining a vision that ensures that the framework of the multilateral trade regime does not degenerate into a self-serving instrument that increases the gap between the rich and the poor nations, as has been happening in the past decades.

The main task of the trade negotiating committee would be to launch fresh negotiations on issues like investment, competition, government procurement and measures facilitating trade, as well as the link between trade and the environment. Since these negotiations have been put off for another two years, India has now an opportunity to shape the agenda. The real gain in the area has been limiting the scope of possible negotiations on government procurement, as well as the introduction of the words "explicit consensus" on the modalities of negotiations. India has also been successful to keep labour standards out of the TWO.

Further, the Doha agenda calls for trade liberalization in all sectors: industry, agriculture and services. Given the urgent need to jump-start India's trade reform, expected benefits to its farmers from increased access to the European market and the need to eliminate tariff peaks in developed countries in products such as textiles and clothing, footwear and fisheries, India stands to benefit from the proposed liberalization agenda. India also believes the protection of geographical indications offered to products like champagne must be extended to basmati. The Doha ministerial decided that the question of extending the protection of geographical indications will be addressed by the council of TRIPS. It further instructed the council of TRIPS to agreement and the convention on Biological Diversity as well as protecting traditional knowledge.

India's key concern is that the WTO regime talks about freer movement of trade and investment but is not so enthusiastic about cross-border movement of labour. After all, labour is a key component of trade in services, which is expected to drive economic growth in the 21st century. So a barrier to movement of people is the biggest barrier to trade.

India does not have global competitiveness in technology intensive goods, simply because it does not have enough resources to acquire high-end technology that originates in the West. But India has great competitiveness in labour intensive services. A simple example will illustrate this point. A barber—described as a 'hair designer' abroad—charges anything between $ 20 and $ 25 in the US for a plain hair cut. A good Indian 'hair designer', on the other hand, charges Rs. 50 to Rs. 75. Thus the Indian 'hair designer' is cheaper than his counterpart by over Rs. 600.

In the end, all the 143 countries that are members of the WTO, agreed on an agenda for negotiations. The agenda is yet another long list of subjects of more than a dozen. Some are old like import duties, some are new like rules on environment and trade and some are on a slow boil like how much freedom individual countries should have in laying down the rules for foreign investors. At Doha they only decided on the agenda. The negotiations themselves are expected to be completed only in 2005, which is when new treaties will be signed.

Every country claims "a victory" at Doha. But the result of what some call the Doha Development Agenda, will depend on how governments are able to negotiate with their trading partners. In the WTO, every member-country is supposed to have the same rights as the other. But that is not how it works, since power comes from how big an exporting nation one is. So while the new round is supposed to have a "development" feel to it, the proof of the Doha pudding will be in its eating. This is one pudding which will see intense fights, which will take years to bake and which many in the end be bitter to taste for some, perhaps many, countries.

Food Security Box

India has proposed a Food Security Box in the ongoing negotiations on WTO Agreement on Agriculture as a safeguard mechanism for farmers. A majority of farmers in India and other developing countries are engaged in subsistence farming and they need protection from surge in imports. The food security in India was becoming increasingly vulnerable to the dynamics of trade liberalization and during the last six years international prices of agricultural commodities were steadily declining and agricultural exports were decreasing. This had adversely affected the farming sector as it resulted in both production losses due to vagaries of weather and low prices. The Food Security Box is likely to safeguard the interest of the farmers, under such situations.

PERFORMANCE OF THE DEVELOPING COUNTRIES

It is argued that developing countries are losing ground in the world trading system, and risk further impoverishment and marginalisation if a new trade round is launched. The developing countries share of world trade is declining that their exports face the highest tariffs and the most protected markets in the world and that they lack the ability to influence or change a system inherently biased in favour of the rich and powerful. It is told that the developing nations are losing out in world trade. Over the past decade, developing countries have consistently outperformed industrialised countries in terms of export growth—an average increase of almost 10 per cent a year, compared to 5 per cent for the industrialised countries. And trade among developing countries is growing more quickly than the trade with the industrialised North. During 2000, developing-country exports rose by 15 per cent—three times their GDP growth—the best in five decades. Even with the current economic slowdown, developing countries are expected to show much stronger trade growth in 2001 than the industrialised economies.

These numbers demonstrate the average performance among developing countries; some are doing better, some worse. Even so, claims about poor-country "marginalisation" distort the facts. For example, the 49 Least-Developed Countries saw the dollar value of their exports rose by 28 per cent in 2000—some $34 billion—the second year in a row where they exceeded the world average. Bangladesh, Cambodia, Madagascar and Nepal saw their exports soar in the 1990s—matching or even exceeding China's impressive performance.

2. Rich-country markets are more closed and protected, while developing countries are being forced to open up. It is true that many developing-country exports continue to face significant barriers in rich country markets. Often the products in which developing countries are highly competitive are the ones that confront the highest protection. However, what is not true is the assertion that industrialised countries are more closed or more protected than developing countries. The average bound tariff for the U.S. is just 3 per cent, for Europe it's 3.6, and for the industrialised countries as a whole it's under 4 per cent. In comparison, the average bound tariff for developing countries is over 12 per cent. While developing countries slashed their tariffs by 20 per cent during the Uruguay Round, developed nations cut theirs by almost 40 per cent.

This helps explain why, each year, developing countries claim a larger and larger share of the industrialised world's imports—from 15 per cent in 1990 to almost 25 per cent in 2000. Over half of Japan's manufactured imports come from developing countries. For the U.S., the share is 45 per cent which is rising. These trends do not reflect that altruism of the industrialised countries so much as their self-interest—a realisation that imports from the developing world are key to low inflation, rising productivity and increased living standards.

3. Developing countries lack a voice in the WTO. How then to explain that so many "development" issues are now at the top of the WTO's agenda? From being a fringe issue a generation ago, the debate over how to get better integrated development priorities into the trading system became the main issue for the fourth WTO Ministerial Conference—and its resolution largely decided new negotiations held in Doha. Developing countries such as India. Brazil and South Africa are in the forefront of nations defining the parameters of the WTO's future programme—their Ministers, Ambassadors and officials are among the most influential trade-policy practitioners today.

Indeed, the idea that a new round of negotiations must be a "development round" is now almost universally espoused—from

Ms. Clare Short, U.K. Minister of Development to Mr. Kofi Annan, U.N. Secretary. General, Mr. Jim Wolfensohn, World Bank President, and Mr. Hurst Kohler, IMF managing director. This is the evidence of a new, more assertive role for developing countries.

This is because WTO has emerged as one of the most important international institutions for development. Developing countries already account for a third of the world trade, from a fifth in the 1970s. At current trends, their share will grow to well over half of the world trade in the next 25 years. They need stronger multilateral rules, not weaker one; more trade liberalisation, not less. Already a third of the cases before the WTO's dispute settlement body are brought by developing countries. They have gained significantly from trade liberalisation under the Uruguay Round and, according to a study, would realise some $200 billion if the remaining trade barriers were to be halved in a new round. That is three times what the developing world receives in overseas aid, eight times what poor countries have so far been granted in debt relief.

To conclude, it may be pointed out that the biggest change is in attitudes. More and more, developing countries have come to see protectionism as a self-inflicted wound. It not only punishes consumers, grossly inflating the price they pay for necessities such as food or clothing, but it also handicaps exporters and entrepreneurs, who cannot hope to compete in world markets without access to world-priced inputs, efficient services and modern technology. Trade liberalisation is the key to developing countries, not just because it opens markets, but because it makes their own economies stronger. It is a fact that the developing world would be much worse off without the multilateral trading system. It is also a fact that the trading system can be greatly improved.

Defining and refining rules for trade—keeping the system relevant to a fast-changing world economy—will always be work-in-progress. Governments will never stop and say they have finished, that they are satisfied. The challenge is to secure balanced progress that reflects common interests. Governments must feel committed, not coerced. They must see justice in the WTO agenda and national advantage in pursuing it. But they must also be reminded of the achievements. More has been done to address poverty in these last 50 years than in the previous 500. Since 1960, child death rates have been halved in developing countries, malnutrition rates have declined by a third: access to safe water has improved dramatically. While the current U.N. Millennium Declaration targets show that there is still a long way to go and we need to keep in mind that trade is just one contributor to the progress that has been secured, we should not lose sight of the important role the multilateral trading system has played. The question is how we share this gift of opportunity and do a better job as an institution designed to serve our member governments.

PERFORMANCE OF AGRICULTURE IN THE POST-REFORMS PERIOD

As expected, the liberalization of Indian economy which had commenced from around the mid- 1980s and accelerated with the launching of full-fledged macro-economic reforms since the early 1990s, has improved the incentive framework for agriculture. With the liberalization of exchange rate and opening up of the economy, the terms of trade for agriculture have shown a significant improvement. As a result, private investment in agriculture registered a steep rise in the post-reform periods. At 1993-94 prices, private investment in agriculture was over 50 per cent higher in 1999-2000 when compared to 1993-94.

However the growth rate of agricultural production in India has declined in the post-reforms period though there has been marked increase in overall production. For example, the average foodgrains production for ten years during the post-reforms period was 188 million tonnes as against 146 million tonnes during the decade before reforms period. But the annual compound growth was only 1.66 per cent, which was lower than population growth rate, as against 3.19 per cent during the pre-reforms period. Improper sequencing of reforms bearing on supply-side factors, such as irrigation and fertilizer, were allegedly responsible for the poor growth rate of foodgrains production during the post-reforms period.

In fact, policy approach to agriculture, particularly in the 1990s, has been more to secure increased production through subsidies in inputs such as power, water and fertilizer, rather than through building new capital assets in irrigation and power. This has reduced the pace and pattern of technological change in agriculture and effected TFP (total factor productivity) adversely. The equity, efficiency, and sustainability of the current approach thus become debatable. The subsidies also do not improve income distribution and the demand for labour. The boost in output from subsidy-stimulated use of fertilizers, pesticides and water may partly be coming at the expense of deterioration in the aquifers and soil- and environmentally unsustainable approach that may partly explain the rising costs and slowing growth and productivity in agriculture, notably in Punjab and Haryana, Moreover, the deteriorating state finances have meant that subsidies have, in effect:-

(a) crowded-out public agricultural investment in irrigation and roads and expenditure on technological upgrading.
(b) Limited maintenance of canals and roads, and
(c) Contributed to the low quality of rural power.

The growth rate of capital formation is important while judging agricultural performance. This is obvious from the fact that during the post-reforms period the average public gross capital formation at 1980-81 price worked out at Rs. 11,600 million as against Rs. 13,130 million during the pre-reforms period. However, shortfalls in public investment and in the provision of agricultural services account for the failure of agricultural supplies to respond to the favourable incentive framework created by macro-economic reforms, including trade liberalization, in the 1990s. The average annual growth of GDP in agriculture and allied sectors slowed down in the post-reform period of nineties when compared to the preceding decade, while the growth of crop output, especially foodgrains output, decelerated. The experience of the 1990s clearly demonstrates that far from trade liberalization dampening the performance of agriculture, the failure of public investment and effort is responsible for the inability to benefit from trade liberalization by stepping up and diversifying agricultural output in a cost-effective way.

Agricultural exports from India include foodgrains, tobacco, cashew, oilmeals, sesame and niger seeds, groundnut, beverages, oil seed extractions, sugar and molasses, and horticultural and floricultural products. Floriculture and horticulture have received a new boost in recent years.

At the end of the Eighth Plan (1996-97), share of agricultural exports was 20.4 per cent. It declined to 18.5 per cent in 1998-99. Under the Exim Policy, agricultural exports continue to be subjected to selective restrictions. The WTO commitments negotiated under AoA require developed countries to open up their markets faster than developing countries for agricultural exports by undertaking reductions in export subsidies, production subsidies and tariffs. However, the pace of implementation of these commitments has been very tardy and protracted negotiations have not yielded positive results in terms of market access for India and other developing countries. Moreover, developed countries have imposed non-tariff barriers which inhibit exports from India. This has resulted in poor demand for products like groundnut, oil meals, cashew, fresh fruits and vegetables etc.

In addition, agriculture has seen much less reform than other sectors. Agriculture is still constrained by central and state regulations that limit movement and intra-state trade, public procurement, and canalization of trade. For example, simply allowing greater private trade in products would help reduce price fluctuations and improve the productivity of labour and land-use and stimulate agricultural exports. Similarly, removal of small-scale reservation would help the growth of domestic agro-industry, which in some cases is now facing increased competition from larger size offshore producers as a result of lower tariff. According to a recent World Bank study cotton and textile policies effectively tax domestic cotton producers and oilseed producers by 15% and 30% respectively.

In the existing international trading scenario with various WTO restrictions and regulations, the Government of India has initiated a few policy changes to make agricultural exports globally competitive.

A market-determined exchange rate policy has favoured agricultural product exports. Lowering of import duty on capital goods as well as easier availability of credit for exports have also helped. The main stress on raising agricultural exports hinges on the promotion of productivity modernisation and competitiveness. India has probably the worst infrastructure in the world. Our ports are miserably inefficient to clean cargo at ports and foreign ship do not touch Indian shores. This is the time to strengthen export infrastructure and market development efforts in potential markets.

Unfinished Agenda

The Uruguay Round did not bring about trade liberalisation in agriculture to the desired extent. The continuation of the high domestic support to agriculture in many developed countries is a cause of concern as they encourage overproduction in these countries leading to low levels of international prices. Benefits to developing countries in terms of increasing their exports will occur only after complete elimination of export subsidies and substantial reduction in domestic support in the developed countries has been effected.

In fact, when the World Trade Organization (WTO) had taken upon itself to put an end to the multifarious distortions that had plagued the markets for agricultural commodities, countries like India had a sense of *déjà vu*. The proposed lowering of their subsidies by the dominant agricultural trading countries, and the consequent firming up of prices of agricultural commodities, was expected to bring a windfall to the low cost producers in the developing world. The farmers in these countries should thus have received the right signals to exploit the global markets in which the barriers to trade were also expected to be lower.

Much of those expectations have, however, not been realized. In the seven years since the WTO discipline has been imposed through the Agreement on Agriculture, the markets for agricultural commodities look possibly more distorted than ever. Several of the major players in the global agricultural trade have given up even the pretence of meeting their commitments to introduce discipline on their farm sectors. Consequently, subsidies handed over to the farm sector kept rising and the markets remain protected through the use of new-found instruments of control.

Despite its much-professed position on freeing agricultural markets from all forms of distortions, the United States has continued to offer huge cash bags to its farm sector. This is in complete contrast to the situation in 1996 when the enactment of the Federal Agricultural Improvement and Reform (FAIR) Act, prompted the New York Times to declare that US President Bill Clinton had signed a farm Bill that would effectively end the subsidies regime in agriculture. However, since the FAIR Act became operational, in every successive year farm subsidies have increased. Direct payments to farmers by the US government has gone up to an average of $20 billion a year in the past three years (1999 to 2001) as compared to an average of $9 billion that was being spent in the early 1990s. These payments have been made largely to protect farm incomes in times of emergencies. But the emergencies against which the farm sector was being protected were nothing more than the episodes of declining prices of agricultural commodities that have been experienced in recent years.

This was, however, not the only way farm support was doled out. Subsidies on specific commodities were also increased. Interestingly, the commodities that received most attention in this regard were those in which the US also has substantial interests in the international markets. For instance, in corn, a commodity in which the share of the US in the world trade exceeds 50 per cent, the subsidies went up from $32 million in 1995 to more than $1.5 billion in 1998. A more or less similar story is repeated in case of wheat, where subsidies have gone up from less than $5 million in 1995 to more than $500 million in 1998.

All available evidence points to the fact that both the United States and the European Union would do nothing in the next few years to bring any measure of discipline on their farm spending. In the US, the farm Bill that is being discussed by the country's law makers promises further largesse to the farm lobby. The farm policy of the European Union, guided by the Common Agricultural Policy (CAP), indicates quite clearly that no substantial reforms should be expected till 2006, the period for which the current version of CAP (CAP 2000) is valid.

It is quite clearly a case of supply management gone awry; the cost of which has to be borne not only by the tax payers in the countries providing these large volumes of subsidies, but by several other countries as well. The cumulative impact of increased subsidies by not just the US as well has been felt in the international prices of several agricultural commodities. In 1995, when liberalization of agricultural trade was ushered in through the WTO Agreement on Agriculture, India, among other developing countries, was expecting rich gains under the new dispensation since the international prices of most commodities were above ruling domestic prices, thus providing the right incentives to the farmers. Furthermore, these countries were expecting the international prices to remain firm primarily because of the reduction of subsidies that were to be effected by the major players in the market for agricultural commodities, in keeping with their WTO commitments. However, in the period since then international prices of every major commodity has declined to such an extent that the domestic prices in India are quite some distance above the international prices. As a result, not only is it difficult for India to find export markets for these commodities, the domestic market is now facing the threat from cheap imports.

Tariffs still remain very high in certain sectors, specially in cereals, sugar and dairy products. Tariff escalation blocks exports of value-added products from developing to developed countries. Sanitary and phytosanitary measures continue to be a major barrier in diversifying exports in horticulture and meat items. Fresh commitments have, therefore, to be negotiated to substantially improve market access for products of particular interest to developing countries. Since entry of newcomers is difficult in the existing tariff quota regime, India is demanding substantial expansion of TQRs pending their eventual abolition and more transparent administration of tariff quotas.

Overall Impact of Lifting of QRs

Of the 715 items for which QRs were withdrawn in the first phase, i.e. on 1 April 1999, 208 items belonged to the agricultural sector. During the remaining two phases QRs have been lifted on the remaining items. While imports are necessary to take care of domestic deficits, import tariff is the only instrument to protect the interests of the domestic producers, which on some of the items like oilseeds and edible oils warranted an upward revision in the import duties. Although it may be desirable to move away from the cultivation of crops with a comparative disadvantage in terms of domestic resource cost, considering the volatility of international markets and the uncertainty in matching India's deficit with surpluses elsewhere, a large degree of self sufficiency cannot be ignored.

The growth prospects in technological breakthrough in agriculture that ushered the green revolution have reached a plateau barring the existence of some unexploited potential in the western region. Biotechnology has emerged as an area of vast scope. The expenditure on agricultural research in India at 0.5 percent of the GDP is very low compared to developed countries. Moreover, the gap between the potential yield and farm yield of most of the crops in India of around 50 percent indicates the inadequacy of extension network and input support systems. Cotton is a classic example to highlight these shortcomings. Despite having more than one fourth of the cotton-sown area in the world, India produced only 12 percent of the output. India's yield of 278 kg is the lowest in the world compared to 1828 of Israel, 1000 kg of China, 750 kg of US and world average of 585 kg. Surveys have revealed that 70 percent of the cottonseeds used by farmers are non-certified and most of them use multiple varieties of seeds on a single farm. They end up using private hybrid seeds year after year, which costs 50 times the cost of local seeds, without any apparent yield advantage. The extension education on seeds, fertilizers, pesticides, etc. are often, provided by the input dealer himself, which along with reportedly spurious pesticides sold, results in 20 to 30 sprayings in a crop of 120-150 days duration. There is, therefore strong need to revamp the agricultural extension network and strengthen the input support system in the country.

In view of the special provisions agreed to, there should be no serious apprehension that imported agricultural and industrial commodities shall flood the Indian market, nor is the country obliged to abolish non-tariffs restrictions on agricultural imports. Moreover, as mentioned earlier, the high level of bound duties can provide adequate level of protection to its domestic sectors. There was considerable fear that the removal of QRs in April 1999, April 2000 and April 2001, would lead to a large increase in imports of consumer goods in India. However, import data indicate that lifting of quantitative restrictions did not have much impact. Table 24.1 shows import data for products on QRs were lifted in 1999 and 2000.

Table 24.1 Level of Imports in India Before and After the Lifting of QRs

Item	*Category-I*		*Category-II*	
	Products on which QRs were lifted on April, 1999		*Products on which QRs were lifted on April 1, 2000*	
	1998-99 (QR era)	*1999-2000 (Post QR era)*	*1999-2000 (QR era)*	*2000-01 (Post QR era)*
1. Value of imports (Rs. crores)	11,802.00	13,821.00	5,151.56	2,675.00
2. As percentage of total imports	6.6%	6.9%	2.6%	2.3%
3. Number of Products imported	554	622	487	474
4. Value of Agricultural Imports (Rs. crores)	8,123.00	8,619.00	510.00	405.00

SOURCE: Director General, Commercial Intelligence, Ministry of Commerce, GOI

Following the lifting of QRs on the remaining 715 items in April 2001, Government of India had introduced on 2 May 2001 a "port of entry" restrictions on import of 300 sensitive items to 11 entry points and on 8 May eight more ports for import of edible oil were included. However, on 20 May, these restrictions were lifted since the government felt that there was no surge in the imports of items concerned under it. The official data released by the "War Group" consisting of Secretaries from the Ministries concerned monitoring the items indicated, a decline of over 30 percent in imports of these items during April 2001 as compared to April 2000 (Table 24.2). The few exceptions to this trend were tea, coffee, alcoholic beverages, marble and granite. These items accounted for 54 tariff lines out of the 300 monitored by the War Group.

Import of items like edible oil, rice, wheat, sugar, coffee and tea can now take place through any port rather than being restricted to the few designated ports. This will prevent any spurt in the price of these items in the domestic market from higher freight or delays due to longer inland transportation.

Table 24.2 Imports of Sensitive Items in April 2001

(Rs. lakh)

Items	*No. of tariff lines*	*Imports*		
		April 2000	*April 2001*	*% Change*
Milk and milk products	35	609.5	160.24	– 76.79
Fruit and vegetables	48	5,308.6	1,909.96	– 64.02
Tea and coffee	32	0.65	1.07	64.62
Spices	35	710.04	271.96	– 61.70
Foodgrains	12	4.04	0.03	– 99.26
Edible oil	27	42,105.24	24,501.01	– 41.81
Alcoholic beverages	8	152.8	203.1	32.92
Rubber	11	63.06	38.19	– 39.44
Cotton	6	34.3	6.69	– 80.50
Marble and Granite	14	67.05	93.64	– 39.66
Automobiles	32	433.18	125.4	– 71.05
Products of concern to SSIs (Umbrella, locks, toys, etc.)	20	350.2	256.19	– 26.84
Others	20	1,970.67	8,513.27	332.00
Grand total	300	51,890.33	36,080.75	– 30.47

SOURCE: Directorate General of Foreign Trade; Foreign Trade Statistics.

Impact on Manufactured Products

The phase out of all QRs represented a major liberalization of India's trade policies and would allow bound tariffs to set an upper limit to the protection of many manufactured products. However, most of these tariffs (presently maximum 42 percent) are quite high even though they are lower than the prevailing pre-reform rates of 100 percent or more. Furthermore, the bindings offered by India (most 40 per cent or 25 per cent effective in year 2001/02), will not do anything to reduce them further. Moreover, they are systematically escalated according to the degree of processing, and hence are capable of providing high level of effective protection. Finally, many tariff lines are not bound—especially tariffs on consumer goods, which are subject to Indian consumer goods import ban—and in these cases the WTO provides no constraint on the level of protection that can be provided by tariffs. In addition, in recent years local content or "indigenisation" programme is being used with increasing frequency and India has revived its long dormant antidumping duties. All this suggest that realized manufacturing protection i.e. the actual difference between the domestic and international prices of manufactured goods is on the rise again in India.

Nevertheless, since the introduction of quantitative restrictions (QR) free regime in May 2001, the domestic manufacturing industry, especially the small and medium scale and unorganized sector, seems to be faced with competition from the foreign products especially from China and other countries. For instance the manufacturers of toys and electric goods are already feeling the heat. The electrical goods industry apprehends that competition from foreign manufacturing is likely to intensify especially in electrical consumer (white) goods. Already some quick profit making companies have sprung up in Mumbai and Delhi to import white goods particularly microwave ovens, mixer grinders, audio sets and colour TVs. Their aim is to import goods from China through Nepal. Using Nepal as a conduit has become lucrative for all importers since imports from that country into India, under existing Indo-Nepal Trade Treaty, are duty free.

Apart from this, the manufacturers of electrical goods face a number of problems in different States. For example, in West Bengal the manufacturers of air conditioners have to pay 12 percent sale tax, while companies having their units at Noida (UP) and Sylvassa do not have to pay any. Different levels of Octroi levies in various states also make a differential in price of the final product.

Fortunately, so far the domestic markets have not been inundated with imported electric white goods. This seems to be due to a lack of demand for these products. However, domestic small and medium enterprises (SME) manufacturers of industrial electrical goods may have to face difficult time. For instance, there is a possibility of China dumping switches and switchgears once it realizes that India is a good market for low-end industrial electrical products. Some of the SMEs have also to buy the raw material from outside state and there is also a dearth of skilled personnel. Nevertheless, even if imports rise for such products, there may not be much of a change in the scenario for high end products. However, the industry faces a serious threat from the spurious producers of industrial electrical goods, who sell their products under established brands names like Siemens and Larsen & Tubro. This detailed discussion relating to electric goods industry is merely intended to serve as an example of problems faced by most other industries.

The problems are universal to the SMEs, no matter which sector they belong to. Lack of consensus on priority sector lending, collateral-based fund by banks and lack of policy for proper protection measures—which have now become an anathema after the QR phase out—has kept these manufacturers from improving their margins and quality. There is also a lack of standardization of products, which limits the reach of these players.

CONCLUDING REMARKS

The liberal trade regime is not likely to have any dramatic impact (on imports or exports) of agricultural and industrial products during the next few years. Given the bound rates and other non-tariff barrier (phyto-sanitary measures for agricultural products and restriction on consumer goods, etc.) imports are not likely to flood the country. Certain farmers' lobbies are raising boggy that they are facing difficulties due to stiff competition from cheap imports from abroad, for example, of edible oils and fresh fruits. They allege that this is harming the domestic farmers. The problems of Indian agriculture are internal and not external. The farmers and the policy makers need to worry more about domestic issues than liberal trade regime and WTO. Some of the major issues concerning agriculture include stagnant productivity of most crops since 1995, the need for a fundamental change in food policy, opening up the country to internal trade in agricultural commodities and inefficiency in transport infrastructure. In fact the Panel of Experts in their draft Approach Paper for the Tenth Five Year Plan, has recommended a number of measures on these lines. Some of their recommendation include radical changes in the food policy, enactment of an Act to ban controls on movement between states, a policy renouncing the use of export restrictions, complete decontrol of sugar and lifting of ban on future trading and stocking of all agricultural commodities. It is high time that the Central Government should accept and implement these recommendations.

In the changing market scenario of removal of controls and liberalized trading conditions under the WTO, the cost of cultivation is most important. There is an urgent need to lower the costs by increasing the yield through improved seeds, new technology and farm practices. For raising productivity there is need for intensive research and introduction of new biotechnology, provide new technology for the rainfed areas and for commercial crops such as oilseeds, cotton and other crops. There is also need to change some of the government policies if the agricultural production is to increase. One of the reasons for low yields is the fragmentation of land holding due to the Land Ceiling Act. There is a need to consolidate the land so that agriculture can become more productive and remunerative. The government also needs to take measures to improve infrastructure like power and irrigation. With proper infrastructure coupled with high yielding seeds, India can double its agricultural production in the next few years.

As regards the national food policy, the system of using combined subsidy to support farmers and build the Public Distribution System (PDS), worked well in time of deficit foodgrain production. The government could afford to procure all that the farmers gave it, because there was always a demand for grains through the PDS. However, during the current era of food surplus, the procurement of all that is offered has left the government with far more grain stocks than can be distributed to the poor. There is an urgent need for reforming the food policy. It is essential to separate the support system to the farmers from the PDS. Whatever subsidy is to be given to the farmers should be given in a way that reduces costs. This would help him to become competitive in the world market. A PDS that targets the poorest can then be built using a much smaller subsidy such as procuring grains from the market and distributing it on low price concessional rates.

Despite repeated pleas by the Minister of Finance for the last five years or so, states have not yet removed zonal and other restrictions on internal free trade in agricultural commodities. In view of this there is considerable variation in prices between surplus states (low prices) and deficit states (high prices). Apart from the PDS, efficiency requires that price equalization takes place by trading among regions. The current situation is that the government is compelled to mop up the surplus at the procurement price. What is worse, since the government procurement is not time efficient, the poorer farmers sell at low prices to traders who then resell the produce elsewhere at the procurement price. While the traders-politician nexus benefits from these operations, the small farmers reap little advantage.

Finally, the inefficiency of the Indian transportation system is obvious from the fact that the cost of transporting grains from Punjab to Mumbai by road, which is largely used by the traders, is twice the cost of shipping grain from Australia and almost four times the cost from Bangkok. On the other hand, the transport cost by rail is more competitive. Here again, freeing internal trade would reduce price and also generate revenue for the railways. It is once again a politically imposed paradox that the railways find its freight revenue falling while grain traders use expensive road transport. It is absolutely essential for all stake holders i.e. Government officials responsible for policy formation, representative of farmers and traders to recognize the folly of taking policy decisions based merely on political considerations rather than on sound economic grounds. It is no use to blame the free trade regimes and the WTO since the problems of Indian agriculture are internal and not external. More or less it is the same with small and medium scale industrial sector, which have enjoyed a prolonged protection from the state.

It is essential to underline that policy to protect Indian agriculture and industry, irrespective of the level of their inefficiency, has a long-term impact. Growers and manufacturers, who cannot match global standards, realize that they can remain at existing inefficient levels. They have no incentive to either improve their efficiency or abandon activities where they are inefficient and move towards activities where they can be globally competitive. It is high time that Indian agriculture and the manufacturing industry improve their efficiency and become globally competitive rather than continue to hang on for protective support, which cannot be provided for long. The latter is generally inconsistent with the provisions of WTO agreement.

Rather than yielding to political pressures for raising import duties, the Government should adopt a long-term policy and strategy to increase India's share in exports in the world market. With right set of policies India should gear up to take advantage of the opening up of the international market especially for agricultural commodities. There is a need not only to adopt the policies mentioned above but also to set up quality parameters for export of agricultural products. These quality parameters must conform to the world standards. India can also become a leading exporter of organic foods. With the poor farmers having no resources to use fertilizers and pesticides on their farms, this handicap should be converted into an opportunity by developing certification standards for organic food, educating farmers to grow the crop as per these standards, certifying the produce as organic and exporting it to the developed countries. This would help to improve the economic status of the farmers and reduce rural poverty.

Taken as a whole, India is more a gainer than a loser from WTO agreements, particularly in respect of trade in agriculture (including horticulture). The nature and magnitude of the gains will however depend on the policies we pursue, the strategies we adopt, and the determination we show to realize the opportunities available to us in the international market place. In agriculture, we have the freedom to follow our policies; it is the industrialized countries that are required to bring down their domestic support and export subsidies and volume of subsidized exports. Our horticultural exports can become more competitive in the international market. Opportunity to realize international prices can perhaps provide the strongest incentive to our farmers to boost production, productivity and quality improvement.

The government has put highly sensitive items on state trading list as the QRs on these items had to be lifted with caution. The State Trading Enterprises designated for import or export would have to work on commercial terms and in line with market demand. Of the 28 items the import of which has been reserved for state trading enterprises, import would be open only to designed companies except cases where advance licenses are procured for bringing imported raw materials. FCI has been made the designated agency for wheat, rice and coarse grains while import of copra and oil have been left to State Trading Corporation and Hindustan Vegetable Oil Company.

Appendix 24.1

India: Major Agricultural Products; Import Tariffs and Trade Policy Status

Item	Applied tariff as if April 2001	Bound tariff	Trade policy status	
			Exports	Imports
Paddy	0	0	Free	Canalised
Rice				
Common rice	70/80	70/80	Free	Canalised
Basmati rice	0	0	Free	Canalised
Wheat				
Soft Wheat	50	100	Restricted	Canalised
Hard Wheat	50	100	Free	Canalised
Wheat Flours	100	150	Restricted	Canalised
Processed Cereals				
Baby foods	15	17.5	Free	Restricted
Baker's dough	50	55	Free	Restricted
Bakfast cereals	50	55	Free	Restricted
All other	50	150	Free	Restricted
Oilseeds	50	100	Mostly restricted	Canalised
Soya, rapeseed, mustard olive and	45	45	Mostly	Free
colza oils	75	300	restricted	
Other edible oils incl. Coconut and palm oils	85	300	Mostly restricted	Canalized
Oil cakes, meals and fours	50	150	Free	Restricted
Non-edible oils from seeds	75	300,100	Restricted	Canalized
Coarse grains	50	100	Restricted	Canalized
Coarse grains flours	50	150	Restricted	Canalized
Pulses	10	100	Restricted	Free
Live Animals	0,22,42	100	Mostly restricted	Mostly restricted
Meat				
Fresh, chilled, frozen	10	150	Mostly restricted	Restricted
Processed-homog meats, hams	12,50	55	Mostly free	Restricted
Hindes and skins incl. Leather	0	25	Restricted	Free
Milk and cream	40	100	Restricted	Restricted
Powered milk (< 1.5% and > 1.5%)	0	0	Free	Restricted
Powdered milk (> 1.5% sweetened and other dairy products	40	40.50	Free	Restricted except butter oil which is free
Vegetables	10	100	Mostly free	Restricted
Dried mushrooms, onions, potatoes	10	35	Free	Restricted
Fruits	50	100	Mostly free	Restricted
Grapes and plums	30	30	Free	Restricted

India: Major Agricultural Products; Import Tariffs and Trade Policy Status
(Contd.)

Item	*Applied tariff as if April 2001*	*Bound tariff*	*Trade policy status*	
			Exports	*Imports*
Dried prunes	50	55	Free	Restricted
Preparations of fruits	50	100	Free	Restricted
About 13 vegetables	50	100	Free	Restricted
Orange Juice	50	85	Free	Restricted
Other fruit juices	50	85	Free	Restricted
Sugar	60	100	Restricted	Mostly free
Raw Cotton	0	150	Restricted	Free
Wood and Wood products	25,50	25-40	Restricted	Free
Fish and crustaceans	12	150 Free	Free	Mostly restricted
Spices	50	100,150	Mostly free	Restricted
Caraway seeds	35	35	Free	Restricted
Thyme, bay leaves	35	35	Free	Restricted
Tea	12	150	Mostly free	Restricted
Raw Tobacco	50	100	Mostly free	Restricted
Natural Rubber	25	25	Free	Restricted
Coffee (Unprocessed)	10	100	Restricted	Restricted
Coffee beans, processed coffee	12	150	Restricted	Free
Cocoa beans, processed cocoa	42,32	100,150	Free	Restricted
Jute (O)	0	40	Restricted	Free
Sisal, coir (O)	32	40	Free	Restricted
Flex, hemp	12	25	Free	Restricted
Greasy wool	12	25	Free	Restricted

Notes: The products shown in the above table account for more than 95 per cent of rural GDP. They are listed in approximate order of the value of their production. Tariffs separated by commas indicate the rates for different tariff lines under a general heading. Tariffs separated by hyphen indicate a number of rates between minimum and maximum. The tariffs shown are for imports intended for consumption, not for imports of seeds or cuttings etc. intended for planting. Tariffs on the later are generally zero, and in many cases are also exempt or lower than the general level in the other countries. The bound tariffs are the rates that will apply in 2004, at the end of the implementation period. A number of the Indian bindings are being reduced in stages from initially higher base period level "Most restricted" means that most products or product varieties in the category are subject to licensing or other non-tariff controls.

SOURCE:
1. Ministry of Finance: Annual Economic Survey for 1999-2000, 2000-2991 and 2001-2002
2. Ministry of Finance: Finance Bill for fiscal years 1999-2000, 2000-01 and 2001-2002
3. Ministry of Finance: EXIMP Policy documents
4. World Bank/FAO Workshop: Implications of the Uruguay Round Agreement for South Asia: The case of Agriculture: (Kathmandu: May 1996).

Appendix 24.2

Reduction in Domestic Support to Agricultural Producers

(In million US$)

Participant	*Base**	*Final*	*Reduction*
European Union	92390	76903	17
Japan	35472	28378	20
United States	23879	19103	20
Mexico	9669	8387	13
Canada	4650	3720	20
Finland	4186	3349	20
Poland	4160	3329	20
Republic of Korea	4086	3543	13
Switzerland	3769	3016	20
Sweden	3429	2743	20
Austria	2534	2027	20
Norway	2247	1797	20
Venezuela	1305	1131	13
Brazil	1053	912	13
Thailand	856	745	13
Czech Republic	717	574	20
Israel	654	569	13
New Zealand	210	268	20
Hungary	613	490	20
Australia	460	368	20
Slovak Republic	435	348	20
Colombia	398	345	13
Iceland	222	177	20
Cyprus	127	110	13
Morocco	93	81	13
Tunisia	76	66	13
Costa Rica	18	16	13
South Africa	3	2	20
Total	197721	162497	18

* Indicates subsidies in 1986 to 1988

Source: WTO

Appendix 24.3

Export Subsidy Reduction Commitments by Country

(In million US$)

Participant	*Base**	*Final*	*Reduction*	*Product composition of export subsidies*
European Union	13274	8496	– 36	Bovine meal (19%), wheat (17%), Coarse grains (13%), butter (13%) other milk products (10%)
Austria	1235	790	– 36	Live animals (45%), wheat (4%), bovine meat (!#%), cheese (12%)
United States	929	594	– 36	Wheat (61%), skim milk powder (14%)
Poland	774	493	– 36	Meat preparations (39%), fruits and vegetables (21%)
Mexico	748	553	– 26	Sugar (76%), cereal preparations (21%)
Finland	708	453	– 36	Butter (25), coarse grains (22%), other milk products (13%)
Sweden	572	366	– 36	Pig meat (21%), wheat (21%), coarse grains (17%)
Canada	567	363	– 36	Wheat (47%), coarse grains (18%)
Switzerland	487	312	– 36	Other dairy products (65%)
Colombia	371	287	– 23	Rice (32%), cotton (20%), fruits and vegetables (23%)
South Africa	319	204	– 36	Fruits and vegetables (24%), cereal preparations (14%), wheat (13%), sugar (10%)
Hungary	312	200	– 36	Poultry meat (30%), pig meat (26%), wheat (11%), fruits and vegetables (19%)
Czech Republic	164	105	– 36	Other milk products (38%), fruits and vegetables (10%)
Turkey	157	98	– 37	Fruits and vegetables (36%), wheat (23%)
New Zealand	133	0	– 100	Not available
Norway	112	72	– 36	Cheese (54%), pig meat (19%), butter (12%)
Australia	107	69	– 36	Other milk products (32%), skim milk powder (27%), cheese (25%), butter (16%)
Brazil	96	73	– 24	Sugar (56%), fruits and vegetables (30%)
Slovak Republic	76	49	– 36	Other dairy products (19%), cereal preparations (13%), bovine meat (13%)

Appendix 24.4

Share of Agricultural Subsidies (PSE) in Selected Countries and India

(in US $ billion)

Country	*Base year (1986-88)*		*1977*		*1988*		*1999 (Provisional)*	
	Total subsidies	% AGDP	Total subsidies	% AGDP	Total subsidies	% AGDP	Total subsidies	% AGDP
Canada	5.645	34.0	3.113	14.0	3.573	18.0	3.093	20.0
EC	95214	44.0	112.260	38.0	122.946	45.0	114.450	49.0
Japan	53.637	67.0	50.534	57.0	49.962	62.0	58.885	65.0
USA	41.890	25.0	30.459	14.0	48.441	22.0	54.009	24.0
OECD	246.226	40.0	246.167	31.0	270.869	36.0	282.780	40.0
India	1.058	6.2	6.096	7.5	6.707	6.8	7.247	6.5

AGDP = Gross domestic product from agriculture.

Note: 1. Exact comparison of subsidies between India and OECD countries is not possible on account of different in composition of PSE and subsidies as computed in India.

2. Figures relating to India are provisional.

3. In case of India, values in Rupees have been converted into US dollars at exchange rate prevalling in 1999 viz Rs. 43.3 per US dollar.

SOURCE: Agricultural Statistics at Glance—2001, Directorate of Economics and Statistics, Ministry of Agriculture and Cooperation, GOI, New Delhi.

Appendix 11.4

(in US $ billion)

Country	Average (1986–88)		1997		1998		1999 (Provisional)	
	Total subsidies	AGDP	Total subsidies	AGDP	Total subsidies	AGDP	Total subsidies	AGDP
Canada	5,643	34.0	3,117	44.0	[illegible]	75.0	[illegible]	20.0
EC	95,214	44.0	112,260	38.0	127,346	45.0	[illegible]	[illegible]
Japan	54,077	67.0	50,454	57.0	49,962	63.0	59,583	65.0
USA	41,990	25.0	30,259	14.0	46,497	22.0	54,004	24.0
OECD	266,226	40.0	246,[illegible]	31.0	271,509	36.0	[illegible]	39.0
India	1,058	6.2	796	7.3	[illegible]	6.8	[illegible]	4.5

3. In case of India subsidies (in US $) have been converted from Rs at the exchange rate prevailing in 1999 i.e. Rs [illegible] per US dollar.

Index